LEADERSHIP AND ORGANIZATIONAL BEHAVIOR IN EDUCATION

Theory Into Practice

William A. Owings
Old Dominion University

Leslie S. Kaplan
Newport News Public Schools

PEARSON

Boston   Columbus   Indianapolis   New York   San Francisco   Upper Saddle River
Amsterdam   Cape Town   Dubai   London   Madrid   Milan   Munich   Paris   Montreal   Toronto
Delhi   Mexico City   São Paulo   Sydney   Hong Kong   Seoul   Singapore   Taipei   Tokyo

Vice President and Editorial Director: Jeffery W. Johnston
Senior Acquisitions Editor: Meredith Fossel
Associate Editor: Anne Whittaker
Editorial Assistant: Nancy Holstein
Vice President, Director of Marketing: Margaret Waples
Marketing Manager: Christopher Barry
Senior Managing Editor: Pamela D. Bennett
Project Manager: Kerry Rubadue
Senior Operations Supervisor: Matthew Ottenweller

Senior Art Director: Diane Lorenzo
Text Designer: S4Carlisle Publishing Services
Cover Designer: Bryan Huber
Cover Art: fotolia
Full-Service Project Management: S4Carlisle Publishing Services
Composition: S4Carlisle Publishing Services
Printer/Binder: Courier/Westford
Cover Printer: Lehigh-Phoenix Color/Hagerstown
Text Font: Goudy

Credits and acknowledgments borrowed from other sources and reproduced, with permission, in this textbook appear on appropriate page within text.

Every effort has been made to provide accurate and current Internet information in this book. However, the Internet and information posted on it are constantly changing, so it is inevitable that some of the Internet addresses listed in this textbook will change.

Library of Congress Cataloging-in-Publication Data
Owings, William A.
   Leadership and organizational behavior in education : theory into practice / William A. Owings, Leslie S. Kaplan.
     p. cm.
   ISBN-13: 978-0-13-705044-4
   ISBN-10: 0-13-705044-5
  1. Educational leadership. 2. Organizational behavior. 3. School management and organization.
I. Kaplan, Leslie S. II. Title.
   LB2806.O95 2011
   371.2—dc22

               2010044606

10 9 8 7 6 5 4 3 2 1

www.pearsonhighered.com

ISBN-13: 978-0-13-705044-4
ISBN-10:   0-13-705044-5

Dedication

To our colleagues and friends, Charlotte Danielson, Linda Darling-Hammond, Michael Fullan, and Robert J. Marzano—education scholars whose keen insights, practitioner-oriented perspectives, and relentless productivity have made significant contributions to both theory and practice. You continue to inspire and motivate us.

About the Authors

William A. Owings, Ed.D. is currently a professor of educational leadership at Old Dominion University in Norfolk, VA. Owings has worked as a public school teacher, an elementary and high school principal, assistant superintendent, and superintendent of schools. In addition, his scholarly publications, co-authored with Leslie Kaplan, include articles in *National Association of Secondary School Principals (NASSP) Bulletin*, *Journal of School Leadership*, *Journal of Effective Schools*, *Phi Delta Kappan*, *Teachers College Record*, and the *Journal of Education Finance*. Owings has served on the state and international board of the Association for Supervision and Curriculum Development (ASCD), is currently the editor of the *Journal for Effective Schools*, and is on the *Journal of Education Finance* Editorial Advisory Board. He is a frequent presenter at state and national conferences and a consultant on educational leadership, school finance, and instructional improvement. Owings and Kaplan share the 2008 Virginia Educational Research Association Charles Edgar Clear Research Award for Consistent and Substantial Contributions to Educational Research and Scholarship.

Leslie S. Kaplan, Ed.D. a retired school administrator in Newport News, VA, is a full-time education writer. She has provided middle and high school instructional leadership as well as central office leadership as a director of program development. Before becoming a school administrator, she worked as a middle and high school counselor and her articles were frequently published in *The School Counselor*. Kaplan's scholarly publications, co-authored with William Owings', appear in numerous professional journals. She also has co-authored several books and monographs with Owings, including *American Education: Building a Common Foundation*; *American Public School Finance*; *Teacher Quality, Teaching Quality, and School Improvement*; *Best Practices, Best Thinking, and Emerging Issue in School Leadership*; and *Enhancing Teacher and Teaching Quality*. Kaplan is co-editor of the *Journal for Effective Schools*, and also serves on the *NASSP Bulletin* Editorial Board. She is a past president of the Virginia Counselors' Association and the Virginia Association for Supervision and Curriculum Development.

Brief Contents

Contents

Chapter 8   **Leadership, Conflict, Problem Solving, and Decision Making**   290

Preface

Leadership and Organizational Behavior in Education: Theory Into Practice was written to help future school leaders understand what leadership is and recognize the varied opportunities for its expression in schools. This awareness is an essential step in learning to become effective school leaders.

For many K–12 students, an effective school—adding value to what their family provides—can make the difference between having adult opportunities for work and personal satisfaction and a life marked by frustration and need. Substantial research supports the belief that the school leaders' effectiveness affects important school and student outcomes. Yet too often, graduate education coursework leaves the connections between school leadership theory and actual leadership practice implicit, haphazard, or altogether absent. Studying leadership or organizational theory is useful but not sufficient to transform practitioner behavior.

With this in mind, the authors have created a leadership text that systematically integrates leadership and organizational theory with its application in actual school situations. Each chapter begins with a realistic case study that raises critical issues in school leadership and whose theme is woven throughout the text. After each major concept, readers have opportunities to find understanding, personal meaning, and relevance in the content discussed, consider these with their professor and classmates, and apply their readings directly to the case and to their own experiences to better understand the leadership and organizational factors at play. These realistic and socially engaging activities prompt transfer of learning, insights, and skills from the graduate classroom into the schoolhouse.

The authors of *Leadership and Organizational Behavior in Education: Theory Into Practice* and instructors of educational leadership and organizational behavior share many common goals for their students:

◆ A *user-friendly resource* about school leadership and organizational behavior that educators will find readable, interesting, scholarly, relevant, and highly practical
◆ A *deliberate connection of theory to practice* by introducing each chapter with a relevant case study and revisiting it throughout the chapter to help students apply the information to successfully resolving real-world, school-based concerns
◆ *Varied perspectives* on important issues and scholarly contributions so readers can assess their merits and form their own conclusions

- *An insight of how effective school leadership can affect school practice* on organizational dynamics; understanding and implementing change; applying leadership theories; creating a shared vision and mission through language and symbols; motivating employees; building leadership capacity; conflict, problem solving and decision making; allocating resources; conducting formative and summative evaluations; practicing leadership with ethics, integrity, and social justice; and developing a satisfying educational career
- *A practitioner's orientation* from authors who have been successful school leaders in public schools, K–12
- *Many opportunities for educational leadership students to become familiar with and learn how to analyze school documents* containing important data and demographics similar to those school leaders actually use
- *Identification of best practices for educational leadership* behavior that are well supported by the current professional literature
- *Ongoing opportunities for readers to generate personal meaning, workplace relevance,* and collegial teams for improving leadership for teaching and learning in their schools
- *Increased transfer of learning* from graduate classroom to schoolhouse by discussing and using virtual school documents, analyzing actual school leadership issues, and working with a team to make informed decisions about school leadership practices
- *A smoother transition from faculty to school leadership* by addressing and engaging in many leadership issues that future educational leaders need to know and understand so they can plan and successfully enact their school leadership careers

FEATURES OF *LEADERSHIP AND ORGANIZATIONAL BEHAVIOR IN EDUCATION: THEORY INTO PRACTICE*

This text offers special features to help educational leadership students learn the contents of each chapter:

- *Focus Questions.* Each chapter begins with focus questions to help orient readers to the essential ideas discussed in the chapter and provide a purpose for reading.
- *Authentic Case Studies.* Each chapter begins with a realistic case study that illustrates how the chapter's topic might appear in a school setting. The case study includes narrative and documents resembling those that educational leaders actually use for making informed decisions. Readers will develop the capacity to read and analyze important school documents and apply their findings to the case at hand.
- *Case Study Questions.* Case studies are followed by specific questions that relate to the events described. These questions help to focus attention and create a purpose for reading. Students are to consider possible answers to the questions when they first appear, but will have opportunities to provide more complete answers when the questions reappear in the activities immediately following relevant content.
- *Activities.* Located immediately following major concepts in each chapter, these socially-mediated practice exercises help students find meaning and relevance in the

ideas just discussed. Most questions have several correct answers that readers can develop by relating text information to the case studies or to their own experiences. Many questions relate directly to the chapter's case study, asking readers to use the just-discussed concept as a framework to better understand and resolve the case. Several activities provide opportunities for readers to self-assess on leadership dimensions and begin to take steps toward advancing a career as educational leaders. Professors can adapt or revise these activities as they desire to accomplish instructional goals.

ORGANIZATION

The text is organized into 12 chapters.

Chapter 1, Historical Overview of Leadership's Role, defines *leadership*, explains its importance as a topic of study, and briefly describes the leadership role throughout history. Traditional theories of leadership (great man, leadership traits, leadership behavior, leadership and power, leadership and relationship paradigms), the principal as an instructional leader, and the Interstate School Leaders Licensure Consortium (ISLLC) standards for principals are discussed.

Chapter 2, Historical Overview of Leadership in Organizations, focuses on organizations and human behavior as studied from the late 19th century to the present. Classical organization topics include Frederick Taylor's scientific management, Henri Fayol's ideas on administration, and Luther Gulick's and Max Weber's views on bureaucracies. Modern organizational theory includes the human relations and the Hawthorne studies; Chester Barnard, Felix Roethlisberger, William Dickson, and Herbert Simon on organizational management; Abraham Maslow on human needs development; Douglas McGregor's Theories X and Y; William Ouchi's Theory Z; and Lee Bolman and Terrence Deal's structural frames. The chapter concludes by considering rational, natural, and open systems of organizations.

Chapter 3, Change Theory and Leadership in Educational Organizations, explains how contemporary organizational leadership has incorporated the idea of continual change and the need for all employees to keep learning. Topics include the societal changes in the United States since the 1950s, how these affected public schools, and the modern view of adult learning. Change theory in organizations looks at contributions by Chris Argyris (leadership and organizational change, used and espoused theories of action, single- and double-loop learning, and Models I and II), Kurt Lewin (field theory, group dynamics, action research, and the 3-step change model), Edgar Schein (defining and understanding organizational culture), Robert Chin (three strategic orientations), Michael Fullan (leading for change), and Peter Senge (systems thinking and the learning organization).

Chapter 4, Leadership Theories, describes modern leadership in theories and practices, including the Ohio State studies, leadership style theory, leadership contingency theory, situational leadership theory, path-goal theory, transformational leadership theory, and authentic leadership theory. Each theory is assessed for its strengths and weaknesses.

Chapter 5, Leadership, Communication, and Vision, addresses how leadership's effectiveness largely depends on the ability to communicate. Topics include the communication process, leadership and developing a shared vision and mission, how effective leaders use language and symbols to advance their agenda, and research on language and motivation.

Chapter 6, Leadership and Motivation, looks at leadership from the employee's perspective. It defines *motivation* and explores leadership and psychological contracts, motivation, and human needs. Frederick Herzberg's motivation-hygiene theory, David McClelland's work on motivation with the need for achievement and need for autonomy, Victor Vroom's expectancy theory, and motivation and organizational diversity are also explored along with relevant research findings and critiques.

Chapter 7, Leadership as Developing Human Capital, explains capacity building as an essential leadership responsibility. The discussion includes defining and building teachers' leadership capacity, identifying teachers for leadership roles, creating opportunities for teacher leadership, identifying and overcoming obstacles to developing teachers' leadership capacity, and research on building a school's leadership capacity. Attribution theory of motivation is also discussed with supporting research and ways principals can use attribution theory to help teachers grow in their leadership abilities.

Chapter 8, Leadership, Conflict, Problem Solving, and Decision Making, considers conflict as a factor in organizational health. It introduces and defines the concept of conflict in organizations, identifies conflict's functional and dysfunctional outcomes, and explains the differences between conflict resolution and conflict management for organizational well-being. Other topics explored are problem solving and decision making in organizations, leadership and rational decision making (Chester Barnard, Peter Drucker, and Herbert Simon), and a variety of leadership and decision-making models (Victor Vroom, Edwin Bridges, Wayne Hoy and John Tarter, Robert Owens and Thomas Valesky, and Irving Janis and Leon Mann) that have varied implications for school settings. The chapter concludes with a discussion of *groupthink* and research on shared decision making.

Chapter 9, Leadership and Resource Allocation, looks at resource allocation in the school and larger contexts. Issues of equity, equality, adequacy, and leadership resource allocation receive consideration. Topics cover key elements influencing resource allocation decisions; learning-focused resource allocation; types of resources available to support teaching and learning and the practical constraints they bring and exploration of money, people, and time resources available to schools. Finally, the chapter focuses on research supporting resource allocation that has an impact on student achievement, including teacher quality, teacher salaries, class size, school size, professional development, facilities, and continuing dilemmas.

Chapter 10, Formative and Summative Evaluation Issues in Leadership, looks at how evaluating educators can serve both the organization (accountability) and the individuals (professional growth). It identifies key issues and obstacles in evaluating educational personnel. Issues discussed include research on principal and teacher impacts on student achievement, current and emerging formative and summative evaluation practices for assessing principals' and teachers' effectiveness, standards-based educator evaluations, and a review of principal and teacher employment rights. The chapter concludes with a principal quality rubric based on ISLLC standards which readers can use for self-assessment, mentor or peer feedback, and professional growth.

Chapter 11, Ethics, Integrity, and Social Justice in Leadership, places school leadership within an ethical context. The chapter considers how general ethical perspectives and multiple ethical paradigms influence school leaders' decision making, how ethics affects normative leadership theories, and school leadership and social justice. The chapter concludes with a closer look at how school leaders can maintain a moral compass in their understanding and responses to individuals as well as teaching and learning issues.

Chapter 12, Developing as an Educational Leader, views the education profession through the lens of career development. Donald Super's career development theory, stages of adult career development, stages in school leadership, the principal's leadership style at different career stages, and preparing for the next generation of school leaders receive attention. The last section allows readers to plan their own educational leadership career stages and considers the role of professional reflection in building, refining, and establishing a satisfying career in education.

ACKNOWLEDGMENTS

Since 1999, the writing team of Bill Owings and Leslie Kaplan has been contributing to the professional literature on principal quality, teacher and teaching quality, school finance, American educational foundations, and school improvement. Together, we have over 50 years of practitioner experiences as public school teachers, school and central office instructional leaders, and the division superintendency. We draw extensively from these experiences for our perspectives and case studies. Husband and wife since 2003, we energize each other's creativity and work ethic on a daily basis. Our collaboration is an extremely enjoyable, satisfying, and productive one.

At Pearson, we sincerely thank the highly talented Steve Dragin, who first expressed interest in our concept of infusing authentic case studies with leadership theory in a way that would help translate concepts into practice. Steve encouraged and supported us during the contractual and early writing stages. During the production phase, Kerry Rubadue, our project manager, kept us moving forward and welcomed our questions.

At S4Carlisle, Roxanne Klaas, our project editor, always positive and encouraging, capably guided us through the production phase. At every turn, Roxanne kept the book's best interest (and the authors' sanity) in mind, and we relied on her wise and practical judgment. We also thank those individuals at Pearson and S4Carlisle whose professional talents brought this book to readers.

We feel a deep appreciation for the professors who reviewed our manuscript and provided excellent and useful feedback. In the best sense, these colleagues became valued collaborators who prodded us to refine and strengthen this text. They are: Diane Alexander, Governors State University; Dave Dolph, University of Dayton; J. Robert Hendricks, University of Arizona; Lora Knutson, Governors State University; Mary K. McCullough, Loyola

Marymount University; Terry Quinn, Queens College SUNY; Dianne Tracey, Johns Hopkins University; and Donald Wattam, University of Idaho. Thank you all so much.

Finally, Bill's educational leadership graduate students also offered constructive feedback as he taught his class from our manuscript draft. The following graduate students provided useful comments: Mary Beth Blessing, Sharon Bowles, Christie Smith, Terry Farmer, Pamela Hatfield, Brian King, Mark Loiterman, Andy McNeish, Kellie Mason, Melissa Morris, Alison Reddy, Melanie Romano-Mason, Helen Ryan, and George Waldenmaier.

Bill Owings and Leslie Kaplan
June, 2011

CHAPTER 1

Historical Overview of Leadership's Role

Focus Questions

- Why should we study leadership?
- What are the contributions and limitations of traditional theories of leadership?
- What is the relationship between leadership and power?
- How does the relationship theory of leadership affect our understanding and practice of leadership today?
- What is *instructional leadership* and how does it impact student achievement?
- How do school leaders understand, identify resources for, and find solutions for community diversity issues affecting student achievement?
- What are the Interstate School Leaders Licensure Consortium (ISLLC) standards and what are their intended influences on how school leaders should influence their schools and communities?

CASE STUDY: OAKDALE HIGH SCHOOL

We begin with a case study of Oakdale High School and use its data to build a case for the type of leadership needed for today's schools.

The year is 2000, before No Child Left Behind (NCLB) increased school accountability for student achievement. Oakdale, a 1,000-student high school, is located in a suburban area serving mostly White, affluent families. It enjoys an excellent reputation in the community. Located just outside a large city, very little has changed in this suburban community over the last 25 years except for a demographic shift. Ten years ago, Oakdale's student population was 96% White. The school runs smoothly. Faculty meetings consist of distributing and briefly summarizing minor state-mandated curriculum revision reports, scholarship selection committee reports, and reminders of upcoming events. Because students' test scores traditionally have been well above the state averages, the principal and teachers have seen no need to review them or change anything about how the school functions.

Achievement, accountability, and student diversity are watchwords. Changes in the nearby city have become Oakdale's challenges. Life has become more complicated for the school leaders, faculty, and staff if they want to have all children succeed. The following are the school demographics as they appeared in 2000 and today (post-NCLB):

Oakdale High School Data Sheet, 2000 and Today (post-NCLB)

Data		Descriptor
2000	*Today*	*Student Race*
89%	57%	Percentage of students who are White
5%	18%	Percentage of students who are African American
3%	20%	Percentage of students who are Latino
2%	4%	Percentage of students who are Asian/Pacific Islander
1%	1%	Percentage of students who are coded "other"
		Selected Student Data
80%	48%	Percentage of students scoring above state average on standardized testing
78%	43%	Percentage of students taking at least one advanced placement or honors class
82%	39%	Percentage of students participating in at least one extracurricular activity
90%	38%	Percentage of students missing 5 or fewer days of school
86	840	Number of discipline referrals
		Student Socioeconomic Status Information
5%	45%	Percentage of students who qualify for free lunch
3%	17%	Percentage of students who qualify for reduced-price lunch

Special Population Information

6%	15%	Percentage of students eligible for special education services
2%	15%	Percentage of students who are English language learners

Postgraduation Data

85%	45%	Percentage of students who enter college directly from high school
5%	16%	Percentage of students who enter the military directly from high school
10%	39%	Percentage of students who enter the workforce directly from high school

Faculty Data

23.7	7.1	Mean tenure rate (in years)
88%	39%	Percentage of teachers holding a master's degree or higher
99%	46%	Percentage of teachers who are White
1%	34%	Percentage of teachers who are African American
0%	20%	Percentage of teachers who are Latino
55%	32%	Percentage of teachers who are male
45%	68%	Percentage of teachers who are female
95%	17%	Percentage of teachers who grew up in the community
0	58%	Teaching turnover in the last 4 years

Community Data

$93,000	$57,000	Median family income
92%	22%	Percentage of parents who are PTA members
25%	30%	Percentage of jobs in the community that are manufacturing jobs
65%	50%	Percentage of jobs in the community that are high-paying white-collar, professional, or service jobs
10%	20%	Percentage of jobs in the community that are minimum-wage service jobs

For the last 3 years, students who belong to minority groups, students with special needs, and students eligible for free and reduced-price lunch have failed to make adequate yearly progress (AYP), as defined by NCLB. The school administration has remained the same.

Given the changes in accountability and in student demographics, effective leadership for Oakdale High School requires different skill sets today—and from more players—than it did before NCLB.

Although Oakdale is a fictional community, its data are not. Oakdale's updated student demographics mirror the national averages as referenced in the current *Digest of Education Statistics*.[1] This is what school leaders everywhere can expect to find.

Case Study Questions

1. Using the data provided previously, how would you describe the community and the school?
2. How would understanding the theory and practice of leadership help you better identify and address the varied issues affecting teaching and learning at Oakdale High School?
3. How would understanding the personal and interpersonal dynamics that "make" a leader effective help you better understand what leadership is and how to develop these attributes in yourself?

ACTIVITY 1.1 Leadership Questions for Oakdale High School

Consider the changes at Oakdale High School between 2000 and today, and answer the following questions.

Case Study Question 1: Using the data provided previously, how would you describe the community and the school?

- In what ways have the community demographics changed?
- In what ways have the student demographics changed?
- What additional opportunities do these student and community changes bring to Oakdale High School?
- What types of cultural changes will be needed at Oakdale High School to ensure the success of every student?
- How will the school district promote the understanding, appreciation, and use of the community's diverse cultural, social, and intellectual resources?
- What leadership tasks must the principal address to lead Oakdale High School effectively?
- What leadership skills must the principal have to lead Oakdale High School effectively?
- What are the critical instructional problems facing the staff now? How have they changed?
- What are the school climate issues the school must address?
- What are the long-term issues that need to be addressed now? How have they changed?

Case Study Question 2: How would understanding the theory and practice of leadership help you better identify and address the varied issues affecting teaching and learning at Oakdale High School?

Case Study Question 3: How would understanding the personal and interpersonal dynamics that "make" a leader effective help you better understand what leadership is and how to develop these attributes in yourself?

WHY STUDY LEADERSHIP?

American confidence in its leaders has declined sharply.

According to findings from a 2008 survey by the Center for Public Leadership at the Harvard Kennedy School and the Merriman River Group, 80% of Americans believed that the United States faces a leadership crisis, up from 65% in 2005, the study's first year.

TABLE 1–1

Changes in Americans' Confidence in Leadership by Sector, 2005–2009

	2005 Mean	2006 Mean	2007 Mean	2008 Mean	2009 Mean	Mean Change 2008–2009
Business	100.9	98.4	100.0	86.6	90.1	3.5
Education	107.6	105.5	103.0	96.8	96.3	−0.6
Medical	112.0	110.8	109.0	109.1	103.1	−6.0
Military	115.4	114.2	113.3	112.5	119.7	7.3
Local government	100.8	102.6	98.3	99.2	99.2	0.0

Source: Rosenthal, S. A., Moore, S., Montoya, R. M., & Maruskin, L. A. (2009). *National Leadership Index 2009: A National Study of Confidence in Leadership.* Center for Public Leadership, Harvard Kennedy School, Harvard University, Cambridge, Massachusetts. (Appendix 2, p. 16)

Confidence in the leaders of seven sectors—business, the Executive Branch, Congress, religion, education, the Supreme Court, and state government—fell more sharply in 2008 than ever before (see Table 1–1). Military and medical leadership were the only sectors for which Americans expressed at least a moderate amount of confidence.[2]

Leading has never been more challenging. Today's leaders face complicated, turbulent realities. According to Michael Fullan, "The more complex society gets, the more sophisticated leadership must become."[3] Today's big problems are multifaceted, interconnected, fast-moving, and filled with paradoxes and dilemmas. Many problems do not have once-and-for-all answers. Yet we expect our leaders to solve them. Heifetz (1994) described leadership not as mobilizing others to solve problems we already know how to solve, but to help them confront problems that have never yet been successfully addressed.[4]

"We are living in chaotic conditions. Thus leaders must be able to operate under complex, uncertain circumstances."[5] With the world changing at an ever-increasing pace, is it any wonder that citizens question whether their "leaders" can keep their balance?

Fullan observed that leaders have a dilemma. "On the one hand, failing to act when the environment around you is radically changing leads to extinction. On the other hand, making quick decisions under conditions of mind-racing mania can be equally fatal."[6] Leadership is the key to making our government, businesses, and schools better, yet public opinion appears to believe that effective leadership is in very short supply.

Schools require capable leaders who can mobilize faculty, staff, students, and community members to invest their time and efforts in educating all children. All children need a robust education's knowledge and skills if they are to understand and competently make their way in a complex world. For many students, an effective school—adding to what their family provides—can make the difference between having adult opportunities for work and personal satisfaction or a life marked by frustration and need. The quality of a school's leadership and how that leadership affects the school vision, climate, classroom practices, and community can make the difference.

Specifically, educational leadership today demands capable individuals who can enact five common themes.[7] Effective school leaders must:

◆ Be able to express a vision and sense of mission or purposefulness that improve learning outcomes for all students.
◆ Create a culture of positive shared values toward this end, and develop and implement strategies that guide and manage the school as it moves toward achieving these goals.
◆ Be able to collect and analyze data and information pertinent to the educational environment and build and sustain positive relationships with families, caregivers, and community partners.
◆ Develop teachers and staff to be *able* to do what needs to be done.
◆ Motivate and inspire people to *want* to do what needs to be done.

Why study leadership? We cannot practice leadership effectively if we don't know what it is. In a world full of multiple complicated issues, understanding how to lead effectively to improve conditions and outcomes for people is essential to secure our future as a nation and as communities. On a smaller scale, the same is true for schools. Without understanding the parameters and possibilities of leadership, we cannot make sense of—or find solutions for—the many challenges facing us. In short, we study leadership so we can become more effective leaders.

This chapter will briefly review the history of leadership, consider why we study it, and look at the traditional ways of understanding it. We will also think about instructional leadership and its positive effects on schools and student learning. You will see why older and less sophisticated leadership ideas no longer work for today's school leaders.

WHAT IS LEADERSHIP?

Leadership has many definitions. Joseph Rost (1991), a leadership scholar, observed that the leadership literature has identified more than 100 different definitions.[8] Management experts Warren Bennis and Burt Nanus (1985) found 350 definitions from thousands of studies.[9] The word *lead* comes from the Old English *laedan*, meaning "take with one" to "show the way."[10] *Ledere* was the term for a person who shows other people the path to take and guides them to safety along the journey.[11]

Over the centuries, the concept and practice of leadership has changed dramatically as the problems and tools available to study it have increased in complexity, number, and sophistication. Despite many decades of research and thousands of studies, a clear understanding of what leadership is and how it can be achieved still escapes us. Many theories address different aspects of leadership but offer little coherence to help us tie them all together.[12] Nonetheless, building a common understanding of what leadership is and looks like helps frame the issue so we can study it.

Expressed simply, Jerry Patterson (1993) defined leadership as "the process of influencing others to achieve mutually agreed upon purposes for the organization."[13] Similarly, James Burns (1978) described leadership as a political process of a leader satisfying the motives of followers to achieve the mutual goals of both the leader and the follow-ers.[14] Focusing on behaviors, James Belasco and Ralph Stayer (1993) defined leadership as "making it possible for others to follow by thinking strategically and focusing on the right directions, removing the obstacles, developing ownership, and taking self-directed actions."[15] Finally, Joseph Rost (1993, p. 99) called it "an influence relation-ship among leaders and their collaborators who intend real changes that reflect their mutual purposes."[16]

These definitions share common factors. Leadership is a process that involves an influ-ence relationship purposefully directed toward meaningful change and that occurs in a cer-tain context. Let's look at these aspects more closely.

First, leadership is a change process. Effective leaders constantly foster change through focused interaction and problem solving, mobilizing people, providing the appropriate direction, and removing obstacles to cooperatively tackle difficult problems. "A leader is most effective when he/she figures out *how* to achieve *what* needs to be done."[17] To lead is to understand the dynamics of the change process.

Second, leadership is a social process. Leadership involves relationships. Leaders must be consummate relationship builders with diverse people and groups. Since leadership is an influence relationship, both followers and leaders can be leading, depending on the situation. Ideally, leadership is also noncoercive, using persuasion and other "soft" influences rather than hard-edged authority or power. Leadership in this context turns followers into collaborators.

Third, leadership is purposeful. It intends meaningful change in a particular environment. Leaders direct the collection and use of data to identify goals, assess organizational effective-ness, and promote organizational learning. The desired changes are deliberately identified. Ideally, the resulting change is substantive and transforming, and results in continuous and sustainable improvement.

Fourth, leaders and followers share mutual purpose. Their shared goals become a common enterprise because they are developed together through their influence rela-tionship. All people involved support the organization's goals because they share these values and desired ends. They support the leaders, helping them attain these outcomes. One of the leader's jobs is to create the milieu, motivate people, and educate them to identify and solve problems so they eventually will become responsible for their own performances. By developing a sense of commitment, or ownership among the organi-zation's members to achieve better performance, leaders can stimulate self-directed action.

Taken together, these four leadership components produce a dynamic greater than the sum of its parts. Leadership today requires a greater range of emotional, social, and intellectual skills than ever before. It means providing resources and developing people. Leadership is also continuous learning. The rapid pace of change drives the need for ongoing education.

Given the state of national and world events, it is reasonable to wonder if our lead-ers are really up to the job. And how do we best prepare future leaders for success in a world that is rapidly changing—economically, demographically, technologically, and globally?

ACTIVITY 1.2   Seeing Oakdale High School Through the Leadership Definition

Much of leadership's effectiveness is learning to ask and answer the right questions. If leadership means facilitating meaningful change through influencing relationships based on purposeful actions around mutually acceptable goals, the school leader might ask:

1. What are the "big picture" issues affecting Oakdale High School and the community (including success for all children, student and family assets, democracy, citizenship, teamwork skills and future occupations, and living in a diverse and global environment)?
2. Do these Oakdale High School data identify areas of concern and opportunity? What concerns or issues might they identify? What assets and opportunities?
3. Who else might be involved in identifying the issues and solutions affecting Oakdale High School? What groups inside and outside the school are affected by these data?
4. Who are the particular individuals from these interest groups who might be invited to work on these issues with school leaders and teachers? By what criteria do we decide this?
5. How do those involved decide how to focus their attentions and efforts? Which information should be studied first, which next, and which last? By what criteria do we make these choices?
6. If the school practices that used to work well are no longer working well, how might the issue of altering these practices affect teachers, parents, students, and the community?
7. How can the principal help the teachers, parents, students, and community members define a common purpose and direction?

Leadership vs. Management

Sometimes the terms *leadership* and *management* are used to mean different things. At other times they are used interchangeably. Let's briefly consider how they differ and where they overlap.

Generally, leadership involves articulating an organizational vision, introducing major organizational change, providing inspiration, and dealing with highly stressful and troublesome aspects of organizations' external environments. Management involves implementing the leader's vision and changes, and maintaining and administrating organizational infrastructures.[18]

Leaders create new approaches and imagine new areas to explore. Managers maintain the balance of operations.[19] Or, as Bennis and Nanus concluded, "Managers do things right. Leaders do the right things."[20] This distinction works in theory, at least.

In schools, the leadership/management separation is not clear cut. In day-to-day practice, managers can be leaders and leaders can be managers. Managers become leaders by providing vision, direction, strategy, and inspiration to their organizational units, and behaving in a manner that reinforces the vision and its inherent values. Conversely, school leaders often must perform many management functions.[21] Yukl (1994) clarified the issue by noting that leadership and management involve separate processes, but need not involve separate people.[22]

Therefore, depending on their particular task, principals alternately may be leaders of school improvement or managers of building operations. Likewise, teachers may be leaders of classroom instruction and school improvement or managers of student grades and school climate.

> **ACTIVITY 1.3   Identifying and Assigning Leadership and Management Roles at Oakdale High School**
>
> Generally speaking, leaders create new approaches and imagine new areas to explore. Managers maintain the balance of operations. Although leadership and management involve separate processes, they need not involve separate people:
>
> 1. As the principal reviews Oakdale data and anticipates school improvement planning, what leadership roles and what management roles does the principal enact?
> 2. Which *leadership* tasks might the principal assign to interested teachers, assistant principals, parents, students, or community members as they review and address these data, identify concerns, and develop strategies for action?
> 3. Which *management* tasks might the principal assign to interested teachers, assistant principals, parents, students, or community members as they review and address these data, identify concerns, and develop strategies for action?

UNDERSTANDING LEADERSHIP: A BRIEF HISTORY

At its core, leadership is about survival. As environments grow more complex, surviving becomes more complicated. Once, the ability to swing a heavy club to beat off would-be attackers and kill animals for food was sufficient. Over the generations, however, leaders have needed to master increasingly more specialized and subtle intellectual and interpersonal "combat" skills. Given its importance to a community's continued existence, leadership understandably has been a topic of considerable attention.

Leadership Models in Prehistory

Leadership reaches back to the time before recorded history, to humans' first families and tribal groups. From the beginning, survival was touch and go. For hunter-gatherer tribes to stay alive, group members needed constant protection from hazardous weather, wild animals, and violent neighbors. Ferociously democratic, these tribes chose their leaders by the individuals' superior hunting ability and a broader moral perspective.[23] In the heat of the moment, those with the raw instincts to respond quickly and appropriately to danger and with the brute physical strength and agility to fight enemies and kill animals for food became natural leaders. In calmer hours, those who could organize others to find shelter and food, protect the group from hostile outsiders and wild beasts, or help group members make sense of their seemingly random world became natural leaders.

Fearful members wisely selected tribal chiefs for their size, strength, agility, competence, and ability to make decisions that advanced the group's well-being. Within families, leadership depended on effective parenting—teaching children the rudimentary language, tasks, and social skills to maintain themselves and their clan. In all instances, leaders needed the relevant expertise to gain legitimacy and respect from the group.

Over the millennia, civilization grew and survival became less moment to moment. Brute force as a leadership characteristic made way for other necessary qualities, such as intelligence, integrity, and self-discipline. Discussions of leadership appear universally among all people, regardless of culture.[24]

Leadership Models in Early Western History

Early civilizations based their understanding of leadership in a fascination with the persona of kings and conquerors that can be traced back to biblical times. Discussions of leadership appear in the works of early Greeks and Romans, including Plato, Caesar, and Plutarch. Until the Renaissance's Age of Enlightenment, people thought that "the anointed one" in charge was actually ordained by God. Accordingly, Thomas Aquinas (1225–1274), a Roman Catholic theologian and philosopher, believed that unquestioning obedience to those in authority was a moral obligation because God had given the rulers power.

As the birthplace of democracy, ancient Greece gave origin to modern administrative thinking. Plato (427–347 BCE), a classical Greek philosopher, was the first on record to present a systematic political and administrative leadership model.[25] He believed that possession of superior intelligence, not superior physical force, qualified certain individuals for wielding political power, and the state's interests must take priority over the individual's interests.[26] Democracy, rule by the masses, invited change that Plato thought would interfere with the society's structure and would threaten the continuity of justice. As an option, Plato promoted the transcendental abilities of the philosopher-king, who was believed to possess magical skills and superhuman wisdom. Modern leadership theory, even the theory of democratic leadership, is still trying to argue for Plato's philosopher-king.[27]

Renaissance politician and writer Niccolo Machiavelli (1469–1527) was the "ultimate pragmatist" about leadership.[28] Profoundly pessimistic about human nature, Machiavelli wrote insightfully about the hardheaded realities of effectively using power to become great leaders. In *The Prince* (1513), he argued that the social benefits of stability and security can be achieved despite a leader's moral corruption. In political leadership, the ends justify the means. Shocked, the early 16th-century church condemned Machiavelli because he removed leadership from God's realm and placed it with humans. Machiavelli's boldness was to suggest that common people could become princes by virtue of their abilities and the skillful application of specific principles: Successful leaders could be made, not born or anointed.

Leadership Models in Later Western Civilization

To this day, conventional Western leadership theory centers about an image of a powerful, usually male-like leader who sits atop a hierarchical structure and controls all outcomes that stem from that arrangement. The leader's power is based in knowledge, control, and the ability to win (at war and politics). The leader imposes his or her will through the direct or indirect threat of violence. In the industrial world, violence is often economic, relating to the acquisition—or loss—of market share and financial and material assets.[29]

Also since Machiavelli's time, leadership theorists have incorporated dimensions of context and "followers." But for the most part, they have sought to explain leadership as the relationship between the persona (abilities, traits, characteristics, and actions) of the "man in charge" and the outcomes of the social milieu within which he appears to operate (his governance).[30] This presumed cause–effect relationship between the person and the social environment is the source of conventional knowledge about leadership.

Leadership Models in the 19th Century

Our traditional leadership paradigms evolved in the mid- to late-19th century and stressed the leader's responsibility for the organization's results. Reflecting their era, these leadership systems were designed to control relatively uneducated, mostly untrustworthy workers in a very slowly changing environment.[31]

In the late 19th century, scholars believed that organizational leadership, administration, and management were essentially one and the same; management was administrative leadership. In this vein, Henri Fayol's *Principles of Administration* (1892), based on his experience running French coal mines, outlined management functions as planning, organizing, commanding, coordinating, and controlling.[32] Max Weber, studying the German army of approximately the same time, reached similar conclusions.[33]

Joseph Rost, a distinguished leadership scholar, determined that the previous mainstream leadership studies did not clearly and consistently define leadership, did not adhere to their own leadership definition if they did define it, and pervasively confused leadership with management/administration. It is logical, therefore, that the 20th century viewed leadership as good, effective management.[34]

Nonetheless, most present organizational methods are based on Fayol's and Weber's models, even though today's circumstances and organizations are very different. With this century-old and Western perspective, traditional leadership models focus on actions that leaders do *to* the organization and its people to *fix* problems, treating the symptoms but not addressing the root causes.

TRADITIONAL THEORIES OF LEADERSHIP

Leadership as a word and leadership as a subject of inquiry and study are distinctly 20th-century phenomena. Although leadership has been around since humans first formed small communities, the systematic study of leadership did not begin until the early 1930s.[35] The resulting contributions have been cumulative, and much is known now about leadership phenomena.

Leadership studies are largely culture bound. In their review of social science leadership studies, Robert House and Ram Aditya (1997) found that the leadership literature is based on a limiting set of assumptions, mostly reflecting Western industrialized culture. Almost all of the prevailing leadership theories and about 98% of the empirical evidence reflect a distinctly American viewpoint. They are individualistic rather than collective, stress follower responsibilities rather than rights, and assume self-interest rather than commitment to duty or altruism. In addition, they emphasize the centrality of work, democratic values, and rationality rather than asceticism, religion, or superstition.[36] As a result, it is important to remember that these models reflect a particular culture's perspective. Other viewpoints about successful leadership exist.

Regardless of the theory used to explain it, leadership has been closely connected to effective functioning of complex organizations throughout the centuries.

The great man model, the leader trait paradigm, and the leader behavior paradigm offer three traditional ways of understanding leadership.

The Great Man Paradigm

According to Rost, "The belief that leadership is about what great men do, articulated a hundred years ago, is still widely pervasive . . . with the exception that we now add women to the doers of leadership."[37] In this notion, leadership is about the individual and what the individual does. Anyone other than the leader is, by default, a follower.

Over the ages, the "great man" concept's popularity is easy to understand. Exceptional individuals come to prominence at certain times. For example, Pharaoh's daughter pulled the baby Moses from the water, and he grew up to lead the Jewish nation out of Egypt to what is now Israel. Similarly, without British Prime Minister Winston Churchill and U.S. General George Patton, the British and Americans might have lost World War II. Lee Iacocca, then chief of Chrysler Motors, allegedly saved the U.S. auto industry in the 1980s with wise decisions and borrowed taxpayers' money. Mother Teresa, the Catholic nun, ministered to the desperately poor, sick, orphaned, and dying in Calcutta, India; for this, she won the Nobel Peace Prize in 1979. These are just a few examples.

Richard Barker (2001), a business professor, believed that the top-down view of industrial-era leadership theories is an adaptation of the hierarchical view of the universe adopted by the early Christian Church. This view presumes that leadership is about the person at the top of the chain of command, this person's exceptional qualities and abilities to manage the hierarchy's structure, and this person's activities in relation to goal achievement. Familiarity with this top-down perspective provided the conceptual basis for researchers as they investigated secular leadership.

During the era of the great man model of leadership, researchers focused on the impressive men and women in the world's history and suggested that a person who copied their personalities and behaviors would become a strong leader.[38] For a full generation, leadership scholars concentrated on identifying the traits associated with outstanding leadership. At first, investigators assumed that all great leaders were exceptionally intelligent, unusually energetic, and far above the norm in their ability to speak persuasively to followers. None of these assumptions, however, stood up to empirical testing. Great leaders were slightly more intelligent than their followers, but not by a large amount. They were more energetic and forceful, but not significantly more. They were better than average public speakers, but not by a substantially large degree. Under close scientific scrutiny, the great man leadership theory disappeared.[39]

In a pivotal study, Bowden (1927) equated leadership with personality.[40] Other theorists attempted to explain leadership based on inheritance.[41] That process was frustrated, however, when it became clear that many effective leaders had widely differing personalities. For instance, from 1930 to 1950, commanding, world-changing leaders such as Adolf Hitler, Winston Churchill, Franklin Roosevelt, and Mohandas Gandhi appeared to have extremely different personalities and perspectives.[42] Furthermore, personalities are extremely difficult to imitate, offering little value to practicing managers wishing to become leaders.

The great man leadership model served a useful political function: providing a visible rallying point when things were going well and offering someone to blame when they weren't. But individual heroics do not solve intractable problems or help us face up to acute contemporary issues.

The Leadership Trait Paradigm

Centuries ago, the Greek philosopher Aristotle believed that from the hour of birth, some individuals are marked for leadership and others for followership. He assumed that individuals are born with the characteristics that would make them leaders. The idea that certain individuals inherited key leadership attributes produced the **trait theory of leadership.**

Mid-20th-Century Leadership Trait Research.   Bernard Bass (1990) observed that in the early 20th century, leaders were generally regarded as superior individuals whose fortunate inheritance or social situation gave them the qualities and abilities that separated them from people in general.[43] Systematic leadership research first focused on the search for individual characteristics that universally differentiated leaders from nonleaders. This research was largely atheoretical. Researchers investigated a large number of personal characteristics, including gender, height, physical energy, and appearance as well as psychological traits and motives such as authoritarianism, intelligence, need for achievement, and need for power. The dominant part of this literature was published between 1930 and 1950.

In influential reviews of the trait literature, Gibb (1947),[44] Jenkins (1947),[45] and Stogdill (1948)[46] identified several studies in which traits were associated with measures of leader effectiveness, with correlations as high as .50. Ralph M. Stogdill reviewed 124 trait studies of leadership completed between 1904 and 1947 and classified the personal factors associated with leadership into the following five general categories:[47]

Capacity—intelligence, alertness, verbal facility, originality, judgment
Achievement—scholarship, knowledge, athletic accomplishments
Responsibility—dependability, initiative, persistence, aggressiveness, self-confidence, desire to excel
Participation—activity, sociability, cooperation, adaptability, humor
Status—socioeconomic position, popularity

Unfortunately, multiple studies could seldom repeat these findings. To scholars of the time, it appeared that effective leaders shared few, if any, universal traits. Consequently, leadership scholars developed a near consensus that the search for universal traits was futile.[48] Rethinking his approach, Stogdill did not call for a stop to the traits study. Instead, he suggested an interactional approach in which traits would be considered as interacting with situational demands facing leaders.[49] As a result, he added a sixth factor to his list of leadership traits:

Situational—followers' characteristics, goals to be achieved, context variables

R.D. Mann's (1959) later work drew similar conclusions.[50] Substantial progress in developing a personality theory and operationalizing traits has been made since the early 1980s. As a result, trait theory has reemerged with a modest amount of empirical evidence supporting it.

Limitations of Early Trait Research.   The early trait research had many weaknesses. Little empirically supported personality theory was available to guide the research. With a variety of definitions for leadership, few studies replicated the same traits. As a result, research methodology was inadequate and investigators operationalized leadership differently. Measurement instruments had little validity. Situational conditions were not considered. Finally, the trait studies were based on adolescents and lower level managers rather than on leaders in significant positions with overall responsibility for the organization.[51]

Recent Leadership Trait Research.   Industrial psychologists interested in improving managerial selection continue to conduct trait research. They focus the trait studies on the relationship between leader traits and leader effectiveness, rather than on the comparison between leaders and nonleaders. In addition, more recent trait studies use a wider range of improved measurement procedures, including projective tests and assessment centers.

Critics of trait theory argue that traits must be stable and predict behavior over substantial periods of time and across widely varying situations.[52] Schneider (1983) noted that traits are predictive of an individual's characteristic behavior in select situations rather than across all situations.[53] Similarly, House, Shane, and Herold (1996) concluded that individual dispositions may be stable over extended periods of time, but not necessarily for life.[54] Thus, traits can predict behavior in the short term and such behavior often has long-term consequences, even for somewhat unstable traits.

In response to such concerns, the second generation of leader trait studies has produced a more consistent set of findings. In 1970, after reviewing 163 new trait studies, Stogdill construed that a leader is characterized by the following traits:[55]

A strong drive for responsibility and task completion
Vigor and persistence in pursuit of goals
Venturousness and originality in problem solving
Drive to exercise initiative in social situations
Self-confidence and sense of personal identity
Willingness to accept consequences of decision and action
Readiness to absorb interpersonal stress
Willingness to tolerate frustration and delay
Ability to influence other persons' behavior
Capacity to structure interaction systems for the purpose at hand

In the same vein, Immegart (1988) proposed that the traits of intelligence, dominance, self-confidence, and high energy or activity level are commonly associated with leaders.[56]

In sum, the evidence supports the conclusion that possessing certain traits increases the likelihood that a leader will be effective.[57] This does not mean that leaders are "born, not made." It is more reasonable and accurate to believe that leadership involves influences from both personal traits and situations.

To better understand the traits associated with effective leadership, consider the findings in three trait categories: personality, motivation, and skills. Table 1–2 collects and compares these dimensions.

TABLE 1–2

Traits and Skills Associated with Effective Leadership

Personality	Motivation	Skills
Self-confidence	Task and interpersonal needs	Technical
Stress tolerance	Achievement orientation	Interpersonal
Emotional maturity	Power needs	Conceptual
Integrity	High expectations	
Extroversion	Self-efficacy	

Source: Hoy, W. K., & Miskel, C. G. (2008). *Educational administration. Theory, research, and practice* (8th ed., p. 424, Table 12–1). Boston, MA: McGraw-Hill Higher Education. Reprinted by permission of The McGraw-Hill Companies, Inc.

Personality Traits.   Gary Yukl (2002) has defined *personality traits* as relatively stable dispositions that behave in a particular way. Although the list of relevant leadership personality traits is long, five are especially important:[58]

- ◆ *Self-confidence.* Self-confident leaders are more likely to set high goals for themselves and their followers, to attempt difficult tasks, and to persist despite obstacles and setbacks.
- ◆ *Stress tolerance.* Stress-tolerant leaders are likely to make good decisions, to remain calm, and to provide decisive direction to subordinates in difficult situations. Only stress-tolerant individuals can successfully handle the intense and rapid pace, long hours, multitasking, and demands for decisions under pressure.
- ◆ *Emotional maturity.* Emotionally mature leaders tend to have an accurate awareness of their strengths and weaknesses and to be oriented toward self-improvement. They do not minimize or deny their shortcomings or daydream about success. As a result, emotionally mature administrators can develop and keep cooperative relationships with subordinates, peers, and supervisors.
- ◆ *Integrity.* Integrity means that the leaders' behaviors are consistent with their stated values. They are honest and ethical, responsible, and trustworthy. Integrity is an essential component in building and retaining loyalty and gaining others' support and cooperation.
- ◆ *Extroversion.* Extroversion, or being outgoing, sociable, uninhibited, and comfortable in groups, is related to the likelihood that an individual will emerge as a group leader.

Possessing these five traits does not make an individual a leader, however. If a person has the desire, skills, and opportunities to become a leader, these personality characteristics contribute to effectiveness.

Motivational Traits.   Motivation factors play key roles in explaining both the chosen action and its degree of success. Generally, highly motivated leaders are likely to be more effective than individuals with low expectations, modest goals, and a limited sense of their own personal competence. Findings from Fiedler (1967),[59] McClelland (1985),[60]

Yukl (2002),[61] and Bass and Riggio (2006)[62] confirmed that leaders become more effective when they have the following five motivational traits:

- *Task and interpersonal needs.* Effective leaders are characterized by their drive for the task and their concern for people.
- *Power needs.* Effective leaders are motivated to seek positions of authority and to exercise influence over people.
- *Achievement orientation.* Effective leaders have an achievement orientation that makes them want to achieve, a desire to excel, a drive to succeed, a willingness to assume responsibility, and a concern to complete the task.
- *High expectations.* School administrators with high expectations for success have a belief that they can do the job and will receive valued outcomes for their efforts.
- *Self-efficacy.* Effective leaders have a high sense of self-efficacy, the belief in one's ability to organize and complete a course of action.

As we can see, self-confidence, stress tolerance, emotional maturity, integrity, and extroversion are personality traits associated with leadership effectiveness.

In addition to these motivational traits, the physical characteristics of energy and activity levels allow individuals to demonstrate competence through their active engagement with others. Knowing these factors helps individuals and organizations. Individuals can assess their own strengths and weaknesses and then find opportunities to develop their leadership abilities. School organizations can identify individuals with particular traits and skills who will fit within and help lead their organizations.

Skills.   Effective leaders also need certain skills to accomplish the job. To compile a comprehensive list of all the abilities leaders need to solve problems in a variety of situations and advance their organization's interests would probably be exhausting, and the list would probably be incomplete. An array of schemata classify the range of problem-solving skills, social judgment skills, and knowledge that make effective leadership possible.[63] In addition, Yukl (2002)[64] and Peter Northouse (2004)[65] have described three especially important skill categories associated with leader effectiveness: technical, interpersonal, and conceptual. These findings support the view that intellectual or general cognitive ability is perhaps the individual characteristic most often and most consistently associated with leadership.

- *Technical skills.* Technical skills mean having the specialized knowledge about and being competent at a specific type of work activity, procedure, or technique to accomplish the task. Educational leaders, for example, must be familiar with supervising and coordinating improvements in teaching and learning, evaluating personnel, interpreting school data (e.g., rules and regulations, enrollment and staffing levels, programs, and student demographics), managing budgets, implementing standards-based accountability, disaggregating and interpreting achievement test results, and maintaining a positive and orderly school climate.
- *Interpersonal skills.* These are people skills. They include an understanding of others' feelings and attitudes and knowing how to work with people in individual and cooperative work relationships. Effective leaders consistently and naturally display social and human skills. Examples of interpersonal skills include communicating clearly in written and oral presentations; expressing sociability and the ability to get along with all types of people, and showing empathy, consideration, and tact in working with others.

◆ *Conceptual or cognitive skills.* Conceptual or cognitive skills involve the abilities to form and work with abstract ideas, to think logically, and to reason analytically, deductively, and inductively. Conceptual skills help leaders develop and use ideas to analyze, organize, and solve complex, novel, and ill-defined problems; to generate creative alternatives; and to recognize emerging trends, opportunities, and problems. Specific conceptual skills include formulating and communicating a vision for the educational organization, understanding and effectively managing the change process, and predicting how societal trends will affect the school.

Underlying the skills approach is the premise that organizational leadership is a form of skilled performance. At its most basic level, leadership ultimately depends on one's capability to effectively formulate and implement solutions to complex, ill-defined social and technical problems.[66] The effectiveness of leaders' behaviors depends on the leader having the expertise necessary to select and enact the needed behaviors in ways that are consistent with the organizational situation.

ACTIVITY 1.4   Assessing Your Leadership Traits

Leadership trait theory posits that certain personality traits contribute to successful leadership. These traits can be classified as personality traits, motivational traits, and skills.

On a scale of 1–10 (10 highest), rate yourself as a leader as you reflect on your experiences in the past and in your present environment. Next, rate yourself as a leader as if you were suddenly named principal of Oakdale High School and told to improve the school, given the data presented earlier in the chapter.

Traits	Self-Assessment as Leader Today	Self-Assessment as if New Principal of Oakdale High School
	1 ——— 5 ——— 10	1 ——— 5 ——— 10
Personality		
Self-confidence		
Stress tolerance		
Emotional maturity		
Integrity		
Extroversion		
	1 ——— 5 ——— 10	1 ——— 5 ——— 10
Motivational		
Drive for the task		
Concern for people		
Achievement orientation		
High expectations		
Self-efficacy		
	1 ——— 5 ——— 10	1 ——— 5 ——— 10
Skills		
Technical		
Interpersonal		
Conceptual/cognitive		

Discuss:

1. According to this activity, which leadership traits are actively engaged in your present life?
2. How have your prior experiences made a difference in your leadership skills?
3. How has having a mentor—or not having a mentor—influenced your leadership skills?
4. According to this activity, which of your traits deserve additional attention and development?
5. Considering the case study in this chapter, how would you describe the differences between your present leadership traits and those needed to be a high school principal? Which areas—personality, motivation, or skills—need development to be effective in that role?
6. What additional career and educational experiences do you need to develop the leadership skills essential to lead a school?
7. How can a leader use the personalities, motivations, and skills of others in the environment to successfully identify and address areas of mutual concern?
8. How might effective leadership traits operate in a school setting?
9. How do relationships, context, and the change process influence the importance of leaders' traits?

Effective leadership requires all three skill sets. In schools, their relative priority depends on the administrative level in which the leader works.[67] Technical skills are especially important for leaders (administrators) at lower hierarchical levels, such as assistant principals or curriculum coordinators. With the assistant principal's initiative and supervisors' active support and encouragement, lower level administrators can develop and refine higher degrees of interpersonal and conceptual skills necessary for organizational leadership and professional advancement. Principals need high degrees of expertise in interpersonal and conceptual skills. Superintendents and other top-level administrators also need strong conceptual and interpersonal skills as they deal with more novel problems, face a wide range of complex and ambiguous activities, and interact with more diverse groups.

Visualizing Leadership in Context.   Leadership may be easier to understand when viewed graphically. Figure 1–1 illustrates Michael Mumford and colleagues' (2000) view of effective leadership as skills based and operating in a context influenced by the leader's career experiences and relevant environmental influences. This model holds that knowledge and skills represent the most direct determinants of a leader's performance. These are more subtly influenced, in turn, by different environmental factors: the leader's own career experiences and the work, social, and cultural environment in which the leader operates. "Put simply, even the most skilled leader may fail if subordinates are completely incapable of implementing a proposed solution."[68]

Limitations of the Trait Paradigm.   Trait theories are often criticized as inadequate means for understanding leadership.[69] At the same time, leadership scholars are generating hundred of traits. In one literature survey, Fleishman and colleagues (1991) listed 499 traits or dimensions of leader behavior from 65 different systems.[70] Even if effective leaders tend to display certain characteristics, the trait approach is an inefficient way to study leadership.

According to Barker (2001), "Just as geocentric theory was based in the understandable but incorrect perception of the sun and stars circling the earth, leadership theory has been

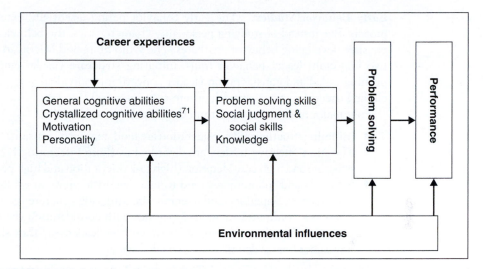

FIGURE 1–1

Influence of Leadership Skills in Leadership Performance (Source: Reprinted from *Leadership Quarterly, 11*(1), Mumford, M. D., Zaccaro, S. J., Harding, F. D., Jacobs, T. O., & Fleishman, E. A., "Leadership skills for a changing world: Solving complex social problems," page 23, figure 2, Copyright © 2000, with permission from Elsevier.)

based in the understandable but incorrect perception of a direct cause–effect relationship between the leader's abilities, traits, actions and leadership outcomes."[72]

Van Seter and Field (1990) concluded that the trait paradigm advanced leadership theory only slightly. Despite the many valid findings connecting individual traits to leadership effectiveness, this approach to understanding leadership has minimal value because most traits cannot be learned. Consequently, both the great man and trait theory perspectives prove too simplistic except as explanatory variables. Instead, the main focus of future leadership theories would be on the leaders' interactions with the people and the situation—their behaviors.[73]

The Leadership Behavior Paradigm

Viewing leadership as behavior emphasizes what leaders *do* as opposed to their traits or sources of power. The behavior paradigm defines leadership as a subset of human performance. Early ideas about leadership typically focus on two types of leader actions. One aspect is concerned with people, interpersonal relations, and group maintenance. The other aspect focuses on production, task completion, and goal achievement.[74]

Focusing on behavior offers a major advance in leadership theory. It enjoys strong research support.[75] It also can easily be adopted by practitioners to improve their leadership effectiveness.[76] Some of the work studying leadership behavior focuses on typical leadership behavior patterns whereas other work analyzes the behavioral differences between ineffective and effective leaders.[77]

Early Behavior Studies.   The early behavior period essentially extends the trait approach. But instead of studying personality characteristics, the behavioral approach emphasizes developing behavior attributes. The Ohio State and Michigan studies identified two important leader behavior traits: **initiating structure** (leader emphasis on accomplishing tasks) and **consideration** (leader concern for individual and group cohesion, including friendship, trust, warmth, interest, and respect).[78]

Four major findings emerged from the Ohio State studies:[79]

♦ Initiating structure and consideration are fundamental dimensions of leader behavior.
♦ The most effective leaders are described as those integrating both high initiating structure and high consideration (high task orientation and high people orientation).
♦ Superiors and subordinates tend to take oppositie views in evaluating the leader's effectiveness. Superiors tend to emphasize initiating structure (getting the job done) whereas subordinates are more concerned with consideration (being treated well).
♦ Only a slight relationship exists between how leaders say they should behave and how subordinates describe that they do behave.

Many scholars have supported these findings.[80] As one would imagine, consideration is typically related to subordinate satisfaction with work and the leader. Consideration has its most positive effect on subordinates' satisfaction when they work in structured situations or when they work on stressful, frustrating, or dissatisfying tasks. In contrast, initiating structure has the greatest impact on group performance when subordinates' tasks are not well defined. Employees want to know what the leader expects them to do, and providing clear directions and expectations helps them perform more effectively. Although the evidence is mixed, initiating structure (clearly defining the task) has been identified as a source of subordinate performance. Situational variables, however, appear to affect the relationship between focusing on the people (consideration) and focusing on the task (initiating structure). They also affect the criteria of organizational effectiveness. Table 1–3 illustrates these relationships.

TABLE 1–3
Leader Behaviors with Most Positive Effect on Worker Performance

Initiating Consideration (People Focus)	Initiating Structure (Task Focus)
Workers are most satisfied if leaders initiate consideration when the:	Workers are most satisfied if leaders initiate structure when the:
♦ Work is structured.	♦ Work is poorly defined.
♦ Work is stressful, frustrating, or disliked.	♦ Expectations for performance are unclear.

Source: Owings & Kaplan.

The meaning for leaders is clear. Leaders must initiate both structure and consideration. Attending to the task without attending to the people doing the task brings poor outcomes. When leaders integrate strength on both dimensions, initiating structure and consideration, they obtain the best results and the most satisfied employees. The relative emphasis will depend on the situation. Matching the appropriate leadership style to the appropriate situation in order to reach the maximum effectiveness is a complex challenge.

Many listings of leadership behaviors are available.[81] Yukl, Gordon, and Taber and colleagues (2002) integrated the many typologies developed over the preceding 50 years into a three-category framework of leader behaviors, as shown in Table 1–4.[82] Their result is a

TABLE 1–4

Integrated Leadership Behavior Framework

Leadership Behaviors	Descriptors	Focus
Task-Oriented Behaviors	Planning short-term activities	Accomplishing tasks
	Clarifying task objectives and role expectations	Using personnel and resources efficiently
	Monitoring operations and performance	Maintaining stable and reliable processes
		Making gradual improvements
Relations-Oriented Behaviors	Providing support and encouragement	Improving relationships
	Providing recognition for achievement and contributions	Helping people
	Developing member skill and confidence	Increasing cooperation and teamwork
	Consulting with members when making decisions	Building commitment to the organization
	Empowering members to take initiative in problem solving	
Change-Oriented Behaviors	Monitoring the external environment for threats and opportunities	Adapting to change in the environment
	Proposing an innovative strategy or new vision	Making major changes in goals, policies, procedures, and programs
	Encouraging innovative thinking	Gaining commitment to changes
	Taking risks to promote necessary changes	

Source: Adapted from Yukl, G., Gordon, A., & Taber, T., "A hierarchical taxonomy of leadership behavior: Integrating a half century of behavior research," *Journal of Leadership and Organizational Studies, 9*(1), pp. 15–32, copyright © 2002. Reprinted by Permission of SAGE Publications.

more comprehensive theory of effective leadership. Task-oriented and relations-oriented behaviors are similar to initiating structure and consideration, respectively, but they are defined more broadly.

Typically, leaders engage in all three types of behaviors. The external environment, however, plays an important role in determining the appropriate balance for leader effectiveness. For instance, in stable environments, task-oriented behaviors are used more often than change-oriented behaviors. If a school's programs are appropriate to its established community, the leader will emphasize task-oriented behaviors such as increasing efficiency and keeping the organization operating smoothly.

In uncertain, changing environments (such as we see in Oakdale High School), change-oriented behaviors are likely to be more effective. Meanwhile, relations-oriented behaviors are easier to enact in stable environments because the people involved know each other; their interpersonal connections are practiced and familiar. Increasing relations-oriented behaviors in unstable environments may be more challenging, but perhaps even more essential as leaders create a community for change. The bottom line: Appropriately applying and balancing different types of behavior for different situations is basic to enhancing leader performance.

Yukl and colleagues (2002) cautioned not to interpret the results of early behavior studies as universal theories of effective leader behavior.[83] The same leadership behavior style is not likely to work well in all situations. If leaders are to be effective, behaviors must be relevant to the situation at hand. Situational factors will have an impact on the effectiveness of the leader's behaviors even when the individual rates high on both people and task dimensions. In later years, scholars would advance these behavioral studies by specifically adapting them for management applications. Chapter 4 will discuss these more contemporary behavior models.

ACTIVITY 1.5   Attending to People and Task Dimensions at Oakdale High School

Oakdale High School is experiencing significant demographic and achievement changes. It appears to be a relatively uncertain—rather than stable—environment.

1. Which behaviors would the principal use to address Oakdale High School's concerns?
2. In this situation, which behaviors merit the most attention?
3. Using Table 1–4, provide examples of how a principal might use task-oriented, relations-oriented, and change-oriented behaviors to successfully address the school's challenges—inside the school and with the larger community.

Leadership and Power Theory Paradigm

Legitimate authorities create and control organizations. They set goals, design structures, hire and manage employees, and monitor activities to ensure behavior is consistent with the organization's goals and objectives. These authorities control the legitimate power of the offices or positions they occupy, but they are not the only sources of power in organizations.

The concepts of *influence*, *power*, and *control* are frequently used interchangeably. The classic definition of power is the ability to get others to do what you want them to do.[84] Power can also be defined as any force that results in behavior that would not have occurred if the force had not been present.[85] Power may be clearly coercive (based on fear of death, maiming, starvation, imprisonment, or other significant personal injury or loss) or based on nonthreatening persuasion and suggestion.

Power is closely related to dependence. To the extent that a person depends on another, he or she is potentially subject to that individual's power. Within organizations, one makes others dependent upon him or her by controlling access to information, persons, and instrumentalities. *Information* includes knowledge of the organization, knowledge about persons, and knowledge of the norms, procedures, and techniques. *Persons* include anyone within or outside the organization upon whom the organization in some way depends. *Instrumentalities* include any aspect of the organization's physical plant or resources (such as equipment, machines, time, and money). Power is a function not only of the extent to which a person controls information, persons, and instrumentalities, but also of the importance of the various attributes he or she controls.[86]

Authority, on the other hand, has a narrower scope than power. Authority is defined as "the probability that certain specific commands (or all commands) from a given source will be obeyed by a given group of persons."[87] Authority does not include exercising power or influence over other persons. People tend to voluntarily comply with legitimate commands from one with organizational standing to issue them.

It is important to understand how to use power and authority effectively so leaders can motivate—rather than demotivate—their employees. How leaders use one type of power can limit or enhance the effectiveness of the other kinds.

Sources of Power in Schools.   Leaders have power because they can get others to comply with their directives or suggestions. Most administrators have power because they represent the organization.

John French and Bertram Raven (1986) described several forms of power: legitimate power, coercive power, reward power, referent power, information power, and expert

TABLE 1–5
Forms of Position Power and Personal Power

Authority (Position Power)	Personal Power
◆ Legitimate power	◆ Psychological reward power
◆ Coercive power	◆ Referent power
◆ Material/financial reward power	◆ Expert power

Source: Reproduced by permission of SAGE Publications, London, Los Angeles, New Delhi and Singapore, from *Theory and practice of leadership* by Roger Gill. Copyright © 2006 by Roger Gill. www.sagepub.co.uk., Copyright Corwin Press, 2006, p. 246.

power.[88] The effectiveness of these forms of power depends on followers' perceptions of their leaders.

In true leaders, power does not so much depend on their authority or right to make things happen as on their *personal power* regardless of their positions, status, or rank. Ultimately, effective leadership depends on personal power—the ability to win others' hearts and minds. Table 1–5 shows how these forms of power might be organized.

Authority can generate legitimate, coercive, or reward power.

Legitimate power.   *Legitimate power* is based on people's perceptions of the administrator's or leader's right or authority to make them do something because of his or her role or position in the organization.

The organization empowers administrators to issue directives, orders, commands, and instructions, and employees are obligated to comply. Employees may respond to their administrators' requests by their commitment or simple compliance, resistance, or alienation depending on the nature and manner of the request.[89] Employees' resistance and alienation are less likely if the leaders make the request politely, clearly explain the reasons for the request, respond to subordinates' concerns, and routinely use legitimate authority.[90]

Legitimate power has nothing to do with personal relationships. Isaac, Zerbe, and Pitt (2001) observed that managers use legitimate power to *push* employees toward desired goals whereas leaders use their influence to *pull* followers toward goals.[91]

For instance, the Oakdale High School principal needs to form a school improvement team (SIT). To recruit teachers to work on this assignment, the principal might tell teachers that they are required to spend 4 hours each month after school on "school business" and that working on the SIT committees is their assigned business. On the other hand, the principal can tell teachers that they have the unique and valued opportunity to help make their school a more satisfying and successful environment for students and teachers. Working on the SIT brings occasions to develop leadership and teamwork skills; to learn more about how their school and students are functioning; to learn best practices for instruction, curriculum, and school climate; to meet colleagues with interests and values similar to theirs; and to make a positive difference in their own and their students' lives. In the first approach, the principal uses the position's legitimate (managerial) authority to require (push) teachers into the task. In the second approach, the principal uses influence (leadership) to make the SIT task more attractive to participants to pull (motivate) them toward this now-appealing assignment.

Coercive power.   Associated with position or authority, *coercive power* is based on the perceived ability of a leader or administrator to bring about undesirable or unpleasant consequences for those who do not comply with expectations, instructions, or directives.

For example, school leaders' coercive power might include the ability to withhold pay raises, bonuses, promotions, or privileges, or to give undesirable tasks or responsibilities. They may include assigning reprimands or disciplinary action, including dismissal. Coercive power might also mean threat or infliction of physical punishment, including pain and death. The least effective leaders use coercive power. Its impact is temporary, and it creates negative attitudes and feelings. Adolf Hitler, Joseph Stalin, and Saddam Hussein are examples of individuals who ruled by using coercive power.

Using coercive power, the Oakdale High School principal might say "no" to teachers' requests for time off, professional leave, or other desired requests or privileges if they do not say "yes" to his or her committee assignments. In addition, teachers refusing to accept the principal's suggestion may find themselves with new student supervisory responsibilities during times when they were expecting to have an extra planning period.

Punishment may have unintended negative effects, however. A teacher who receives an official reprimand for consistently leaving school early may start to take frequent absences, refuse to provide students with extra help unless specified in the contract, and show a tendency to avoid all but essential job requirements. Ironically, the same situation can be viewed as having reward or coercive power. If a teacher obeys a principal through fear of punishment, it is coercive power. If a teacher obeys with the expectation of future benefit, it is reward power.

Most school leaders try to avoid using coercive power because it typically undermines the use of referent power and creates hostility, alienation, and aggression among subordinates. Absenteeism, sabotage, theft, job actions, and strikes are common responses to excessive coercion. Coercion is usually considered suitable for discipline issues and is most appropriate to deter behavior harmful to the organization, such as fighting, stealing, rule breaking, sabotage, and direct disobedience to legitimate directives.[92]

Reward power—material/financial.   *Reward power* is the leader's perceived ability to offer a material or financial benefit in return for cooperation or followership.

The school leader can influence subordinates by rewarding their desirable behaviors. Reward power is likely to produce positive feelings and encourage the development of referent power (liking and respecting the administrator). Employee compliance is most likely when the request is feasible, the incentive is attractive, the administrator is a credible source of the reward, the request is proper and ethical, and compliance to the request can be verified. For example, principals who control allocation of teaching and room assignments, grants for innovative teaching practices, and professional development travel funds have reward power for teachers in that school.

Occasionally, using reward power can bring certain negative consequences. Employees may feel resistance and hostility if they perceive reward power as manipulative. Additionally, administrators who frequently use reward power may be perceived as fostering a purely economic relationship, relying on subordinates receiving tangible benefits in exchange for doing their jobs properly. Conversely, rewards given to express an administrator's personal appreciation for a job well done can become a source of increased referent power. The principal's handwritten thank-you note for a job well done can give significant satisfaction to its recipient and generate increased loyalty toward the giver. Those who repeatedly provide incentives in an acceptable manner gradually become better liked by the reward recipients.[93]

Depending on how the school district funds the school, the Oakdale High School principal probably has few discretionary dollars to offer as incentives. Typically, the school district controls salaries, promotions, and stipends. On the other hand, the principal may have some limited monies available for professional development and can offer these to a few obliging teachers. It is more likely that the Oakdale principal will rely on personal power to influence and reward faculty and staff.

Personal power is the ability to affect others' attitudes, beliefs, and behaviors without using force or formal authority.[94] Personal power comes from many sources: psychological reward power, referent power, and expert power.

Psychological reward power.   *Psychological reward power* is personal rather than positional because it does not require any authority to use it. It takes the form of giving praise and recognition for achievement. Psychological reward power requires perceptual and behavioral skills and a willingness to use them effectively. Followers receive a variety of ego boosts that make them feel satisfied, appreciated, respected, and valued.

When the Oakdale High School principal uses a faculty or PTA meeting to publicly recognize the teachers serving on the school improvement team and asks them to stand so parents and faculty can acknowledge and applaud them, the principal is using reward power to express appreciation and respect for their extra work and ideas to improve their school. This public thanks makes the teachers feel that their energies and contributions are valued.

Referent power.   *Referent power* is the power holder's personal charisma or ideas and beliefs that others greatly admire and that influence them to seek opportunities to be associated with the power holder and, to the extent possible, become more like him or her.

Referent power is something followers give to leaders for whom they feel respect, esteem, and belief in what the leaders are trying to do. People identify with leaders who display insight into their needs, values, and aspirations and who respond positively to followers in a timely fashion. Leaders who show courage, take personal risk and responsibility, and develop credibility through integrity, honesty, and competence build referent power.

The school leader with an extraordinary personality and strong "people skills" has the ability to influence behavior because subordinates like and identify with the leader. School leaders improve their referent power when they demonstrate concern, trust, and affection for subordinates. In return, leaders receive employees' admiration, trust, respect, and loyalty. The employees also desire to emulate the leader. These factors develop over a relatively long period in an exchange process. Referent power is most effective if administrators select subordinates who are most likely to identify with them, make frequent use of personal appeals, and lead by example. Teachers and groups may also hold referent power.

When the Oakdale High School principal sits down at the teachers' lunch table in the cafeteria and spends time visiting informally with them, learning about their interests and families, the principal is building referent power among the faculty. When the principal sends handwritten thank-you notes to teachers for contributing extra time and energy to school and student projects and places birthday cards in their school mailboxes, the principal builds referent power. Likewise, when the principal actively participates in parent-teacher conferences and supports teachers' efforts to work effectively with students and parents, the principal builds referent power. All these actions increase the principal's stature among the faculty and staff, strengthening teachers' desire to support the principal's goals for their school.

Expert power.   Knowledge is a source of power. *Expert power* is a form of personal power based on others' perceptions of a leader's competence, special knowledge, or expertise. People are willing to be influenced by those who they perceive as knowledgeable or skillful.

The school leader's specialized knowledge and skills can influence subordinates' behaviors. Subordinates who believe the leader's information and expertise is relevant and helpful tend to view the leader as having more legitimate power. This is a personal characteristic and does not depend on occupying a formal position of power. In fact, expert power may be power's most stable form. One study found that while changes in an organization's reward structure increased the perceived use of coercive power and reduced the administrator's perceived use of reward, legitimate, and referent power, expert power remained stable.[95]

Since it takes time to become expert and known, new principals must show that they can enact their administrative and leadership functions skillfully before subordinates are willing to accept their attempts to implement new practices and procedures. By itself, however, expertise is not enough to guarantee employee commitment. Administrators must convincingly demonstrate their knowledge by maintaining credibility, keeping informed, acting decisively, recognizing subordinate concerns, and avoiding threats to employees' self-esteem.

Being able to disaggregate the student demographic and achievement data gives the principal of Oakdale High School the ability to influence the teachers and community members to conscientiously address the school's needs. Without clear and compelling facts that the data disaggregation present, the principal's vision for change that benefits all students is merely an opinion, easily countered by teachers' and parents' opinions that everything is fine and no reviews of the curriculum, instructional practices, student placement in courses, or school climate are necessary.

ACTIVITY 1.6   Using Personal Power at Oakdale High School

The Oakdale High School principal can use personal power to influence teachers, staff, parents, and students to join in problem solving to benefit the school and those within it.

1. Identify at least three ways that the principal can use psychological reward power to influence teachers, staff, students, and parents to join the school improvement team (SIT) to work on improving school climate and student performance.
2. Identify at least three ways the principal can use referent power to influence teachers, staff, students, and parents to participate in the SIT activities.
3. Identify at least three ways the principal can use expert power to influence teachers, staff, students, and parents to participate in the SIT activities.
4. Which aspects of power can the principal use to engage the parents and larger community in school improvement activities?

Formal leaders do not have a monopoly on power.   Leaders are not the only organization members with power. The most effective way for participants to achieve power is to obtain, maintain, and control access to persons, information, and instrumentalities. To the extent that this can be done, organization members make higher ranking members and formal leaders dependent upon them. For an employee who is not a formal leader, dependence and manipulation of the dependency relationship can be a key to holding power.[96]

If, for instance, the new Oakdale High School principal does not know the faculty members or how to collect and disaggregate test data but the assistant principal knows both, the assistant principal gains power as the principal comes to depend on the assistant for insight into the teachers and to interpret the school achievement data. The principal might rely on the assistant principal to deliver high-visibility presentations about the changing demographics and student achievement to teachers, parents, and community members. While these opportunities raise the assistant principal's profile and career options, they may reduce the principal's stature in the community's eyes. Similarly, if the principal does not understand how to construct the master schedule to correctly allocate teachers, students, space, and time to achieve maximum learning gains—but the school counselor does—the principal may depend on the counselor to make the master schedule work. How the assistant principal and the counselor handle the principal's dependence on them can affect their relationship with the principal and have an impact on school climate, school effectiveness, and their own professional futures. In these examples, access to information and essential skill sets bring subordinates power over their titular boss.

Likewise, access to people and information can give a subordinate power over an organizational superior. If a school superintendent wants to remove a high school principal who takes unauthorized professional leave to play golf with his buddies during the school day, removing the principal from his position will be difficult if the golfing buddies include the school board chairperson. The principal's access to the influential golfing buddy and access to information that the school-day golf outings are acceptable to the superintendent's "boss" give the principal more power over this situation than his nominal superior.

The Leadership and Relationship Paradigm

The traditional belief that "leaders lead and all others follow" views followers as passive, submissive, subordinate, controlled, and directed. With this time-honored perspective, leaders are active; followers are passive. Leaders are intelligent; followers are not very smart. Leaders are productive; followers are unproductive unless directed by a leader. Running parallel to leadership, followership is a separate process. But like two railroad tracks going in the same direction, they never meet. In this paradigm, leadership remains individualistic, with the leader as top dog.[97] And unless you are lead dog, the scenery never changes.

In studying leadership theory's evolution, David Van Seter and Richard Field (1990) found two trends.[98] The first, which we have already discussed, is leader focused. It attempts to explain individual, group, and organizational performance by identifying and examining specific leader traits, behaviors, and power directly related to them. The second perspective is more relationship based. It focuses explicitly on how one-on-one reciprocal social exchanges between leaders and followers evolve, nurture, and sustain the dyadic

FIGURE 1–2
Leadership's Three Domains (Source:
Reprinted from *The Leadership Quarterly, 6,*
No.2, Graen, G. B., & Uhl-Bien, M.,
"Relationship-based approach to leadership:
Development of leader-member exchange
(LMX) theory of leadership over 25 years:
Applying a multi-level multi-domain
perspective," pages 219–247 Copyright
1995, with permission from Elsevier.)

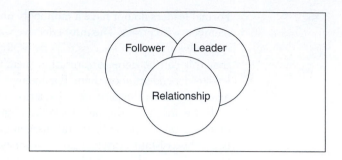

relationship.[99] Understanding leadership as a relationship brings attention to followers and their essential role in leadership effectiveness.

Likewise, George Graen and Mary Uhl-Bien (1995) argued that leadership studies also needed to include followers and the leader-follower dyad if we were to more fully understand the leadership process. Leadership, they proposed, included all three domains, as depicted in Figure 1–2.[100]

As Figure 1–2 indicates, leadership domains include the leader, the follower, and the relationship. One can study leadership from any or all of the domains. In addition, this model is compatible with studies of leadership traits, behavior, power, relationships, and the interactions among and between them. According to this perspective, the quality of the relationship that develops between a leader and a follower is predictive of outcomes at the individual, group, and organizational levels of analysis.[101] After more than 35 years of empirical research and theoretical development, the leader-member dyad continues to provide an operable alternative to the traditional leadership traits and behaviors approaches.[102]

With the relationship perspective, leadership is not about what an individual leader does. Rather, leadership is about what leaders and collaborators do together. Leadership is a band of leaders and collaborators who imagine a better future and go after it. Table 1–6 illustrates a comparison of the traditional and emerging leadership paradigms.

With this emerging perspective, leadership is now considered as:[103]

◆ A relationship rather than an individual
◆ A process entirely distinct from management
◆ A relationship in which people other than managers can be leaders
◆ A focus on the interactions of both leaders and collaborators rather than a focus only on leaders' traits and behaviors
◆ A relationship that aims at mutual purposes rather than the leader's wishes
◆ A relationship in which only influence behaviors are acceptable rather than one in which authority and other forms of coercion are acceptable
◆ An episodic process rather than something that people in organizations do all the time

People need both leadership and management in their organizations and societies to survive and prosper. But Rost argued that people need to keep the two roles conceptually separate so they can know which is which and so both leadership and management can develop in organizations. Building collaborative and noncoercive relationships based on

TABLE 1–6

The Leadership Paradigm Shift: From Individual to Relationship

Traditional Paradigm *Leadership viewed as:*	Emerging Paradigm *Leadership viewed as:*
Individual	Relationship
Good management	Process separate from management, good or bad
Influencing followers	Influencing collaborators, who, in turn, influence leaders
Focusing on leadership traits and behaviors	Focusing on leaders and collaborators interacting in a relationship
Followers do leaders' wishes	Do what both leaders and collaborators wish
Pursuing all organizational goals	Pursuing purposes that intend real, substantive, and transforming change
Using any legitimate behaviors	Using influence behaviors only
Leadership and leaders are the same	Leadership and leaders are NOT the same
Practiced continuously	Practiced episodically

Source: Adapted from Rost, J. C., "Leadership development in the new millennium," *Journal of Leadership and Organizational Studies, 1*(1), p. 100, copyright © 1993. Reprinted by Permission of SAGE Publications; Rost, J. C. (1997). Moving from individual to relationships: A postindustrial paradigm of leadership. *Journal of Leadership and Organizational Studies, 4*(4), 14.

persuasive strategies and the desire to achieve mutually important goals may be a more effective leadership model to successfully meet 21st-century challenges.

If the Oakdale High School principal believes in leadership as a relationship in which teachers and staff can be leaders who collaborate with formal leaders for mutual purposes to address specific needs, then deciding where to begin identifying and solving problems becomes clearer. With this view, the entire task of conducting school improvement does not rest on the principal's shoulders, alone. Responsibility for analyzing the situation and enacting solutions can be shared. Seeing leadership as relationships, the principal can create the environment that motivates teachers, students, parents, and community members to work with the school to meet their own as well as the school's needs. Such collaboration would develop a more successful, equitable, and satisfying school experience for all concerned.

THE PRINCIPAL AS AN INSTRUCTIONAL LEADER

Societal shifts and nationally driven school reform efforts have changed the principal's role. The school restructuring reforms of the 1980s and 1990s identified the principal as a transformational leader who must be involved in school problem finding and problem solving, shared decision making, decentralized leadership, and systemic change.[104] If finding ways to improve *every* student's learning and achievement has become the school's central purpose, then improving teaching and learning has become the principal's central orientation.

Instructional leadership is a particular type of school leadership that emphasizes the improvement of teaching and learning. This leadership strand has two touchstones. One includes the leaders' ability to stay consistently focused on the core technology of schooling: learning, teaching, curriculum, and assessment. The second touchstone is to make all the other dimensions of schooling (e.g., administration, organization, finance) work in the service of a more robust core technology and improved student learning.[105]

Principal as Instructional Leader in Successful Schools

Three decades of research provides ample evidence that principals' effective leadership positively affects school and student outcomes. From early research into school effectiveness[106] which institutionalized the term *instructional leadership* and an early review of school leadership studies,[107] the effective principal appears as an instructional or educational leader who affects school climate and student achievement. Scholars conducting research in effecting change,[108] school improvement,[109] and program improvement[110] have consistently found that school success in a variety of change-related variables is linked to skillful leadership from school principals. Later researchers agree with this conclusion.[111]

The Chicago Panel on School Policy's study of 5 years of their school reform found that "the most distinguishing feature of improving [as compared to stable or declining] schools was [that] they were led continuously by strong principals who had a vision of improvement for their school."[112] According to Hallinger and Heck's (2000) national analysis of 15 years of research on school leadership, an outstanding principal exercises a "measurable though indirect effect" on school effectiveness and student achievement.[113] Leithwood and colleagues (2004) found that leadership is second only to classroom instruction among all school-related factors that influence student outcomes. They reported that direct and indirect leadership effects account for about one quarter of total school effects on student learning.[114]

Although the principal's impact on student achievement may be indirect, it is critical. The principal controls the most important factors affecting a school's teaching and instructional quality, including attracting, selecting, and keeping outstanding teachers; working with the school community to establish a common mission, instructional vision, and goals; creating a school culture grounded in collaboration and high expectations; facilitating continuous instructional improvement; finding fair, effective ways to improve or remove low-performing teachers; and producing excellent academic results for all students as gauged by external tests aligned with state academic standards. In addition, principals have increased responsibilities for traditional areas such as politics, security, public relations, finances, personnel, and technology.[115]

Principals' Leadership Responsibilities and Student Achievement

Similarly, Marzano, Waters, and McNulty's (2005) meta-analysis on 30 years of research on the effects of principals' practices on student achievement found a significant, positive correlation of .25 between effective school leadership and student achievement. For an average school, having an effective leader can mean the difference between scoring at the 50th percentile on a given achievement test and achieving a score 10 percentile points higher.[116]

In addition, the study identified 21 leadership responsibilities, practices, knowledge areas, strategies, and tools that seemed to be linked to changes in students' test scores.

TABLE 1–7

Instructional Leadership Responsibilities with Highest Impact on Student Achievement

Responsibility	The Extent to Which the Principal . . .	Average Correlation with Student Academic Achievement
Situational awareness	Is aware of the details and undercurrents in running the school and uses this information to address current and potential problems	.33
Flexibility	Adapts his or her leadership behavior to the current situation's needs and is comfortable with dissent	.28
Monitoring/evaluating	Monitors the effectiveness of school practices and their impact on student learning	.27
Outreach	Is advocate and spokesperson for the school to all stakeholders	.27
Discipline	Protects teachers from issues and influences that would detract from their teaching time or focus	.27
Knowledge of curriculum, instruction, and assessment	Is knowledgeable about current curriculum, instruction, and assessment practices	.25
Change agent	Is willing to challenge and actively challenges the status quo	.25
Input	Involves teachers in the design and implementation of important decisions and policies	.25
Order	Establishes a set of standard operating procedures and routines	.25
Resources	Provides teachers with materials and professional development necessary for them to successfully execute their jobs	.25
Intellectual stimulation	Ensures faculty and staff are aware of the most current theories and practices and makes the discussion of these a regular aspect of the school's culture	.24

Source: Adapted from Marzano, R., Waters, T., & McNulty, B. A. (2005). *School leadership that works. From research to results* (pp. 42–43). Alexandria, VA: Association for Supervision and Curriculum Development. Reprinted by permission of Mid-Continent Research for Education in Learning (McREL).

Table 1–7 shows Marzano and colleagues findings regarding the principal's responsibilities with the highest measured impact on student achievement.

Even this partial list shows that effective principals perform a broad range of actions. As instructional leaders, principals must continually know what is going on in their schools, formally and informally. This includes being aware of issues that have surfaced and those that are about to, and deliberately addressing them. Principals must be flexible so they can adapt their leadership behaviors to the current situation's needs and have the mental agility to accept diverse opinions, protecting and encouraging those with different viewpoints. They must involve teachers in designing and enacting important decisions and policies. Strong instructional leaders systematically consider new and better ways of doing things, and they are willing to lead change initiatives with uncertain outcomes.

As instructional leaders, principals establish strong communication with and between teachers and students, fostering a school culture and smoothly structured environment that positively influences student achievement. They engage teachers in meaningful dialog about research, theory, and practice about curriculum, instruction, and assessment. They build "teacher learning into the everyday fabric of school life."[117] Together, they design, conduct, and evaluate a comprehensive, rigorous, and coherent curricular program. They find ways to personalize and motivate each student's learning. Finally, principals understand that their school is not an island; it functions in a complex context. Accordingly, principals must effectively advocate and be a spokesperson for the school to all its stakeholders—inside and outside the school.

Arguably, effective professional relationships are central to successfully conducting many of these instructional leadership responsibilities. Fullan (2001) described the importance of school leaders forming emotional bonds with and among teachers that help staff and administrators stay aligned and focused during uncertain times.[118] But for instructional leadership, relationships mean more than face-to-face awareness of others' personal lives. Relationships are the thread connecting many of these responsibilities, the means by which many of these other responsibilities become possible and fruitful.

In sum, instructional leaders use their personalities, motivation for success, and professional skills to accomplish improvements by interpreting internal and external events, changing the organization and the substance of work practices, and improving individual motivation and abilities, power relations, and shared beliefs. Full awareness and use of the leader, follower, and relationship domains provide the springboard for successful instructional leadership. Clearly, although the principal's impact on student achievement may be indirect, it is critical.

While authors vary widely about how leaders should improve educational outcomes, they do not question the ability of principals to improve educational outcomes per se.[119] It is clear that principals as instructional leaders have a profound influence and play a critical role in shaping their schools' environments and instructional climates. This, in turn, influences the quality of teaching and learning for students.

ACTIVITY 1.7   Applying the Instructional Leadership Responsibilities Related to Increased Student Achievement

Marzano, Waters, and McNulty's research identified 21 instructional leadership responsibilities that are empirically related to increased student achievement.

Using Table 1–7, identify ways that the Oakdale High School principal might use each of these responsibilities to address school needs identified in the case study data or to influence the climate and practices at Oakdale High School that the data suggest.

Use Table 1–7 to identify principal behaviors that you have witnessed or experienced in your own school during your role as a student, teacher, or administrator.

THE EFFECTS OF GOOD PRINCIPAL LEADERSHIP

Any true picture of a principal's workday includes many managerial and leadership tasks. But central to all of these responsibilities is a strong focus on instruction and the behaviors most likely to promote better learning. "The most important change that has occurred in education leadership in decades is the priority placed on the work that leaders do to guide and support the improvement of teaching and learning."[120]

During the mid-1990s, the educational community—states, professional associations, and universities—came together to develop a blueprint to rebuild school leadership in the United States. In 1994, under direction of the Council of Chief State School Officers (CCSSO), the National Association of Elementary School Principals (NAESP), the National Association of Secondary School Principals (NASSP), and the National Policy Board for Educational Administration formed the Interstate School Leaders Licensure Consortium (ISLLC). Produced in 1996 and revised in 2008 to reflect the updated research base,[121] the ISLLC standards intend to define and guide school leaders' practice. Not meant to be all-inclusive, these research-based standards focus on indicators of knowledge, dispositions, and performances (now called *functions*) important to effective school leadership. The standards present a comprehensive vision of what education leadership should look like and strive to accomplish.

Since then, 43 states have used the 1996 ISLLC Standards for School Leaders in their entirety or as a template for developing their own standards for practicing administrators and as the foundation for leadership preparation programs.[122] The National Council for the Accreditation of Teacher Education (NCATE) scaffolded the ISLLC standards into their accreditation process for educational administration programs. At present, all NCATE-accredited principal preparation programs in the United States have adopted the ISLLC standards.[123] By 1998, the Educational Testing Service (ETS) had developed the complementary School Leaders Licensure Assessment (SLLA) to assess beginning principal candidates. As a result, the ISLLC standards are now a fundamental part of both principal practice and preparation.

Redefining School Leadership

Traditionally, principals' leadership focus was managerial and administrative. From this starting point, the ISLLC standards redefine school leadership in two ways. First, they define school leadership as instructional leadership centering on enhancing teaching and learning and creating powerful learning environments. Today, the principal is an instructional leader, not merely an educational leader. As Murphy and Shipman (2002) noted, ISLLC's goal was to rebuild and reculture schooling's leadership infrastructure,[124] shifting principals' primary attention from "busses, budgets, and buildings" to classroom teaching and learning.

Next, the six standards represent broad themes and priorities that a variety of education leaders—superintendents and other district leaders, principals, teacher leaders, and mentors—must keep focal in their efforts to promote the success of every student. The standards recognize that effective leadership depends not on one individual but on the support system of leadership, the core group of individuals and what they know and do in the school to increase student learning. Instructional leadership is a collaborative responsibility and a collaborative set of activities.

Despite ISLLC's inclusive definition of instructional leaders, the ISLLC standards have been enthusiastically supported and adopted by states, principal preparation programs, and principals' professional associations because principal leadership is key to a school's success. These standards help states and districts target, anchor, and provide instructionally directed professional development. The standards' overall objective is to help policy makers and practitioners recognize that school leaders' career development never ends. Over time, standards can guide school leadership development all the way through mastery.

The Six Standards and Functions

Each of the six ISLLC standards includes several functions that describe actions leaders should take to promote the success of every student.[125]

Standard 1: An education leader promotes the success of every student by facilitating the development, articulation, implementation, and stewardship of a vision of learning that is shared and supported by all stakeholders.

Functions: The instructional leader collaboratively develops and implements a shared vision and mission; collects and uses data to identify goals, assess organizational effectiveness, and promote organizational learning; creates and implements plans to achieve goals; promotes continuous and sustainable improvement; and monitors and evaluates progress and revises plans.

Standard 1 recognizes the complex processes within schools and the need to have one individual or a small group of leaders consistently focused on educational goals/vision and able to translate that vision into specific actions or behaviors by the stakeholders.

Standard 2: An education leader promotes the success of every student by advocating, nurturing, and sustaining a school culture and instructional program conducive to student learning and staff professional growth.

Functions: The instructional leader nurtures and sustains a culture of collaboration, trust, learning, and high expectations; creates a comprehensive, rigorous, and coherent curricular program; creates a personalized and motivating learning environment for students; supervises instruction; develops assessment and accountability systems to monitor student progress; develops the instructional and leadership capacity of staff; maximizes time spent on quality instruction; promotes the use of the most effective and appropriate technologies to support teaching and learning; and monitors and evaluates the impact of the instructional program.

Standard 2 understands that educational leadership is a collaborative enterprise. The vast amount of information available, the increasing research-based knowledge about the connections between a well-designed curriculum and effective teaching, and ever-changing student needs require leaders who are willing and able to surround themselves with individuals who possess a depth of knowledge and experience in the issues at hand. One leader cannot possibly be an expert in all areas. One leader can, however, be skilled in seeking individuals who can provide input into the process.

Standard 3: An education leader promotes the success of every student by ensuring management of the organization, operation, and resources for a safe, efficient, and effective learning environment.

Functions: The instructional leader monitors and evaluates the school's management and operational systems; obtains, allocates, aligns, and efficiently utilizes human, fiscal, and technological resources; promotes and protects the welfare and safety of students and staff; develops the capacity for distributed leadership; and ensures teacher and organizational time is focused to support quality instruction and student learning.

Standard 3 reinforces the traditional school administrative and managerial role as necessary but not sufficient conditions for successful instructional leadership.

Standard 4: An education leader promotes the success of every student by collaborating with faculty and community members, responding to diverse community interests and needs, and mobilizing community resources.

Functions: The instructional leader collects and analyzes data and information pertinent to the educational environment; promotes understanding, appreciation, and use of the community's diverse cultural, social, and intellectual resources; builds and sustains positive relationships with families and caregivers; and builds and sustains productive relationships with community partners.

Standard 4 acknowledges the instructional leader's facility with effectively using school data—including familiarity and appreciation of the diverse community and available resources—to build and sustain positive relationships with families, caregivers, and the community as they work together to support all students' learning.

Standard 5: An education leader promotes the success of every student by acting with integrity, fairness, and in an ethical manner.

Functions: The instructional leader ensures a system of accountability for every student's academic and social success; models principles of self-awareness, reflective practice, transparency, and ethical behavior; safeguards the values of democracy, equity, and diversity; considers and evaluates the potential moral and legal consequences of decision making; and promotes social justice and ensures that individual student needs inform all aspects of schooling.

Standard 5 focuses on creating systemic accountability for oneself and school staff for student academic and social achievement, professional and ethical behavior, democratic and equitable practices, and attention to individual needs.

Standard 6: An education leader promotes the success of every student by understanding, responding to, and influencing the political, social, economic, legal, and cultural context.

Functions: The instructional leader advocates for children, families, and caregivers; acts to influence local, district, state, and national decisions affecting student learning; and assesses, analyzes, and anticipates emerging trends and initiatives in order to adapt leadership strategies.

Standard 6 recognizes the school leader's active advocacy and proactive role in supporting the students and families in school and in the wider community.

ACTIVITY 1.8   Using the ISLLC Standards at Oakdale High School

The six ISLLC standards identify the broad themes and priorities that instructional leaders must keep central in their efforts to promote the success of every student.

1. Read each standard, its functions, and descriptions carefully.
2. Identify principal behaviors related to the Chapter 1 case study which attempt to meet each standard.
3. Which other persons would the principal have to involve to make the most effective decisions regarding each standard?
4. Which standards are not directly relevant to the case study? What are situations involving the schools for which they might be relevant?

Outcomes of Leadership Standards

The ISLLC standards alone won't improve student achievement, but they do help to establish policies and practices that can help all students achieve at higher levels. Research shows that education leadership quality is second only to classroom instruction in school-related factors that have an impact on student achievement.[126] Research also finds that teachers rarely improve student achievement without effective leaders.[127] Therefore, these standards can be used to develop and promote policies to improve education leadership—a critical step toward transforming schools and classrooms.

Education leadership standards can help keep education leaders—particularly principals—in step with their teachers' priorities, skills, and curricular focus. Lack of such alignment can undermine the efforts of both school leaders and teachers. The 2008 education leadership standards emphasize both goal and vision setting, which helps align the expectations of education leaders, teachers, and students. The standards also call for leaders to take an active role in creating, monitoring, and evaluating instructional programs that are conducive to student learning and staff professional growth.

At the university level, ISLLC 2008 establishes principal preparation performance expectations and facilitates curriculum development, candidate assessment, and program/candidate accountability. Certainly ISLLC 2008 is already informing the National Council for the Accreditation of Teacher Education (NCATE) process and program standards that guide NCATE's work.

Criticism of ISLLC.   The ISLLC standards have drawn criticism. English (2000) has argued that the 1996 standards are not anchored in a professional knowledge base or rigorous research.[128] Achilles and Price (2001) have said they overly reinforce the status quo, and that they lack enough specificity or operational guidance to help school leaders use them for action.[129] Pitre and Smith (2004) have contended that the standards' 1996 language is ambiguous and occasionally contradictory, assuming that the principal is the school leader while calling for collaborative leadership at the same time.[130] They add that the standards are so important that vesting their successful implementation and execution in one person (or at best a few people) is unrealistic.

Addressing these concerns, the revised 2008 standards see school leadership as more than the principal. Most schools still perceive the principal as head of a top-down hierarchy within the school; for administrative and managerial functions, this remains true. Increasingly, however, the means and practices by which schools strengthen teaching and learning and boost student achievement require the collaboration of stakeholders. The ISLLC standards provide a framework for proactive and real-time behaviors as well as professional development linked by research to increasing student achievement. School leaders can use this framework to develop the attitudes and skills that make appropriate collaboration possible and productive, and academic and social growth for all students a reality.

Our understanding of leadership has evolved, along with our appreciation for its complexity. This is as true for our culture as for our schools. Today, with clear and measurable connections evident between effective school leaders and successful schools, developing clarity about what leadership is and how it works in the daily practice of schooling is essential if educators are to meet their commitment to educating all children.

SUMMARY

Leadership is a process that involves an influence relationship purposefully directed toward meaningful change and that takes place in a certain context. A leader facilitates change. Whether family, business, school, or nation, the leader must organize, educate, team build, and facilitate transformation from one existence to another.

Leadership theory began as a one-dimensional, internal, and individualistic process. Only a leader's personality, traits, or behaviors mattered. Eventually, scholars considered the leader's relationships with others. Situational elements outside the leader-member dyad would be added to the leadership equation later.

Leadership relationships use power and influence to move others toward identified goals. Power is the ability to get others to do what you want them to do. Position power and personal power either push or pull members, respectively, toward advancing identified goals. Leaders use different kinds of power to exercise that influence: legitimate, reward, coercive, expert, and referent.

Contemporary leadership theory focuses explicitly on the leader's relationships with group members: how one-on-one reciprocal social exchanges between leaders and followers evolve, nurture, and sustain the dyadic relationship. With the relationship perspective, leadership is about what leaders and collaborators do together. Understanding leadership as a relationship brings attention to followers and their essential role in leadership effectiveness.

Instructional leadership emphasizes the improvement of teaching and learning in the school. Three decades of research provides ample evidence that principals' effective leadership positively affects school and student outcomes.

Produced in 1996 and revised in 2008 to reflect the updated research base, the Interstate School Leaders Licensure Consortium (ISLLC) standards redefine school leadership to reflect principals' current role centering on enhancing teaching and learning and creating powerful learning environments. ISLLC standards are now a fundamental part of both principal practice and preparation.

Leadership theory continues to evolve as a complex, interactive process with behavioral, relational, and situational elements. Today, we understand that leadership belongs not only to the person in the leader position. To be effective, leadership must be collaborative.

ENDNOTES

1. Snyder, T. D., Dillow, S. A., & Hoffman, C. M. (2008). *Digest of education statistics 2007* (NCES 2008-022, p. 70). Washington, DC: National Center for Education Statistics, Institute of Education Sciences, U.S. Department of Education.

2. Rosenthal, S. A., Pittinsky, T. L., Moore, S., Ratcliff, J. J., Maruskin, L. A., & Gravelin, C. R. (2008). *National leadership index 2008: A national study of confidence in leadership.* Cambridge, MA: Center for Public Leadership, Harvard Kennedy School, Harvard University.

3. Fullan, M. (2001). *Leading in a culture of change* (p. ix). San Francisco, CA: Jossey-Bass.

4. Heifetz, R. (1994). *Leadership without easy answers.* Cambridge, MA: Harvard University Press.

5. Fullan. (2001). Op. cit., p. xiii.

6. Fullan. (2001). Op. cit., p. ix.

7. Gill, R. (2006). *Theory and practice of leadership.* Thousand Oaks, CA: Sage.

8. Rost, J. C. (1991). *Leadership for the twenty-first century.* Westport, CO: Praeger. Rost found 221 definitions in 587 books and articles written from 1900 to 1990.

9. Bennis, W., & Nanus, B. (1985). *Leaders: The strategies for taking charge.* New York, NY: Harper-Collins.

10. Hoad, T. F. (Ed.). (1988). *The concise Oxford dictionary of English etymology.* Oxford, United Kingdom: Oxford University Press.

11. Kets De Vries, M., & Florent-Treacy, E. (1999). AuthentiZoptoc organizations: Global leadership from A to Z. (Working Paper No. 99/62/ENT, INSEAD, Fontainblue, France). In R. Gill. (2006). *Theory and practice of leadership* (p. 8). Thousand Oaks, CA: Sage.

12. Graen, G. B., & Uhl-Bien, M. (1995). Relationship based approach to leadership: Development of leader-member exchange (LMX) theory of leadership over 25 years: Applying a multi-level

multi-domain perspective. *Leadership Quarterly,* 6(2), 219–247.

13. Patterson, J. L. (1993). *Leadership for tomorrow's schools* (p. 3). Alexandria, VA: Association for Supervision and Curriculum Development.

14. Burns, J. M. (1978). *Leadership.* New York, NY: Harper & Row.

15. Belasco, J. A., & Stayer, R. C. (1993). *The flight of the buffalo. Soaring to excellence, learning to let employees lead.* New York, NY: Warner Books.

16. Rost, J. L. (1993). Leadership development in the new millennium. *Journal of Leadership and Organizational Studies,* 1(1), 91–110.

17. Belasco & Stayer. (1993). Op. cit.

18. House, R. J., & Aditya, R. N. (1993). The social science study of leadership. Quo Vadis? *Journal of Management,* 23(3), 409–473.

19. Zaleznik, A. (1977). Managers and leaders: Are they different? *Harvard Business Review,* 55(3), 67–78.

20. Bennis, W., & Nanus, B. (1985). *Leaders: The strategies for taking charge* [on the dust jacket]. New York, NY: Harper & Row.

21. House & Aditya. (1993). Ibid.

22. Yukl, G. (1994). *Leadership in organizations* (3rd ed.). Englewood Cliffs, NJ: Prentice Hall.

23. Boehm, C. (1999). *Hierarchy in the forest.* Cambridge, MA: Harvard.

24. Bass, B. M. (1990). *Bass and Stogdill's handbook of leadership.* New York, NY: Free Press.

25. Takala, T. (1998). Plato on leadership. *Journal of Business Ethics,* 17(7), 785–798.

26. Plato's Republic. (2000). Ablemedia. Retrieved from http://ablemedia.com/ctcweb/netshots/republic.htm

27. Barker, R. (2001). The nature of leadership. *Human Relations,* 54(4), 469–494.

28. Kellerman, B. (2008, December 15). Machiavelli's advice. *The Washington Post.* Retrieved from http://

views.washingtonpost.com/leadership/panelists/
2008/12/what-would-machiavelli-say.html

29. Barker, R. (2001). Op. cit.

30. We prefer to use gender-neutral terms. We use *he* in this case because most leaders until recent Western civilization were men, with a few exceptions.

31. Belasco & Stayer. (1993). Op. cit., pp. 49–52.

32. Fayol, H. (1937). *Papers on the science of administration*. L. Gulick & L. Urwick (Eds.). New York, NY: Columbia University, Institute of Public Administration; Fayol, F. (1949). *General and industrial administration*. New York, NY: Pitman.

33. Fry, B. R., & Nigro, L. G. (1996). Max Weber and US public administration. The administrator as neutral servant. *Journal of Management History, 2*(1), 37–46.

34. Rost, J. C. (1997). Moving from individual to relationship. A postindustrial paradigm of leadership. *Journal of Leadership and Organizational Studies, 4*(4), 3–16.

35. Bass, B. M. (1990). *Bass and Stogdill's handbook of leadership: Theory, research and managerial applications* (3rd ed.). New York, NY: Free Press; House, R. J., & Aditya, R. N. (1997). The social science study of leadership: Quo Vadis? *Journal of Management, 23*(3), 409–473.

36. House & Aditya. (1997). Ibid.

37. Rost. (1997). Op. cit., p. 7.

38. Borgotta, E. G., Rouch, A. S., & Bales, R. F. (1954). Some findings relevant to the great man theory of leadership. *American Sociological Review, 19*, 755–799; Galton, F. (1869). *Hereditary genius*. New York, NY: Appleton.

39. Sashkin, M., & Rosenbach, W. E. (2001). A new vision of leadership. In M. Sashkin & W. E. Rosenbach (Eds.), *Contemporary issues in leadership* (5th ed., pp. 19–41). Boulder, CO: Westview Press.

40. Bowden, A. O. (1927). A study on the personality of student leadership in the United States. *Journal of Abnormal Social Psychology, 21*, 149–160.

41. Jennings, E. E. (1960). *An anatomy of leadership: Princes, heroes, and supermen*. New York, NY: Harper.

42. Van Seter, D. A., & Field, R. G. (1990). The evolution of leadership theory. *Journal of Organizational Change Management, 3*(3), 29–45.

43. Bass, B. M. (1990). *Bass and Stogdill's handbook of leadership* (3rd ed.). New York, NY: Free Press.

44. Gibb, C. A. (1947). The principles and traits of leadership. *Journal of Abnormal and Social Psychology, 42*, 267–284.

45. Jenkins, W. O. (1947). A review of leadership studies with particular reference to military problems. *Psychological Bulletin, 44*, 54–79.

46. Stogdill, R. M. (1948). Personal factors associated with leadership: A survey of the literature. *Journal of Psychology,25*, 35–71.

47. Stogdill. (1948). Ibid.

48. House & Aditya. (1997). Op. cit.

49. Stogdill. (1948). Op. cit.

50. Mann, R. D. (1959). A review of the relationship between personality and performance. *Psychological Bulletin, 56*, 241–270.

51. House & Aditya. (1997). Op. cit.

52. Davis-Blake, A., & Pfeffer, J. (1988). Just a mirage: The search for dispositional effects in organizational research. *Academy of Management Review, 14*(3), 385–400.

53. Schneider, B. (1983). Interactional psychology and organizational behavior. In L. L. Cummings & B. M. Staw (Eds.), *Research in organizational behavior* (Vol. 5, pp. 1–31). Greenwich, CT: JAI Press.

54. House, R. J., Shane, S., & Herold, D. (1996). Rumors of the death of dispositional theory and research in organizational behavior are greatly exaggerated. *Academy of Management Review, 21*(1), 203–224.

55. Stogdill, R. M. (1981). Traits of leadership: A follow-up to 1970. In B. M. Bass (Ed.), *Stogdill's handbook of leadership* (pp. 73–97). New York, NY: Free Press.

56. Immegart, G. L. (1988). Leadership and leader behavior. In N. J. Boyan (Ed.), *Handbook of research on educational administration* (pp. 259–277). New York, NY: Longman.

57. Yukl, G. A. (2002). *Leadership in organizations* (5th ed.). Upper Saddle River, NJ: Prentice Hall.

58. Yukl. (2002). Ibid.

59. Fiedler, F. E. (1967). *A theory of leadership effectiveness*. New York, NY: McGraw-Hill.

60. McClelland, D. C. (1985). *Human motivation*. Glenview, IL: Scott, Foresman.

61. Yukl, G. A. (2002). *Leadership in organizations* (5th ed.). Upper Saddle River, NJ: Prentice Hall.

62. Bass, B. M., & Riggio, R. E. (2006). *Transformational leadership* (2nd ed.). Mahwah, NJ: Erlbaum.

63. Mumford, M. D., Zaccaro, S. J., Harding, F. D., Jacobs, T. O., & Fleishman, E. A. (2000). Leadership skills for a changing world: Solving complex social problems. *Leadership Quarterly, 11*(1), 11–35.

64. Yukl. (2002). Op. cit.

65. Northouse, P. G. (2004). *Leadership: Theory and practice* (3rd ed.). Thousand Oaks, CA: Sage.

66. Mumford et al. (2000). Op. cit.

67. Yukl. (2002). Op. cit.

68. Mumford et al. (2000). Op. cit., p. 23.

69. Bass, B. M. (1981). *Stogdill's handbook of leadership* (Rev. ed.). New York, NY: Free Press; Bennis, W. G. (1959). Leadership theory and administrative behavior: The problem with authority. *Administrative Science Quarterly, 4,* 259–301; Mintzberg, H. (1982). If you're not serving Bill and Barbara, then you're not serving leadership. In J. G. Hunt, U. Sekaran, & C. A. Schriesheim (Eds.), *Leadership: Beyond establishment views* (pp. 239–250). Carbondale, IL: Southern Illinois University Press; Rost, J. C. (1991). *Leadership for the twenty-first century.* New York, NY: Praeger; Stogdill, R. M. (1948). Personal factors associated with leadership: A survey of the literature. *Journal of Psychology, 25,* 35–71.

70. Fleishman, E. A., Mumford, M. D., Zaccaro, S. J., Levin, K. Y., Korotkin, A. L., & Hein, M. B. (1991). Taxonomic efforts in the description of leadership behavior: A synthesis and functional interpretation. *Leadership Quarterly, 2,* 245–287.

71. Mumford et al. (2000, p. 22) consider crystallized cognitive abilities those specific skills that allow general intelligence to translate into real-world performance. These crystallized abilities, or skills, include effective written and oral communications, and the ability to analyze, synthesize, evaluate, and create new solutions.

72. Barker. (2001). Op. cit.

73. Van Seter & Field. (1990). Op. cit.

74. Cartwright, D., & Zander, A. (1953). *Group dynamics: Research and theory.* Evanston, IL: Row, Peterson.

75. Fleishman, E. A., & Harris, E. F. (1962). Patterns of leadership behavior related to employee grievances and turnover. *Personnel Psychology, 15,* 43–56.

76. Van Seter & Field. (1990). Op. cit.

77. Yukl, G. A. (1989). *Leadership in organizations* (2nd ed.). Englewood Cliffs, NJ: Prentice Hall.

78. Griffin, R. W., Skivington, K. D., & Moorhead, G. (1987). Symbolic and international perspectives on leadership: An integrative framework. *Human Relations, 40,* 199–218.

79. Halpin, A. W. (1966). *Theory and research in administration.* New York, NY: Macmillan.

80. House, R. J., & Baetz, M. L. (1979). Leadership: Some empirical generalizations and new research directions. *Research in Organizational Behavior, 1,* 341–423; Leverette, B. B. (1984). *Professional zone of acceptance: Its relation to the leader behavior of principals and socio-psychological characteristics of teaching* (Doctoral dissertation). Rutgers University, New Brunswick, NJ; Kunz, D., & Hoy, W. (1976). Leader behavior of principals and the professional zone of acceptance of teachers. *Educational Administration Quarterly, 12,* 49–64; Mitchell, T. R. (1979). Organizational behavior. *Annual Review of Psychology, 30,* 243–281; Vroom, V. H. (1976). Leadership. In M. D. Dunnette (Ed.), *Handbook of industrial and organizational psychology* (pp. 1527–1551). Chicago, IL: Rand McNally.

81. Bass, B. M. (1990). *Handbook of leadership: A survey of theory and research.* New York, NY: Free Press; Yukl, G. (2002). *Leadership in organizations* (5th ed.).Upper Saddle River, NJ: Prentice Hall.

82. Yukl, G., Gordon, A., & Taber, T. (2002). A hierarchical taxonomy of leadership behavior: Integrating a half century of behavior research. *Journal of Leadership and Organizational Studies, 9*(1), 15–32.

83. Yukl et al. (2002). Ibid.

84. Hoy, W. K., & Miskel, C. G. (2008). *Educational administration. Theory, research, and practice* (8th ed., p. 219). Boston, MA: McGraw-Hill.

85. Mechanic, D. (1962). Sources of power of lower participants in complex organizations. *Administrative Science Quarterly, 7*(3), 349–364.

86. Mechanic, D. (1962). Ibid.

87. Weber, M. (1947). *The theory of social and economic organizations* (p. 324). T. Parsons (Ed.), A. M. Henderson & T. Parsons (Trans.). New York, NY: Free Press.

88. French, J. P., & Raven, B. H. (1986). The bases of social power. In D. Cartwright & A. F. Zander (Eds.), *Group dynamics: Research and theory* (3rd ed.). New York, NY: Harper & Row; Raven, B. H. (1993). The bases of power: Origins and recent developments. *Journal of Social Issues, 49*(4), 227–251.

89. *Commitment* means the person is enthusiastic about the request and exerts the maximum effort

to do it effectively. *Compliance* means the person is indifferent about the request and makes only a minimum effort. *Resistance* means the person is opposed to carrying out the request and tries to avoid doing it. Employee commitment is desirable for requests involving taking initiative in solving problems and persisting in the face of difficulties—such as serving as a school improvement team member. Compliance is often sufficient for simple routine requests—such as completing student attendance accurately and on time. See: Yukl, G. (2000). Use power effectively. In E. A. Locke (Ed.), *The Blackwell handbook of principles of organizational behavior* (2nd ed., pp. 241–256). Hoboken, NJ: Blackwell.

90. Yukl, G. (2002). *Leadership in organizations* (5th ed.). Upper Saddle River, NJ: Prentice Hall.

91. Isaac, R. G., Zerbe, W. J., & Pitt, D. C. (2001). Leadership and motivation: The effective application of expectancy theory. *Journal of Managerial Issues, 13*(2), 211–226.

92. Yukl. (2002). Op. cit.

93. French, J. R. P., & Raven, B. H. (1968). Bases of social power. In D. Carwright & A. Zander (Eds.), *Group dynamics: Research and theory* (pp. 259–270). New York, NY: Harper & Row.

94. Dent, F., & Brent, M. (2001, July). Influencing: A new model. *Training Journal,* 14–17.

95. Greene, C. N., & Podsakoff, P. M. (1981). Effects of withdrawal of a performance contingent reward of supervisory influence and power. *Academy of Management Journal, 24*(3), 527–542.

96. Mechanic. (1962). Op. cit.

97. Rost. (1997). Op. cit.

98. Van Seter & Field. (1990). Op. cit.

99. Wang, H., Law, K. S., Hackett, R. D., Wang, D., & Chen, Z. X. (2005). Leader-member exchanges as a mediator of the relationship between transformational leadership and followers' performance and organizational citizenship behavior. *Academy of Management Journal, 48*(3), 420–432.

100. Graen, G. B., & Uhl-Bien, M. (1995). Development of leader-member exchange (LMX) theory of leadership over 25 years: Applying a multilevel multi-domain perspective. *Leadership Quarterly, 6,* 219–247.

101. This model describes a theoretical approach to studying leadership called leader-member exchange, or LMX. See: Graen, G. B., & Uhl-Bien, M. (1995).

Development of leader-member exchange (LMX) theory of leadership over 25 years: Applying a multi-level multi-domain perspective. *Leadership Quarterly, 6,* 219–247; Gerstner, C. R., & Day, D. V. (1997). Meta-analysis review of leader-member exchange theory: Correlation and construct issues. *Journal of Applied Psychology, 82,* 827–844.

102. Bass, B. M. (1990). *Bass and Stogdill's handbook of leadership* (3rd ed.). New York, NY: Free Press; Mintzberg, H. (1973). *The nature of managerial work.* New York, NY: Harper & Row; Stogdill, R. M. (1948). Personal factors associated with leadership: A survey of the literature. *Journal of Psychology, 25,* 35–71.

103. Rost. (1997). Op. cit.

104. Hallinger, P. (1992). The evolving role of American principals: From managerial to instructional to transformational leaders. *Journal of Educational Administration, 30*(3), 35–48; Leithwood, K. A. (1992). The move toward transformational leadership. *Educational Leadership, 49*(5), 8–12; Murphy, J., & Hallinger, P. (1992). The principalship in an era of transformation. *Journal of Educational Administration, 30*(3), 77–88; Murphy, J., & Louis, K. S. (1994). *Reshaping the principalship: Insights from transformational reform efforts.* Thousand Oaks, CA: Corwin.

105. Knapp, M. S., Copland, M. A., & Talbert, J. F. (2003, February). *Leading for learning: Reflective tools for school and district leaders.* Seattle: Center for the Study of Teaching and Policy, University of Washington.

106. Brookover, W. B., Beady, C., Flood, P., Schweitzer, J., & Wisenbaker, J. (1979). *School social systems and student achievement. Schools can make a difference.* New York, NY: Praeger; Edmonds, R. R. (1979). *A discussion of the literature and issues related to effective schooling.* Cambridge, MA: Harvard Graduate School of Education, Center for Urban Studies; Rutter, M., Maugham, B., Mortimore, P., Ouston, J., & Smith, A. (1979). *Fifteen thousand hours. Secondary schools and their effects on children.* Somerset, United Kingdom: Open Books.

107. Leithwood, K., & Montgomery, D. (1982). The role of the elementary principal in program improvement. *Review of Educational Research, 52,* 309–339.

108. Fullan, M. (1982). *The meaning of educational change.* New York, NY: Teachers College Press; Hall, G., & Hord, S. (1987). *Change in schools.* Albany, NY: SUNY Press; McLaughlin, M. (1990). The Rand change agent study revisited. *Educational Researcher, 5,* 11–16.

109. Fullan. (1982). Op. cit.; Purkey, S., & Smith, M. (1983). Effective schools: A review. *Elementary School Journal, 83,* 427–452.

110. Leithwood & Montgomery. (1982). Op. cit.

111. Goldhaber, D. (2007, December). *Principal compensation. More research needed on a promising reform.* Washington, DC: Center for American Progress; Hallinger, P., & Heck, R. (2000, October). Exploring the principal's contribution to school effectiveness, 1980–1995. In *Leadership for student learning: Reinventing school leadership for the 21st century.* Washington, DC: Institute for Education Leadership; Heck, R. H., Larsen, T. J., & Marcoulides, G. A. (1990). Instructional leadership and school achievement: Validation of a causal model. *Educational Administration Quarterly, 26*(2), 94–125; Leithwood, K., Harris, A., & Hopkins, D. (2008). Seven strong claims about successful school leaders. *School Leadership and Management, 28*(1), 27–42; Leithwood, K., Louis, K. S., Anderson, S., & Wahlstrom, E. (2004). *How leadership influences student learning.* New York, NY: Wallace Foundation; Levine, D. U., & Lezotte, L. W. (1990). *Unusually effective schools: A review and analysis of research and practice.* Madison, WI: National Center for Effective Schools Research and Development; Marzano, R. J., Waters, T., & McNulty, B. A. (2005). *School leadership that works. From research to results.* Alexandria, VA: Association for Supervision and Curriculum Development; Sammons, P., Hillman, J., & Mortimore, P. (1995). *Key characteristics of effective schools: A review of school effectiveness research.* London: OFSTED; Schnur, J. (2002, June 18). *An outstanding principal in every school: Using the new Title II to promote effective leadership.* National Council on Teacher Quality. Retrieved from http://www.nctq.orgt/press/2002_consumers_guide/schnur.htm

112. Hess, A. G., Jr. (1998, September). Strong leadership is no. 1. *Catalyst.* Voices of School Reform. Chicago, IL.

113. Hallinger, P., & Heck, R. (2000, October). Exploring the principal's contribution to school effectiveness, 1980–1995. In *Leadership for student learning: Reinventing school leadership for the 21st century.* Washington, DC: Institute for Educational Leadership.

114. Leithwood et al. (2004). Op. cit.

115. Kaplan, L. S., Owings, W. A., & Nunnery, J. (2005, June). Principal quality: A Virginia study connecting interstate school leaders licensure consortium standards with student achievement. *NASSP Bulletin, 89*(643), 28–44.

116. Marzano, R. J., Waters, T., & McNulty, B. A. (2005). *School leadership that works. From research to results.* Alexandria, VA: Association for Supervision and Curriculum Development.

117. Lashway, L. (2001). Leadership for accountability. *Research Roundup, 17*(3), 1–14. Eugene, OR: Clearinghouse on Education Policy and Management.

118. Fullan, M. (2001). *Leading in a culture of change.* San Francisco, CA: Jossey-Bass.

119. Leithwood, K., Tomlinson, D., & Genge, M. (1996). Transformational leadership. In K. Leithwood, J. Chapman, D. Corson, P. Hallinger, & A. Hart (Eds.), *International handbook of educational leadership and administration* (pp. 785–840). Dordrecht, the Netherlands: Kluwer Academic; Marzano, Waters, & McNulty. (2005). Op. cit.

120. The Wallace Foundation. (2009, March). *Assessing the effectiveness of school leaders: New directions and new processes* (p. 4). New York, NY: Author. Retrieved from http://www.wallacefoundation.org/KnowledgeCenter/KnowledgeTopics/CurrentAreasofFocus/EducationLeadership/Documents/Assessing-the-Effectiveness-of-School-Leaders.pdf

121. Council of Chief State School Officers (CCSSO). (2008). *Educational leadership policy standards: ISLLC 2008.* As adopted by the National Policy Board for Educational Administration. Washington, DC: Author. Retrieved from http://www.wallacefoundation.org/SiteCollectionDocuments/WF/Knowledge%20Center/Attachments/PDF/ISLLC%202008.pdf; Council of Chief State School Officers (CCSSO). (1996). *Interstate School Leaders Licensure Consortium standards for school leaders.* Washington, DC: Author.

122. Toye, C., Blank, R., Sanders, N. M., & Williams, A. (2007). *Key state education policies on PK-12 education, 2006* (p. 29). Washington, DC: Council of Chief State School Officers. Retrieved from http://www.ccsso.org/ publications/details.cfm?PublicationID=348; To look at the empirical research data base supporting the 2008 ISLLC standards, see: http://www.ccsso.org/content/pdfs/ISLLC% 202008%20Empirical%20Research% 20Database%20final.pdf and http://www.ccsso.org/ projects/isllc2008research/documents/ISLLC% 202008%20Citation%20References%20by% 20Standard%20Function.pdf

123. Fossey, R., & Shoho, A. (2006). Educational leadership preparation programs. In transition or crisis? *Journal of Cases in Educational Leadership, 9*(3), 3–11; Murphy. (2005). Op. cit.

124. Murphy, J., & Shipman, N. J. (2002). The Interstate School Leaders Licensure Consortium (ISLLC) story: A brief narrative. In K. Hessel & J. Holloway, *A framework for school leaders. Linking the ISLLC standards to practice* (pp. 4–9). Princeton, NJ: Educational Testing Services.

125. Council of Chief State School Officers. (2008). *Educational Policy Leadership Standards*: ISLLC 2008. Washington, DC: Author.

Retrieved from http://www.ccsso.org/content/ pdfs/elps_isllc2008.pdf

126. Leithwood, K., Seashore, K. L., Anderson, S., & Wahlstrom, K. (2004). *How leadership influences student learning* (p. 5). New York, NY: Wallace Foundation.

127. Leithwood et al. (2004). Ibid., p. 70.

128. English, F. W. (2000, April–June). Psst! What does one call a set of non-empirical beliefs required to be accepted on faith and enforced by authority? [Answer: A religion, aka the ISLCC Standards]. *International Journal of Leadership in Education: Theory and Practice, 3*(2), 159–168; Hale, E. L., & Moorman, H. N. (2003, September). *Preparing school principals: A national perspective on policy and program innovations.* Washington, DC: Institute for Educational Leadership. Retrieved from http://www.iel.org/ pubs/PreparingSchoolPrincipals.html

129. Achilles, C. M., & Price, W. J. (2001, Winter). What is missing in the current debate about educational administration (EDAD) standards! *AASA Administrator*, pp. 8–13. Retrieved from http:// www.aasa.org/publications/tap/Winter_2001.pdf

130. Pitre, P., & Smith, W. (2004). ISLLC standards and school leadership: Who's leading this band? *Teachers College Record, 106*(10).

CHAPTER 2

Historical Overview of Leadership in Organizations

Focus Questions

- How does understanding organizational theory help improve leadership practice?
- How does classical organizational theory—scientific management and administrative management—contribute to our understanding of organizational behavior?
- How does modern organizational theory contribute to our understanding of organizational behavior?
- How does the focus on human motivation contribute to our understanding of organizational behavior?
- How does reflecting on organizations as production and human environments contribute to our understanding of organizational behavior?

CASE STUDY: HERITAGE COUNTY

In the 1930s, Heritage County was a rural, politically and religiously conservative community encompassing a land mass of just over 500 square miles. Agriculture was its main business. Located 30 miles north of a large, urban, eastern seaboard city, Heritage County had all three of its schools built in the 1930s under the Works Progress Administration (WPA), a financial stimulus package started in the Great Depression. At the time of completion, the three new brick school buildings housed a primary school with students in grades 1–3, an intermediate school housing grades 4–7, and a high school housing grades 8–12. The total student enrollment was 1,200 students.

Over the years, the three school buildings have had additions and renovations in keeping with their original classic schoolhouse design. Today, the three schools comfortably house 2,000 students, and county growth projections indicate that student population will double over the next 10 years. As the city to the south has grown, more commuters with young families, retirees, and small business owners have moved north to Heritage County, to the disappointment of the board of supervisors, the county's governing body. The five members of the board of supervisors appoint the five members to the school board for a 4-year term. The school board reflects the conservative, antigrowth sentiment of the aging supervisors, whose average age is 82.

In the past 10 years, the school board has hired three superintendents from outside the county who were appointed to 3-year terms. Their contracts were not renewed after the initial appointment because the school board felt they were "weak, spineless leaders who tried to dilute the power of the school board and the superintendent's office." The new superintendent, Dr. Smith, comes from a Heritage County family that predates the Revolutionary War. Dr. Smith, hired 35 years ago as a history teacher, has also been an elementary and high school principal, and was assistant superintendent in Heritage County before being named superintendent on July 1. Dr. Smith's sentiments reflect the feelings of the school board and the board of supervisors who feel the superintendent should run the schools with an iron fist by establishing a chain of command and holding the subordinates accountable for their clearly defined job roles.

The younger and nonnative county residents are at odds with the county officials for their rather parochial views of management, and tensions have become evident. Under the three previous superintendents, the newer members of the county lobbied to have community members on the interview teams when new principals were hired. During that time frame, all three principals who were hired were recommended unanimously by the community members on the interview team. As a result, the principals feel a loyalty to the community members and practice a leadership philosophy that solicits input from the staff and parents as decisions are being made that have an impact on their schools. The three principals have become popular in the community for their collaborative leadership approaches.

Now that Dr. Smith is superintendent, however, he has been directed by the school board to get control back of the schools and initiate a "no-nonsense, top-down management style" that requires subordinates to do what they are told to do. Dr. Smith was appointed by the school board due to his understanding of the county and because he is the only employee of the system with a doctorate. The school board has told the superintendent that they will listen to his suggestions, but they know what is needed in the schools and will direct him to take specific actions. The first action Dr. Smith is directed to take is to reengineer the organizational chart so that specific job functions will be overseen by central office staff and communication will follow a strict chain of command.

Second, Dr. Smith has been instructed to eliminate the ineffective and inefficient teaching practice of cooperative learning which they see as having the more capable students do the work for the less capable students. Third, ability grouping is to be reinstated so the advanced students can excel without being burdened by students who are less capable and all can work at their optimal pace. Fourth, the curriculum will be set for the teachers and uniform goals will be established for student achievement in each classroom. Fifth, merit pay will be awarded for teachers whose students meet the achievement goals. Sixth, principals are to make certain that teachers follow these new directives. Last, Dr. Smith is to ensure that teachers are trained in these new methods and willingly accept the changes in management.

Case Study Questions

1. What is the dilemma Dr. Smith faces as he attempts to enact the directives that the school board has assigned?
2. How might the school board's directives about a no-nonsense, top-down management style—and their instructional proposals—compromise Dr. Smith's ability to be an effective educational leader?
3. In what ways does the Heritage County School Board neglect to consider the school district and community's informal organization when designing their directives for Superintendent Smith?

INTRODUCTION

Organizations are not tangible structures. They are concepts that exist in our minds as we try to create order out of complexities related to groups of otherwise unrelated individuals with diverse skills, backgrounds, and resources coming together for a common purpose.

Thinking about leading and managing organizations has ancient origins. Writing itself is evidence of this. About 5,000 years ago, the Sumerians developed the script (cuneiform) in order to manage the first developing cities. These city-societies generated administration problems absent in small tribal communities: orderly recording of taxes on social and economic activity. Script enabled administrators to control complex and long-running affairs.

Large human organizations have been with us for 4,000 years. Although a modern army uses entirely different physical technology than that used by Alexander the Great, the processes that people used in these ancient armies to make decisions or to manage people appear familiar to us, having changed little over the centuries.

The Industrial Revolution of the mid to late 18th century greatly accelerated the development of large organizations. The factory system's massive production scale reflected the larger economic, social, and cultural changes that occurred when mechanized manufacturing prompted a tectonic shift from home workshops to factory production. The factory provided a large-scale work organization for thousands of recent farm workers accustomed to laboring independently or in small groups.

Since educational leaders work with and through other people, understanding the relationship between people's behavior at work and organizational productivity and effectiveness is essential to organizational—and leaders'—success. This chapter reviews the key milestones in organizational theory's development from the late 19th century to the present. This brief history reflects the evolution of thought from viewing workers as specialized adjuncts of the industrial machinery to recognizing the organization as a human environment that significantly affected productivity. Similarly, organizational leaders' and managers' roles shifted from measuring and standardizing the workers' practices to finding ways to simultaneously meet both human needs and organizational purposes by addressing organizational goals.

ORGANIZATIONS AND HUMAN BEHAVIOR

Most jobs occur within organizations—schools, industries, retail stores, government, the military services, or businesses. Organizations are not buildings with brick and mortar foundations. They cannot be touched, measured, or weighed. Instead, organizations are people interacting to produce discernible cultures, goods, and services.

William Ouchi, a management professor, has defined *organizations* as "any stable pattern of transactions between individuals or aggregations of individuals."[1] Organizations are social systems, people brought together for a common purpose. Although purposes and products differ, as schools differ from car manufacturers or the Marine Corps, organizations share common dimensions that affect how those working within them behave.

Understanding Organizations

Organizational behavior is defined as the study of human behavior in the context of an organization and its application to administrative and leadership practices that seek to understand and use knowledge of human behavior in social and cultural settings to improve organizational performance.[2] Organizational behavior is typically applied to the study of behavior of people at work. It is a field of scientific inquiry and a field of applied practice.

Organizational theory is the study of the design, structure, and process of decision making in organizations.[3] Organizational theory is based on a set of interrelated concepts, assumptions, definitions, and generalizations that systematically describe and explain patterns of regularities in organizational life. The purposes of a theory are to explain, to guide research, to predict phenomena, and to inform practice. Theories provide analytical tools and a frame of reference to help practitioners label and analyze problems they face and offer a means for reflective decision making. We all use theories to guide our actions, whether they are explicit or implicit, personal beliefs or formal ones. Theories are not substitutes for thought but are frameworks for making decisions and solving problems.

By their nature, theories are abstract and general. They are not strictly true or false. Rather, they are useful or not useful. Theories are valuable to the degree that they generate accurate predictions about events and help us understand and influence behavior. Actual organizations are much more complex than any theory can represent. As a result, theories may distort reality, but they provide mental maps that helps us navigate what is otherwise unknown and unknowable territory. In practice, we do not choose between reality and theory, but rather between alternative theories that best fit a given situation.

Organizational Study and Social Sciences

Scholars in the social science disciplines of cultural anthropology, sociology, social psychology, political science, and economics each design, conduct, and analyze research that helps make sense of people's behaviors in organizations. Each discipline frames the problems and selects research methods according to its own traditions. Political scientists typically focus on how people in organizations tend to form coalitions and use power. Social psychologists prefer to study the behaviors of people as influenced by the organization's social milieu. In the real world, boundaries separating disciplines' ideas and methods may overlap. Collaborative interdisciplinary inquiry is common. As you will later see, while studying human motivation, psychologist Abraham Maslow developed a theory and hierarchy of human needs that management professor Douglas McGregor applied in developing his organizational theories.

As an applied science, *organizational behavior* is a field of professional practice that seeks to apply knowledge from the social sciences to solve practical problems in organizations to improve their performance. For instance, both undergraduate and graduate students in business administration at U.S. universities study organizational behavior. The purpose is to improve leadership, management, and performance of business organizations in today's highly competitive global environment. Military colleges and graduate institutions study this topic to improve leadership and outcomes in their professional domains.

Much of the logic underpinning organizational concepts came from military tradition. These organizational concepts tended to strongly emphasize the linear, logical, hierarchical, authoritarian, and disciplinary structure that reflected the military, monarchical, and church configurations. During the late 19th and early 20th centuries, large-scale business and industrial organizations uncritically adopted these concepts. Typically, engineers were in charge of leading, designing, and managing these organizations. Their interest in human factors was focused largely on fitting people into the machine system to create a more efficient and manageable operation and a more profitable enterprise.

Organizations as Human Environments

During the 20th century, social scientists believed that the organizational life all around them required a critical study as human environments. In the 1930s, scientific studies of organizations' human side began. The Great Depression and industry's upsurge in labor-management conflicts prompted the study of human relations to address urgent societal needs. By the late 1940s, social and behavioral scientists had largely displaced engineers as organizational theorists.

Reflecting this changing perspective, the study of organizations moved from the exclusive focus on product, profit, and workers as extensions of machines to include a more multifaceted attention on organizations as individuals with personal motives. Accordingly, questions arose regarding how to best balance the organization's needs and its humans' needs in a sustainable successful endeavor.

ACTIVITY 2.1   Looking at Heritage County's Organizational Structure

Case Study Question 1: What is the dilemma Dr. Smith faces as he attempts to enact the directives that the school board has assigned?

Much of the rationale supporting organizational concepts came from military tradition that strongly emphasized the linear, logical, hierarchical, authoritarian, and disciplinary structures that reflected the military, monarchical, and church institutions. Later, large-scale business and industrial organizations uncritically adopted these concepts. Discuss as a class:

1. In what ways does the Heritage County School Board and school district reflect this traditional organizational structure?
2. Which of the school board's expectations for Superintendent Smith reflect this linear and authoritarian view of organizations?
3. Which of the school district's and newly hired principals' practices disregard this linear, authoritarian organizational structure?
4. How does this case study depict a dynamic tension between the school board on one hand and the younger, nonnative county residents and newly hired principals on the other?

School Leaders and Organizational Behavior

Future school leaders benefit from studying organizational behavior. Leadership occurs not in a vacuum, but with people in organizations. As instructional leaders, principals have a measurable but indirect impact on student achievement.[4] By consistently communicating and reinforcing the school's purpose in words and deeds, and by developing and sharing leadership with teachers, the principal creates a professional environment in which teachers can thrive and contribute to the overall school goals and climate.

Principals have very different responsibilities—and very different skill sets—than even the most accomplished teachers. The change from teacher to principal is a major career shift, even though both roles perform within schools. Working as a school leader with and through other adults—conferring with people individually or in small groups; planning and running meetings; motivating teachers, students, and parents to act in certain ways; developing an effective team in the school and community; and dealing with emergencies—requires substantial knowledge and skills for addressing the human dimension of organizations. Leadership effectiveness depends on developing the mental maps of what work to do and how to do it. In this context, understanding and facilitating human concerns is a critical factor influencing organizational effectiveness.

Business and educational models of organizations are similar only to a degree. Both models have chain of command, bureaucratic rules, specialized labor, and formal and informal networks of interpersonal influence, among other factors. Yet, many differences are obvious. Business tends to deal with production of inanimate goods or paid interpersonal services among consenting adults. In contrast, schools are responsible for working with actual children who are legally required to attend. Businesses answer to their board of directors and shareholders for generating high financial profits. Schools are answerable to students, parents, and taxpayers for showing respect for students as individuals and for generating satisfactory student learning as demonstrated on report cards, standardized tests, and other measures. Such legal, maturational, and practical differences in purposes and clientele between businesses and schools mean varying expectations for leaders' and workers' ethical behaviors and allowable practices. Therefore, using business models to analyze educational organizations can be useful but may not be totally appropriate for every comparison.

CLASSICAL ORGANIZATIONAL THEORY

By the 17th century, European agricultural methods had improved; surpluses were common and commerce became possible. Trade routes expanded on a global scale, including east to Asia and west to the Americas. The stirrings of the Industrial Revolution were at hand.

By the 18th century, technical advances had improved hygiene and diet. Populations were expanding. Technological developments, increasing business and markets, and growing populations created opportunities for merchants and entrepreneurs to invest in new factories. The Industrial Revolution had begun. With it came the need to improve work methods, quality, and productivity. Adam Smith (1723–1790), a Scottish moral philosopher and economist, advocated specialization to make labor efficient. In his book, *The Wealth of Nations* (1776), he proposed breaking the work into simple tasks. Developing workers' skills, saving time, and using specialized tools would bring business advantages. Changes in the manufacturing process soon appeared. Before long, machines would replace traditional manual labor and markedly boost productivity.

Classical organizational theory emerged during the early 20th century. It included two different perspectives: scientific management and administrative management. Generally, scientific management focused on the management of work and workers. Technically, its goal was to engineer maximum worker productivity, starting on the shop floor. Alternately, administrative management concerned itself with how an organization should be structured and operated. Its attention was on overall organizational efficiency, addressing the top executive, down the hierarchy.

Frederick W. Taylor developed scientific management principles and practices. Henri Fayol, Luther Gulick, and Max Weber primarily contributed to administrative management theory and application. Together, these industrial engineers, chief executives, public officials, and sociologists designed complementary views of how to best lead organizations to maximum efficiency and effectiveness.

Scientific Management

As the 19th century was ending, business leaders in the United States and Western Europe were escalating their efforts to increase industrial profits. The assembly lines' mass production innovations promised efficiency and wealth by lowering the unit cost of producing goods. In this era of manufacturing expansion, engineers and mechanically savvy scientists led the technical revolution, building machines and assembling them on the production line. The focus was on making the work and the work setting sufficiently specialized and standardized to promote worker efficiency and industry prosperity.

Frederick W. Taylor and Principles of Scientific Management.   Frederick W. Taylor became known for the principles of scientific management. *Scientific management* can be understood as the rational determination of purpose and the intelligent organization and use of manpower, technology, and other means to accomplish that end.[5] Although no precise and universally agreed upon dates bookend the scientific management era, it is generally considered to have held sway from 1910 to 1935.

From around 1900 to 1915, Taylor became a top engineering consultant and worked to solve practical production problems in factories across the United States. As a mechanical engineer, Taylor understood that much of the "inefficiency" in craftsmen's labors resulted from their efforts to deal with contingencies resulting from variations in machinery and materials. He realized that he had to remove these workplace inconsistencies and make the work area itself more rational by breaking each step into its component parts. The concept of "working smarter" rather than "working harder" originated with Taylor.[6]

Through his intensive involvement in engineering work systems using measurement and scientific procedures to find the one best way to do each job, Taylor developed his four principles of scientific management:[7]

1. *Scientific job analysis.* Eliminate the guesswork of "rule of thumb" (a rough practical rule not based on science or exact measurement) approaches to deciding how each worker is to do a job. Instead, adopt scientific measurements to break the job into a series of small, related tasks.
2. *Selection of personnel.* Use more scientific, systematic methods of selecting workers and training them for specific jobs instead of allowing workers to choose their own tasks and train themselves as best they could.
3. *Management cooperation.* Develop a spirit of hearty cooperation between workers and management to ensure that work is carried out in accordance with scientifically devised procedures.
4. *Functional supervision.* Establish a clear division of responsibility between management and workers. Management does the goal setting, planning, and supervising. Workers execute the required tasks.

Taylor's goal was to increase worker productivity. He taught that there was one best method of work that maximized efficiency that could be discovered through scientific study and analysis. Scientific management required careful investigation of why traditionally used procedures developed. Next, time-and-motion studies would determine the speed attainable with each step, unifying the best points of each procedure into a single standard practice that would be faster and easier than possible before. This new practice would stay in use until a better one (as determined scientifically by another time-and-motion study) replaced it. Gradually, managers and employees on the shop floor would substitute science for rule of thumb. Scientific management practices eliminated waste in human energy and in equipment and machine power while they improved work schedules and recorded individual effort. Specialization and standardization were key.[8]

Taylor's methods were directed primarily toward the largely uneducated factory employees. At that time, lower level supervisors and the workforce had limited education—an average of 3 years of formal schooling.[9] Recent immigrants who lacked English literacy comprised much of the factory population. In addition, Taylor's attitudes toward workers reflected his view that most workers were lazy, willing to do as little work as they safely could.[10] Additionally, he could extract increased labor productivity and exercise intensive control over the work environment because cheap labor was available, workers were not protected by unions, and workers feared unemployment.[11]

To Taylor, supervisors and workers with such low education levels and questionable work habits were not qualified to plan how work should be done. To solve this problem, Taylor separated planning from implementation by creating planning departments, staffed with engineers who had the responsibility to:

1. Develop scientific methods for doing work.
2. Establish goals for productivity.
3. Establish systems of rewards for meeting the goals.
4. Train the personnel in how to use the methods and thereby meet the goals.

Implicit in this approach, organizations were hierarchical, impersonal relationships, and systems of abstract rules. Nonetheless, Taylor saw his approach bringing justice for both managers and workers. The division of work between workers and managers in almost equal shares, each group taking over the work for which it was best suited, improved the situation in which responsibility largely rested with the workers.

Taylor also urged consideration of worker motivation, namely money. He saw the motivation to work as a simple economic transaction between the individual worker and the employer. Accordingly, pay should be closely tied to the job difficulty and achieved productivity. In Taylor's mind, the scientific management system would prevent employers from focusing only on making money by refusing to do their share of the work, and by driving workers harder for low pay. It would also prevent labor from making increasing and continual demands for more pay and shorter work hours instead of becoming more efficient.

Although Taylor's work had a narrow physiological focus and ignored psychological and sociological variables, he demonstrated that many jobs could be performed more efficiently. Scientific management also benefited unskilled workers by improving productivity enough to raise their pay nearly to that of skilled labor, allowing workers to earn middle-class wages, greater purchasing power, and a higher standard of living.[12]

Indirectly, Taylor also contributed to organizational theory. He advocated clear delineation of authority and responsibility, separation of planning from operations, incentive schemes for workers, management by exception (where managers delegate as much responsibility as possible to those below them and only intervene when workers fail to meet their performance standards), and task specialization. These concepts were universal in nature and were widely adopted in all kinds of organizations throughout the United States and the world.

Scientific Management in Schools. In the early 1900s, educators tried using scientific management in public schools. It was not a natural fit. Managing labor on an assembly line was not the same as educating dissimilar children. In making a factory model work in schools, teachers had to identify actual learning outcomes and take periodic measurements to determine whether students had reached them. Taylor's approach began the science of school measurement: finding supposedly objective and numerical ways to demonstrate student achievement. Other efficiency reforms required teachers to document their teaching activities in order to minimize "waste." However, since many of Taylor's education disciples were not educators themselves, they seldom tried to tell teachers what or how to teach.[13]

Scientific management in schools had curricular, instructional, and social implications. The factory model idea for education reached its peak in 1908 in Gary, Indiana, where "platoon" schools became popular. Organized like factories, these schools ran on tight schedules. After each bell, students moved from room to room in an orderly fashion. Hundreds of cities adopted this plan, thinking it made better use of school facilities, using a bell schedule to organize learning time, providing a varied curriculum, organizing academic departments to guide instruction in separate disciplines, and outfitting certain rooms for special uses. Many of these practices still appear in schools today.

Scientific management also had an impact on school leaders. Between 1900 and 1930, school administrators began to see themselves as managers, rather than as educators. They used scientific management ideas to help their schools accommodate the large numbers of immigrant children at low cost. Children entered school and moved through the grades with their age peers, changing classes at predetermined intervals to ringing bells. Today we know that children grow and develop at different and variable rates, so moving students in lockstep with those of their chronological age rewarded students with quicker development. Those who developed more slowly fell behind and dropped out.[14]

Scientific management had an intense and long lasting impact on how schools were organized and administered. In *Education and the Cult of Efficiency* (1964),[15] Raymond E. Callahan clearly described how U.S. school superintendents quickly adopted the business and industrial values and practices of their time. Responding to shared cultural norms, managers in all organizations had a mania for efficiency (low cost per unit), rigid application of uniform work procedures, and detailed accounting practices. Although some held doubts, many school administrators clamored to take on the jargon and practices of those with higher status in society.[16]

During the period from approximately before World War I until almost World War II, scientific management was widely believed to be a relevant model for schools. Professors of educational administration commonly conducted studies to determine, for instance, the cheapest and most efficient methods of maintaining floors—mopping or sweeping, oiling or waxing—so they could provide future school superintendents with the necessary knowledge and skills to train janitorial workers.[17]

In addition, scientific management influenced how school leaders viewed others in the school setting. Educators understood Taylor's views to mean that managers needed the brains and workers did not. Managers set the rules, and workers followed them. In the resulting division of labor, individuals with high intelligence were assumed to be inherently more important to the country's economic well-being than those less blessed, intellectually and socially.[18] To principals as school managers, this perspective applied to their treatment of teachers as well as students.[19]

Criticism of Scientific Management.   Although Taylor's concept of rationality in pursuit of organizational goals and his innovations in the workplace led to dramatic improvements in productivity, his ideas were widely misinterpreted. Employers used time-and-motion studies simply to obtain more work from employees at less pay. Unions condemned speedups and the lack of voice in their work that "Taylorism"[20] consigned them. Quality and productivity declined when administrators instituted his principles simplistically.[21]

Mainly, critics decried scientific management as reductionist and dehumanizing to workers. Taylor's methods specifying "not only what is to be done but how it is to be done and the exact time allowed for doing it"[22] assigned managers responsibility for all the thinking while workers did all the doing. Although this practice may have been appropriate for supervising an uneducated workforce, it left no scope for the individual worker to excel or to reason.[23] Likewise, critics saw standardization and specialization as authoritarianism, provoking industrial unrest and conflict, higher employment turnover and absenteeism, industrial sabotage, low employee morale, and other managerial problems.[24] Some critics further objected to Taylor's lack of concern for social and psychological problems that affected the workplace.[25]

Scientific management's impact on schools made them bureaucratic, impersonal, departmentalized, and increasingly isolated from the larger society. School codes and procedures spelled out exactly how to address every detail of school life. Students moved through the fragmented curriculum, and standardized tests purported to measure the quality of their learning. As learning became less meaningful to students, misbehavior increased and absences and dropouts went up. Academic quality and student achievement declined.[26]

ACTIVITY 2.2   Scientific Management in Heritage County

Case Study Question 2: How might the school board's directives about a no-nonsense, top-down management style—and their instructional proposals—compromise Dr. Smith's ability to be an effective educational leader?

In the late 1800s, Frederick Taylor's scientific management theory and practices strengthened industry's organizational efficiency by eliminating waste in human energy and equipment while improving work schedules and individual effort. Specialization and standardization were key. Scientific management approaches were especially productive with the minimally educated, unskilled workers on the shop floor. Discuss as a class:

1. In what ways did scientific management influence the culture and structure of public schools?
2. In the case study, how do the school board's directives to Superintendent Smith regarding a reengineered organizational chart, communication following a strict chain of command, uniform curriculum goals, specific job functions, merit pay, and teacher training clearly reflect Taylor's scientific management principles?
3. How might Taylor's separating the organization's management and planning functions from the implementation functions succeed in late-19th-century factories but fail in 21st-century public schools?

Administrative Management Theory

Unlike scientific management's spotlight on the unique particulars of the production floor, administrative management considered the general processes common to all organizations. Administrative management recommended how to structure an organization's leadership and identified the managerial tasks necessary to keep the enterprise working efficiently, from the top executives down to the middle managers and supervisors.

Henri Fayol (1841–1925), a French industrialist, looked at increasing efficiency by concentrating on the entire organization's management. As the managing director (chief executive officer) of a mining firm and a very successful businessman, Fayol believed that his experiences in managing people and in organizing a company—rather than his competence as an engineer—were primary contributors to his business's prosperity.[27] His most notable work, *General and Industrial Management*,[28] established Fayol as the first modern organizational theorist.

Henri Fayol's Ideas on Administration.   Taylor and Fayol viewed the organization from two contrasting perspectives. Taylor, the engineer-technician, addressed the organization from the bottom up, addressing task efficiency and viewing the workers as extensions of the factory machinery. Fayol, the top-level executive, looked at the organization from the top down, concentrating attention on the general highest level administrators with overall control and organizational efficiency.[29]

Fayol advanced the following ideas on administration:[30]

1. Rather than stressing specialization and standardization, as Taylor had, Fayol emphasized the common elements in administrative processes across organizations. These included controlling the organization with authority, discipline (rules of budgeting and behavior), and coordination of activities. As industries grew in size, geographic locations, and endeavors, vertically integrating and organizing operations by senior management with strong central control became essential to prevent bankruptcy or hostile takeovers.

2. Rather than focusing on the manager, worker, and tasks, as Taylor had, Fayol clearly separated the processes of administration from the actual work of organizations, such as production. Building the product was a separate and distinct set of organizational functions from the planning, budgeting, coordinating, and hiring functions.

3. Rather than seeing managers' expertise and authority coming from the technical skills needed on the assembly line, as Taylor had, Fayol viewed administrators as experts in organizational leadership who needed professional training. Unlike the materials engineers who dominated production through analysis and calculations originally developed on inanimate machines to find the one best way to produce and make a profit, organizational leaders needed education in management and accounting.

While Taylor argued that specialization was the most efficient form of management, Fayol emphasized that administration consists of a set of principles to direct management that are common to all organizations. Domains as diverse as politics, religion, commerce, industry, and families all had administrative or governing principles that resembled each other. Since organizations were so much alike, managers' actual work shared many similarities. This awareness made it possible to develop a common code of administrative knowledge and principles. The rules that held true for one organization held true for another.[31]

Fayol analyzed administrative work into five responsibilities:[32]

1. **Forecasting and planning:** examining the future and laying out the actions to be taken
2. **Organizing:** laying out the lines of authority and responsibility
3. **Commanding:** putting the plan into action
4. **Coordinating:** laying out timing and sequencing activities; binding and harmonizing all
5. **Controlling:** monitoring and adjusting, ensuring conformity with rules, evaluating results

Fayol's administrative responsibilities were more nuanced than authoritarian. For instance, *commanding* included putting the plan into action and energizing employees, while *controlling* included adapting the overall plan to changing circumstances.

Fayol also identified 14 principles: division of work, authority and responsibility, discipline, unity of command, unity of direction, subordination of the individual interest to the common good, centralization, chain of command, remuneration (wages), order, equity, stability of personnel, initiative, and esprit de corps (Table 2–1). He admitted that the number of principles was arbitrary, the list was not exhaustive, and the principles were flexible and adaptable to every need.[33]

Planning and flexibility were essential to Fayol's view of administration. While planning was management's most important job, strategies needed to be flexible enough to accommodate the unexpected. Good administrators should prepare for surprises. Fayol extended the importance of contingency to the entire management process. Administrators had to be intelligent and experienced, and have a sense of proportion if they were to be able to adapt to changing circumstances.[34]

In addition, human relations within the organization concerned Fayol. As he saw it, administration was a relationship between an organization's head and other members who together comprised the entire enterprise's social structure.[35] Administration was not an exclusive privilege but a responsibility that comes with authority. Fayol made the distinction between authority that stemmed from a manager's official title and that which came from the manager's experience and personality. He continually stressed the need for fairness in industrial relations and the impact of stability on the labor force's morale. Real management talent was needed to coordinate effort, encourage dedication, use each worker's abilities, reward each one's merit without arousing jealousies, and maintain harmonious relations. He also observed that workers' attitudes and behaviors were influenced by their lives outside the factory and suggested "benevolent collaboration" for their welfare.

TABLE 2–1

Fayol's 14 Management Principles

Management Principle	Definition
Division of labor	Specialization increases the organization's output by making employees more efficient as they build up experience and continuously improve skills.
Authority	The right to give orders and the power to secure obedience. Responsibility, a corollary of authority, is the obligation to carry out assigned duties.
Discipline	Implies respect for the rules that govern the organization. Good discipline is the result of effective leadership.
Unity of command	An employee should receive orders only from one supervisor with no other conflicting lines of command.
Unity of direction	Similar activities directed toward a particular goal should be grouped together under one manager using one plan to ensure coordination of an enterprise.
Subordination of individual interests	The interests of individuals and groups within the organization should not take precedence over the interests of the organization as a whole.
Remuneration	Workers must be paid a fair and satisfactory wage for their services.
Centralization	Managers must retain final responsibility, but they should give subordinates enough authority to make decisions that will successfully complete the task. The appropriate degree of centralization will vary with the condition of the business and the quality of the personnel.
Scalar chain	The chain of command is the sequence of supervisors ranging from the ultimate authority to the lowest ranks. The exact lines of authority should be clear and followed at all times. However, if following the chain creates delays, cross-communications can be allowed if agreed to by all parties and if superiors are kept informed.
Order	People and materials should be coordinated to be at the right place at the right time.
Equity	Managers should be kind and fair to their subordinates.
Stability of personnel	High employee turnover is inefficient. Successful organizations need a stable workforce. Management should provide orderly personnel planning and ensure that replacements are available to fill vacancies.
Initiative	Employees who are allowed to originate and carry out plans will exert high levels of effort. Managers should encourage them to do so.
Esprit de corps	Managers should promote and maintain teamwork, team spirit, and morale to build harmony and unity within the organization.

Sources: Adapted from Fayol, H. (1949). *General and industrial administration* (pp. 20–41). New York, NY: Pitman. Originally published in 1916 in French, entitled *Administration industrielle et generale*. See also: Robbins, S. P., & Coulter, M. (2000). *Management*. Australia: Prentice Hall. Retrieved from http://everything2.com/title/Fayol%2527s%252014%2520Principles%2520of%2520Management; Marino, V. (2009). *14 management principles (Henri Fayol). 12 manage. The executive fast track*. Retrieved from http://www.12manage.com/methods_fayol_14_principles_of_management.html

Taylor and Fayol saw the Western world becoming an organizational society. Fayol was the first to recognize management as a continuous process. Although Taylor's ideas about management are more widely known in the United States than Fayol's, Fayol's principles are compatible with later management studies and continue in practice to the present day.[36]

Luther Gulick and POSDCoRB.   As the study of organizations, management, and administration received increased scholarly attention, academics and practitioners amplified their concerns about the principles of scientific management. Increasing conflict arose between the organization's demands for workers' submissiveness and discipline and the individuals' needs to experience a realistic sense of reward and satisfaction from their work. The 1920s and 1930s witnessed increasing labor unrest, public displays of dissatisfaction with top-down management, and qualms about the outcomes for employees. During this era, Luther Gulick, a highly regarded practitioner and scholar, found a way to synthesize those elements that could make organizations more effective and functional.

Gulick (1892–1993) was among the first scholars to study the role of the executive in modern government, and he helped to devise and put into effect the concepts of budgeting and management training for public officials.[37] As a young man, he had met Frederick Taylor. Impressed with the man and his ideas, Gulick expanded Taylor's somewhat limited conception of the use of science in management into a more evolved science of administration.[38] Gulick saw the value of applying scientific management principles to public affairs. In 1936 and 1937, he worked with President Franklin D. Roosevelt on reorganizing the executive branch of government to strengthen the president's administrative power and capacity.

During his work on Roosevelt's Committee on Administrative Management, Gulick built upon Fayol's theory. Using his own acronym, POSDCoRB, to delineate an executive's activities and duties, Gulick included Planning, Organizing, Staffing, Directing, Coordinating, Reporting, and Budgeting (Table 2–2). His list provides a template of administrative actions intended for any competent administrator to follow.[39]

TABLE 2–2

Comparing Fayol's Administrative Functions to Gulick's Functions

Fayol's Administrative Functions	Gulick's Administrative Functions
Planning	Planning
Organizing	Organizing
[No equivalent]	Staffing—involves the whole personnel function of selecting, training, and developing the staff, and maintaining favorable working conditions
Commanding	Directing
Coordinating	Coordinating
Controlling	Reporting
[No equivalent]	Budgeting—concerns all activities that accompany budgeting, including fiscal planning, accounting, and control

Source: Adapted from Gulick, L., & Urwick, L. (Eds.). (1937). *Papers on the science of administration.* New York, NY: Institute of Public Administration, Columbia University; Fells, M. (2000). Fayol stands the test of time. *Journal of Management History, 6*(8), 345–360.

Even while expanding the administrative functions to include a human resources dimension, Gulick's model met criticism. In his attempt to "take politics out of administration," POSDCoRB in later years appeared overly technical and less humanistic. Gulick did not intend to omit administrative ethics, values, and human relations from administrative theory.[40] Nonetheless, his model has become incorrectly characterized as an administrative design that is logically and rigidly rational and does not include humanistic guidelines.

ACTIVITY 2.3   Fayol's and Gulick's Theories Applied to Heritage County

Henri Fayol and Luther Gulick looked at organizations from the top down. They believed in a vertically integrated organization with strong centralized control to promote organizational efficiency; controlling the organization through authority, discipline, rules, and coordinated activities; separating planning and production functions; and applying administrative principles to govern management. Discuss as a class:

1. In the case study, how does the Heritage County School Board's concept of their relationship to Dr. Smith reflect Fayol's and Gulick's administrative principles?
2. Which directives to Dr. Smith exhibit Fayol's ideas regarding centralization, division of labor, unity of command, authority, discipline, scalar chain of command, subordination of individual interests, and esprit de corps?
3. Which of Fayol's management principles do the Heritage County School Board appear to neglect?
4. Which of Fayol's management principles do the three newly hired principals appear to be using?

Max Weber and Bureaucratic Organizational Theory.   In the early 1900s, individuals were becoming an increasingly larger consideration in organizations. The relatively simple social and political structures of an earlier time no longer seemed adequate in an urban industrial society. Mixing people of diverse backgrounds, values, beliefs, talents, and even languages in urban communities and inside factories led to wide-ranging tensions—social, political, and economic. The escalating sense of conflict between people and organizations became a critical factor in the struggle to successfully adapt to this new industrialized world. In the years before World War I, labor unrest, revolution, and Communism's rise put communities and nations on edge.

Today, *bureaucracy* is often used as a pejorative word for all public administration or any large-scale formal organization epitomized by impersonal inefficiency. Ironically, in the early 20th century, German sociologist Max Weber[41] (1864–1920) conceived of bureaucracy as an analytical concept, an administrative form, and a set of ideas and observations that brought efficiency and effectiveness to public administration and formally organized institutions.[42] Relying on rationality, legitimate authority, and the procedurally correct application of rules to ensure evenhanded operations, Weber expected well-run bureaucracies to be fairer, more impartial, more predictable, more rational, and more capable than large organizations that operated on powerful industrialists' whims or entrenched politicians' biases.[43]

Weber was the first to describe the concept of bureaucracy based on a set of rational guidelines. Writing at about the same time as Taylor and Fayol (about 1910 to 1920), Weber's work was not translated into English until the 1940s. Similar in concept to many of Fayol's 14 principles, Weber's guidelines were believed to comprise an ideal structure for organizational effectiveness. Together they laid the foundation for contemporary organizational theory.[44]

According to Weber, highly trained technical specialists, each skilled in a specific, limited part of the administrative task, would make a bureaucracy the most efficient form of organization yet designed. The bureaucratic apparatus would be very impersonal, minimizing irrational personal and emotional variables, and leaving bureaucratic employees free to work with a minimum of friction or confusion. This would result in expert, impartial, and unbiased service to the organization's clients. Almost all modern organizations, including schools, have these characteristics.

Ideally, Weber's well-run bureaucracy can be characterized by:[45]

◆ *Impersonal social relations*. The bureaucratic employee is expected to make decisions based on facts, not feelings. Impersonality by administrators increases the probability for equality and rational treatment.

◆ *Appointment and promotion based on merit/technical competence*. Employees think of their work as a career based on specialized competencies. Promotions are based without favoritism on seniority, achievement, or some combination of both.

◆ *Rules and regulations covering employees' rights and duties*. A consistent system of abstract rules intentionally established and applied covers the rights and duties inherent in each position, helps coordinate the organization's activities, and ensures the probability of uniformity and stability of employee action.

◆ A *well-defined hierarchy of authority*. Each office is under the control and supervision of a higher one. The organizational chart illustrates these vertical relationships. In schools, superintendents are at the top; principals, teachers, and students are lower on the hierarchy.

◆ A *division of labor based on functional specialization*. A division of labor among positions allows the organization to handle large, complex tasks by a variety of knowledgeable and expert employees who have been hired based on their technical qualifications. This increases efficiency.

◆ *Efficiency*. The organization maximizes rational decision making and administrative efficacy. Division of labor and specialization produce experts. Experts with impersonal orientations make technically correct, rational decisions based on facts and in accordance with the organization's rules and regulations.

Weber's bureaucracy was also characterized by the separation of policy and administrative decisions, and acting in the client's rather than the organization's best interest. Additionally, it also expected employees to separate work from private life.[46]

Weber's theoretical model speaks to the ideal, which may or may not occur in the real world. He assumed that the organization deals primarily with uniform events and with occupations stressing traditional areas of knowledge rather than social skills. By "uniform," Weber meant that the identified tasks recur in time, among many people, and are important. Therefore, he assumed that problems are standard and unsurprising and that the environment changes very slowly.

In reality, however, problems arise from actions occurring outside of the approved flow charts, from underperforming production rates, or from external changes. For example, as the telegraph was coming into widespread use, the Pony Express business might have attempted to overtake this new competition by purchasing faster horses, hiring younger riders, and placing change stations more strategically instead of adapting to the larger change issues. In such cases, Weber's model has clear limitations.

While recognizing its merits in ideal situations, Weber showed sensitivity to the dangers of bureaucracy. While he applauded its efficiency, Weber recognized that bureaucracy can become *bureaucratization*, leading to the "iron cage" of mindless routine and mechanization.[47] He even warned that massive, uncontrollable bureaucracy could be the greatest threat to both Communism and free-enterprise capitalism.[48]

Criticism of Administrative Management.   Although Weber understood his model as an ideal type, a concept to offer guidance for organizational efficiency, critics have challenged his ideas. These include not being sensitive enough to the ways the model's rules can become dysfunctional, its neglect of the informal organization, its internal contradictions, and its inherent gender bias. These criticisms can be useful for seeing the limitations in all classical organizational theories. Let's consider these critiques.

Functional Can Be Dysfunctional.   In administrative theory—as in Weber's bureaucracy—the same principle that promotes efficiency and goal attainment can also have dysfunctional outcomes. Predesigned rules that work fairly, efficiently, and effectively in predictable and ideal conditions may not be so fair, efficient, or effective in unique situations. Table 2–3 illustrates how a functional dimension in one context can become dysfunctional in another. What begins with positive expectations for efficiency and effectiveness may have some unintended consequences.

Although Weber's bureaucracy and the classical organizational models in general are based on the ideal of uniform events, the real world is full of exceptions. The larger the organization, the more likely it will include various situations and people. If each unique situation requires a general rule, there will be too many rules for employees to learn. Yet, without rules for unique or ambiguous situations, administrators will likely make decisions that may be inappropriate or substitute their own private value systems. Efficiency is likely to drop when general rules are used and the task is not uniform just as it will when no consistent rules apply.

Similarly, division of labor and specialization can produce expertise and efficiency, but they can also create problems when the environment changes. In a new situation, having the wrong specialty may lead to organizational error or inflexibility and obsolescence. Consider the armed forces where a rapidly changing technology makes traditional specialties outdated. For example, a well-equipped, high-tech modern military has difficulty fighting overseas against ideologically-driven insurgents who use stealth, improvised explosive devices (IEDs), and easy blending with the local population in asymmetrical warfare. Clinging to the traditional specialties and practices can lead to a dangerous lag in military preparedness as well as wasteful conflict between specialties.[49]

Impersonality may improve rationality in decision making, but it may also produce an atmosphere in which people feel invisible, like faceless cogs in a machine, resulting in low morale which frequently harms organizational efficiency. Hierarchy in organizations may strengthen coordination, but it might also limit communication. Every level of the hierarchy brings the potential for communication distortions and blockages. Employees tend to want to look good to their superiors: they tend to tell only those things that make them appear highly competent and with unlimited potential or say what they think their supervisors want to hear.

TABLE 2–3
Administrative Theory's Functions and Dysfunctions

Bureaucratic Characteristic	When Functional	When Dysfunctional (Unintended Consequences)
Expects uniform events	Uniform events permit consistent rules, predictability, consistent responses, and increased efficiency.	The real world has exceptions. It is impractical to make rules for all unique or ambiguous situations. Administrators use rules that are inappropriate or rely on personal values. This reduces efficiency.
Specialization and division of labor	Creates expertise and efficiency.	In a new situation, having the wrong specialty may lead to organizational error or inflexibility and obsolescence (for example, the Pony Express).
Impersonality	Improves rationality in decision making.	May produce an atmosphere in which people feel invisible, resulting in low morale, reducing organizational efficiency and effectiveness.
Hierarchy and chain of command	Strengthens coordination.	Limits communication, increases potential for distortion and blocked communication, reducing efficiency and effectiveness.
Rules and regulations	Supports continuity, coordination, stability, and uniformity.	Produces rigidity and goal displacement in which the employee works to satisfy the organization rather than the client, e.g., "red tape."
Informal organization	**Not considered in Weber's or administrative theory models.**	Informal groups' status, rules, and norms may either support or undermine the formal organization's goals and practices.
Internal contradictions	**Not considered in Weber's or administrative theory models.**	Is authority based on technical competence or compliance with rules? Does authority come from the formal position held or the professional expertise developed?
Gender bias	**Not considered in Weber's or administrative theory models.**	Emphasis on rationality, dominance, and expertise disadvantage women who face conflicting responsibilities for work and family and lack of educational or training opportunities.

Source: Based on Hoy, W. K., & Miskal, C. G. (2008). *Educational administration. Theory, research, and practice* (8th ed., pp. 92–97). Boston, MA: McGraw-Hill. Used with permission.

Finally, rules and regulations can provide for continuity, coordination, stability, and uniformity but they can also produce rigidity and *goal displacement* (the rules become ends in themselves). When this happens, employees may become so rule oriented that they work to serve the organization instead of their clients. They forget that rules and regulations are means to help achieve certain goals; they are not ends in themselves. The iconic "bureaucratic red tape" illustrates this dysfunction in action.[50]

Neglects the Informal Organization. The *informal organization* is a system of interpersonal relations that form spontaneously within all formal organizations—off the organizational chart. It evolves from employees' needs to interact in the workplace. It includes informal structure, informal norms, and informal leadership.[51] In schools as in other organizations, employees and administrators typically construct their own networks of informal relations, systems of status and power, communications (the "grapevine"), and working arrangements. All these connections and relationships shape individual behavior. Informal organizations reduce impersonality and foster an atmosphere of cordiality, belonging, friendliness, and cohesion. Differences in social relations, respect, and status among group members result. Some members become informal leaders, others followers, and a few are isolated.

These informal interactions produce subgroups or cliques. Clique membership provides prestige and status in the larger group. Cliques develop norms for their behavior; common values describe what individuals should do in different situations and the consequences of not meeting these expectations. Generally, *values* define the goals of human behavior while *social norms* provide the legitimate and clear means for pursuing those ends.[52] As such, the informal group has a set of shared values and beliefs, behaviors, and social structure that operate apart from—and occasionally against—the organization's formal structure and rules. This informal organization will influence the formal organization, enhancing or retarding its effectiveness.

In schools, the informal organization allows teachers to keep a sense of personal integrity, self-respect, and independence. These informal groups can be a useful vehicle for improving school efficiency. Effective principals frequently use the grapevine to stay on top of school concerns and preempt potential problems. Teachers and administrators often acknowledge the school's informal organization, laughing knowingly about regular faculty meetings in which no teacher volunteers a comment or question, although they get together afterwards in the parking lot to fully express their opinions about what just occurred.

Neglects the Internal Contradictions.   According to Weber, all characteristics of the ideal type are logically consistent and interact for maximum organizational efficiency. Other administrative theorists assume the same. Both theoretical and empirical analysis show this is not always so.

Talcott Parsons (1947) and Alvin Gouldner (1954) questioned whether bureaucracy's authority is based on technical competence or on legal powers and discipline.[53] Weber (1947, p. 339) affirmed that "bureaucratic administration means fundamentally the exercise of control on the basis of knowledge,"[54] asserting the central importance of discipline as well as expertise. The unanswered question—Is bureaucratic administration based on expertise or compliance with directives?—provides the basis for future organizational conflict and contradiction.

Similarly, Weber did not separate bureaucratic discipline from professional principles.[55] Discipline reduces the scope of uncertainty (follow the rules) whereas professional expertise provides the knowledge to handle it (solve the problem). Since professionals frequently work in bureaucracies, these two alternate modes of rationality may produce strain and conflict. Does an administrator's authority reside in the office held or in the expertise learned? Again, with no clear answer, this seeming duality provides the basis for future organizational conflict.

Neglects Gender Issues.   Weber's ideal model is gender neutral and universal—as is classical organizational theory—but feminists such as Joanne Martin (1990; with

Knopoff, 1999) often believe that this model disadvantages women.[56] The emphasis on full-time employment and extensive training as job qualifications hinders women who often lack equal access to training programs and face the conflicting demands of job and family responsibilities. By default, bureaucracies may be considered as gender biased in their hiring and promotion criteria.[57] Bureaucracies also perpetuate systems in which men control the organization and prioritize masculine virtues of authority, rationality, rules, regulations, dominance, and impersonality, thereby devaluing alternative ways of organization that are allegedly more characteristic of women's values of interdependence, affect, and cooperation.[58]

When assessing classical organization theory, historical context remains important. Freund (1972) reminded us that Weber intended his model to be a starting point for further research, not true or false, complete or incomplete, but something to be evaluated as useful or not.[59] The same may be true for other early organizational theorists. Nevertheless, the administrative theorists understood that an organization is greater than the human-machine interface. Instead, it is a complex network of social relationships and interdependencies. Worker motivations include ideals, values, beliefs, and the need for personal satisfactions. Scientific management and administrative management theorists provided the first steps to organizational efficiency and effectiveness. Time, maturing organizational thought, and new experiences in the workplace would suggest additional ones.

ACTIVITY 2.4   Assessing the Bureaucracy in Heritage County

Case Study Question 3: In what ways does the Heritage County School Board neglect to consider the school district and community's informal organization when designing their directives for Superintendent Smith?

Max Weber described bureaucracy as a set of rational guidelines for organizational effectiveness. In theory, the bureaucratic apparatus would be socially impersonal, depend on rules and regulations in a well-defined hierarchy of authority, use a specialized division of labor, and result in efficient, expert, impartial, and unbiased service to the organization's clients. Discuss as a class:

1. Which of Weber's bureaucracy characteristics did the Heritage County School Board use when giving Dr. Smith their directives?
2. Using Table 2–3, identify the areas of possible dysfunction in the Heritage County School Board's expectations for their superintendent, principals, and teachers.
3. How do the informal organization's values and social norms for leadership and education differ from the formal organization's values and social norms? How do these differences appear in the case study?
4. In what areas do the case study's contradictions between bureaucracy based on expertise on the one hand and compliance with directives on the other appear? In the short term, who will likely struggle the most with this contradiction? Who will likely struggle the least?
5. What gender issues may be masked by the school board's administrative management practices?
6. Using Weber's definition, in what respect is a public school or college a bureaucracy?

MODERN ORGANIZATIONAL THEORY

Modern organizational theory expands the administrative focus from the organization as an impersonal whole to include human variables as essential factors affecting organizational productivity. The human relations approach is considered to have started with a series of studies conducted at Western Electric's Hawthorne plant near Chicago. Using scientific and administrative management principles, the Western Electric Company, a relatively enlightened industrial employer, cooperated with the National Research Council on a simple experiment designed to determine the optimum level of lighting in a shop for maximum production efficiency. Well designed and executed, the experiments revealed that the relationship between the lighting level and worker productivity was neither direct nor simple.

Since Taylor's principles of scientific management strongly suggested a relationship would exist between illumination and optimal worker output, the studies raised more questions than they answered. In the process, the human element entered the equation, and organizational theory moved from classical to modern.

Human Relations and the Hawthorne Studies

After the preliminary experiments from 1924 to 1927, Western Electric retained Harvard professors Elton Mayo, an industrial psychologist, and Fritz Roethlisberger, a social psychologist, to continue the studies between 1927 and 1933. These investigations are popularly known as the Hawthorne studies. Researchers stumbled upon a principle of human motivation that would help to revolutionize management theory and practice. By paying attention to workers and their needs, management could expect increases in performance and productivity.

The Hawthorne studies consisted of several experiments and interviews with 21,126 Western Electric workers to learn what employees liked and disliked about their work environment. Researchers examined the workplace's physical and environmental influences (such as brightness of lights, humidity) and its psychological aspects (such as work breaks, group pressure, working hours, managerial leadership).

The Experiments.   Two experiments highlight what the workers experienced. In the Relay Assembly Test Room experiments, Mayo designated two female work groups. Each group performed the same task. The groups were located in two separate rooms, each lighted equally. One group, the control group, had no changes made in the lighting or other work environment factors. The experimental group had lighting and other environmental factors varied at stated intervals. Mayo put the experimental group with a supervisor who was more a friendly observer than disciplinarian. Mayo made frequent changes in their working conditions, always discussing and explaining the changes in advance. He changed the hours in the work week, the hours in the workday, the number of rest breaks, and the time of the lunch hour. Occasionally, he would return the women to their original, harder working conditions.

Throughout the series of experiments, an observer sat with the women in the workshop noting all that occurred, keeping the women informed about the experiment, asking for advice or information, and listening to their complaints. The experimental group had considerable freedom of movement. They were not pushed around or bossed by anyone. Under these conditions, they developed an increased sense of responsibility. Instead of discipline from higher authority being imposed, it came from within the group itself.[60]

Researchers then measured and analyzed changes in the two groups' productivity. Results were puzzling. Regardless of light levels, adjustments in rest periods, or workday or workweek lengths, productivity in both control and experimental groups improved. In fact, the worse the situation became, the higher the productivity rose. The experiments did not confirm any of the hypotheses being tested.

Another experiment also produced unexpected findings. In the Bank Wiring Observation Room experiments, a group of nine men were paid on a piecework incentives system. Their wages increased as their productivity increased. Researchers expected that worker productivity would rise over time, but this did not happen. Instead, the group informally set an acceptable level for its members' output. Most workers, the "regulars," ignored the incentive system and voluntarily conformed to the group's standard level of acceptable amount, called a *group norm*. The group disciplined those who did not conform, the "deviants," using social pressure to bring their output closer in line to the group's standard. Workers who produced too much, called "rate-busters," sometimes received physical threats to make them conform with the rest of the group. Finally, employees who under-produced were labeled "chiselers" and received group pressure to increase their output.

The Informal Organization.   To understand the complicated and confounding results, Mayo and Roethlisberger interviewed over 20,000 employees who had taken part in the experiments. One thing became clear: The workers' behavior did not conform to the official job specifications. The interviews and observations during the experiments suggested that a human-social element operated in the workplace.

An informal organization emerged that affected performance. An *informal organization* is an unofficial social structure that operates within the organization with informal leaders; informal norms, values, and feelings; and functional communication patterns. Informal cliques with their own interaction patterns existed on and off the job. The research conclusions: Increases in productivity were more an outcome of group dynamics and effective management than any set of employer demands or physical factors.

The Novelty Effect.   In the lighting experiment, Mayo concluded that the workers enjoyed receiving the researchers' attention, also known as the "novelty effect."[61] He believed that employees' needs for recognition, security, and sense of belonging were more important in determining workers' morale and productivity than the physical condition under which they worked. Likewise, effective management's interpersonal skills such as motivating, leading, participative decision making, and effective communications also led to increased productivity. From the results of the incentive pay group, researchers concluded that informal work groups emerged with their own norms for group members' appropriate behavior. The social norms held more sway than the economic incentives. Investigators realized that human variability is an important determinant of productivity.

These findings challenged the basic assumptions of human engineers and scientific managers. Although these studies date from the 1930s, they established the foundations for modern human relations theory and practice. The importance of understanding human behavior, especially group behavior, became firmly established.[62]

Criticism of the Human Relations Approach.   The human relations approach to management had its detractors. Sociologist Amitai Etzioni (1964) suggested that the human relations approach grossly oversimplified the complexities of organizational life by glossing over work realities. Organizations have conflicting values and interests as well as shared ones. Worker dissatisfaction may be a symptom of actual underlying conflicts of interests. An organization is not one big happy family.[63] More recent critics of the human relations movement have argued that the concern for workers was not genuine but a management tool or strategy to manipulate subordinates.[64]

Nonetheless, the human relations approach tempered the administrative manager's emphasis on organizational structure with attention on the worker as an individual employee whose motivation, satisfaction, and group morale contributed to organizational efficiency and productivity. It would become the basis for developing effective educational leadership.

Organizational Management Theory

Classical and bureaucratic approaches to organizations tend to emphasize organizational structure and the highly rational logic of top-down hierarchical control over people. Additionally, they tend to treat the organization as a tangible, concrete, almost living entity. Early studies of organization called this the *formal organization*. Today, we call this *structuralism*. Structuralists tend to think that a properly structured organization will improve organizational performance. When we merge small school districts into larger ones, adopt school-based management, or conduct articulation activities between high schools and colleges, structuralist thought is influencing our administrative practice—seeing school components as part of complex systems of interrelated parts.

The Hawthorne studies bridge the gap between two types of organizational thinking and theory. For all its formal structure, rules, and regulations, the organization consists of human beings and their personal beliefs, attitudes, assumptions, hopes, fears, and histories. The organization has both *formal* (structural) and *informal* (human) *organization*. These two dimensions continually interact. As a result, changes in the relations between human beings in the organization have tremendous power to affect the organization's performance. When we involve people more fully in decisions that affect them, attend more conscientiously to their motivational needs, or increase the collegiality and collaboration through teamwork, we are using people approaches to organizational problems.

Between 1937 and 1942, three significant books appeared that provided the groundwork for the influential post–World War II era in organizational thought and practice. Chester Barnard, Felix J. Roethlisberger and William J. Dickson, and Herbert A. Simon all contributed ideas that clarified the dynamic mutual interactions between the workers' needs and aspirations and the organization's goals.

ACTIVITY 2.5   Applying Hawthorne Study Findings to Heritage County

The Hawthorne studies found that organizations have both formal (structural) and informal (human) organizations. An informal organization is an unofficial social structure that operates within the organization. It has informal leaders; informal norms, values, and feelings; and functional communication patterns. Research found that increases in productivity were more an outcome of group dynamics and effective management than any set of employer demands or physical factors. Discuss as a class:

1. How do the Heritage County School Board's expectations reflect their indifference to (or lack of awareness of) the community's and schools' informal organizations?
2. How will awareness of these informal organizations influence the way Dr. Smith carries out his responsibilities?
3. Which of the new superintendent's actions suggest that his leadership philosophies allow him to effectively use the schools' and community's informal organizations?

Chester Barnard.   Chester Barnard was not an academic; he constructed his theories painstakingly from decades of organizational experience. As president of the New Jersey Bell Telephone Company, Barnard was in close communication with the scientists who conducted the Western Electric studies. In *The Functions of the Executive* (1938),[65] he underscored the critical importance of better understanding the relationship between the formal and the informal organizations. He believed that organization comes not from above but from the cooperation of work groups.[66]

Barnard's best known idea is the cooperative system, an attempt to integrate human relations and classical management principles into one coherent framework. He argued that the executive must meet two conditions if organizations are to realize cooperation and long-term financial success: effectiveness and efficiency. While *effectiveness*, or the degree to which the organization's common purpose is achieved, is important, satisfying the employees' personal desires, or *efficiency*, is equally important.[67]

Likewise, according to Barnard's theory of equilibrium, each employee receives inducements from the organization (wages, other benefits) for which the employee makes contributions (or sacrifices, depending on one's viewpoint). An employee will continue his or her participation so long as the inducements offered are as great or greater (measured in terms of the employee's values and satisfactions) than the sacrifices the employee is asked to make. Therefore, to Barnard, an enterprise can operate and survive only when it keeps the satisfaction/sacrifice trade-offs in balance and satisfies both its participants' motives and the organization's explicit goals. To effect this balance depends on successful management communication.[68]

Felix J. Roethlisberger and William J. Dickson.   In 1939, scholars Felix J. Roethlisberger and William J. Dickson published *Management and the Worker*,[69] a comprehensive and definitive account of the Hawthorne experiments. In it, they presented a new view of the mutual interactions between the formal and the informal organizations.

Based on evidence gathered from the earlier Western Electric Company research, Roethlisberger and Dickson described and documented the informal organization's surprising sophistication and power to influence the workers', supervisors', and managers' behaviors. The authors argued for an increased role for personnel managers in shop floor organization and in their employees' lives.[70] Their emphasis on individual needs, informal groups, and social relationships among employees quickly found support among other social scientists and led to a "philosophy of management" devoted primarily to human relationships in formal organizations.[71]

Herbert A. Simon.   Finally, Herbert A. Simon's *Administrative Behavior* (1947)[72] brought a fresh approach to understanding administrative practice. As a 25-year-old without much practical experience in administration, Simon mocked the classical management principles as "proverbs," essentially useless as guides to practical action because of their vagueness and contradictions.[73] He believed that the social scientist's empiricism was more relevant to understanding organizations than the businessman's experiences.[74] With his strong background in political science, psychology, and business administration, Simon drew upon Barnard's emphasis on the organization as a social system and moved ahead.

Simon asserted that each participant in the organization (owner, employee, and client) brings one's own motivations for involvement in the organization. Decision making, as portrayed in *Administrative Behavior*, is purposeful, but not rational. Simon believed that the boundary between rational and nonrational aspects of human social behavior is administrative theory's central concern. Acknowledging the realities of working in a human environment, Simon stressed that behavior can never be completely rational, in the scientific sense, because of knowledge limitations (facts) and ethical concepts (values). Nonetheless, he argued that effective organizations can be powerful tools for human rationality in pursuit of collective goals.[75] He also pointed to the distinction between a fact and a value as the basis for making decisions.

Simon agreed with Barnard's concept of the organization as a system of exchange, in which both the employees and the organization cooperate on goals as long as the organization continues to meet employees' needs.[76] With his insightful and powerful vision of the organization as a human enterprise seeking internal and external equilibrium, Simon's *Administrative Behavior* moved beyond its original roots in public administration to achieve its status as a contributor to generic organizational theory.[77] It established a new concept for administration which brought interdisciplinary social and behavioral perspectives together after World War II with the promise of a new viewpoint. In fact, most administrative research in the 1950s and beyond considered psychology and social psychology, sociology, anthropology, political science, and management.

Challenges to Simon's views.   Simon's perspective has elicited both intellectual and theoretical challenges, mainly from various scholars arguing the finer details from standpoints of their own disciplines.[78] Reid (1995b) observed that the elasticity and apparent contradictions in classical management theory that bothered Simon were, in fact, advantages that gave managers the flexibility to maneuver and to incorporate the findings of social scientists (like Simon), not as social facts but as practical tools.[79] Other critics have argued around the margins about Simon's fact-value distinction in making decisions,[80] as well as Simon's treatment of "ultimate values."[81] Some have debated the issue of efficiency values versus democratic values in public administration[82] or challenged Simon's "rational man" perspective from the position of humanistic or self-actualization theory.[83] Ironically, understanding these debates is now a part of any strong theoretical grounding in public administration, and Simon's writings are still in print after more than 50 years.[84]

ACTIVITY 2.6   Engaging Formal and Informal Organizations in Heritage County

Roethlisberger and Dickson described and documented the informal organization's sophistication and power to influence the workers', supervisors', and managers' behaviors. Barnard and Simon saw the organization as a system of exchange, in which both the employees and the organization cooperated on goals as long as the organization continued to meet employees' needs. Discuss as a class:

1. Describe the lessons about formal and informal organizations that the Heritage County School Board has yet to learn if they want to create a high-achieving school district.
2. Identify the various informal organizations inside and outside the schools that are likely to be affected by the school board's directives to Superintendent Smith. How might each group respond to their lack of participation in developing these directives as well as to the content of these expectations?
3. What steps would Superintendent Smith have to take in order to have teachers "willingly accept the changes in management" as the school board requested?
4. What steps might Superintendent Smith take to persuade the school board to increase stakeholder participation in designing and implementing school improvement changes? What are the risks to the school board, Dr. Smith, and the school personnel in taking a more participative approach?

Focus on Human Motivation

By the mid-20th century, the informal organization and human needs as key factors in an enterprise's success had gained widespread acceptance. Developing a greater understanding of human purpose became critical. In *Motivation and Personality* (1954), Abraham Maslow, an American psychologist, attempted to synthesize a large body of research related to human motivation.[85] Prior to Maslow, researchers generally focused separately on such factors as biology, achievement, or power to explain what energizes, directs, and sustains human behavior. Maslow integrated these varied perspectives in a unique theory of human drive.

Abraham Maslow's Hierarchy.   Maslow posited a hierarchy of human needs based on two groupings: those necessary to preserve life (food, water, and shelter) and those more essential to promote social connections and development (need to be loved, to be appreciated, and to experience personal growth). He suggested that such hierarchies of need ranged on a continuum from "deficiency" needs to "being" needs, representing a demand system in which the more basic needs must be fulfilled before higher order ones can be achieved.

Maslow's hierarchy identifies the deficiency needs (physiological and social, items 1–4), and the growth needs (self-actualization, item 5):[86]

1. Physiological: hunger, thirst, bodily protection
2. Safety/security: out of danger (physical, psychological)
3. Belonging and love: affiliate with others, be accepted
4. Esteem: to achieve, be competent, gain approval and recognition
5. Self-actualization: Consists of cognitive: to know, to understand, and explore; aesthetic: symmetry, order, and beauty; self-actualization: to find self-fulfillment and realize one's potential; and self-transcendence: to connect to something beyond the ego or to help others find self-fulfillment and realize their potential

Once individuals satisfy their life-or-death physiological needs, more social, intellectual, aesthetic, and self-actualization or growth needs emerge and require attention. According to Maslow, an individual is ready to act upon the growth needs if and only if the deficiency needs are met. If at some future time, one of these earlier needs again becomes unsatisfied (if the person loses a job, lacks money to buy food and pay rent), the individual will act to fulfill the unmet need.

Fundamentally, however, the person's basic striving is for self-fulfillment, self-actualization, or "peak experience." Unlike the physiological and safety/security needs and the social needs for belonging and love which can be met, the higher needs for self-esteem and self-actualization are rarely satisfied. Yet just as depriving the physiological and safety needs has behavioral consequences, the same is true for the higher level needs. Not meeting individuals' needs for belonging, esteem, and personal growth has unanticipated costs.

Maslow and the organization.   Although Maslow was not writing specifically for the organizational environment, his theories hold crucial implications for administrators. Employees need more than Taylor's adapted shovels, Western Electric's enhanced lighting and rest breaks, and Fayol's fair wages in order to work enthusiastically or productively. People are complicated individuals with increasingly sophisticated ranges of unmet needs that they seek to meet in their environments, including work. Although earning a decent living wage is necessary to provide the basic food, shelter, and clothing for themselves and their families, they also want work environments that keep them safe and out of physical or emotional danger. They want job security. Even more, employees want to satisfy social, self-esteem, and self-fulfillment motives. They want the respect and acceptance of being part of a supportive group working for a common goal. Some want the high regard gained from becoming more knowledgeable, skilled, and proficient at their work. Still others want the cognitive satisfactions that come with accepting and meeting intellectually challenging assignments and responsibilities that generate new, innovative, and useful outcomes.

In part, administrators' jobs are to help identify and provide avenues for employees to satisfy their needs in ways that also support the organization's goals. Managers should find and remove obstacles that block employees' fulfillment and cause frustration, negative attitudes, and behaviors at odds with the organization's purposes. They should also locate or create opportunities within the organization to allow interested and capable workers to meet their own social and individual requirements through their work. Douglas M. McGregor would adapt Maslow's theories of a human needs hierarchy and successfully advance them into the work environment.

Criticism of Maslow.   Although Maslow's ideas have intuitive appeal, academic psychology has criticized him for his lack of scientificity.[87] His study of self-actualizers has been criticized on methodological grounds, and his theoretical constructs have been characterized as overly vague, equivocal, and untestable.[88] This does not mean Maslow was wrong—his subject was highly complex and not easily studied by traditional psychological experimentation—but it does mean that his opinions are not validated in the normal scientific way, by finding independent sources of evidence.

Maslow's hierarchy of emerging needs has been researched, but the results are mixed, at best. The specific order in which needs emerge in his theory appears to be ambiguous. Additionally, the concept of self-actualization is not clearly defined. The human system is too multifaceted to allow discrimination between "potential" developments and "impossible" ones. Then too, the definition of self-actualization as fulfillment of basic needs does not always correspond with observed self-actualization which occasionally results from frustration of certain needs—as one might observe with Nazi death camp survivors—rather than from their gratification.[89]

Lastly, Maslow's subjectivity and uniquely American bias of his criteria for psychological health are open to question. Other societies and cultures with a more collectivist orientation might not view an individualistic, autonomous personality as healthy or well adapted.[90]

Theories X, Y, and Z.   Douglas M. McGregor was a management professor at the MIT Sloan School of Management and president of Antioch College (1948 to 1954). His 1960 book, *The Human Side of Enterprise*,[91] examined human motivation at work and illustrated the inadequacy of conventional management concepts to inspire employees' behaviors.[92] Extending this perspective, management professor William Ouchi's 1981 book, *Theory Z: How American Management Can Meet the Japanese Challenge*,[93] defined an effective leader as one who facilitates people in organizations to form a common culture of shared values, beliefs, priorities, experiences, and traditions. Both authors believed that integrating the human and organization's needs can increase worker satisfaction and organizational productivity.

McGregor and Theories X and Y.   McGregor theorized that management views workers from two different perspectives, Theory X and Theory Y. Theory X managers believe the following:[94]

1. The average worker naturally does not like work and will avoid it whenever possible.
2. Managers must always control, motivate, and direct their employees to perform well.
3. Most workers prefer being directed, avoid responsibility, and seek job security.

In Theory X, management's responsibility is to organize the elements of productive enterprise—money, materials, equipment, and people—in the interest of economic ends. Management must "firmly but fairly" direct, motivate, control, and modify people's behavior to fit the organization's needs, or else the workers will be passive. Workers, in this view, lack ambition, and are lazy by nature, inherently self-centered, resistant to change, and gullible. A "carrot-and-stick" management approach is necessary for organizational productivity.

On the other hand, Theory Y managers assume that:[95]

1. Employees enjoy working.
2. Managers do not need to control and punish workers to accomplish organizational goals.
3. Workers will be committed to an organization if their work is satisfying.
4. Managers should arrange organizational conditions and methods of operation so that people can achieve their own goals best by directing their efforts toward organizational objectives.

Theory Y's central tenet, the integration principle, is based on the belief that workers can achieve their goals best by working toward organizational success. It assumes that organizations can only be profitable if they adjust to workers' needs and goals. In this way, both the organization's and the individuals' needs are recognized and met.

According to McGregor, Theory Y is based on more adequate assumptions about human nature and human motivation and will best stimulate employee enthusiasm toward accomplishing organizational goals. Theory X assumptions about workers reflect classical management theory. Theory Y assumptions, on the other hand, reflect Maslow's upper level needs hierarchy (esteem and self-actualization), providing workers with opportunities to meet their social and growth needs as they fulfill the organization's purposes. In that way, both individuals and organizations prosper. By arranging organizational conditions, climate, and methods of operation, management's job is to allow people to achieve their own goals by directing their best efforts toward organizational objectives.

The major difference between Theory X and Theory Y is that Theory X places exclusive reliance upon external control of human behavior whereas Theory Y relies heavily on self-control and self-direction. Theory X lacks confidence in human capacities, viewing workers as lazy, passive, and needing managers to push them to work. In contrast, Theory Y has confidence in human capacities. If workers become passive or resistant to organizational needs, it is because of their negative experiences with management's philosophy, policy, and practice rather than a consequence of human nature. Theory X, according to McGregor, confuses cause (ineffective management philosophy, policy, and practices) and effect (worker resistance to organizational needs).

McGregor claimed that the traditional carrot-and-stick approach to management—rewards, promises, incentives, or threat and other coercive devices—will not work once persons have reached an adequate subsistence level and are motivated primarily by higher needs. Management cannot provide employees with self-respect or respect of coworkers. It can, however, create such conditions that individuals are encouraged and enabled to seek such satisfaction for themselves or it can thwart them by failing to create those conditions.

Therefore, according to McGregor, unless there are opportunities at work to satisfy these higher level social and growth needs, people will feel deprived and their behavior will reflect this deprivation: indolence, passivity, resistance to change, lack of responsibility, willingness to follow a demagogue, and unreasonable demands for economic benefits. Management should try to develop a relationship based on two-way trust between management and employees, which can enable self-direction and increased productivity. Furthermore, McGregor pointed out that management should not expect to see significant changes when first initiating his theory. Change comes slowly, but in the long run, companies will see improvements in employee motivation toward their work.

Although McGregor depicted them as sharp opposites, Theory X and Theory Y in practice are not necessarily all-or-nothing models. Tannenbaum and Schmidt (1973) considered leadership as existing on a continuum of leadership behaviors.[96] Figure 2–1 illustrates how Theory X and Theory Y might appear graphically if integrated into this continuum. This image suggests that boss-centered (Theory X) and participant/subordinate-centered (Theory Y) leadership may be a matter of degree.

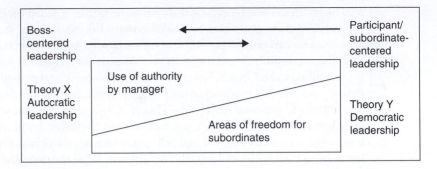

FIGURE 2–1
McGregor's Theory X and Theory Y Leadership Continuum (Source: Adapted from
Boss-Participant/Subordinate-Centered Leadership continuum by Marc Bowles. Retrieved from
http://www.marcbowles.com/courses/adv_dip/module1/chapter1/amc1_ch1_two2.htm) Reprinted
by permission of Marc Bowles.

William Ouchi and Theory Z.   William G. Ouchi provided a slightly different perspective for organizing human effort. During the 1980s, Ouchi's work drew attention to
comparisons between Japanese and North American management styles and how that
affected organizational effectiveness. He believed that his model would simultaneously
produce individual freedom and group cohesion in a shared commitment to organizational productivity.[97]

Ouchi concured that while a formal organization relies on individuals purposefully
working together toward a common and explicitly recognized goal, developing such
cooperation is difficult unless individuals within the organization share a common understanding of its goals. Creating such cohesion is a challenge in today's society. Before the
Industrial Revolution, people learned their shared values and beliefs from family, kinship,
church, and community. Since increasing technology brings rapid urbanization and
mobility, modern industries include varied individuals representing an array of prior
experiences, backgrounds, and norms.

Ouchi saw contemporary work organization as a social institution that provides a place
for new associations and cooperation among individuals. Theory Z focuses on the quality
of work life for employees, consensual decision making, and a team approach to organizational processes and change. The organization's leadership is responsible for creating an
organizational culture that fosters open communications, trust, and commitment to
organizational goals. An effective leader develops these shared values, beliefs, priorities,
experiences, traditions, and practices among employees by using informal controls (e.g.,
relying on self-control, peer pressure, identification with superiors, shared values, and lack
of bureaucratic pressure to follow rules).

For instance, if all members of the organization have an apprenticeship or other socialization experiences, they are more likely to share personal goals that are compatible with
those of the organization.[98] Likewise, *quality circles*—groups consisting of rank-and-file

workers who exchange information for mutual professional improvement—are examples of such open communication, trust, and commitment. Leaders who advance consensual decisions foster the broad dissemination of information and values within the organization. The quality circles also serve the symbolic role of clearly signaling the firm's respect for employees and its cooperative intent.

Lee Bolman and Terrence Deal: Multiple Frames.   In *Reframing Organizations: Artistry, Choice, and Leadership* (2008), educational leadership and organizational behavior professors Lee G. Bolman and Terrence E. Deal observed that individuals tend to examine issues and organizations through one predominant mental model or lens. Unfortunately, relying on one or even two lenses restricts individuals' ability to see the whole picture and to consider the issues' complexity.[99]

Bolman and Deal contended that in an increasingly multifaceted and ambiguous world, the best leaders use multiple frames or lenses to view common challenges and to influence the most difficult problems. In this context, it is important to look "beyond narrow and mechanical thinking" to "a more expressive, artistic conception that encourages flexibility, creativity, and interpretation"[100] and "pinpoint what is really going on."[101] Bolman and Deal also believed that leadership is contextual: Different situations require different patterns of thinking. Framing, and then *reframing*—the conscious effort to size up a situation from multiple perspectives and then find a new way to handle it—helps leaders (or anyone) clarify, anticipate, and comprehensively resolve dilemmas. Especially in times of crisis or overload, having more than one option provides reasonable alternatives that lead to solutions.

Like everyone else, leaders view their experiences through a set of preconditioned filters. They often resist questioning their view of how an organizations works—or how it might work better. When their frames of reference accurately fit the circumstances, they can understand and shape human experience. In contrast, when their frames of reference do not correctly define the situation, their perspectives freeze into a distorted picture that traps them in misconceptions. A faulty diagnosis leads to faulty action. Frustrated, leaders explain failure by blaming circumstances rather than questioning their own inability to comprehend and respond accurately to the situation at hand.[102]

To these ends, Bolman and Deal distilled theories of organizations into four categories or traditions:[103]

◆ *Structural frame*. The structural frame emphasizes rationality, coordination, efficiency, structure, and policies. The structural frame maintains that classrooms and schools work best when goals and roles are clear and when individuals' and groups' efforts are highly coordinated through authority, rules, policies, and more informal strategies. Structural leaders value analysis and data, keep their eye on budgeting, set clear direction and measurable standards, hold people accountable for results, and try to solve organizational problems with new policies and rules.

◆ *Human resource frame*. The human resource frame stresses the interaction between individual (and related feelings, needs, preferences, or abilities) and organizational needs. Showing concern for others and providing sufficient occasions for participation and shared decision making are among the ways to enlist people's commitment and involvement. Human resource leaders value relationships and emotions and seek to lead by facilitating and empowering employees in a win-win collaboration. This frame is a favorite among principals and teachers.

◆ *Political frame*. The political frame focuses on conflict or tensions among different groups and agendas competing for scarce resources. It points out the limits of authority. Political leaders are advocates and negotiators who invest much of their time and energy networking, creating coalitions, building a power base, resolving disputes over resource allocations, and working out compromises.

◆ *Symbolic frame*. The symbolic frame emphasizes a chaotic world in which meaning and predictability are socially constructed and facts are interpretive rather than objective. Every school and classroom creates symbols to encourage commitment, hope, and loyalty. Symbols govern behaviors through shared values, informal agreements, and implicit understandings. Addressing issues including institutional identity, vision, organizational culture, and image, symbolic leaders pay strict attention to myth, ritual, ceremony, stories, and other symbolic forms.

Each frame offers new possibilities for generating positive outcomes. The structural frame promotes clear organizational standards and goals, which often give rise to greater productivity. The human resource frame involves sharing individual needs and motives, which nurture a sense of ownership and commitment to the organization. The political frame illuminates conflict and compromise, which can be a constant source of renewal. And the symbolic frame focuses on the organizational culture, rituals, and beliefs, which cultivate shared values and meaning. All four cognitive perspectives enhance a leader's insight and options.

Bolman and Deal applied their four-frame leadership model to organizations as diverse as schools, families, factories, and religious institutions. Likewise, the Bolman and Deal framework has received wide acceptance over the past quarter century and has demonstrated utility in a range of cultural contexts.[104] In addressing leadership challenges, most educators rely on the human resource or structural lenses. Yet many school situations are politically charged and emotionally symbolic. Reframing helps individuals see what they had once overlooked with a more meaningful and holistic appreciation for what is happening so they can respond with more versatility and effectiveness.

Research supports Bolman and Deal's four cognitive frames as related to leadership and managerial effectiveness among different populations.[105] Studies have shown that more experienced leaders acquired greater cognitive complexity and were able to utilize multiple frames in their managerial and leadership experiences while the new leaders were more likely to use frames emphasizing managerial effectiveness but not leadership effectiveness.[106] For U.S. school administrators, effective managers were perceived to be highest on structural and symbolic frames whereas effective leaders were perceived highest on symbolic and political frames. Effectiveness as leaders and managers is not the same thing, and what works well depends on the culture and context. Notably, men and women in comparable educational leadership positions are more alike than different, showing almost no significant differences. These studies contain several methodological limitations, however, which reduce their widespread generalizability.[107]

Criticism of Bolman and Deal's four-frame theory points to their unclear theoretical roots (other than drawing from the social sciences). Choosing the correct level of analysis is difficult since the same activity might be logically considered under several different frames at the same time. For instance, meetings can be viewed from structural, human resources, political, and symbolic frames.[108] Others have noted that most of these studies did not consider gender differences as the research's primary focus—even though no significant differences appeared in male and female leaders' behaviors.[109]

It is important to remember that the model is not meant to imply that abstract organizational domains can be neatly divided into exclusive categories. Instead, using the four frames is intended to broaden perspective on organizations' problems, situations, challenges, and data that can be best understood by viewing them from varying perspectives.

ACTIVITY 2.7   Applying Motivational Theories in Heritage County

Theories of human motivation help us understand what drives individuals' efforts at work. According to Maslow, McGregor, and Ouchi, integrating human and organizational needs increases worker satisfaction and organizational productivity. Bolan and Deal proposed four cognitive frames by which leaders can better understand and effectively respond to situations. To this end, administrators should locate or create opportunities within the organization to allow interested and capable workers to meet their own social and individual requirements through their work—and remove obstacles that block employees' fulfillment. Discuss as a class:

1. Which of the groups in the Heritage County School District support McGregor's Theory X, and what evidence can you find in the case study to support your answer?

2. Which of the groups in the Heritage County School District support McGregor's Theory Y and Ouchi's Theory Z, and what evidence can you find in the case study to support your answer?

3. How might Superintendent Smith apply Bolman and Deal's four cognitive frames—structural, human resource, political, and symbolic—to better identify what is occurring and decide how best to respond?

4. Using these theories of human motivation in the workplace, how can Superintendent Smith help persuade the school board to rethink both their management model and their process for making instructional and curricular decisions?

5. What are the likely outcomes for Heritage County Public Schools if Dr. Smith follows the school board's directives as delivered? Use Maslow's hierarchy of needs, McGregor's Theory X and Theory Y, Ouchi's Theory Z, and Bolman and Deal's four frames to support your answer.

6. What are the possible outcomes for Superintendent Smith if he practices Theory Y leadership with his principals and community while his bosses (the school board) subscribe to Theory X?

7. If you were Superintendent Smith, how would you successfully resolve this dilemma?

REFLECTING ON ORGANIZATIONS AS PRODUCTION AND HUMAN ENVIRONMENTS

As industrial engineers, managers, and scholars learned more about how organizations functioned, they built upon their own experiences and insights as well as those of practitioners and scholars who came before. Theorists try to make sense of events by looking for commonalities and patterns, for systems of relationships and outcomes. Organizational theorists continue in this tradition.

A Systems Perspective

A variety of ways exist to understand institutions and organizations. The systems perspective is one. Three competing systems perspectives exist, each with its own advocates. W. Richard Scott (1987, 1992, 1998) called these perspectives the rational-systems, natural-systems, and open-systems perspectives.[110] Each approach considers a slightly different—yet complementary—view of organizations.

Rational System: A Machine Model.   A rational-systems perspective sees organizations as formal instruments designed to achieve specific organizational goals. *Rationality* is the degree to which a set of actions is organized and implemented to achieve predetermined goals with maximum efficiency. Behavior in rational systems is assumed to be purposeful, disciplined, and logical. The rational systems' early roots extend to the classical organizational thought of the scientific and administrative managers.

Frederick Taylor looked for ways to use people effectively in industrial organizations. His technical background and work experiences reinforced his beliefs that individuals could be programmed to be efficient machines. The machine metaphor graphically captures the scientific management concepts. Taylor's time-and-motion studies, his passion for specialization and standardization, and his quest for efficiency reflected his logical view that science and technology could improve worker and industrial practices.

Henri Fayol also took a scientific, rational approach to organizational study, identifying the administrative behaviors common to all organizations. His division of labor permitted work tasks to become specialized and standardized. Limiting span of control, or the number of workers directly supervised, infused a linear logic to administrative organizations with authority flowing uniformly from the top to the bottom. Luther Gulick applied similar rationality to administrative tasks in the public sphere. Max Weber further developed and extended the rational-systems view with his theory of bureaucracies.

Both the human engineers and the scientific managers emphasized the formal organization. They were concerned with the division of labor, the allocation of power, formal authority, rules and regulations, and each position's specifications. They neglected the individual differences and the social dynamics of people at work. This viewpoint, termed the *machine model*, implies that an organization can be constructed according to a blueprint, as one might build a bridge or an engine.[111]

Perhaps the rational-systems perspective's greatest shortcoming, however, is its adherence to a rigid conception of organization. An organization's structure and functioning may be greatly affected by outside and internal events, neither of which can be planned for in advance.[112] Additionally, Bolman and Deal (1991, 1992, 2002) saw the rational—or structural—perspective as important but only as part of the whole. Placing undue emphasis on parts rather than the whole is shortsighted.[113]

Natural Systems: An Organic Model.   With its roots in the early human relations approach of the 1930s, the natural-systems perspective offers a more contemporary view of organizations. It developed in part as a reaction to the scientific managers and perceived limitations of the rational-systems model.

The Hawthorne studies showed the importance of the informal organization's norms, values, sentiments, and communications patterns in an organization's productivity. Friendships and well-defined work groups formed, and much of their activity countered the formal job descriptions. These experiments were the first to challenge many of the human engineers' and scientific managers' basic assumptions that organizations were structural and rational arrangements designed to achieve specific goals. Instead, natural-systems advocates saw organizations as primarily social groups trying to adapt and survive in their particular situations. Although goal specificity and formalization characterize organizations, they may actually have little to do with what is actually happening in them.[114] Or, as Bolman and Deal asserted, the human organization is an essential part of what is occurring within the organization.[115]

The natural-systems model focuses on similarities among social groups, primarily motivated by survival rather than by the institution's goals. Formal organizations are viewed as vehicles for individuals to satisfy their human needs, rather than as a means for achieving specific ends. People are valuable resources for the organization. In addition, behavior in organizations is typically regulated by informal structures that emerge to transform the system. People enter the organization with their own needs, beliefs, values, and motivations. They interact with others and generate informal norms, status structures, power relations, communication networks, and working arrangements.[116] Whereas the rational-systems perspective emphasizes structure over individuals, the natural-systems approach emphasizes individuals over structure.

Open Systems: An Integration.   The open-systems perspective formed in reaction to the unrealistic assumptions that organizational behavior could be isolated from external forces. The external environment's competition, resources, and political pressures affect the organization's internal functioning. Organizations take inputs from the environment, transform them, and produce outputs. The open-systems model views organizations as not only affected by environments but also dependent on them.

The rational-systems approach (and especially scientific management) and the natural-systems approach are both limited and incomplete. The first ignores the impact of individual needs and social relations, and the second discounts the formal structure's importance. Obviously, both formal and informal components as well as structure and people are essential to understanding organizations. An open-systems position offers such a perspective. Barnard and Simon saw the organization as an exchange system in which inducements are exchanged for work. Employees remain as long as they perceive they are receiving at least as much as their work efforts are contributing.

Although sharing many views with scientific managers and administrative theorists, Max Weber articulated a view of bureaucracies as social systems that interact with and are dependent on their environments. Talcott Parson (1960) advanced this concept still further with his view of the organization as an open system—a social system dependent on and influenced by its environment.[117] Organizations have planned and unplanned features, rational and irrational characteristics, formal and informal structures, rational concerns and social relationships—all coexisting within a system that is open to its environment. Likewise, Bolman and Deal's four frames offered a way to conceptualize these various rational, social, political, and symbolic dynamics occurring within the organization.

Although some scholars insist that contemporary organizations are either rational, natural, or open systems adapting to different environments, it is reasonable to believe that organizations are open systems with rational and natural constraints that change as the environment changes. To neglect either the rational or the natural elements would be myopic—and unproductive.

ACTIVITY 2.8   Applying a Systems Perspective in Heritage County

Three competing systems perspectives exist: the rational-systems, natural-systems, and open-systems perspectives. Each approach considers a slightly different, yet complementary, view of organizations. At the same time, each approach provides a discrete mental model from which individuals make sense of their experiences and derive a framework for action. Discuss as a class:

1. Which systems perspective does the Heritage County School Board appear to adopt? What evidence from the theory and the case study supports this view?
2. Which systems perspective do the new principals and the community appear to adopt? What evidence from the theory and the case study supports this view?
3. What difficulties arise when people in the same organization base their understanding, beliefs, and behaviors on contradictory mental models?
4. What evidence suggests that Superintendent Smith does or does not subscribe to one of these three system perspectives?
5. Why would it be difficult to challenge the school board's beliefs and values about their preferred systems perspective?

Considering Theorists' Contributions

Each of the individuals described in this chapter appeared at a singular historical, economic, and cultural time. Each brought distinctive professional backgrounds and skill sets that influenced how they perceived organizations. Their insights helped administrators move from a narrow focus on product, profit, and workers as extensions of machines to a wider view of organizations as social and business endeavors, employees as idiosyncratically motivated, and the necessity of balancing organizations and human needs in a sustainable, successful enterprise.

Table 2–4 summarizes each theorist's contribution to more completely understanding organizations as production and human environments. Figure 2–2 presents a timeline of the organizational theories.

TABLE 2–4

From Organization as Machine to Organization as Human Environment

Contributor, Work Background, Theory	View of Organization	View of Worker
Classical Organizational Theory: Focus on production and formal organization		
Frederick W. Taylor Engineer Scientific management	Focus on production.	Specialized, standardized work to increase efficiency.
Classical Organizational Theory: Focus on formal organization; separate production from administration		
Henri Fayol French chief executive of mining industry Administrative management	Common elements in all organizations. Governance structures: planning, organizing, commanding, coordinating, controlling.	Separated administration from production; impersonal.
Luther Gulick Executive administrator to government agency Scholar Administrative management	Common elements in all organizations. POSDCoRB acronym delineates an executive's activities and duties: planning, organizing, staffing, directing, coordinating, reporting, and budgeting.	Deliberate reference to "staffing" and importance of selecting, training, and developing the staff, and maintaining favorable working conditions.
Max Weber German sociologist Bureaucracy theory	Bureaucracy as ideal structure for organizational effectiveness.	Treated more fairly in impersonal, impartial, rational, and efficiency organization.
Modern Organizational Theory: Focus on formal and informal organization; workplace as a human environment; need to satisfy both employee needs and organization's goals		
Elton Mayo Industrial psychologist Hawthorne studies	A human-social element operated in the workplace: informal structure. Organizations as human environments.	Recognized that workers are individuals with motives that have an impact on their satisfaction and productivity.
Chester Barnard President of NJ Bell Telephone Company Organizational theory	Organization as a social system. A successful organization needed to keep in balance and satisfy both its employees' motives and the organization's explicit goals.	Employees' individual needs must find satisfactory expression in the process of meeting organizational goals.
Felix J. Roethlisberger, William J. Dickson Scholars Hawthorne studies Organizational theory	Organization as a social system. A successful organization needed to keep in balance and satisfy both its employees' motives and the organization's explicit goals.	Employees' individual needs must find satisfactory expression in the process of meeting organizational goals.
Herbert A. Simon Professor with a strong background in political science, psychology, and business administration Organizational theory	Organization as a human enterprise seeking internal and external equilibrium. Decision making is purposeful but not rational.	Individuals and effective organizations can pursue collective goals.
Modern Organizational Theory: Considers how to integrate human motives with organizational needs		
Abraham Maslow Psychologist Humanistic psychology Human motivation theory	Did not write specifically for the organizational environment. Focused on individuals' needs and motives: physiological, social, and personal.	People are complicated individuals with an increasingly sophisticated range of unmet needs that they seek to meet in their environments, including at work.

(continued)

TABLE 2–4   *(continued)*

From Organization as Machine to Organization as Human Environment

Contributor, Work Background, Theory	View of Organization	View of Worker

David McGregor
  Management professor
  Human motivation theory
    within organizations
	Organizations can be successful only if they adjust to workers' needs and goals. Management's task is to allow people to achieve their own goals by directing their best efforts toward organizational objectives. Favored participative management style.	Theory Y's integration principle believes that workers can achieve their personal goals best by working toward organizational success.

William Ouchi
Management professor
  Human motivation theory, sociology,
    within organizations
	Explicitly addresses organizations' structural governance issues.
	
	Defines leaders' responsibilities to develop an organizational climate of trust and cooperation. Participative management, organizational productivity, and workplace community.
		Theory Z places more reliance on the attitude and responsibilities of the workers (than does theory Y) to participate in making their organizations more productive and effective.

Lee Bolman and Terrence Deal
  Educational leadership and
  organizational development professors
Four frames of an organization
	Provides four cognitive frames of reference by which to understand and intervene in organizational issues: structural, human resources, political, and symbolic.	Gives leaders four separate but integrated viewpoints with which to accurately identify and respond to what is occurring in organizations.

Source: Owings & Kaplan.

Remembering Context.   Organizations are not tangible structures. They are concepts that exist in our minds as we try to create order out of complexities related to groups of otherwise unrelated individuals of diverse skills, backgrounds, and resources coming together for a common purpose. As America's Industrial Revolution brought people into complex associations to manufacture products, no model yet existed for how to coordinate the relationships needed to make the nascent enterprise efficient and effective.

Scientific management's concepts grew from a practical, technical focus on the shop floor's specialized tasks into administrative management's more sophisticated understanding of the authority and responsibility networks that influenced the entire undertaking. The Hawthorne studies led to a more complete appreciation for the informal organization and its impact on the formal organization's effectiveness. Barnard, Roethlisberger and Dickson, Simon, and Bolman and Deal brought additional dimensions to understand the worker–organization interactions. Maslow and McGregor looked even more closely at individual workers' motivations and the need for organizational managers to integrate employees' personal drives with the industrial goal for mutual benefit. In short, as the organizations matured, so did the thinking about how to best structure, manage, and lead them. Each approach contributed additional insights and practices to the preceding one, appreciating the organization's complexity and advancing its efficiency and effectiveness.

While all theories deserve rational critiques, it is important to remember that concepts about organizations are anchored in their particular era and culture. Attacks on Frederick

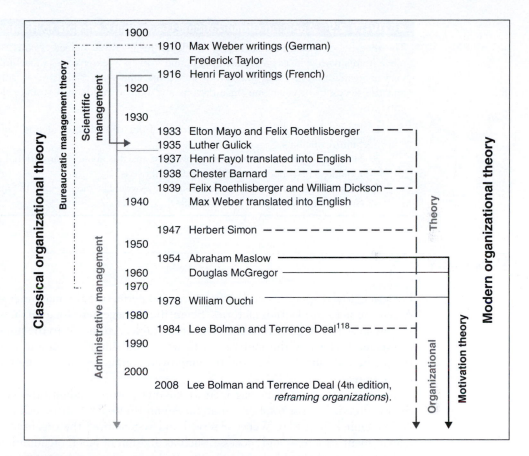

FIGURE 2–2
Organizational Theories Timeline, 1900–2008 (Source: Owings & Kaplan.)

Taylor, Henri Fayol, Luther Gulick, Max Weber, and other classicists; on the Hawthorne studies; or on more contemporary theorists ignore the reality that all intellectual progress is historically grounded. Where and when an event or idea occurs significantly affects its character. Sensitivity to time and place contexts is essential not only to understanding "what," "how," and "why," but also for gaining insights into the continuing flow of events and ideas. In this respect, an understanding of both the past and present requires the study of context.[119] For example, disparaging Taylor's work for ignoring the intricacies of modern motivation theories is much like attacking Isaac Newton because he failed to discover the theory of relativity.[120] Organizational theorists must be viewed and judged within their historical contexts.

In the years ahead, other administrative and leadership theorists would follow, designing increasingly detailed models of how to best integrate the informal and formal organizations, balancing human motives with organizational purposes in ways that would fulfill both.

ACTIVITY 2.9   Applying Organizational Leadership Concepts to Heritage County

The theorists discussed in this chapter developed insights that helped organizational leaders move from a narrow focus on product, profit, and workers as extensions of machines to a wider view of organizations as social and business endeavors, employees as idiosyncratically motivated, and the necessity of balancing organizations and human needs in a sustainable, successful enterprise.

1. Using the information and perspectives from this chapter, define Superintendent Smith's dilemma.
2. How can Superintendent Smith apply these insights about organizational effectiveness to address his school district's dynamics and needs?
3. Which organizational theorists do you believe would be most helpful to Superintendent Smith in addressing his dilemma, and why?

SUMMARY

Frederick Taylor spent his career designing and perfecting the machines and machine systems of mass production factories. Scientific management focused on ways to make individuals at work more reliable, more predictable. Attending to the human-machine interface, Taylor saw the motivation to work as a simple economic transaction between the individual worker and the employer, connecting worker motivation to job performance.

In contrast to scientific management's focus on the worker, administrative management theory attended to the total organization. Administrative theorists such as Henri Fayol, Luther Gulick, and Max Weber observed and systematized the organization's common management structures and processes such as division of labor, organizational hierarchy and power, and defined lines of authority. Weber's concept of bureaucracy attempted to reduce the frustrations and irrationality between management and workers where relationships were based on traditions of class and privilege.

The Hawthorne experiments bridged the gap between classical and modern organizational thinking. Researchers at the Western Electric plant in Illinois determined that increases in productivity were more an outcome of informal worker group dynamics and effective management than any set of employer demands or physical factors. These studies led to a focus on the worker as an individual employee whose motivation, satisfaction, and group morale contributed to efficiency and productivity.

Chester Barnard, Felix J. Roethlisberger and William J. Dickson, and Herbert A. Simon all contributed ideas that clarified the relationship between the workers' needs and aspirations and the organization's goals. Attempting to integrate human relations and classical management principles into one coherent framework, Barnard affirmed that an enterprise can operate and survive only when it keeps the satisfaction/sacrifice trade-offs in balance and satisfies both its participants' motives and the organization's explicit goals.

Roethlisberger and Dickson documented the informal organization's sophistication and power to influence the workers', supervisors', and managers' behaviors. Simon asserted that decision making within organizations was purposeful but not rational because it was influenced by individuals' responsibilities, beliefs, and values. Simon, like Barnard, saw the organization as a system of exchange in which both the employees and the organization cooperated on goals as long as the organization continued to meet employees' needs.

By the mid-20th century, the informal organization and human needs as key factors in an enterprise's success had gained widespread acceptance. Abraham Maslow synthesized a large body of research related to human motivation and developed a hierarchy of human needs that drove human behavior.

Applying Maslow's ideas, Douglas M. McGregor examined human motivation at work and created Theory X and Theory Y to illustrate the inadequacy of conventional management concepts to inspire employees' behaviors. Extending this perspective, William Ouchi defined an effective leader as one who facilitates a common culture in organizations by helping people develop and share similar values, beliefs, priorities, experiences, and traditions. McGregor and Ouchi believed that integrating the human and organization's needs can increase worker satisfaction and organizational productivity. Moving still further, Bolman and Deal integrated a variety of cognitive frames into a comprehensive and holistic perspective on organizational functioning.

A systems perspective is one way to understand the development of organizational theory. Rational systems, natural systems, and open systems describe various ways of conceptualizing how organizations function. While useful, these approaches are not totally separate, and each has its limitations.

Insights from classical and modern organizational theorists and practitioners helped organizational leaders and managers move from a narrow attention to product, profit, and workers as extensions of machines to considering organizations as social and business environments, employees as having individual motives that influence their behaviors, and the need to balance and integrate organizational and human needs in a sustainable, successful enterprise.

ENDNOTES

1. Ouchi, W. G. (1980). Markets, bureaucracies, and clans. *Administrative Science Quarterly, 25*(1), 129–141.

2. Owens, R. G., & Valesky, T. C. (2011). *Organizational behavior in education. Adaptive leadership and school reform* (p. 64). Boston, MA: Pearson.

3. Organizational theory. (2006). *A dictionary of business and management*. Retrieved from http://www.encyclopedia.com

4. Goleman, D., Boyatzis, R., & McKee, A. (2002). *Primal leadership: Realizing the power of emotional intelligence*. Boston, MA: Harvard Business School Press; Hallinger, P., & Heck, R. (2000, October). Exploring the principal's contribution to school effectiveness, 1980–1995. In *Leadership for student learning: Reinventing school leadership*

for the 21st century. Washington, DC: Institute for Educational Leadership; Marzano, R. J., Waters, T., & McNulty, B. A. (2005). *School leadership that works. From research to results*. Alexandria, VA: Association for Supervision and Curriculum Development; McColl-Kennedy, J. R., & Anderson, R. D. (2002). Impact of leadership style and emotions on subordinate performance. *Leadership Quarterly, 13*(5), 545–559.

5. Van Riper, P. P. (1995). Luther Gulick on Frederick Taylor and scientific management. *Journal of Management History, 1*(2), 6–7.

6. Drucker, P. (1991). The new productivity challenge. *Harvard Business Review, 69*(6), 69–79.

7. Taylor, F. W. (1911). *The principles of scientific management*. Elibron Classics. New York, NY: Harper & Brothers. Republished (1964). New York, NY: Adamant Media, pp. 36–37; Hartley, N. T. (2006). Management history: An umbrella model. *Journal of Management History, 12*(3), 278–292.

8. Brunsson, K. H. (2008). Some effects of Fayolism. *International Studies of Management and Organization, 38*(1), 30–47; Nyland, C. (2000). An early account of scientific management as applied to women's work with comment by Frederick W. Taylor. *Journal of Management History, 6*(6), 248–271.

9. Davis, L. E. (1980). Individuals and the organization. *California Management Review, 22*(2), 5–14.

10. Taylor. (1911). Op. cit., p. 13.

11. Parker, L. D., & Lewis, N. R. (1989). Classical management control in contemporary management and accounting: The persistence of Taylor and Fayol's world. *Accounting, Business, and Financial History, 5*(2), 211–236.

12. Bedeian, A. (1998). Exploring the past. *Journal of Management History, 4*(1), 4–15; Drucker, P. F. (1968). *The age of discontinuity*. New York, NY: Harper & Row. Drucker noted that the application of scientific management to the study of work has enabled many of the world's less developed and poor countries—South Korea, for instance, after the Korean conflict—to become world-class competitors within a single generation.

13. Kaplan, L. S., & Owings, W. A. (2011). *American education: Building a common foundation*. Boston, MA: Cengage.

14. Gray, K. (1993). Why we will lose Taylorism in America's high schools. *Phi Delta Kappan, 74*(5), 370–374.

15. Callahan, R. E. (1962). *Education and the cult of efficiency*. Chicago, IL: University of Chicago Press.

16. Greenberg, N. C. (1964). Callahan, Raymond E., Education and the cult of efficiency. Book review. *Journal of Teacher Education, 15*(3), 342–343.

17. Tyack, D. B., & Cummings, R. (1977). Leadership in American public schools before 1954: Historical configurations and conjectures. In L. L Cunningham, W. G. Hack, & R. O. Nystrand (Eds.), *Educational administration:*

The developing decades (pp. 46–66). Berkeley, CA: McCutchan.

18. Gray. (1993). Op. cit.

19. Silva, D. Y., Gimbert, B., & Nolan, J. (2000). Sliding the doors: Locking and unlocking possibilities for teacher leadership. *Teachers College Record, 102*(4), 779–804; Frymier, B. (1987). Bureaucracy and the neutering of teachers. *Phi Delta Kappan, 69*(1), 9–16.

20. "Taylorism" is a pejorative term used to describe scientific management.

21. Freedman, D. H. (1992). Is management still a science? *Harvard Business Review, 70*(6), 26–38.

22. Taylor. (1911). Op. cit., p. 39.

23. Morgan, G. (1986). *Images of organization*. Newbury Park, CA: Sage.

24. Sewell, G., & Wilkinson, B. (1992). Someone to watch over me: Surveillance, discipline, and the just-in-time labour process. *Sociology, 26*(2), 271–289.

25. Morgan. (1986). Op. cit.

26. Wilms, W. W. (2003, April). Altering the structure and culture of American public schools. *Kappan, 84*(8), 606–615.

27. Wren, D. A. (1995). Henri Fayol: Learning from experience. *Journal of Management History, 1*(3), 5–12.

28. Fayol, H. (1916/1984). *General and industrial management*. New York, NY: IEEE Press. Fayol's work was published in French in 1916 and received widespread recognition in Europe. Translations of his work appeared in English in the 1940s. See: Fayol, H. (1937). *Papers on the science of administration*. L. Gulick & L. Urwick (Eds.). New York, NY: Columbia University, Institute of Public Administration.

29. Cuthbert, N. (2002). Fayol and the principles of organization. In J. C. Wood & M. C. Wood. (Eds.), *Henri Fayol. Critical evaluations in business and management* (pp. 3–25). London, United Kingdom: Taylor & Francis.

30. Parker, L. D., & Lewis, N. R. (1989). Classical management control in contemporary management and accounting: The persistence of Taylor and Fayol's world. *Accounting, Business, and Financial History, 5*(2), 211–236.

31. Reid, D. (1995a). Fayol: From experience to theory. *Journal of Management History, 1*(3), 21–36.

32. Fells, M. (2000). Fayol stands the test of time. *Journal of Management History, 6*(8), 345–360.

33. Fayol, H. (1949). *General and industrial management* (translation by Constance Storrs). London: Sir Isaac Pitman & Sons Ltd.

34. Parker, L. D., & Ritson, P. (2005). Fads, stereotypes, and management gurus: Fayol and Follett today. *Management Decision, 43*(10), 1335–1357.

35. Baker, R. (1972). *Administrative theory and public administration* (pp. 23–27). London, United Kingdom: Hutchinson & Company.

36. Fells. (2000). Op. cit.

37. Steinberg, J. (1993, January 11). Dr. Luther H. Gulick, 100, dies: Adviser to Roosevelt and Mayors. *The New York Times*. Retrieved from http://www.nytimes.com/1993/01/11/nyregion/dr-luther-h-gulick-100-dies-adviser-to-roosevelt-and-mayors.html

38. Van Riper. (1995). Op. cit.

39. Blumberg, S. K. (1980). Notes on the art of administration. *American Review of Public Administration, 14*(3), 191–199; Fitch, L. C. (1990). Luther Gulick. *Public Administration Review, 50*(6), 604–608.

40. Blumberg, S. K. (1981). Seven decades of public administration: A tribute to Luther Gulick. *Public Administration Review, 41*(2), 245–248.

41. Weber, a German surname, pronounced **"Vay**–ber."

42. Olsen, J. P. (2006). Maybe it's time to rediscover bureaucracy. *Journal of Public Administration Research and Theory, 16*(1), 1–24.

43. Fry, B. R., & Nigro, L. G. (1996). Max Weber and US public administration. The administrator as neutral servant. *Journal of Management History, 2*(1), 37–46.

44. Leithwood, K., & Duke, D. L. (1999). A century's quest to understand school leadership. In J. Murphy & K. S. Louis (Eds.), *Handbook of research on educational administration* (2nd ed., pp. 45–72). San Francisco, CA: Jossey-Bass.

45. Litwak, E. (1961). Models of bureaucracy which permit conflict. *American Journal of Sociology, 67*(2), 177–184.

46. Litwak. (1961). Ibid.

47. Ritzer, G. (1974–1975). Professionalization, bureaucratization, and rationalization: The views of Max Weber. *Social Forces, 53*(4), 627–634.

48. Mayer, J. P. (1943). *Max Weber and German politics* (p. 128). London, United Kingdom: Faber & Faber.

49. Wilensky, H. L., & Lebeaux, C. N. (1958). *Industrial society and social welfare* (pp. 235–265). New York, NY: Russell Sage Foundation.

50. Merton, R. (1957). *Social theory and social structure*. New York, NY: Free Press.

51. Scott, W. R. (1992). *Organizations: Rational, natural, and open systems* (3rd ed.). Englewood Cliffs, NJ: Prentice Hall.

52. Blau, P. M., & Scott, W. R. (2003). *Formal organizations: A comparative approach*. Stanford, CA: Stanford Business Books.

53. Gouldner, A. (1954). *Patterns of industrial bureaucracy*. New York, NY: Free Press; Parsons, T. (1947). Introduction. In *Max Weber, The theory of social and economic organization* (pp. 3–86). A.M. Henderson & T. Parsons (Trans.). New York, NY: Free Press.

54. Weber, M. (1947). *The theory of social and economic organization*. T. Parsons (Ed.), A. M. Henderson & T. Parsons (Trans.). New York, NY: Free Press.

55. Blau & Scott. (2003). Op. cit.

56. Martin, J. (1990). *Rereading Weber: Searching for feminist alternatives to bureaucracy*. Annual Meeting of the Academy of Management. San Francisco, CA; Martin, J., & Knopoff, K. (1999). The gendered implications of apparently gender-neutral theory: Rereading Weber. In E. Freeman & A. Larson (Eds.), *Ruffin lectures series. Vol. 3: Business ethics and women's studies*. Oxford, United Kingdom: Oxford University Press.

57. Scott, W. R. (1992). *Organizations: Rational, natural and open systems* (3rd ed.). Englewood Cliffs, NJ: Prentice Hall.

58. Scott. (1992). Ibid.

59. Freund, J. (1972). *The sociology of Max Weber*. Hammondsworth, United Kingdom: Penguin.

60. Accel. (2008). *Employee motivation, the organizational environment, and productivity*. Cambria, United Kingdom: Accel Team Development. Retrieved from http://www.accel-team.com/motivation/hawthorne_02.html

61. This phenomenon of improved performance without obvious intervention is now also known as the "Hawthorne effect" in honor of the initial Hawthorne studies.

62. Dobuzinskis, L. (1997). Historical and epistemological trends in public administration. *Journal of Management History, 3*(4), 298–316.

63. Etzioni, A. (1964). *Modern organizations.* Englewood Cliffs, NJ: Prentice Hall.

64. Clark, D. L., Astuto, T. A., Foster, W. P., Gaynor, A. K., & Hart, A. W. (1994). Organizational studies: Taxonomy and overview. In W. K. Hoy, T. A. Astuto, & P. B. Forsyth (Eds.), *Educational administration: The UCEA document base.* New York, NY: McGraw-Hill Primus; Scott, W. R. (1998). *Organizations: Rational, natural, and open systems* (4th ed.). Englewood Cliffs, NJ: Prentice Hall.

65. Barnard, C. (1938). *The functions of the executive.* Cambridge, MA: Harvard University Press.

66. Reid, D. (1995b). Reading Fayol with 3D glasses. *Journal of Management History, 1*(3), 63–71.

67. Barnard defined *organizational effectiveness* as being able to accomplish the organization's explicit goals. *Organizational efficiency*, however, is defined as the degree to which that organization is able to satisfy the motives of the individuals.

68. McMahon, D., & Carr, J. C. (1999). The contributions of Chester Barnard to strategic management theory. *Journal of Management History, 5*(5), 228–240; Roehling, M. V. (1997). The origins and early development of the psychological contract construct. *Journal of Management History, 3*(2), 204–217.

69. Roethlisberger, F. J., & Dickson, W. J. (1939). *Management and the worker.* Cambridge, MA: Harvard University Press.

70. The Hawthorne experiments showed that no universal rules existed to the problems of fatigue and monotony; personnel managers had to study each situation in context and solve them on a case-by-case basis. See: Gillespie, R. (1993). *Manufacturing knowledge: A history of the Hawthorne experiments* (pp. 203–204). Cambridge, United Kingdom: Cambridge University Press.

71. Cartwright, D. (1965). Influence, leadership, control. In J. G. March (Ed.), *Handbook of organizations* (p. 2). Chicago, IL: Rand McNally.

72. Simon, H. A. (1947). *Administrative behavior.* Cambridge, MA: MIT Press.

73. Wren. (1995). Op. cit.; Wolf, W. B. (1995). The Barnard-Simon connection. *Journal of Management History, 1*(4), 88–97; Reid. (1995b). Op. cit.

74. Wren. (1995). Op. cit.; Reid. (1995b). Ibid.

75. Augier, M., & March, J. C. (2002). A model scholar: Herbert A. Simon. *Journal of Economic Behavior and Organization, 49*(1), 1–17.

76. Cruise, P. L. (1997). Are proverbs really so bad? Herbert Simon and the logical positivist perspective in American public administration. *Journal of Management History, 3*(4), 342–359.

77. Sherwood, F. P. (1990). The half-century's "great books" in public administration. *Public Administration Review, 50*(2), 249–264.

78. Argyris, C. (1973a). Some limits of rational man organization theory. *Public Administration Review, 33*(3), 253–267; Argyris, C. (1973b). Organization man: Rational and self actualizing. *Public Administration Review, 33*(4), 354–357; Chisholm, R. F. (1989). The Storing critique revisited: Simon as seen in the science of politics. *Public Administration Quarterly, 12*(4), 411–436; Cooper, P. J. (1990). Public Administration Review: The first fifty years. *Public Administration Review, 50*(2), 293–309; Golembiewski, R. T. (1988). Nobel laureate Simon "looks back": A low frequency mode. *Public Administration Quarterly, 11*(3), 275–300; Harmon, M. M. (1984). The Simon-Waldo debate: A review and update. *Public Administration Quarterly, 12*(4), 437–451; Lovrich, N. P. (1989). The Simon/Argyris debate: Bounded rationality versus self-actualization conceptions of human nature. *Public Administration Quarterly, 12*(4), 452–483; Storing, H. J. (1962). The science of administration: Herbert A. Simon. In Herbert J. Storing (Ed.), *Essays in the scientific study of politics.* New York, NY: Holt, Reinhart & Winston; Waldo, D. (1952). Development of theory of democratic administration. *American Political Science Review, 46*(1), 81–103.

79. Reid. (1995b). Op cit.

80. Storing. (1962). Op. cit.

81. Chisholm. (1989). Op. cit.; Cooper. (1990). Op cit.

82. Cooper. (1990). Op. cit.; Harmon. (1989). Op. cit.; Golembiewski. (1988). Op. cit.; Waldo. (1952). Op. cit.

83. Argyris. (1973a). Op. cit.; Argyris. (1973b). Op. cit.; Cooper. (1990). Op. cit.; Golembiewski. (1988). Op. cit.; Loverich. (1989). Op. cit.

84. Simon, H. A., & Thompson, V. A. (1991). Reissue of Simon, Smithberg, and Thompson's *Public Administration*. *Journal of Public Administration Research and Theory, 1*(1), 75–88.

85. Maslow, A. (1954). *Motivation and personality*. New York, NY: Harper; Maslow, A. H. (1970). *Motivation and personality* (Rev. ed.). New York, NY: Harper & Row.

86. Maslow, A. (1971). *The farther reaches of human nature*. New York, NY: Viking Press; Maslow, A., & Lowery, R. (Ed.). (1998). *Toward a psychology of being* (3rd ed.). New York, NY: Wiley & Sons.

87. Heylighen, F. (1992). A cognitive systematic reconstruction of Maslow's theory of self-actualization. *Behavioral Science, 37*(1), 39–58.

88. Ewen, R. B. (1980). *An introduction to theories of personality*. New York, NY: Academic Press.

89. Heylighen. (1992). Op. cit.

90. Heylighen. (1992). Op. cit.

91. McGregor, D. M. (1960). *The human side of enterprise*. New York, NY: McGraw-Hill.

92. McGregor, D. M. (1995). The human side of enterprise. In D. A. Kolb, I. M. Rubin, & J. S. Osland (Eds.), *The organizational behavior reader* (5th ed., pp. 41–50). Englewood Cliffs, NJ: Prentice Hall.

93. Ouchi, W. G. (1981). *Theory Z: How American management can meet the Japanese challenge*. Reading, MA: Addison Wesley.

94. McGregor. (1995). Op. cit.

95. McGregor. (1995). Op. cit.

96. Tannenbaum, R., & Schmidt, W. H. (1973). How to choose a leadership pattern. *Harvard Business Review, 51*(3), 162–164.

97. Ouchi, W. G., & Jaeger, A. M. (1978). Type Z organization: Stability in the midst of mobility. *Academy of Management Review, 3*(2), 305–314.

98. Ouchi. (1980). Op. cit.

99. Bolman, L. G., & Deal, T. E. (2008). *Reframing organizations: Artistry, choice, and leadership* (4th ed.). Thousand Oaks, CA: Corwin Press. First published in 1991.

100. Bolman, L. G., & Deal, T. E. (1997). *Reframing organizations: Artistry, choice, and leadership* (2nd ed., pp. 16–17). Thousand Oaks, CA: Corwin Press.

101. Bolman & Deal. (1997). Ibid., p. 29.

102. Bolman, L. G., & Deal, T. E. (1991). Leadership and management effectiveness: A multiframe, multisector analysis. *Human Resource Management, 30*(4), 509–534.

103. Bolman, L. G., & Deal, T. E. (1992). Leading and managing: Effects of context, culture, and gender. *Educational Administration Quarterly, 28*(3), 314–329; Bolman, L. G., & Deal, T. E. (1991). *Reframing organizations: Artistry, choice and leadership*. San Francisco, CA: Jossey-Bass; Bolman, L. G., & Deal, T. E. (1984). *Modern approaches to understanding and managing organizations*. San Francisco, CA: Jossey-Bass; Bolman, L. G., & Deal, T. E. (2008). *Reframing organizations. Artistry, choice and leadership* (4th ed.). San Francisco, CA: Jossey-Bass; Deal, T. E., & Bolman, L. G. (Eds.). (2002). *Reframing the path to school leadership: A guide for teachers and principals*. Thousand Oaks, CA: Corwin Press.

104. Lueddeke, G. R. (1999). Toward a constructivist framework for guiding change and innovation in higher education. *Journal of Higher Education, 70*(3), 235–260; Swiercz, P. M., & Ross, K. T. (2003). Rational, human, political and symbolic text in Harvard Business School cases: A study of structure and content. *Journal of Management Education, 27*(4), 407–430; Bolman, L., & Granell, E. (1999, December 9–11). *Versatile leadership: A comparative analysis of reframing in Venezuelan managers*. Paper presented at the meeting of the Ibero American Academy of Management, Universidad Carlos III, Madrid, Spain.

105. Bensimon, E. M. (1989). The meaning of "good presidential leadership": A frame analysis. *Review of Higher Education, 12*(2), 107–123; Bolman, L. G., & Deal, T. E. (1991). Leadership and management effectiveness: A multiframe, multisector analysis. *Human Resource Development, 30*(4), 509–534; Bolman, L. G., & Deal, T. E. (1992). Leading and managing: Effects of context, culture, and gender. *Educational Administration Quarterly, 28*(3), 314–329; Thompson, M. D. (2000). Gender, leadership orientation, and effectiveness: Testing the theoretical models of Bolman and Deal. *Sex Roles, 42*(11–12), 969–992.

106. Bolman & Deal. (1991). Op. cit.

107. Bolman & Deal. (1991). Op. cit., Mabey, C. (2003). Reframing human resources development.

Human Resource Development Review, 2(4), 430–452.

108. Bolman, L. G., & Deal, T. E. (1984). *Modern approaches to understanding and managing organizations* (p. 237). San Francisco, CA: Jossey-Bass; Mabey. (2003). Op. cit.

109. Thompson. (2000). Ibid.

110. Scott, W. R. (1987). The adolescence of industrial theory. *Administrative Science Quarterly, 32*(4), 493–511; Scott, W. R. (1992). *Organizations: Rational, natural, and open systems* (3rd ed.). Englewood Cliffs, NJ: Prentice Hall; Scott, W. R. (1998). *Organizations: Rational, natural, and open systems* (4th ed.). Englewood Cliffs, NJ: Prentice Hall.

111. Worthy, J. C. (1950). Factors influencing employee morale. *Harvard Business Review, 28*(1), 61–73.

112. March, J. G., & Simon, H. (1958). *Organizations.* New York, NY: Wiley.

113. Bolman & Deal. (1991, 1992). Op. cit.; Deal & Bolman. (2002). Op. cit.; Kofman, F., & Senge, P. M. (1993). Communities of commitment: The heart of learning organizations.

Organizational Dynamics, 22(2), 5–23; Senge, P. M. (1990). *The fifth discipline: The art and practice of the learning organizations.* New York, NY: Doubleday.

114. Scott. (1998). Op. cit.; Etzioni, A. (1975). *A comparative analysis of complex organizations.* New York, NY: Free Press; Perrow, C. (1978). Demystifying organization. In R. Saari & U. Hasenfeld (Eds.), *The management of human services* (pp. 105–120). New York, NY: Columbia University Press.

115. Bolman & Deal. (1991, 1992). Op. cit.; Deal & Bolman. (2002). Op. cit.

116. Scott. (1992). Op. cit.

117. Parsons, T. (1960). *Structure and process in modern societies.* Glencoe, IL: Free Press.

118. Bolman, L. G., & Deal, T. E. (1984). *Modern approaches to understanding and managing organizations.* San Francisco, CA: Jossey-Bass.

119. Bedeian, A. G. (1998). Exploring the past. *Journal of Management History, 4*(1), 4–15.

120. Drucker, P. F. (1976). The coming rediscovery of scientific management. *Conference Board Record, 13*(6), 23–27.

CHAPTER 3

Change Theory and Leadership in Educational Organizations

Focus Questions

◆ How have societal changes occurring from 1960–2010 influenced educators' and communities' views about how schools educate *all* of their students?

◆ How does understanding adult learning contribute to our understanding of organizational learning?

◆ How has the study of change theory and leadership influenced how leaders view and affect organizational culture, organizational learning, and organizational change?

◆ How can leaders create the conditions that best promote organizational learning and sustained change?

CASE STUDY: ALFRED E. NEWMAN HIGH SCHOOL

The 2,500-student Alfred E. Newman High School is located in an urban area of a medium-sized city. It was built in 1958 as the city's only high school. Today's student demographics reveal a much more diverse student body than when the school opened. Stable over the past 10 years, Newman High School's student characteristics are:

58% African American (*n* = 1,450)
27% Caucasian (*n* = 675)
11% Latino (*n* = 275)
 4% Asian (*n* = 100)
71% eligible for free or reduced-price lunch (*n* = 1,775)
16% eligible for special education services (*n* = 400)
26% of graduating seniors attend college after graduation (*n* = 650)
62% of those going to college obtain full academic scholarships (*n* = 403)
26% of ninth graders do not graduate within 4 years
29:1 average pupil-to-teacher ratio in core subjects
Two assistant principals—one assigned to the Academically Talented Newman Students (ATNS) program and one to the regular program

The school is very proud of the approximately 400 students who obtain full academic scholarships when they go off to college. To assist in meeting this goal, the school began the Academically Talented Newman Students (ATNS) program more than 20 years ago. Those students admitted to the ATNS program in the ninth grade are placed in courses with no more than 14 students in a class. Newman's best teachers teach the ATNS students. Two of the six school counselors are assigned to deal with ATNS achievement, testing, and college placements. The faculty is quite pleased with the ATNS program and its results for students, and the school culture reflects this. Pictures, trophies, and honors awarded to ATNS individuals are prominently displayed throughout the school.

Just last year, however, a small group of parents became aware of the ATNS's low pupil-to-teacher ratio and began to express concern that the less academically talented students were not receiving the help they needed to be successful in school. They spoke to the school board in the January meeting, but the board took no action.

As of July 1, you are the new principal of Alfred E. Newman High School and new to the community. The superintendent and assistant superintendent recommended you for the job. Although both are retiring at the end of your first year in the principalship, they have pledged their support to you. The faculty held a reception for you, and they were eager to share their pride in student accomplishments. Several ATNS graduates attended the reception and spoke to you. Among them were the head of neurosurgery at Johns Hopkins, the state attorney general, and the Speaker of the House in the state legislature.

The previous principal had been a teacher, department chair, and assistant principal in the school. He became the principal in 1975, was highly regarded in the community, and the faculty loved him. When the school demographics began to change in the early 1970s, the ATNS program was his idea. Through the years, he nurtured the program and made certain that the talented students received the highest quality education. The previous principal "tapped" and mentored the two current assistant principals. In fact, they are almost his clones. One even sports the previous principal's crewcut hairstyle. Both had applied for the principalship.

As you disaggregate the data, one item becomes very clear. The school barely made Adequate Yearly Progress (AYP) last year. The school has been relying on the ATNS group to ensure the school meets its annual achievement goals. After analyzing the test scores, you look at how the school has used its assets.

You begin to notice disturbing facts about the allocation of resources. Two school counselors serve the ATNS program, and the remaining four counselors service the remaining 2,100 students. The average pupil-to-teacher ratio for ATNS is 14 to 1. For the other students the ratio is more than double that of ATNS. The highest quality teachers are assigned to the ATNS group. ATNS students attend seven field trips each year while the remaining student body is allowed only one field trip.

At your first administrative meeting with the two assistant principals, head of the guidance department, and the department chairs you find overwhelming support for the ATNS program. You are surprised by the negative, almost hostile reaction to your suggestion that the number of pupils in ATNS classrooms be increased so the students with academic needs can have a lower pupil-to-teacher ratio.

One or two new teachers have approached you about how long they would have to wait for their turn to teach in the ATNS program. When you mention that all students need high-quality teachers, they moan and mention another job offer they have. At your next meeting with the superintendent, you make him aware of this situation. He mentions that he is retiring soon and advises you not to rock the boat in your first year as principal.

As you leave the superintendent's office, you meet one of the parents who spoke to the school board about the school's resource imbalance favoring the talented over the regular students. With considerable emotion, she relates to you that her son dropped out of school at the end of last year and has joined a gang. Since then, he has been arrested twice. He was an average student who did not cause trouble. Most schools would have been happy to have him, she tells you through her tears, but unless you are in the ATNS program, you are nothing at this school. She begs you to change things at Newman so something like this does not happen to other children.

Case Study Questions

1. What is the imperative for change? Why?
2. Should the principal take the superintendent's advice? Explain.
3. Where might the principal start the change process?
4. What first steps might the principal take to unfreeze this culture?
5. What leadership strategies might the principal use to start the change process?
6. How would you describe the culture of Alfred E. Newman High School?
7. What steps might the principal take to create a vision of what the school could become for the students and the community?

INTRODUCTION

Since World War II, Americans from all backgrounds have experienced significant changes in every sphere of life: social relationships, politics, civil rights, economics, national security, technology, education, and respect for traditional authority.

Today, planning for manageable and beneficial change and responding appropriately to unexpected external events—rather than working to maintain stability—have become necessary for organizational survival. The challenge for school leadership is to understand the change process and recognize the opportunities to help move their organizations forward in constructive and sustainable ways that help students, teachers, and their wider communities.

SOCIETAL CHANGES AND EDUCATION SINCE THE 1950s

In 1945, America emerged from World War II as a great world power, untouched by the physical destruction that shattered so many of its enemies and allies. Its capital infrastructure remained intact. Nevertheless, the immediate postwar years challenged the nation to provide leadership and policies not only for rebuilding a war-ravaged world but also for creating a more normal situation at home.

Ideas about leadership reflect their eras. The social, political, economic, technological, and cultural shifts in the United States after World War II had a distinct impact on organizational behavior and leadership practices. Theories about change and effective leadership would also have to evolve.

The 1950s

The 1950s was a time of national self-reflection and improvement. Civil rights, scientific advances, international competition for control of outer space, and a flood of postwar baby boomers would forever change American education.

Brown v. Board of Education, 1954.   After World War II, public attitudes against educating White and African American children in "separate-but-equal" schools began to grow.[1] In the unanimous 1954 *Brown v. Board of Education* decision, the U.S. Supreme Court wrote that "separate-but-equal" was "inherently unequal." Separating children from others of similar age and qualifications only because of their race generated feelings of inferiority about their status in the community—and limited their educational and mental development—in ways that could not be repaired. Giving African American children access to racially mixed classrooms would help to equalize their educational resources and improve their academic outcomes. The case became a watershed for American education and its impact on the larger society.

Baby Boomers and School Construction.   After the war, American GIs took their honorable discharges, veterans' benefits, and Veterans Administration loans, and wed their sweethearts. Marriages and birth rates skyrocketed. Demands on government for education, health care, and other social services increased dramatically. Between 1946 and 1964, approximately 79 million babies were born in the United States.[2] The increase in school construction between 1950 and 1969 corresponds to the years when the baby boom generation attended school. In 1998, 45% of all public schools had been built between 1950 and 1969.[3]

Sputnik and the Space Race.   On October 4, 1957, the Soviet Union successfully launched *Sputnik I*, the world's first artificial satellite. This feat introduced the Space Age and caught Americans off guard. Not only was the Soviets' technological achievement superior to the planned U.S. satellite, but the U.S. public feared that Soviets had the capacity to launch warhead-topped intercontinental ballistic missiles from Europe to attack the United States.

Sputnik forced a national self-appraisal of American educational, scientific, technical, industrial, and moral strength. Education critics recommended greater emphasis on higher academic standards, especially in math and science.

Congress and the National Defense Education Act.   Concerned that Soviet schools were more advanced than American schools, Congress passed the National Defense Education Act (NDEA) in 1958, providing $887 million to support national security by stimulating educational advancements in science, mathematics, and modern foreign languages. Additionally, NDEA gave financial assistance—largely through the National Defense Student Loan program—for thousands of 1960s college students to become teachers.

The 1960s

The 1960s was a decade of head-spinning changes for the United States. Electing a young John Fitzgerald Kennedy as president, landing a man on the moon, and passing landmark civil rights legislation occurred in the same decade as drafting American youths for faraway wars and experiencing nation-wrenching political assassinations. If the present was turbulent, the future looked uncertain.

Education did not escape this era of protest. The Coleman Report unintentionally encouraged the idea that school differences had little relationship to student achievement. The titles of books from this period clearly express the educational protest: *Compulsory Mis-Education* (Goodman, 1964),[4] *Death at an Early Age* (Kozol, 1967),[5] *Our Children Are Dying* (Hentoff, 1966),[6] and *How Children Fail* (Holt, 1964).[7] Previously financed and managed locally, education after the 1960s became increasingly influenced by Congress and by the Supreme Court. Meanwhile, many college-attending baby boomers were becoming student radicals and "hippies" who rebelled against political and cultural authority. The younger generation questioned the wisdom of traditional authority in all areas, creating a bitter chasm between the generations.

Vietnam War.   In July 1954, a defeated France signed a peace agreement with Vietnam, temporarily partitioning its former colony at the 17th parallel. Wanting to limit Communist influence by avoiding reunification, the United States helped create a new nation in southern Vietnam. In 1955, massive amounts of American military, political, and economic aid began to arrive in South Vietnam. In December 1969, the U.S. government instituted the first U.S. draft lottery since World War II, calling as many as 40,000 young men into service monthly.[8]

By February 1965, American public opinion had begun to question the U.S. government's assertion that it was fighting a democratic war to liberate the South Vietnamese people from Communist aggression. By November 1967, American troop strength in Vietnam approached 500,000, and U.S. casualties reached 15,058 killed and 109,527 wounded.[9]

By 1968, the antiwar movement had spread nationwide. In late April 1970, after days of anti-war protests, National Guardsmen called out to preserve order at Kent State University in Ohio killed four students on campus. Students at Jackson State in Mississippi were shot and killed in a similar event. On April 30, 1975, America's involvement in the war ended with approximately 58,148 American soldiers dead.[10]

Counterculture.   In the 1960s, thousands of White, middle-class, college-aged youths began to criticize established American priorities of achievement, rationality, and economic growth in pursuit of "the good life." Their rebellion targeted the Vietnam War, race relations, sexual mores, traditional authority, women's rights, and the materialist interpretation of the American dream. Sometimes called hippies or flower children, their counterculture lifestyle asserted itself in long hair, rock music, colorful and innovative attire, casual sex outside committed relationships, recreational drug use, and occasional violence. In the first 6 months of 1968, more than 200 major demonstrations occurred at 100 American colleges and universities, involving more than 40,000 students.[11]

The Coleman Report.   Investigating the nationwide availability of educational opportunity, Johns Hopkins University Professor James Coleman and colleagues surveyed over 640,000 students in grades 1, 3, 6, 9, and 12 and approximately 60,000 teachers in more than 4,000 schools.[12] Their 1966 report, *Equality of Educational Opportunity* (the "Coleman Report"), concluded that family background, not the school, was the major determinant of student achievement and life outcomes,[13] affirming the statistical correlations between socioeconomic status and school achievement. The controversial findings made schools appear unable to overcome or equalize the gaps in students' academic achievement stemming from environmental factors.

In response, the federal government created compensatory education programs such as Head Start and Title I to strengthen economically disadvantaged students' academic and social behaviors. The report also stimulated researchers and educators who believed that effective schools *could* make a difference in student learning *regardless* of students' family backgrounds or socioeconomic status. These researchers of effective schools developed a body of data affirming that the school controls the factors needed to ensure student mastery of the core curriculum, and acknowledging the family's crucial role in promoting student learning.

Lyndon Johnson's Great Society.   Lyndon Johnson was a masterful politician with an extraordinary ability to get things done. To help our society's most vulnerable citizens, President Johnson submitted, and Congress enacted, more than 100 major proposals which came to be called the "Great Society."

Above all else, Lyndon Johnson saw the Great Society as an instrument to create racial justice and eliminate poverty. From 1963 until 1970, the Great Society's impact reduced the portion of Americans living below the poverty line from 22.2% to 12.6%.[14] Great Society programs included aid to education, attack on disease, Medicare (health insurance for the elderly), Medicaid (health assistance for the poor), urban renewal, beautification, conservation, development of economically-depressed regions, money to support medical research, wide-scale programs to reduce poverty, control and prevention of crime and delinquency, food stamps, and the school breakfast programs.The Voting Rights Act of 1965 opened the way for African Americans to participate at every level of government.

Elementary and Secondary Education Act (ESEA).   In 1965, Congress passed President Johnson's Elementary and Secondary Education Act (ESEA), parent of the No Child Left Behind Act of 2001. ESEA was the first federal government funding commitment to help local school districts level the playing field between middle-class and economically disadvantaged children.

ESEA introduced the federal Head Start programs to give children from economically disadvantaged homes a "head start" on school success. Title I intended to supplement academic resources for low-income children who needed extra reading and math help in the early grades. Additionally, ESEA provided scholarships, grants, and work-study programs to able but financially needy college students and bilingual education.

The 1970s

Many of the 1960s' "radical" ideas gained wider acceptance in the new decade. Civil rights, distrust of government, the women's movement, and concern for the environment became mainstream American life. The 1963 U.S. and U.S.S.R.'s test ban treaty signaled a more secure political environment. Meanwhile, American culture experienced increasingly rapid changes.

In education, the 1970s saw a return to more traditional curriculum and instruction. Congress made free and appropriate public education available to all children with disabilities, and the federal Department of Education became a Cabinet-level post. Independent researchers also began to identify public schools that could successfully educate low-income and minority students by using certain principles and practices.

Back-to-Basics Movement.   In the mid-1970s, the back-to-basics movement epitomized public and policy discontent about education. Academic standards appeared to have dropped. The well-publicized decline in SAT scores, the lagging achievement of low-income students, the sense that schools were not "accountable" for sufficiently advancing student learning, the "watered-down" 1960s academic curriculum made "relevant" to students' social and political concerns, and the apparent lack of respect for adult authority in schools pressed policy makers to rethink the school standards and curriculum.[15]

The back-to-basics movement involved curriculum, testing, and standards. It required schools to teach students the subjects as separate disciplines. Many districts adopted a "basic skills" or "essential skills" curricula. School boards and administrators pushed for improved student test scores as proxies for higher achievement. Many districts adopted tests that aligned with their curricula and focused teaching and learning to the tests. Vocational studies, art, music, and physical education received reduced status with less time in the school day.

Many states added courses to high school graduation requirements and mandated that students pass minimum competency tests for promotion or to earn a high school diploma. Policy makers believed that standards, published evidence on performance, and required passing marks would create incentives for teachers to teach more effectively and for students to study hard.

Public Law 94-142—IDEA.   In 1970, U.S. schools educated only one in five children with disabilities. Many states had laws excluding children who were deaf, blind, emotionally disturbed, or mentally disabled.[16] In 1975, more than half of the over 8 million U.S. children with disabilities did not receive appropriate educational services or access to full equality of opportunity. One million children with disabilities were excluded entirely from the public school system.[17] Courts and Congress would soon remake this educational landscape.

Courts in Pennsylvania (1971) and the District of Columbia (1972) established the right of all children labeled as "mentally retarded" to a free and appropriate education. In 1973, the Rehabilitation Act, Section 504, and later amendments guaranteed the rights of individuals with disabilities in employment settings and in schools that receive federal monies. Finally, parental pressure, court decisions, and legislative actions swayed Congress to pass the Education for All Handicapped Children Act (Public Law 94-142) in 1975, the first law to clearly define the rights of children with disabilities to free appropriate public education. Over the years, additional amendments extended and clarified these rights.[18]

New Federal Department of Education.   Since the mid 19th century, responsibility for educating America's children has had a national presence. First established in 1838 for gathering statistics on schools and teaching, federal education offices usually were housed in separate Cabinet-level departments. The federal education office remained small until the 1950s and 1960s, even as the national education budgets grew to overshadow those of other large Cabinet departments.

In 1979, President Jimmy Carter signed the law creating the U.S. Department of Education as a Cabinet-level agency. Over the years, the Department of Education has become a major policy engine in primary, secondary, and higher education at national, state, and even local levels. Today, the department's elementary and secondary programs annually serve nearly 14,000 school districts and 56 million students attending approximately 99,000 public and 34,000 private schools. Department programs also provide grant, loan, and work-study assistance to more than 13 million postsecondary students.[19]

The 1980s

Science and technology accelerated its impact on people's lifestyles in the 1980s. Columbia, America's first reusable spacecraft was launched in 1981. Large numbers of Americans began using personal computers in their homes, offices, and schools. Video games, aerobics, minivans, camcorders, and talk shows became part of our culture.

Families changed drastically during these years. The 1980s continued the trends of the 1960s and 1970s: more divorces, more unmarried couples living together, and more single-parent families. The two-earner family became more common than in previous decades. More women earned college and advanced degrees, married, and had fewer children.

American public education came under attack in a new report. Advocating for setting and meeting world-class standards for public schools became a popular political activity. At the same time, Congress gave parents of students with disabilities more resources to challenge disagreements they had with their schools about students' education.

A Nation at Risk.   In 1983, the National Commission on Excellence in Education's report, *A Nation at Risk*, sharply criticized public schools.[20] It claimed that world competitors were challenging the United States' former preeminence in commerce, industry, science, and technological innovation. Our schools, once a source of justifiable pride, were "presently being eroded by a rising tide of mediocrity that threatens our very future as a Nation and as a people."[21] Our students were scoring poorly on international tests, not taking enough science and math courses, and showing weak critical thinking skills.

The authors of *A Nation at Risk* advocated high expectations for all students by completing a reasonably demanding academic curriculum and meeting high standards for receiving a high school diploma. Textbooks and standardized tests would drive the improvement.

As a report, *A Nation at Risk* generated much controversy. Some questioned the assumed cause-and-effect relationship between public schooling and market dominance or industrial productivity, asking whether schools could either cause or cure America's social, economic, and political dilemmas.[22] Critics challenged the fallacy of comparing the highly dissimilar U.S. with European and Asian education systems.[23] Some observed that the report's narrow definition of *excellence* did not consider learning's intrinsic value of building cooperation and community, or that its recommendations placed educationally and economically disadvantaged students at greater risk of failure.[24] Others saw *A Nation at Risk* as propaganda meant to advance a political agenda.[25]

A Nation at Risk spurred policy makers to increase public schools' accountability and educational rigor. By 1985, 35 states required statewide minimum competency tests; 11 required students to pass such tests to graduate from high school. Many believe that the emphasis on students mastering basic skills plus the new public accountability of published "school report cards" were important reasons why African American students' NAEP (National Assessment of Educational Progress) scores rose during the 1970s (for 9-year-olds) and during the 1980s (for 17-year-olds).[26]

1986 Handicapped Children's Protection Act (HCPA).   In 1986, Public Law (PL) 99-372, the Handicapped Children's Protection Act, allowed parents or guardians to be reimbursed for reasonable legal costs if they successfully sued the school district in state or federal court over the school's special education decisions affecting their child.

Parents of children with disabilities could choose to have an attorney represent them during both administrative hearings and court proceedings and could receive reimbursement from state or local education agencies for some or all of their lawyers' fees if they won in all or part of the hearings or proceedings. The law also provided some safeguards for school districts.

America 2000.   Since American schools' basic governance is decentralized with most power wielded at the state level, we actually have 50 school systems, one for each state. In 1989, the National Governors Association (NGA) Education Summit met in Charlottesville, Virginia.

Originally published in a report, *America 2000: An American Educational Strategy*,[27] the group developed national education goals for all schools to meet by the year 2000:

1. All children will start school ready to learn by participating in preschool programs.
2. The high school graduation rate will increase to at least 90%.
3. All students will leave grades 4, 8, and 12 having demonstrated competency in English, mathematics, science, foreign languages, civics and government, economics, art, history, and geography.
4. Teachers will have opportunities to acquire the knowledge and skills needed for preparing students for the 21st century.
5. Students will be first in the world in mathematics and science achievement.
6. Every adult will be literate and will possess the knowledge and skills necessary to compete in a global economy.
7. Every school will be free of drugs, violence, and the unauthorized presence of firearms and alcohol.
8. Every school will promote partnerships to increase parental involvement in the social, emotional, and academic growth of children.

The National Center for Education Statistics (NCES) developed a set of performance benchmarks, and collects ongoing data to allow states and policy makers to determine how successfully schools are meeting these goals.

The 1990s

In 1992, the World Wide Web began altering the ways we communicate (e-mail), spend our money (online retail, gambling), and do business (e-commerce). The number of people online increased from 3 million in 1994 to 100 million by 1998.[28] The booming economy led to record low unemployment. Minimum wage increased to $5.15 an hour. The stock market reached an all-time high, as individuals learned to buy and trade via the Internet. Americans enjoyed the country's affluence by traveling more (up 40% from 1986), enjoying sporting events such as the 1996 Atlanta Summer Olympics, and energetically spending consumer dollars.[29]

Despite the general economic well-being, violence remained a part of life. In 1992, South-Central Los Angeles residents rioted after jurors acquitted four White police officers of assault charges for beating an African American motorist, Rodney King. In 1993, foreign terrorists detonated a bomb in the garage beneath the New York City World Trade Center. Domestic terrorists bombed the Alfred P. Murrah Federal Building in Oklahoma City on April 19, 1995. Schools were not immune to the bloodshed. Between February 1996 and April 1999, America witnessed at least 14 school shooting incidents, the most deadly occurring on April 20, 1999, when 14 students and 1 teacher were killed and 23 wounded at Columbine High School in Littleton, Colorado.

In education, policy makers continued their push for standards-based education and school accountability.

Goals 2000.   In 1994, President Bill Clinton and Secretary of Education Richard Riley attempted to update *America 2000* with *Goals 2000*. Its purposes: to raise expectations for parents, teachers, and students with high academic standards; and to give state and local reform efforts greater flexibility and more support. *Goals 2000* expanded *America 2000* with the goals to improve teacher preparation and promote parents' involvement in all aspects of their children's growth.

With its emphasis on standards-based reform, *Goals 2000* marked a major shift in federal education policy away from concerns about the process and quality of program implementation toward a focus on outcomes and accountability for programs.

The New Century

The new century brought additional changes to public education. For the first time, the federal government held public schools accountable for increasing achievement of traditionally underserved students.

No Child Left Behind Act of 2001. The No Child Left Behind (NCLB) Act of 2001, a reauthorization of the 1964 Elementary and Secondary Education Act, tied federal monies to rigorous and highly visible public school accountability. Seeking equity and excellence, NCLB was the federal government's first serious attempt to hold states, districts, and schools accountable for remedying the unequal achievement among different populations, especially low-income students, minority students, English language learners, and students with disabilities.

According to the legislation, all student subgroups must be "proficient" in both reading and math—be performing at grade level—by the end of the 2013–2014 school year. The law also required schools to guarantee that only "highly qualified teachers"—individuals with documented subject matter knowledge in the content they were teaching—be available in each core subject classroom.

Operating under the slogan "what gets measured gets done," NCLB required every state to develop a comprehensive system of standards and assessments in language arts and math. Students were tested in grades 3–8 and once in high school in language arts and math to measure student progress toward proficiency and to determine school accountability.[30] States were required to disaggregate the test scores by race, socioeconomic status, disability, and English proficiency to prevent schools from "hiding" or glossing over underserved students' low achievement by averaging their scores with those from higher achieving, more economically advantaged peers. NCLB made schools' failure to move each student subgroup closer to proficiency liable for a range of penalties.

Obama Administration and Education. Elected in 2008 during the most severe economic recession since the Great Depression, President Barack Obama committed policy and funding to cash-strapped states to support widespread educational improvements and to prevent teacher layoffs. Signing an economic stimulus into law in early 2009, President Obama's American Recovery and Reinvestment Act (ARRA) directed historic levels of federal dollars into education. The focus of funding went to improving teacher and principal effectiveness and turning around chronically underperforming schools.

Additionally, the Recovery Act supported the $4.35 billion Race to the Top competitive grant program to provide monies to states for large-scale educational reforms that result in improved student achievement, narrowed achievement gaps, and increased graduation and college enrollment rates. Grant applications required states to incorporate student achievement data into teacher and principal evaluations and obligated states to ensure their equitable distribution in high-poverty and/or high-minority schools. All but 10 states applied for the award during the first round of competition.[31] Chronically underperforming schools also received Department of Education attention, with $3.5 billion intended to boost state and district efforts to overhaul their worst-performing schools. An extra $650 million in Investing in Innovation grants was allotted for districts, groups of schools, and their nonprofit partners to pursue and scale up innovative reform strategies through three tiers of grants with the biggest awards going to the proposals with the strongest research evidence of past success.

Reprise: Change in American Culture.   If Rip Van Winkle[32] had gone to sleep in 1950 and awoken in 2000, he would not have recognized the United States or the rest of the developed world. Ways of understanding and acting in the world have shifted the once-solid ground from under our feet. The world no longer resembles the one in which our parents and grandparents came of age. In today's culture, planning for manageable and beneficial change and responding appropriately to unexpected external events—rather than working to maintain stability—have becomes a business and lifestyle necessity.

Since organizations are groups of people, understanding and responding appropriately to these significant and rapidly occurring societal transformations requires major mental, emotional, and behavioral adjustments. Change theory came to influence how leaders viewed and led their industries and businesses in shifting environments.

ACTIVITY 3.1   Analyzing and Interpreting the Data from Alfred E. Newman High School

Case Study Question 1: What is the imperative for change? Why?

The new principal of Alfred E. Newman High School (ANHS) enters a school with a highly diverse student population. All the administrators and most of the teachers have been working there for years. The staff is very proud of their successful Academically Talented Newman Students (ATNS) program. At the same time, the data show that the school barely made Adequate Yearly Progress last year. Sixteen percent of the students, those in the ATNS program, receive an overwhelming share of school resources. A group of teachers are complaining. Are changes necessary? Working in small groups:

1. Identify all the factors that suggest ANHS is doing certain things well for certain students—and those factors that suggest ANHS is not doing things well for all its students.
2. What do the current practices at ANHS say about what and who they value and what and who they don't value?
3. From the variety of feedback the new principal is receiving, what does the majority of the school faculty and community seem to believe about the need for changes at ANHS?
4. How can the new principal use the collected data and information to analyze their meaning for the educational environment?
5. How can the new principal use these collected data to identify goals, assess organizational effectiveness, and promote organizational learning?
6. How can the new principal use these data to better obtain, allocate, align, and efficiently use human, fiscal, and technological resources?
7. From the new principal's point of view, what is the imperative for change?

THE ADULT LEARNING FRAMEWORK

Learning involves change. Learning implies an alteration in the individual due to the interaction of that individual with the environment. It entails acquiring the habits, knowledge, and attitudes that enable the individual to make cognitive, personal, and social adjustments. Since learning is inherent to the concept of change, any change in behavior implies that learning is occurring or has occurred.[33]

For organizational change to happen, employees must learn. Understanding how adults learn can help educational leaders create the environment that motivates and supports employees' personal and professional growth—and that, in turn, produces organizational learning and change.

Although adult learning as a field of study has been a focus of scholars and practitioners since the 1920s, it still has no single theory. Rather, it has a mosaic of theories, models, sets of principles, and explanations that comprise its knowledge base.[34]

Early research on adult learning investigated whether adults *could* learn. Today, it is recognized that adults score better on some aspects of intelligence as they get older and worse on others, resulting in a fairly stable composite measure of intelligence until very old age.[35] Until the mid 20th century, the information available on adult learning was limited. It came from research in psychology and educational psychology with understanding gained from behaviorist-designed research and insights extrapolated from research with children. Eventually, researchers began asking: What was different about adult learning?

Andragogy and self-directed learning emerged as appropriate conceptual frameworks to describe adult learning. With andragogy providing a learner-centered focus and self-direction describing the learning process, these twin anchors reflect a philosophy of lifelong education and the position of the mature person in the education process.

Andragogy

Andragogy became a new organizing concept for adult learning to distinguish it from pre-adult schooling.[36] Andragogy has six underlying assumptions that describe the adult learner as someone who:[37]

◆ Has a need to know what, why, and how
◆ Has an independent self-concept and can direct own learning
◆ Has accumulated a reservoir of life experiences that is a rich resource for learning
◆ Has learning needs closely related to changing social roles and developmental tasks
◆ Is problem centered and interested in immediate application of knowledge
◆ Is motivated to learn by internal rather than external factors

These assumptions provide the basis for designing, implementing, and evaluating educational experiences with adults. Accordingly, the most effective organizational climate for adult learning is one in which adults feel accepted, respected, safe, supported, and trusted, and in which they sense a spirit of mutuality existing between leaders and learners as "joint inquirers."[38] The ambiance is informal and "mature." The physical environment provides for creature comforts (i.e., temperature, comfortable chairs, adequate light, good acoustics, refreshments, and a layout that favors interaction) to support learning. Resources include books, computers with Internet access, journals, and other media that can be used proactively. Hypothesis testing, prompt honest and detailed feedback, and tolerance of mistakes are useful practices. Any situation in which adults are not allowed to be self-directing and in which they perceive they are being treated as children interferes with learning. Because adults manage other aspects of their lives, they are capable of directing—or at least helping to plan—much of their own learning.

Critics challenge the andragogy assumptions, noting that these characteristics are not unique to adult learners. Some adults are highly dependent on a teacher for structure, and some children are independent, self-directed learners. Likewise, adults may be externally motivated to learn, such as attending training sessions to keep their jobs, while children may be motivated by curiosity or learning's internal satisfaction. Certain life experiences may impede learning,[39] while children in certain situations may have a range of experiences qualitatively richer than some adults.[40]

This critique led to reconceptualizing learning on a continuum ranging from teacher directed to student directed rather than assuming that pedagogy as only for children and andragogy only for adults. Both approaches are appropriate with children and adults, depending on the situation. Andragogy, however, remains as the most learner-centered education pattern, involving learners in as many aspects of their education as possible and creating the climate in which they learn best.[41]

Self-Directed Learning

While the andragogy concept contributes to our understanding of adults as learners, the idea of self-directed learning helps expand and clarify our understanding of the learning process. Emerging at the same time that scholars introduced andragogy to North American adult educators, self-directed learning appeared as another model to help define adult learners as different from children. Instead of depending on an instructor or a classroom, self-directed learning is widespread and occurs as part of adults' everyday life. Self-directed learning can be categorized into three dimensions: the goals, the process, and the learner.[42]

The goals of self-directed learning include developing the learner's capacity to be self-directed and act responsibly,[43] fostering critical reflection to increase self-knowledge,[44] and promoting political action for social justice.[45] According to Abraham Maslow, the ultimate goal of learning is self-actualization.[46]

The process for self-directed learning can be linear—moving step-by-step from diagnosing needs to identifying resources and instructional formats to evaluating outcomes.[47] Or the process can be more interactive, considering the learner, the context of learning, and the nature of the learning itself.[48] Generally, the difference between a content learning model appropriate for children and a process learning model appropriate for adults is that the content model is concerned with transmitting information and skills whereas the process model is concerned with providing procedures and resources for helping learners acquire information and skills.[49] The first model is for dependent learners, the second for more autonomous learners.

The learner dimensions include allowing the adult to have substantial input regarding the content to be learned and the manner in which it is to be learned and assessed. Not all adult learners are alike in needs or preferred learning approach. Research suggests that educators should not assume that because a person has been self-directed in one situation that he or she will be successful in a new area. Orientation, support, and guidance may all be needed in the first stages of any learning project.[50]

Critics note that adult learning theory's assumptions are untested and may largely be a product of the environment in which adults find themselves rather than any innate differences between adults and children. Also, self-directed learning does not ensure greater competence.[51] Such criticism, however, serves to strengthen the argument that organizational climate and practices are essential factors in supporting employee learning and organizational growth.

Implications for Organizational Learning

Knowledge about adult learning has implications for the organization's educational quality. Every organization is not only a place to get things done but also a social system that serves as a means for helping people meet human needs and achieve human goals: developing the work and personal competencies that will enable employees to meet their own survival and growth needs as well as serving organizational ends.

The organization's culture and environment affect the quality of learning that takes place within it. The culture and environment either facilitate or inhibit learning. For example, if graduate students in educational leadership are taught to involve subordinates in decision making, but their own principals never involve them in making decisions, which leadership practice are they likely to adopt? If an adult church member is taught to "love thy neighbor" but the overall church life is characterized by discrimination and intolerance, which value is more likely to be learned?

Organizations that expect to continue growing and adapting to market, societal, and technological realities need to build an educative environment that supports leadership and employee learning. Characteristics of such a learning environment for adults include four basic qualities: (1) respect for personality; (2) participation in decision making; (3) freedom of expression and availability of information; and (4) mutuality of responsibility in defining goals, planning and conducting activities, and evaluating outcomes. If the growth of people conflicts with the accomplishment of things, precedence goes to the former. Existing within organizations that hold such a democratic philosophy is a spirit of mutual trust, an openness of communications, a general attitude of helpfulness and cooperation, and a willingness to accept responsibility. This ethos stands in contrast to paternalism, regimentation, restriction of information, suspicion, and enforced dependence on authority.[52]

An organization that values adult learning values adults. The organization sees human beings as its most precious assets and their development as its most productive investment. The climate and educational activities are based on participants' real needs and interests.

Participants will have input into policies that affect them, and they will have shared responsibility for making and implementing decisions and evaluating strategies for continuous organizational and personal self-renewal. Likewise, in actual learning situations, the adults' experiences will count for as much as the teacher's knowledge. Shared learning reflects shared authority. In sum, the organization's most effective instrument of persuasion is its own behavior, serving as a role model for those it influences.

Throughout the rest of this chapter as we learn about change theory, organizational culture, change leadership, and learning organizations, it is important to remember that effective implementation of adult learning concepts underlies them all.

ACTIVITY 3.2   Considering Adult Learning as a Factor in Changing Newman High School

Case Study Question 3: Where might the principal start the change process?

Discuss as a class:

1. How might the new principal begin to collaboratively develop and implement a shared vision and mission that supports the success of each student?
2. How might the new principal begin the process of initiating, nurturing, and sustaining a culture of collaboration, trust, learning, and high expectations that promotes the success of every student?
3. Which adult populations at ANHS will have to evolve their perceptions, ideas, and instructional practices so that each student will have high-quality teaching and learning experiences?
4. What new perspectives and skills will different teacher groups have to learn so they can support high achievement for all students?
5. What key ideas about adult learning will the new principal need to remember when building a school culture and professional development that support adult learning at ANHS?

CHANGE THEORY AND LEADERSHIP IN ORGANIZATIONS

How people view change depends upon the society in which it occurs. Different cultures hold different theories of change. In the early 20th century and before, U.S. culture viewed organizational life as relatively stable and bureaucratic. After World War II, a cascade of events deeply undermined the U.S. sense of security—at home and in the world. Understandably, these unsettling events also had an impact on ideas about organizational functioning. As a result, since the mid-20th century, U.S. and Western European organizational change models have increasingly addressed not only how to deal with continuous change but how to create change.[53]

Organizational theorists in the mid- to late 20th century would study more complex dynamics of modern organizations and people's interactions within them. Scholars such as Chris Argyris, Kurt Lewin, Edgar Schein, Robert Chin, Michael Fullan, and Peter Senge would provide insights to help us better understand such forces. Their findings would offer new perspectives on topics including theories of action, organizational learning, and overcoming barriers to organizational change.

Chris Argyris: Leadership and Organizational Change

Chris Argyris, a Harvard Graduate School of Business professor and an organizational psychologist has used empirical and theoretical research to study how formal organizational structures, control systems, and management affect individuals (and how they respond and adapt to them). Argyris has also investigated how people actually behave in organizations, and how organizations can increase their learning capacity. His theories of action help practitioners and organizations make informed decisions in rapidly shifting and often uncertain contexts and overcome barriers to organizational change. His work emphasizes the need to develop greater harmony and consistency between the organization's goals and human needs of people who work in them.

Theory of Personality and Organizations.   To Argyris, organizations do not hire "hands"; they hire whole human beings. Using psychology and sociology, he believes that individuals are themselves complex organizations. In individuals' attempts to live, mature, and seek self-acceptance, they tend to live out their biological and interpersonal predispositions in their social environments. Individuals produce energy for an organization (effort) if they perceive some gain for themselves by doing so. The type of gain desired depends on the individual's predispositions.[54]

Accordingly, employees mentally sign a "psychological work contract" that commits them to give a fair, full day's work in exchange for wages, job security, lack of harassment from management or other employees, and having superficial, friendly relationships with everyone. This psychological contract governs relationships within the organization and maintains the employee culture. The psychological contract also influences the amount of personal growth available to workers and the productivity levels possible from the organization.[55]

Argyris has suggested that individuals mature along a developmental continuum. Infants are dependent and submissive to parents or other adults, have few and shallow abilities, and hold a short-time perspective. Their behavior is mostly present centered. By contrast, adults strive toward relative independence, autonomy, and a degree of control over their immediate world. They develop many abilities with a few in-depth, and they acquire a longer time perspective. Both past and future influence their behavior.[56] The most productive and satisfied employees, therefore, are those with jobs that allow them to apply and develop their maturing abilities, independence, and choices over work tasks.

Argyris believes that when an incongruity exists between the healthy individual's needs and the formal organization's requirements, the individual will tend to experience frustration, psychological failure, a short time perspective, and conflict. Addressing this dilemma requires replacing directive administrative styles with more participative styles and creating opportunities for job enrichment. By increasing employees' autonomy over what they do, how they do it, and how they assess their effectiveness, organizations create more meaning for employees and more productivity for the organization.[57]

Types of Reasoning: Defensive and Productive.   Argyris has defined *reasoning* as the process that human beings use to move from what they know to what they do, from thought to action. There are two primary types of reasoning: defensive and productive. Defensive reasoning is tacit and unvoiced; the individual does not make his or her assumptions explicit. Defensive reasoning uses data that are not subject to verification. It is also self-protective and anti-learning. In contrast, productive reasoning makes inferences explicit and tests their validity in practice. Also, it consciously designs activity to help self and others understand what is going on around them. Productive reasoning is central to initiating and sustaining action or change.[58]

Productive reasoning is especially difficult for people in dynamic environments because it requires them to reexamine their basic assumptions and to test their judgments against changing conditions. Reasoning productively requires time, attention, and focus. In contemporary organizations where people operate under the stress of time constraints and multiple and conflicting demands on limited resources, time, attention, and focus are scarce commodities.[59] Leadership effectiveness, therefore, depends on individuals using and encouraging productive reasoning.

Theories of Action: Espoused and Used.   Argyris and collaborator, Massachusetts Institute of Technology (MIT) professor Donald Schön, have posited that our culture socializes individuals with theories of action (reasoning)—or skills and values for dealing with other people—that generally are counterproductive to individual growth and organizational effectiveness.[60] These same theories are used to design organizations. As a result, Argyris and Schön have proposed two theories of action—what people say or intend (espoused theories of action) and what they do (theories in use). These theories reflect the reasoning processes that people use to generate behavior.

The first theory of action includes the assumptions, values, and skills that individuals consciously adopt. *Espoused theories of action* are the words we use to convey what we do or what we would like others to think we do.[61] People often fail to look beyond their initial reactions to events to consider the issue at deeper levels. Espoused theories of action involve the way people plan, implement, and review their actions.

People's actual behaviors (theories in use) are shaped by an implicit desire to win (and to avoid embarrassment), to control the environment and task, and to protect self and others. This second theory of action is when people act upon assumptions, values, and skills that they have not consciously adopted. "Do as I say, not as I do" reflects this approach. These *theories in use* or mental maps—rather than theories they explicitly articulate—govern people's real behaviors. They contain assumptions about self, others, and the environment in everyday life. People are rarely aware of this type of theory because it is ingrained from early childhood.[62]

For example, an espoused theory of communicating difficult information may be to express one's concerns to the person openly and honestly. Conversely, the theory in use may be for the individual to avoid the embarrassment or threat of engaging in a face-to-face confrontation with someone who might become angry, humiliated, or vengeful. Instead, the person with the concern might hide the mismatch between espoused and in-use behavior through rationalization, calling the indirect or avoidance actions "diplomatic" or "thoughtful." While the actual behaviors used to bypass or cover up may vary with the occasion, the motives producing the behaviors—to avoid embarrassment, threat, or loss of control—remain the same.[63] Incongruence between thought and action results: the individual says one thing but does another.

Argyris (1980) made the case that productive reasoning and effectiveness come from developing congruence between theory in use and espoused theory—narrowing the gap between the person's intention (espoused theory) and the outcome (actual behavior).[64] This increasing congruence requires individuals to engage in mature reflection with a lack of personal defensiveness and openness to new viewpoints.

Model for Action Theory. Argyris and Schön created a model to illustrate the theory-in-use process. They considered three elements (Figure 3–1):[65]

Governing variables: dynamics which sustain the status quo, such as underlying values and assumptions and organizational rules that people are trying to keep within acceptable limits. Any action is likely to have an impact upon a number of such variables—thus any situation can trigger a trade-off among governing variables.

Action strategies: the moves and plans people use to keep their governing values within the acceptable range.

Consequences: what happens as a result of an action. These can be both intended—those that the actor believes will result—and unintended. In addition, consequences may affect the self or others.[66]

Figure 3–1 shows the movement among governing variables, action strategies, and consequences. In a continuous cycle, the status quo reinforcing governing variables and change oriented action strategy affect the consequences, and the consequences, in turn, provide feedback to the strategy (Did intended outcomes result?) and governing variables (Are the assumptions and values correct?). When a used strategy's outcomes (consequences) are what the person wanted, it confirms a match between intention and outcome. When a mismatch occurs between the person's intention and the resulting outcome, the consequences may be unintended and may even work against the person's governing values. Argyris and Schön suggested two responses to correct this mismatch: single-loop and double-loop learning.

FIGURE 3–1
Argyris and Schön's Theory-in-Use Action Model (Source: From "Models of theories-in-use" by Bob Dick, http://www.scu.edu.au/schools/gcm/ar/arp/argyris.html. Reprinted by permission of Bob Dick.)

Learning: Single loop and double loop.   For Argyris and Schön (1978), *learning* involves detecting and correcting a problem or error. In *single-loop learning*, when something goes wrong, many people look for another strategy that will address and work within the same governing variables. They tweak their responses to the problem's symptoms rather than look more intensively for its underlying causes. In other words, people typically do not question the given or chosen goals, values, plans, and rules.[67] They emphasize making the overt strategy or the techniques more effective rather than challenging the underlying norms and assumptions upon which their actions rest. If people tested their assumptions, they might be proven wrong and lose control of the situation.[68] As seen in Figure 3–2, in *single-loop learning*, feedback from consequences returns to the action strategy and not to the governing variables.

Double-loop learning, in contrast, involves questioning the organization's norms, values, and assumptions (the governing variables) that support goals and strategies. With double-loop learning, people first challenge and change the underlying governing values and norms and then amend the actions (Figure 3–2).[69] The consequence's feedback goes to governing variables and their underlying assumptions which then influence the action strategy and affect the resulting consequences.

Argyris has compared single-loop learning to a thermostat that "learns" or is set to turn on the heat if the room temperature drops below 68 degrees (takes in information about the room temperature, determines when it is too cold, and takes corrective action to turn on the heat). Double-loop learning occurs when an error is detected and corrected in ways that involve modifying the organization's underlying norms, values, assumptions, policies, and objectives. Imagine an "intelligent" thermostat that can evaluate whether 68 degrees is the right temperature for optimum efficiency.[70]

An educational parallel to single-loop learning would be for a fifth grade math teacher to require a failing student to spend more time practicing the unit's math problems before a test. Double-loop learning might have the teacher assesses the student's math skills to identify the specific skill and knowledge deficits apparent on the failed test and then re-teach the relevant math skills to the student at the appropriate level of difficulty using suitable resources and providing the correct level of support—regardless of the grade level at which the content allegedly belongs.

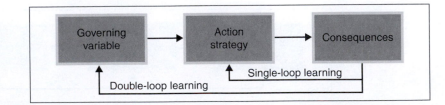

FIGURE 3–2
Argyris and Schön's Theory-in-Use Action Model (Source: From "Argyris and Schon's Theory in Use Action Model" by Bob Dick, http://www.scu.edu.au/schools/gcm/ar/arp/argyris.html. Reprinted by permission of Bob Dick.)

Organizational learning.   Single- and double-loop learning theories help us understand organizational learning. Organizations learn through individuals who act as their agents. In turn, the individuals' learning activities are facilitated or inhibited by an ecological system of factors in what Argyris and Schön have called an organizational learning system. When the learning system is only adequate enough to enable the organization to implement its existing policies and meet its stated objectives, single-loop learning is the process at work. In contrast, an organizational environment that permits comprehensive questioning of underlying goals, values, and assumptions (its governing variables) permits double-loop learning.[71] In the double-loop learning example above, the fifth grade math teacher works in a school environment where he or she feels free to use resources and approaches outside the traditional fifth-grade curriculum if it means helping each student successfully master the material.

Single-loop learning leads to changes in practice; the organization stays unchanged. Double-loop learning leads to changes in the organizational values, beliefs, norms, and practices; the organization changes, or "learns." Single-loop learning is less risky for the individual and the organization, and it affords greater control. Double-loop learning is more creative and critically reflective, and it involves weighing what "good" means. Individuals confront the basic assumptions behind ideas or policies, they face and publicly test hypotheses, and they can end practices that do not hold up to critical scrutiny.[72]

To Argyris, learning is more than problem solving. If learning is to persist, managers and employees must look inward and think critically about their own behavior, identify the ways they inadvertently contribute to an organization's problems, and then change how they think and act. The differences between the two reasoning approaches reflect the leaders' and employees' values about honest self-awareness, openness to new ideas, the credibility of interpersonal communications, and lack of defensiveness about change and control in the organization.

Argyris believes that effective leadership and effective learning are intimately connected.[73] Double-loop learning is rare in most organizations. If it is to be nourished, according to Argyris, it requires leaders who continually model and reward it, especially under conditions where the problems are difficult, embarrassing, and threatening. Unless the leaders behave consistently with double-loop learning when it requires courage to do so, double-loop learning will not be credible.

Model I and Model II.   Going a step further, Argyris has described two models of theories in use that either inhibit or enhance double-loop learning. These models resemble McGregor's Theory X and Theory Y. Model I (similar to Theory X) inhibits double-loop learning. Model I theories in use resemble those presently embedded in formal pyramidal structures and management theory. In Model II (similar to Theory Y), the governing values associated with theories in use can enhance double-loop learning (Table 3–1).[74]

Model I involves "making inferences about another person's behavior without checking whether these assumptions are valid and advocating one's own views abstractly without explaining or illustrating one's reasoning."[75] Model I often leads to deeply entrenched defensive routines that can operate at individual, group, and organizational levels. Exposing actions, thoughts, and feelings make people vulnerable to others' reactions. "Consequently, individuals become skillfully incompetent."[76] They limit their opportunities for learning in order to reinforce their existing beliefs, which are familiar and grant some measure of certainty and sense of control, even if wrong.

TABLE 3–1
Characteristics of Model I and Model II

Model I Characteristics Governing Variables (Defensive Reasoning)	Model II Characteristics Governing Variables (Productive Reasoning)
Control the purpose of the meeting or encounter.	Valid (and verifiable) information.
Maximize winning; minimize losing.	Free and informed choice.
Suppress negative feelings.	Internal commitment to the choice.
Emphasize rationality.	Monitor actions in order to prevent thoughts that are counterproductive to learning.
Model I Action Strategies	**Model II Action Strategies**
Advocate your position to be in control and win; control the task and environment unilaterally.	Share control; advocate your position and combine with inquiry and public testing.
Protect self and others unilaterally; maximize saving face.	Participate in design and implementation of action; minimize unilateral face saving.
Usually Operationalized By:	**Usually Operationalized By:**
Unillustrated attributions and evaluations: "You seem unmotivated."	Attribution and evaluation illustrated with relatively direct observable data.
Advocating courses of action that discourage inquiry: "Let's not rehash the past. It's over."	Surfacing conflicting views.
Treating one's views as obviously correct.	Encouraging public testing of evaluations.
Face-saving moves, such as omitting potentially embarrassing facts.	Acting in ways that produce valid information.
Consequences Include:	**Consequences Include:**
Miscommunication.	Effective communication and problem solving.
Defensive relationships.	Minimally defensive relationships.
Low freedom of choice.	High freedom of choice.
Reduced production of valid information.	Increased likelihood of double-loop learning.
Little public testing of ideas.	Open inquiry and public testing of ideas.
Escalating error.	Reducing error.
Self-fulfilling prophecies.	Reducing self-fulfilling prophecies.
Decreased effectiveness.	Increased effectiveness.
Consequences on Learning Include:	**Consequences on Learning Include:**
Single-loop learning.	Double-loop learning.

Source: Model I based on Argyris, C., Putnam, R., & McLain Smith, D. (1985). *Action science, concepts, methods, and skills for research and intervention* (p. 89). San Francisco, CA: Jossey-Bass. Model II based on Anderson, L. (1997). *Argyris and Schön's theory on congruence and learning.* Retrieved from http://www.scu.edu.au/schools/gcm/ar/arp/argyris.html. Also used: Argyris, C. (1993). Education for leading-learning. *Organizational Dynamics, 21*(3), 5–17; Argyris, C. (1976). Leadership, learning, and the changing status quo. *Organizational Behavior, 4*(3), 29–43; Argyris, C. (1982). The executive mind and double-loop learning. *Organizational Dynamics, 11*(2), 12, 19; Smith, M. K. (2001). Chris Argyris: Theories of action, double-loop learning and organizational learning. *The encyclopedia of informal education.* Retrieved from http://www.infed.org/thinkers/argyris.htm

Model I organizations cannot learn how to improve. Model I creates organizational learning systems characterized by "defensiveness, self-fulfilling prophecies, self-fuelling processes, and escalating error."[77] Its feedback loops "make organizational assumptions and behavioral routines self-reinforcing, inhibiting detection and correction of error, and giving rise to mistrust, defensiveness and self-fulfilling prophecy."[78]

Ironically, defensive routines lock out the very information needed to overcome the sense of inadequacy that influences organizational members to develop such protective behaviors in the first place. Acting defensively seriously impairs one's potential for growth and learning. If an employee's behavior is motivated by not wanting to *appear* incompetent, the person may hide things from self and others in order to avoid looking or feeling incompetent. If, on the other hand, the employee is motivated to *be* competent, honest evaluations of behavior by self and others would be welcome and useful.

Model II includes the ability to call upon good-quality data and to make inferences. It includes participants' authentic views and experiences rather than seeks to impose a preselected perspective upon the situation. In Model II, theories are made explicit and tested; positions are reasoned and open to exploration by others. In other words, Model II can be seen as a dialogue and is more likely to be found in settings and organizations that look to shared leadership. It emphasizes common goals and mutual influences and combines advocacy with inquiry.[79] Argyris looks to move people from a Model I to a Model II orientation and practice—to foster the double-loop learning essential to individual and organizational growth (Table 3–1).

Nevertheless, Model I practices are not all bad. Argyris has noted that Model I practices can be useful in routine situations and for emergencies such as natural disasters when prompt, preplanned responses are critical. Model II is preferable in those situations that would benefit from productive reasoning, inquiry, testing ideas, views, and feelings that lead to effective problem solving for the long term.[80]

Model II arguably makes organizational development possible. The process entails looking for the maximum participation of employees, minimizing the risks for candid participation, starting where people want to begin (often with fixable, clear-cut problems), and designing methods that value rationality and honesty. Edmondson and Moingeon (1999) concluded that employing Model II in difficult interpersonal interactions "requires profound attentiveness and skill for human beings socialized in a Model I world."[81] Although individuals are not being asked to relinquish control altogether, they do need to share that control.

Criticism of Argyris's Work.   Argyris's work has its critics. Some have argued that it is questionable to assume that "good" learning occurs in a climate of openness where political behavior is minimized because organizations are inherently political.[82] An organization can be seen as a coalition of various individuals and interest groups who bargain and negotiate to determine the organization's goals, structure, and policies.[83] Perhaps we need to develop theory that looks to the political nature of structures, knowledge, and information.

Next, critics claim that is not wise to trust bipolar models like Model I and Model II which tend to set up an either-or orientation. Although they are useful as teaching or sensitizing devices, alerting us to various important aspects of organizational life, they are more likely points on an extensive continuum that might contain other valid and useful models.[84] In addition, Argyris's model is described as a linear model whereas it may be possible for certain organizational and interpersonal events to operate at the same time.

Nonetheless, thinking about theory in action, the educative power of the models, and the concept of organizational learning has made, and continues to make, significant contributions to understanding the organizational learning processes. With his concepts and models, Argyris makes it possible to learn by reflecting critically on theory in action, rather than learn by trial and error.

ACTIVITY 3.3   Psychological Contract and Theories of Action at Newman High School

Case Study Question 2: Should the principal take the superintendent's advice? Explain.

Discuss as a class:

1. How does a psychological contract play a role in how the new principal approaches this job?
2. How does a psychological contract influence how the school's long-term teachers and assistant principal approach their job?
3. How are the superintendent's "mixed" messages to the new principal an example of the gap between the superintendent's *espoused* and *used* actions?
4. Which advice should the new principal take: "I'll support you" or "Don't rock the boat"?
5. Are changes needed at the school? What should the new principal do?

ACTIVITY 3.4   Models I and II, Single- and Double-Loop Learning at Newman High School

Case Study Question 3: Where might the principal start the change process?

1. How would you describe the governing variables, action strategies, and consequences currently operating in Alfred E. Newman High School?
2. How is the present action model creating single-loop learning?
3. Using the information in Model I and Model II for general strategies, what would the new principal have to do in order to have the school membership engage in double-loop learning?
4. How might double-loop learning affect the school culture in ways that support the success of every student?

Kurt Lewin and Change Theory

German-born psychologist Kurt Lewin, a former University of Iowa and MIT professor, was one of the modern pioneers of social and organizational psychology. Providing an early model of the change process, Lewin synthesized change into three stages—unfreezing, moving, and refreezing—to provide a foundation for building a theory.[85] Lewin believed that the key to resolving social conflict was to facilitate planned change through learning and to enable individuals to understand and restructure their perceptions of the world around them. His contributions to our understanding of individual and group behavior and the role these play in organizations and society continue to be relevant.

Lewin viewed his planned approach to change (including field theory, group dynamics, action research, and the three-step model) as four concepts forming an integrated and unified approach to analyzing, understanding, and initiating change at the group, organizational, and societal levels.[86]

Field Theory and the Change Process.　Lewin's theory conceptualizes a system's present condition or activity level as a dynamic social equilibrium, a state of balance maintained by forces favorable to change and forces resisting it. For change to happen, the equilibrium must be disturbed, either by adding forces favoring the desired change or by removing forces opposed to it.[87]

Lewin defined a *field* as "a totality of coexisting facts which are conceived of as mutually interdependent" (1946, p. 240).[88] He believed that a field was in a continuous state of adaptation. Change and constancy were relative concepts, and differences existed merely in the amount and type of change.[89]

Lewin believed that if one could identify and plot the strength of these forces, it would be possible to understand why individuals, groups, and organizations act as they do. It would also be possible to recognize which forces would need to be diminished or strengthened to bring about change. In this way, well-designed and executed interventions could produce transformations. Although Lewin saw behavioral modifications as a slow process, he also accepted that under certain circumstances—such as a personal, organizational, or societal crisis—various forces in the field can shift quickly and radically. In such situations, established routines and behaviors break down, and the status quo no longer works. New patterns of activity can rapidly emerge and form a new equilibrium.[90]

Group Dynamics.　Lewin was the first psychologist to write about group dynamics and the group's importance in shaping its members' behavior.[91] Lewin saw group behavior as an intricate set of symbolic interactions and forces that not only affect group structures but also modify individual behaviors. Individual behavior is a function of the group environment, or "field."[92] As a result, any changes in individual behaviors result from changes, large or small, in the forces within the field (or group).[93]

Lewin maintained that it is futile to concentrate on changing individuals' behaviors because the isolated individual is constrained by group pressures to conform.[94] Consequently, the focus of change must be at the group level and should concentrate on factors such as group norms, roles, interactions, and socialization processes to create "disequilibrium" and change.[95]

Action Research.　Lewin conceived of *action research* as a repeating, two-pronged process whereby research leads to action, and action leads to evaluation and further action.[96] Its theoretical foundations lie in Gestalt psychology, which stresses that change can only successfully be achieved by helping individuals to reflect on and gain new insights into the totality of their situation.[97] Lewin stated that action research "proceeds in a spiral of steps each of which is composed of a circle of planning, action, and fact finding about the results of the action."[98]

Action research draws on both field theory (to identify the forces that focus on the group to which the individual belongs) and group dynamics (to understand why group members behave in the way they do when subjected to these forces). Action research stresses that for change to be effective, it must be a participative and collaborative process that involves all concerned.[99]

FIGURE 3–3

Lewin's Three-Stage Model of Change in Organizational Development (Source: Marshak, R. J., "Lewin meets Confucius: A review of the organizational development model of change," *Journal of Applied Behavioral Science*, 29(4), p. 397, copyright © 1993. Reprinted by Permission of SAGE Publications.)

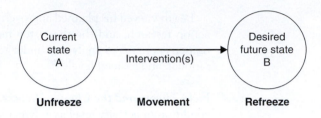

The Three-Step Change Model.   Lewin conceived of the three-step model as one part of an integrated approach to analyzing, understanding, and bringing about planned change at the group, organizational, and societal levels. Analyzing driving and restraining forces could help shift the balance in the direction of the planned change.[100]

Lewin conceptualized successful change as a process with three stages (Figure 3–3):

Stage 1—Unfreezing: Motivate people to change. For Lewin, human behavior was based on a quasi-stationary equilibrium supported by a complex field of forces. Before old behavior can be discarded (unlearned) and new behavior successfully adopted, the equilibrium needs to be destabilized (unfrozen). Lewin's insight was that equilibrium would change more easily if restraining forces such as personal defenses, group norms, or organizational culture were unfrozen.[101]

People's basic tendency is to seek a context in which they have relative safety and feel a sense of control. They attach their sense of identity to their environment, creating a comfortable stability from which any shift, even beneficial ones, causes discomfort. Their equilibrium must be undermined (unfrozen) before old behavior can be ended (unlearned) and new behavior successfully adopted (refrozen). Significant effort may be required to "unfreeze" them and get them moving, and the process may stir many emotions.[102]

Stage 2—Moving: Change what needs to be changed. This means altering the magnitude, direction, or number of favorable and resisting forces, shifting the equilibrium to a new level. Although unfreezing creates motivation to learn, it does not predict the direction of learning or change. Once group members feel sufficient dissatisfaction with the current conditions and really desire to make some change, it is necessary to specify exactly what needs to be altered. People need a clear and concise view of the new state so they can plainly see the gap between the present conditions and the proposed one. Without reinforcement, any change would be short-lived.

Stage 3—Refreezing: Make the change permanent. Refreezing seeks to stabilize and maintain the group at a new social equilibrium to ensure that the new behaviors are relatively safe from backsliding. Here, the new behavior becomes a habit. The person develops a new self-concept and identity and establishes new interpersonal relationships.

To some degree, the new behavior must be congruent with the rest of the learner's behavior, personality, and environment or it will simply lead to a new round of unfreezing, movement, and refreezing.[103] This is why Lewin saw successful change as a group activity, because unless organizational culture, group norms, policies, and practices are also transformed, individual behavior changes will not be sustained.[104]

Lewin also suggested that although common sense might lean toward increasing driving forces to induce change, in many instances this might arouse an equal and opposite increase in resisting forces, the net effect being no change and greater tension than before.[105]

Influenced by his experiences as a Nazi refugee in the early 1930s, Lewin's work stemmed from his desire to find an effective approach to resolving social conflict by changing group behavior (whether these conflicts occur at the group, organizational, or societal level). Lewin promoted an ethical and humanist approach to change. He saw learning and involvement as the key processes for achieving behavioral change needed to develop and strengthen democratic values in society as a whole. Only in this way could its members act as a buffer against the racism and totalitarianism that so dominated events in his lifetime.[106]

Criticism of Lewin's Change Theory.   Lewin's approach to change, particularly the three-step model, has attracted substantial criticism.

Many have argued that Lewin's planned approach is too simplistic and mechanistic for a world where organizational change is a continuous and open-ended process.[107] Bernard Burnes (2004), professor at University of Manchester Institute of Science and Technology, Manchester, United Kingdom, responded to these challenges as a simplistic misreading of Lewin's work when it is studied in isolation rather than as a whole.[108] Lewin viewed change as a complex learning process where stability was always fluid, only quasi-stationary, and where outcomes could not be predicted but emerged as trial and error.[109] What is more, Elrod and Tippett (2002) compared a wide range of change models and found that a substantial body of evidence in the social and physical sciences supported Lewin's three-step perspective on change.[110]

Other critics have asserted that Lewin's work was only relevant to incremental and isolated change projects and was not able to incorporate radical, transformational change.[111] This criticism appears to relate to the speed—rather than the size—of the change, because over time, small incremental changes can lead to radical transformations.[112] Also, Lewin was concerned with behavioral change at the individual, group, organizational, and societal levels, a slow process,[113] whereas rapid transformational change is seen as only being applicable to situations requiring major structural change.[114] Additionally, Lewin recognized that under certain crisis conditions, organizational transformations can be rapidly achieved.[115]

Next, Lewin has been accused of ignoring the role of power and politics in organizations or that organizational life is often conflictual.[116] Given Lewin's personal history as a refugee from Nazi Germany, this accusation is difficult to support. Lewin, a Jew, seriously addressing racism and religious intolerance in his own life could not easily ignore these issues in his professional one. Lewin's approach to change required accounting for differences in value systems and power structures of all the parties involved.

Lastly, critics have charged Lewin with advocating a top-down, management-driven approach to change and ignoring situations requiring bottom-up change.[117] This claim, too, is mistaken. Lewin clearly recognized that change could be initiated from the organization's top, middle, or bottom but could not succeed unless those concerned experienced a "felt need" and everyone participated actively and willingly.[118]

In spite of the critiques, the last few decades have seen a renewed interest in understanding and applying Lewin's approach to change.[119] Planned change (field theory, group dynamics, action research, and the three-step model) provides a rigorous and insightful approach to developing organizations. Lewin's three stages of change—unfreeze, change, and refreeze—continue to be a generic recipe for organizational development.[120] As Hendry (1996) noted, "Scratch any account of creating and managing change and the idea that change is a three-stage process which necessarily begins with a process of unfreezing will not be far below the surface. Indeed it has been said that the whole theory of change is reducible to this one idea of Kurt Lewin's" (p. 624).[121]

ACTIVITY 3.5   Applying Lewin's Ideas about Change to Newman High School

Case Study Question 4: What first steps might the principal take to unfreeze this culture?

Work in small groups to develop answers and then discuss responses as a large group:

1. Using Lewin's ideas about field theory, identify the forces presently aligned in Alfred E. Newman High School for and against change. Depict them graphically. At present, which side appears to have more strength?
2. How can the principal collect and use school achievement data and other information to identify goals, assess organizational effectiveness, and promote organizational learning in ways that would promote the success of every student?
3. What might collaboratively developing a shared vision and mission help the principal do to create more momentum and sway for making constructive changes in the school program and practices?
4. How do Lewin's ideas about group dynamics provide a suggested direction for the new principal's efforts to create positive change in this school?
5. Describe the three-step change process. What might be the first steps the new principal may use to "unfreeze" the restraining forces of personal defenses, group norms, and organizational culture in the current situation?

Edgar Schein and Organizational Culture

During the 1990s, understanding organizational culture became critically important as increasing global competition, shrinking resources, and a rapidly changing international context stressed American organizations to "learn to adapt faster and faster or be weeded out in the economic evolutionary process" (Schein, 1993, p. 85).[122] Edgar H. Schein, Sloan Fellows Professor of Management Emeritus at MIT's Sloan School of Management and an expert on organizational development, introduced the concept of organizational psychology (apart from industrial psychology). He applied social psychology, sociology, and anthropology to develop a more integrated view of group and organizational phenomena than simply focusing on the individual.[123] By studying organizational culture, Schein was able to identify the psychological factors that either promoted or inhibited organizational change and why people in organizations behave the way they do.[124]

According to Schein, the dynamic processes of culture creation and management are leadership's core responsibilities. Leadership and culture are two sides of the same coin. The "ability to perceive the limitations of one's own culture and to evolve the culture adaptively are the essence and ultimate challenge of leadership."[125] He observed that if leaders do not become conscious of the cultures in which they are embedded, these cultures will manage them.[126]

Understanding Organizational Culture. Schein identified *organizational culture*—a set of shared, taken-for-granted assumptions that a group holds and that determines how it perceives, thinks about, and reacts to its various environments—as one of the most powerful and stable forces operating in organizations.[127] Cultural norms knit a community together. An organizational culture develops through three different but closely linked concepts:

◆ A body of solutions to external and internal problems that has worked consistently for a group is taught to new members as the correct way to perceive, think about, and feel in relation to those problems.
◆ These eventually come to be assumptions about the nature of reality, truth, time, space, human nature, human activity, and human relationships.
◆ Over time, these assumptions come to be presumed, unchallenged, and finally drop out of awareness. Culture's power lies in the fact that it operates as a set of unconscious, unexamined assumptions that is taken for granted.[128]

Learning an organization's culture is simultaneously a behavioral, cognitive, and emotional process. The unique culture is taught to new members as the correct way to perceive, think, and feel in relation to organizational problems.[129] For instance, schools have learned spoken and unspoken patterns of agreement among teachers, administrators, and others about how to make decisions and solve problems: "the way we do things around here." These understandings reinforce thoughts and behaviors in ways that powerfully shape people's experiences.

Once a group has learned to hold common assumptions, the resulting automatic patterns of perceiving, thinking, feeling, and behaving provide meaning, stability, and comfort. The shared learning helps reduce the group's anxiety that results from the inability to understand or predict events happening around them. In part, reducing members' anxiety strengthens the culture. One can think of some aspects of culture as being for the group what defense mechanisms are for the individual.[130]

Characteristics of an Organization's Culture. An organization's *culture* is defined as shared philosophies, ideologies, beliefs, feelings, assumptions, expectations, attitudes, norms, and values.[131] Although exact definitions may vary, Schein observed that most organizational cultures contain the following characteristics:[132]

◆ *Observed behavioral regularities.* When organizational members interact, they use common language, terminology, rituals, and ceremonies related to respect and conduct.
◆ *Norms.* Standards of behavior evolve in work groups, such as "a fair day's work for a fair day's pay." The impact of work-group action, endorsed by group norms, results in standards and benchmarks.
◆ *Dominant values.* An organization supports and expects its members to share major values. Typically, school values include high performance levels, low absentee and dropout rates, and high efficiency by staff and students.

- *Philosophy.* Policies guide an organization's beliefs about how employees and clients are to be treated. For example, most school districts have mission statements that articulate their philosophy.
- *Rules.* Guidelines exist for getting along in the organization or the "ropes" that a newcomer must learn to become an accepted member.
- *Feelings.* This is an overall atmosphere or emotional climate that an organization communicates by the physical layout and way in which members interact with clients or other outsiders.

Levels of Organizational Culture.   Schein's model (Figure 3–4) illustrates how people can see, hear, touch, and feel an organization's culture in its facilities, art, technology, and human behaviors. He outlines three levels of culture. At the first level, artifacts can be seen and touched, but these signs are merely cultural symbols, often below most people's awareness. Next, below the publicly visible level, the organization's cultural values lie in its written mission statement, its philosophy, or its credo. These documents or slogans help articulate the organization's basic assumptions.

Finally, the assumptions that are taken for granted, invisible, and outside consciousness rest at the third and lowest level. These are the culture's essence. They are concerned with individuals' relationships to the environment; the nature of reality, time, and space; the character of human nature; the characteristics of human activity; and the qualities of human relationships. Organization members are unaware of these assumptions, but they

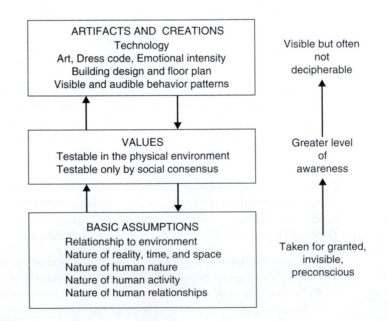

FIGURE 3–4

Schein's Three Levels of Culture (Source: Adapted from Schein, E. H. (1985). *Organizational culture and leadership* (p. 14, Figure 1). San Francisco, CA: Jossey-Bass; and Schein, E. H. (1990). Organizational culture. *American Psychologist, 45*(2), 109–119 (p. 114, Table 2).)

form implicit, unconscious patterns that members uncritically accept unless some questioning process calls them to the surface.

Paradoxes of Organizational Learning.   Schein wrote that human change, whether at the individual or group level, is "a profound psychological dynamic process that involved painful unlearning without loss of ego identity and difficult relearning as one cognitively attempted to restructure one's thoughts, perceptions, feelings, and attitudes" (1996b, p. 27).[133] As a result, Schein found that an inherent paradox surrounds learning: Anxiety inhibits learning, but anxiety is also necessary if learning is going to happen at all.[134] This psychological dynamic helps explain why meaningful organizational change is so difficult.

As Schein saw it, learning is associated with two kinds of anxiety: *learning anxiety* and *survival anxiety*. Learning anxiety comes from being afraid to try something new for fear that it will be too difficult, that we will look foolish in the attempt, or that we will have to give up old habits that have worked for us in the past. Learning something new can make us appear to be the deviant in our groups. It can threaten our self-esteem and, in extreme cases, even our identity. People's learning anxieties underlie their resistance to change.

Survival anxiety is the second type of anxiety. This is the uncomfortable realization that in order to continue living, one will have to change. Like prisoners of war, potential learners experience so much stress and hopelessness through survival anxiety that they eventually become open to the possibility of learning. But this disquiet is no guarantee that they will learn.

Evidence suggests that real organizational change does not begin until people in it experience a real threat of pain that destroys their expectations or hopes and forces them to open themselves to the possibility of change. Threats may come from the organization's leaders or from outside competitors. The basic principle is that learning only happens when survival anxiety is greater than learning anxiety. Learning can be accomplished in two ways: Increase the survival anxiety by threatening people with loss of jobs or valued rewards, or decrease learning anxiety by creating a safer environment for unlearning and new learning.[135]

Creating psychological safety at the same time that organizations are pushing for greater workforce productivity is very difficult. Psychological safety is also dramatically absent when a company is downsizing or undergoing a major structural change, such as reorganizing into flatter networks. In this respect, it's important to distinguish between forcing people to learn something they can see the need to accept—such as new computer skills—and asking them to learn something that seems questionable to them. Learning anxiety will always exist, but if the employee accepts the need to learn, then good training, coaching, group support, feedback, and positive incentives can greatly facilitate the process.[136]

Schein concluded that unless leaders become learners themselves and can acknowledge their own vulnerabilities and uncertainties, transformational learning will never take place. When leaders become genuine learners, they set a good example and help to create a psychologically safe environment for others.

In spite of all the attention and resources devoted to educating employees for organizational change, most people end up doing the same old things in superficially modified ways. Organizational change requires people to give up long-held assumptions and to adopt radically new ones. This unlearning and relearning process is painful and slow.

Major cultural change can take 25 years because it can take that long to forge new identities and relationships throughout all levels of the organization. According to Schein, an imposed cultural change either needs to start with a whole new population of people who already hold the desired new assumptions or will require painful periods of coercive persuasion.[137]

Criticism of Schein.   Critics have challenged the political source of Schein's views on change management and his application of anthropology to understanding culture. Cooke (2002) criticized Schein for seeing the cruel and coercive North Korean Communists' "brainwashing" techniques used on American POWs as being benevolent—instead of cruel or coercive—when applied to management applications.[138] Cooke has not challenged Shein's ideas on their validity or usefulness.

Iavari and Abrahamsson (2002) noted that cultural anthropology has criticized Schein's conception of three levels of culture—artifacts, values, and basic assumptions—and his conclusions about shared beliefs.[139] Anthropologists argue that cultures are always interpreted through subjective realities and cannot be viewed as a fixed set of shared beliefs but instead as fragmented, pluralistic phenomena.[140] In addition, anthropology definitions of culture have moved away from specifying the content or properties of culture (e.g., artifacts, values, basic assumptions), toward a view of culture as an emergent process of reality creation.[141] Since anthropologists also assert that this "reality creation" includes socially transmitted patterns for a particular group's behavior characteristics, sense of collective social identity, and common frames of reference for interpreting and negotiating meaning, non-anthropologists may suspect that the discipline's scholars are engaging in word play rather than making an actual distinction about Schein's model's validity for understanding organizational culture.

ACTIVITY 3.6   Using Schein's Ideas About Organizational Culture at Newman High School

Case Study Question 5: What leadership strategies might the new principal use to start the change process?

Working in small groups, answer the following questions and discuss your findings with the rest of the class:

1. Give specific examples of how the new principal can come to understand the school's culture by observing and analyzing the school's behavioral regularities, norms, dominant values, philosophy, rules, and emotional climate.
2. How can the principal use data, observations, and other information to help the school faculty and staff understand their organizational culture?
3. Give specific examples of where and how the new principal might find information about the school's culture by examining its:
   ◆ Visible artifacts and creations (including student achievement and demographic data).
   ◆ Less visible cultural values but generally within-awareness.
   ◆ Invisible basic assumptions.
4. In what ways is learning an organization's culture a behavioral, cognitive, and emotional process?

ACTIVITY 3.7   Identifying Examples, Values, and Assumptions of Newman High School's Culture

Case Study Question 6: How would you describe the culture at Alfred E. Newman High School? Complete the following chart with information given and suggested from the case study to compile data about the school's culture.

Levels of Culture (Figure 3–4)	What might the new principal see, hear, touch, or sense that would give information about these aspects of the school's culture:	What might YOU as a student see, hear, touch, or sense in your present or former school that would give you information about these aspects of the school's culture:
Artifacts and Creations		
Technology		
Art in halls, offices, classrooms		
Dress code for students		
Dress code for faculty, administrators, staff		
Building design and floor plan		
Actual student behavior patterns		
Actual teacher behavior patterns		
Student achievement data (disaggregated)		
Values		
Observable in physical environment		
Observable through social Consensus		
Basic Assumptions		
Relation to the environment		
Nature of reality, time, space		
Nature of human nature		
Nature of human relations		

Robert Chin and Strategic Orientations

Robert Chin was a Chinese American psychologist and Boston University professor for 32 years. In 1943, Chin joined the U.S. Army and was assigned to the Office of Strategic Services. Along with other psychologists, he served in counterintelligence, working in both Washington, D.C. and China. A master of organizational theory, Chin was an early leader among social psychologists interested in applying their ideas about intergroup behavior. His work on minority students' intelligence was part of the psychological foundation that contributed to the *Brown v. Board of Education* decision.[142]

Although Lewin's change model identifies the major elements of organizational development, it does not address the interventions' underlying strategic orientations or the underlying assumptions about the change process, or provide an appropriate toolkit of intervention techniques to effect organizational change.[143] Robert Chin added to our understanding of how to lead organizational change when he proposed that there are three major *strategic orientations* to organizational change interventions: empirical-rational, power-coercive, and normative-reeducative strategies.[144]

Empirical-Rational Strategies.   This strategy assumes that people are rational beings who will follow their own self-interest once it is revealed to them. When rational and reasonable people receive new knowledge (about a product, technique, or good idea), they will accept the change because it is in their own best interest. Organizational development and change, then, is the process of rational persuasion about the benefits of change for those affected by it. Successful change is based on communicating information and offering incentives. This strategy comfortably fits within the Western traditions and values of our scientific-technological culture.

Receiving new ideas in practical form facilitates adoption. For instance, when schools can obtain relatively complete staff development packages based on demonstrably effective concepts and best practices that address an identified school need, such as helping teachers learn differentiated instruction, teachers more easily accept the learning and change their teaching practices. Similarly, another empirical-rational strategy would involve creating educational research and development centers linked to state education departments and regional educational laboratories and developing school and university consortiums to spread the best practices. Empirical-rational strategies to recruit new teachers might include early retirement programs, school transfers, and changing credentialing and employment criteria.

Power-Coercive Strategies.   This strategy focuses on using legitimate power and threat of sanctions as a way to influence behavior. Sanctions may be political, economic, or moral. To the power-coercive viewpoint, rationality, reason, and human relations are secondary to the ability to effect change by exercising power. Political-coercive power can come from legislation, executive orders, and court decisions that pose penalties for not following the ruling. Closer to home, power-coercive strategies may include threats of embarrassment, transfer, demotion, salary cut, or dismissal.

For example, the No Child Left Behind Act of 2001 (NCLB) assumes that only public humiliation and punishment will motivate educators to invest significant instructional time and resources to raise traditionally underserved children's academic achievement. According to NCLB, schools that do not meet Adequate Yearly Progress face a range of public sanctions as "failing" schools. Congressional lawmakers appeared to be using a political-coercive change strategy in applying NCLB.

Normative-Reeducative Strategies.   Both empirical-rational strategies and power-coercive strategies assume that organizations must be made to change (because they are naturally resistant to change). In contrast, the normative-reeducative strategies assume that organizations can change from within if they have an ethos of continual learning and self-renewal. While the empirical-rational strategies depend on the proposed change making cognitive sense, and power-coercive strategies depend on threat of punishment for not making the change, the normative-reeducative strategies rely on appealing to listeners' emotions and ideals in addition to organizational values as keys to effecting organizational change.

With normative-reeducative strategies, successful change is based on collaboratively redefining and reinterpreting existing norms and values and developing commitment to new ones. Here, a change agent attempts to modify, influence, persuade, manipulate, and strengthen the individual or group's self-awareness, self-understanding, and self-control.[145] Going beyond empirical-rational strategies, normative-reeducative strategies presume that knowledge is necessary but not sufficient to solve problems or to change behavior. The motivation to change behavior must come from inside, not outside. The users must believe that the current system is not satisfactory and that the proposed change is the right method for fixing those inadequacies. Similarly, this strategy assumes that intelligence is social rather than strictly rational, and organizational change cannot happen unless the change appeals to organizational values.

For example, if superintendents want to entice their best principals to leave their current high-achieving schools to lead the district's most high-needs schools—and to view these transfers as a desired challenge—superintendents can: openly announce a competition to identify the most effective principals (based on growth in student achievement scores); meet privately with the winners before publicizing their award and offer them the professional, moral, and ethical "opportunity" to turn around one of the district's failing schools; provide incentives of a 10% raise, more freedom from district rules, the chance to pick an eight-person transition team (each of whom would also receive a raise); and "transfer out" up to five teachers from their new school, including obstructionists, underperformers, and toxic influencers.[146]

According to Nickols (2006), Chin proposed no right or wrong strategy. They may be combined into a larger master strategy that works across the entire organization. Any given initiative is usually best served by a mix of approaches.[147]

Chin emphasized that planned change is most effective when human systems are an integral part of the change process. Whether change is based on introducing new personnel or new technologies, planned change must be anchored in knowledge and must incorporate strategies derived from this knowledge.[148]

ACTIVITY 3.8   Using Chin's Strategic Orientations at Newman High School

Case Study Question 5: What leadership strategies might the principal use to start the change process?

Chin emphasized that normative-reeducative strategies presume that knowledge is necessary but not sufficient to solve problems or to change behavior because the motivation to change behavior must come from inside, not outside.

1. How might the new principal use each of the following—empirical-rational strategies, power-coercive strategies, and normative-reeducative strategies—to facilitate school change? Give examples of what the principal might do to enact each approach.
2. Which approach seems most appropriate to create a new school culture that supports high achievement for all students—and the means to make it happen? Why?
3. Which approach seems the least appropriate to create a new school culture that supports high achievement for all students? Why?

Michael Fullan and Change Leadership

Michael Fullan, currently professor emeritus at the Ontario Institute for Studies in Education and the special advisor on education to the premier of Ontario, Canada, is a recognized international authority on educational reform. Fullan sees change as a journey, a never-ending proposition under conditions of dynamic complexity; it is not a blueprint. He believes that leaders cannot *make* people change. Rather, leaders can create the conditions that enable and press people to consider personal and shared visions, and develop skills through practice over time.[149] In this way, Fullan's approach to leading change resembles Chin's normative-reeducative strategies.

Leading for Change.   Fullan believes that leaders must work with others to change their organizational culture if they are to implement any meaningful transformation. Such leadership requires high levels of cognitive, communication, and personal skills. In *Leading in a Culture of Change* (2007), Fullan broadly describes how successful leaders can mobilize other people's commitment to actions designed to improve things, individually and collectively, by:[150]

- ◆ *Having a moral purpose:* acting with the intention of making a positive difference in the lives of employees, customers, and society as a whole. For schools, the moral purpose is to make a difference in the lives of students regardless of background, and to help produce citizens who can live and work productively in increasingly dynamic and complex societies.
- ◆ *Understanding the change process:* appreciating the difficulties of trying something new, the "implementation dip," redefining resistance as a potential positive force, and reculturing the organization with expanded norms and values.
- ◆ *Building relationships:* being skillful relationship builders with diverse people and groups, being wary of easy consensus that pleasantly masks serious disagreements.
- ◆ *Creating and sharing knowledge:* turning information into knowledge through a social process, generated upon solid relationships.
- ◆ *Making coherence:* clarifying, prioritizing, focusing, and connecting the multiple priorities into a sensible whole.

Fullan observes that transformation requires messiness. Change "*is* rocket science."[151] Fullan states, "Change cannot be managed. It can be understood and perhaps led, but it cannot be controlled."[152]

Looking more specifically at schools, Fullan views leadership's role in generating collective capacity as the means to infuse systemwide emotional commitment and technical expertise into every classroom, every year. Sustained school reform shows that improved student outcomes requires a persistent effort to change teaching and learning practices in every classroom. To give every child the opportunity to work with an effective teacher every year, every educator throughout the school system and its partnering communities needs higher order skills. This can only occur in a true systemic approach within schools, across school districts, and beyond.[153]

To make "all systems go," Fullan continues, leaders throughout the school system need to remember and do "only five things" (and avoid doing the wrong things):[154]

◆ *Moral purpose and high expectations*: acting upon the "no excuses" belief that, given the right approach and amount of time, all (95%) children and youth can learn the dispositions and skills—literacy, numeracy, higher-order thinking, reasoning, and problem solving—essential for surviving and thriving in a complex, interdependent global society.[155]

◆ *Resolute leadership*: focuses on steadfastly holding a clear vision for improving instruction (a small number of ambitious goals relentlessly pursued), building the core guiding group who meets frequently around the shared purpose, progress, and corrective action, and developing positive working relationships with teachers to keep them highly motivated to practice effective teaching every day.

◆ *Intelligent accountability*: increases individual and collective capacity for instructional improvements and shared responsibility for positive student outcomes. This accountability is held internally and reinforced externally. Peer interaction, identifying and spreading best practices, and transparency of data help develop a culture of continuous adult learning and internal accountability. Teachers generally become more motivated as they are helped to become more effective and see positive results.

◆ *Collective capacity building*: "the breakthrough concept to make all systems go."[156] Collective capacity building is the learning process in which teachers are helped, individually and collectively, to focus on instruction and then collaborate for mutual benefit. This process makes the knowledge about effective practice more widely available and accessible on a daily basis, generates teacher commitment, enhances teachers' awareness of moral purpose, and increases the speed of change.

◆ *Individual capacity*: a necessary but not a sufficient solution to improving schools' ability to increase student learning. Individual and collective strategies are compound resources that work in synergy to make the system go.

    Fullan argues that these five components represent a complex resource that build and multiply its effect through interrelated use. Improving student and teacher learning is difficult work; strong and effective school leadership is key to making it happen.

Keenly interested in both theory and practice, Fullan's quarter century of study and writing about successful leadership connects both big picture concepts and daily behaviors.

He believes that leading in a culture of change is about understanding, insight, and relationships. Educators must continually learn, and principals must grow other leaders in their schools. The dilemma: Complexities may be understood, but they cannot be controlled. Although coercive strategies may appear to work in emergencies, in the long run, effectiveness depends on developing members' internal commitments. Leadership in authoritative ideas, democratic empowerment, affiliative connections, and coaching will all be needed. Knowing when and how to use various skills is part of leadership's repertoire.

ACTIVITY 3.9   Applying Fullan's Change Ideas at Newman High School

Case Study Question 7: What steps might the principal take to create a vision of what the school could become for the students and the community?

Work in small groups to complete the following activities and then share your responses with the entire class:

1. How can the new principal of Alfred E. Newman High School use each of Michael Fullan's ideas about successful leadership to begin creating the climate for change? Respond to each of the following bullets with a possible statement that the new principal might use to express his or her vision to teachers, parents, and community leaders.
    ◆ By having a moral purpose:
    ◆ By understanding the change process:
    ◆ By building relationships:
    ◆ By creating and sharing knowledge:
    ◆ By making coherence:
2. As the new principal begins to plan for change, how might each of Fullan's five components of "All Systems Go" affect his or her thinking, planning, and doing? Given each bulleted point, what might the new principal think and do to help the school move forward?
    ◆ Moral purpose and high expectations
    ◆ Resolute leadership
    ◆ Intelligent accountability
    ◆ Collective capacity building
    ◆ Individual capacity

Peter Senge and Systems Thinking

Peter R. Senge, a senior lecturer at MIT's Sloan School of Management, agrees with Fullan's press for capacity building but views organizational learning from the system's perspective. "Increasingly, successful organizations are building competitive advantage through less controlling and more learning—that is, continually creating and sharing new knowledge."[157] Organizations that excel will be those that discover how to develop people's commitment and capacity to learn at *all* organizational levels. Organizations learn only through individuals who learn. While individual learning does not guarantee organizational learning, without it, no organizational learning occurs.

To Senge, *learning organizations* are those where people continually expand their capacity to create their desired results. These organizations nurture new and expansive thinking patterns, where collective aspiration motivates and directs work, and where people are continually learning how to learn together. However, Senge observed that most organizations learn poorly. The way they are designed and managed, the way people's jobs are defined, and the way individuals have been taught to think and interact create fundamental "learning disabilities."

As described in his book, *The Fifth Discipline. The Art & Practice of the Learning Organization*, Senge identified five "component technologies"—or disciplines (bodies of theory and technique that must be studied before they can be put into practice)—that work together to enhance an organization's ability to "learn":[158]

- ◆ *Personal mastery:* a process; the lifelong discipline of continually clarifying and deepening individual vision, focusing energies, developing patience, and seeing reality objectively—including continually clarifying what is important to us. People with a high level of personal mastery integrate reason with intuition. They see "current reality" as an ally and have learned how to perceive and work with forces of change rather than resist them. This is the learning organization's spiritual foundation. An organization's commitment to and capacity for learning can be no greater than that of its members. Personal mastery fosters the personal motivation to continually learn how our actions affect the world.

- ◆ *Mental models:* deeply ingrained assumptions, generalizations, or images that influence how we understand and act in the world. Frequently operating unconsciously, our mental models affect our beliefs about what can and cannot be done in life or in organizations. Many insights into outdated organizational practices fail to be implemented because they conflict with powerful, hidden, but widely shared mental models. Making our thinking open to rigorous scrutiny and challenge allows us to balance inquiry and advocacy, identify shortcomings in our present ways of seeing the world, and become receptive to change.

- ◆ *Building a shared vision:* a critical leadership role; creates a shared vision of goals, values, and missions that motivates people in organizations to a common identity and collective advancement of their agenda. This sense of a common destiny galvanizes individuals to excel and learn because they want to, rather than because they are told to. Building a shared vision fosters individuals' commitment to the long term and generates a focus and energy for learning.

- ◆ *Team learning:* occurs when the intelligence of the team exceeds the intelligence of the team's members, and the team develops extraordinary capacities for coordinated action. Through their shared focus, openness, and interactions—especially using reflection, inquiry, and dialogue—individual team members grow more rapidly than they would otherwise. Suspending assumptions and overcoming defensive routines, team members enter a genuine dialogue of "thinking together"—looking for the larger picture that lies beyond individual perspectives—while avoiding the defensive interaction patterns than undermine learning.

- ◆ *Systems thinking:* a holistic conceptual framework by which understanding the whole depends on recognizing the contributions of its individual parts. Businesses and other human enterprises are systems bound by invisible connections of interrelated actions. Sometimes, it takes years for these links to fully impact each other. Only by thinking holistically of systems, rather than of separate parts, can individuals effectively impact organizational change. By making the subtlest organizational facets understandable, systems thinking gives individuals a "mind shift": new ways to perceive themselves and their world.

Ideally, these five learning disciplines develop as an ensemble. Systems thinking, however, is the "fifth discipline," integrating the other learning disciplines into a coherent body of theory and practice. The systems perspective keeps the focus on the whole. All five learning disciplines are necessary for an organization to realize its potential. For Senge, the fifth discipline is lifelong generative learning. In this context, "learning" does not mean acquiring more information but expanding the ability to produce the life results we truly want. And learning organizations cannot happen unless they have people at every level who practice it.

The template for effective systems thinking is identifying the patterns of behavior that control events and leveraging—seeing where actions and changes in structures can lead to significant, enduring improvements. Identifying patterns of behavior which control events means recognizing the circles of causality—seeing interrelationships rather than linear cause–effect chains, and recognizing processes of change rather than isolated, static, "true-for-one-moment" snapshots—highlights the systems thinking mind shift. Likewise, identifying behavior patterns means discovering the organization's sources of stability and resistance—the traditional norms that support current practices—so artful leaders can jujitsu the organization's resistance to change by focusing directly on the implicit rules, values, and power relationships which hold the embedded norms. At the same time, leveraging suggests the principle of economy: getting the best results from small, well-focused actions. In short, systems thinking includes seeing both the forest *and* the trees.

In Senge's view, tomorrow's leadership will be distributed among diverse individuals and teams who share responsibility for creating the organization's future. Building a community of leaders within an organization requires three types of leadership:

◆ Local line leaders and managers with significant bottom-line responsibility introduce and implement new ideas
◆ Top-level executive leaders recognize, develop, and mentor local line leaders; become their "thinking partners"; steward cultural change through shifts in their own behavior; and use their authority to invest in new knowledge infrastructures
◆ Internal networkers, including internal consultants and frontline workers, move about the organization spreading and fostering commitment to new ideas and practices

In knowledge-creating organizations, these three types of leaders rely on one another to create an environment that ensures continual innovation and knowledge diffusion.[159] This context integrates research, capacity building, and practice—rather than hierarchically fragmenting them within different facets of the organization.

The leader's task is designing the learning process in which organizational members can deal productively with the critical issues they face and develop their mastery in the learning disciplines. Leadership's core strategy is to be a role model. When leaders commit themselves to personal mastery, they work tirelessly to foster a climate in which members can practice the principles of personal mastery in daily life. Many of the behaviors most helpful to increasing one's own personal mastery—developing a more systemic worldview, learning how to reflect on implicit assumptions, expressing one's vision and listening to others' ideas, and jointly inquiring into various people's view of current reality—are inherent in the disciplines for building learning organizations. Effective leaders develop an organization where it is safe for people to create vision, where inquiry and commitment to truth are expected, and where challenging the status quo is predictable and encouraged. Such an organizational climate strengthens personal mastery in two ways: It continually reinforces the idea that the organization values personal growth, and it provides on-the-job training to those individuals who welcome what is offered.

To Senge, the virtues of life and business success are not only compatible but also they enrich one another.

Reviewing the Contributions

Throughout this chapter, scholars have asserted that human systems are integral parts of the organizational change process. Table 3–2 highlights each theorist's or author's contributions and identifies what each added to our understanding about leadership for organizational change.

TABLE 3–2

Reviewing Change Scholars / Theorists' Contributions

Change Scholar/Theorist	Contributions	What They Added to Understanding Organizational Change
Chris Argyris		Used empirical and theoretical research to study how people actually behave in organizations.
	"Psychological contract."	Psychological beliefs which guide employees' relationships within the organization.
	Defensive and productive reasoning (using implicit rather than testable reasoning to make decisions).	Employees must look inward and reflect honestly and critically on their own behaviors—and change them if necessary.
With Donald Schon	Espoused and in-use theories of action (what people say they believe as compared with what they actually do).	People typically behave on the basis of unspoken assumptions and beliefs.
	Theories in use action model (shows relationship among governing variables, action strategies, and consequences).	Effective leadership and effective learning are closely connected.
	Single-loop and double-loop learning (explains how organizational change can be "tweeking" or systemic).	Describes how organizations "learn."
	Model I and Model II	Describes organizational functioning that either inhibits or enhances organizational learning.

(continued)

Change Scholar/Theorist	Contributions	What They Added to Understanding Organizational Change
Kurt Lewin	Field theory.	Describes dynamics of why organizations change or remain the same.
	Group dynamics.	Leaders can change individuals by changing the group's behavior.
	Action research.	Change occurs by helping individuals reflect on and gain new insights into situations; effective change is participative and collaborative.
	Three-step change model (unfreezing, moving, refreezing).	Leaders should motivate people to change by addressing personal defenses, group norms, organizational culture; providing clear direction and reinforcement to help the new behaviors become habitual.
Edgar Schein	Essence of leadership: cultural creation and management.	Identifies the psychological factors in organizations that either promote or inhibit organizational change.
	Defined organizational culture's characteristics.	Explains why people in organizations behave as they do.
	Learning an organization's culture is a behavioral, cognitive, and emotional process that powerfully reinforces thoughts, behaviors, and experiences.	Shared organizational culture leads to shared assumptions and automatic patterns of perceiving, thinking, feeling, and behaving and provides members with meaning, stability, and psychological comfort. These may not be visible to outsiders.
	"Paradoxes" of organizational learning: learning anxiety and survival anxiety.	Leaders must provide psychological safety if employees are to learn new attitudes, values, behaviors.
Robert Chin	Three strategic orientations for organizational change:	Provided psychological insight to leaders about ways to best approach introducing and conducting organizational change.
	empirical-rational strategies.	
	power-coercive strategies.	
	normative-reeducative strategies.	
Michael Fullan	How change leaders can mobilize people's commitment to invest in change.	Change is about understanding and insight, not merely action.
	Five components create systemic educational change that builds collective capacity and effectiveness within the school and throughout the educational system.	Leadership is essential to building the moral purpose, high expectations, intelligent accountability, and collective and individual capacity essential to ensuring every child an effective teacher every year.
Peter Senge	The learning organization.	Successful organizations develop all members' commitment and capacity to learn continuously.
	Five disciplines work together to enhance an organization's ability to learn: systems thinking, personal mastery, mental models, building a shared vision, team learning.	Understanding an organization requires a holistic perspective; everything is interconnected.
	Three types of organizational leaders work and interact as a community: top-level executives, local line leaders, and internal networkers.	Effective leaders are role models and build an organizational climate where creating vision, challenging the status quo and implicit assumptions, and seeking truth are safe and expected activities.

SUMMARY

The cascade of international, legal, social, technological, and educational events following World War II affected ideas about organizational functioning. As a result, since the mid 20th century, the U.S. and Western European organizational change model has increasingly addressed not only how to deal with continuous change but how to create and sustain meaningful change.

For organizational change to happen, employees must learn. Andragogy and self-directed learning are concepts that reflect a philosophy of lifelong education and the position of the mature person in the education process. Organizations that expect to continue adapting to market, societal and technological realities need to build an educative environment that supports adult learning.

Organizational psychologist Chris Argyris proposed that a "psychological contract" governs relationships within the organization and maintains the employee culture. Argyris and his colleagues' ideas about individual maturity, types of reasoning, theories of action, and single- and double-loop learning help leaders better understand group behavior in institutions and take appropriate actions to make the workplace more effective and satisfying.

Psychologist Kurt Lewin synthesized change into three stages—unfreezing, moving, and refreezing. His field theory, group dynamics, action research, and three-step change model integrate an approach to analyzing, understanding, and initiating change at the group, organizational, and societal levels. Lewin believed that the key to resolving social conflict is to facilitate planned change through learning and to enable individuals to understand and restructure their perceptions of the world around them.

Management professor Edgar Schein saw the dynamic processes of culture creation and management as the essence of leadership. Schein identified organizational culture as one of the most powerful and stable forces operating in organizations and knowable through an organization's facilities, art, technology, and human behaviors.

Psychologist Robert Chin emphasized that planned change is most effective when human systems are an integral part of the change process. He proposed three major "strategies" to organizational change interventions: empirical-rational strategies, power-coercive strategies, and normative-reeducative (organizational self-renewal) strategies.

Organizational change and educational reform scholar Michael Fullan believes that leaders can create the conditions that can mobilize others' commitment to act. Change cannot be managed or controlled, but it can be understood and led. Likewise, management scholar Peter Senge believes that organizations that excel will be those that discover how to develop people's commitment and capacity to learn at *all* organizational levels. Effective leaders are role models and build an organizational climate where creating vision, challenging the status quo and implicit assumptions, and seeking truth are safe and expected activities.

ENDNOTES

1. Several court cases challenging "separate-but-equal" began making their way through the lower courts, eventually reaching the U.S. Supreme Court in 1952. These cases came from Kansas, Virginia, South Carolina, and Delaware.

2. Rosenberg, M. (2009, March 26). *Baby boom. The population baby boom of 1946–1964 in the United States.* About.com: Geography. Retrieved from http://geography.about.com/od/populationgeography/a/babyboom.htm

3. About one fourth (28%) of all public schools had been built before 1950, 17% of public schools had been built between 1970 and 1984, and 10% were built after 1984. See: Rowand, C. (1999). How old are America's public schools? *Education Statistics Quarterly, 1*(1), 53–56. Retrieved from http://nces.ed.gov/pubs99/1999626.pdf

4. Goodman, P. (1964). *Compulsory mis-education.* New York, NY: Horizon Press.

5. Kozol, J. (1967). *Death at an early age.* Boston, MA: Houghton Mifflin Harcourt.

6. Hentoff, N. (1966). *Our children are dying.* New York, NY: Viking Press.

7. Holt, J. (1964). *How children fail.* New York, NY: Pitman.

8. Heavyweight boxer Muhammad Ali was one of the more prominent Americans who resisted the draft system, declaring himself a conscientious objector and earning a prison sentence (later overturned) and a 3-year ban from boxing. See: History.com. (n.d.). *Vietnam War. Vietnam War protests.* The History Channel. Retrieved from http://www.history.com/states.do?action=detail&state=Vietnam%20War&contentType=State_Generic&contentId=56741&parentId=1968

9. History.com. (n.d.). *Vietnam War. Government involvement in Vietnam.* The History Channel. Retrieved from http://www.history.com/states.do?action=detail&state=Vietnam%20War&contentType=State_Generic&contentId=56757&parentId=1968

10. CACF (Combat Area Casualty File), November 1993. Center for Electronic Records, National Archives, Washington, DC. As found on The History Channel. (n.d.). *Statistics about the Vietnam War.* History.com. Retrieved from http://www.vhfcn.org/stat.html

11. The counterculture in the United States peaked between 1966 and the early 1970s. In April 1968, a Columbia University rally, attended initially by some 150 students, soon escalated into taking three school officials hostage for 24 hours inside a campus building, forcing the university's president to resign. See *1968.* New York University Library (n.d.). Retrieved from http://www.nyu.edu/library/bobst/collections/exhibits/arch/1968/Index.html

12. Marzano, R. (2000). *A new era of school reform: Going where the research takes us* (p. 2). Aurora, CO: Mid-continent Research for Education and Learning.

13. Coleman, J. S., Campbell, E. Q., Hobson, C. J., & McPartland, J. (1966). *Equality of educational opportunity.* Washington, DC: U.S. Government Printing Office.

14. Califano, J. A., Jr. (1999, October). What was really great about the great society. *The Washington Monthly OnLine.* Retrieved from http://www.washingtonmonthly.com/features/1999/9910.califano.html

15. Cohen, D. K., & Barnes, C. A. (1993). Pedagogy and policy. In D. K. Cohen & C. A. Barnes (Eds.), *Teaching for understanding: Challenges for policy and pedagogy* (pp. 207–239). San Francisco, CA: Jossey Bass.

16. U.S. Department of Education. (2007). *History. Twenty-five years of programs educating children with disabilities through IDEA.* Ed.gov. Retrieved from http://www.ed.gov/policy/speced/leg/idea/history.html

17. McCarthy, M. M. (1991). Severely disabled children: Who pays? *Phi Delta Kappan, 73*(1), 66–71.

18. By 1976, all states had laws subsidizing public school programs for students with disabilities. IDEA amendments of 1997 (PL 105-171) addressed the need for high educational performance standards for all students and teachers, including those in special education. By the early 1980s, students considered to have mild or moderate disabilities were usually integrated into general education classrooms on at least a part-time basis. In addition, many students not served in the past—including those with severe

disabilities—increasingly started receiving educational services in their local neighborhood schools, participating in regular cafeteria, playground, library, halls, buses, and restroom activities.

19. U.S. Department of Education. (2009). *Federal role in education*. Retrieved from http://www.ed .gov/about/overview/fed/role.html

20. *A nation at risk*. (1983, April). Washington, DC: U.S. Department of Education, National Commission on Excellence in Education.

21. *A nation at risk. The imperative for educational reform. An open letter to the American people.* (1983, April). Retrieved from http://www.ed.gov/ pubs/NatAtRisk/risk.html

22. Yeakey, C. C., & Johnston, G. S. (1985, February). High school reform: A critique and a broader construct of social reality. *Education and Urban Society, 17*(2), 157–170.

23. Husen, T. (1983, March). School standards in America and other countries. *Phi Delta Kappan, 64*, 455–461.

24. Yeakey & Johnson. (1985). Op. cit.

25. Writer Gerald Bracey concluded that *A Nation at Risk* was not intended to objectively examine the condition of American education, but to document the terrible things that Terrell Bell, President Ronald Reagan's secretary of education, had heard about schools. In his memoir, *The Thirteenth Man*, Bell recalled that he had sought a "*Sputnik*-type occurrence" that would dramatize all the "constant complaints about education and its effectiveness" that he kept hearing. To better press their case for public school reform, *A Nation at Risk*'s writers incorrectly assumed that high scores indicated global competitiveness. See: Bracey, G. (2001, May 21) The propaganda of *A Nation at Risk*. Education Disinformation Detection and Reporting Agency. Retrieved from http://www.america-tomorrow.com/bracey/ EDDRA/EDDRA8.htm

26. Ferguson, R. F., & Mehta, J. (2004). An unfinished journey: The legacy of *Brown* and the narrowing of the achievement gap, *Phi Delta Kappan, 85*, 656–669.

27. U.S. Department of Education. (1990). *America 2000*. Washington, DC: U.S. Government Printing Office. These referred to national goals for public schools to reach by the year 2000. Retrieved from http://www.answers.com/topic/ department-of-education

28. Whitley, P., Bradley, B., Sutton, B., & Goodwin, S. (2007). *American cultural history. 1990–1999*. Kingwood College. Retrieved from http://kclibrary .lonestar.edu/decade90.html

29. Whitley, Bradley, Sutton, & Goodwin. (2007). Ibid.

30. Beginning in 2007–2008, states were required to also include science assessments at least once during each of these three grade spans.

31. McNeil, M. (2010, March 3). Reviewers winnow Race to Top hopefuls. *Education Week, 29*(23), 1, 20.

32. "Rip Van Winkle" is a short story and fictional character created by American author Washington Irving in 1819. The setting is the New York Catskill Mountains.

33. Crow, L. D., & Crow, A. (1963). Meaning and scope of learning. In L. D. Crow & A. Crow (Eds.), *Readings in human learning* (pp. 1–3). New York, NY: McKay; Burton, W. H. (1963). Basic principles in a good teaching-learning situation. In L. D. Crow & A. Crow (Eds.), *Readings in human learning* (pp. 7–19). New York, NY: McKay.

34. Merriam, S. B. (2001). Andragogy and self-directed learning: Pillars of adult learning theory. *New Directions for Adult and Continuing Education, 89*(1), 3–13.

35. Shaie, K. W., & Willis, S. L. (1986). *Adult development and aging* (2nd ed.). Boston, MA: Little, Brown.

36. Knowles, M. S. (1968). Andragogy, not pedagogy. *Adult Leadership,16*(10), 350–352, 386. *Pedagogy* comes from the same stem as *pediatrics*—the Greek word meaning "child." Pedagogy literally means the art and science of teaching children. To speak of "the pedagogy of adults" is a contradiction in terms. Pedagogy and andragogy make different assumptions about the learners. See: Knowles, M. (1973). *The adult learner: A neglected species* (p. 42). Houston, TX: Gulf Publishing.

37. Merriam. (2001). Op. cit.; Knowles, M. S. (2005). *The adult learner: The definitive classic in adult education and human resource development* (6th ed.). Burlington, MA: Elsevier.

38. Knowles. (1980). Op. cit., p. 47.

39. Merriam, S. B., Mott, V. W., & Lee, M. (1996). Learning that comes from the negative interpretation of life experience. *Studies in Continuing Education, 18*(1), 1–23.

40. Hanson, A. (1996). The search for a separate theory of adult learning: Does anyone really need andragogy? In R. Edwards, A. Hanson, & P. Raggatt (Eds.), *Boundaries of adult learning* (pp. 99–108). New York, NY: Routledge.

41. Houle, C. O. (1996). *The design of education* (2nd ed.). San Francisco, CA: Jossey-Bass; Knowles, M. S. (1980). *Modern practice of adult education: From pedagogy to andragogy.* Revised and updated. Chicago, IL: Follett, Association Press.

42. Merriam, S. B., & Caffarela, R. S. (1999). *Learning in adulthood* (2nd ed.). San Francisco, CA: Jossey-Bass.

43. Knowles, M. S. (1975). *Self-directed learning.* New York, NY: Association Press; Tough, A. (1967). *Learning without a teacher. Educational Research Series No. 3.* Toronto, Canada: Ontario Institute for Studies in Education; Tough, A. (1971). *The adult's learning projects: A fresh approach to theory and practice in adult learning.* Toronto, Canada: Ontario Institute for Studies in Education; Brockett, R. B., & Hiemstra, R. (1991). *Self-direction in adult learning: Perspectives on theory, research, and practice.* London and New York: Routledge.

44. Mezirow, J. (1985). A critical theory of self-directed learning. In S. Brookfield (Ed.), *Self-directed learning from theory to practice. New directions for continuing education, 25* (pp. 17–30). San Francisco, CA: Jossey-Bass.

45. Andruske, C. L. (2000). Self-directed learning as a political act: Learning projects of women on welfare. *Proceedings of the 41st Annual Adult Education Research Conference,* Vancouver, British Columbia; Brookfield, S. (1993). Self-directed learning, political clarity, and the critical practice of adult education. *Adult Education Quarterly, 43*(4), 227–242; Collins, M. (1996). On contemporary practice and research: Self-directed learning to critical theory. In R. Edwards, A. Hanson, & P. Raggatt (Eds.), *Boundaries of adult learning: Adult learners, education and training* (pp. 21–36). New York, NY: Routledge.

46. Maslow, A. (1970). *Motivation and personality.* New York, NY: Harper & Row.

47. Tough, A. (1971). *The adult's learning projects: A fresh approach to theory and practice in adult learning.* Toronto, Canada: Ontario Institute for Studies in Education; Knowles. (1975). Op. cit.

48. Danis, C. (1992). A unifying framework for data-based research into adult self-directed learning. In H. B. Long et al. (Eds.), *Self-directed learning: Application and research.* Norman: Oklahoma Research Center for Continuing Professional and Higher Education, University of Oklahoma.

49. Knowles, M. (1973). *The adult learner: A neglected species.* Houston, TX: Gulf Publishing.

50. Candy, P. C. (1991). *Self-direction for lifelong learning.* San Francisco, CA: Jossey-Bass.

51. Norman, G. R. (1999). The adult learner: A mythical species. *Academic Medicine, 74*(8), 886–889.

52. Knowles. (1973). Op. cit.

53. Marshak, R. J. (1993). Lewin meets Confucius: A review of the organizational development model of change. *Journal of Applied Behavioral Science, 29*(4), 393–415.

54. Argyris, C. (1973). Personality and organization theory revisited. *Administrative Science Quarterly, 18*(2), 141–167.

55. Argyris, C. (1958). The organization: What makes it healthy? *Harvard Business Review, 36*(6), 107–116. Argyris observed that as long as a minimum standard of skin-surface human relationships is maintained, the "rational man relationship" as described by Herbert Simon can easily flourish.

56. Argyris. (1973). Op. cit.

57. Argyris. (1973). Op. cit. Argyris, C. (1974). Personality vs. organization. *Organizational Dynamics, 3*(2), 3–17; Argyris, C. (1957). The individual and the organization: Some problems of mutual adjustment. *Administrative Science Quarterly, 2*(1), 1–24.

58. Argyris, C. (1994). Initiating change that perseveres. *Journal of Public Administration Research and Theory, 4*(3), 343–365.

59. Argyris. (1994). Ibid. Argyris believes that emotions also play an important role in generating change. The productive reasoning necessary to design and implement actions that lead to effective change generates strong feelings. Progress toward change requires constructively expressing those feelings as well as respecting them.

60. Argyris, C., & Schön, D. (1978). *Organizational learning: A theory of action perspective.* Reading, MA: Addison Wesley.

61. Argyris, C. (1982). The executive mind and double-loop learning. *Organizational Dynamics, 11*(2), 5–22.

62. Argyris, C. (1980). *Inner contradictions of rigorous research.* New York, NY: Academic Press; Argyris. (1982). Ibid.; Argyris, C., & Schön, D. (1974). *Theory in practice: Increasing professional effectiveness.* San Francisco, CA: Jossey-Bass.

63. Argyris, C. (1997). Learning and teaching: A theory of action perspective. *Journal of Management Education, 21*(2), 9–27.

64. Argyris. (1993). Op. cit.

65. Argyris & Schön. (1974). Op. cit.

66. Anderson, L. (1997). *Argyris and Schön's theory on congruence and learning.* Retrieved from http://www.scu.edu.au/schools/gcm/ar/arp/argyris.html

67. Argyris, C., & Schön, D. (1978). *Organizational learning: A theory of action perspective.* Reading, MA: Addison Wesley.

68. Argyris. (1982). Op. cit.

69. Argyris observed that the knowledge and skills required for double-loop learning can be used, with easy modification, for single-loop learning. The opposite is not true. See: Argyris. (1993). Op. cit., p. 5.

70. Argyris. (1993). Op. cit.

71. Argyris, C. (1990). Managers, workers, and organizations. *Society, 27*(6), 5–48.

72. Argyris, C. (1982). *Reasoning, learning, and action: Individual and organizational.* San Francisco, CA: Jossey-Bass.

73. Argyris, C. (1976). Leadership, learning, and the changing status quo. *Organizational Dynamics, 4*(3), 29–43; Argyris, C. (1996). Teaching smart people how to learn. *Harvard Business Review, 69*(3), 99–109.

74. Argyris. (1976). Ibid.

75. Edmondson, A., & Moingeon, B. (1999). Learning, trust and organizational change. In M. Easterby-Smith, L. Araujo, & J. Burgoyne (Eds.), *Organizational learning and the learning organization.* London: Sage.

76. Argyris. (1994). Op. cit., p. 348.

77. Argyris, C. (1982). *Reasoning, learning, and action: Individual and organizational* (p. 8). San Francisco, CA: Jossey-Bass.

78. Edmondson & Moingeon. (1999). Op. cit., p. 161.

79. Argyris, C., & Schön, D. (1996). *Organizational learning II: Theory, method and practice.* Reading, MA: Addison Wesley.

80. Argyris. (1997). Op. cit.

81. Edmondson & Moingeon. (1999). Op. cit., p. 162.

82. Easterby-Smith, M., & Araujo, L. (1999). Current debates and opportunities. In M. Easterby-Smith, L. Araujo, & J. Burgoyne (Eds.), *Organizational learning and the learning organization.* London: Sage.

83. Bulman, L. G., & Deal, T. E. (1997). *Reframing organizations. Artistry, choice and leadership.* San Francisco, CA: Jossey-Bass.

84. Smith. (2001). Op. cit.

85. Miner, J. B. (2005). Kurt Lewin. From social psychology and personality theory (pp. 37–45). *Organizational behavior I: Essential theories of motivation and leadership.* Armonk, NY: M. E. Sharpe.

86. Burnes, B. (2004). Kurt Lewin and the planned approach to change: A reappraisal. *Journal of Management Studies, 41*(6), 977–1002.

87. Lewin, K. (1943). Psychological ecology. In D. Cartwright (Ed.), *Field theory in social science.* London: Social Science Paperbacks.

88. Lewin, K. (1946). Action research and minority problems. In G. W. Lewin (Ed.), *Resolving social conflict.* London: Harper & Row.

89. Lewin, K. (1947a). Frontiers in group dynamics. In D. Cartwright (Ed.), *Field theory in social science.* London: Social Science Paperbacks.

90. Kippenberger, T. (1998a). Planned change: Kurt Lewin's legacy. *The Antidote, 14,* 10–12; Lewin. (1947a). Op. cit.

91. Lewin, K. (1939). When facing danger. In G. W. Lewin (Ed.). (1948). *Resolving social conflict.* London: Harper & Row; Allport, G. W. (1948). Foreword. In G. W. Lewin (Ed.), *Resolving social conflict.* London: Harper & Row; Cartwright, D. (1951). Achieving change in people: Some applications of group dynamics theory. *Human Relations, 6*(4), 381–392; Bargal, D., Gold, M., & Lewin, M. (1992). The heritage of Kurt Lewin—introduction. *Journal of Social Issues, 48*(2), 3–13.

92. Lewin, K. (1947b). Group decisions and social change. In T. M. Newcomb & E. L. Hartley (Eds.), *Readings in social psychology.* New York, NY: Henry Holt.

93. Lewin, K. (1947a). Frontiers in group dynamics. In D. Cartwright (Ed.), *Field theory in social science.* London: Social Science Paperbacks.

94. Lewin. (1947b). Op. cit.

95. Schein, E. H. (1988). *Organizational psychology* (3rd ed.). London: Prentice-Hall.

96. Lewin, K. (1946). Action research and minority problem. In G. W. Lewin (Ed.). (1948). *Resolving social conflict*. London: Harper & Row; Bennett, R. (1983). *Management research*. Management Development Series, 20. Geneva, Switzerland: International Labour Office.

97. Smith, M. K. (2001). Kurt Lewin: Group, experimental learning and action research. *The Encyclopedia of Informal Education*, 1–15.

98. Lewin. (1946). Ibid., p. 206.

99. Lewin. (1947b). Op. cit.

100. Lewin. (1947a). Op. cit.

101. Weick, K. E., & Quinn, R. E. (1999). Organizational change and development. *Annual Review of Psychology, 50*(1), 361–386.

102. Lewin. (1947a). Ibid.

103. Schein. (1996). Op. cit.

104. Cummings, T. G., & Huse, E. F. (1989). *Organization development and change* (4th ed.). St. Paul, MN: West Publishing; Cummings, T. G., & Worley, C. G. (2001). *Organization development and change* (7th ed.). Mason, OH: South-Western College Publishing.

105. Zand, D. E., & Sorensen, R. E. (1975). Theory of change and the effective use of management science. *Administrative Science Quarterly, 20*(4), 532–545.

106. Burnes, B. (2004). Kurt Lewin and the planned approach to change: A reappraisal. *Journal of Management Studies, 41*(6), 977–1002.

107. Dawson, P. (1994). *Organizational change: A processual approach*. London: Paul Chapman; Garvin, D. A. (1993, July–August). Building a learning organization. *Harvard Business Review*, 78–91; Kanter, R. M., Stein, B. A., & Jick, T. D. (1992). *The challenge of organizational change*. New York, NY: Free Press; Nonaka, I. (1988, November–December). Creating organizational order out of chaos: Self-renewal in Japanese firms. *Harvard Business Review*, 96–104; Pettigrew, A. M. (1990a). Longitudinal field research on change: Theory and practice. *Organizational Science, 3*(1), 267–292; Pettigrew, A. M., Hendry, C. N., & Sparrow, P. (1989). *Training in Britain: Employers' perspectives on human resources*. London: HMSO; Stacey, R. D. (1993). *Strategic management and organisational dynamics*. London: Pitman; Wilson, D. C. (1992). *A strategy of change*. London: Routledge.

108. Burnes. (2004). Ibid.

109. Burnes. (2004). Op. cit.; Kippenberger, T. (1998). Planned change: Kurt Lewin's legacy. *The Antidote, 14*, 10–12; Lewin, K. (1947a). Frontiers in group dynamics. In D. Cartwright (Ed.), *Field theory in social science*. London: Social Science Paperbacks.

110. Elrod, P. D., II, & Tippett, D. D. (2002). The "Death Valley" of change. *Journal of Organizational Change Management, 15*(3), 273–291.

111. Dawson. (1994). Op. cit.; Dunphy, D. D., & Stace, D. A. (1992). *Under new management*. Sydney, Australia: McGraw-Hill; Dunphy, D. D., & Stace, D. A. (1993). The strategic management of corporate change. *Human Relations, 46*(8), 905–918; Harris, P. R. (1985). *Management in transition*. San Francisco, CA: Jossey Bass; Miller, D., & Friesen, P. H. (1984). *Organizations: A quantum view*. Englewood Cliffs, NJ: Prentice Hall; Pettigrew, A. M. (1990a). Longitudinal field research on change: Theory and practice. *Organizational Science, 3*(1), 267–292; Pettigrew, A. M. (1990b). Studying strategic choice and strategic change. *Organizational Studies, 11*(1), 6–11.

112. Quinn, J. B. (1980). *Strategies for change: Logical incrementalism*. Homewood, IL: Irwin; Quinn, J. B. (1982). Managing strategies incrementally. *Omega, 10*(6), 613–627.

113. Dickens, L., & Watkins, K. (1999). Action research: Rethinking Lewin. *Management Learning, 30*(2),127–140.

114. Allaire, Y., & Firsirotu, M. E. (1984). Theories of organizational culture. *Organization Studies, 5*(3),193–226; Beer, M., & Nohria, N. (2000, May–June). Cracking the code of change. *Harvard Business Review*, 133–141; Burnes, B. (2000). *Managing change* (3rd ed.). Harlow: FT/Pearson Educational; Cummings, T. G., & Worley, C. G. (1997). *Organization development and change* (6th ed.). Cincinnati, OH: South-Western College Publishing.

115. Lewin. (1947a). Op. cit.

116. Dawson. (1994). Op. cit.; Hatch, M. J. (1997). *Organization theory: Modern, symbolic and postmodern perspectives*. Oxford: Oxford University Press; Pettigrew, A. M. (1980). The politics of

organisational change. In N. B. Anderson (Ed.), *The human side of information processing.* Amsterdam: North Holland; Wilson, D. C. (1992). *A strategy of change.* London: Routledge.

117. Dawson. (1994). Op. cit.; Kanter et al. (1992). Op. cit.; Wilson. (1992). Op. cit.

118. Lewin. (1947b). Op. cit.; Bargal, D., Gold, M., & Lewin, M. (1992). The heritage of Kurt Lewin— Introduction. *Journal of Social Issues,* 48(2), 3–13; Dickens, L., & Watkins, K. (1999). Action research: Rethinking Lewin. *Management Learning,* 30(2), 127–140; French, W. L., & Bell, C. H. (1984). *Organization development* (4th ed.). Englewood Cliffs, NJ: Prentice-Hall.

119. Bargal, D., & Bar, H. (1992). A Lewinian approach to intergroup workshops for Arab-Palestinian and Jewish youth. *Journal of Social Issues,* 48(2), 139–154; Elrod, P. D., II, & Tippett, D. D. (2002). The "Death Valley" of change. *Journal of Organizational Change Management,* 15(3), 273–291; Hendry, C. (1996). Understanding and creating whole organizational change through learning theory. *Human Relations,* 48(5), 621–641; Kippenberger, T. (1998). Planned change: Kurt Lewin's legacy. *The Antidote,* 14, 10–12; MacIntosh, R., & MacLean, D. (2001). Conditioned emergence: Researching change and changing research. *International Journal of Operations and Production Management,* 21(10), 1343–1357; Wooten, K. C., & White, L. P. (1999). Linking OD's philosophy with justice theory: Postmodern implications. *Journal of Organizational Change Management,* 12(1), 7–20.

120. Weick, K. E., & Quinn, R. E. (1999). Organizational change and development. *Annual Review of Psychology,* 50(1), 361–386.

121. Hendry, C. (1996). Understanding and creating whole organizational change through learning theory. *Human Relations,* 49, 621–641.

122. Schein, E. H. (1993). How can organizations learn faster? The challenge of entering the green room. *Sloan Management Review,* 34(2), 85–92.

123. Schein, E. H. (1965). *Organizational psychology.* Englewood Cliffs, NJ: Prentice-Hall.

124. Coutu, D. L. (2002). Edgar H. Schein. The anxiety of learning: The darker side of organizational learning. *Harvard Business Review,* 80(3), 100–106.

125. Schein, E. H. (2004). *Organizational culture and leadership* (3rd ed). New York, NY: John Wiley p. 2.

126. Schein. (2004). Ibid.

127. Schein, E. H. (1992). *Organizational culture and leadership* (2nd ed.). San Francisco, CA: Jossey-Bass.

128. Schein, E. H. (1985). How culture forms, develops, and changes. In R. H. Kilmann, M. J. Saxton, & R. Serpa (Eds.), *Gaining control of the corporate culture* (pp. 19–21). San Francisco, CA: Jossey-Bass.

129. Schein, E. H. (1990). Organizational culture. *American Psychologist,* 45(2), 109–119.

130. Hirschhorn, L. (1987). *The workplace within.* Cambridge, MA: MIT Press; Menzies, I. E. P. (1960). A case study in the functioning of social systems as a defense against anxiety. *Human Relations,* 13, 95–121; Schein, E. H. (1985). Organizational culture: Skill, defense mechanism or addiction? In E. R. Brush & J. B. Overmier (Eds.), *Affect, conditioning, and cognition* (pp. 315–323). Hillsdale, NJ: Erlbaum.

131. Mats, A. (2002). *Understanding organizational culture.* Thousand Oaks, CA: Sage.

132. Schein, E. H. (2004). *Organizational culture and leadership* (3rd ed., pp. 12–13). New York, NY: John Wiley.

133. Schein, E. H. (1996b). Kurt Lewin's change theory in the field and in the classroom: Notes toward a model of managed learning. *Systemic Practice and Action Research,* 9(1), 27–47.

134. Schein. (1996b). Ibid.

135. Schein. (1996b). Op. cit. Coutu. (2002). Op. cit.

136. Schein. (1996b). Op. cit.

137. Coutu. (2002). Op. cit.

138. Cooke, B. (1999). Writing the left out of management theory: The historiography of the management of change. *Organization,* 6(1), 81–105. This is a critical theorist's view of management history.

139. Avison, D. E., & Myers, M. D. (1995). Information systems and anthropology: An anthropological perspective on IT and organizational culture. *Information Technology & People,* 8(3); Borofsky, R. (1994). *Assessing cultural anthropology.* New York, NY: McGraw-Hill; Clifford, J., & Marcus, G. E. (1986).*Writing culture: The poetics and politics of ethnography.* Berkeley: University of California Press; Goodenough, W. H. (1994). Toward a working theory of culture. In R. Borofsky (Ed.), *Assessing*

cultural anthropology. New York, NY: McGraw-Hill; Goody, J. (1994). Culture and its boundaries: A European view. In R. Borofsky (Ed.), *Assessing cultural anthropology*. New York, NY: McGraw-Hill; Vayda, A. P. (1994). Actions, variations, and change: The emerging anti-essentialist view in anthropology. In R. Borofsky (Ed.), *Assessing cultural anthropology*. New York, NY: McGraw-Hill. As cited in Iavari, N., & Abrahamsson, P. (2002). *The interaction between organizational subcultures and user-centered design—A case study of an implementation effort*. Paper presented at the Proceedings of the 35th Hawaii International Conference on System Sciences—2002 (pp. 3260–3268). IEEE Computer Society. Retrieved from http://ieeexplore.ieee.org/xpl/freeabs_all.jsp?arnumber=994362

140. Iavari, N., & Abrahamsson, P. (2002). *The interaction between organizational subcultures and user-centered design—A case study of an implementation effort*. Paper presented at the Proceedings of the 35th Hawaii International Conference on System Sciences—2002 (Vol. 8., pp. 3260–3268). IEEE Computer Society. Retrieved from http://ieeexplore.ieee.org/xpl/freeabs_all.jsp?arnumber=994362

141. Berger, P. L., & Luckmann, T. (1967). *The social construction of reality: A treatise in the sociology of knowledge*. New York, NY: Doubleday.

142. Saxe, L., & Kubansky, P. E. (1991). Robert Chin (Chin Yuli) (1918–1990). Obituary. *American Psychologist, 46*(12), 1343.

143. King, N., & Anderson, N. (2002). *Managing innovation and change. A critical guide for organizations*. Belmont, CA: Cengage Learning.

144. Chin, R. E., & Benne, K. D. (1984). General strategies for effecting change in human systems. In W. G. Bennis, K. D. Bennis, & R. Chin (Eds.), *The planning of change* (4th ed.). New York, NY: Holt, Rineholt, & Winston.

145. Fischman, S. H. (1973). Change strategies and their application to family planning programs. *American Journal of Nursing, 73*(10), 1771–1774.

146. Wingert, P. (2010. October 18). An offer they wouldn't refuse. *Newsweek*, 38–39. This is the empirical-rational change strategy used by Peter Gorman, the school superintendent in Charlotte, N.C. Every winning principal accepted the challenge.

147. Nickols, F. (2006). *Change management 101. A primer*. Distance Consulting. Retrieved from http://www.jeslen.com/change2003.pdf

148. Chin & Bennis. (1969). Op. cit.

149. Fullan, M. (1993). *Change forces. Probing the depths of educational reform* (pp. 23–25). New York, NY: Falmer Press.

150. Fullan, M. (2007). *Leading in a culture of change*. San Francisco, CA: Jossey-Bass.

151. Fullan. (2007). Op. cit., p. 31.

152. Fullan. (2007). Op. cit., p. 33.

153. Fullan, M. (2010). *All systems go. The change imperative for whole system reform*. Thousand Oaks, CA: Corwin and Ontario Principals' Council.

154. Fullan. (2010). Ibid., p. 61.

155. Those who are seriously physically or mentally disadvantaged can lead effective lives through inclusionary developmentally-based programs within this system.

156. Fullan. (2010). Op. cit., p. 71.

157. Senge, P. (1997). Communities of leaders and learners. *Harvard Business Review, 75*(5), 31.

158. Senge, P. M. (1990). *The fifth discipline. The art & practice of the learning organization*. New York, NY: Doubleday.

159. Senge. (1997). Op. cit.

CHAPTER 4

Leadership Theories

Focus Questions

- ◆ What is leadership?
- ◆ What is a leadership model?
- ◆ How can using models increase leadership effectiveness?
- ◆ What are the strengths and limits to how trait theory explains leadership?
- ◆ What are the strengths and limits of the contingency theory of leadership?
- ◆ What are the strengths and limits of transactional leadership?
- ◆ What are the strengths and limits of transformational leadership?
- ◆ What are the strengths and limits of authentic leadership?
- ◆ What factors determine the effectiveness of a leadership style?

CASE STUDY: FRANKLIN CITY HIGH SCHOOL

As of January 1, Dr. Ed Smith is the newly appointed principal of Franklin City High School, a suburban 2,000-pupil school outside a major metropolitan area. Prior to this, Ed had served for 1 year as an assistant middle school principal and for 12 years as an English teacher and English department chair in the neighboring school district. His first few months as principal are uneventful as he gets acquainted with the school, its staff and students, and the community. Ed is forming the impression that the academic program at Franklin could be offering much more to the students and to the community. The school still uses the traditional seven-period day. It offers only honors classes and no advanced placement (AP) classes. It has no dual enrollment program with the local community college where the high school students can take community college classes at the high school and earn both high school and college credits. Further, the school is tracking students into academic, general, and vocational courses. The faculty appears pleased with the tracking and with the seven-period schedule; Ed's alternative suggestions bring teacher resentment and resistance to change.

Ed is not impressed with the four assistant principals. They have all been assistant principals at the school for at least 20 years, have little instructional knowledge, and seem less than eager to help. Ed learned that all four had applied for the principalship, and he believes this accounts for their "less than willing" attitudes.

In April, the superintendent who hired Ed announces that he is retiring at the end of the school year. After a quick, closed session meeting, the school board proclaims that the long-serving assistant superintendent, Mr. Jones, will assume the superintendency on July 1.

Ed does not know Mr. Jones well, but has heard both positive and negative comments about him. In May, Ed decides to schedule an appointment with Mr. Jones to discuss the situation at Franklin City High School. At the brief meeting, Ed shares some of his ideas about proposed changes at the high school. Mr. Jones tells Ed that they should schedule another meeting when they have more time to discuss the ideas, and Ed can bring data supporting his suggestions. In leaving, Mr. Jones tells Ed that he was the principal of Franklin City High School 15 years ago before moving to the assistant superintendent's job. Ed wonders how Mr. Jones will receive his suggestions for change—especially if Jones established the high school program currently in use.

Ed meets with Mr. Jones in July to share the data he has collected and his suggested changes laid out in a timetable format as follows:

Action #1: Transition to a four-by-four block schedule (four periods each semester) where a minimum of 12 dual enrollment courses will be offered to juniors and seniors.

Rationale: All five surrounding school systems' high schools use a four-by-four block schedule and offer dual enrollment classes authorized by the state more than 10 years ago. The dual enrollment classes will fit in well with the block schedule format. This will provide our students a competitive educational opportunity compared to the surrounding school systems. It will save parents significant tuition when their children go to college. The PTA voted 78 to 22 in favor of offering dual enrollment classes and 62 to 38 in favor of exploring the move to a block schedule. The faculty was evenly split on offering dual enrollment classes and voted against moving to a block schedule by a 66% majority. All four assistant principals voted against the move to dual enrollment and to the block schedule.

Time Frame: Year One

August–October: An exploratory committee of teachers, parents, students, the local community college academic dean, business representatives, and the director of secondary education for the school district will be established once school starts. They will visit surrounding high schools using the block schedule and offering dual enrollment programs (all the other surrounding high schools). They will report back in October with a recommendation regarding moving to the block schedule and offering dual enrollment classes. A steering committee will be formed from this group to oversee the transition.

October–December: The faculty and staff will examine what training, funding, and accommodations need to be made to make the transition.

January–June: Professional development activities on teaching in the block schedule, differentiated instruction, and cooperative learning for the staff will be provided. Parents and students will be informed of the changes and what advantages the changes will offer students and families.

April–June: Student registration and orientation will be held. Parent and community orientations will be presented to inform the public of the changes and to answer their questions.

September: Implement block scheduling and dual enrollment courses for students.

Action #2: In year two, explore the use of advanced placement (AP) classes for Franklin City High School.

Rationale: Four of the five surrounding school systems' high schools offer AP classes for students. After 1 year of working with the block schedule and dual enrollment classes, there may be a need for AP classes.

Time Frame: Year Two

Summer: Survey students, teachers, and parents about the need for AP courses at the high school.

September: Discuss the potential need for AP classes with faculty and with the PTA. Share results of the summer survey.

October–December: Establish an exploratory committee to examine the cost/benefit options of offering AP classes. If there is no interest, stop. If interest exists, establish a steering committee for planning purposes.

January–March: The planning committee reports back on requirements for starting AP classes. Information is shared with faculty, PTA, and community members. The budget will be established and funding sought.

Time Frame: Year Three

Professional development activities will be provided for teachers who will work with AP classes. The curricula will be developed and materials ordered.

Time Frame: Year Four

Implement AP courses.

Action #3: Increase the instructional focus of the administrative staff at Franklin City High School.

Rationale: None of the four assistant principals uses the clinical supervision process to help teachers improve instruction. Teacher evaluations consist of checklists that reflect class control, classroom cleanliness, up-to-date bulletin boards, inventory control, and grade book organization.

Time Frame: Ongoing

I will work with the assistant principals to develop their skill level in classroom observation, formative and summative assessment, and instructional leadership.

Mr. Jones commends Ed on his thoughtful presentation of the action plan, but asks if too much is being planned too quickly. Mr. Jones wonders if the faculty can be prepared for the changes in such a short time. Next, he suggests delaying Action #2 since the dual enrollment classes provide the same benefit to the students as AP classes. Jones says that amount of change in that brief time frame is not good for the school community. Last, Mr. Jones questions the third action plan. Student achievement does not appear to be a problem at Franklin City. Why would Ed want to risk alienating his assistant principals by refocusing them solely on instruction?

Ed tells Mr. Jones that he can see the point about AP classes, but he asserts that the third action plan is vital for the students' and school's success. Mr. Jones allows Ed to proceed with his third action plan, but tells him that he does not fully support the change. Ed will be on his own leading that initiative.

Case Study Questions

1. How does the lack of faculty motivation to change influence how Ed leads the school?
2. How does the assistant principals' lack of willingness to help and their lack of instructional expertise affect Ed's leadership style as he works with them?
3. How will Superintendent Jones's lack of support for some of Ed's action plans affect how Ed leads the faculty and community?
4. What personality or physical traits will help Ed be more effective in leading his proposed changes?
5. What situational factors should Ed consider as the leader of Franklin City High School?

LEADERSHIP AND LEADERSHIP THEORIES

In our culture, children grow up learning about leadership. Hollywood movies and television celebrate leaders—for example, Harry Potter, Jack Bauer, Captain James T. Kirk, Jack Ryan, Superman, and Iron Man. Perhaps we idolized specific persons who changed history—Thomas Jefferson, Abraham Lincoln, Franklin D. Roosevelt, Martin Luther King, John F. Kennedy, Mohandas Gandhi, Winston Churchill, Mikhail Gorbachev, Sandra Day O'Connor, and Hillary Clinton, to name a few. Many first gain interest in leadership from reading Greek and Roman mythology or the biographies of great military leaders—the tales of Odysseus, Napoleon, George Washington, and other heroes sparked interest. What qualities made these figures noteworthy leaders? Did their intellect, fluency with words, or another trait make them so effective?

If you were to enter the term *leadership studies* in Google Scholar, you would find more than 2 million academic citations. Enter the word *leadership* in Google, and you find more than 136 million hits. Obviously, educators are not the only ones interested in leadership.

What is leadership? Why study leadership models? A *model* can be defined as a representation of a system, theory, or phenomenon that explains how and why something works the way it does. In this chapter, we will use the terms *model* and *theory* interchangeably.

Leadership has many definitions that have evolved over time. An early definition of leadership was "the ability to impress the will of the leader on those led and induce obedience, respect, loyalty, and cooperation" (Moore, 1927).[1] Twenty years later, leadership was defined as "the act of guiding or directing the behavior of one or more individuals" (Jenkins, 1947, p. 54).[2] Within two decades, the concept of leadership changed from authoritarian rule to one of influence through social interaction.

Since then, definitions of leadership have grown to include leader characteristics or traits and behaviors—the leader's charisma and his or her concerns for coworkers, for accomplishing the task, and for transforming the organization's culture. Different leadership models appear to explain how the leader has an effective impact on the organizational climate and productivity.

When school leaders can explain how and why leadership works in various situations or what leadership model applies in a given circumstance, they increase the probability of successful outcomes. A *theory* is a result of a tested hypothesis over time producing consistent results. A model or theory of leadership can frame our understanding of how situations can be understood and engaged for successful results. When we can understand, explain, and predict, we become able to manipulate certain variables to increase the likelihood of certain ends occurring (see Figure 4–1).

As the old saying goes, if the only tool you have is a hammer, everything looks like a nail. When leaders learn to conceptualize, explain, predict, and intervene in the variety of challenging situations that occur in organizations, they increase their abilities to successfully anticipate and solve problems. Understanding leadership models provides a framework for thinking about and thoughtfully addressing leadership issues.

FIGURE 4–1
EPM Model Schematic
(Source: Owings & Kaplan.)

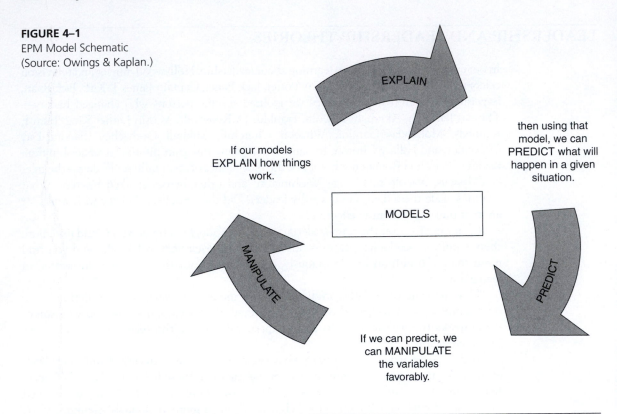

MODERN LEADERSHIP THEORIES

In many ways, modern leadership differs greatly from the ways it has been historically practiced and viewed. As Chapter 1 describes, the leader in ancient times was the tribe's strongest or the village's best hunter. Physical strength, skills, and deeds earned him (and it usually was a he) the right to lead. As civilizations developed, leadership extended into societal roles. Kings were assumed to rule by divine right. Generals were renowned for their strategic and tactical fighting abilities. Religious leaders were identified by both charisma and metaphysical factors. This chapter examines the evolution of modern leadership theory.

The modern leadership studies began in the early 1900s with Alfred Binet, a French psychologist. Around that time, the French government enacted laws requiring all children to attend schools. The French government asked Binet to help identify students who would need special educational assistance under these new compulsory attendance laws. He and his research partner, Theodore Simon, developed the concept of "mental age" by determining the average abilities and knowledge of children of various age groups and testing what an individual child knew or could do in comparison with the averages they had determined. The test became known as the Binet–Simon test. It quickly came to the attention of Stanford University researcher Lewis Terman, who standardized it for an American population where it became known as the Stanford–Binet Intelligence Scale. Eventually, the mental age and chronological age were used to compute an IQ (Intelligence Quotient) score by dividing the mental age by the chronological age and multiplying by 100.[3]

The IQ concept caught the interest of the U.S. military. With the advent of World War I, the U.S. government had the overwhelming task of screening millions of new recruits to determine the military positions for which they would be best suited. Robert Yerkes, then the American Psychological Association (APA) president, received commission as an army major (in the psychological service) and was placed in charge of administering intelligence tests to recruits for classification and placement. During the war, almost 2 million recruits were tested for military assignments. Those with higher tested IQs were posted in higher level executive and leadership jobs. Those with lower tested IQs were designated for infantry, custodial, and menial jobs.

While the older officers did not trust the unfamiliar intelligence testing, the younger officers recognized its merit.[4] Intelligence testing and leadership study returned with World War II and provided the genesis for some of the major leadership investigations of the time.[5] As a means of "providing a summary of techniques and results that would be of value to psychologists dealing with the problems of selecting leaders, particularly in the military field," Indiana University professor William Jenkins (1947, p. 54) reviewed leadership research findings in five areas: industry and government, scientists and professionals, children, education, and the military. He concluded that, "it is reasonably clear that above a certain desirable minimum, intelligence has little relevance to combat performance" (p. 72).

Dismissing the trait research that had dominated thinking for some time, Jenkins found little to support a systematic theory of leadership since the concept lacked a workable definition to guide research in isolating leadership traits, and few of the leadership hypotheses could be empirically tested. Leadership study in the military would continue, however.

TRAIT THEORIES OF LEADERSHIP

Most of the individuals—fictional or real—who kindled our interest in leadership were strong, ethical, driven, persuasive, intelligent, responsible, and eloquent. Early-20th-century scholars studied traits of great leaders. Sometimes called "great man" theories, these *trait theories* investigations examined leaders' innate personal characteristics. At first, researchers assumed that leaders were born with these qualities. Later, it was believed that these traits could be learned to an extent.

Leadership trait study lasted for more than 100 years. As Alfred Binet was examining French children's intelligence, America's Lewis Terman was examining leadership in children. Terman concluded that the youthful leaders "are on the average larger, better dressed, of more prominent parentage, brighter, more noted for daring, more fluent of speech, better looking, greater readers, and less selfish" than their peers.[6] Terman's study may also have confirmed a relationship between a child's socioeconomic status and later leadership behaviors.

The Ohio State Leadership Studies

After World War II, the U.S. Congress enacted the GI Bill, partly to defer millions of returning soldiers from entering the workforce at the same time. Economists were uncertain if the postwar economy could safely absorb so many workers without creating an economic calamity like the Great Depression. Carroll Shartle was among those studying or teaching GIs in college classrooms. Shartle had worked at the U.S. Department of Labor and the War

Manpower Commission where General George Marshall, former army chief of staff and later U.S. secretary of state, inspired his interest in leadership.[7] At Ohio State University, Shartle received support for an interdisciplinary study of leadership, and he later invited Ralph Stogdill to work with him, supported by the Office of Naval Research.

The Ohio State leadership studies were the first to examine leadership from a multidisciplinary approach that included psychology, sociology, economics, and education. Equally important, and another first in research, the study shifted from a trait approach to a situational and behavioral-based approach or style. Overcoming the methodological criticisms leveled earlier by Jenkins, the Ohio State leadership studies provided a model of construct validation and investigation that led to the development of leadership research instruments.[8]

Ralph Stogdill stands out for his insight as a member of the Ohio State leadership team. In 1948, when certain personal traits were believed to be associated with effective leadership, Stogdill reviewed 100 leading leadership studies and posited that leadership might be situational in nature and should be considered "in terms of the interaction of variables which are in constant flux and change."[9] This and other investigations led to a new study of leadership—leaders' behavior and its impact on individuals, groups, and the organizational outcomes.

In 1949, John Hemphill made a profound contribution to leadership study with his dissertation highlighting the importance of interpersonal and social factors in leadership.[10] He wrote, "The popular idea that leaders are born, not made, stresses the importance of individual traits which make for the successful leadership but ignores another factor of equal importance: the characteristics of the social group which is to be led. It is the interaction of the leader who possesses a given set of personal attributes and the group whose efficient functioning demands that particular combination of attributes which results in successful leadership."[11] Hemphill addressed the leader's behavior interacting with specific demands of the group to be led for one of the first times in the literature.

Stogdill's Contributions to Trait Theory

In 1948, Ralph Stogdill summarized trait leadership theory to that date.[12] He examined 28 traits identified in the literature as associated with leadership and concluded that:

a. The average person who occupies a leadership position exceeds the average group member in: (1) intelligence; (2) scholarship; (3) dependability in exercising responsibilities; (4) activity and social participation; and (5) socioeconomic status.

b. The qualities, characteristics, and skills required in a leader are determined to a large extent by the demands of the situation in which he is to function as a leader.[13]

After Stogdill's study, publications about trait theories of leadership decreased in number.[14] In the late 20th century, interest in transformational and charismatic leadership began to gain momentum. In 1985, Bernard Bass's book, *Leadership Beyond Expectations*, integrated trait study with transformational leadership by including charisma as a quality of transformational leadership, initiating a revived interest in traits.[15] Impetus for additional trait study came from industrial psychologists who were applying knowledge of leadership traits to improve managers' selection and effectiveness.[16] Accordingly, the research at this time shifted to focus on examining the relationship between leader traits and leader effectiveness instead of comparing traits of those in leadership and those not in leadership positions.

ACTIVITY 4.1   Traits and the Case Study

Considering the case study and Table 4–1 (below), what personality traits will help Dr. Ed Smith accomplish his goals for Franklin City High School?

Discuss as a class:

1. What are the most important traits that Ed will need to lead these initiatives successfully?
2. Why won't these traits be enough for him to accomplish the goals?
3. What traits do you need to develop more fully to enhance your leadership skills?

Trait Theory in Practice

Many trait theory ideas are based on survey research and anecdotal comments. While the methodology used in this approach is simplistic and less rigorous than a mixed-methods design, the concept of trait theory has useful benefits. We expect first-rate educational leaders to have traits including honesty, integrity, intelligence, knowledge of curriculum and instruction, and advocacy of social justice. Daniel Goleman's work in emotional intelligence—EQ (as compared with IQ)—is one example of a trait that effective leaders have or develop.[17] In this way, trait theory will always have new components for researchers and practitioners to study and implement.

No one person can have all the traits studied (see Table 4–1). Nevertheless, these traits provide benchmarks or goals of what we may want to see in our leaders and—if we choose to become leaders—in ourselves.

TABLE 4–1

Leadership Traits Studied

Researcher, Year	Traits Studied
Stogdill, 1948[18]	Intelligence, scholarship, knowledge, judgment and decision, insight, originality, adaptability, introversion/extroversion, dominance, initiative, persistence, ambition, responsibility, integrity and conviction, self-confidence, mood control, mood optimism, emotional control, social and economic status, social activity and mobility, biosocial activity, social skills, popularity and prestige, cooperation, transferability, and persistence of leadership
Mann, 1959[19]	Intelligence, masculinity, adjustment, dominance, extroversion, conservatism
Stogdill revisited, 1974[20]	Achievement, persistence, insight, initiative, self-confidence, responsibility, cooperativeness, tolerance, influence, sociability
Lord, DeVader, and Alliger, 1986[21]	Intelligence, masculinity, dominance
Kirkpatrick and Locke, 1991[22]	Drive, motivation, integrity, confidence, cognitive ability, task knowledge
Zaccaro, Kemp, and Bader, 2004[23]	Cognitive abilities, extroversion, conscientiousness, emotional stability, openness, agreeableness, motivation, social intelligence, self-monitoring, emotional intelligence, problem solving

Source: Adapted from Stogdill, R. M. (1948). Personal factors associated with leadership: A survey of the literature. *Journal of Psychology, 25,* 35–72; Northouse, P. (2010). *Leadership: Theory and practice* (5th ed.). Thousand Oaks, CA: Sage.

ACTIVITY 4.2   How Identifiable Are Your Traits?

Early leadership studies focused on identifying traits necessary for successful leadership. Today, we know that leadership also includes situational factors of people and environment as well as the leader's personality.

Which of these leadership traits are in your repertoire and to what extent do others observe them in your behaviors? Using the following list of leadership traits, identify which characteristics you believe are readily observable in your current behaviors and which are less noticeable. Also survey other faculty and staff in your school to get anonymous feedback about the extent to which they observe these behaviors in you. Compare your self-assessment with the survey findings. What do these differences or similarities suggest regarding your professional development?

Trait	Self-Assessment Trait Is Observable			Survey of Others Trait Is Observable		
	Yes	Somewhat	No	Yes	Somewhat	No
Achievement						
Adaptability						
Cognitive ability/intelligence						
Confidence/self-confidence						
Conscientiousness/dependability						
Cooperation						
Dominance/assertiveness						
Emotional intelligence						
Emotional stability						
Extroversion						
Influence						
Initiative						
Insight						
Integrity						
Judgment/decision making						
Knowledge/scholarship						
Motivation/drive						
Openness						
Optimism						
Persistence						
Problem solving						
Responsibility						
Social and economic status						
Social intelligence/skills						

Source: Owings & Kaplan.

LEADERSHIP STYLE THEORIES

While the trait theory emphasizes personal characteristics, *leadership style* theory examines the leader's behavior. Examining leadership style involves looking at how leaders act or behave in an organization. Style theories mark a major conceptual step in the evolution of leadership theory. Before this, leadership was examined as a trait or a characteristic—such as intelligence, extroversion, dominance, and the like. Style theories look more broadly and examine specific leadership behaviors.

Basic Leadership Behaviors: Task and People

As mentioned, the Ohio State studies in the late 1940s examined leadership traits and later, leadership behaviors—or leadership styles. John Hemphill and Alvin Coons, two Ohio State University professors, studied leader behavior by having subordinates complete questionnaires about their leaders' behaviors and how many times leaders exhibited those actions. From an original list of almost 2,000 behaviors, Hemphill and Coons developed the 150-item *Leader Behavior Description Questionnaire* (LBDQ).[24] They found that the LBDQ centered around two basic leader behaviors: initiating structure and consideration.

Initiating structure is defined as leader behavior that deals with operational tasks such as having concern for getting the job done, organizing and scheduling the work, maintaining lines of communication, and following procedures with subordinates. *Consideration* is defined as the relationship aspect of work—that is, building respect, trust, friendship, and concern for coworkers. These two behaviors can be described as the two essential dimensions of a leader's activities, namely, structuring the tasks and caring about the relationships at work.

The LBDQ was widely studied in business, military, and education settings. In 1966, Andrew Halpin, professor of education at Montana State University, described the four major findings from the LBDQ studies.[25] First, initiating structure and consideration are the essence of leader behaviors. Leaders provide the structure and define the nature of the interpersonal relationships in the workplace. Second, the most effective leaders exhibit high initiating structure and high consideration. Third, workers and leaders tend to evaluate the leader's effectiveness differently. Leaders see initiating structure as more valuable. Workers tend to value consideration more in assessing leader effectiveness. Fourth, little correlation appears between how leaders say they behave and how subordinates describe leader behavior.

Blake and Mouton's Leadership Grid

In the 1960s, Robert Blake and Jane Mouton, two University of Texas management scholars, developed a well-known business model for understanding managers' behavior.[26] Similar to the LBDQ, the Blake and Mouton model uses concern for both production and people. The similarity between concern for production and initiating structure is as obvious as the similarity between concern for people and consideration. Blake and Mouton's model adds to our understanding of leadership behavior by providing a dual axis for examining these two key factors.

Consider a four-quadrant grid, with the *x* axis representing concern for production/initiating structure and the *y* axis representing concern for people/consideration, both with

FIGURE 4–2
A Dual-Axis Leadership Matrix (Source: Based on Blake, R., &
Mouton, J. (1964). *The Managerial Grid*. Houston, TX: Gulf
Publishing.)

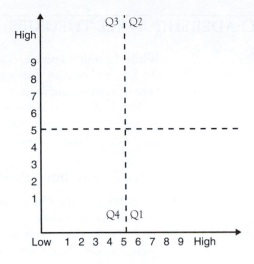

a range of 1 through 9. A plot of 9,1 describes high concern for production/initiating
structure and low concern for people/consideration, whereas a plot of 1,9 depicts high
concern for people and low concern for results. The Q1, Q2, Q3, and Q4 represent the
four quadrants (see Figure 4–2).

According to a two-axis leadership model, five leadership styles are possible.

The first style, *control-compliance*, is plotted at 9,1. It places heavy emphasis on concern
for production/structure and little concern for people/consideration. The name,
control-compliance, reflects this style. Here the leader's style is seen to be hard-
driving and is results oriented with little attention for anything else.

The second style, *people and results*, is plotted at 9,9. It places a heavy emphasis on concern for production and for people. Here the leader's style is seen to be results oriented with a high concern for people in the process. The leader focuses on building
a team where everyone shares the goals for production and finds satisfaction through
the work.

The third style, *people over results*, is plotted at 1,9. It places heavy emphasis on people
and little concern for results. Much attention goes to making certain the organization's
members' personal needs are met. "Friendly" is the word to describe this style.

The fourth style, *weak management*, is plotted at 1,1. It places little emphasis on results
or on the people involved. The leader may be seen as an absentee, and the style
might well be described as indifferent.[27]

The fifth style, *moderate management*, is plotted at 5,5. It places moderate concern for
results and for people. This style finds an equilibrium between the two factors, results
and people. The style may be considered as a balanced compromiser.

Blake and Mouton contend that leaders have a dominant style that they use most of the
time in organizational settings. This model also speculates that leaders have a "backup"
style that they use when under intense pressure or when the dominant style is not working
in a given situation.

ACTIVITY 4.3 Leadership Style and the Case Study

Considering a dual axis leadership matrix, discuss as a class: What leadership style should Ed use in working with the superintendent? What leadership style should Ed use in dealing with the faculty and school community? Are two different styles needed? Explain your answers.

Leadership Style Theory in Practice

One's leadership style is defined from the behaviors displayed around the factors of initiating structure (concern for results) and consideration (concern for people). If a high concern for initiating structure and a high concern for consideration are the leader's dominant behaviors, then that would be labeled as that person's leadership style. In style theory, it is important to know one's leadership style—understanding that at times one style may be more effective than another. If you know your leadership style, you have a better understanding of how you lead and how your coworkers perceive you.

LEADERSHIP CONTINGENCY THEORIES

It is logical to ask whether one "best" style works well all the time or whether certain styles work better in given situations. Matching a style to a situation is highly complex.

Contingency theory expands on leadership style by trying to match the appropriate leadership style with the particular situation's characteristics. It is called *contingency theory* because it suggests that the leader's effectiveness is contingent upon how well the leader's style fits the particular situation's characteristics. Fred Fiedler's contingency theory is the most widely known.[28]

In studying leadership styles, Fiedler, professor of management and research sociologist at the University of Illinois and later at the University of Washington, developed the Least Preferred Coworker (LPC) scale. To Fiedler, leadership style was fixed, and the LPC scale measured one's leadership orientation. The LPC scale asks respondents to think of all the people with whom they have worked and then describe the person with whom they have worked the least well. The scale ranks items on an ordinal scale of 1–8 for 18 adjectives (e.g., unfriendly to friendly; uncooperative to cooperative). A high LPC score indicates a relationship-motivated person. A low score indicates a task-motivated person.

Fiedler suggested that there is no ideal leader type. Leaders can be effective if their leadership orientation fits the particular situational characteristics. Fiedler's model predicts the characteristics of the appropriate circumstances in order for the leader to be effective. According to the model, three factors characterize situations: leader-member relations, task structure, and position power.

Leader-member relations refers to the level of mutual trust, respect, and confidence that the group has for its leader. If the group atmosphere is favorable and the leader is trusted, is respected, and holds the group's confidence, then the leader–member relations are good. If not, they are defined as poor.

Task structure refers to the extent to which the task requirements are clear and communicated effectively. When tasks are clear, leader control increases. When tasks are vague and not clearly communicated, leader control decreases. The task structure can be either high or low.

Position power refers to the amount of legitimate power or authority inherent in the leader's position to provide rewards or punishments to the group or individuals within the group. Position power is seen as high if the leader has the authority to hire or fire, promote or demote, or provide pay increases, bonuses, or pay cuts to individuals. Position power is considered weak if the leader has little or no power to implement these actions.

All three factors determine the favorableness of organizational situations. When leader–member relations are good, task structure is clear, and position power is strong, the situation is defined as favorable. In contrast, situations are least favorable when leader–member relations are poor, task structure is low, and position power is weak. Situations that are rated in the middle areas are known as moderately favorable.

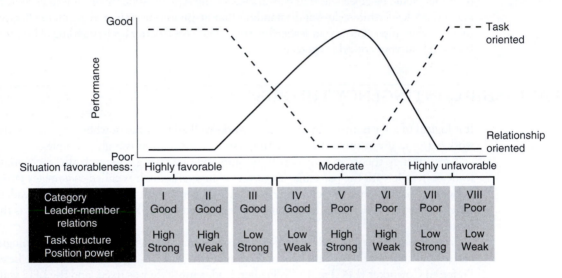

FIGURE 4–3
Contingency Theory Model (Source: Fiedler, F. E. (1967). *A Theory of Leadership Effectiveness* New York: McGraw-Hill.) Reprinted by permission of the author.

Contingency theory research suggests that certain styles are more effective in different situations. The two major findings conclude:

◆ Task-motivated leaders (low LPC scores) will be effective when situations are very favorable and very unfavorable.
◆ Relationship-motivated leaders (high LPC scores) will be effective in moderately favorable conditions.

Figure 4–3 shows graphically how this works. The *x* axis represents the situation's favorableness from high to low. The *y* axis represents the leader's effectiveness. The dotted line represents the task-oriented leader doing well in highly favorable and unfavorable situations, whereas the solid line represents the relationship-oriented leader doing well in moderately favorable situations. Low LPC score leaders (task oriented) will be effective in categories I, II, III, and VIII. High LPC score leaders (relationship oriented) will be effective in categories IV, V, VI, and VII.

Contingency Theory in Practice

Contingency theory represents a major evolution in leadership theory and deserves consideration from that point alone. Nonetheless, contingency theory is not used widely in education settings, and interest in contingency theory has diminished over the years for several reasons. First, situational leadership models surfaced with more explanatory power, allowing for leaders to adapt their leadership style to fit the situation. Second, the LPC scale had validity problems with what it actually measured and how it is measured. Third, contingency theory requires that when a mismatch occurs between the leader and the situation, either the leader is changed or the situation is engineered to fit the leader. The practicality of such situational engineering is problematic, to say the least. Contingency theory does provide an evolutionary bridge to situational leadership theory, however.

ACTIVITY 4.4   Contingency Theory and the Case Study

As a class, answer the following three questions that apply Contingency Theory to the case study. Then, in pairs, discuss answers to the Case Study Questions. Finally, discuss your answers as a class.

1. How would you describe the leader–member relations?
2. How would you consider the task structure?
3. How would you consider the position power Ed has?

Case Study Question 1: How does the lack of faculty motivation to change influence how Ed leads the school?

Case Study Question 2: How does the assistant principals' lack of willingness to help and their lack of instructional expertise affect Ed's leadership style as he works with them?

Case Study Question 3: How will Superintendent Jones's lack of support for some of Ed's action plans affect how Ed leads the faculty and community?

Case Study Question 4: What personality or physical traits will help Ed be more effective in leading his proposed changes?

Case Study Question 5: What situational factors should Ed consider as the leader of Franklin City High School?

SITUATIONAL LEADERSHIP THEORY

Situational leadership theory represents another evolutionary step forward in thinking. In this model, the task and relationship orientations are still present from the Ohio State studies, the leadership style model, and the contingency model. With situational leadership, however, the leadership style is not fixed. Rather, leadership styles can and should change with the situation. The leadership style is situational.

Situational leadership is most closely associated with Paul Hersey and Ken Blanchard, American management experts, and is frequently used in training business executives.[29] In fact, Blanchard's situational leadership (SL) II model training has been used in 318 of the current Fortune 500 companies.[30]

The situational leadership model continues to use the dual axis format with the x axis depicting task orientation, called *directive behavior*. The y axis shows the relationship orientation, called *supportive behavior*. The dual axis model allows for four quadrants similar to Figure 4–2, without the moderate management (5,5) designation. The leadership styles (Ss) and the employees' developmental or maturity levels (Ds) are equivalent to quadrants (Qs) 1–4.

The first quadrant (Q1), S1, or *directing behaviors*, depicts a leadership style that is high directive (high task orientation) and low supportive (low relationship orientation). Behaviors in this style stress how the job is to be accomplished, the importance of achieving the organizational goals, and frequently monitoring progress.

The second quadrant (Q2), S2, *coaching behaviors*, depicts a leadership style that is high directive (task oriented) and high supportive (relationship oriented). Leadership behaviors in this style emphasize meeting organizational goals while also encouraging and supporting team collegiality.

The third quadrant (Q3), S3, or *supporting behaviors*, shows a leadership style that is low directive (task) and high supportive (relationship). This style's behavior emphasizes listening, sustaining, encouraging teamwork, seeking group input, and providing recognition.

The last quadrant (Q4), S4, *delegating behaviors*, represents a leadership style characterized by low directive (task) and low supportive (relationship) behaviors. This style's behaviors provide little task direction and little social support or feedback. Much of the control for the task is assigned to the group or individual. The S4 leadership style works with the group to set direction and then allows the group to carry out the tasks as they see fit.

It is important to note that "low level" does not equate to "no level" of a particular behavior. Each of these styles should be used with a particular situation as determined by the individual's or group's maturity or development level.

There is no one correct leadership style. The correct style depends on the situation. Deciding under what situations to use each of these leadership styles involves assessing the individual's or group's maturity or developmental level. *Developmental level* is the degree to which an individual or group has the competence (sometimes called ability) and commitment (or willingness) to accomplish the task. Four developmental levels, D1 through D4, match the four leadership styles, S1 through S4, of this model.

Developmental level 1 (D1). Level D1 individuals are low in competence and low in commitment. This might be new teachers fresh out of college with only 8 weeks of student teaching experience. Their commitment to education and teaching may be low due to the newfound difficulties all beginning teachers experience with student discipline, paperwork, deadlines, and unsupportive parents. Moreover, new teachers may not yet be well versed in school policies and procedures, or have knowledge of what organizing the year instructionally with state testing mandates entails (competence issues).

Developmental level 2 (D2). Level D2 individuals are somewhat competent, but low in commitment. This might be a teacher who has a degree of job mastery, but some of the initial excitement and motivation to excel has worn off—perhaps due to a violation of the psychological contract (see Chapter 6).

Developmental level 3 (D3). Level D3 individuals are those with moderately high to high levels of competence, but they may be somewhat lower on the commitment level. They might be seen as having the skills to do the job but, like some veteran educators nearing retirement, require active and ongoing support to boost their willingness to continually invest the effort and time necessary to perform at their best

Developmental level 4 (D4). Level D4 individuals are those at the apex of the developmental scale. They have confidence in their competence to complete the task, and they exhibit a high level of commitment to the task. A D4 individual might be the master teacher who continues to inspire younger teachers with his or her classroom expertise and enthusiastic talk about education's many benefits to society.

The job of an effective leader is to match the leadership style with the individual's or group's developmental level. The challenge of the situational leadership theory is to correctly identify this developmental level. Once accomplished, the leader matches the leadership style with the corresponding developmental level. For example, if a teacher is identified as D1 (low competence, high commitment), the most effective leadership style is S1. The new teacher with little experience (competence) and high enthusiasm (commitment) for the job would fit the D1 level. According to the situational leadership model, the correct leadership style to use is S1—high directive behavior and low supportive behavior.

Situational Theory in Practice

The situational model has an intuitiveness and logic, matching the leader's behaviors to the employee's developmental level (see Table 4–2). Let's consider the new teacher (D1) and what leadership style the principal might use. It makes sense for the principal to take a more directive and less socially supportive role. The new teacher needs guidance on how to increase his or her competence; that should be the principal's goal. As the teacher matures in the job (D2)—increased competence but a lower level of commitment—the principal

TABLE 4–2
Applying Leadership Style

Developmental Level	Characteristics of Individual or Group	Appropriate Leadership Style to Use	Rationale
D1	Low competence and low commitment levels	**S1**	Workers have low competence and commitment levels and need high levels of direction.
D2	Somewhat more competence but still lower commitment levels	**S2**	Workers' competence is increasing and commitment remains low. They still need high level of direction, but increased support is called for.
D3	Moderately high competence and somewhat moderate commitment levels	**S3**	Workers are competent and commitment is increasing. They need less direction, but still need a high level of support to enhance commitment.
D4	High competence and high commitment levels	**S4**	Workers' levels of competence and commitment are high. High levels of direction and support tend to be distracting. Lower levels of direction and support are called for.

Source: Based on Hersey, Paul, and Blanchard, K. H. (1988). *Management and Organizational Behavior*. Englewood Cliffs, NJ: Prentice Hall.

can still exhibit directive behavior, but increase the supportive behavior to bolster the teacher's commitment level. As the teacher matures and shows high to moderately high competence and commitment (D3), the principal can reduce the directive behaviors and continue the supportive behavior to maintain the commitment level. Once the teacher has become a "master teacher" with high levels of both competence and commitment (D4), the principal needs lower levels of directive and supportive behaviors. This teacher may have more competence in teaching than the principal. Directive behaviors from the principal would not be helpful. Moreover, the master teacher may perceive the principal's high levels of supportive behavior as a waste of time or the principal's lack of respect for the teacher's competence and autonomy. A D4, therefore, would be best served by an S4 leadership style.

Situational leadership theory has been researched for more than 40 years, albeit mostly in doctoral dissertations.[31] It is popular in practice due to its sensible application. Using this situational leadership model provides a convenient tool for educational leaders and a useful frame of reference for dealing with leadership issues.[32]

ACTIVITY 4.5   Situational Theory and the Case Study

Consider Ed's situation in the case study. Discuss in pairs:

1. How would you describe the developmental level of the Franklin City High School faculty (D1–D4)? Defend your answer with a colleague. Do the two of you agree? If so, what would be the appropriate leadership style for Ed to use with the faculty? Explain your answer to your colleague.
2. How would you describe the developmental level of the assistant principals (D1–D4)? Given your answer, explain what the appropriate leadership style would be to use with that group of individuals. After all pairs have finished, share answers with the entire class.

PATH-GOAL THEORY

Robert House, professor of organizational studies and management at Wharton School, University of Pennsylvania, developed the path-goal theory of leadership in the early 1970s.[33] Northouse (2010) stated, "The underlying assumption of path-goal theory is derived from expectancy theory, which suggests that subordinates will be motivated if they think they are capable of performing their work, if they believe their efforts will result in a certain outcome, and if they believe that the payoffs for doing their work are worthwhile."[34] Although House refined his path-goal theory in 1996, we will discuss his original leader behaviors.[35]

People constantly hold certain expectations for their future, both personally and professionally. Expectancy theory, discussed fully in Chapter 6, is basically a presumption of what motivates individuals' behavior. Expectancy theory holds that motivation is a combination of three factors:

Valence. What is the value of the expected outcome? What do I get out of it?

Instrumentality. The belief that if certain actions are completed, the outcome will be achieved. Is there a clear path for me to achieve the goal?

Expectancy. The belief that one has the ability to complete the actions. Am I capable of achieving the goal?

In path-goal theory, the leader uses a leadership style that matches the workers' motivational needs in a particular situation. The leader behaviors depend on two situational factors—the subordinate conditions and the task characteristics. House and Mitchell examined four leader behaviors that meet these needs: directive, supportive, participative, and achievement oriented.[36] Using these behaviors helps workers move along the *path* toward the *goal* (path–goal), avoiding obstacles that might obstruct them.

The four leader behaviors in the original path-goal theory can be viewed as task or relationship behaviors. *Directive-oriented leadership* is similar to the task orientation in the situational leadership theory. Here, the leader clearly directs, instructs, and monitors workers in the time, quality, and expectations for how the task is to be accomplished. The leader is quite prescriptive in directing worker behavior and training.

Supportive-oriented leadership resembles the relationship orientation in situational leadership theory. The leader behavior is seen as respectful, caring, and approachable. Here, the leader takes a genuine interest in the workers' well-being and their working conditions.

Participative-oriented leadership can be seen as working with a group developmentally high in capacity and cooperation. The leader consults and shares information with the group to obtain their input into the decision-making process as a means to implement a superior solution.

Finally, *achievement-oriented leadership* is a high level of task orientation and relationship orientation. Here, the leader expresses challenging goals with a high standard for excellent performance. Moreover, the leader expresses a high level of confidence that workers are competent and willing to meet these expectations.

The concept behind path-goal theory is to match the leadership style to the situation. Researchers have focused on subordinates' needs for affiliation, preferences for structure, desire for control, and self-perceived level of task ability.[37] These factors and others determine the level to which workers find leader behavior a source of satisfaction.

ACTIVITY 4.6   Path-Goal Theory and the Case Study

Apply the path-goal theory to consider Ed's situation in the case study. Discuss as a class:

1. What are the obstacles that Ed must overcome to achieve the goals he has given to the superintendent?
2. List at least three leader behaviors that Ed must use for defining goals, clarifying the path, removing obstacles, and providing support. Which of these does Ed list in his action plans?
3. Read the next section, "Path-Goal Theory in Practice." Using the information provided in this section, justify which leadership behavior Ed should use in Action #1 to accomplish the goal he has submitted to the superintendent.

Path-Goal Theory in Practice

The purpose of using path-goal theory is to increase worker effort, performance, and job satisfaction in each situation. Table 4–3 illustrates how this operates as it identifies (1) a situation, (2) the specific leadership behavior recommended according to path-goal theory, (3) the impact of this leadership behavior on the follower, and (4) the outcome. For instance, supportive behavior is used in situations when the followers lack self-confidence and need

TABLE 4–3
Path-Goal Theory in Practice

Situation	Leadership Behavior	Impact on Follower	Outcome
Followers lack self-confidence and need affiliation and support. Task is menial, boring, and repetitive.	Supportive (cultivating)	Increases self-confidence in achieving the outcome as well as increases support for working conditions.	**Increased worker effort, performance, and job satisfaction.**
Followers prefer authoritarian leadership. Task is complex and ambiguous, and the rules and regulations are unclear about how to complete the task.	Directive (guiding and structuring)	Clarifies path to the reward.	
Followers have high expectations and a need for task accomplishment. Task is complex, ambiguous, and challenging (or it may have a lack of challenge).	Achievement oriented (challenging)	Increases high expectations and goals for performance.	
Followers have a high level of competence and cooperation and a need to excel. Task may be unclear or unstructured and the reward may not be appropriate to the goal.	Participative (involving)	Clarifies worker needs and goals and correctly articulates and aligns reward structures.	

Source: Adapted from Northouse, P. (2010). *Leadership: Theory and practice* (5th ed.). Los Angeles, CA: Sage; Hoy, W., & Miskel, C. (2008). *Educational administration: Theory, research, and practice* (8th ed.). New York, NY: McGraw-Hill.

affiliation and support, and the task is menial, boring, and repetitive. A supportive behavior tends to increase the worker's confidence in achieving the outcome as well as providing support for the working conditions.

Directive leadership is used in situations when the followers prefer authoritarian leadership, the task is complex and ambiguous, and the rules and regulations are unclear about how to complete the task. A directive behavior tends to clarify the path to the reward for the followers.

Supportive leadership resembles the relationship orientation in situational leadership theory. The leader behavior is seen as respectful, caring, and approachable. Here, the leader takes a genuine interest in the workers' well-being and their working conditions. The workers have internal locus of control, are highly competent to successfully complete the task, and do not want authority leadership.

Achievement-oriented leadership is used in situations when the followers have high expectations and a need for task accomplishment, and in situations where the task is complex, ambiguous, and challenging (or it may lack challenge). Achievement-oriented leadership tends to help workers set high goals and high expectations for their performance.

Participative leadership is used in situations when the followers have a high level of competence and cooperation along with a need to excel, the task may be unclear or unstructured, and the reward may not be appropriate to the goal. A participative leadership style tends to clarify workers' goals and correctly articulate and align reward structures by securing worker input in the decision-making process.

Additionally, workers with a high level of *internal locus of control* (those who believed their outcomes were a result of their own hard work and good decisions) tend to be more satisfied working with leaders who use participative leadership styles. On the other hand, workers with a high level of external locus of control (see outcomes as a result of external factors or luck) tend to be more satisfied working with leaders using directive leadership styles. Here, educational leaders need to work with teachers, other administrators, and staff to build their relevant knowledge and skillls if they are to increase employees' internal locus of control (see Chapter 7 for a discussion of attribution theory and building capacity).

Path-goal theory can be practical and complex at the same time. Educational leaders should be able to apply path-goal theory by assessing the needs of workers in the school and the particular situation and then apply the correct leadership style. By using path-goal theory and correctly assessing the situation, school leaders increase the probability of increased worker effort, performance, and job satisfaction. They also build staff capacity to confront and solve new tasks.

TRANSFORMATIONAL LEADERSHIP THEORY

Transformational leadership is a current hot topic in leadership research. In 1978, James MacGregor Burns, a historian and political scientist, developed this concept. As a leadership theory, transformational leadership sits on the opposite end of the continuum from laissez-faire leadership.[38] Although Kurt Lewin and colleagues had earlier (1939) identified laissez-faire as a leadership style, Burns brought this to a more elegant construct.[39] Figure 4–4 shows an early model of authoritarian leadership use.

Background Information

Earlier leadership theory development identified laissez-faire, democratic, and autocratic as three distinct leadership styles based on the leader's use of authority. Laissez-faire leadership is on the low use end of the authority continuum, democratic leadership is in the middle, and autocratic leadership is on the high use end of the authority continuum.

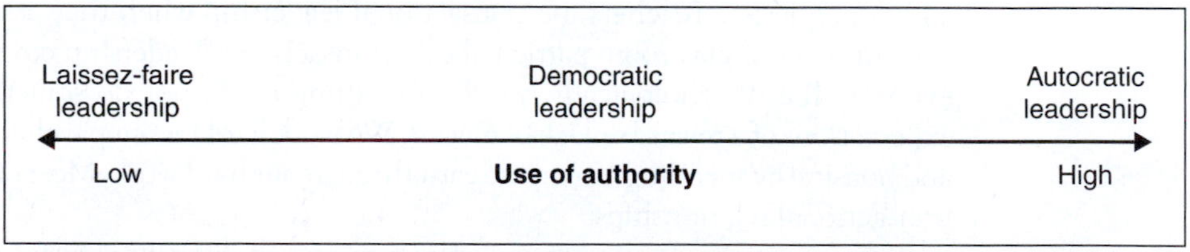

FIGURE 4–4
Use of Authority Continuum in Leadership Styles (Source: Owings & Kaplan.)

Laissez-faire leadership (from the French, "let it be") is characterized by the leader's minimal use of authority. This type of leadership was considered optimal for capable and committed workers who needed little oversight—similar to S4 and D4 in the situational leadership model—where there is little need for initiating structure and supportive behavior.

Democratic leadership style is characterized by worker involvement in the decision-making process. The level of worker involvement depends on how far to the left or right one moves on the authority dimension. As in the situational leadership model, using a democratic leadership style may be problematic if a wide range of viewpoints exists on how the goal is to be accomplished or if a wide range in workers' capacity or commitment to accomplish the goal is present. Lewin, however, found democratic leadership to be the most effective style.[40]

Autocratic leadership style is characterized by low levels of worker involvement in the decision-making process. It is akin to S1 in the situational leadership model where the leadership style is characterized by high task and low relationship behaviors. Although this may be an appropriate leadership style for workers at the lowest developmental stages, Lewin's research found that the autocratic leadership style was associated with the highest levels of worker discontent.[41]

Transformational Leadership's Concept

Burns's concept of *transformational leadership* is defined as a process where "leaders and followers help each other to advance to a higher level of morale and motivation."[42] To more fully understand transformational leadership, however, we must examine it in comparison to another concept Burns discussed—transactional leadership.

Figure 4–4 shows a continuum of leadership styles based on the use of authority. Transactional and transformational leadership may also be conceived as a continuum. In 1985, Bass expanded on Burns's work and developed a continuum that ranged from transformational to transactional to laissez-faire leadership.[43] For clarity, however, we will compare and contrast transactional and transformational leadership as if they were opposite ends of one continuum.

On the one end stands transactional leadership, a type of *quid pro quo* (Latin meaning "this for that") style of leading people. This style is frequently associated with autocratic leadership. Here the leader gives something to get something or withholds something to get something. Transactional leadership involves the use of power—of punishments and rewards—to achieve a goal. Principals use transactional leadership when they give teachers exceptionally high evaluations for volunteering to serve on committees or take on additional duties. Teachers use transactional leadership when they assign high grades for student work or classroom participation. Transactional leadership covers a broad array of everyday life. Psychologically, we do something or do not do something based on the expectations of a reward or lack of reward. We work hard for our paychecks. We obtain food and housing by spending money we earn through our hard work. Most of life is built around transactional relationships.

Transformational leadership, in contrast, is a much different concept. Instead of a power-based "give and take" exchange process, transformational leadership encompasses three concepts. First, the leader is a moral exemplar of the organization's mission, personally epitomizing the organization's goals and vision. By visibly symbolizing the organization's mission, leaders make the workers aware of the attractive potential and specific details of the organizational change. Second, the leader articulates a vision and builds awareness of this vision while also attending to the followers' needs, concerns, and motives. Third, the leader helps followers by building the team's capacity, both morally and technically.[44] Understanding transformational leadership's three components helps clarify the differences between a transactional and a transformational leader. Transformational leadership is gauged by the influence on the followers above and beyond a simple transactional (exchange) level.

Examples of transformational leaders continue to inspire. India's Mohandas Gandhi, the founder of nonviolent protest, displayed transformational leadership. Gandhi built awareness of an independent India and civil rights for all Indians through nonviolent demonstrations. Through his own moral example, he showed others how to accomplish the task of changing an empire. His leadership stirred competent believers to carry out his vision.

Other researchers (Bass & Riggio, 2006; Bass & Bass, 2008) have identified four common factors associated with transformational leadership: idealized influence, inspirational motivation, intellectual stimulation, and individualized consideration.[45] Cited frequently in the literature, these four factors are commonly referred to as the "four I's" of transformational leadership.

Idealized Influence. Also known as *charisma* (from the Greek, meaning "gift"), *idealized influence* describes the leader's ability to affect followers' loyalty to the leader and to the organization by the power of his or her person. These leaders have a deep conviction about the direction the organization needs to take. They serve as a moral example for the organization's "cause." As such, they share their vision and mission, engendering loyalty in the process, as they attempt to change the organization.

Interestingly, Bass observed that the extent to which followers are ready to view their leaders as having this idealized influence depends on the followers' personality.[46] Followers who have previously experienced psychological distress may be open to perceive an effective leader's idealized influence.[47] In other words, the charismatic leader (who has this idealized influence) is "the right person in the right place at the right time" when the old way of doing things has failed and a new order is required. Carrying this to school contexts, leaders who come into a failing school and who garner sufficient staff buy-in to successfully turn it around may be seen to have charisma. After all, a persistently failing school that now has become successful gives followers a euphoric experience of "mission accomplished." Having fulfilled a challenging and important goal, followers share a camaraderie of success which builds pride, respect, and trust for their leader.

Weber pointed out that charisma remains unstable, dependent on the situation. For charisma to endure, it must be "routinized" by establishing policies and protocols.[48] Using Lewin's terms, when the school is "turned around," the organization must develop policies and procedures to stabilize (refreeze) the new culture and behaviors after the prior culture has been unfrozen and moved to the now well-functioning place.

Inspirational Motivation. The term *inspirational motivation* describes the leader who is able to communicate a vision that motivates workers to increasingly higher levels of accomplishment by increasing shared expectations. This is closely related to Vroom's expectancy theory (see Chapter 5), which says if someone believes their increased job effort will result in the desired performance, it likely will lead to that end. By increasing what can be accomplished, workers gain confidence in their capacities to successfully solve other concerns as well. This process energizes workers to create better and more productive work environments which enhances team spirit, optimism, creativity, and vision. As in the prior example of the persistently failing school that experiences a successful turnaround, the staff now sees that they can create a better climate for learning. This realization strengthens their belief that they have the capacity to make even greater changes to the school.

With transformational leadership, leaders encourage grade level or subject area teams to boost their expectations for student achievement in class and in important ways that may or may not appear on local or state tests. Teachers then provide students with effective instruction, appropriate and personalized assistance, and ongoing encouragement. As a consequence, higher percentages of students learn the curricula, learn to see and understand the world in deepened ways, and pass formal assessments. Inspirational motivation carries over from staff to students. The process enhances the culture for motivation for everyone in the school community.

Intellectual Stimulation.   *Intellectual stimulation* involves the degree to which leaders challenge traditional organizational assumptions and have followers confront their own beliefs and behaviors. Intellectual stimulation also involves the leader encouraging workers to be creative problem solvers who can reframe issues and use fresh insights to solve problems. Intellectual stimulation values employee learning and resourcefulness as a means to professional and organizational growth. As leaders encourage employee development, open consideration of issues, and creative problem solving, leaders elicit and take guidance from followers' informed input.[49]

Leaders educate teachers about the organization and the issues, help them challenge familiar assumptions that may block problem solving, solicit teachers' ideas, and act on them. By helping the staff to mature their capabilities and collaboration skills, the leader enhances and makes full use of the organization's human capital.

Individualized Consideration.   The degree to which leaders attend to the followers' individual needs through coaching or mentoring is called *individualized consideration*. This factor is most closely associated with S3—high relationship, low task behavior. Bass observed that there are really two separate factors associated with consideration.[50] Consideration is displayed in group settings—consulting with groups, participative decision making with groups, and treating group members alike. Individualized consideration also occurs where individuals are treated differently according to their needs and capabilities. This may take many forms, such as congratulating an individual on having done a good job, privately and constructively pointing out weaknesses, and assigning projects to heighten the individual's confidence and capability.[51]

Bass noted that Andrew Carnegie, a 19th-century American industrialist and philanthropist, exemplified individualized consideration when he gave responsibility to employees at all management levels to avail themselves of whatever talents the individuals around them had—and this was done at a time when autocratic leadership was the rule.[52] Given his own experiences as a child laborer, Carnegie was sensitive to the needs of both blue-collar and white-collar workers.

In transformational leadership, the leader creates a supportive and nurturing climate for mentoring where concern for both individuals and task is high. Not all transformational leaders display individualized consideration, however. They may depend on their charisma or intellectual stimulation to compensate for a lack of individual consideration.[53]

Situational theory and transformational leadership have certain commonalities. According to Bass, transformational leadership theory downplays the importance of situational variables.[54] More recently, Bass stated that situational factors may influence leadership effectiveness and there may be no best leadership style in all circumstances.[55]

> **ACTIVITY 4.7 Transformational Leadership and Case Study**
>
> Reflect on the case study. Consider the four factors associated with transformational leadership: idealized influence, inspirational motivation, intellectual stimulation, and individualized consideration. As a class, discuss what Ed can do in relation to these factors to become the transformational leader needed at Franklin City High School.

Transformational Leadership Theory in Practice

Leaders seeking to transform a school or a school district would fare well to think of transformational leadership as a goal and not necessarily as a leadership style. Although the four factors of idealized influence, inspirational motivation, intellectual stimulation, and individualized consideration comprise the theory's essence, these distinct factors build over time in dealing with people and issues. They cannot be worn all at once like a newly tailored suit.

Gary Yukl, professor of management at the State University of New York at Albany, has offered ideas to help school leaders become transformational leaders:[56]

- ◆ Develop a challenging vision with followers.
- ◆ Link the vision with a strategy for achievement.
- ◆ Develop a specific vision and translate it into actions.
- ◆ Express confidence and optimism about the vision and its implementation.
- ◆ Accomplish the vision through small, planned successes moving toward its full implementation.

> **ACTIVITY 4.8 Are You a Transformational Leader?**
>
> Individually reflect on the following statements about transformational leadership and then answer whether each of these statements is true for you.
>
> 1. My faculty and staff would tell you that they know what I stand for.
> 2. My students, parents, and community will tell you that they know what I stand for.
> 3. My faculty and staff will tell you that I have important goals for our school and know how to reach them.
> 4. I know that I have the ability to inspire others to greater effort for a desired end.
> 5. My faculty and staff tell me that my confidence and optimism motivates them in positive ways.
> 6. My faculty and staff would say that I am genuinely interested in their needs and concerns.
> 7. I often delegate tasks (that I could easily do myself) to others to develop my faculty and staff's capacity.
> 8. I believe that team collaboration, creativity, and innovation are essential for success.
> 9. I encourage my faculty and staff to question the assumptions upon which our school practices and school culture rest.
>
> Note: Items 1, 2, and 3 deal with idealized influence; items 4 and 5 deal with inspirational motivation; items 6 and 7 deal with individualized consideration; and items 8 and 9 deal with intellectual stimulation.
>
> 1. Which transformational leadership area is your strongest?
> 2. Which transformational leadership area needs additional growth?
> 3. How and where do you expect to develop leadership skills in your areas needing the most growth?

Source: Owings & Kaplan.

AUTHENTIC LEADERSHIP THEORY

Authentic leadership theory is a relatively new theory and is still under construction. It concerns congruence between what leaders say and what they do.

Authenticity is not a new concept. Probably the best known reference is from Shakespeare's *Hamlet* when Polonius advises Laertes, his son, "To thine own self be true, and it must follow, as the night the day, thou canst not then be false to any man."[57] The phrase was not original to Shakespeare, however. It comes from an ancient Greek saying— Να είσαι αυτός Που είσαι—literally, "be the one that you are." Another translation is, "Be true to your better self."

Background Information

Basically, individuals want their leaders to be good people. We want the confidence of knowing our leaders are being true to their better selves. No one appreciated Enron's leader encouraging his employees to buy more company stock when he knew the organization's dire financial predicament. Quite a few U.S. investment bankers put the world into the Great Recession of 2008 by selling subprime mortgage-backed securities based on mortgages of home buyers who could not afford to pay for them, and inflated home assessments that would soon be "under water" (worth less than the mortgage). The public was shocked to learn after the 2010 *Deepwater Horizon* oil rig explosion in the Gulf of Mexico that BP had a history of taking shortcuts to save money while compromising worker and environmental safety. To their corporate mind, paying fines for malpractice cost the company less than the money lost by taking time to operate prudently.

Education is not immune to scandal. Examples each year show school leaders embroiled in high-stakes test cheating, financial improprieties, and inappropriate relationships.

Such instances and many others have generated a demand for authentic leadership:[58] ethical leaders who have the integrity to match their deeds to their words. Although many definitions of authentic leadership exist, they share several common threads: a desire to serve, integrity and ethics, a strong moral compass and core values, a pursuit of worthy objectives, a desire to empower workers for the good of the organization, and positive organizational citizenship. Fred Walumbwa, an Arizona State University associate professor of management, and colleagues defined *authentic leadership* as:

> a pattern of leader behavior that draws upon and promotes both positive psychological capacities and a positive ethical climate, to foster greater self-awareness, an internalized moral perspective, balanced processing of information, and relational transparency on the part of leaders working with followers, fostering positive self-development.[59]

Authentic Leadership's Concept

Authentic leaders achieve genuineness through self-awareness, self-acceptance, and dependable actions and relationships.[60] As those authentic relationships develop they are characterized by the following:

- ◆ Transparency, openness, and trust
- ◆ Guidance toward worthy objectives
- ◆ An emphasis on follower development[61]

Authentic leaders foster their followers' development into authentic leadership roles. Authentic leadership centers around relationships built on honesty, trust, and the pursuit of a moral purpose.

Figure 4–5 presents a conceptual representation for authentic leadership.[62] *Antecedent events* are those events that have previously taken place in our lives that shape us into who we are now. The two types of antecedent events come from our personal history and key trigger events. *Personal history* comes from how we were raised, the role models who influenced us, and our education and work experiences. *Trigger events* are those significant and usually crisis-centered personal and occupational events that have spurred personal growth and self-concept development. Our upbringing and those life-shaping events are what we bring to the table as leaders.

Authentic leadership is composed of two components: self-awareness and self-regulation. *Self-awareness*, or self-knowledge, results from self-reflection. It is only as we understand

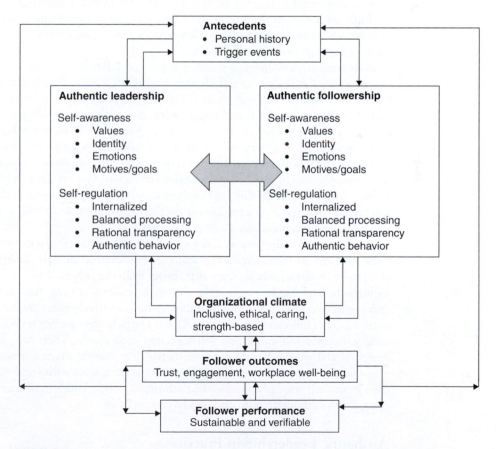

FIGURE 4–5

Conceptual Framework for Authentic Leader and Follower Development (Source: Adapted from Walumbwa, F., Avilio, B., Gardner, W., Wernsing, T., & Peterson, S. (2008). Authentic leadership: Development and validation of a theory-based measure. *Journal of Management, 34*(1), 89–126; Kearnis, M. (2003). Toward a conceptualization of optimal self-esteem. *Psychological Inquiry, 14*, 1–26.)

ourselves—our motivations, values, and goals—that we become truly self-aware. Kearnis (2003) suggested that self-awareness is a vital component of authentic leadership where leaders are self-reflective and trust in their values, identity, emotions, and goals.[63]

As leaders become increasingly self-aware, they internalize and integrate their identity, values, emotions, and goals as part of their being. This ongoing self-knowledge allows the leader to become more comfortable with *self-regulation*. As a consequence, this self-knowledge guides and limits the leader's behavior to those which are in sync with those same values, emotions, and goals. This congruence between the leader's being and actions leads to a balanced processing of information and situations. In theory, full self-awareness and self-regulation allow the leader to act without bias, prejudice, or maladaptive behaviors associated with inauthentic behaviors resulting from a leader who is not self-aware and self-regulated.

As the leader exhibits this maturity in balanced processing of information, he or she is able to present a coherent and unified self to followers. Through self-disclosure, the leader is open and truthful in interpersonal dealings and in the decision-making process. This truthfulness is seen in dealings with others, but also in being true to the leader's values, identity, emotions, and goals. This is known as *rational transparency*. Rational transparency leads to the leader's authentic behaviors.

Authentic leadership has a positive impact on followers and the organization. As the leader makes the organizational climate a more inclusive, ethical, caring, and strength-based environment, it has a positive impact on the *follower outcomes*. These outcomes include enhanced levels of trust, engagement, and workplace well-being. According to the model, the positive work environment allows *follower performance* to become sustainable and verifiable. In this way, authentic leadership creates a two-way loop. The follower outcomes and follower performances become part of the antecedents for future behaviors, their own personal history and trigger events enhanced by interaction with authentic leadership. Authentic leadership and authentic followership augment each other in every interaction that has a positive impact on the organizational climate, follower outcomes, and follower performance in a continuous cycle.

Authentic leadership theory is not without flaws. Theoretically, it contains many of the same qualities as transformational and other leadership models, making it difficult to practically or empirically separate this theory from the others. Also, authentic leadership requires the leader to be a consistent, authentic leader over time. A lack of authentic leadership engenders a lack of authentic followership, negatively affecting the climate, follower outcomes, and follower performance. All too often, leaders are not reflective and therefore cannot become self-aware and self-regulated individuals. Then too, leaders may hold dysfunctional values that do not benefit the organization or its followers. Additionally, many leaders behave defensively, in response to their insecurities and weaknesses, rather than from their strengths. Just as the performance cycle builds from each positive experience, it can deteriorate from one negative experience.

Authentic Leadership in Practice

Authentic leadership is a relatively new topic in leadership studies. Definitions of authentic leadership vary from author to author. As such, it is difficult to translate into a coherent theory. Only recently have models been developed which can be quantified and tested. Nevertheless, practicing authentic leadership requires a leader who is self-confident and has reflected extensively about his or her own values, goals, ethics, and philosophy and how these apply to the work setting. It requires a leader who genuinely values developing positive, professional relationships with followers and a willingness to lead based on his or her positive role modeling for others in the organization.

On the other hand, we know that certain behaviors minimize authentic leadership. These include unethical, manipulative, and highly transactional conduct. Leaders who have not reflected about what they believe and value have few core standards upon which they act consistently. As a result, they may act from convenience and not conscience. Their "walk and talk" may be at odds with each other. Acting from conscience and not merely convenience—as well as having a high level of emotional maturity—may be the crux of authentic leadership.

ACTIVITY 4.9   Considering Leadership in Action

Discuss the following in pairs:

1. Considering the case study, if you were Ed, would you be prepared to be the authentic leader to guide the changes he has laid out?
2. What are the limits to leadership's transparency? When should you not practice transparency?
3. Does your "talk match your walk" on a consistent basis? Give an example.
4. Describe the circumstances under which there was incongruity between your talk and your walk.
5. Have you recently reflected on and written out your evolving philosophy of leadership? After considering the leadership theories described in this chapter, write your philosophy of leadership in 250 words or less and share it with the class.

SUMMARY

Leadership theories and models provide us a means to examine organizational situations through different lenses. Theories help us explain, predict, and manipulate variables in leadership, providing us with tools to frame and solve problems.

Modern leadership studies began in the early 1900s when Binet began investigating intelligence. The military applied these findings during World Wars I and II for effective personnel selection and placement. After World War II, Ohio State University expanded these studies to investigate leadership traits. Trait theory evolved into a behavioral theory of leadership based on the leader's dual concern for accomplishing the task and for building and maintaining relationships. Most researchers at the time believed high task, high relationship to be the optimal leadership style.

In the 1960s, Blake and Mouton developed a four-quadrant leadership matrix which used almost identical factors—concern for production and concern for people (task and relationship orientation). Blake and Mouton posited that individuals have a dominant leadership style and that awareness of leadership style is key to leadership effectiveness.

Contingency theory expands on leadership style by trying to match the appropriate leadership style with the characteristics of the particular situation. It is called contingency theory because it suggests that the leader's effectiveness is contingent upon how well the leader's style fits the situation's characteristics. Fiedler's contingency theory is the most widely known and posits that no one ideal leadership style exists. One's leadership style must fit the situation.

Hersey and Blanchard's situational leadership theory incorporates the task and relationship thinking from the Ohio State studies, the leadership style model, and the contingency model. With situational leadership, however, the leadership style is not fixed. Leadership styles can and should change with the situation based on the maturity level of the group or individual with whom the leader is working.

House developed the path-goal theory of leadership in the early 1970s. Path-goal theory affirms that the leader behaviors depend on two situational factors: the subordinate conditions and the task characteristics. Four leader behaviors that meet workers' needs include directive, supportive, participative, and achievement-oriented behaviors. The focus of path-goal theory is to match the leadership style to the situation.

In 1978, Burns developed the concept of transformational leadership. He posited a continuum from transactional leadership to transformational leadership. Transactional leadership uses power to reward or punish to achieve a goal and gain compliance. In contrast, transformational leadership changes the organization into a more productive, satisfying, and functioning whole by advancing three concepts: The leader is a moral exemplar of the organization's mission; the leader builds awareness and articulates a vision while being attentive to the followers' needs; and the leader helps followers by building team capacity, both morally and technically.

Finally, authentic leadership is a relatively new and untested concept. While it has many definitions, all include the leader's desire to serve, integrity and ethics, a strong moral compass and core values, a pursuit of worthy objectives, a desire to empower workers for the good of the organization, and positive organizational citizenship. Basically, authentic leadership expects congruence between what the leader says and does. This requires self-examination, reflection, and clearly articulated vision.

Leadership theories frame our understanding of situations, help us explain what is happening, predict what will happen, and manipulate the situational variables to increase the probability of a successful outcome.

ENDNOTES

1. Moore, B.V. (1927). The May conference on leadership. *Personnel Journal*, 6, 124–128. The quote is from General Stewart, superintendent of West Point Military Academy, at the joint conference on leadership of the Taylor Society and the Personnel Research Foundation.
2. Jenkins, W. (1947). A review of leadership studies with particular reference to military problems. *Psychological Bulletin, 44*(1), 54–79.
3. For example, the IQ of a 10-year-old with a mental age of 12 would be computed as $12/10 \times 100 = 120$.
4. Kevles, D. (1968). Testing the army's intelligence: Psychologists and the military in World War I. *Journal of American History, 55*(3), 565–581. This article provides an excellent overview of IQ testing and how it was used in World War I.
5. Jenkins, W. (1947). A review of leadership studies with particular reference to military problems. *Psychological Bulletin, 44*(1), 54–79.
6. Terman, L. (1904). A preliminary study in the psychology and pedagogy of leadership. *The Pedagogical Seminary, 11,* 433.

7. For an excellent, name-dropping, and insightful historical account of World War II to the Ohio State leadership studies, see Shartle, C. (1979). Early years of the Ohio State leadership studies. *Journal of Management, 5*(2), 127–134.

8. Schriesheim, C., & Bird, B. (1979). Contributions of the Ohio State studies to the field of leadership. *Journal of Management, 5*(2), 135–145.

9. Stogdill, R. M. (1948). Personal factors associated with leadership: A survey of the literature. *Journal of Psychology, 25,* 35–72, p. 64.

10. Hemphill, J. K. (1949b). The leader and his group. *Educational Research Bulletin, 28*(9) 225–229, 245–246; Hemphill, J. D. (1949a). *Situational factors in leadership.* Columbus: Ohio State University, Bureau of Educational Research.

11. Hemphill. (1949b). Ibid., p. 225.

12. Stogdill, R. (1948). Personal factors associated with leadership: A survey of the literature. *Journal of Psychology, 25,* 35–71.

13. Stogdill (1948), Ibid., p. 63.

14. Lord, R. G., DeVader, C. L., & Alliger, G. M. (1986). A meta-analysis of the relation between personality traits and leadership perceptions: An application of validity generalization procedures. *Journal of Applied Psychology, 71*(3), 402–410.

15. Bass, B. (1985). *Leadership beyond expectations.* New York, NY: Free Press.

16. Yukl, G. (2002). *Leadership in organizations* (5th ed.). Upper Saddle River, NJ: Prentice Hall.

17. Goleman, D. (1995). *Emotional intelligence.* New York, NY: Bantam; Goleman, D. (2002). *Primal leadership: Realizing the power of emotional intelligence.* Boston, MA: Harvard Business School Press.

18. Stogdill, R. (1948). Personal factors associated with leadership: A survey of the literature. *Journal of Psychology, 25,* 35–71.

19. Mann, R. (1959). A review of the relationships between personality and performance in small groups. *Psychological Bulletin, 62,* 177–183.

20. Stogdill, R. (1974). *Handbook of leadership: A survey of theory and research.* New York, NY: Free Press.

21. Lord, R., DeVader, C., & Alliger, G. (1986). A meta-analysis of the relations between personality traits and leadership perceptions: An application of validity generalization procedures. *Journal of Applied Psychology, 71,* 402–410.

22. Kirkpatrick, S., & Locke, E. (1991). Leadership: Do traits matter? *Academy of Management Executive, 5*(2), 121–139.

23. Zaccaro, S., Kemp, C., & Bader, P. (2004). Leader traits and attributes. In J. Antonakis, A. Cianciolo, & R. Sternberg (Eds.), *The nature of leadership* (pp. 101–124). Thousand Oaks, CA: Sage.

24. Hemphill, J., & Coons, A. (1950). *Leader Behavior Description Questionnaire.* Columbus: Personnel Research Board, Ohio State University.

25. Halpin, A. (1966). *Theory and research in administration.* New York, NY: MacMillan.

26. Blake, R., & Mouton, J. (1964). *The managerial grid.* Houston, TX: Gulf Publishing.

27. It may also be reflected in the *Mad* magazine character Alfred E. Newman with his comment, "What, me worry?"

28. Fiedler, F. (1964). A contingency model of leadership effectiveness. In L. Berkowitz (Ed.), *Advances in experimental social psychology* (Vol. 1, pp. 149–190). New York, NY: Academic Press.

29. Hersey, P., & Blanchard, K. (1969). Life cycle theory of leadership. *Training and Development Journal, 23,* 26–34. Also see Hersey, P., & Blanchard, K. (1969). *Management of organizational behavior: Utilizing human resources.* Englewood Cliffs, NJ: Prentice Hall. Hersey and Blanchard based their model on Bill Reddin's 3-D theory. See: Reddin, W. (1967, April). The 3-D management style theory. *Training and Development Journal,* pp. 8–17.

30. Personal communication with Nick Peterson, director of marketing for the Ken Blanchard Companies, May 1, 2010. Companies included in the Fortune 500 listing change from time to time. The total number of Fortune 500 companies having used SL II training is above the 400 range.

31. A January 4, 2011, Google Scholar search of "situational leadership" turned up nearly 353,000 results.

32. It should be noted that there are subtle differences between the Hersey and Blanchard situational leadership model and the revised theory by Ken Blanchard, SL II. Differences center mostly in differentiating between the maturity level or developmental level of the group or individual and in descriptors.

33. See House, R. (1971). A path-goal theory of leader effectiveness. *Administrative Science Quarterly, 16,* 321–339; also, House, R., & Mitchell, R. (1974).

Path-goal theory of leadership. *Journal of Contemporary Business, 3,* 1–97.

34. Northouse, P. (2010). *Leadership: Theory and practice* (5th ed., p. 125). Los Angeles, CA: Sage.

35. House, R. (1996). Path-goal theory of leadership: Lessons, legacy, and a reformulated theory. *Leadership Quarterly, 3*(2), 323–352.

36. House, R., & Mitchell, R. (1974). Op. cit.

37. Northouse, P. (2010). Op. cit., p. 129.

38. Bass, B. (1998). *Transformational leadership: Industrial, military, and educational impact.* Mahwah, NJ: Erlbaum.

39. Lewin, K., Lippit, R., & White, R. K. (1939). Patterns of aggressive behavior in experimentally created social climates. *Journal of Social Psychology, 10,* 271–301.

40. Lewin, Lippit, & White. (1939). Ibid.

41. Lewin, Lippit, & White. (1939). Op. cit.

42. Burns, J. M. (1978). *Leadership* (p. 18). New York, NY: Harper & Row.

43. Bass, B. (1985). *Leadership and performance beyond expectations.* New York, NY: Free Press.

44. Bass, B., & Aviolo, B. (1990). The implications of transactional and transformational leadership for individual, team, and organizational development. *Research in Organizational Change and Development, 4,* 232–272.

45. Bass, B., & Riggio, R. (2006). *Transformational leadership* (2nd ed.). Mahwah, NJ: Erlbaum; Bass, B., & Bass, R. (2008). *The Bass handbook of leadership: Theory, research, and managerial applications* (4th ed.). New York, NY: Free Press.

46. Bass, B. (1985). Op. cit., p. 36.

47. Galanter, M. (1982). Charismatic religious sects and psychiatry: An overview. *American Journal of Psychiatry, 139,* 1539–1548.

48. Weber, M. (1947). *The theory of social and economic organizations* (T. Parsons, Trans.). New York, NY: Free Press.

49. Avolio, B. (1999). *Full leadership development.* Thousand Oaks, CA: Sage.

50. Bass, B. (1985). Op. cit., pp. 82–83.

51. Bass (1985). Op. cit., p. 83.

52. Bass, B. (1985). Op. cit., p. 81.

53. Bass (1985). Op. cit., p. 83.

54. Bass, B. (1997). Does the transactional-transformational paradigm transcend organizational and national boundaries? *American Psychologist, 52,* 130–139.

55. Bass, B., & Riggio, R. (2006). Op. cit.

56. Yukl, G. (1999). An evaluation of conceptual weaknesses in transformational and charismatic leadership theories. *Leadership Quarterly, 10*(2), 285–305.

57. *Hamlet,* Act 1, Scene 111.

58. The journal *Leadership Quarterly* believed *authentic leadership* to be such an important emerging subject that they devoted the entire June 2005 issue to the topic.

59. Walumbwa, F., Avilio, B., Gardner, W., Wernsing, T., & Peterson, S. (2008). Authentic leadership: Development and validation of a theory-based measure. *Journal of Management, 34*(1), 89–126.

60. Garner, W., Avolio, B., Luthans, F., May, D., & Walumbwa, F. (2005). "Can you see the real me?" A self-based model of authentic leader and follower development. *Leadership Quarterly, 16*(3), 345.

61. Garner, et al. (2005). Ibid.

62. Garner, et. al. (2005). Op. cit.

63. Kearnis, M. (2003). Toward a conceptualization of optimal self-esteem. *Psychological Inquiry, 14,* 1–26.

CHAPTER

Leadership, Communication, and Vision

Focus Questions

- In what ways is communication a process rather than an event?
- How does organizational culture affect communications, and vice versa?
- What is *vision* and how is it important to leadership and organizational change?
- How can leaders' use of language and symbols have an impact on organizational effectiveness?

CASE STUDY: SHAKY GROUND MIDDLE SCHOOL

Tim Jones is finishing his fifth year as principal of the 1,000-student Shaky Ground Middle School (SGMS), which has not made Adequate Yearly Progress (AYP) in the past 4 years. The superintendent of schools has given Tim 5 years to turn around the school's culture so high expectations for all students' achievement becomes the norm. Currently, an external evaluation described the school's culture as "apathetic." In his yearly evaluation conferences with the superintendent, Tim has shared what he has tried to do (in his words) "to make the faculty" achieve his vision for the school. Yearly principal evaluation ratings are unacceptable, unsatisfactory, satisfactory, good, and excellent. Three consecutive years of unsatisfactory ratings, 2 consecutive years of unacceptable ratings, or 3 years of unsatisfactory/unacceptable ratings in a 5-year period result in dismissal. The superintendent sets the principal's goals. Tim's yearly goals, results, superintendent's evaluations, and ratings are listed as follows.

Year 1

Goal. Get to know the school, the culture, the curriculum, and the teachers. Restart the parent-teacher-student association (PTSA) group, which has not functioned for the past 11 years.

Result. Mr. Jones has accurately assessed the culture, agreeing with the external evaluation, and ended the school year with a PTSA meeting with a turnout of six parents, four students, and five teachers. The school did not make AYP.

Evaluation. It appeared to take too long to understand the culture and act to improve the situation. No mention was made of the PTSA until 4 weeks before the end of school. Only two faculty meetings were held this year. It is reported that the principal stays in the office much of the day engaged in paperwork.

Rating. Satisfactory

Year 2

Goal. Increase the number of faculty meetings as a way to provide two-way communication with the staff toward establishing a vision of excellence in teaching and learning. Develop a vision for Shaky Ground Middle School with the teachers, parents, and students. Initiate the motto of "Solid Achievement at Shaky" with teachers, students, and parents. Increase attendance at PTSA meetings. Establish interdisciplinary teams for all grades.

Result. Mr. Jones held four faculty meetings and developed some communication. He still tended to read his notes to the faculty and considered this a meeting. He distributed the vision statement and the motto, and he instructed teachers to establish interdisciplinary teams at each grade level and share the vision and school motto with students and parents. A 1-hour videotape on interdisciplinary instruction was purchased and played at one of the faculty meetings, after which he dismissed the group. The principal assigned names to the interdisciplinary teams. Attendance at PTSA increased to eight parents, four students, and six teachers. The school made AYP by less than 1 point.

Evaluation. The school made AYP. Teachers, parents, and students were not involved in developing the vision statement, the motto, or the interdisciplinary team concept. Interdisciplinary teams functioned poorly with no guidance from the principal. A 1-hour in-service activity on the first day back to school is insufficient professional development and poorly timed. The principal needs to monitor classrooms during the day to monitor progress of interdisciplinary teaching and learning.

Rating. Unsatisfactory

Year 3

Goals. Involve teachers, parents, and students in reshaping the vision statement to increase community buy-in. Increase PTSA involvement. Provide effective, sustained professional development on interdisciplinary teaching during the year and monitor classrooms closely for progress. Work to increase the effectiveness of two named teachers or document shortcomings sufficiently to recommend dismissal.

Result. PTSA meetings increased in attendance to 25 parents, 15 students, and 18 teachers. The vision and mission statements were discussed at faculty and PTSA meetings. A local university professor was brought in to provide six 90-minute professional development activities (one each 6-week marking period) on interdisciplinary teaching during the school year. Teachers report more comfort with teaming. Although the school did not make AYP this year, there was significant growth in scores from grade 6 to grade 7. Two named teachers were placed on "plan of improvement" status with specific benchmarks for improvement.

Evaluation. Goals were met. Professional development activities were implemented. The principal needs to work on communication skills. Simply having a discussion at faculty and PTSA meetings does not meet the standard of involvement or of having the school vision adopted. The principal should monitor classroom practices to check on teacher use of effective interdisciplinary teaching methods provided in the professional development. It is still reported that the principal spends too little time monitoring classrooms. The faculty and parents have no sense of mission or vision. This must be a priority for next year.

Rating. Satisfactory

Year 4

Goals. Continue to increase involvement in the PTSA. The faculty, staff, and PTSA cannot be given a vision statement and then discuss it. There must be involvement to develop a shared sense of mission and vision. Once this has been accepted, build consensus around it. The two teachers on plan of improvement status need to have demonstrated significant progress toward the established goals or there should be sufficient documentation provided to the superintendent for dismissal. Student achievement should increase for the school to make AYP.

Result. Involvement in the PTSA remained static from last year. At three faculty meetings, the principal delegated the discussion of the school mission and vision to the new assistant principal, who was not certain what direction she should take, and he left the meetings. Teachers are uncertain and frustrated about what direction the school should be taking in improving student achievement. The two teachers on plan of improvement were recommended for dismissal, but insufficient documentation was forwarded to the superintendent's office for action. While the principal was certain he had told the teachers he was recommending their dismissal, the teachers thought that Mr. Jones told them they would be reappointed. Nothing about recommending termination was placed in writing.

Evaluation. None of the goals have been met. The principal appears to have abandoned involvement in shaping the school mission and vision for faculty and the community. He has apparently turned the matter over to a new assistant principal who states that she was not aware that she was to be given this responsibility prior to the faculty meeting. The two teachers placed on plan of improvement status had insufficient documentation for the superintendent to recommend dismissal to the board. This created an embarrassing situation when the superintendent notified the two teachers of a dismissal hearing, and they were unaware of the situation. AYP has not been made.

Rating. Unacceptable

Year 5

Goals. Year 4 goals are still in place as they were not met last year. Mr. Jones is reminded that should an unsatisfactory or unacceptable rating be made this year, his contract will not be renewed per school board policy regarding 3 years of unsatisfactory/unacceptable ratings within a 5-year period.

Result. PTSA involvement declined. The principal held monthly faculty meetings and demanded the faculty adopt the vision and mission statements. Professional development on interdisciplinary teaching stopped. The two teachers on plan of improvement were rated as satisfactory, although there are no records of the teachers being observed this year and no documentation of improved teaching behaviors.

Evaluation. AYP was not achieved. The principal was seen as being hostile to the faculty and parents, blaming them for the school's lack of improvement. Four faculty meetings were held and described as negative, with the principal blaming teachers for the school's failure to rally around the need to increase student achievement. The new assistant principal resigned in the middle of the year. She claimed that the principal blamed her for not getting the school to adopt the vision and mission; he recommended that her contract not be renewed and advised her to return to the classroom where she had tenure. Mr. Jones visited very few classes—only two documented observations existed in writing. PTSA involvement dropped off to year 1 levels.

Rating. Unacceptable. Mr. Jones's contract will not be renewed.

Case Study Questions

1. What appears to be Mr. Jones's primary problem?
2. What leadership behaviors would have made him more effective in his job?
3. What could Mr. Jones have done differently to develop a school vision that the various school communities could have accepted?
4. If you were the principal, what would you do differently given the circumstances?

INTRODUCTION

Communication is the organization's lifeblood, providing direction and meaning to focus employees' attention and energies on the overall mission and the tasks at hand. School leaders' effectiveness with speaking, writing, and presenting information and ideas to employees, students, parents, and community members has a tremendous impact on the organization's success. Yet language is highly complex and ambiguous; listeners respond to messages with their own idiosyncratic interpretations influenced by the organizational culture and their own prior experiences. While communication breakdowns cannot always be avoided, having a better understanding of the communication process and enhancing one's language skills can make misunderstandings less likely to occur.

Defining and articulating a compelling vision for what the school can be and expressing this idea in words and actions that connect with employees' values can increase motivation, commitment, and effectiveness. It can also strengthen organizational culture. Understanding the power of effective communications can help school leaders more skillfully use language and behavior to increase their own and their organization's success.

THE COMMUNICATIONS PROCESS

Leaders, managers, employees, and clients all rely on speaking, listening, reading, and seeing as key ways to convey expectations, relay directions, ask questions, and receive feedback. They expect effective word choices to deliver a clear message that can be easily and accurately understood and that can prompt the appropriate behaviors. Since language is inherently ambiguous, however, occasional miscommunications are unavoidable.

Communication can be defined as "the transmission and/or reception of signals through some channel(s) that humans interpret based on a probabilistic system that is deeply influenced by context."[1] We transmit information by talking, writing, texting, drawing, demonstrating, and touching. We receive information by listening, reading, watching, smelling, or touching. Signals can be verbal, nonverbal, or visual. The array of channels can include face to face, cell phones, memos, videos, skype, and e-mails. Simply having access to these resources, however, does not help people communicate more effectively.

Recognizing how communication works in organizations and understanding its opportunities and limitations can help leaders develop both a heightened awareness and keener tools with which to promote organizational effectiveness.

Language Is Ambiguous

Language is inherently ambiguous. Words can have a variety of meanings. One researcher noted that for the 500 most frequently used words in the English language, more than 14,000 definitions exist.[2] For example, politicians run races but not necessarily with their legs. A customer may intend to bring a deposit to the bank, but unless we know whether the "deposit" is cash and bonds or bait and tackle, we cannot be certain whether the destination is a large commercial building on Main Street or the river on the town's outskirts. Even simple, everyday words can bring confusion unless they have additional details.

Given language's elusiveness, we can assign probabilities to the various likely interpretations. Context clues, such as adding "to deposit a check," help us to determine the bank's true meaning. Communicators who do not grasp the probabilistic nature of interpretations may create difficulties for themselves and others. Different listeners may interpret the message in varying ways. Context information increases the likelihood of some interpretations while it decreases the odds of others.

Context is more than helpful environmental clues needed to decode a message's meaning. It includes corporate culture and ethics. Context is also individualistic. Each person creates a highly idiosyncratic perspective of past experiences, values, assumptions (accurate and inaccurate), and personal sensitivities. As a result, context emerges from complex interactions among people, situations, and personal relationships.[3] These factors are mostly beyond the speaker's control.

Contexts develop through a dynamic process. Past communication experiences build a very powerful set of background cues. For example, repeating certain experiences under similar circumstances and comparable settings—such as greeting colleagues each morning with a cheery, "Good morning. How are you doing?" or receiving frequent and credible praise from one's supervisor—prompts persons to make certain interpretations more likely and others less likely. After many similar brief impersonal salutations, the first context is construed as a ritual greeting rather than as a request for a health update. Likewise, the second context is understood as a positive work environment, and future messages from the supervisor are likely to be (at least initially) experienced as positive. Therefore, correctly understanding a message's context helps speakers reasonably assume that meanings will be shared.

Without a doubt, construing meaning is a complicated process. Leaders can, however, achieve a more reasonable certainty that the meaning will be received as intended when leaders fully understand how people interpret messages. Every person uses a similar process to construct meaning. Becoming an effective communicator requires inferring how the content and context will interact in the receiver's mind. The more familiar leaders are with the contexts in which employees interpret actions and words—the more they learn about employees' attitudes, environment, needs, and wants—the greater the likelihood that leaders can appropriately construct their message and accurately predict the probable interpretations. Getting to know employees and colleagues as workers and as persons not only builds relationships but also helps leaders gain valuable cues about the employees' daily realities. Similarly, "management by wandering around" (MBWA) helps administrators develop an intuitive understanding of the varied milieus that employees use to influence their interpretation.[4] Effective communicators know their audience and the influences that actively shape the meaning that the listeners actually hear.

Preventing Communication Breakdowns

Messages can be misunderstood and communication can fail in a variety of ways. Speaking clearly, precisely, and believably is essential to achieve the desired results—but it does not guarantee them. Communication is not like selecting arrows from a quiver, accurately aiming, and deliberately releasing them at the target. Communication depends on more than the sender's skill. Message receivers are not passive information receptors who react as intended if the words hit "on the mark."

What is clear and precise to one person is not always clear and precise to another. Figure 5–1 illustrates a model designed to help engineers decide how to most efficiently transmit electrical impulses from point A to point B.[5] This model reflects a simplistic view of communication as moving in one direction. More sophisticated models using social-psychological factors would develop from this schema.[6]

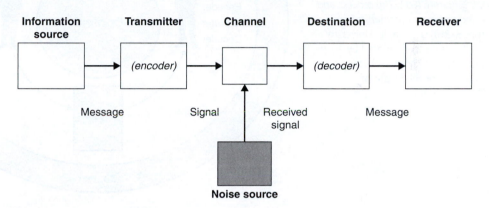

FIGURE 5–1

One-Way Communication Model (Source: From Clampitt, Phillip G. (2009). *Communicating for managerial effectiveness*. Thousand Oaks, CA: Sage Publications. Copyright 2009 by Sage Publications Inc. Books. Reproduced with permission of Sage Publications Inc. Books in the format Textbook via Copyright Clearance Center.)

Whether using an industrial or humanistic frame of reference, the one-way communication model assumes that the message sent equals the message received. Words are assumed to contain all the meaning necessary to ensure the receivers' appropriate responses. Today, we know that this view is naive. Given language's inherent vagueness and the array of personal and organizational contexts within which receivers may (mis)interpret the message, communication failures are to be expected. Communication is not an event. Rather, it is a process in which the message receivers actively construct meaning from the message's content and context. Yet the sender will not recognize that any message distortions occurred unless some type of feedback is received.[7]

In contrast to the one-way arrow approach illustrated in Figure 5–1, the circuit approach in Figure 5–2 involves networking and making connections. This more complex communication model stresses feedback and response, relationship as well as content variations, and understanding over compliance. This circuit model views communication as a two-way process involving a dynamic interplay of active senders and receivers.

FIGURE 5–2

The Circuit Model of Communications (Source: Based on Clampitt, P. G. (2010). *Communicating for managerial effectiveness. Problems, strategies, solutions* (p. 34). Thousand Oaks, CA: Sage. Originally from Schramm, W. L. (1954). How communication works. In W. Schramm (Ed.), *The process and effects of mass communications* (pp. 3–26). Urbana, IL: University of Illinois Press. Reprinted by permission of Mary Coberly executor for the Estate of W.L. Schramm.)

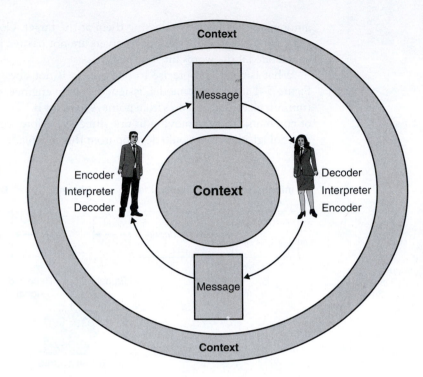

Leaders who understand communication as a two-way interactive process recognize the importance of rapport building and creating a team environment. Listening to employees, receiving feedback, and generating interaction are important contextual factors that reduce message ambiguity. Communicators who follow this model focus on delivering a clear message and also pay attention to the meaning that the listeners may impose. The communicator's goal is not to increase employees' productivity by making them feel happy and valued, but to increase their accurate understanding and thereby prompt appropriate actions. In addition, building strong relationships, encouraging people to speak openly about their concerns, and providing constructive feedback literally fosters healthier employees. Researchers have found that positive social interactions at work are associated with instant and lasting effects on the cardiovascular, immune, and neuroendocrine systems.[8]

Even with careful attention to context and content, communication failures may still occur. People do not always interpret a message in the same way. Many people are poor listeners who misinterpret remarks. Then too, understanding a message does not automatically lead to agreement or compliance. Teachers may accurately understand, for example, that they are expected to meet with parents in the evenings after a long school day but may resent doing so because they are exhausted and have family obligations.

Constructing an Effective Organizational Culture

Leaders' communication practices shape "the way we do things around here." *Culture* refers to the intellectual, emotional, and physical environment that influences the values, beliefs, and actions of a group, a society, or organization members. *Corporate culture*, therefore, is an organization's underlying belief and value structure that employees collectively share and that it expresses symbolically in a variety of ways.[9] Both a process and a condition, an organization's culture is relatively stable as well as continually evolving as it meets new challenges. Organizational leaders' implicit and explicit decisions and the ways they express these encourage certain values and discourage others to become part of the organization's culture.

Organizational culture influences how its members process stimuli, focus attention to certain cues and not to others, and regulate day-to-day activities. It directs employee attention to tasks the organization prizes and ignores the rest. At the same time, the organizational culture fosters ties between employees and the organization, encouraging individual members to identify with what the organization stands for.

An organization's culture matters. It influences the organization's functioning in many ways. Culture affects effectiveness and productivity, shapes how the organization analyzes and solves problems, impacts how the group will respond to change, and inspires employee motivation and client satisfaction.

Culture exerts a powerful force on an organization's effectiveness and productivity. In one study of 207 companies over an 11-year period, James Kotter (1992) found that the companies that live by their stated values experienced four times more growth in revenues than did their peers.[10] Another eye-opening study of 160 companies over a 10-year period found that culture was one of four business fundamentals that high-performing companies must master.[11] These organizations design and support a culture that encourages outstanding individual and team contributions and holds all employees responsible for success. The right culture with the correct strategy, structure, and incentives provides employees with focus, purpose, and motivation. The expectations for all are clear, and employees have direction and personally meaningful reasons to efficiently coordinate their actions for a common goal. The result is less waste, more innovation, and higher productivity. Measured in school terms, a positive culture means greater student achievement and increased teacher and staff satisfaction.

Culture also influences how an organization makes and carries out decisions. Once established, the culture prescribes certain ways of believing, thinking, and acting. It may encourage active exploration of important alternatives to solve problems or it can discourage meaningful interaction, making it difficult for people to conceptualize their dilemmas in a way that makes them solvable. Likewise, culture determines whether all important planning and decision making occurs unilaterally in the leader's office or whether it is shared with other organizational members who can apply their varying perspectives and insights to correctly define the problem and find and implement workable solutions.

In addition, culture influences how the organization will respond to change—actively encouraging it or consistently inserting obstacles to prevent it. Public school culture offers a case in point. In the late 19th century, America's public schools adopted industrialization's culture of organizational efficiency to make them "more productive." Between 1900 and 1930, school administrators began to see themselves as managers, rather than as educators, using scientific management ideas to help their schools accommodate the large numbers of immigrant children at low cost. These "industrial schools" were structured to maximize competition between students and to reduce the relationships between teachers and pupils. Children entered school and moved through the grades with their age peers, changing classes at predetermined intervals to ringing bells. Academic subjects became departmentalized, artificially separating subjects that appeared integrated in the real world. Students competed with peers for grades, class rank, and access to further education. Students who could not keep up dropped out, usually finding employment in the low-skill, labor-intensive economy.

Today we know that children grow and develop at different rates. Moving students with their chronological age peers rewards those with quicker development and extra educational opportunities outside school. Likewise, the modern workplace relies on high-level knowledge, reasoning, problem solving, and teamwork. As a result, the public school culture, which is relatively unchanged from the early 1900s, might actually be contributing to today's "achievement gap"—shorthand for the many learning and achievement difficulties faced in educating today's highly diverse student populations for work and life in an information-rich and global economy.[12]

Finally, culture affects employee motivation and client satisfaction.[13] Although public schools do not have customers, they do have administrators, faculty, and staff as well as students, their parents, communities, and local businesses who care about how well schools are performing. Employees who believe in what they are doing, what their organization does, and the essential purpose it stands for can become highly motivated to work for these ends. When schools make the policy and practice changes necessary to effectively educate all students to high levels and treat all employees with respect and fairness, the school culture nurtures and sustains this positive momentum. In these situations, the stated school culture as ideally expressed in its mission statement is congruent with the unstated culture of tangible practice.

In contrast, when the school culture speaks of "educating all students to their fullest potential" but visibly provides only certain students with quality teachers, rigorous and coherent curricula, and detailed and ongoing feedback to support learning, then the culture espouses one philosophy but practices another. Faced with such a disconnect between philosophy and practice, employees, students, parents, and the community can become discouraged, disillusioned, and cynical. Poor performance all around may result.

No organization—or individual—can always practice what it preaches. The larger the gaps between the stated and practiced culture, the greater the discouragement, cynicism, and poor performance. Organizational culture needs to be consistent with organizational strategy and the marketplace demands.[14] When the external realities change, organizational cultures must also change. In business and commerce, organizations with dysfunctional cultures either adapt or fail. When public school cultures do not adapt sufficiently to external realities, students and teachers fail.

ACTIVITY 5.1   Communication and Culture at Shaky Ground Middle School

Case Study Question 1: What appears to be Mr. Jones's primary problem?

Mr. Jones's behaviors as a leader suggest that he is a very poor communicator. Discuss as a class:

1. What examples from the case study suggest that Mr. Jones is not an effective listener, is not an effective speaker, may not be comfortable interacting with other people, and does not have a deep understanding of the communication process?

2. In what ways does the superintendent suggest that Mr. Jones might positively transform the apathetic school culture and increase student achievement? How were the superintendent's annual goals for Mr. Jones supposed to increase both the principal's and teachers' understanding of important school outcomes and motivate their behaviors toward these ends?

3. How might Mr. Jones use "management by wandering around" and frequent classroom visits to change the school's culture by developing open and respectful relationships with the teachers and providing clarity about the school vision and mission?

4. How might developing strong and respectful relationships with teachers assist Mr. Jones in gaining their support for better teaching and learning at Shaky Ground Middle School?

5. How is the school's culture affecting its functioning and productivity, how the organization makes and carries out decisions, how the organization analyzes and solves problems, how the organization influences and motivates employees and clients to make changes?

LEADERSHIP AND VISION

The effective leader teaches employees what the organization values, why it is valued, and how to transform values into action. Like students, employees do not always see the worth of what they are doing. They may become tired, discouraged, or even resistant. Far-sighted leaders help employees build commitment to the organizational values and translate these ideals from mission-statement rhetoric into personal dedication and actions.

According to Conger (1991), the "language of leadership" can be broken into two distinct skill categories. The first is the process of defining the organization's purpose in a meaningful way. This is the leader's message—the vision—and this process is called *framing*. The second skill is the leader's ability to use symbolic language to give emotional power to his or her message. This is a process of *rhetorical crafting*. While the message provides a sense of direction, rhetoric heightens its emotional and motivational appeal and determines whether it will be sufficiently memorable to influence the organization's day-to-day decision making.[15] This section will discuss vision, and the next will consider rhetorical crafting.

Before the 1980s, *vision* was mostly a research concept for scholars studying political leadership of social or religious movements. Rarely was it considered within the business or educational leadership literature.[16] Since the 1980s, the leadership focus has shifted from traits and leader behaviors to the need for leaders to articulate a vision to their followers, especially in organizations undergoing major change.[17] Shared vision is also basic to complex organizations of the future.

Defining Vision

Throughout the years, *vision* has been thought of either as a faddish, trendy, and charismatic concept or as a fundamental attribute of effective leadership, the basis of one's power to lead.[18] Vision's importance has been emphasized by theoretical[19] and research[20] leadership scholars. Specifically, researchers have asserted that an organization with a well-articulated vision can achieve sustained competitive advantage over those organizations lacking such a vision. Direction setting and organizational management are the two essential ways in which leaders add value to their organization.

As Bennis and Nanus (1985) defined it, vision refers to a cognitive image of a desired future state.[21] In leadership, vision is a mental model of an ideal future state which offers a picture of what could be—a realistic, credible, attractive future for the organization.[22] An effective leader creates a compelling image that guides people's behavior.

Bennis and Nanus observed, "A vision is a target that beckons."[23] Thomas Jefferson, Henry Ford, and Martin Luther King Jr. each had a unique vision that powered great change efforts and achievements. When President John Kennedy (in 1961) set the almost unimaginable goal of placing a man on the moon by 1970, and when Microsoft founder Bill Gates aimed at putting a computer on every desk and in every home, they were concentrating attention on worthwhile, highly challenging, and attainable changes. A vision provides a bridge from the present to the future. Only when you know where you want to go can you plan how to get there. Conversely, if you don't know where you are going, any road will take you there.

Leaders bring vision into action by sharing it with others and by championing a particular image of what is possible, desirable, and intended for the enterprise's future. An essential leadership skill is the capacity to influence and organize meaning for the organization's members. Leaders articulate and define what has previously remained unsaid. They invent images, metaphors, and mental models that help direct attention and shape action.[24] Bennis and Nanus confirmed, "This image . . . may be as vague as a dream or as precise as a goal or mission statement."[25] By doing this, leaders bring together or challenge the prevailing wisdom.

Ultimately, vision can be defined as a cognitive construction or a specific mental model, a conceptual representation used both to understand system operations and to guide actions within it.[26]

Characteristics of Vision

Because vision is essential to leadership, understanding vision is a critical part of becoming an effective leader. Research on visionary leadership suggests that organizational visions have five characteristics:[27]

- ◆ A *picture*. A vision creates a picture of a future that is better than the present, an ideal image of where a group or organization should be going. This picture may be an outline not fully developed but inspiring and attractive when presented effectively.
- ◆ A *change*. A vision represents a change in the status quo and moves an organization or system toward a more positive future. Changes may be in rules, procedures, goals, values, or rituals. They take the best features of the prior system and strengthen them in pursuit of a new goal.
- ◆ *Values*. A vision is grounded in values, and advocates for positive transformations in organizational and individual principles. A school leader who emphasizes that every student is important expresses the dominant ideal of human dignity and worth. A school leader who emphasizes that every student should have access and support for success in high-status courses expresses the dominant values of fairness and justice.

◆ *A map.* A vision provides a clearly marked path or direction to follow, a guiding philosophy that offers meaning and purpose. When people know an organization's overarching goals, principles, and values, it is easier for them to recognize who they are and how they contribute to the organization.

◆ *A challenge.* A vision challenges people to transcend the status quo to do something to benefit others. Vision dares and inspires people to commit themselves to worthwhile causes.

When widely shared throughout the organization, vision can help the entire enterprise make sense to its employees. It creates coherence out of separate parts and encourages individuals to commit and work toward important common goals.

How Vision Affects the Organization

Bert Nanus, professor of business administration at the University of Southern California, and a well-known leadership expert and author, explained that vision is so powerful because it grabs attention and provides focus by:[28]

◆ *Creating meaning for everyone in the organization.* Vision cuts through confusion and makes the world understandable. It helps explain why things are done the way they are, why some things are considered good and rewarded while others are not. Once people see the big picture, they can understand how their own jobs, skills, and interests relate to it.

◆ *Providing a worthwhile challenge.* Vision stretches people by showing them a collaborative accomplishment in which they can be part. Being part of a team with a positive goal generates pride and makes people feel important, urging them to higher levels of commitment and performance.

◆ *Energizing members.* Vision gives people something to believe in. Being committed to a shared goal is exhilarating and exciting. It encourages risk taking, experimentation, and new ways to think, behave, and learn.

◆ *Bringing the future into the present.* Vision allows one to imagine and name what can be, making it real right now. Imagining and naming a compelling vision can be genuine enough to alter perceptions and attitudes, to concentrate and direct resources, to modify today's decisions, to define what is essential, and to filter out distractions.

◆ *Creating a common identity.* Vision encourages people to work together with a sense of common ownership and purpose. A common identity fosters cooperation and promotes synergy, aligning people's interests in a shared direction.

Vision is the main tool leaders use to guide from the front, showing the way. The positive and potent image of the organization as it might be allows leaders to inspire, attract, align, and energize others, empowering them to become part of a collective endeavor dedicated to achieving an attractive and valuable end. Organizations without vision begin to stagnate. Managers cannot agree on priorities and become less willing to take risks. Forces for the status quo go unchallenged. The initiatives for innovation fade, conflicts become difficult to resolve, and a downward spiral begins.[29]

How Leaders Articulate a Vision

Leaders must be able to explain and describe their vision to others. They do this by adapting the vision to their audience, highlighting its ideals, selecting the correct language and symbols, using inclusive language, and providing proper task and goal specificity.

Leaders adapt the vision to their audience. Most people have a drive for consistency and will not change unless the required adjustment is not too different from their present state.[30] Leaders articulate the vision to fit within others' latitude of acceptance by modifying it to their listeners.[31] If the vision demands too big a transformation, it will be rejected. If it is articulated as fitting closely with the members' values and ideals, and does not demand too great an adjustment, it will be accepted.

Leaders highlight the vision's values by emphasizing how the image presents ideals worth following. Understanding the vision's values helps individuals and group members find meaning for their own work, allows them to identify with something larger than themselves, and connects them to a larger community.

Articulating a vision also requires *selecting the right language*. Effective leaders use words and symbols that motivate and inspire listeners. Words describing a vision should be affirming, uplifting, hopeful, and worthy. Symbols can also express a vision and bring group cohesion. For example, Uncle Sam is the national personification of the United States, and more specifically, of the American government. He is shown as an elderly White man with white hair and a goatee, dressed in clothing that recalls the U.S. flag—a top hat with white stars on a blue band and red and white striped trousers. The well-known "I Want You" poster of Uncle Sam pointing directly at the viewer was used extensively during World Wars I and II to recruit soldiers. At that time, the government used Uncle Sam as a symbol with whom most Americans could identify—and follow his suggestion to enlist. Likewise, a college football team is more likely to energize its students and alumni with mascots such as Bruins, Monarchs, Cavaliers, or Volunteers rather than have their symbol be an aardvark, sloth, or bunny.

Next, leaders need to describe vision to others using inclusive language that links people to the vision and makes them part of the process. Words like *we* and *our* are inclusive words that enlist participation and build community around a shared goal.

Finally, leaders must describe their vision with enough task and goal specification that individuals understand what they are to do if they are to accomplish their goal. Direction needs to become increasingly clearer and concrete the closer the leader (or the leader's agents, the managers) gets to those who will actually put the vision into play through implementation.

If leaders can clearly express a vision that is tailored to their audience, emphasize the vision's intrinsic worth, choose uplifting words and symbols, use inclusive language, and provide enough detail that group members know what they are to do, leaders increase the chances for the vision's adoption and eventual goal achievement.

How Leaders Implement a Vision

In addition to creating and expressing a vision, leaders must translate the vision into an organizational reality. This requires significant and sustained leadership effort. Leaders must not only "talk the talk" but also "walk the walk." They must model to others the attitudes, values, and behaviors the vision expresses. In this way, the leader becomes a living embodiment or symbol of the vision's ideals. If the vision is to promote the success of every student by understanding, appreciating, and using the community's diverse cultural, social, and intellectual resources, then the leader must be seen inviting and securing diverse community participation on school improvement committees, in parent-teacher-student associations, and on curriculum advisory committees. The leader must build and sustain positive relationships with families and caregivers. When people see the leader living the vision, he or she builds credibility that inspires others to convey and live out similar values.

Making a vision into a reality is a step-by-step process that takes continuous attention and effort, supporting others' actions in the day-to-day activities that lead to accomplishing the larger goal. Vision implementation is not a solitary act. It requires collaboration. Leaders must work together with others to accomplish their common purpose.

ACTIVITY 5.2   Defining a Vision for Shaky Ground Middle School

Case Study Question 2: What leadership behaviors would have made Mr. Jones more effective in his job?

An essential leadership skill is the capacity to influence and organize meaning for the organization's members by creating and expressing a vision using positive images, metaphors, and mental models.

Given the five characteristics of vision and the goals suggested by the superintendent, write one or two sentences that Mr. Jones might use to articulate a vision to promote the success of each student at Shaky Ground Middle School.

Working first in pairs, and then sharing answers with the entire class, compose vision sentences for:

1. A picture—an ideal image of where the group is going.
2. A change—a transformation from the status quo to a positive future.
3. Values—advocate for positive changes in organization and individual principles and standards.
4. A map—a clearly marked direction, a guiding philosophy with enough task and goal specificity.
5. A challenge—a dare that inspires people to commit themselves to worthwhile causes.

How might Mr. Jones use these vision statements to engage and motivate his faculty and community in defining and implementing the new direction and goals for Shaky Ground Middle School?

"Clock Building, Not Time Telling"[32]

Leadership for change is more than tapping into organizational and employees' ideals and communicating a vision for a better future. The most successful leadership is focused on creating a growing and sustainable organization as much as (if not more than) on designing a more marketable product or process.

For their book, *Built to Last* (2004), Jim Collins, management researcher, educator, and writer in Boulder, Colorado, along with Jerry Porras, professor at Stanford University's Graduate School of Business, investigated what visionary leadership looked like in well-established, healthy companies. During a 6-year study comparing 18 thriving organizations with less successful business counterparts, Collins and Porras developed a set of guidelines and principles that all organizations can use to keep themselves growing.[33] In the process, they clarified the role of vision in organizational success and longevity.

Collins and Porras likened a company's longevity to time telling and clock building. According to the authors, "time telling" is having a great idea or being a charismatic visionary leader while "clock building" is creating a company that can flourish far beyond the presence of any single leader and through many product life cycles. Collins and Porras explained the importance of building an organization's "core value system" and sense of purpose rather than relying on great product ideas or charismatic leaders, and paying too much attention to profit. "Clock building" is Collins and Porras's metaphor for developing organizational culture and capacity.

To these authors, no "right" set of core values exists. The crucial variable is not the content of the organization's ideology but how deeply it believes—and how consistently it lives—its ideology. These core values form a rock-solid foundation that doesn't bend with trends or fashion but instead guides the organization for decades. Visionary companies focus primarily on outperforming themselves, continuously improving to be better tomorrow than they are today.

Collins and Porras found that the most successful companies were not those that started with a "great idea" with the company built as a vehicle for the product, but rather those that saw the product as a vehicle for the company. Examples of "be a clock builder, not a time-keeper" are instructive. Henry Ford was able to take advantage of the Model T concept because he already had a company in place as a launching pad. Sam Walton started in 1945 with a single Ben Franklin franchise five-and-dime store in small-town Newport, Arkansas. He was confident that if employees did their work well and were good to their customers, the company would grow. The concept of rural retail discount store jumped out almost 20 years later.[34]

In schools, "clock building, not time telling" means creating a robust culture, employee capacity, and instructional processes that support every student's success and every educator's growth. To accomplish such clock building, the principal collaborates with teachers and others to build a shared vision and mission. All staff members develop their leadership and instructional knowledge and skills aligned with the vision and mission. Harnessing timely and detailed feedback to inform decisions and practices, they implement plans to collect and use data to identify goals, assess organizational effectiveness, promote organizational learning, and ensure accountability for every student's academic and social success. They monitor and evaluate the impact of the instructional program, revising strategies as necessary in a cycle of continuous and sustainable improvement. Focused on the goal of supporting every student's success, the "clock building" school has the ability to constantly assess its effectiveness and make necessary adjustments to keep advancing its purpose.

In short, building the organization (building the clock, culture, or employee capacity)—not the product (telling the time or reporting achievement test scores)—is the ultimate creation. All products, services, and great ideas eventually become obsolete. But a visionary company (or school) does not become outdated if it has the organizational ability to continually adjust and evolve beyond its existing product line. Similarly, all visionary leaders eventually move on, retire, or die. But a visionary company—or school—does not necessarily fail if it has the strength and culture to survive beyond any individual leader.[35]

Research on Leadership and Vision

Despite vision's importance to leadership and organizational effectiveness, few studies on leadership and vision exist.[36] Those that do tend to be anecdotal,[37] qualitative, and case analysis based rather than empirical.[38] The few empirical studies typically have methodological limitations, such as occurring in training contexts rather than being observed and assessed in the workplace. Agreeing on a common definition for *visionary leadership* also creates difficulties operationalizing the vision construct in any empirical study.

Nonetheless, vision has been studied as a blend of charismatic leadership in a wide variety of samples and industries, with generally positive findings between this kind of leadership and followers' performance, attitudes, and perceptions.[39] Likewise, research has demonstrated vision's significant contributions to organizational effectiveness.[40] Attention to vision was found to be a key strategy used by 90 leaders who enlisted others in a common endeavor.[41] Lack of vision appears to be associated with failed attempts to manage organizational change.[42] In short, research has found that vision presents a value-based direction for an organization and provides a rationale for strategic decision making.

Vision is not only associated with increased competitive performance, but it is also essential to sustaining it. One study hypothesized that European sustainable enterprises adopted the long-term perspective for managing their organizations because it allowed them more time to communicate and enact a vision and also offered a cognitive map to assign organizational resources.[43] Another study was among the first to find positive relationships between executive vision and attributes of brevity, challenge, future orientation, aspirations, abstractness, clarity, stability and vision content, and organizational performance in business firms.[44] These features have also been found positively but indirectly related to customer satisfaction, and directly related to staff satisfaction.[45]

The theoretical literature reports few studies on the critical components of effective visions or how such visions are formed. However, these available investigations do indicate positive relationships between vision attributes and content and organizational performance. Again, effective organizational vision is vital to its success.[46]

ACTIVITY 5.3   Expressing Vision and Mission at Shaky Ground Middle School

Case Study Question 2: What leadership behaviors would have made Mr. Jones more effective in his job?

Transforming a vision into organizational reality requires a leader who can live the vision and work with others. Discuss as a class:

1. If Mr. Jones were to enact the following leadership behaviors, what would he be doing or saying?
   a. Setting high performance expectations for students and teachers
   b. Modeling vision-related behaviors in his everyday activities
   c. Expressing confidence and empowering administrators, teachers, and staff
   d. Taking innovative and courageous actions
   e. Mentoring and coaching administrators and teachers
2. If Mr. Jones effectively enacted the above leadership behaviors, what would Shaky Ground Middle School administrators, teachers, parents, and community members be doing or saying regarding the following?
   a. Identifying with the school's vision
   b. Experiencing higher efficacy and motivation
   c. Feeling confidence, trust, and loyalty toward their leader
   d. Exhibiting high levels of effort and persistence
   e. Showing good organizational citizen behaviors
   f. "Clock building, not time telling"

Since ancient times, vision has been essential to managing people to achieve a goal. While the vision concept has critics, the empirical findings suggest that effective vision makes a positive impact on performance outcomes in practice, directly or indirectly. Vision will continue to play an essential role in improving and sustaining organizational performance.

LEADERSHIP, LANGUAGE, AND SYMBOLS

Across time, cultures, and geography, people want events in their lives to make sense. *Making sense* is the process of arranging our understanding of experience so we can know what has happened, what is happening, and what likely will happen. Making sense of our experience means constructing knowledge of our world and ourselves.

Each day, we experience large amounts of information through our five senses. To make these data meaningful, we create mental maps to guide our behavior based on our images of what the world is about.[47] To a large degree, these maps determine how we perceive the world and what our choices and behaviors will be.

We unconsciously store information and experiential memories as symbols and images. These silent, invisible ciphers create the assumptions that guide our thoughts and actions. Values and beliefs mediate between our inner world of symbols and the external, observable world of everyday life. For instance, all things being equal, we would rather have a job that pays $$$$$ than a job that pays $$. We express our values and beliefs through our language and our choices.

Arguably, if the era of managing by dictate has ended and an era of managing by inspiration is replacing it—that is, leading by pull rather than by push—chief among the new leadership skills will be the ability to rhetorically craft and articulate a highly motivational message.[48] A critical link exists between a leader's ability to powerfully communicate and the ability to connect employees' values and beliefs with the organization's vision. Leaders have to be not only effective strategists but also successful rhetoricians who can energize others through the words and images they choose. "Let's go! Our students need us to help them become smarter!" is more likely to motivate colleagues than "Get started! The buses are arriving."

Leadership, Language, and Metaphor

A leader must be able to detect opportunities in the environment and describe them in ways that amplify their significance. This ability to describe is captured by a simple story:

> Two stone masons, while working on the same project, were asked what they were doing. The first replied, "I am cutting stone." The second said, "I am building a great cathedral." The latter was able to describe his work in a more sweeping and meaningful way that excited the listener about the intended outcome. To this mason, work had a higher purpose.[49]

Leadership today must embody this same ability to articulate an organization's vision and mission and communicate it in ways that inspire—that is, figuratively make the vision visible and real for the listener. In fact, *inspirational motivation*—the creation and presentation of an attractive vision of the future, the use of symbols and emotional arguments, and the demonstration of optimism and enthusiasm—is an essential characteristic of transformational and charismatic leadership.[50]

Previous research has shown that these behaviors are related to leadership effectiveness and high employee performance.[51] Further, a review of the charismatic leadership literature highlights "articulating a value based vision of the future" as one of its four essential qualities.[52]

Using Language to Frame a Vision

Vision is the way a leader describes the future purpose of his or her organization. *Frames* then are essentially snapshots that leaders take of their organization's purpose which provide a map for action. By framing an organization's mission or state of affairs, leaders interpret reality for followers. If we believe and describe the world as flat or square—or that an effective teacher can create a personalized and motivating learning environment for students—we will frame our understanding of reality through that perspective and act accordingly. Simply framing or wording an opportunity in a certain way influences our perceptions of its outcomes. In one research study, participants were told of a project having an 80% chance of success and of another project having a 20% chance of failure; then they were asked to choose one. They all chose the former, yet both outcomes are the same.[53]

Effectively framing an organizational mission ensures emotional impact, building a sense of confidence and excitement about the future. For example, a regional telephone company undergoing separation from its parent organization, AT&T, during deregulation worried about the lost revenue and product support from its parent. Fear of failure ran high until the company president cautiously reframed the organization's future from one of great uncertainty and turmoil to one of unusual and highly promising opportunity: The future is positive. We are strong and viable. Take the best from what we were, innovate to be even better, and cast off those things that could be cumbersome. With effective framing, leaders can use vision to build a sense of security and future possibilities.[54]

By selecting and amplifying specific values and beliefs, the leader further frames interpretations of events, problems, or issues as they relate to the vision. *Value amplification* is the process of identifying and elevating certain values as basic to the overall mission.[55] Research on transformational leadership confirms that the creation of values that inspire, provide meaning for, and instill a sense of purpose in an organization's members lies at the core of effective leadership.[56] When describing the organization's mission, a skillful leader will use language that highlights values or stories that illustrate ideals that employees find strongly appealing and justify their activities in highly desirable ways. For example, in his "I Have a Dream" speech, Martin Luther King Jr. framed his movement's values in terms of the nation's ideals and their protection. In this way, he heightened the significance of the African American's struggle for every American, optimizing its potential acceptance across the country by people of all races.[57]

Playing up the employees' beliefs about achieving their desired values and stressing the mission's importance as the most viable and attractive pathway to the future, leaders' language brings an emotional resonance that motivates employees. Likewise, stressing the need for the mission, stereotyping antagonists of the mission, and expressing beliefs in the organization's effectiveness build cohesion, commitment, and confidence in the organization's purpose.[58]

While framing presents leaders with an opportunity to construct an appealing and stirring force for organizational transformation, the process by which leaders communicate it is just as important. We know from research in political science that it is not uncommon for two leaders to present the same message and yet receive different responses.[59] The style of verbal communications is a critical distinguishing factor in whether the message will be remembered and endorsed or fall flat.

Rhetorical Techniques of Inspirational Leaders

A leader's words often assume their greatest impact as symbols rather than as literal meanings. Inspiring leaders use a number of rhetorical techniques such as metaphors and analogies, stories, symbolic acts, different language styles, or rhythmic devices to ensure that their message's symbolic content has a profound impact.[60]

Metaphors and analogies draw a relationship of likeness between two things—often very unlike things—and provide vividness, offer clarification, express certain emotions, or interpret reality. The power of metaphors and analogies comes from their ability to capture and illustrate a reality by appealing simultaneously to the listeners' various senses, ensuring a more vibrant experience. In 1979, when Lee Iacocca, then Chrysler Motors president, explained a decision to cut his salary to $1 after accepting U.S. government loans to save his failing auto company from bankruptcy, he used the war metaphor of a commander joining his troops in the trenches: "I didn't take $1 a year to be a martyr. I took it because I had to go into the pits." He then drew an analogy to the family, calling for "equality of sacrifice" for everyone involved, like a family getting together to pay back a loan from their rich uncle. As for those who would challenge his approach to saving Chrysler Motors, Iacocca presented himself to the American public as a four-star general going into battle, daring, "Lead, follow, or get out of the way!" With his analogy and metaphor, Iacocca implied that he and his fellow Chrysler workers were all members of a common family working hard to prove their worth.[61] And with taxpayer help, Iacocca argued, they would prevail.

Stories, too, convey more vividly the values and behaviors that are important to an organization. The story of an MBA candidate's inability to cope with the unexpected offers a case in point. The MBA candidate was being recruited by a hard-charging firm. At the end of a day full of excellent interviews, she had met with everyone except the charismatic woman who was the company's chief executive officer (CEO). At 5:30 P.M., the candidate met with the CEO who promptly invited her for drinks and dinner with another manager. At the restaurant, the group had drinks but the interview never began. Dinner ended at midnight—with still no interview conducted. The CEO then asked the candidate back to her office for the actual interview. Surprised, the young woman balked, saying she was tired and needed to return home. She was not offered the position. The company CEO repeated this story often: Company qualifications required being able to "roll with the punches" and "go the extra mile."[62] The story was a far more powerful and dramatic way of showing what the leader saw as important values and behaviors than simple statements that employees should be willing to demonstrate greater flexibility and commitment.

In addition to analogies, metaphors, and stories, leaders can advance their vision by engaging in various symbolic, verbal, and expressive acts aimed at the group. A skillful use of slogans and symbols (e.g., flags, logos, company-insignia lapel pins), rituals (e.g., singing the organizational songs, "hail-and-farewells" to newly arriving or departing organization members), labels, metaphors, and ceremonies,[63] and the creation of attractive organizational images[64] can affect not only the individual but also the shared group orientation. Using slogans, symbols, rituals, and ceremonies can give relevance to the group's ideals, wishes, and aspirations; elicit a collective sense of a forward-looking orientation; and contribute to forming an innovation-oriented culture.[65] In fact, the principal can become a living symbol by modeling and continually articulating the school's valued purposes and behaviors.[66] By emphasizing common ground, stressing communal principles and ideology, connecting followers' personal goals to the group's interests, and using symbols and symbolic language (graphic or oral), leaders can frame and communicate the common purpose and organizational unity as a desired challenge.

Paralanguage and Motivation

Paralanguage, or the sound of speech, is an additional crucial factor in effective communications. Through appropriate paralanguage, one can convey an image of self-confidence and power or just the opposite. For example, when speakers are nervous and lack confidence, they speak at a lower volume and make more speech errors such as incomplete sentences, long pauses between words, and omitted portions of words or sentences.[67] Unpolished public speakers also use speech hesitations such as *ah, um, er,* and *you know,* which interfere with the message and reduce the listeners' confidence in the speaker. These paralanguage weaknesses lessen employees' motivation to follow this leader. A more poised and practiced speaking style will avoid these mistakes and more effectively motivate followers.

Research on Language and Motivation

Inspirational motivation has been empirically linked to a range of outcomes such as extra effort,[68] ethical behavior, learning orientation, and project success.[69] Two areas of research support and explain the greater impact of metaphors and analogies over rational discourse. In the field of speech communications, research shows that these devices appear to excite the listeners' imagination and create consecutive states of tension (puzzlement and recoil) and tension release (insight and resolution).[70] No longer a passive information receiver, the listener is triggered into a state of active thinking as he or she puzzles over the meaning of the analogy, metaphor, or story, and attempts to make sense of it, usually in light of the listener's own situation. This meaning-making process is so engaging that it fosters listener attention and interest.

Studies from social psychology explain why these rhetorical devices are a more persuasive and effective means of imparting ideas. They find that people treat statistical summaries as if they were uninformative and without impact because of their abstract, impersonal nature. In contrast, brief, face-to-face comments have a substantial impact on decision making.[71] It might be concluded that information is used in proportion to its vividness and meaning to the receiver.

Recent research has also found differences between what are perceived as powerful and powerless speech styles resulting from paralanguage and using certain words. The powerless style includes speech hesitations such as *ah, you know,* and *uh;* polite phrases like *please* and *thank you;* questioning voice tones at the end of declarative statements; and hedging phrases such as *I think, I guess,* and *kinda.* The powerful style without these factors portrays the speaker as more assertive, more goal directed, and straightforward. In a study of these two styles, participants rated speakers using the powerful style as more potent, more attractive, and more credible.[72]

Through vision and rhetorical crafting, leaders convey their message of challenging and worthy standards and portray an idealized future. Leaders use mental images to focus their followers' attention and heighten their motivation for accomplishing the desired outcomes. An attractive and shared vision pulls employees toward its realization.

ACTIVITY 5.4   Rhetorical Crafting at Shaky Ground Middle School

Case Study Question 2: What leadership behaviors would have made Mr. Jones more effective in his job?

A leader's communication style is an important influence in generating and directing employees' interest and commitment to the organizational goals. Discuss in pairs:

1. Framing and value amplification are methods that the principal highlights and uses to play up the values most important to teachers in ways that resonate and motivate them. Identify examples of how Mr. Jones could have framed or amplified teacher values toward their school improvement objectives.
2. Give examples of metaphors, analogies, stories, and symbolic acts that Mr. Jones might have used to motivate and direct teacher interest and effort toward creating a better teaching and learning environment at Shaky Ground Middle School.
3. Describe paralanguage examples that might have undermined Mr. Jones's efforts rhetorical crafting.

ACTIVITY 5.5   Developing a Vision at Shaky Ground Middle School

Case Study Question 3: What could Mr. Jones have done differently to develop a school vision that the various school communities could have accepted?

Discuss as a class how Mr. Jones could have used the following occasions differently to encourage teacher and community buy-in to a shared vision and appropriate behaviors for teaching and learning that support all students?

1. Developing and sharing a vision with teachers, parents, and community
2. Planning for and conducting faculty meetings
3. Initiating the interdisciplinary team concept and practices
4. Planning for and conducting PTSA meetings
5. Mentoring and coaching his assistant principals
6. Choosing his preferred activities during the school day

What would Mr. Jones and the superintendent see and hear at Shaky Ground Middle School to know if the school culture were changing in positive directions?

ACTIVITY 5.6   Message and Rhetorical Crafting at Shaky Ground Middle School

Question 4: If you were the principal, what would you do differently given the circumstances?

Discuss questions in pairs and then discuss findings as a class:

1. What would you have done differently, starting from your first meeting with the superintendent about his goals for the school and continuing through year 5?
2. As a prospective school leader, which of the communication skills discussed do you believe you have developed most fully? Which communication skills do you still need to develop more fully? What opportunities would you like to have in order to develop these capacities?

SUMMARY

Effective communication is an important factor in an organization's success. Because language is inherently ambiguous, communication breakdowns are likely. Context information increases the probability of some interpretations while decreasing the probability of others. Context emerges from complex interactions between people, situations, and personal relationships. Communication is a two-way dynamic process in which the message receivers actively construct meaning from the message's content and context.

Leaders' communication practices shape the organization's values, beliefs, and climate. Both a process and a condition, organizational culture directs employees' attention to tasks that the organization values and regulates day-to-day activities. The larger the gaps between the stated and practiced cultures, the greater the employee discouragement, cynicism, and poor performance.

The language of leadership consists of two parts: message (vision) and rhetorical crafting (selecting words with emotional appeal). The effective leader teaches employees what the organizational values, why it is valued, and how to transform values into action. School leaders articulate an image for a more effective school by adapting the vision to their audience, highlighting its values, selecting the correct language and symbols, using inclusive language, and providing enough task and goal specificity. Once organizational members find the vision meaningful, they let it energize and direct their attention, shape their action, and create a sense of common purpose and ownership. In this way, effective communication creates an effective organizational culture. Research supports the significance of vision's contributions to organizational effectiveness.

Effective communication requires rhetorical crafting. Simply framing or wording an opportunity in a certain way influences its outcomes. Inspiring leaders use a number of rhetorical techniques such as metaphors and analogy, stories, varied language styles, symbols, rituals, and paralanguage to ensure that their message's symbolic content has a powerful impact. Research supports the effect of metaphors, analogies, and rhetorical devices over rational discourse in motivating employees' productivity.

ENDNOTES

1. Clampitt, P. G. (2010). *Communicating for managerial effectiveness. Problems, strategies, solutions* (4th ed., p. 4). Thousand Oaks, CA: Sage.
2. Haney, W. V. (1979). *Communication and interpersonal relations: Text and cases.* Homewood, IL: Irwin.
3. Clampitt. (2010). Op. cit.
4. Peters, T. J., & Waterman, R. H., Jr. (1982). *In search of excellence.* New York, NY: Harper & Row.
5. Shannon, C., & Weaver, W. (2008). The mathematical theory of communication. In R. Dawkins (Ed.), *The Oxford book of modern science writing*

(pp. 297–304). Oxford, United Kingdom: Oxford University Press.
6. See, for example: Lasswell, H. D. (1948). The structure and function of communication in society. In L. Bryson (Ed.), *The communication of ideas* (pp. 37–51). New York, NY: Knopf; Gerbner, G. (1956). Toward a general model of communication. *Audio-Visual Communication Review, 4*(3), 171–199; Shannon, C., & Weaver, W. (1949). *A mathematical theory of communication.* Urbana, IL: University of Illinois Press.

7. Clampitt. (2010). Op. cit.

8. Heaphy, E. D., & Dutton, J. E. (2008). Positive social interactions and the human body at work: Linking organizations and physiology. *Academy of Management Review, 33*(1), 137–163; see also: DiSalvo, V. S. (1980). A summary of current research identifying communication skills in various organizational contexts. *Communication Education, 29*(3), 283–290.

9. Clampitt. (2010). Op. cit.

10. Kotter, J. P., & Heskett, J. L. (1992). *Corporate culture and performance*. New York, NY: Free Press. See also Collins, J., & Porras, J. (1994). *Built to last: Successful habits of visionary companies* (p. 87). New York, NY: Harper Business.

11. Nohria, N., Joyce, W., & Roberson, B. (2003). What really works. *Harvard Business Review, 81*(7), 42–52.

12. Kaplan, L. S., & Owings, W. A. (2011). *American education: Building a common foundation*. Belmont, CA: Wadsworth/Cengage Learning.

13. Clampitt. (2010). Op. cit.

14. Awal, D., Klinger, J., Rongione, N., & Stempf, S. A. (2006, January 1). Issues in organizational culture change: A case study. *Journal of Organizational Culture, Communications and Conflict, 10*(1), 79–97.

15. Conger. (1991). Op cit.

16. Kantabutra, S. (2008). What do we know about vision? *Journal of Applied Business Research, 24*(2), 127–138.

17. Bass, B. M. (1990). *Bass & Stogdill's handbook of leadership: Theory, research, and managerial applications* (3rd ed.). New York, NY: Free Press; Conger, J. A. (1991). Inspiring others: The language of leadership. *Academy of Management Executive, 5*(1), 31–45; Conger, J. A., & Kanungo, R. N. (1987). Toward a behavioral theory of charismatic leadership in organizational settings. *Academy of Management Review, 12*, 637–647; Lucey, J., Bateman, N., & Hines, P. (2005). Why major lean transitions have not been sustained. *Management Services, 49*(2), 9–13.

18. Kouzes, J. M., & Posner, B. Z. (1987). *The leadership challenge: How to get extraordinary things done in organizations*. San Francisco, CA: Jossey-Bass; Zaccaro, S. J., & Banks, D. (2004). Leader visioning and adaptability: Bridging the gap between research and practice on developing the ability to manage change. *Human Resource Management, 43*(4), 367–380.

19. Maccoby, M. (1981). *The leader*. New York, NY: Simon & Schuster; Peters, T. (1987). *Thriving on chaos*. New York, NY: Harper & Row; Slater, R. (1993). *The new GE: How Jack Welch revived an American institution*. Homewood, IL: Business One Irwin.

20. Kotter, J. P. (1990). *A force for change: How leadership differs from management*. New York, NY: Free Press; Larwood, L., Falbe, C. M., Kriger, M. R., & Miesling, P. (1995). Structure and meaning of organization vision. *Academy of Management Journal, 85*, 740–769; Westley, F., & Mintzberg, H. (1989). Visionary leadership and strategic management. *Strategic Management Journal, 10*, 17–32.

21. Bennis, W. G., & Nanus, B. (1985). *Leaders: The strategies for taking charge*. New York, NY: Harper & Row.

22. Nanus, B. (1992). *Visionary leadership* (p. 8). San Francisco, CA: Jossey-Bass.

23. Bennis, W., & Nanus, B. (1997). *Leaders. Strategies for taking charge* (p. 82). New York, NY: HarperCollins.

24. DeBono, L. (1984). *Tactics—The art and science of success* (p. 4). Boston, MA: Little, Brown.

25. Bennis & Nanus. (1997). Ibid., p. 82.

26. Kantabutra. (2008). Op. cit.

27. Nanus, B. (1992). *Visionary leadership: Creating a compelling sense of direction of your organization*. San Francisco, CA: Jossey-Bass; Zaccaro, S. J., & Banks, D. J. (2001). Leadership, vision, and organizational effectiveness. In S. J. Zaccaro & R. J. Klimoski (Eds.), *The nature of organizational leadership: Understanding the performance imperatives confronting today's leaders* (pp. 181–218). San Francisco, CA: Jossey-Bass.

28. Nanus, B. (1996). Why does vision matter? In J. S. Osland, D. A Kolb, & I. M. Rubin (Eds.), *The organizational behavior reader* (7th ed., pp. 381–383). Upper Saddle River, NJ: Prentice Hall.

29. Nanus. (1996). Ibid.

30. Festinger, L. (1957). *A theory of cognitive dissonance*. Stanford, CA: Stanford University Press.

31. Conger, J. A., & Kanungo, R. N. (1987). Toward a behavioral theory of charismatic leadership in organizational settings. *Academy of Management Review, 12*(4), 637–647.

32. "Clock Building, Not Time Telling" is the title of Chapter 2 (pp. 22-42) in Collins, J., & Porras, J. I.

(2002). *Built to last. Successful habits of visionary companies.* New York, NY: HarperCollins.

33. Collins, J., & Porras, J. I. (2004). *Built to last. Successful habits of visionary companies.* New York, NY: HarperCollins.

34. Collins & Porras. (2004). Ibid., pp. 25–27.

35. Collins & Porras. (2004). p. 31.

36. Kantabutra, S. (2008). What do we know about vision? *Journal of Applied Business Research, 24*(2), 127–138.

37. Bowman, M. A. (1997). Popular approaches to leadership. In P. G. Northhouse (Ed.), *Leadership: Theory and practice* (pp. 239–260). Thousand Oaks, CA: Sage.

38. Benson, Y., Shamir, B. M., Avolio, B. J., & Popper, M. (2001). The relationship between vision strength, leadership style, and context. *Leadership Quarterly, 12*(1), 53–73.

39. Kantabutra. (2008). Op. cit. For a thorough, detailed discussion of leadership vision research—theoretical and empirical—see Kantabutra, 2008.

40. Zaccaro, S. J. (2001). *The nature of executive leadership: A conceptual and empirical analysis of success.* Washington, DC: APA Books.

41. Bennis, W. G., & Nanus, B. (1985). *Leaders: Strategies for taking charge.* New York, NY: Harper & Row.

42. Collins & Porras. (1994). Op. cit.; Lucey et al. (2005). Op. cit.

43. Avery, G. C. (2004). *Understanding leadership.* London, United Kingdom: Sage.

44. Baum, I. R., Locke, E. A., & Kirkpatrick, S. A. (1998). A longitudinal study of the relation of vision and vision communication to venture growth in entrepreneurial firms. *Journal of Applied Psychology, 83*, 43–54.

45. Kantabutra, S. (2003). *An empirical examination of relationships between customer and staff satisfaction in retail apparel stores in Sydney, Australia* (Unpublished doctoral dissertation). Macquarie Graduate School of Management, Macquarie University, Sydney, Australia.

46. Bennis, W. G., & Nanus, B. (1985). *Leaders. The strategies for taking charge.* New York, NY: Harper & Row; Benson et al. (2001). Op. cit.; Gailbraith, J. R., & Lawler, E. (1993). *Organizing for the future: The new logic for managing complex organizations.* San Francisco, CA: Jossey-Bass; Gardner, J. W. (1990). *On leadership.* New York,

NY: Free Press; Kantabutra. (2008). Op. cit.; Tichy, N. M., & Devanna, M. A. (1990). *The transformational leader* (2nd ed.). New York, NY: Wiley.

47. Wilbur, K. (1982). *The holographic paradigm and other paradoxes.* Boulder, CO: Shambala Press.

48. Conger, J. A. (1991). Inspiring others: The language of leadership. *The Executive, 5*(1), 31–45.

49. Adapted from: Girard J.P. & Lambert S. (2007). The story of knowledge: Writing stories that guide organisations into the future" *The Electronic Journal of Knowledge Management, 5*(2), 161–172.

50. Yukl, G. (1998). *Leadership in organizations.* Englewood Cliffs, NJ: Prentice-Hall; Bass, B. M., & Avolio, B. J. (1994). *Improving organizational effectiveness through transformational leadership.* Thousand Oaks, CA: Sage; Ehrhart, M. G., & Klein, K. J. (2001). Predicting followers' preferences for charismatic leadership: The influence of follower values and personality. *Leadership Quarterly, 12*(2),153–179. The three other characteristics of charismatic leadership are communicating high performance expectations, exhibiting confidence in followers' ability to reach goals, and taking calculated risks that oppose the status quo.

51. Lowe, K. B., Kroeck, K. G., & Sivasubramaniam, N. (1996). Effectiveness of correlates of transformational and transactional leadership: A meta-analytic review of the MLQ literature. *Leadership Quarterly, 7*(3), 385–425.

52. Ehrhart, M. G., & Klein, K. J. (2001). Predicting followers' preferences for charismatic leadership: The influence of follower values and personality. *Leadership Quarterly, 12*(2),153–179.

53. Conger. (1991). Op cit., p. 32.

54. Conger. (1991). Op. cit.

55. Snow, D. A., Rochford, E.B., Worden, S. K. & Benford, R. D. (1988). Frame alignment processes, micromobilization, and movement participation. *American Sociological Review, 51*(4), 464–481.

56. Bennis, W., & Nanus, B. (1985). *Leaders.* New York, NY: Harper & Row; Selznick, P. (1957). *Leadership in administration.* New York, NY: Harper & Row; Zaleznik, A. (1977). Managers and leaders: Are they different? *Harvard Business Review, 15*(3), 67–78.

57. Conger. (1991). Op. cit., p. 34.

58. Conger. (1991). Op. cit.

59. Wilier, A. R. (1984). *The spellbinders.* New Haven, CT: Yale University Press.

60. Conger. (1991). Op. cit., p. 38.

61. Conger. (1991). Op. cit., pp. 39–40.

62. Conger. (1991). Op. cit., pp. 40–41.

63. Ashforth, B. E., & Mael, F. (1989). Social identity theory and the organization. *Academy of Management Review, 14*(1), 20–39; Shamir, B., Zakay, E., Breinin, E. B., & Popper, M. (1998). Correlates of charismatic leader behavior in military units: Subordinates' attitudes, unit characteristics, and superiors' appraisals of leader performance. *Academy of Management Journal, 41*(4), 387–409.

64. Dutton, J. E., Dukerich, J. M., & Harquail, C. V. (1994). Organizational images and member identification. *Administrative Science Quarterly, 39*(2), 239–263.

65. Kark, R., & vanDijk, D. (2007). Motivation to lead, motivation to follow: The role of self-regulatory focus in leadership. *Academy of Management Review, 32*(2), 500–528.

66. Sergiovanni, T. J. (1984). Leadership and excellence in schooling. *Educational Leadership, 41*(5), 4–13.

67. Conger. (1991). Op. cit., p. 42.

68. Bass, B. M., & Avolio, B. J. (1990). *Manual for the multifactor leadership questionnaire.* Palo Alto, CA: Consulting Psychologists Press; Hater, J. J., & Bass, B. M. (1988). Supervisors' evaluations and subordinates' perceptions of transformational leadership. *Journal of Applied Psychology, 73*(4), 695–702.

69. Banerji, P., & Krishnan, V. R. (2000). Ethical preferences of transformational leadership: An empirical investigation. *Leadership & Organizational Development Journal, 21*(8), 405–413; Coad, A. F., & Berry, A. J. (1998). Transformational leadership and learning orientation. *Leadership & Organizational Development Journal, 19*(3), 164–172; Thite, N. M. (1999). Identifying key characteristics of technical project leadership. *Leadership & Organizational Development Journal, 20*(5), 253–261.

70. Osborn, M. M., & Ehninger, D. (1962). The metaphor in public address. *Speech Monograph, 29*(3), 223–235.

71. Seminal studies of psychological impact of rhetorical practices were conducted by Borgida, E., & Nisbett, R. E. (1977). The differential impact of abstract vs. concrete information on decisions. *Journal of Applied Technology, 7*(3), 258–271; Bowers, J. W., & Osborn, M. M. (1966). Altitudinal effects of selected types of concluding metaphors in persuasive speeches. *Speech Monographs, 33*(2), 147–155; Osborn, M. M., & Ehninger, D. (1962). The metaphor in public address. *Speech Monographs, 29*(3), 228.

72. The original findings concerning these two styles were made in courtroom settings. See Erickson, B., Find, E. A., Johnson, B. C., & O'Barr, W. M. (1978). Speech style and impression formation in a court setting: The effects of "powerful" and "powerless" speech. *Journal of Experimental Social Psychology, 14*(3), 266–279. See also Schlenker, B. R. (1980). *Impression management.* Monterey, CA: Brooks/Cole for an in-depth discussion of research on language and impression management.

CHAPTER 6

Leadership and Motivation

Focus Questions

- What is motivation and how does it influence leaders and employees in the work environment?
- How do employees' "psychological contracts" affect their work motivation and commitment to the organization?
- How does the study of motivation and human needs influence leadership behaviors that keep employees satisfied and productive?
- How does expectancy theory influence employees' work motivation?
- How does organizational diversity affect employees' motivation?

CASE STUDY: PSYCHOLOGICAL CONTRACT VIOLATION STORY

Ed Graves had been an English teacher in the Millstone Public Schools for 9 years and department chair for the last 2 years. In December, Ed finished his master's degree in educational leadership from the local university. He was eager to put his new training to use, but there were no anticipated vacancies in Millstone. The neighboring district, Spring Valley, had posted three assistant principal positions for the coming year. In February, Ed applied and interviewed for an assistant principalship.

On March 3, Ed opened the e-mail from Spring Valley Public Schools. His contract would be in the mail and must be accepted, signed, and returned by April 1. The interview had gone very well. The assistant superintendent had told Ed that he would be offered the job at Spring Valley Middle School—the one school he wanted of the three openings. Two days later, the contract arrived and the position description said "assistant principal." Ed called the Spring Valley School Board office to ask why the contract did not state the school where he would become the assistant principal. He was told that teacher contracts stated "teacher" and principal contracts stated "principal." That was the way it was done in Spring Valley.

Ed had a flash of uncertainty, but the explanation sounded reasonable, and he had a good feeling about the assistant superintendent. Ed signed the contract and went home to draft a letter of resignation that he would give to his principal the next day. When Ed handed the letter to his principal, he stated how much Ed would be missed. The principal also stated that if Ed had waited for a couple of years, he could have been the assistant principal at Millstone.

Reluctantly, Ed put his house up for sale because Spring Valley had a residency clause for administrators—a fact he learned after signing the contract. He loved his home, which he had renovated. With the downturn in the economy, he made a much smaller profit on his home than he had hoped, but he was moving to a more affluent community for a job he really wanted. He bought a small condo in Spring Valley for more money than his house had sold for, but the condo was less than a mile away from Spring Valley Middle School, and he would save money on gasoline and time on the road. Ed was psyched up for the new job.

On July 7, the Spring Valley new administrator workshop was held. As the assistant superintendent was introducing the new administrators, he announced that Ed would be the new assistant principal at Pittsville Elementary School—not Spring Valley Middle School. Pittsville was not what he had been told, and he would not have left his teaching job at Millstone for the assistant principalship at Pittsville Elementary. Ed heard nothing of the rest of what was said during the morning orientation meeting. At the break, Ed approached the assistant superintendent and asked what had happened to the job at Spring Valley Middle School. The assistant superintendent looked a bit awkward and replied that "something came up just yesterday that made the Spring Valley job impossible." When Ed asked what that something was, the assistant superintendent said that it was a confidential personnel matter. Two other administrators overheard the conversation which made the assistant superintendent visibly upset.

At lunch Ed was introduced to the Pittsville elementary principal. Both appeared awkward and ill at ease. At the end of the day's meetings, Ed walked to the parking lot with his new boss and asked if he knew that the assistant superintendent had promised him the job at Spring Valley Middle School. The principal responded rather curtly and said, "Welcome to Spring Valley Public Schools. Get used to it and you better do a good job for me at Pittsville."

Ed drove home to his little condo and walked slowly up the three flights of stairs to his unit.

Case Study Questions

1. What beliefs about the mutual obligations, values, expectations, and aspirations does Ed have for his employment relationship with the Spring Valley School District? Which of these has been met so far?
2. What contributions has Ed made that lead him to think the new school district has certain reciprocal obligations to him?
3. How have the events that have occurred affected Ed's level of trust toward the school district and its personnel?
4. Explain the legal, emotional, and organizational implications in dealing with implicit expectations based on individuals' perceptions.
5. How long do you think Ed will remain in his job until he starts looking for a new position?

INTRODUCTION

One of a leader's primary tasks is motivating employees to perform at their best. In fact, motivation has been described as "one of the most pivotal concerns of modern organizational research."[1]

Worker motivation is a complex process and crosses many disciplinary boundaries, including economics, psychology, organizational development, human resource management, and sociology. While organizational resources and worker competencies are essential, they are not sufficient in themselves to ensure that the employee delivers high quality performance. Worker performance also depends on the level of drive stimulating them to come to work regularly, work diligently, and be flexible and willing to carry out the necessary tasks in an agreeable and competent manner.

Motives—both as conscious representations of desired conditions or as unconscious or implicit strivings—represent the purposes which guide our behaviors. In the end, the leaders' motives determine the goals to which employees' attention and efforts will be mobilized and directed. Motivation generates the energy and focus for both leaders and followers.

Effective leaders recognize how to encourage their employees' investment of energies and skills on behalf of the organization's goals, products, and services. Understanding how workers perceive their relationship with the organization gives leaders insight into building satisfying and productive work environments.

DEFINING MOTIVATION

Defining motivation of people at work depends on one's frame of reference: the individual, the context, or the interaction between the two. *Motivation in the work environment* can be defined as an individual's degree of willingness to exert and maintain an effort toward organizational goals.[2] *Work motivation* is a set of energetic forces that originate both within as well as beyond an individual's being to initiate work-related behavior and to determine its form, direction, intensity, and duration.[3] Thus, *motivation* is a psychological process resulting from the interaction between the individual and the environment. The environment may include factors such as national culture, organization climate and culture, job design characteristics, person-environment fit, leadership, and group and team norms.[4]

More narrowly, *job satisfaction* is defined as an affective or emotional response to one's work.[5] Job satisfaction is related to motivators in the work or work situation itself that make the work intrinsically fulfilling.

Most contemporary theories of motivation assume that people initiate and persist at behaviors to the extent that they believe their actions will lead to desired outcomes. Employee performance is frequently described as a joint function of ability and motivation.

George A. Miller (1962), Princeton psychology professor and former president of the American Psychological Association, has said, "The study of motivation is the study of all those pushes and prods—biological, social, and psychological—that defeats our laziness and moves us, either eagerly or reluctantly, to action." Unless we are motivated, we will do nothing.[6]

Personal Values and Motivation

Work motivation is an invisible, internal, hypothetical construct. We cannot actually see work motivation nor can we measure it directly. Instead, we rely on established theories to guide us in measuring its observable signs.

Values influence motivation. Rooted in needs, values provide a principal basis for goals. Similar to needs in their capacity to arouse, direct, and sustain behavior, yet unlike needs which are inborn, values are acquired through thought and experience. Values are a step closer to action than needs. They influence conduct because they are normative standards used to judge and choose among alternative behaviors. The compatibility between individuals' values and those inherent in their organization's culture becomes the footing for a social or psychological contract with the organization.[7]

Our values determine how much commitment we feel toward an organization or the products and services it offers. For example, having interesting work, being treated with respect, and receiving a reasonable salary and recognition for quality performance matter to many people. Other values include having the chance to develop skills, abilities, and creativity; working for people who listen to one's ideas about how to do things; and having a chance to think for oneself rather than simply carry out instructions. For some, job security and financial incentives are the highest values they want from an organization.

Personal values affect organizational life in three ways. First, a person's values influence his or her desire to join and remain with a particular organization. Second, once in the organization, the degree of value compatibility affects a person's use of discretionary effort, and thus determines the extent to which the person uses his or her full competencies at work. Third, since people appear to hold beliefs consistent with the era in which they grew up (especially through adolescence), inevitable conflicts will arise as managers, subordinates, and colleagues of different ages and generations find themselves interacting but having substantially varying values about the nature of work, employee commitment, and life.[8]

National Culture, Values, and Motivation

Context matters when studying motivation and values. Organizational and societal cultures create a climate for individual values. Globalization has prompted research on values within the context of a person's culture and job as well as person-environment fit. National culture determines three key sets of motivation sources:[9]

- ◆ People's self-concept, including personal beliefs, needs, and values
- ◆ Norms about work ethic and variables including the nature of "achievement," tolerance for ambiguity, and locus of control
- ◆ "Environmental factors" such as education and socialization experiences, economic prosperity, and political/legal systems

These culture-dependent factors influence leaders' and employees' self-efficacy beliefs, work motivation levels, and goals, as well as the nature of incentives and disincentives to perform. Projecting one's own values onto people from other cultures that differ on key dimensions can create dysfunctional consequences for employee motivation, interpersonal communication, and overall performance.[10] As a result, motivational strategies vary in effectiveness depending on the culture in which they are used.

Not all motivation-related values vary across cultures, however. A study of more than 19,000 participants from 25 countries found a high degree of consistency in the psychometric properties of a scale assessing general self-efficacy, an important concept related to goal setting and self-regulation.[11] Nevertheless, context and culture always matters when discussing motivation or other psychological dimensions.

ACTIVITY 6.1 Values and Commitment in Case Study

Our values determine how much commitment we feel toward an organization or the products and services it offers. Job satisfaction is related to motivators in the work or work situation that make work intrinsically fulfilling. Ed Graves finds himself in a situation that challenges his values and potential job satisfaction. Discuss as a class:

1. As a successful English teacher and department chairperson with a new master's degree in educational leadership, what values might Ed Graves hold and expect to live out in an assistant principal position?
2. In the process of seeking and obtaining the assistant principal position with Spring Valley School District, what actions has Ed taken that illustrate some of his values?
3. Using incidents from the case study, describe the extent of value compatibility evident so far between Ed and the Spring Valley School District.
4. How might these events have an impact on Ed's motivation to give his best efforts to the Spring Valley School District?

LEADERSHIP AND THE PSYCHOLOGICAL CONTRACT

Central to a modern understanding of the workplace is the idea that some form of exchange occurs between parties in an employment relationship,[12] and that the nature of the exchange process can have a strong influence on organizational outcomes.[13] Leaders must identify a range of appropriate incentives to induce employees to give their best efforts at work. Over the last two decades, academics and practitioners alike have been searching for the factors likely to contribute to sustained employee motivation and commitment.

Daniel Yankelovich, former New York University psychology professor and a leading interpreter of American social trends and the global economy, concluded that a person's commitment to the organization is the key factor in determining how much discretionary effort the person uses in those tasks that allow personal choices in performance.[14] Understanding how employees develop implicit psychological contracts with their organizations can help leaders provide the right incentives to motivate individual employees as well as understand the mutual obligations these entail.

The Psychological Contract

The compatibility we feel between our values and those inherent in the organization's culture forms the basis for the psychological contract. Our *psychological contracts* are mental models that help explain our interactions with organizations.

Chris Argyris (1960), professor emeritus at Harvard Business School, first coined the notion of the "psychological contract" to refer to employer and employee expectations of the employment relationship: beliefs about the mutual obligations, values, and expectations and aspirations that operate over and above the formal employment contract.[15]

Defining Psychological Contract.   Despite an increasing interest and abundance of literature pertaining to the psychological contract, no one accepted universal definition exists.[16] Researchers have used the concept of the psychological contract in a variety of different ways. Nevertheless, all significant definitions of the psychological contract include:[17]

1. Incorporation of beliefs, values, expectations, and aspirations of employer and employee, including beliefs about *implicit promises and obligations*, the extent to which these are *perceived to be met or violated*, and the extent of trust within the relationship.
2. Awareness that these expectations are not necessarily made explicit. Rather, it is the *implicit deal* between employers and employees. It implies fairness and good faith.
3. Understanding that a psychological contract can be *continually renegotiated*, changing with an individual's and an organization's expectations and in shifting economic and social contexts. It is not static, but dynamic. However, most research provides only a snapshot of one point in time, thereby capturing only one stage in this social process.
4. Understanding that because it is based on individual perceptions, persons in the same organization or job may perceive different psychological contracts, which will, in turn, influence the ways in which they perceive—and respond to—organizational events.

Influenced by family upbringing, societal mores, and past experiences, people create *mental maps* or *models* that frame events at work, including promises, assumptions, and expectations about future payoffs for their contributions.[18] Organizational documents, discussions, and practices also influence employees' mental models. These multiple information sources plus individuals' cognitive and perceptual differences shape the psychological contract's particular nature.[19] These highly subjective models frame and occasionally distort our vision, determining what we see and how we act. One way to understand our behavior is to make these mental maps visible.

Similar to legal contracts—except seldom written or openly expressed—our psychological contracts imply mutual obligations. Psychological contracts with the organization emerge when an individual *perceives* that the contribution he or she makes *obligates* the organization into reciprocity.[20] They also include the limits of what we will do and describe conditions that we see as fair, exciting, synergistic, and desirable, or conversely, as unfair, tedious, and unpleasant.

These implicit contracts reflect our beliefs or assumptions *about* work and life obligations, not the obligations themselves. Although typically undocumented and unspoken, we invest our psychological contract with the power of our commitment. Being a subjective construct, however, the parties to the relationship do not have to agree on, or even discuss, the contract's terms. Given its subjective and dynamic nature, a psychological contract is difficult to manage.

Although the promise that a psychological contract implies has no objective meaning, the perceptions of what was understood become the holder's reality. Rather than passive interpretations, people's perceptions are actively meaningful to them.[21] As a result, the psychological contract serves both the employee and the employer. Shore and Tetrick (1994) argued that while psychological contracts afford employees a sense of control and security in their relationship with employers, they provide employers a way to manage and direct employee behavior without heavy-handed surveillance.[22]

The Psychological Contract: Theoretical Roots. Psychological contract theory has its roots in social exchange theory. Reciprocity is central to this theory: Individuals enter into social relationships to maximize their benefits (monetary, material, or socioemotional), and social relationships have always consisted of unspecified obligations and unequal power resources. To the extent that both partners possess and are willing to supply assets strongly desired by the other, reciprocation of increasingly valued resources strengthens the exchange relationship over time. Social exchange theory highlights the importance of understanding employees' motivation and its relation to achieving organizational goals within employees' and employers' mutual obligations.[23]

Both social exchange theory and psychological contract theory assume that employees increase their efforts carried out on behalf of the organization to the degree that they perceive the organization to be willing and able to respond by giving them desired impersonal and socioemotional resources. Employees who receive highly valued resources (e.g., pay raises, promotions, and training opportunities) would feel obligated, based on the reciprocity norm, to help the organization reach its objectives through such behaviors as increased performance and reduced absenteeism. Some believe the two theories to be mutually interdependent or possibly two ways of defining the same dynamic.[24]

Factors that Develop the Psychological Contract.   Denise Rousseau, professor of organizational behavior at Carnegie Mellon University, has suggested that employees derive the terms of their psychological contract in three main ways.[25] First, individuals may receive persuasive communications from others. Recruiters or interviewers may give the prospective employees implicit or explicit promises which may or may not match those which coworkers and supervisors share. Second, employees' observations about how their coworkers and supervisors behave and how the organization treats them act as social cues that inform employees of their contractual obligations. Third, the organization provides structural signals such as human resource policies, formal compensation systems and benefits, performance reviews, and organizational literature, including handbooks and mission statements that all play a role in creating the employee' psychological contract.

Individual determinants of the psychological contract also may vary according to individual differences in factors such as age, gender, education level, union membership, and lifestyle commitments.[26] Employees' employment goals would also shape the psychological contract. Employees seeking to build a career with the organization would be inclined to seek information conveying extensive mutual obligations. Conversely, employees with only a short-term interest in working for the organization would seek information about and form contracts with limited mutual obligations.

Age Cohorts and Psychological Contracts.   One's age cohort also influences the psychological contract. Some contend that today's workers experience a "new psychological contract" reflecting their own experiences and expectations, societal attitudes, and changing work situations. Current employment trends, characterized by an increase in short-term employment contracts and a loss of job security, have resulted in redefined career expectations and employment relationships. The traditional prospect of lifelong employment with the same organization in exchange for loyalty and commitment is no longer valid.[27]

While many older workers have expected to grow and sustain their careers with one employer over their working lives, many younger employees expect to have several jobs in a variety of work settings over their careers while living full and satisfying lives outside their jobs. Older employees may view their organizational membership and the number of years invested in their companies as important parts of who they are, and unmet expectations or perceived promises for advancement or for supporting work-life needs may lead to a sense of violated psychological contract. For younger workers, self-respect comes from making a strong and valued contribution rather than the passing of years.[28] They identify with their work and their compensation rather than with their employer. Accordingly, some evidence suggests that perceptions of contract violations have decreased as people have more realistic (fewer) expectations and the nature of reciprocal obligations is communicated more explicitly.[29] Young adults' assumptions appear to reflect the changing labor market and employment relationship realities. Clearly, each age group's psychological contract implies a unique but unspoken set of reciprocal obligations.

Although the role of gender within psychological contract theory has received little attention, some suggest that women view the contract differently than men, expecting less in terms of pay and promotion and trading these benefits for flexibility.[30] Nonetheless studies of young adults have shown little gender difference in psychological contract expectations, suggesting that as women's and men's expectations of work converge, so may their experiences of the psychological contract.[31]

In addition, many organizations operate with a cultural lag from the old psychological contract.[32] They want the new contract's flexibility, but they want to retain the traditional contract's artifacts such as career paths and benefits. This suggests that organizational leaders need to be more explicit and clear about mutual obligations and communicate them unambiguously to reduce the likelihood of misunderstandings and perceived violations.

Types of Psychological Contracts. Two types of psychological contracts have been evaluated: relational and transactional.[33] The more traditional *relational contracts* imply obligations that depend on the socioemotional factors (such as trust, loyalty) and a degree of job security rather than purely financial issues. Conversely, *transactional contracts* are short-term monetary agreements with little close involvement of the parties. For example, employees may work in exchange for high pay and training opportunities. Transactional definitions recognize that an organization may not be able to provide job security but can still provide employability, or may be perceived as offering high levels of personal support.

Rousseau and Parks (1993) proposed that these contract types differ with respect to focus, time frame, stability, scope, and tangibility.[34] Relational contracts tend to describe perceived obligations that are emotional and intrinsic in nature, while transactional contracts describe obligations that are economic and extrinsic. Relational contracts appear to have an open-ended, indefinite duration whereas transactional contracts have a more specific and short-term time frame. As a result, transactional contracts seem to be static whereas relational contracts are dynamic and evolving. Additionally, the scope of relational contracts is more general and enveloping, subject to clarification and modification as circumstances evolve. Relational contracts are, therefore, more subjective and less explicit in comparison to transactional contracts—and more likely to involve extensive psychological contracts.

In reality, individuals do not necessarily have one type of psychological contract or the other. More accurately, the exchange relationship contains varying degrees of *both* relational and transactional elements. Individuals can have elements of both types in their own psychological contract.[35]

Violating Psychological Contracts

It is easy to understand how psychological contracts can be violated. Since psychological contracts are typically implicit and unspoken, the employer and employee may not agree about what the contract actually involves. This can lead to feelings that promises have been broken or ignored. Contract violation erodes trust and undermines employment relationships. It lowers employee contributions (such as performance or attendance) and lowers employer investments (such as retention or promotion) in employees.

The literature shows substantial agreement in its focus on psychological contract violation. Numerous studies concentrate on attitudinal reactions to contract violation in terms of organizational commitment,[36] work satisfaction,[37] work-life balance,[38] job security,[39] motivation,[40] and stress.[41] Others have assessed violation in terms of behavioral consequences, such as organizational citizenship behavior,[42] employee turnover,[43] and job performance.[44] Ultimately, many of these studies show that employees with dissimilar understandings of their psychological contracts respond differently to contract violation and to organizational change.

Psychological contract violations may run the continuum from slight misunderstandings to stark breaches of good faith. Given the subtle nature of psychological contracts, how people interpret the circumstances of this failure to meet their expectations and assumptions affects whether they experience a violation.

ACTIVITY 6.2   The Psychological Contract Between Ed and Spring Valley District Schools

The psychological contract refers to employer and employee *implicit* (unwritten) expectations of the employment relationship: beliefs about the mutual obligations, values, expectations, and aspirations that operate over and above the formal employment contract. Psychological contracts emerge when an individual *perceives* that the contribution he or she makes *obligates* the organization or employee into reciprocity. Discuss this as a class:

1. What concrete actions by Ed and Spring Valley School District personnel helped Ed create his psychological contract with the school district?
2. **Case Study Question 1:** What beliefs about the mutual obligations, values, expectations, and aspirations does Ed have for his employment relationship with the Spring Valley School District? Which of these have been met so far?
3. **Case Study Question 2:** What contributions has Ed made that leads him to think the new school district has certain reciprocal obligations to him?
4. **Case Study Question 3:** How have the events that have occurred affected Ed's level of trust toward the school district and its personnel?
5. Would you consider Ed's psychological contract with the Spring Valley School District to be relational or transactional, and why?
6. **Case Study Question 4:** Explain the legal, emotional, and organizational implications in dealing with implicit expectations based on individuals' perceptions.
7. **Case Study Question 5:** How long do you think Ed will remain in his job until he starts looking for a new position?

Types of Psychological Contract Violations.   Denise Rousseau has described the three forms that psychological contract violations take.[45] Table 6–1 illustrates these sources.

TABLE 6–1
How People Experience the Circumstances of Psychological Contract Violations

Inadvertent	Able and willing (divergent interpretations made in good faith)
Disruption	Willing but unable (inability to fulfill contract)
Breach of contract	Able but unwilling (reneging)

Source: Rousseau, D. M. (2001a). Psychological contracts: Violations and modifications. In Osland, Joyce S., Kolb, David A., & Rubin, Irwin M., *The Organizational Behavior Reader* (7th ed.). © 2001. Printed and Electronically reproduced by permission of Pearson Education, Inc., Upper Saddle River, New Jersey.

Inadvertent violation occurs when both parties are able and willing to keep their agreement but differing interpretations lead one party to act in a way at odds with the other's understanding and interests. For instance, two people who misunderstand the time of a meeting will inadvertently fail to honor their mutual commitment to attend.

Disruption to the contract occurs when the circumstances make it impossible for one or both parties to fulfill their end of the agreement, despite the fact that they are willing to do so. For example, a Category 3 hurricane forces a school district to close all its schools until the electric power returns and shattered facilities are repaired. This decision prevents the employer from providing work. Likewise, a car accident can prevent a teacher from arriving in school on time. Although parties in both instances are willing to uphold the psychological contract, outside events disrupt their ability to do so.

Breach of contract happens when one side, otherwise capable of performing the contract, refuses to do so. One party is seen as reneging on a deal where obligations owed are knowingly left unmet due to unwillingness to fulfill a promise. For instance, a high school principal who wants to spend more time with her family leaves a high-demand, relatively well-compensated position to take one at a small private elementary school. Within a few weeks of taking the job, the principal learns that the school's trustees are starting a major marketing campaign to raise funds to build a new gymnasium. In addition to leading the school, the principal is expected to direct the marketing and head the fund drive. These additional responsibilities will keep her away from her family for even longer hours than before. The new school's trustees have breached the new principal's psychological contract with them by imposing new unnegotiated expectations upon her. Costs to the principal include increased stress, family conflict, and diminished professional reputation if she tries to change jobs again soon.

Responses to Psychological Contract Violations.   Whether the "violated" individual understands the source of breach as inadvertent, inability, or unwillingness to comply has a tremendous impact on the person's experience and reaction. Violating the psychological contract has implications for employee trust,[46] performance,[47] and behavior.[48] Various factors influence how individuals respond to psychological contract violations. Research finds that people differ in their willingness to tolerate unfair or inequitable exchanges.[49] Situational factors also promote certain behaviors and inhibit others in response to psychological contract violations. Additionally, social learning and the presence of behavioral role models tend to induce certain types of behavior. For instance, employees in organizations where others with perceived psychological contract violations have resigned their positions might tilt toward leaving. Individuals who have witnessed others successfully complain about their treatment might be inclined to make a complaint.[50]

Responses to psychological contract violations reflect two essential behavioral dimensions: active-passive and constructive-destructive. These behaviors have been categorized as voice, loyalty, neglect, and exit,[51] and may involve attempts to reestablish balance in the exchange.[52] Figure 6–1 reflects their relationship.

Voice refers to active, constructive actions victims take to remedy the violation. Any attempts to change the situation's objectionable features—such as complain to one's supervisor or human resources—are efforts to fix or compensate for the violation while

FIGURE 6–1

Responses to Psychological Contract Violations (Source: Rousseau, D. M. (2001a). Psychological contracts: Violations and modifications. In Osland, Joyce S., Kolb, David A., & Rubin, Irwin M., *The Organizational Behavior Reader* (7th ed.). © 2001. Printed and Electronically reproduced by permission of Pearson Education, Inc., Upper Saddle River, New Jersey.)

	Constructive	Destructive
Active	Voice	Neglect/destruction
Passive	Loyalty/silence	Exit

remaining in the relationship. As a method to register dissatisfaction, research has found voice used in filing grievances,[53] willingness to vote for unions,[54] whistle-blowing,[55] talking with superiors, making threats, and changing behaviors.[56] Talking with superiors was the most frequent type of voice.[57] For instance, a novice teacher who expects school leaders to treat him fairly and supportively may ask the assistant principal who conducts the instructional observations to reschedule and return at another time if the assigned class is "having a bad day" (rather than have the assistant principal visit the class and possibly give the teacher an unsatisfactory evaluation). As a means of remediating psychological contract violations, voice can reduce losses and restore trust.[58]

Voice is most likely when:

◆ A positive relationship and trust exist;
◆ Voice channels exist;
◆ Other people are using voice; and
◆ People believe that they can influence the other contract party.[59]

Silence is a passive, constructive response that serves to keep the existing relationship. Seen as loyalty or as avoidance, silence reflects a willingness to endure or accept unfavorable circumstances. Silence can imply pessimism as one believes no alternatives are available. Alternatively, the silence can reflect loyalty as the individual optimistically waits for conditions to improve.[60] For instance, a teacher who disagrees with the principal about giving "lazy students" opportunities to earn extra credit may not publicly express this contrary opinion during a faculty meeting even though she knows that several colleagues also disagree with the principal on this issue.

Silence is likely when:

◆ No voice channels or established ways of complaining or communicating violations exist, and
◆ No available alternative opportunities exist elsewhere.[61]

Neglect involves behaviors ranging from inactive negligence to active destruction. It can involve inattention to one's duties to the detriment of others' interests. Employee behaviors, such as work slowdowns, not promptly returning parent e-mails or phone calls, or giving poor customer service are all forms of neglect. An organization's failure to invest in certain employees while developing others is another form of neglect. Even when less visible, neglect reflects erosion of the relationship between parties. Moving further along the continuum, *destruction* involves more active behaviors, including vandalism, theft, and violence at work. Neglect and destruction are most likely responses when:

- There is a history of conflict, mistrust, and violation;
- No voice channels exist; or
- Most of the other employees demonstrate neglect and destruction.[62]

Exit is voluntary termination of the relationship. While employers can fire workers whose performance does not meet standards (i.e., frequently tardy, absent, or careless), workers can quit an untrustworthy or unreliable employer (such as one who fails to deliver promised training or promotions). The largest majority of people who quit their jobs within the first 2 years of employment report that their employer violated commitments it had made.[63]

Exit is the most likely action following a contract violation when:

- The contract is transactional and many other potential jobs or employees are available;
- The relationship is relatively brief;
- Other people are also exiting; and
- Attempts to remedy a violated contract have failed.[64]

For instance, employees are more likely to voluntarily exit the organization in settings in which employees seek "a fair day's work for a fair day's pay," in employment agencies that specialize in temporary hires, and in seasonal work. In these situations, the focus is on short-term limited commitments, conditions are well specified, and money exchanges are more clearly specified and less subject to be part of a psychological contract.

Organizational culture likely shapes the type of violation responses available to frustrated employees. A highly bureaucratic culture that inhibits communication and deviant behaviors probably generates little voice and more neglect and disloyalty whereas an open, communal organization might foster more outward complaints and attempts to repair the contract by communicating with superiors.

Psychological contract violations, however, do not always lead to exit. Robinson and Rousseau (1994) found that although 79% of leavers reported violated contracts, 52% of stayers did too.[65] While enduring the violation, stayers can respond with voice, loyalty, or neglect.

Responses to psychological contract violation are culturally sensitive. Culturally different people learn different sets of values which develop cognitive frameworks used to organize information about various situations, including employment relationships. Cultural differences affect the characteristics of the psychological contract, the perception of contract violations, and the varying cognitive scripts that individuals use to guide their behavioral responses to such breaches.

For example, when the U.S. Disney company was building its European theme park outside Paris, employees in the Euro-Disney hotel had very different ideas about the promises their employer had made and their obligations due in return. After one weekend of orientation (or "brainwashing," as one 22-year-old French medical student called it), the entire Fantasyland gift shop personnel had turned over by the next weekend. The medical student quit after a dispute with his supervisor over the time of his lunch break.[66]

Other cultural differences reflect the value orientations of individualism and collectivism. Thus, in addition to cognitive effects, characteristic differences in social exchange motives between cultural groups will influence behavioral responses to violations and to situational variables (such as the quality and availability of job alternatives). Awareness of such cultural differences in employee expectations about mutual obligations is especially important when working in a globalized context.

Violating, Not Ending, the Contract.   The fact that so many people with violated psychological contracts remain with their employers suggests that although breaches may be based on a specific event (such as an employer reneging on an assumed promise), fulfilling a contract is a matter of degree. The extent of contract keeping is affected by what benefits the employee receives (i.e., if not the promotion as scheduled, then a title change with increased status) as well as whether the violation is an isolated event or part of a larger pattern. Job fulfillment is a continuum shaped by both the quality of the relationship and postviolation behaviors by the victim and the violator. In short, violating the employee's psychological contract does not necessarily mean ending the contract.[67]

How individuals respond to violations of their psychological contracts largely depends on the attributions made regarding the violator's motives, the violator's behaviors, and the amount of losses incurred. The victim's perspective about the violation determines its impact and later responses. From the victim's viewpoint, the experience of violation increases when:

- ◆ Losses seem greater; the experience of violation is a matter of degree rather than a specific event (all or nothing).
- ◆ The event occurs in a context where it poses a threat to the parties' relationship (such as a history of previous rift or conflict).
- ◆ The violation event appears to be voluntary as compared to inadvertent, accidental, or because of forces beyond the violator's control.
- ◆ The victim perceives no evidence of good faith efforts to avoid violation (the appearance or irresponsibility or neglect).[68]

For example, workers in Singapore—with an unstructured labor market, many short-term employment contracts, and "transactional" psychological contracts—show a lower sense of obligation to employers than U.S. workers, and less perceived violation when changes are introduced.[69]

ACTIVITY 6.3   Responses to Psychological Contract Violations

Responses to psychological contract violations can be constructive or destructive, active or passive. What possible behavior choices does Ed Graves have in the present situation in response to his perceived psychological contract violation? Complete the following table with possible behavior alternatives that fit each category and the factors that might prompt Ed to act in this manner: and then discuss answers as a class.

Category	Possible Behavior Responses	Prompting Factors for that Response
Voice (active/constructive)		
Silence (passive/constructive)		
Neglect (passive/destructive)		
Exit (active/destructive)		

ACTIVITY 6.4   Ed's Potential Responses to Violations of His Psychological Contract

How individuals respond to violations of their psychological contracts largely depends on the attributions made regarding the violator's motives, the violator's behaviors, and the score of losses incurred.

From Ed's perspective:

1. To what extent is the psychological contract violation inadvert? Voluntary? Beyond the violator's control?
2. Can Ed find evidence of good faith efforts to avoid the psychological contract violations?
3. How might the answers to the above questions influence Ed's work motivation, his job satisfaction, his trust in his employer, and his decisions about what to do next?

Maintaining Psychological Contracts During Organizational Change

The employment relationship's strength and quality affect the extent to which employees can tolerate a psychological contract violation or move toward dissolving the employment contract. Employees' perceptions are their reality and influence their emotions and behaviors. Therefore, introducing changes into the work setting may provoke the employee to believe that the new practices will jeopardize old promises.

In times of organizational change, leaders and managers can take certain steps to maintain their relationships and reduce employees' sense of violation, anger, and mistrust:

- ◆ Recognize that any departure from the status quo can involve losses and painful consequences for those who have enjoyed the present condition's benefits. Leaders can manage these losses by first identifying and accepting the forms these losses might take and then adopting steps to offset or accommodate them.
- ◆ Actively try to understand how the employees interpret the leader's and the organization's commitment to them when designing work-life policies and practices. This understanding makes it easier to honor existing commitments and to identify how to effectively modify a psychological contract or create a new one.
- ◆ Be more clear and explicit about mutual obligations and expectations, and communicate them unambiguously. For example, are people valued by time put in, by outputs achieved, or by other measures? Do flexible working times jeopardize the opportunities for promotion?

During times of organizational change, understanding specifically how each employee views his or her reciprocal arrangements and relationships with the organization can help leaders can take steps to prevent breaches of trust. Acting in good faith, anticipating concerns, and addressing issues directly with employees in joint problem solving can lead to stronger relationships, respect, and commitment by those involved.

Research on Psychological Contracts

Investigators have studied employees' responses to perceived psychological contract violations. Studies show that perceived psychological contract violations negatively impacted employees' feelings and actions toward their employers and organizations.

- ◆ Managers who shared their organizations' values to high extent had greater feelings of personal success, clearer perspective on ethical dilemmas, lower levels of work/home stress, better understanding of others' values, greater us of discretionary effort, and greater commitment to organizational goals than managers who shared their organizations' values to a low or moderate extent. [70]
- ◆ Approximately 75 percent of employees in a 1985 study said they could increase their job output's quantity and quality if organizational conditions were ideal—over half (51 percent) said by more than 20 percent—but the organizational conditions did not encourage them to give their best effort,[71]

Other investigations on the impact of psychological contract violations on employees' feelings and actions toward their employers and organizations show:

- ◆ Reduced employee trust in the employer, less satisfaction with their job and organization, increased intent to leave the employer, and a positive association with actual job turnover.[72]
- ◆ Lower trust in their employers and more likely to look for incidents of violation, while those with higher trust were likely to overlook, forget, or not recognize the violation.[73]
- ◆ Increased levels of exit, increased whistle-blowing and grievance filings, decreased work effort, and decreased levels of loyalty to the organization.[74]
- ◆ Reduced commitment and willingness to engage in organizational citizenship behavior.[75]
- ◆ Decreased relational and transactional obligations, with significantly greater harm to relational obligations.[76]

Relational orientation appears to have an important mediating effect on the consequences of psychological contract fulfillment.[77] This suggests that those people with a greater degree of relational-type expectations in their psychological contracts are more disappointed by contract violations than those with a greater degree of transactional-type expectations.

Criticism of Psychological Contract Theory.   Psychological contract theory is not without its critics. Cullinane and Dundon (2006) pointed to the important conceptual and methodological limitations that compromise the construct's research and evaluation. Variables tend to be subjective and unspecific. Some researchers attempt to measure factors directly through survey questionnaires or indirectly through related variables such as commitment or loyalty. Some consider context, such as studying the concept in another country and culture, while others make the psychological contract part of a wider analytical framework for the employment relationship.[78] These varied methodologies make comparisons and conclusions problematic.

Critics have challenged Rousseau's one-sided consideration of the employee perspective without the employer's viewpoint, necessary to assess fully the notion of mutual and reciprocal obligations.[79]

At the same time, focusing upon mutuality between employee and employer presents its own difficulties, especially where a large power differences exist between them. This allows multiple psychological contracts to emerge, some imposed rather than mutual, with employees unable to incorporate their own expectations and hopes.[80] Such sets of possibly conflicting implied expectations make the concept unwieldy and empirical study difficult.

In addition, some critics claim that the psychological contract literature has refashioned the employment relationship in ways that ignore important structural, institutional, and class-based dimensions of social relationship. The implicit meanings of *mutual obligations*, delivering a *fair deal* to employees, *shared understandings*, and *reciprocity* detract from the degrading nature of daily work for many people. The system, rather than individuals' misunderstood expectations or ill-considered management practices, may be the cause of violations.[81]

Boxall and Purcell (2003) concluded that if the psychological contract is entirely subjective and constructed only in the individual employee's mind, it cannot in any meaningful way be considered contractual.[82] As Guest (1998, p. 652) observed, "where the implicit encounters the implicit, the result may be two strangers passing blindfold and in the dark, disappointed at their failure to meet."[83] Cullinane and Dundon agreed, concluding that its highly subjective, unspoken, and ambiguous nature contributes conceptual blinders to outstanding theoretical issues. Instead of a "contract," they see it as a social exchange interaction, and suggest researchers and theorists focus on the sociopolitical interpretations of the messages employees receive, not only internally from management but also externally from the wider political economy of capitalism.[84]

Psychological contract is a well-researched and studied concept. We now have considerable knowledge concerning the implications and outcomes of unspecified and unmet expectations and obligations. In fact, the construct has become a metaphor for making sense of the employment relationship and for planning ways to improve employee motivation and commitment.[85] However, much work remains if the psychological contract is to become a viable framework capable of understanding the complex and uneven social interactions of both employer and employee.

LEADERSHIP, MOTIVATION, AND HUMAN NEEDS

As previously discussed, Abraham Maslow viewed motivation as fulfilling an increasingly complex hierarchy of human needs. Once individuals meet their primary survival needs for food, shelter, and safety/security, other motives become prominent incentives. Belongingness and love; affiliation with others; gaining esteem through increasing competence and approval of others; and self-actualizing through increased cognitive understanding, finding fulfillment, and realizing one's potential are highly powerful motivators for human action.[86]

Just as depriving the physiological and safety needs has behavioral consequences, the same is true for the higher level needs. Not meeting individuals' needs for belonging, esteem, and personal growth has unanticipated costs. This also holds within the work environment.

Frederick Herzberg's Motivation-Hygiene Theory

Extending Maslow's work, Frederick Herzberg, a Case Western Reserve University psychology professor, developed a two-factor motivation-hygiene theory.[87] Herzberg saw human beings as having two distinct types of needs: survival (biological plus learned drives related to them) needs and growth (psychological) needs. Rather than looking for needs energized within the individual, he focused attention on the job environment to identify factors that arouse in people either positive or negative attitudes toward work.

Like Maslow's needs hierarchy theory, Herzberg's motivation-hygiene theory seeks to identify factors that cause motivation. After studying accountants and engineers, Herzberg distinguished between factors that prevent or cause job dissatisfaction—*hygiene factors*[88]— and factors that cause job satisfaction—*motivation factors*. In Herzberg's view, the growth or motivator factors are intrinsic to the job. These include achievement, recognition for achievement, the work itself, responsibility, and growth or advancement. The dissatisfaction-avoidance or hygiene factors are extrinsic to the job. These include company policy and administration, supervision, interpersonal relationships, working conditions, salary, status, and employment security.[89]

Herzberg's motivation-hygiene theory has several basic assumptions:

◆ People at work have two distinct sets of needs that explain work satisfaction and dissatisfaction.
◆ Motivators tend to produce satisfaction, and absence of hygiene factors tends to produce dissatisfaction.
◆ Work satisfaction and dissatisfaction are not opposites, but are separate and distinct dimensions.

Only factors that cause job satisfaction can be motivators. Herzberg's hygiene factors closely resemble Maslow's lower level needs: physiological, safety, and social. Hygiene factors such as salary, working conditions, supervision, interpersonal relations, policy and administration, status, and security can reduce dissatisfaction, but they are neither satisfiers nor motivators. Meeting these needs reduces employees' dissatisfaction yet leads only to minimal job satisfaction. It does not motivate. Conversely, his motivational factors are analogous to Maslow's upper level needs: esteem and self-actualization.

To Herzberg, job satisfiers and job dissatisfiers did not represent opposite ends of the same continuum, but instead represent two distinct continua. A few job characteristics actually functioned in both directions.[90] As Herzberg (1987, p. 112) concluded, "The opposite of job satisfaction is not job dissatisfaction but, rather, *no* job satisfaction; and similarly, the opposite of job dissatisfaction is not job satisfaction, but *no* job dissatisfaction."[91]

Job Satisfiers as Motivators. According to Herzberg, removing dissatisfiers may ensure that the employee will perform at minimum levels, but only job satisfiers can motivate individuals and contribute to superior performance. As Table 6–2 illustrates, job satisfaction and motivation are more likely to come from the work itself (challenging), autonomy, responsibility, recognition (for achievement), advancement (promotion), personal growth, and development derived from doing the job. Meeting job satisfiers such as these provides a context for motivated behavior in the workplace.

Herzberg suggested that administrators can increase employee motivation by enriching jobs in the organization.[92] Table 6–3 depicts the principle of job enrichment applicable to most worker roles. Increasing employee motivation by allowing more control, more task variety, less task routine, and opportunities to move task performance to higher levels also create additional work motivators.[93]

TABLE 6–2
Herzberg's Motivation-Hygiene Theory

Hygiene Factors	Motivation Factors
◆ Interpersonal relations (with subordinates or peers)	◆ Achievement
	◆ Recognition
◆ Supervision (technical)	◆ Autonomy
◆ Policy and administration	◆ Challenge
◆ Working conditions	◆ Work itself
◆ Job security and salary	◆ Responsibility
◆ Personal life	◆ Advancement
↓	↓
Prevent Dissatisfaction	**Provide Satisfaction**

Source: Adapted from Hoy, W. K., & Miskel, C. G. (2008). *Educational administration. Theory, research, and practice* (8th ed., p. 142). Boston, MA: McGraw-Hill Higher Education. Used with permission.

TABLE 6–3
Herzberg's Principles and Motivators to Increase Employee Satisfaction and Performance[94]

Principle	Motivators Involved
Removing some controls while retaining accountability	Responsibility and personal achievement
Increasing individuals' accountability for their own work	Responsibility, achievement, and recognition
Giving a person a complete natural unit of work	Responsibility, achievement, and recognition
Granting additional authority to employees in their activity and job freedom	Responsibility, achievement, and recognition
Making periodic reports directly available to workers themselves rather than to supervisors	Internal recognition
Introducing new and more difficult tasks not previously handled	Growth and learning
Assigning individuals specific or specialized tasks, enabling them to become experts	Responsibility, growth, and advancement

Source: Reprinted by permission of *Harvard Business Review*. From "One more time: How do you motivate employees?" by Herzberg, F. J., Volume 65, Issue 5. Copyright © 1986 by the Harvard Business School Publishing Corporation; all rights reserved.

Research on Motivation-Hygiene Theory in Schools.   Extensive research followed the motivation-hygiene theory during the 1970s and early 1980s, but not much has occurred since then. Thomas Sergiovanni, education professor at Trinity University in San Antonio, Texas, replicated Herzberg's study with teachers. His findings suggest that achievement, recognition, and responsibility contribute to teachers' motivation. Dissatisfaction appears to result from poor interpersonal relations with students, inadequate styles of supervision, rigid and inflexible school policies and administrative practices, and poor interpersonal relations with colleagues and parents.[95]

Sergiovanni's study differed from Herzberg's in at least two important ways. First, the work itself accounted for both teachers' satisfaction and dissatisfaction. Explaining his findings, Sergiovanni noted that teachers found certain job elements "inherently less satisfying."[96] Tasks such as routine housekeeping, attendance taking, completing paperwork, or supervising study hall, or lunch seemed to balance out teaching's more satisfying aspects. Second, Sergiovanni's teachers did not view "advancement" as motivating. According to Sergiovanni, teaching as an occupation offered little opportunity for advancement as it was currently structured.[97]

Studies with other teacher samples (in Georgia and in Saskatchewan, Canada)[98] and with college and university faculty found support for Herzberg's two-factor theory.[99] A separate investigation compared teachers, principals, and central office administrators' responses using a questionnaire version of Herzberg's method. The researcher found that teachers have a lower tolerance for work pressure than do principals. Teachers also have greater desire for security than do central office administrators, except for those teachers who aspire to become administrators themselves. The would-be administrators also expressed a greater desire for the motivators.[100]

A different study found that teachers, school administrators, and industrial managers hold varied conceptual frameworks for motivation, hygiene, and risk factors. All the groups equally desire opportunities for creativity and responsibility. They diverge in their preference for hygiene factors and risk taking. Teachers show high concern for hygiene factors with low preference for risk, managers in business settings show low concern for hygiene factors with high propensity for risk, and educational administrators place in the continuum's middle. School administrators were similar to teachers in their high concern for hygiene factors and security but resemble industrial managers in their willingness to take risks.[101]

ACTIVITY 6.5   Hygiene and Growth Factors in the Case Study

In Herzberg's view, growth or motivator factors are intrinsic to the job. These include achievement, recognition for achievement, the work itself, responsibility, and growth or advancement. The dissatisfaction-avoidance or hygiene factors are extrinsic to the job. These include company policy and administration, supervision, interpersonal relationships, working conditions, salary, status, and security. Work in pairs and then discuss findings as a class:

1. Explain how Herzberg might view Ed's psychological contract violations as largely the result of hygiene factors.
2. What responsibilities and conditions (job satisfiers) might the Pittsville Elementary School principal include in Ed's assistant principal role to provide motivators for him?
3. What responsibilities and conditions (job dissatisfiers) might the Pittsville Elementary School principal include in Ed's assistant principal role to decrease his work motivation?
4. How might Ed's responsibilities and conditions as assistant principal influence his feelings about his psychological contract with the Spring Valley School District? With his principal and school?

Criticism of Motivation-Hygiene Theory.   Critics have identified four weaknesses in Herzberg's theory. First, critics cite the procedural limitation that Herzberg's theory is "methodologically bound"—that is, the techniques he used to measure motivation-hygiene factors determined the results. When given directions to "think about a time when you felt exceptionally good or exceptionally bad about your job. . . . [and] tell me what happened,"[102] people tend to give socially acceptable answers, saying what they think the interviewer wants to hear.[103] In a review of more than 20 studies that used a method different from Herzberg's critical incident technique, one researcher found only 3% that supported the theory.[104] Others have challenged the coding procedures that require rater interpretation of data which might contaminate results.[105] Additional procedural criticisms about data reliability, time sampling, and drawing inferences have also been expressed.[106]

Second, some critics say the theory is based on faulty research. Inadequate operational definitions confound the investigations and lead to flawed findings and conclusions. Critics also question whether satisfaction and dissatisfaction are really two separate dimensions, challenging their mutual exclusiveness.[107] For instance, some researchers have found that motivators—such as salary, status, security, and interpersonal relationships—appear frequently as satisfiers as well as dissatisfiers.[108]

Third, critics of Herzberg's model say that it is inconsistent with past evidence concerning satisfaction and motivation. Herzberg and colleagues (1959) cited 27 studies in which there was a quantitative relationship between job attitude and productivity. Of these, only 14 revealed a positive relationship between job attitudes and productivity.[109] Nor does the model find support from other studies.[110]

Finally, questions exist regarding the links among study variables. Little research focused on the connections between satisfying job experiences, favorable performance effects, dissatisfying experiences, and unfavorable performance effects.[111] Miner (2002), for example, found that salary was not just a dissatisfier but could be a motivator for some people.[112] Understanding these relationships would clarify the differences between motivation and attitude. Miner claimed that Herzberg's work addresses employee satisfaction rather than the employee's actual motivation and performance.[113]

Nevertheless, Herzberg's distinction between intrinsic and extrinsic factors continues to have considerable intuitive appeal, particularly in organizational settings (such as schools) in which managers have limited access to financial motivators.[114] He extended Maslow's needs hierarchy theory and made it more relevant to the work environment. He advanced a theory that is simple to grasp, is based on empirical data, and offers specific recommendations to administrators. Instead of focusing solely on hygiene factors such as salary, security, and working conditions, Herzberg's theory expands thinking to include intrinsic job factors such as job enrichment, quality of work life, and shared leadership, which are designed to increase work satisfaction and performance. His theory has meaningfully contributed to school leaders' views about what motivates faculty and staff.

Criticisms noted, Herzberg's theory has been widely used as a management tool in disciplines such as engineering management, manufacturing, nursing, health care management, consumer satisfaction, library construction, tourism, and education.[115] By building motivational factors into the job content and allowing employees to take on responsibilities traditionally reserved for managers, organizations have been able to downsize, flatten their hierarchy, and increase productivity and profitability.[116]

School leaders should be aware of both sets of factors as they try to design and enrich teaching and school staff jobs to make them inherently challenging and interesting in addition to eliminating those job aspects that are most likely to produce dissatisfaction. Both hygiene and motivational factors are important but for different reasons.

Motivation and Need for Achievement

The *need to achieve*—the act of successfully accomplishing something to a high standard of excellence—varies with the culture and the individual. Not everyone has the need to accomplish challenging tasks, to triumph over difficulties and barriers, and to excel. Persons who strive for excellence in any field for the sake of achievement rather than for some other rewards are thought to have a high need for achievement.

Many believe that the need for achievement is a learned motive, culturally rather than biologically determined. As people develop, they learn to associate positive and negative feelings with certain things that happen to and around them. If a child is raised in an environment that stresses competition and receives positive reinforcement for performing well on various tasks and negative reinforcement or punishment for failure, the child's drive to achieve can become relatively high. As a result, the achievement value is learned when opportunities for competing with standards of excellence become connected with positive outcomes.[117]

Others believe that achievement motivation is a set of conscious beliefs and values shaped by recent experiences with success and failure and by immediate situational factors such as the task difficulty and the available incentives.[118] In this way, a teacher may be highly motivated to work with her advanced placement (AP) history class because the class is enthusiastically learning, but be less motivated with her world geography class because the students are frequently disinterested, off task, and academically struggling. Of course, both explanations—that achievement orientation is learned early and that certain situations evoke its expression—have merit.

David McClelland and Need for Achievement.   In his 1961 book, *The Achieving Society*,[119] David McClelland, a Harvard and Boston University psychology professor, defined *achievement motivation* as a learned motive, unconscious in nature, resulting from reward or punishment of specific behavior. He also asserted that human motivation comprises three dominant needs: the need for achievement, the need for power, and the need for affiliation. The subjective importance of each need varies from individual to individual and depends on an individual's family and cultural background. Likewise, McClelland claimed that this motivational complex is an important factor in the social change and societal evolution.

For those with a high need to achieve, accomplishment appears to be an end in itself. Although the achievement-motivated person does not turn down tangible rewards, the incentives do not drive the effort. Competing successfully brings a special joy in winning and meeting a taxing standard. This can be more meaningful to high achievement need individuals than money (unless they view money as a measure of success) or public recognition. In this way, achievement can be a motivator in Herzberg's framework.

McClelland hypothesized that individuals who are high in achievement motivation have three key characteristics:

◆ *They have a strong desire to assume personal responsibility.* These persons want to perform a task or solve a problem and receive personal credit for the outcomes. They tend to work alone rather than with others. If the job requires others, they tend to choose coworkers based on their competence rather than their friendship. They tend to be attracted to reward for performance systems (as compared with others having low motives for achievement).

◆ *They tend to set moderately difficult goals and take intermediate levels of risk.* Risk depends more on skill than on chance. Where tasks are too hard, the chance of succeeding and probability of satisfaction are low. Easy tasks represent things that anyone can do, so accomplishing them gains little satisfaction. High achievers tend to calculate the risks and select situations in which they expect to feel slightly, but not too, overextended by the challenges.

◆ *They have a strong desire for concrete performance feedback.* These individuals want to know how well they have done and are eager to receive information about results, regardless of whether they have succeeded or failed. Without feedback, a person cannot tell success from failure and gains little opportunity for achievement satisfaction.

From his research, McClelland concluded that the achievement motivation probably is learned at an early age, largely affected by child-rearing practices and other parental influences. Parents who teach independent mastery, a sense of competition, and reward values give their children "achievement training."[120] Parents set moderately high achievement goals and are warm, encouraging, and nonauthoritarian in helping their children reach these. Children who are taught that actions influence their success and who learn how to recognize good performance are more likely to grow up with the desire to excel. The need for achievement seems to grow stronger the more the individual accomplishes.[121]

In addition, McClelland provided some evidence that training programs that concentrate on developing achievement needs can produce entrepreneurial behavior among adults where it previously did not exist. Education and training remain a general strategy for changing motives.[122] Attempts to infuse achievement motivation should have the following factors:

◆ Establish situations in which individuals can succeed.
◆ Set reasonable and achievable goals.
◆ Accept personal responsibility for performance.
◆ Provide clear feedback on performance.

Individuals with high achievement needs tend to single-mindedly focus on task accomplishment. As a result, the achievement need is an important motive in schools because students, teachers, and administrators who are absorbed in increasing student learning and achievement, and who take personal responsibility for making it happen, are often successful.

Research on Need for Achievement.   Research on the need for achievement usually examines the relationship between need for achievement (or achievement striving) and work behavior. Research on motives relies primarily on individuals' self-reported preferences for job attributes and has found few consistent differences between groups in preference patterns.[123]

Research demonstrates that achievement striving is related to sales performance[124] and in-role behavior,[125] and to parental achievement pressure in the first 2 years of life.[126] Achievement also interacts with other variables such as time management to influence performance.[127] Research also finds that cognitive ability moderates the relationship between need for achievement and performance.[128]

In addition, the research examining the need for achievement has begun to use more sophisticated research designs permitting the examination of interactive and longitudinal effects on performance.[129] Longitudinal studies on achievement motivation demonstrate that achievement at younger ages predicts future performance.[130]

ACTIVITY 6.6   Need for Achievement and Case Study

McClelland called the need for achievement a learned motive with three characteristics: a strong desire to assume personal responsibility, a tendency to set moderately difficult goals and take intermediate levels of risk, and a strong desire for concrete performance feedback. Discuss in pairs and then as a class:

1. What evidence in the case study suggests that Ed Graves has a need for achievement?
2. How can the Spring Valley School District and the Pittsville principal use Ed's need for achievement to motivate his efforts and help him grow professionally?
3. What might the Spring Valley School District and the Pittsville principal do to discourage and frustrate Ed's need for achievement?
4. How will the school district's and principal's actions regarding Ed's need for achievement influence his work motivation and commitment to his school and continued employment in the district?

Criticism of McClelland's Need for Achievement.   Because of its extensive influence on behavior in organizations, the need for achievement has been an area of frequent research.[131] As with other psychological testing, many methodological problems complicate these studies.[132] Some critics have concluded that as a construct, need for achievement may not even be a single unitary trait or attribute.[133] Others have found that McClelland made the unwarranted leap from finding correlation with need for achievement to assuming need for achievement as causality because of his lack of social or historical perspective,[134] leading to gross and unsupportable generalizations.[135]

Some have argued that the achievement motivation is situational or specific rather than global "achievement for achievement's sake."[136] For example, an individual may be motivated to achieve in sports but not in the classroom. This criticism may reflect a misunderstanding because McClelland believed that the need for achievement motive predicts behavior only in the presence of appropriate incentives.[137] Without the appropriate achievement incentives for the individual in a given situation, the achievement motivation in that circumstance would be low. The situational argument does have worth along with expected group differences as a partial explanation of why research on race, sex, and class variations in achievement motivation remains inconclusive.[138]

In addition, feminist critics have taken aim at achievement motivation theory and research. Much motivation research occurred before the women's movement of the late 20th century altered our culture's view of women's achievement in the workplace and in society. McClelland's study of achievement need did recognize women's desire for autonomy and success as an important intermediary variable in their development.[139] Making a finer point, Griscom (1992) observed that although McClelland published the first significant work on women and power,[140] and expressed awareness of some societal constraints on women's use of their achievement and power needs, McClelland did not analyze the historical, institutional, and social-structural barriers that limit and shape women's achievement and power behaviors.[141] In fact, studies find that race, gender, and class exercise a great influence on specific types of achievement behaviors.[142]

Motivation and Autonomy

The need for independent thought and action may be a basic human need. *Autonomy* or self-determination is the desire to have choice in what we do and how we do it. It is the desire to act independently, be self-regulating and coherent in directing our own actions rather than have outside pressures and rewards determine our behavior.[143] People chafe against other-imposed rules, regulations, directives, orders, and deadlines because they interfere with their need for autonomy. At times, persons may reject help so they can remain in control.[144] Results of some studies show that when individuals feel like they have autonomy in their environments, they have higher self-esteem, feel more competent, and perform at higher levels of accomplishment.[145]

Characteristics of Job Autonomy.   Between 1970 and 1990, more than 200 studies conducted on job characteristics tried to determine attitudinal and behavioral outcomes.[146] Job autonomy can facilitate the time necessary for learning and development, which in turn improves job performance.[147] Jobs have three different autonomy dimensions:

◆ *Method control:* the amount of discretion one has over the way in which work is performed
◆ *Timing control:* the influence one has over scheduling of work
◆ *Discretion in setting performance goals:* influence over identifying and setting work objectives[148]

Four interrelated dimensions affect job autonomy. These are the extent to which the supervisor:

◆ Provides clear attainable goals,
◆ Exerts control over work activities,
◆ Ensures that the needed resources are available, and
◆ Gives timely, accurate feedback on progress toward goal attainment. These influence employee perceptions of autonomy.[149]

Autonomy is important even in those jobs where the work is routine or predictable. Routine jobs without opportunities for employee input and control can result in depression.[150]

Of course, having high autonomy on the job does not necessarily suggest that an individual will have major control over the work outcomes. A number of factors in the work environment over which the worker has little meaningful control may affect the final results. For example, a football quarterback has high autonomy in selecting plays but only a moderate level of personal control over the consequences from executing them. Therefore, work autonomy is probably best viewed as a necessary but not sufficient condition for feeling personal responsibility for work results.[151]

Professional Autonomy and the Organization.   Since 1939, an extraordinary amount of research has examined whether organizational employment is compatible with professional autonomy and, perhaps, with professionalism itself. Not surprisingly, given the theoretical disagreements in the field, no single finding answers this question.[152] One common conclusion is that organizational employment necessarily involves a degree of conflict between the professional's desire for self-direction and the organization's need to constrain its employees.[153] In fact, restricted autonomy and the existence of organizational/professional conflict may be the central experience of contemporary organizational professionals.[154]

Other scholars of contemporary professions have emphasized the professionals' ability to maintain high levels of autonomy in organizational settings. Organizations may grant salaried professionals several degrees and types of autonomy depending upon the nature of the organization, the products and services they produce,[155] and the position they occupy within it.[156] Some have noted that many professions have always been based in organizations; professionalism and bureaucracy may, to a degree, be mutually reinforcing rather than antagonistic.[157] Others suggest that, even in conventional organizations, good reasons exist why professionals are likely to maintain their self-sufficiency. In particular, the fact that professional work may involve solutions with more than one right answer makes it difficult for organizations to "routinize" professional functions and deny professionals their usual autonomy.[158] Some have argued that more work will be professionalized as society becomes increasingly dependent on information, knowledge, and reasoning.[159]

Despite these disagreements, all sides concur that professionals value independence and self-regulation.[160] Implicitly and often explicitly, it is assumed that the absence of autonomy will cause professionals to respond negatively. Responses to lost autonomy can range from quitting the job and high levels of absenteeism to less dramatic actions such as producing an inferior product or service. Similarly, frustration about lessening autonomy at work may appear as low levels of job satisfaction, dissatisfaction with career progress, or low levels of commitment to the employing organization.[161]

At the same time, the relationship between autonomy and professionals' job satisfaction is more complex than one might expect. Professionals accept certain constraints as legitimate work realities, and these do not necessarily reduce work satisfaction. They may be willing to accept managerial authority that does not directly affect their professional expertise and be willing to accept restraints on job assignments or time limits. Work limitations may be accepted as inevitable and a predictable professional trade-offs in exchange for interesting and well-paying work.[162]

Research on Autonomy and Motivation. Autonomy's positive effects on motivation have been well documented, especially regarding students' intrinsic motivation to learn and increased learning effectiveness.[163] Self-determination (autonomy) may actually lead to intrinsic motivation.[164]

- ◆ A strong link exists between autonomy and intrinsic motivation. Studies have found that intrinsic motivation promoted in circumstances in which the learner has a measure of self-determination (autonomy) and locus of control leads to more effective learning.[165]
- ◆ Studies have found that adult supportiveness of learners' autonomy dramatically increases students' intrinsic motivation, engagement, conceptual learning and creative thinking, and academic achievement relative to that of students in settings that foster extrinsically oriented learning.[166]

- Laboratory experiments as well as field studies in several domains have shown that autonomy motivation is associated with more effective performance on relatively complex tasks, whereas there is either no difference or a short-term advantage for controlled motivation when mundane tasks are involved.[167]

- Consistent findings across different samples (e.g., elementary school children and children with learning disabilities) indicate that intrinsic motivation is greater among children whose parents' and teachers' autonomy-supportive interaction styles encourage children to choose and initiate activities to help promote mastery rather than a performance orientation (working for the "A" or high test score) toward learning.[168]

- College students' experiences with classroom autonomy were more closely related to motivational factors than to performance (course grades). Autonomy does seem to foster intrinsic goal orientation, greater student interest in the material, and greater persistence in the face of difficulty.[169]

- Some studies have found that autonomy promotes identity development and mental health in adolescence and adulthood.[170]

- Other important motivational factors found to be related to the experience of autonomy include perceived competence, perceptions of control, and academic coping.[171]

The relationship between autonomy, intrinsic motivation, and learning/achievement appears well supported by the research on students. Research on these factors in adult employees is not currently available.

ACTIVITY 6.7   Need for Autonomy in the Case Study

The need for autonomy at work is the desire to have choice over what one does and how one does it. It is the degree to which a job provides freedom, independence, and discretion in scheduling and conducting the work. Organizations often place restrictions on job autonomy. Discuss in pairs and then as a class:

1. What are the ways that Ed might want autonomy as an assistant principal?
2. Given Ed's newness to the assistant principal role, to the Spring Valley School District, and to Pittsville Elementary School, what are the areas in which the Pittsville principal may place reasonable restraints on Ed's autonomy?
3. At which point might constraints on Ed's job autonomy adversely affect the degree of job enrichment and satisfaction he receives?

Criticism of Need for Autonomy.   Social scientists and psychologists from varied theoretical traditions have challenged this understanding of the autonomy construct.[172] As a result, differing definitions of the autonomy concept lead to methodological problems in studying it.[173]

Historical and cultural contexts also have an impact on our understanding of autonomy. Critics of the autonomy construct assert that it reflects the socialized gender difference within our society. Behaviors reflect socialization patterns, and males and females in American society receive different lessons about how to act.[174] Before the mid 20th century, our society traditionally considered autonomy to be a masculine quality. Accordingly, feminist theory disputes the definition of autonomy, defining it as separateness and contrasting the female development toward relatedness with the male development toward independence.[175]

In addition, national cultures affect the presence and expression of human needs, such as autonomy, in unique ways. In the United States, individual independence is a cherished value reflected in popular psychology from parent education courses to self-help books. As a social science, psychology reflects the individualistic ethos of Western Europe and its former North American colonies. Even within the United States, however, different ethnic groups value autonomy differently; some cultures emphasize meeting familial and collective rather than individual goals. While all societies manage to meet basic human needs such as autonomy at least to some extent, varying cultures or subcultures control the ways in which this need is permissibly expressed.[176] In fact, psychology has been criticized for contributing to the preoccupation with and the exaltation of the individual (for which autonomy is a proxy), unfettered by any loyalties to others.[177]

LEADERSHIP AND EXPECTANCY

Values are inherent in most work motivation theories.[178] Expectancy theory uses the social exchange concept—"a fair day's effort for a fair day's wage"—to examine workers' values to predict and understand work-related behavior. In its general form, expectancy theory predicts that individuals will engage in behaviors that they perceive as eventually leading to desired rewards. Higher motivation is associated with greater perceived values for the various job rewards and greater perceived likelihoods that effort will bring these outcomes. When leaders recognize and understand that employees have expectancies and the organization's response to these affects workers' motivation to work hard and well, leaders can better address employees' personal preferences in ways that also meet organizational goals.

Victor Vroom and Expectancy Theory

Victor Vroom is usually credited with developing the first complete version of the expectancy theory relevant to organizational settings.[179] Expectancy theory is based on four assumptions:

- ◆ People join organizations with expectations about their needs, motivations, and past experiences that influence how they react to the organization.
- ◆ An individual's behavior results from conscious choice. People are free to choose those behaviors suggested by their own expectancy calculations.
- ◆ People want different things from the organization—salary, job security, advancement, and challenge.
- ◆ People will choose among alternatives so as to optimize outcomes for themselves.

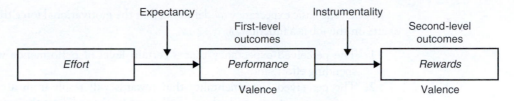

FIGURE 6–2

Basic Expectancy Model (Source: From Lunenburg, & Ornstein. *Educational Administration, 5E.* © 2008 Wadsworth, a part of Cengage Learning, Inc. Reproduced by permission. www.cengage.com/permissions.)

Elements of Expectancy Theory.   The expectancy theory based on these assumptions has four key elements: outcomes, expectancy, instrumentality, and valence (see Figure 6–2).

◆ **Outcomes** are the end results of certain work behaviors. *First-level outcomes* refer to various aspects of performance that result from spending some effort on the job. *Second-level outcomes* are consequences to which first-level outcomes are expected to lead (reward, such as salary, promotion, peer acceptance, supervisor recognition, and sense of accomplishment).

◆ **Expectancy** is the strength of the individual's subjective perception that job-related effort will result in a certain performance level. Expectancy is based on probabilities ranging from 0 to 1. If an employee sees no chance that effort will lead to the desired performance level, the expectancy is 0. If the employee is entirely certain that the task will be completed, the expectancy has a value of 1. Most expectancies fall between these two extremes.

◆ **Instrumentality** is the individual's subjective estimate of probability that performance (first-level outcomes) will lead to certain results and rewards (second-level outcomes). Similar to expectancy, instrumentality ranges from 0 to 1. If an employee sees that a good performance rating will always end in a salary increase, the instrumentality value is 1. If no perceived relationship exists between the first-level outcome (good performance rating) and the second-level outcome (salary increase), then the instrumentality rating is 0.

◆ **Valence** is the strength of an employee's preference for a particular result or reward. Salary increase, promotion, peer acceptance, supervisor recognition, or other second-level outcomes might have more or less value to individual employees. The valence of a first-level outcome depends on the degree to which it ends in a valuable second-level outcome. Valence can be either positive or negative, depending on the outcome's attractiveness to the employee. If the employee has a strong preference for it, valence is positive. If the employee has a strong dislike for it, valence is negative. If the employee is indifferent to the outcome, the valence is 0. The total valence range is from −1 to +1. Valence provides a connection to the content theories of motivation.

In brief, the basic expectancy model shows that the motivational force that an employee exerts on the job is a function of:

1. The perceived expectancy that a certain level of performance will result from spending effort, and
2. The perceived instrumentality that rewards will result from a certain level of performance, both of which are moderated by the valences the employee attaches to these outcomes.

Combining these three factors—expectancy, instrumentality, and valence—produce different levels of motivation. The strongest motivation is high positive valence, high expectancy, and high instrumentality. If any key elements are low, weaker motivation will result.

Research on Expectancy Theory.   For the most part, research supports expectancy theory. It has been able to explain the relationship between salary and managerial performance,[180] predict individuals' occupational choices,[181] and suggest that differential performance determines rewards and that rewards increase the individual's satisfaction.[182]

Research studying expectancy theory in the 1990s reported the following:

◆ It can be integrated with other theories to provide a clearer understanding of motivation.[183]
◆ Differences were found between public and private sector employees on the importance of extrinsic factors.[184]
◆ Differences were found between supervisory and nonsupervisory employees on the degree they perceive they are receiving desired job rewards (such as security, salary, or opportunities for personal and professional growth).[185]
◆ Public sector professionals' social relations on the job and the fulfillment of intrinsic needs were the best predictors of attitudes.[186]
◆ Although no significant differences were found on 20 motivational needs between public and private sector employees, there was a lower need to compete, a lower need for autonomy, and a higher need for serving the community among employees of nonprofit organizations.[187]
◆ Opportunities for promotion and job challenge were the most important factors influencing the job satisfaction of individuals in nonprofit and public agencies.[188]
◆ Motivation and hygiene factors varied according to national culture.[189]

Expectancy theory has research support as a concept explaining how employees determine their work motivation. School administrators can use this model when framing assignments for employees. Informing subordinates of likely outcomes and rewards, building skills and confidence in their abilities to successfully accomplish an assigned task, and identifying results that they find desirable will help motivate individuals to commit their attention and energies to the important projects at hand.

Criticism of Expectancy Theory.   Although research evidence validates expectancy theory, it still has three major problems. First, expectancy theory has become so complex that it has exceeded the capacity of leaders to use it and empirical measures to adequately test it,[190] even with improved instruments.[191]

Second, research does not support the idea that many individuals actually conduct conscious, detailed cognitive arithmetic before deciding at what level to perform. For instance, researchers find that upwardly mobile employees tend to engage in the complex multiple calculations the model requires while less ambitious employees simply make gut-level decisions before exerting effort.[192]

Finally, some investigators question whether the model is complete in its present form. Expectancy and commitment may be two independent motivating behavior-stabilizing forces.[193] Therefore, employees' behavior may be the result of high expectancy or high commitment, or a combination of both.[194]

Expectancy theory has become a standard in understanding motivation. Studies appear to show that expectancy theory can accurately predict an employee's work effort, satisfaction, and performance. In addition, expectancy theory has been linked to several important leadership practices including goal setting. Individuals consistently express preferences for intrinsic job attributes, and individuals' preference patterns may eventually contribute to our understanding of employees' occupational and organizational choices.

ACTIVITY 6.8   Expectancy Theory at Work in the Case Study

Expectancy theory predicts that individuals will engage in behaviors that they perceive as eventually leading to prized rewards. Although Ed Graves has not yet begun actual work as an assistant principal, the expectancy theory model can describe the employment events leading to his present motivation for the job.

Using the expectancy model with the case study, discuss as a class how Ed's thoughts and actions fit into the model:

1. What efforts did Ed direct toward securing an assistant principal position at Spring Valley Middle School?
2. Given the information he received from the Spring Valley School District and their assistant superintendent, what was Ed's expectancy of getting the middle school position: high, medium, or low?
3. What performances outside the classroom did Ed accomplish to show his commitment to his new school district and expected new position?
4. What level of instrumentality did Ed expect that his demonstrated commitment and acceptance of the contract would bring regarding the middle school assistant principal position: high, medium, or low?
5. What were the strengths of Ed's valences for his preferred outcomes: high, medium, or low?
6. What desired rewards did Ed actually receive?
7. How do these events and responses affect Ed's motivation to work for Spring Valley School District and Pittsville Elementary School?

Motivation and Organizational Diversity

Leaders are responsible for ensuring the motivation of all employees. Effectively addressing diversity and inclusion often challenge leaders in meeting in this responsibility. *Diversity* typically refers to workforce composition, including race, gender, disability, ethnicity, and age cohorts, and how this creates personal and practical heterogeneity.[195] Looking at these employees *inclusively* means removing obstacles to organizational members' full participation, work motivation, and contributions.[196] Both sets of lenses help leaders more deeply understand and create the conditions necessary to energize varied employees' efforts within the organization.

The U.S. workforce—generally ages 25 to 64—is rapidly changing as increasing numbers of minority employees enter the job market. From 1980 to 2020, the White working age population is projected to decline from 82% to 63% while the minority workforce is projected to double from 18% to 37%. In 2014, women are projected to comprise 47% of the total labor force.[197] Viewing employee diversity as a "positive core" of organizational life[198] and creating workplace environments receptive to these individuals in ways that each feels a valued part of the group bring positive outcomes to the individuals and to the organization.[199]

The existing literature describing diversity's impact on organizational functioning and employee motivation has produced inconsistent conclusions. Some studies find diversity beneficial with increased creativity, productivity, and quality[200] while others find it detrimental to organizational outcomes, increasing conflict, decreasing social integration, and inhibiting decision making.[201] Nonetheless, organizational leaders can draw upon gender, racial, ethnic, age, and disability diversity as resources for building on employee strengths; cultivating a climate that encourages respect, compassion, openness, and opportunities for learning; and eventually gaining a competitive advantage by generating feelings of inclusion of both minority and nonminority employees. The question, however, remains, "How?"

Addressing Diversity in Organizations. Organizations nurture and manage diversity in a variety of ways, usually by using either the colorblind approach or the multicultural approach. The colorblind approach is the dominant model in mainstream American culture and organizations.[202] "Treating all people the same," the colorblind style reflects the American cultural ideals of individuality, equity, meritocracy, and the "melting pot" assimilation of different cultures. Colorblind practices focus on ignoring cultural group identities or realigning them with an overarching identity, such as being an American or employee of a certain company.[203] Stressing individual accomplishment and qualifications over other factors, the colorblind approach discourages diverse employees from thinking and acting in the unique ways associated with their social categories, discouraging them from fully using their distinctive viewpoints within the organization, and reducing their motivation to do their best at work.

Evidence suggests that minorities commonly interpret the colorblind approach as exclusionary;[204] frustration, dissatisfaction, and conflict likely appear in minority employees when they perceive that their organizations ignore or devalue racial differences.[205] Although a colorblind ideology may appeal to White employees, this approach to diversity may not only alienate and de-motivate minority employees but also allow a culture of racism to develop.[206]

Next, the multicultural approach to diversity emphasizes the benefits of a diverse workforce and clearly recognizes employee differences as a source of strength. Minorities are attracted to organizations that use multicultural approaches because these institutions recognize diverse racial, ethnic, religious, and other group identities as being different and valuable.[207] Multicultural initiatives might include networking and mentoring programs, "diversity days" that celebrate employees' backgrounds, and diversity training workshops designed to diminish bias and increase cultural awareness among nonminority employees.

Instead of fostering a lasting climate of inclusion and acceptance, however, multicultural diversity initiatives often fall short of their goals or fail completely because nonminority employees meet them with noncompliance and resistance.[208] Ironically, despite the overt attempts to advance workplace inclusion, multicultural activities may instead result in skepticism, resentment, and significant backlashes of biased language, silence about inequities, stereotyping, and discriminatory culture and practices.[209]

Despite the positive intentions, a colorblind approach does not motivate minority employees, and a multicultural approach does not motivate nonminority employees. A third method—using an all-inclusive approach—is a more successful way to manage organizational diversity and motivate all employees. Neither group resists an approach that recognizes and values everyone's unique characteristics and contributions. All-inclusive multiculturalism (AIM) recognizes and acknowledges the importance of individual differences; this perspective is essential for gaining minority and majority support. At the same time, the AIM approach explicitly acknowledges the important role that nonminorities play in workplace diversity, speaking to their concerns about exclusion and disadvantage.[210]

The all-inclusive approach explicitly endorses the vision that the demographic groups to which people belong have important consequences for individuals, and this is true across members of all groups. This viewpoint fits comfortably within the American ethos of equality and egalitarianism. Now, demographic groups can maintain their subgroup identities within the context of an overarching shared identity. The emerging empirical evidence supports this all-inclusive method as having the potential to enhance rather than impede positive intergroup relations as well as motivate individual and organizational performance.[211]

A key facet in creating a truly inclusive work climate requires moving beyond the tactics that superficially appreciate diversity. Instead, inclusive work environments must inspire individuals to integrate diversity into their work lives by recognizing themselves and others in their organization. At its foundation, all-inclusive organizations focus on forming high-quality relationships among dissimilar employees that encourage positive emotions, ongoing learning, resilience, longevity, and the capacity for individuals to confidently engage, challenge, and support each other. By nurturing an environment where individual differences are not ignored (as with the colorblind approach) and where feelings of inclusion are commonplace (unlike the exclusion of nonminorities with multiculturalism), leaders can encourage all employees to participate in open, honest, and respectful conversations about their individual differences and common goals. In such a culture, individuals can develop authentic relationships without the prejudice and stereotyping typically associated with "diversity" programs.[212]

School leaders can foster all-inclusive work climates by communicating their expectations to all employees and to the larger community in clear words and deeds. For example, language that celebrates the unique contributions of all faculty, students, and community members should appear in school newsletters, newspaper articles, and mission statements. Language that appears exclusive must be avoided—for example, it is more inclusive to ask for "family recipes from all employees" rather than request "ethnic recipes that reflect your heritage" to compile an organization cookbook. Also, the school's leadership should visibly reflect minority and majority members, with their participation evident on the school's improvement team, in the parent-teacher-student association, among department chairpersons, and on the school's social committee. In addition, every employee should be expected to develop and refine intercultural competence.

By explicitly including all demographic groups within the diversity concept, organizational leaders make it clear that everyone will enjoy the same opportunities, recognition, and respect. In such environments, individuals feel free to innovate, knowing that their unique experiences and contributions are valued and positive human relations facilitated, especially across demographic lines. By encouraging employees to feel included and valued, the all-inclusive approach fosters organizational commitment and trust, internal motivation, and personal satisfaction for all individuals to reach their fullest potential.

SUMMARY

Motivation is a psychological process resulting from the interaction between the individual and the environment. While organizational resources and worker competencies are essential, worker performance also depends on employees' level of drive stimulating them to come to work regularly, work diligently and competently, and be flexible and willing to carry out the necessary tasks. Motivational strategies vary in effectiveness depending on the cultures in which they are used.

People working in organizations may feel more or less commitment to the business, its people, or its products and services depending on their internal values, personal histories, and societal mores. The compatibility individuals feel between their values and those inherent in their organization's culture affects the degree to which people apply themselves to the business's products or services and forms the basis for the psychological contract.

Psychological contract refers to employer and employee beliefs about the mutual obligations, values, expectations, and aspirations that operate over and above the formal employment contract. Seldom written or openly expressed, our psychological contracts with the organization implicitly spell out what we expect to give and what we expect to get from the organization. The psychological contract will change over time. Psychological contract is a well-researched and studied concept.

As a subjective construct, the parties to the psychological contract's relationship do not have to agree on, or even discuss, the terms of any individual contract. This makes them difficult to manage, and violations may occur. Psychological contract violations erode trust and undermine employment relationships.

Herzberg identified workplace factors that arouse people's positive or negative attitudes toward work. Hygiene factors prevent or cause job dissatisfaction; motivation factors cause job satisfaction. Motivation factors are intrinsic to the job; dissatisfaction-avoidance or hygiene factors are extrinsic to the job. According to Herzberg, removing dissatisfiers may ensure that the employee will perform at minimum levels, but only job satisfiers can motivate individuals and contribute to superior performance. The motivation-hygiene theory has been extensively researched.

Persons who strive for excellence in any field for the sake of accomplishment rather than for some other rewards are thought to have a high need for achievement. McClelland found that individuals with a high need for achievement set moderately difficult but potentially achievable goals, set challenges to make them stretch, and favor working at a problem rather than leaving the outcome to chance or to others. For these persons, successful accomplishment is motivating in itself.

Autonomy or self-determination is the desire to have choice in what we do and how we do it. Workplace autonomy includes the freedom to decide how to pursue work goals and control over the resources (materials, time) necessary to do the job. Results of some studies confirm the connection between individuals' autonomy in their environments and higher self-esteem, competence, and accomplishment. Research also suggests that autonomy leads to intrinsic motivation.

Vroom's expectancy theory predicts that individuals will engage in behaviors that they perceive as eventually leading to prized rewards. Higher motivation is associated with greater perceived values for the various rewards in one's job and greater perceived likelihoods that effort will lead to these rewards. Research largely supports the expectancy theory concept.

Organizational diversity provides opportunities to strengthen the organization. An all-inclusive approach—rather than a colorblind or multicultural framework—motivates all individuals to contribute their unique talents and perspectives to their common purpose.

ENDNOTES

1. Baron, R. A. (1991). Motivation in work settings: Reflections on the core of organizational research. *Motivation and Emotion, 15*(1), 1–8 (p. 1).

2. Franco, L. M., Bennett, S., & Kanfer, R. (2002). Health sector reform and public sector health worker motivation: A conceptual framework. *Social Science and Medicine, 54*(8), 1255–1266.

3. Pinder, C. C. (1998). *Work motivation in organizational behavior* (p. 11). Upper Saddle River, NJ: Prentice Hall.

4. Latham, G. P., & Pinder, C. C. (2005). Work motivation theory and research at the dawn of the 21st century. *Annual Reviews of Psychology, 56*(1), 485–516.

5. Kreitner, R., & Kinicki, A. (1998). *Organizational behavior* (4th ed., p. 158). Boston, MA: Irwin, McGraw-Hill.

6. Atkinson, R. L., Atkinson, R. C., & Hilgard, E. R. (1990). *Introduction to psychology* (10th ed., p. 361). San Diego, CA: Harcourt Brace Jovanovich.

7. Boyatzis, R. E., & Skelly, F. R. (1991). The impact of changing values on organizational life. In D. A. Kolb, I. M. Rubin, & J. S. Osland (Eds.), *The organizational behavior reader* (pp. 1–15). Englewood Cliffs, NJ: Prentice Hall.

8. Boyatzis, R. E., & Skelly, F. R. (1991). The impact of changing values on organizational life. In D. A. Kolb, I. R. Rubin, & J. S. Osland (Eds.), *The organizational reader* (5th ed., pp. 1–15). Englewood Cliffs, NJ: Prentice Hall.

9. Steers, R. M., & Sanchez-Runde, C. J. (2002). Culture, motivation, and work behavior. In M. J. Gannon & K. L. Newman (Eds.), *The Blackwell handbook of principles of crosscultural management* (pp. 190–216). Bodmin, United Kingdom: MPG Books.

10. Earley, C. P. (2002). Redefining interactions across cultures and organizations: Moving forward with cultural intelligence. In B. M. Staw & R. M. Kramer (Eds.), *Research in organizational behavior: An annual series of analytical essays and critical reviews* (pp. 271–299). Kidlington, United Kingdom: Elsevier; Roe, R. A., Zinovieva, I. L., Diebes, E., & TenHorn, L. A. (2000). A comparison of work motivation in Bulgaria, Hungary, and the Netherlands: Test of a model. *Applied Psychology: International Review, 49,* 658–687.

11. Scholz, U., Dona Sud, S., & Schwarzer, R. (2002). Is general self-efficacy a universal construct? Psychometric findings from 25 countries. *European Journal of Psychological Assessment, 18*(3), 242–251.

12. Hecker, R., & Grimmer, M. (2006). The evolving psychological contract. In P. Holland & H. De Cieri (Eds.), *Contemporary issues in human resource development: An Australian perspective* (pp. 183–207). Frenchs Forest, Australia: Pearson Education Australia, Frenchs Forest, NSW.

13. Rousseau, D. M. (1989). Psychological and implied contracts in organizations. *Employee*

Responsibilities and Rights Journal, 2,
121–139.

14. Yankelovich, D. (1981). *New rules: Searching for self-fulfillment in a world turned upside down.* New York, NY: Random House.

15. Argyris, C. (1960). *Understanding organizational behavior.* Homewood, IL: Dorsey Press.

16. Anderson, N., & Schalk, R. (1998). The psychological contract in retrospect and prospect. *Journal of Organizational Behavior, 19,* 637–647.

17. Smithson, J., & Lewis, S. (2003). Psychological contract. History and definitions of the concept. *References and research encyclopedia.* Boston, MA: Boston College Sloan Work and Family Research Network. Retrieved from http://wfnetwork.bc.edu/encyclopedia_entry.php?id=250

18. Rousseau, D. M. (2001b). Schema, promise and mutuality: The building blocks of the psychological contract. *Journal of Occupational and Organizational Psychology, 74*(4), 511–541.

19. Shore, L., & Tetrick, L. E. (1994). The psychological contract as an explanatory framework in the employment relationship. In C. L. Cooper & D. M. Rousseau (Eds.), *Trends in organizational behavior* (Vol. 1, pp. 91–109). Chichester, United Kingdom: Wiley.

20. Rousseau, D. M. (1989). Psychological and implied contracts in organizations. *Employee Responsibilities and Rights Journal, 2*(2), 121–139.

21. Rousseau, D. M. (2001a). Psychological contracts: Violations and modifications. In J. S. Osland, D. A. Kolb, & I. M. Rubin (Eds.), *The organizational behavior reader* (7th ed.). Saddle Brook, NJ: Prentice Hall.

22. Shore, L. M., & Tetrick, L. E. (1994). The psychological contract as an explanatory framework in the employment relationship. In C. Cooper & D. Rousseau (Eds.), *Trends in organizational behavior* (Vol. 1, pp. 91–109). New York, NY: Wiley.

23. Aselage, J., & Eisenberger, R. (2003). Perceived organizational support and psychological contract: A theoretical interpretation. *Journal of Organizational Behavior, 24*(5), 491–509; Blau, P. (1964). *Exchange and power in social life.* New York, NY: Wiley; Homans, G. (1974). *Social behavior: Its elementary forms* (Rev. ed.). New York, NY: Harcourt Brace Jovanovich; Cullinane, N., & Dundon, T. (2006). The psychological contract:

A critical review. *International Journal of Management Reviews, 8*(2), 113–129.

24. Aselage & Eisenberger. (2003). Op. cit. For a discussion of how social exchange theory and psychological contract theory compare and contrast, see Aselage & Eisenberger's article.

25. Rousseau, D. M. (1995). *Psychological contracts in organizations.* Thousand Oaks, CA: Sage.

26. Guest, D., & Conaway, N. (1998). *Fairness at work and the psychological contract.* London, United Kingdom: Institute of Personnel and Development.

27. Herriot, P. (1992). *The career management challenge.* London, United Kingdom: Sage Publications; Herriot, P., Manning, W. E. G., & Kidd, J. M. (1997). The content of the psychological contract. *British Journal of Management, 8*(2), 151–162; Smithson, J., & Lewis, S. (2000). Is job insecurity changing the psychological contract? Young people's expectations of work. *Personnel Review, 29*(6), 680–702; Turnley, W. H., & Feldman, D. C. (1999b). The impact of psychological contract violations on exit, voice, loyalty and neglect. *Human Relations, 52*(7), 895–922.

28. Guss, E., & Miller, M. C. (2008, October). *Ethics and generational differences: Interplay between values and ethical business decision* [SHRM white paper]. Retrieved from http://www.shrm.org

29. Harwood, R. (2003, January). The psychological contract and remote working. An interview with Denise Rousseau. *Ahoy Magazine,* January 2003. Retrieved from http://www.odysseyzone.com/news/hot/rousseau.htm

30. Herriot, P., Manning, W. E. G., & Kidd, J. M. (1997). The content of the psychological contract. *British Journal of Management, 8,* 151–162.

31. Smithson, J., & Lewis, S. (2000). Is job insecurity changing the psychological contract? Young people's expectations of work. *Personnel Review, 29*(6), 680–702.

32. Noer, D. (2000). Leading organizations through survivor sickness: A framework for the new millennium. In R. Burke & C. L. Cooper (Eds.), *The organisation in crisis.* Oxford, United Kingdom: Blackwell.

33. See: Rousseau, D. M. (1990). New hire perceptions of their own and their employer's obligations: A study of psychological contracts. *Journal of Organizational Behavior, 11*(5), 389–400;

Herriot, P., Manning, W. E., & Kidd, J. M. (1997). The content of the psychological contract. *British Journal of Management, 8*(2), 151–162; Anderson, N., & Schalk, R. (1998). The psychological contract in retrospect and prospect [Special issue]. *Journal of Organizational Behavior, 19*, 637–647; Millward, L. J., & Hopkins, L. J. (1998). Psychological contracts, organizational and job commitment. *Journal of Applied Psychology, 28*(16), 1530–1556. Rousseau, D. M., & Wade-Benzoni, K. A. (1995). Changing individual-organizational attachments: A two-way street. In A. Howard (Ed.), *The changing nature of work*. Jossey Bass Sparrow, P. (2000). The new employment contract: Psychological implications of future work. In R. Burke & C. L. Cooper (Eds.), *The organisation in crisis*. Oxford, United Kingdom: Blackwell.

34. Rousseau, D. M., & Parks, J. M. (1993). The contracts of individuals and organizations. In L. L. Cummings & B. M. Staw (Eds.), *Research in organizational behavior* (Vol. 15, pp. 1–43). Greenwich, CT: JAI Press.

35. Millward, L. J., & Herriot, P. (2000). The psychological contract in the UK. In D. M. Rousseau & R. Schalk (Eds.), *Psychological contracts: Cross-national perspectives* (pp. 231–249). London, United Kingdom: Sage.

36. Lemire, L., & Rouillard, C. (2005). An empirical exploration of the psychological contract violation and individual behaviour. *Journal of Managerial Psychology, 20*(2), 150–163.

37. Sutton, G., & Griffin, M. (2004). Integrating expectations, experiences and psychological contract violations. A longitudinal study of new professionals. *Journal of Occupational and Organizational Psychology, 77*, 493–514.

38. Sturges, J., & Guest, D. (2004). Working to live or living to work? Work/life balance in the early career. *Human Resource Management Journal, 14*(4), 5–20.

39. Kramer, M. L., Wayne, S. J., Liden, R. C., & Sparrowe, R. T. (2005). The role of job security in understanding the relationship between employee's perceptions of temporary workers and employee performance. *Journal of Applied Psychology, 90*(2), 389–398.

40. Lester, S. W., Claire, E., & Kickull, J. (2001). Psychological contracts in the 21st century: What employees value most and how well organizations are responding to these expectations. *Human Resource Planning, 24*(1), 10–21.

41. Gakovic, A., & Tetrick, L. E. (2003). Psychological contract breach as a source of strain for employees. *Journal of Business and Psychology, 18*(2), 235–246.

42. Othman, R., Arshad, R., Hashim, N. A., & Rosmah, M. (2005). Psychological contract violation and organizational citizenship behaviour. *Gadjah Mada International Journal of Business, 7*(3), 325–349.

43. Sturges, J., Conway, N., Guest, D., & Liefooghe, A. (2005). Managing the career deal: The psychological contract as a framework for understanding career management, organizational commitment and work behavior. *Journal of Organizational Behavior, 26*(7), 821–838.

44. Lester, S. W., Turnley, W. H., Bloodgood, J. M., & Bolino, M. C. (2002). Not seeing eye to eye: Differences in supervisor and subordinate perceptions of an attribution for psychological contract breach. *Journal of Organizational Behavior, 23*(1), 39–56.

45. Rousseau. (2001a). Op. cit.

46. Robinson, S., & Rousseau, D. (1994). Violating the psychological contract: Not the exception but the norm. *Journal of Organizational Behavior, 15*(2), 289–298.

47. Robinson, S., & Wolfe-Morrison, E. (1995). Psychological contracts and organizational citizenship behavior: The effect of unfulfilled obligations on civic virtue behavior. *Journal of Organizational Behavior, 16*(2), 289–298.

48. Nicholson, N., & Johns, G. (1985). The absence culture and the psychological contract. *Academy of Management Review, 10*(3), 397–407.

49. Walster, E., Bercheid, E., & Walster, G. (1973). New directions in equity research. *Journal of Personality and Social Psychology, 25*(2), 151–176.

50. Robinson, S. L. (1992). *Responses to dissatisfaction* (Unpublished doctoral dissertation). Evanston, IL: Northwestern University School of Management.

51. Rousseau. (2001a). Op. cit.; Rusbult, C. E., Farrell, D., Rogers, G., & Mainous, A. G., III. (1988). Impact of exchange variables on exit, voice, loyalty, and neglect: An integrative model of responses to declining job satisfaction. *Academy of Management Journal, 31*, 599–627;

Thomas, D. C., & Au, K. (2002). The effect of cultural variation on the behavioral response to low job satisfaction. *Journal of International Business Studies, 33*(2), 309–326; Turnley, W. H., & Feldman, D. C. (1999). The impact of psychological contract violations on exit, voice, loyalty and neglect. *Human Relations, 52*(7), 895–922.

52. Thomas, D. C., Au, K., & Ravlin, E. D. (2003). Cultural variation and the psychological contract. *Journal of Organizational Behavior, 24*(5), 451–471.

53. Allen, R., & Keaveny, T. (1981). Correlates of faculty interests in unionization: A replication and extension. *Journal of Applied Psychology, 66*(5), 582–588.

54. Getman, J., Goldberg, S., & Herman, J. (1976). *Union representation elections: Law and reality.* New York, NY: Russell Sage.

55. Near, J., & Miceli, M. (1986). Retaliation against whistleblowers: Predictors and effects. *Journal of Applied Psychology, 71*(1), 137–145.

56. Rousseau, D. M., Robinson, S. L., & Kraatz, M. S. (1992, May). *Renegotiating the psychological contract.* Paper presented at the meeting of the Society for Industrial Organizational Psychology, Montreal.

57. Rousseau, Robinson, & Kraatz. (1992). Ibid.

58. Rousseau. (2001a). Op. cit., p. 6.

59. Rousseau. (2001a). Op. cit., p. 7.

60. Rusbult, C., Farrell, D., Rogers, G., & Mainous, A. (1988). Impact of exchange variables on exit voice, loyalty, and neglect: An integrative model of response to declining job satisfaction. *Academy of Management Journal, 31*(3), 599–627.

61. Rousseau. (2001a). Op. cit., p. 7.

62. Sparrow, P., & Cooper, C. L. (2003). *The employment relationship: Key challenges for HR.* Burlington, MA: Butterworth-Heinemann.

63. Robinson, S. L., & Rousseau, D. M. (1994). Violating the psychological contract: Not the exception but the norm. *Journal of Organizational Behavior, 15*(3), 245–259.

64. Rousseau. (2001a). Ibid.

65. Robinson & Rousseau. (1994). Op. cit.

66. Thomas, D. C., Hu, K., & Rastin, E. C. (2003). Cultural variation and the psychological contract. *Journal of Organizational Behavior, 24*(5), 451–471.

67. Rousseau. (2001). Op. cit.

68. Rousseau. (2001a). Op. cit. pp. 7–8.

69. Ang, S., Tan, M. L., & Ng, K. Y. (2000). Psychological contracts in Singapore. In D. Rousseau & R. Schalk (Eds.), *Psychological contracts in employment: Cross-national perspectives.* Newbury Park, CA: Sage.

70. Schmidt, W. H. & Posner, B. A. (1983). Managerial values in perspective. *American Management Associations' Survey Report,* New York, NY; Similar findings in: Yankelovich. (1981). Op. cit; and Yankelovich, D. and Immerwahr, J. (1983). *Putting the work ethic back to work: A public agenda report on restoring America's competitive vitality.* New York: The Public Agenda Foundation.

71. Boyatzis & Skelly (1991). Op. cit.

72. Robinson, S. L., & Rousseau, D. M. (1994). Violating the psychological contract: Not the exception but the norm. *Journal of Organizational Behavior, 15*(3), 245–259; Grimmer, M., & Oddy, M. (2007). Violation of the psychological contract: The mediating effects. *Australian Journal of Management, 32*(1), 153–174; Kickul, J. (2001). Promises made, promises broken: An exploration of employee attraction and retention practices in small business. *Journal of Small Business Management, 39*(4), 320–335.

73. Robinson, S. L. (1996). Trust and breach of the psychological contract. *Administrative Science Quarterly, 41*(4), 574–599.

74. Turnley, W. H., & Feldman, D. C. (1999). The impact of psychological contract violations on exit, voice, loyalty, and neglect. *Human Relations, 52*(7), 895–922.

75. Coyle-Shapiro, J., & Kessler, I. (2000). Consequences of psychological contract for the employment relationship: A large scale survey. *Journal of Management Studies, 37*(7), 903–930; Van Dyne, L., & Ang, S. (1998). Organizational citizenship behavior of contingent workers in Singapore. *Academy of Management Journal, 41*(6), 692–703.

76. Robinson, S. L., Kraatz, M. S., & Rousseau, D. M. (1994). Changing obligations and the psychological contract: A longitudinal study. *Academy of Management Journal, 37*(1), 137–146; Grimmer & Oddy. (2007). Op. cit.

77. Grimmer & Oddy. (2007). Op. cit.

78. Cullinane & Dundon. (2006). Op. cit. p. 119.

79. Guest, D. (1998). Is the psychological contract worth taking seriously? *Journal of Organizational*

Behavior, 19(6), 649–664; Guest, D. (2004). Flexible employment contracts, the psychological contract and employee outcomes: An analysis and review of the evidence. *International Journal of Management Reviews, 5/6*(1), 1–19. Guest (1998) also suggests that the conceptual distinctions between "obligations" and "expectations" are somewhat obscure.

80. Cullinane & Dundon. (2006). Op. cit.

81. Cullinane & Dundon. (2006). Op. cit. p. 124; Ackroyd, S., & Thompson, P. (1999). *Organizational misbehavior*. London, United Kingdom: Sage; Hollway, W. (1991). *Work psychology and organization behavior: Managing the individual at work*. London, United Kingdom: Sage.

82. Boxall, P., & Purcell, J. (2003). *Strategy and human resource management*. Basingstoke, United Kingdom: Palgrave Macmillan.

83. Guest, D. (1998). Is the psychological contract worth taking seriously? [Special issue]. *Journal of Organizational Behavior, 19*, 649–664.

84. Cullinane & Dundon. (2006). Op. cit., pp. 117, 122.

85. Guest, D., & Conaway, N. (1998). *Fairness at work and the psychological contract*. London, United Kingdom: Institute of Personnel and Development.

86. Maslow, A. (1971). *The farther reaches of human nature*. New York, NY: Viking Press; Maslow, A., & Lowery, R. (Ed.). (1998). *Toward a psychology of being* (3rd ed.). New York, NY: Wiley & Sons.

87. Herzberg, F., Mausner, B., & Snyderman, B. S. (1993). *The motivation to work*. New Brunswick, NJ: Transaction.

88. Herzberg named dissatisfiers "hygiene" factors by using a medical metaphor: Although hygiene is very important in preventing serious infection, hygiene alone typically does not produce a cure just as hygiene factors by themselves cannot produce high levels of job satisfaction.

89. Herzberg, F. J. (1987). One more time: How do you motivate employees? *Harvard Business Review, 65*(5), 109–120.

90. House, R. J., & Wigdor, L. A. (1967). Herzberg's dual-factor theory of job satisfaction and motivation: A review of the evidence and a criticism. *Personnel Psychology, 20*(4), 369–389.

91. Herzberg, F. J. (1987). One more time: How do you motivate employees? *Harvard Business Review, 65*(5), 109–120.

92. Herzberg. (1987). Ibid.

93. Gill, T. G. (1996). Expert systems usage: Task change and intrinsic motivation. *MIS Quarterly, 20*(3), 301–329.

94. In an experiment using these motivators in a business setting, at the end of 6 months, Herzberg found the members of the achieving unit to be outperforming their counterparts in the control group, and in addition indicated a marked increase in their liking for their jobs. Other results showed that the achieving group had lower absenteeism and, later, a much higher promotion rate. See: Herzberg. (1987). Op. cit.

95. Sergiovanni, T. J. (1967). Factors which affect satisfaction and dissatisfaction of teachers. *Journal of Educational Administration, 5*(1), 66–82.

96. Sergiovanni, T. J., & Carver, F. D. (1980). *The new school executive* (p. 108). New York, NY: Harper & Row.

97. Sergiovanni & Carver. (1980). Ibid.

98. Savage, R. M. (1967). *A study of teacher satisfaction and attitudes: Causes and effects* (Unpublished doctoral dissertation). Auburn University, Auburn, AL; Wickstrom, R. A. (1971). *An investigation into job satisfaction among teachers* (Unpublished doctoral dissertation). University of Oregon, Eugene.

99. Moxley, L. (1977). *Job satisfaction of faculty teaching higher education: An examination of Herzberg's dual factor theory and Porter's need satisfaction research.* (ERIC Document No. ED 139-349)

100. Miskel, C. G. (1973). The motivation of educators to work. *Educational Administration Quarterly, 9*(1), 42–53.

101. Miskel, C. G. (1974). Intrinsic, extrinsic, and risk propensity factors in the work attitudes of teachers, educational administrators, and business managers. *Journal of Applied Psychology, 59*(3), 339–343.

102. Herzberg, Mausner, & Snyderman. (1993). Op. cit., p. 141.

103. Vroom, V. H. (1964). *Work and motivation*. New York, NY: John Wiley & Sons.

104. Solimon, H. M. (1970). Motivator-hygiene theory of job attitudes: An empirical investigation and attempt to reconcile both the one- and

two-factor theories of job attitudes. *Journal of Applied Psychology, 54*(5), 452–461.

105. Vroom. (1964). Op. cit.; Graen, G. (1966). Motivator and hygiene dimensions for research and development engineers. *Journal of Applied Psychology, 50*(6), 563–566.

106. House & Wigdor. (1967). Op. cit.

107. Miner, J. B. (2005). *Organizational behavior 1. Essential theories of motivation and leadership.* Armonk, NY: M.E. Sharpe; Malinowsky, M. R., & Babby, J. R. (1965). Determinants of work attitude. *Journal of Applied Psychology, 49,* 446–451; Burke, R. (1966). Are Herzberg's motivators and hygienes unidimensional? *Journal of Applied Psychology, 50*(4), 317–321; Ewen, R. B. (1964). Some determinants of job satisfaction: A study of the generality of Herzberg's theory. *Journal of Applied Psychology, 48*(3), 161–163; Dunnette, M. D. (1965, May). *Factor structure of unusually satisfying and unusually dissatisfying job situations for six occupational groups.* Paper presented at Midwestern Psychological Association, Chicago, IL.

108. House, R. J., & Wigdor, L. A. (1967). Herzberg's dual-factor theory of job satisfaction and motivation: A review of the evidence and a criticism. *Personnel Psychology, 20*(4), 369–389.

109. Herzberg, F., Mausnek, B., & Snyderman, B. (1959). *The motivation to work* (2nd ed.). New York, NY: John Wiley & Sons.

110. Vroom. (1964). Op. cit.

111. Campbell, J. P. (1990). *Managerial behavior, performance, and effectiveness.* New York, NY: McGraw-Hill.

112. Miner, J. B. (2002). *Organizational behavior: Foundations, theories, and analysis.* New York, NY: Oxford University Press.

113. Miner. (2002). Ibid.

114. Ambrose, M. L., & Kulik, C. T. (1999). Old friends, new faces: Motivation research in the 1990s. *Journal of Management, 25*(3), 231–292.

115. Gnoth, J. (1997). Tourism and motivation and expectation formation. *Annals of Tourism Research, 24*(2), 283–304; Mcneesesmith, D. K. (1999). The relationship between managerial motivation, leadership, nurse outcomes and patient satisfaction. *Journal of Organizational Behavior, 20*(2), 243–259; Poppleton, P. (1999). Teacher morale, job-satisfaction and motivation, by L. Evans. *Teaching and Teacher Education,*

15(3), 325–331; Stamatoplos, A., & Mackoy, R. (1998). Effects of library instruction on university-students' satisfaction with the library: A longitudinal study. *College and Research Libraries, 59*(4), 323–334; Tuten, T. L., & August, R. A. (1998). Understanding consumer satisfaction in service settings—A bidimensional model of service strategies. *Journal of Social Behavior and Personality, 13*(3), 553–564.

116. Zhang, P., & Van Dran, G. M. (2000). Satisfiers and dissatisfiers: A two-factor model for website design and evaluation. *Journal of the American Society for Information Science, 51*(14), 1253–1268.

117. Pinder, C. C. (1984). *Work motivation: Theory, issues, and applications.* Dallas, TX: Scott, Foresman.

118. Stipek, D. J. (1993). *Motivation to learn* (2nd ed.). Boston, MA: Allyn & Bacon.

119. McClelland, D. C. (1961). *The achieving society.* Princeton, NJ: D. Van Nostrand.

120. Castenell, L. A. (1983). Achievement motivation: An investigation of adolescents' achievement patterns. *American Educational Research Journal, 20*(4), 503–510.

121. McClelland, D. C. (2001). Op. cit; Stipek, D. J. (1993). Motivation to learn. (2nd edition). Boston, MA: Allyn & Bacon; Wood, S. E., & Wood, E. G. (1999). *The world of psychology.* Boston, MA: Allyn & Bacon.

122. Katzell, R. A., & Thompson, D. E. (1990). Work motivation: Theory and practice. *American Psychologist, 45*(2), 144–153.

123. Ambrose, M. L., & Kulik, C. T. (1999). Old friends, new faces: Motivation research in the 1990s. *Journal of Management, 25*(3), 231–292.

124. Bluen, S. D., Barling, J., & Burns, W. (1990). Predicting sales performance, job satisfaction, and depression by using the achievement strivings and impatience-irritability dimensions of type A behavior. *Journal of Applied Psychology, 75*(2), 212–216.

125. Lee, C. (1995). Prosocial organizational behaviors: The roles of workplace justice, achievement striving, and pay satisfaction. *Journal of Business and Psychology, 10*(2), 197–206.

126. McClelland, D. C., & Franz, C. E. (1992). Motivational and other sources of work accomplishments in mid-life: A longitudinal study. *Journal of Personality, 60*(4), 697–707.

127. Barling, J., Kelloway, E. K., & Cheung, D. (1996). Time management and achievement striving interact to predict car sales performance. *Journal of Applied Psychology, 81*(6), 821–826.

128. Wright, P. M., Kacmar, K. M., McMahan, G. C., & Deleeuw, K. (1995). P = f(M × A): Cognitive ability as a moderator of the relationship between personality and job performance. *Journal of Management, 21*(6), 1129–1139.

129. McClelland & Franz. (1992). Op. cit.; Wright et al. (1995). Op. cit.

130. Stein, J. A., Smith, G. M., Guy, S. B., & Bentler, P. M. (1993). Consequences of adolescent drug use on young adult job behavior and job satisfaction. *Journal of Applied Psychology, 78*(3), 463–474; Miner, J. B., Smith, N. R., & Bracker, J. S. (1994). Role of entrepreneurial task motivation in the growth of technologically innovative firms: Interpretations from follow-up data. *Journal of Applied Psychology, 79*(44), 627–630.

131. Cassidy, T., & Lynn, R. (1989). A multifactorial approach to achievement motivation: The development of a comprehensive measure. *Journal of Occupational Psychology, 62,* 301–312.

132. Entwisle, D. R. (1972). To dispel fantasies about fantasy-based measures of achievement motivation. *Psychological Bulletin, 77*(6), 377–391; Fineman, S. (1977). The achievement motive and its measurement: Where are we now? *British Journal of Psychology, 68*(1), 1–22; Klinger, E. (1966). Fantasy need achievement. *Psychological Bulletin, 66,* 291–306; Scott, W. A., & Johnson, R. C. (1972). Comparative validities of direct and indirect personality tests. *Journal of Consulting and Clinical Psychology, 38*(3), 301–318; Weinstein, M. S. (1969). Achievement motivation and risk preference. *Journal of Personality and Social Psychology, 13*(2), 153–172; Schatz, S. O. (1961). Achievement and economic growth: A critique. *Quarterly Journal of Economics, 79*(2), 234–245; Tekiner. (1980). Op. cit.

133. Ray, J. J. (1980). The comparative validity of Likert, projective, and forced-choice indices of achievement motivation. *Journal of Social Psychology, 111*(1), 63–72; Bernstein, H. (1971). Modernization theory and the sociological study of development. *Journal of Development Studies, 7*(2), 141–160.

134. Rhodes, R. I. (1968). The disguised conservatism in evolutionary development theory. *Science and Society, 32*(3), 383–412.

135. Bernstein. (1971). Op. cit.

136. Maehr, M. (1974). *Sociocultural origins of achievement.* Monterey, CA: Brooks/Cole.

137. McClelland, D. C. (1980). Motive dispositions: The merits of operant and respondent measures. In L. Wheeler (Ed.), *Review of personality and social psychology, 1* (pp. 10–41). Beverly Hills, CA: Sage; McClelland, D. C. (1985). How motives, skills, and values determine what people do. *American Psychologist, 40,* 812–825. Such incentives might include the inherent lure of the activity's content; the degree of risk the activity represents; having the appropriate knowledge, skills, and experience to succeed at the activity; and the time pressure and desirable social or material rewards available for effectively completing the activity. For a more detailed analysis and discussion, see Spangler (1992).

138. Castenell. (1983). Op. cit.

139. Jacquette, J. S. (1982). Reviewed: Women and modernization theory. A decade of feminist criticism. *World Psychology, 34*(2), 267–284. Need for achievement was viewed as intermediary in that women who could not act out this desire in their own lives would inculcate "need achievement" in their sons.

140. McClelland, D. (1975). *Power. The inner experience.* New York, NY: Irvington.

141. Griscom, J. L. (1992). Women and power. Definition, dualism, and differences. *Psychology of Women Quarterly, 16*(4), 389–414.

142. Castenell, L. A. (1983). Achievement motivation: An investigation of adolescents' achievement patterns. *American Educational Research Journal, 20*(4), 503–510.

143. Deci, E., & Ryan, R. M. (1985). *Intrinsic motivation and self-determination in human behavior.* New York, NY: Plenum; Deci, E., Vallerance, R. J., Pelletier, L. G., & Ryan, R. M. (1991). Motivation and education: The self-determination perspective. *Educational Psychologist, 26*(3), 325–346; Ryan, R. M., & Deci, E. L. (2000). Intrinsic and extrinsic motivation: Classroom definitions and new directions. *Contemporary Educational Psychology, 25*(1), 54–67.

144. deCharms, R. (1976). *Enhancing motivation.* New York, NY: Irvington; deCharms, R. (1983). Intrinsic motivation, peer tutoring, and cooperative learning practical maxims. In J. Levine & M. Wang (Eds.), *Teacher and student perceptions: Implications for learning* (pp. 391–398). Hillsdale, NJ: Erlbaum.

145. deCharms. (1976). Op. cit.; Ryan, R. M., & Grolnick, W. S. (1986). Origins and pawns in the classroom: Self-report and projective assessments of individual differences in the children's perceptions. *Journal of Personality and Social Psychology, 50*(3), 550–558.

146. Ambrose, M. L., & Kulik, C. T. (1999). Old friends, new faces: Motivation research in the 1990s. *Journal of Management, 25*(3), 231–292.

147. Wall, T. D., & Jackson, P. R. (1995). New manufacturing initiatives and shop floor job design. In A. Howard (Ed.), *The changing nature of work* (pp. 139–174). San Francisco, CA: Jossey-Bass.

148. Cordery, J. (1997). Reinventing work design theory and practice. *Australian Psychology, 32*(3), 185–189.

149. Cordery. (1997). Ibid.

150. Latham & Pinder. (2005). Op. cit.

151. Hackman, J. R., & Lawler, E. (1971). Development of the Job Diagnostic Survey. *Journal of Applied Psychology, 55*(3), 259–286.

152. Meiksins, P. F. & Watson, J. M. (1989). Professional autonomy and organizational constraint. *The Sociological Quarterly, 30*(4), 561–585.

153. Hall, R. H. (1972). Professionalization and bureaucratization. In R. H. Hall (Ed.), *The formal organization* (pp. 143–163). New York, NY: Basic Books; Miller, G. A. (1972). Professionals in bureaucracy: Alienation among industrial scientists and engineers. In R. H. Hall (Ed.), *The formal organization* (pp. 213–235). New York, NY: Basic Books; Scott, W. R. (1966). Professionals in organizations: Areas of conflict. In H. Vollmer & D. Mills (Eds.), *Professionalization* (pp. 265–275). Englewood Cliffs, NJ: Prentice-Hall.

154. Meiksins & Watson. (1989). Op. cit.

155. Perrow, C. (1967). A framework for the comparative analysis of organizations. *American Sociological Review, 32*(2),194–208.

156. Bailyn, L. (1985, Summer). Autonomy in the industrial R & D lab. *Human Resource Management, 24,* 129–146.

157. Freidson, E. (1986). *Professional powers.* Chicago, IL: University of Chicago Press; Larson, M. S. (1977). *The rise of professionalism: A sociological analysis.* Berkeley: University of California Press; Engel, G. (1969). The effect of bureaucracy on the professional authority of physicians. *Journal of Health and Social Behavior, 10,* 30–41.

158. Jamous, H., & Peloille, B. (1970). Professions or self-perpetuating systems? Changes in the French University hospital system. In J. A. Jackson (Ed.), *Professions and professionalization* (pp. 111–152). Cambridge, MA: Cambridge University Press; Larson, M. S. (1980). Proletarianization and educated labor. *Theory and Society, 9*(1), 131–175; Freidson. (1986). Op. cit.

159. Freidson, E. (1973). Professions and the occupational principle. In E. Freidson (Ed.), *The professions and their prospects* (pp. 19–38). Beverly Hills, CA: Sage.

160. Meiksins & Watson. (1989). Op. cit.

161. Raelin, J. (1985). *The clash of cultures: Managers and professionals.* Boston, MA: Harvard Business School Press.

162. Meiksins & Watson. (1989). Op. cit.

163. Dickenson, L. (1995). Autonomy and motivation: A literature review. *System, 23*(2), 165–174.

164. Deci, E. L., & Ryan, R. M. (1985a). *Intrinsic motivation and self-determination in human behavior.* New York, NY: Plenum; Deci, E. L., & Ryan, R. M. (1985b). The general causality orientations scale: Self-determination in personality. *Journal of Research in Personality, 19*(2) 109–134; Deci, E. L., & Ryan, R. M. (2000). The "what" and "why" of goal pursuits. Human needs and the self-determination of behavior. *Psychological Inquiry, 11*(4), 227–268; Gague, M., & Deci, E. L. (2005). Self-determination theory and work motivation. *Journal of Organizational Behavior, 26*(4), 331–362; Ryan, R. M., & Deci, E. L. (2000). Self-determination theory and the facilitation of intrinsic motivation, social development, and well-being. *American Psychologist, 55*(1), 68–78.

165. Deci & Ryan. (1985a). Op. cit.; Deci, E. L., Hodges, R., Pierson, L., & Tomassone, J. (1992). Autonomy and competence as motivational factors in students with learning disabilities and emotional handicaps. *Journal of Learning Disabilities, 25*(7), 457–471; Grolnick, W. S., & Ryan, R. M. (1987).

Autonomy in children's learning: An experimental and individual difference investigation. *Journal of Personality and Social Psychology, 52*(5), 890–898; Grolnick, W. S., Ryan, R. M., & Deci, E. L. (1991). Inner resources for school achievement: Motivational mediators of children's perceptions of their parents. *Journal of Educational Psychology, 83*(4), 508–517; Skinner, E. A., & Belmont, M. J. (1993). Motivation in the classroom: Reciprocal effects of teacher behavior and student engagement across the school year. *Journal of Educational Psychology, 85*(4), 571–581.

166. Deci et al. (1992). Op. cit.; Deci & Ryan. (1985a). Op. cit., p. 261; Grolnick & Ryan. (1987). Op. cit.; Grolnick et al. (1991). Op. cit.; Skinner & Belmont. (1993). Op. cit.

167. Amabile, T. M. (1983). The social psychology of creativity: A componential conceptualization. *Journal of Personality and Social Psychology, 45*(2), 357–376; Grolnick & Ryan. (1987). Op. cit.; McGraw, K. O., & McCullers, J. C. (1979). Evidence of a detrimental effect of extrinsic incentives on breaking a mental set. *Journal of Experimental Social Psychology, 15*(3) 285–294.

168. Deci, Hodges, Pierson, & Tomassone. (1992). Op. cit.; Grolnick, Ryan, & Deci. (1991). Op. cit.; Rosenholtz, S. J., & Simpson, C. (1984). Classroom organization and student stratification. *Elementary School Journal, 85*(1), 21–37; Skinner & Belmont. (1993). Op. cit.

169. Garcia, T., & Pintrich, P. R. (1996). The effects of autonomy on motivation and performance in the college classroom. *Contemporary Educational Psychology, 21*(4), 477–486. Researchers measured classroom autonomy here by asking students about the degree of choice they had over selecting paper topics and of readings and about the degree to which students were able to negotiate course policies with the instructor.

170. Frank, S. J., Pirsch, L. A., & Wright, V. C. (1990). Late adolescents' perceptions of their relationships with their parents: Relationships among deidealization, adolescent adjustment and ego identity status. *Journal of Youth and Adolescence, 19*(6), 571–588; Turner, R. A., Irwin, C. E., Jr., & Millstein, S. G. (1991). Family structure, family process, and experimenting with substances during adolescence. *Journal of Research on Adolescence, 1*(1), 93–104; Turner, R. J., & Lloyd, D. A. (1999).

The stress process and the social distribution of depression. *Journal of Health and Social Behavior, 40*(4), 374–404.

171. Deci et al. (1992). Op. cit.

172. For a thorough discussion of how varied social and physical science "schools of thought" view autonomy, see: Bandura, A. (1989). Human agency in social cognitive theory. *American Psychologist, 44*, 1175–1184; Mischel, W., & Shoda, Y. (1995). A cognitive-affective system of personality: Reconceptualizing situations, dispositions, dynamics, and invariance in personality structure. *Psychological Review, 102*, 246–268; Gergen, K. J. (1993). *The saturated self.* New York, NY: Basic Books.

173. Kagiticibasi, C. (2005). Autonomy and relatedness in cultural context: Implications for self and family. *Journal of Cross-Cultural Psychology, 36*(4), 403–422.

174. Rosenfield, S., Vertefuille, J., & McAlpine, D. (2000). Gender stratification and mental health: An exploration of dimensions of the self. *Social Psychology Quarterly, 63*(3), 208–223.

175. Gilligan, C. (1982). *In a different voice.* Cambridge, MA: Harvard University Press; Jordan, J. V. (1997). Do you believe that the concepts of self and autonomy are useful in understanding women? In J. V. Jordan (Ed.), *Women's growth in diversity: More writings from the Stone Center* (pp. 29–32). New York, NY: Guilford; Van Gundy, K. (2002). Gender, the assertion of autonomy, and the stress process in young adulthood. *Social Psychology Quarterly, 65*(4), 346–363.

176. Kagiticibasi, C. (2005). Autonomy and relatedness in cultural context: Implications for self and family. *Journal of Cross-Cultural Psychology, 36*(4), 403–422; Keller, H., Papaligoura, Z., Kunsemuller, P., Voelker, S., Papaeliou, C., Lohaus, A., et al. (2003). Concepts of mother-infant interaction in Greece and Germany. *Journal of Cross-Cultural Psychology, 34*(6), 677–689; Killen, M., & Wainryb, C. (2000). Independence and interdependence in diverse cultural contexts. In S. Harkness, C. Raeff, & C. M. Super (Eds.), *Variability in the social construction of the child. New directions in child and adolescent development* (pp. 5–22). San Francisco, CA: Jossey-Bass.

177. Baumeister, R., & Leary, M. R. (1995). The need to belong: Desire for interpersonal attachments as

a fundamental human motivation. *Psychological Bulletin, 117*, 497–529; Capps, D., & Fenn, R. (1992). *Individualism reconsidered: Bearing on the endangered self in modern society* (Princeton Theological Seminary Monograph Series No. 1). Princeton, NJ: A & A Printing; Schwartz, B. (1986). *The battle for human nature: Science, morality, and modern life*. New York, NY: Norton; Smith, M. B. (1994). Selfhood at risk: Post-modern perils and the perils of postmodernism. *American Psychologist, 49*, 405–411; Wallach, M. A., & Wallach, L. (1983). *Psychology's sanction for selfishness: The error of egoism in theory and therapy*. New York, NY: Freeman.

178. Locke & Henne. (1986). Op. cit.

179. Vroom, V. H. (1994). *Work and motivation*. San Francisco, CA: Jossey-Bass.

180. Lawler, E. E. (1990). *Strategic pay: Aligning organizational strategies and pay systems*. San Francisco, CA: Jossey-Bass.

181. Wanous, J. P., Keon, T. I., & Latack, J. C. (1983). Expectancy theory and occupational/organizational choices: A review and test. *Organizational Behavior and Human Performance, 32*(1), 66–86.

182. Pecotich, A., & Churchill, G. A. (1981). An examination of the anticipated satisfaction importance valence controversy. *Organizational Behavior and Human Performance, 27*(1), 137–156.

183. Ambrose & Kulik. (1999). Ibid. See Ambrose and Kulik for the specific studies that integrate expectancy theories with other theories to provide a clearer understanding of motivation.

184. Maidani, E. A. (1991). Comparative study of Herzberg's two-factor theory of job satisfaction among public and private sectors. *Public Personnel Management, 20*(4), 441–448.

185. Jurkiewicz, C. L., & Massey, T. K., Jr. (1997). What motivates municipal employees: A comparison study of supervisory vs. non-supervisory personnel. *Public Personnel Management, 26*(3), 367–376.

186. Emmert, M. A., & Taher, W. A. (1992). Public sector professionals: The effects of public sector jobs on motivation, job satisfaction and work involvement. *American Review of Public Administration, 22*(1), 37–48.

187. Gabris, G. T., & Simo, G. (1995). Public sector motivation as an independent variable affecting career decisions. *Public Personnel Management, 24*(1), 33–50.

188. Vinokur-Kaplan, D., Jayaratne, S., & Chess, W. A. (1994). Job satisfaction and retention of social workers in public agencies, non-profit agencies, and private practice: The impact of workplace conditions and motivators. *Administration in Social Work, 18*(1), 93–121.

189. Leviatan, U. (1992). Determinants of work motivation and work satisfaction among kibbutz aged workers. *Canadian Journal of Community Mental Health, 11*(2), 49–64; Savery, L. K., & Wingham, D. L. (1991). Coping with the career plateau: Motivators for directors of child-care centers. *Leadership and Organization Development Journal, 12*(2), 17–19; Charles, K. R., & Marshall, L. H. (1992). Motivational preferences of Caribbean hotel workers: An exploratory study. *International Journal of Contemporary Hospitality, 4*(3), 25–29.

190. Campbell, J. P., & Pritchard, R. D. (1976). Motivation theory in industrial and organizational psychology. In M. D. Dunnette (Ed.), *Handbook of industrial and organizational psychology* (pp. 63–130). Chicago, IL: Rand McNally; Mitchell, T. R. (1974). Expectancy models of job satisfaction, occupational preference and effort: A theoretical, methodological, and empirical appraisal. *Psychological Bulletin, 81*(12), 1053–1077; Lord, R. G., Hanges, P. J., & Godfrey, E. G. (2003). Integrating neural networks into decision making and motivational theory: Rethinking VIE theory. *Canadian Psychology, 44*(1), 21–38.

191. Ilgen, D. R., Nebeker, D. M., & Pritchard, R. D. (1981). Expectancy theory measures: An empirical comparison in an experimental simulation. *Organizational Behavior and Human Performance, 28*(1), 189–223.

192. Staw, B. M., & Cummings, L. I. (Eds.). (1990). *Research in organizational behavior* (Vol. 12). Greenwich, CT: JAI Press.

193. Commitment may be defined as an employee attitude or set of behavioral intentions, such as a desire to remain with the organization, an intention to exert high levels of effort on behalf of the organization, and an identification with the organization's goals. See Scholl, R. W. (1981). Differentiating organizational commitment from

expectancy as a motivating force. *Academy of Management Review, 6*(4), 589–599.

194. Scholl, R. W. (1981). Differentiating organizational commitment from expectancy as a motivating force. *Academy of Management Review, 6*(4), 589–599.

195. Jehn, K. A., Northcraft, G. B., & Neale, M. A. (1999). Why differences make a difference: A field study of diversity, conflict, and performance in workgroups. *Administrative Science Quarterly, 44*(4), 741–763.

196. Robertson, Q. M. (2006). Disentangling the meanings of diversity and inclusion in organization. *Group Organizational Management, 31*(2), 212–236.

197. Bureau of Labor Statistics. (2007). *Demographic characteristics of the labor force (current population survey)*. Retrieved from http://www.bls.gov/

198. Cooperrider, D. L., & Sekerka, L. E. (2003). Toward a theory of positive organizational change. In K. S. Cameron, J. E. Dutton, & R. E. Quinn (Eds.), *Positive organizational scholarship: Foundations of a new discipline* (pp. 225–240). San Francisco, CA: Berrett-Koehler.

199. Stevens, F. G., Plaut, V. C., & Sanchez-Burks, J. (2008). Unlocking the benefits of diversity: All-inclusive multiculturalism and positive organizational change. *Journal of Applied Behavioral Science, 44*(1), 116–133.

200. Earley, P. C., & Mosakowski, E. (2000). Creating hybrid team cultures: An empirical test of transnational team functioning. *Academy of Management Journal, 43*(1), 26–49; Ely, R. J., & Thomas, D. A. (2001). Cultural diversity at work: The effects of diversity perspectives on work group processes and outcomes. *Administrative Science Quarterly, 46*(2), 229–273; Polzer, J. T., Milton, L. P., & Swann, W. B., Jr. (2002). Capitalizing on diversity: Interpersonal congruence in small work groups. *Administrative Science Quarterly, 47*(2), 296–324; Swann, W. B., Jr., Kwan, V. S. Y., Polzer, J. T., & Milton, L. P. (2003). Fostering group identification and creativity in diverse groups: The role of individuation and self-verification. *Personality and Social Psychology Bulletin, 29*(11), 1396–1406.

201. See: Chatman, J. A., Polzer, J. T., Barsade, S. G., & Neale, M. A. (2006). Being different yet feeling similar: The influence of demographic composition of organizational culture on work processes and outcomes. *Administrative Science Quarterly, 43*(4), 749–780; Jehn et al. (1999). Op. cit.; Morrison, E. W., & Milliken, R. J. (2000). Organizational silence: A barrier to change and development in a pluralistic world. *Academy of Management Review, 25*(4), 706–725; Westphal, J. D., & Milton, L. P. (2000). How experience and network ties affect the influence of demographic minorities on corporate boards. *Administrative Science Quarterly, 45*(2), 366–398.

202. Plaut, V. C., & Markus, H. R. (2007). *Basically we're all the same? Models of diversity and the dilemma of difference* (Unpublished manuscript). University of Georgia.

203. Markus, H. R., Steele, C. M., & Steele, D. M. (2000). Colorblindness as a barrier to inclusion: Assimilation and non-immigrant minorities. *Daedalus, 129*, 233–259; Plaut, V. C. (2002). Cultural models of diversity: The psychology of difference and inclusion. In R. Shweder, M. Minow, & H. R. Markus (Eds.), *Engaging cultural differences: The multicultural challenge in a liberal democracy* (pp. 365–395). New York, NY: Russell Sage; Hogg, M. A., & Terry, D. J. (2000). Social identity and self-categorization processes in organizational contexts. *Academy of Management Review, 25*(1), 121–140.

204. Markus et al. (2000). Op. cit.

205. Chrobot-Mason, D., & Thomas, K. M. (2002). Minority employees in majority organizations: The intersection of individual and organizational racial identity in the workplace. *Human Resource Development Review, 1*(3), 323–344.

206. Bonilla-Silva, E. (2003). *Racism without racists: Color-blind racism and the persistence of racial inequality in the United States.* Lanham, MD: Rowman & Littlefield.

207. Plat & Markus. (2007). Op. cit.; Verkuyten, M. (2005). Ethnic group identification and group evaluation among minority and majority groups: Testing the multiculturalism hypothesis. *Journal of Personality and Social Psychology, 88*(1), 121–138.

208. Brief, A. P., Umphress, E. E., Dietz, J., Burrows, J. W., Butz, R. M., & Scholten, L. (2005). Community matters: Realistic group conflict theory and the impact of diversity. *Academy of Management Journal, 48*(5), 830–844;

Kalev, A., Dobbin, F., & Kelly, E. (2006). Best practices or best guesses? Assessing the efficacy of corporate affirmative action and diversity policies. *American Sociological Review, 71*(4), 589–617; Mannix, E. A., & Neale, M. A. (2006). What differences make a difference? The promise and reality of diverse teams in organizations. *Psychological Science in the Public Interest, 6*(2), 32–55; Thomas, K. M. (2008). *Diversity resistance in organizations: Manifestations and solutions.* Mahwah, NJ: Lawrence Erlbaum.

209. Linnehan, F., & Konrad, A. M. (1999). Diluting diversity: Implications for intergroup in organizations. *Journal of Management Inquiry, 8*(4), 399–413; Thomas, K. M., & Plaut, V. C. (2008). The many faces of diversity in the workplace. In K. M. Thomas (Ed.), *Diversity resistance in organizations: Manifestations and solutions* (pp. 1–22). Mahwah, NJ: Lawrence Erlbaum.

210. Stevens, Plaut, & Sanchez-Burks. (2008). Op. cit.

211. Plaut et al. (2007). Op. cit.; Stevens et al. (2008). Op. cit.; Markys et al. (2000). Op. cit.

212. See: Davidson, M. N., & James, E. J. (2006). The engines of positive relationships across difference: Conflict and learning. In J. E. Dutton & B. R. Ragins (Eds.), *Exploring positive relationships at work: Building a theoretical and research foundation* (pp. 137–158). Mahwah, NJ: Lawrence Erlbaum; Wolsko, C., Pak, B., Judd, C. M., & Wittenbrick, B. (2000). Framing interethnic ideology: Effects of multicultural and color-blind perspectives on judgments of groups and individuals. *Journal of Personality and Social Psychology, 78*(4), 635–654.

CHAPTER **7**

Leadership as Developing Human Capital

Focus Questions

◆ In what ways is leadership "capacity building" and why is it important in schools?
◆ In what ways can principals develop teachers' leadership capacity?
◆ How can principals use attribution theory to help develop teacher leadership in their schools?

CASE STUDY: A TALE OF TWO PRINCIPALS

It was the most enabling of times. It was the least enabling of times. Mr. Jones was principal of Alpha High School. Mrs. Smith was principal of Omega High School. Both high schools enrolled approximately the same number of students and each had similar student and community demographics. Prudence Johnson, an educational leadership student, shadowed both principals for 2 weeks as part of her 1-month paid internship. Prudence is in her tenth year of teaching at Alpha High School where she is a ninth-grade team leader. One of the internship requirements was to document how the principal handled certain issues that included the following seven situations:

1. Personal conflict between teachers
2. Curriculum decisions
3. Faculty meeting planning
4. Developing teacher leadership
5. Working with or developing the master schedule
6. Parent conferences
7. Student achievement issues

The following passages are Prudence's log documenting the seven situations.

Log of Alpha High School Shadowing

Mr. Jones is in his eleventh year as principal of Alpha High School. Prior to this assignment, he was an assistant principal for 6 years in a middle school in the same school district. He was a classroom teacher for 9 years before that. I viewed the seven situations required in the internship and provide the following log. I have been a teacher at this school for 10 years.

1. ***Personal conflict between teachers.*** *Adam Pernell and Joe Landon, in the same grade-level team, have been having problems getting along with each other. Adam feels as if Joe is not pulling his weight on the team. Adam reports that Joe frequently does not follow through on the weekly team planning. Joe feels that Adam is being too bossy with him and objects to Adam's directives. The team leader, Lorne Cartwright, has not dealt with the issue even though Adam and Joe have brought this to his attention numerous times. Finally, Adam goes to the principal for assistance. Mr. Jones allows me to sit in on all the meetings.*

   Meeting #1. Adam Pernell approaches the principal in the hallway and mentions that he has "had it" with Joe Landon. There is no use in wasting time in the team planning session if Joe is not going to follow through with the planned activities. The principal says he will meet with the two teachers a bit later on in the week.

   Meeting #2. Joe Landon approaches the principal the next day saying he heard that Adam Pernell has made derogatory comments about him, and he is tired of Adam's bossy attitude toward him. Joe requests a meeting with the principal and Adam as soon as possible. The principal agrees to meet with the two teachers a bit later in the week.

Meeting #3. *Adam and Joe both approach the principal the following week about the meeting. Mr. Jones says he will meet with both teachers as soon as he can. I ask the principal how he plans to deal with the situation. He tells me that the conflict will blow over. He has seen similar problems in the past with the two and the problems always resolve themselves.*

Meeting #4. *Two weeks later Adam tells the principal he wants to be transferred to a different team. The planning sessions have stopped and no one on the team is talking to each other.*

Meeting #5. *The principal sees Adam Pernell at the counter in the main office at the start of the first lunch period and asks him to come in and chat for a minute. Mr. Jones asks permission from Mr. Pernell for me to sit in. Adam agrees. Mr. Jones then sits behind his desk and asks me to stand while bidding Adam to sit in the chair facing the principal's desk. Mr. Jones's countenance changes as he says that he is tired of hearing about the problems between Adam and Joe. They are both adults and professionals. Both need to do their work; and if they cannot be friends, they must at least be professionals and work together. He does not want to hear anything more about this issue again. Mr. Jones hits his fist on the desk and asks if there are any questions. Adam says he understands and leaves the office.*

Meeting #6. *The principal sees Joe Landon at the main office counter at the end of the first lunch period and asks to see him for a minute in the office. He asks if it is permissible for me to sit in on the meeting. Joe has no objection. Mr. Jones then sits behind his desk and asks me to stand while bidding Joe to sit in the chair facing the principal's desk. Mr. Jones's countenance changes as he says that he is tired of hearing about the problems between Adam and Joe. They are both adults and professionals. Both need to do their work; and if they cannot be friends, they must at least be professionals and work together. He does not want to hear anything more about this issue again. Mr. Jones hits his fist on the desk and asks if there are any questions. Joe says he understands and leaves the office.*

2. ***Curriculum decisions.*** *I talk with Mr. Jones about how curriculum decisions are made at the school. He mentions that this is a good time to discuss this since the new reading textbook adoptions are due next week. He gives me four reading textbook series to review and asks me to tell him which is the best one. I feel rather honored to provide this input. Two days later I give him my recommendation. He says that is his favorite series as well. He then calls the curriculum director and places the order for next year's textbooks. I ask him if we should have consulted the teachers about the change. He says they are busy enough with all they have to do and they appreciate being told what to do.*

3. ***Faculty meeting planning.*** *Mr. Jones and I review the ideas necessary to discuss at tomorrow's faculty meeting. He says that he likes to send the agenda out the morning of the faculty meeting so teachers will know what they are meeting about that afternoon. He tells me that he has placed the following items on the agenda:*

   ◆ *Reminder of the state testing in 6 weeks. He will be sending out memos of curriculum areas that need to be addressed from the benchmark testing results.*

- *Next month's duty assignments—hall duty, morning and afternoon bus duty, lunch supervision assignments, bathroom supervision assignments during change of classes, and others as needed.*
- *Reminder of progress reports being sent out next week. Make certain there are at least four letter grades in the grade books at progress report time.*
- *Parent conference night is 9 days away. Please make certain to have student work posted in your rooms.*
- *Several teachers (Mrs. Sing, Mr. Blocker, and Miss Candy) have allowed students out of class without hall passes this past week. School policies must be followed—there are safety reasons for the policies.*
- *Dr. Roy Coffee, superintendent of schools, will be touring the building on Thursday. Please make certain your bulletin boards are current and that the superintendent sees active teaching as he walks by the rooms.*
- *Finally, a reminder about team planning time. Please use the time wisely to plan. If this is not working well, the planning time will revert to duty assignments.*
- *Other items from the faculty.*

Mr. Jones asks if I can think of anything else for the agenda. I can't.

4. **Developing teacher leadership.** *I am not quite certain what this is. I ask Mr. Jones what he thinks this is. He says that my graduate work in an educational leadership master's degree is what teacher leadership is. The school system paying for my 1-month shadowing experience is what this is all about. I seem to remember something else about developing teacher leadership from my Introduction to Educational Leadership class, however. I must get my notes on this and review them.*

5. **Working with or developing the master schedule.** *I ask Mr. Jones about the master schedule part of my shadowing experience. He shows me the master schedule and asks me to look it over. It was developed more than 25 years ago and is the best schedule he has ever seen. He says he will use it and make it work as long as he is principal. On Wednesday, one teacher asks Mr. Jones if math classes for his grade level could be moved to a period before lunch next year. The teacher feels that having math last period hurts math scores as students' attention and energy levels are low last period. Mr. Jones responds that a perfectly good schedule was built more than 25 years ago and has worked well for all that time. Perhaps the teacher needs to examine his own teaching techniques. Reading classes are always placed earliest in the day as reading is fundamental in student success. I mention to Mr. Jones that as a science teacher, I think the math teacher has a valid concern. I am told that one day, I will see the beauty of our master schedule and how difficult it is to change to anything better.*

6. **Parent conference.** *Early in the day, Mr. Jones is approached by Dan Hoss, a student who says another student is picking a fight with him. Mr. Jones tells Dan to see the school counselor. I think Mr. Jones forgot the school counselor is absent today. Later, two students are referred to the office for fighting in the hallway. The school policy is to suspend any student for 10 days if they are involved in a fight. Dan Hoss, who had come to see Mr. Jones earlier, says that he was not fighting. He tried to get away; but the other student backed him into a corner, and the*

crowd that gathered around would not let him out. Dan says that he never took the offensive—he only tried to defend himself by blocking any punches. The teacher who brought the students to the office agrees with Dan's statement. I ask Mr. Jones what he is going to do. He says that he has to meet with the parents of both students that afternoon and will suspend both students for 10 days as that is the rule.

At the parent conference, Mr. and Mrs. Hoss state that their son should not be suspended because he was not fighting—just trying to get away. Mr. Jones states that there was a fight that involved their son, and he will be suspended. Order must be maintained in the school; for that to happen, there are strict consequences for fighting. The parents leave, saying they are going to see the superintendent about the matter. Mr. Jones tells them to have a good day.

7. ***Student achievement issues.*** *Toward the end of my 2 weeks with Mr. Jones, we discuss student achievement issues. Mr. Jones and I review the latest benchmark tests in math that are given 6 weeks before the state tests. Mr. Jones tells me that the tests indicate students have not mastered three content areas that are on the state tests and asks if I draw the same conclusions. (Truthfully, I am not certain what the tests show as this is the first time I have seen test data like these.) Mr. Jones then calls for his secretary to come in to take a memo. The secretary then types and prints a memo and copies it to an e-mail sent to all math teachers. The memo reads, "After reviewing the benchmark pacing tests, it is obvious that more emphasis needs to be placed on the following three math competencies." The memo then directs the teachers to spend the next 6 weeks addressing the three areas and to suspend what they had planned to do.*

Log of Omega High School Shadowing

Mrs. Smith is in her fourth year as principal of Omega High School. Prior to this assignment, she was an assistant principal for 6 years in a neighboring school district. She was a classroom teacher for 7 years before that. I viewed the seven situations required in the internship and provide the following log. This is the first time I have been to Omega High School and it has a different "feel" from my school, Alpha. I am interested to see what makes this school feel different.

1. ***Personal conflict between teachers.*** *My 2 weeks are almost up here at Omega High School, and I have not seen many conflicts between teachers. Today, I hear of the first one, and I ask Mrs. Smith if I may sit in. Two teachers in the 11th grade are having a dispute about an assignment. Carl Petrie is an English teacher and Robert Reiner is a history teacher. Mr. Petrie is teaching* The Red Badge of Courage *and has assigned the class to write a diary from Henry Fleming's perspective of the story with particular attention given to historical details of the Civil War. Mr. Reiner teaches U.S. history and has given the same assignment to his students. Both teachers share many of the same students. Mr. Petrie, the English teacher, wants to give an F to all students who turned in the identical assignment to each teacher. Mr. Reiner feels this is unfair to the students.*

Mrs. Smith, the principal, hears of the disagreement and asks to talk with both teachers together. I sit in as the principal meets with the two teachers immediately after the last bell. She starts out by asking what the problem is. They both agree that a lack of communication has caused a problem with both teachers requiring the same project. Mr. Petrie is adamant that the students used one assignment to count for two grades, and that the students knew it was wrong to turn in one assignment for two grades. Mrs. Smith then asks if it is fair to penalize the students for the teachers' lack of communication. Mr. Petrie eventually agrees that his actions are unfair. Mrs. Smith then asks Mr. Petrie what he can do to make the situation fair to the students and fair to his sense of right and wrong. A compromise is worked out so that Mr. Petrie grades more heavily on writing mechanics and Mr. Reiner grades more heavily on historical accuracy. Mrs. Smith then asks how incidents of this nature can be avoided in the future. Both teachers volunteer to cochair a committee to improve interdisciplinary communication at the school. I am impressed at how she handles this matter—much different than Mr. Jones who basically told the teachers to make sure this did not happen again!

2. ***Curriculum decisions.*** *I talk with Mrs. Smith about how curriculum decisions are made at this school. She tells me that a group of excellent English teachers representing each of the grade levels are currently reviewing a variety of literature texts and will make recommendations for the next textbook adoption. Mrs. Smith gives me the date and location of their next meeting and invites me to visit with them and see how they make such judgments. I like that since teachers are the ones who will be using these resources, they will have a say in selecting the materials that will work best with their students.*

3. ***Faculty meeting planning.*** *I ask Mrs. Smith how she plans for faculty meetings. She offers to let me sit in on the next SLT meeting. She explains that SLT is the school leadership team composed of department chairs and key teachers in the school. They work with the principal to examine test data and help plan for faculty meetings and professional development activities. Impressive! As the team of 14 teachers meets with the principal after school, there is soda, pizza, veggies and dip, coffee, and candy on a side table. The team gets right into the calendar, testing schedules, and reminders about upcoming events. They suggest that an e-mail outlining upcoming events will be sufficient and the faculty meeting scheduled for 10 days from now will not be necessary. The e-mail is worded and sent out so the teachers can make arrangements for child care and planning. Nothing like this happens at Alpha High School. All the teachers on the SLT seem to be aware of so many details about operating the school.*

4. ***Developing teacher leadership.*** *Mrs. Smith seems to "poke and prod" all the teachers to think with leadership of the school in mind. I sit in with her on Friday afternoon when she meets with all the first-year teachers. She meets with this group every Friday afternoon to discuss what is going well, what is going wrong, and what can be done to improve. She does not tell them what to do or what is going wrong. She sort of facilitates the meeting and asks the group to draw conclusions, offer ideas, and suggest ways to improve. I could have used that experience in my first year of teaching! As I think about this, the principal is developing*

the first-year teachers' leadership capacity by making them think reflectively and not making them dependent on her to tell them what to do. Impressive!

5. ***Working with or developing the master schedule.*** *This is perfect timing! The SLT has a meeting scheduled to discuss the master schedule. I sit in on the meeting that lasts for about 35 minutes. Mrs. Smith has sent out an e-mail asking the faculty what some of the problems are with the master schedule this year so the SLT can consider midyear changes. I tell her about what happens at my school, Alpha High School, and the "sacred" master schedule. She gets tears in her eyes laughing so hard. She says there is no such thing as a sacred schedule—they must evolve as changes are made in curriculum, teaching methods, and individual needs of the school. This year many of the athletes have their advanced placement (AP) classes after lunch. This is becoming problematic in that when there are away games, students miss important classes that are difficult to make up. Apparently this was not a problem last year as all AP classes were scheduled in the morning. In making some refinements, this detail got lost, and AP classes ended up after lunch. Three of the teachers on the SLT make suggestions and the problem is resolved. I am learning a lot in this shadowing experience.*

6. ***Parent conference.*** *Two students, Alan Brady and Morey Sorrell, get into an altercation over a girl, Mary Moore. Alan has been dating Mary, but apparently he has become somewhat abusive. Morey and Mary have been friends for a long time, and Mary confides to Morey that Alan has hit her several times. Morey speaks with the school counselor, Mrs. Rogers, about the situation. Mrs. Rogers goes to Mrs. Smith to report suspected abuse. The principal briefly talks with Mary and then calls Mary's mother for a conference. I am invited to sit in with Mary, her mother, the counselor, and Mrs. Smith.*

   Mrs. Smith starts the conference by asking Mary to share what she mentioned about Alan's behavior. Mary admits that Alan has hit her at least three times when she disagreed with him over trivial matters. Mary feels that his reaction is partly her fault for not agreeing with Alan. Mary's mother becomes quite upset at this news and demands that Alan be suspended. Mrs. Smith kindly tells Mrs. Moore that she cannot discuss another student's discipline with her, but she should rest assured that the right action will be taken. By the end of the conference, Mary agrees to talk with a counselor about the abuse and begins to understand that the hitting was not her fault, and she had every right to end a relationship where the other person repeatedly hit her, regardless of the reason.

   Later, Mrs. Smith meets with Alan and his father, Mr. Brady. Alan admits pushing Morey for trying to break up his relationship with Mary. Mr. Brady defends his son's actions and says that if Mary was disrespectful to his son, she deserved to be shown who was the boss. Mrs. Smith quickly tells Mr. Brady that hitting is abusive behavior, and she believes that Alan has a problem that needs to be dealt with by a professional counselor. She will have to check to see if Alan's behavior has to be reported to a social service agency. Mr. Brady becomes very defensive, but Mrs. Smith's calm and caring demeanor and genuine concern for Alan defuses the situation. Mrs. Smith explains that Mary's parents could file legal charges against Alan, and that Alan will need to be suspended for at least 3 days. She suggests that during that time, Mr. Brady seek counseling for Alan and himself—that this is a family issue that needs to be addressed. Mr. Brady leaves, agreeing to seek family counseling. He asks Mrs. Smith to try to persuade Mrs. Moore not to file charges.

Finally, Mrs. Smith meets with Morey and his father. Morey is concerned that he will be suspended as he was involved in an altercation at school. Mrs. Smith tells Morey how proud she is of him for reporting what happened to the school counselor. He is a good friend to Mary. Since Morey did nothing but receive Alan's pushes and taunts, there will be no disciplinary action taken against him. Instead, Mrs. Smith tells Morey that she wishes more students had the sense of responsibility Morey displayed.

Boy, did I learn a lot! This would have been handled so much differently at Alpha!

7. ***Student achievement issues.*** *I am able to sit in on the next SLT meeting. The benchmark test results have come back for Omega High School. The principal has sent the information out to the entire faculty and asked departments and teams to discuss the results and forward suggestions to the SLT for consideration at the next meeting. The SLT talks about mining the data—something I learned last semester in a graduate class and honestly had never heard before or after the class. Here the teachers are talking about mining data just like the professor had. Interesting!*

Just like at Alpha, the math scores are low, but mining the data indicates that 14 students' scores brought the average down rather substantially. It is decided that those 14 students will receive extra assistance in math skills before the state tests. I suggest the same course of action that Alpha uses, but the SLT members say that to change everyone's schedule would be an intrusion on many people when providing extra help to 14 students could take care of the problem. That makes a lot of sense to me.

Case Study Questions

1. How would you characterize Mr. Jones's leadership?
2. How would you characterize Mrs. Smith's leadership?
3. What are the major differences in how Mr. Jones and Mrs. Smith handle the seven issues the internship student observes?
4. What impact does Mr. Jones's leadership have on developing teacher leadership at Alpha High School? Cite specific examples of how Mr. Jones's leadership affects the faculty?
5. What impact does Mrs. Smith's leadership have on developing teacher leadership at Omega High School? Cite specific examples of how Mrs. Smith's leadership affects the faculty?
6. What impact do you believe the leadership of each principal will have on how the faculty works to enhance student achievement?
7. What is the impact of Mr. Jones's leadership style on the faculty, students, and community?
8. What is the impact of Mrs. Smith's leadership style on the faculty, students, and community?

INTRODUCTION

Kenneth Leithwood, an educational leadership and policy professor at OISE/University of Toronto and colleagues write, "Leadership serves as a catalyst for unleashing the potential capacities that already exist in the organization."[1] Researchers and policy makers agree that leadership's central task is to help improve employee performance. Such performance is a function of employees' beliefs, values, motivations, skills, knowledge, and working conditions. Understanding and developing people is a core component of a leader's charge.

Leadership in today's schools is not simply about the principal. Organizations cannot long flourish by the top leader's actions alone. Schools depend on leadership throughout the organization to shape productive futures through a process of self-renewal. The commitment needed for sustainable improvement must be nurtured every day and up close in the ordinary behaviors that make schools run. This means helping teachers develop the knowledge, skills, and willingness to take on leadership roles within their schools. Roland Barth (2001), education author and founder of the Harvard Principals' Center, predicted that the future of public education depends upon the majority of teachers extending their work as educators to the entire school, not just the classroom.[2]

While remaining the central agents of change, principals recognize teachers as essential partners in this process, acknowledging their professionalism and capitalizing on their knowledge and skills. In the complex workings of today's schools, principals' success will be "determined by their ability to inspire a culture of empowerment by acting as 'hero-makers' rather than heroes."[3] Principals are expected not only to lead their schools but to build leadership capacity among faculty and staff. Developing and drawing upon colleagues' resources is essential for making improvements to teaching and learning.

LEADERSHIP AS CAPACITY BUILDING

Leaders primarily work through and with other people. Effective educational leaders influence the development of their schools' human resources by offering intellectual stimulation, providing individualized support, and presenting an appropriate model.[4] Effective principals encourage teachers to reflect and challenge their assumptions about work and rethink how they can perform it. Educational leaders provide incentives, structures, and opportunities to promote change and individual adult learning along with appropriate means for monitoring progress toward improvement. And principals set examples for faculty to follow that are consistent with the school's values and goals.

Capacity is a general term, referring to the power or ability to accomplish some particular task. Theorists define *capacity building* as helping people to acquire skills and dispositions to learn new ways of thinking and acting. When leaders recognize and nurture capacity in others, they provide the opportunity for staff to cultivate leadership skills. By helping teachers develop their instructional and leadership skills, schools increase their organizational capacity.

Why Build Leadership Capacity?

Principals cannot do it all alone. Principals play managerial, political, instructional, human resource, and symbolic leadership roles in their schools. Critics have long asserted that for principals to focus narrowly on their instructional leadership role in an effort to improve student achievement would be dysfunctional for both the principal and the school.[5] At the same time, principals must adjust their leadership role to the needs, opportunities, and limits that the school's context imposes. For instance, the direct involvement in teaching and learning that principals can enact in small elementary schools—where one study reported that the principal knew the reading level of each of the school's 450 students[6]—is an unrealistic possibility for principals working in larger schools.

Then too, many secondary school principals have less instructional and curricular expertise than the teachers they supervise. Even if principals have the necessary "will and skill" to enact hands-on instructional leadership, they may find their schools' basic structural and normative conditions work against it.

In short, it is unrealistic to think that the principal can carry the burdens of school leadership and school improvement by themselves. Such an approach is neither sustainable nor does it promote organizational improvement. Instead, if leadership for school improvement is to reach every corner of the school, it needs to be spread more widely throughout the organization.

A growing body of evidence within the school improvement field points toward the importance of capacity building as a means to sustain improvement.[7] One of the most consistent findings from recent studies of effective leadership is that authority to lead need not be located only in the person of the leader but can be dispersed within the school among people.[8] From this perspective, leadership resides in the human potential available to be released from within the organization.

Why Build Teachers' Leadership Capacity?

With the proper development and support, teachers can help improve schools. In part, recognizing teacher leadership stems from awareness that active involvement by individuals at all organizational levels and domains is necessary if change is to take hold. Research has found that teacher leadership far outweighs principal leadership in school improvement because it has a significant impact on student engagement.[9] In addition, research highlights that an organization's ability to improve and continue improvement depends on its ability to foster and nurture professional learning communities or "communities of practice."[10] Teacher leadership is central to generating a school-wide culture where all educators participate in leadership activities and decision making, have a shared sense of purpose, engage in collaborative work, and accept joint responsibilities for their outcomes.[11] Teacher leadership is central to both classroom and school improvement.

Leadership *as* Capacity Building

Various literature strands discuss the idea of leadership *as* capacity building among a wider group of people. Related terminology and concepts include increasing leadership density by expanding leadership capital;[12] distributed leadership and systemic leadership;[13] transformational leadership;[14] teacher leadership;[15] relational or post-heroic leadership;[16]

shared leadership, dispersed leadership, collective leadership, parallel leadership, and a leader-rich culture;[17] or creating "leaderful organizations."[18] The basic notion: Leadership does not belong to an individual but is expanded throughout the organization with leadership roles and functions being performed by various people who do not necessarily hold formal leadership positions.

Leadership as capacity building is about creating opportunities for others to learn. Ann Lieberman, emeritus professor at Teachers College, Columbia University and a senior scholar at the Carnegie Foundation for the Advancement of Teaching, affirms, "Leadership is about contributing to, learning from, and influencing the learning of others."[19] Similarly, Linda Lambert, professor emeritus at California State University and herself a former principal, observes, "Learning and leading are deeply intertwined, . . . Indeed, leadership can be understood as reciprocal, purposeful learning in a community."[20]

Understanding leadership as capacity building requires rethinking what leadership means. More than a formal position of authority or a collection of certain "heroic" personality traits, leadership involves creating conditions and opportunities that are conducive to collective, reciprocal learning directed toward a shared purpose and productive change. In practice, this entails bringing people together so they can construct and negotiate meanings and arrive at a common intent. It also means enabling more individuals in the school to build their own informal authority and display leadership behaviors in vision creating, planning and implementing strategies to improve teaching and learning, and assessing and revising tactics that lead to continuous improvement. Finally, leadership requires accepting the redistribution of power and authority within the school. Creating occasions for collective purpose, action, and responsibility in school aligns with democratic ideals and brings a realignment of power and authority.[21]

ACTIVITY 7.1   Capacity Building at the Two High Schools

Case Study Question 1: How would you characterize Mr. Jones's leadership as it relates to developing his school's capacity?

Case Study Question 2: How would you characterize Mrs. Smith's leadership as it relates to developing her school's capacity?

Discuss in pairs or small groups:

1. Using the chapter's definitions of *capacity building as helping people to acquire skills and dispositions to learn new ways of thinking and acting*, give examples from the case study for each of the following situations in which one principal's actions appear to be developing teachers' leadership capacity and the other principal's actions do not:
   ◆ Personal conflict
   ◆ Curriculum decision
   ◆ Faculty meeting planning
   ◆ Developing teacher leadership
   ◆ Master schedule development
   ◆ Parent conference
   ◆ Using student achievement data
2. Which mode of principal leadership reflects the working environment of your present school? Which of the seven case study situations resemble principal and teacher practices in your own school?
3. How can Prudence use this internship experience to develop her own leadership capacity?

DEFINING AND BUILDING TEACHERS' LEADERSHIP CAPACITY

Developing teacher leadership benefits the organization. Teachers possess critical information about their students and how they learn. They have experiences inside and outside the classroom which can significantly contribute to improved student achievement and enhanced work life quality. Educational reform has a greater likelihood of success when teachers are actively involved. While functioning in leadership capacities such as lead teacher, staff developer, or school improvement team chair, teachers can shape their schools' goals and culture while retaining ties to their classrooms. In these ways, teachers develop greater legitimacy as leaders, and the principal becomes "the leader of instructional leaders."[22]

In addition, developing human potential invites people to grow professionally and enjoy their work. By expanding their perspectives and increasing their skills, teachers can experience broadened autonomy, greater job enrichment, opened achievement opportunities, and widened affiliations. Shared activities in which individuals learn, lead, and influence others by building on their personal strengths and passions may satisfy higher level cognitive and social needs and tap higher degrees of personal motivation and competence. Job satisfaction results when individuals feel energized and purposeful in their work.

Defining Teachers' Leadership Capacity

Varying definitions of teacher leadership exist.[23] Perspectives range from the conceptual to the practical.

Looking at ways of institutionalizing teacher leadership, Lambert (1998) defined building "leadership capacity" as "the broad-based, skillful involvement in the work of leadership."[24] This viewpoint addresses participants in two essential dimensions—breadth and skillfulness.

Broad-based participation means involving many people—administrators, teachers, parents, students, community members, district personnel, university faculty—in the work of leadership. *Skillful participation* refers to participants' comprehensive understanding of and demonstrated proficiency in leadership's dispositions, knowledge, and skills.[25] Accordingly, for schools to develop broad-based and skillful participation to advance this shared leadership capacity, a school must meet at least two critical conditions:[26]

◆ The school needs a significant number of skillful teacher leaders who understand the school's shared vision and the full extent of the work under way to achieve it, and who have the abilities to carry out the school's strategies and plans.

◆ The school staff needs to be committed to the central work of school improvement. This means the professional behaviors of reflection, inquiry, conversations, and focused action are made integral parts of daily work.

Looking more pragmatically, leadership development consultants and authors Marilyn Katzenmeyer and Gayle Moller (2001) proposed teacher leadership as viable in three main areas:[27]

◆ *Leadership of students or other teachers:* serving as facilitator, coach, mentor, trainer, curriculum specialist, or union representative; creating new approaches; and leading study groups

◆ *Leadership of operational tasks:* keeping the school organized and moving toward its goals, through roles such as department head, action researcher, and task force member

◆ *Leadership through decision making or partnership:* serving on school improvement teams and committees; instigating partnerships with businesses, higher education, local educational agencies (LEAs), the school districts, and parent-teacher-student associations

Also addressing the specific ways that teachers enact leadership within their schools, Day and Harris (2003) suggested four different processes:[28]

◆ *Teachers translate school improvement into classroom practice.* As they work with students, teachers ensure school links between planning and behavior and maximize opportunities for meaningful teacher development and positive student outcomes.

◆ *Teachers in participative leadership feel ownership of the change.* Teacher leaders may help other teachers come together around a particular development—such as creating a comprehensive, rigorous, and coherent curricular program—and foster more collaborative ways of working. They act with colleagues to shape school improvement efforts and take some lead in guiding teachers toward a shared goal.

◆ *Teacher leadership as mediating.* Teachers are important sources of expertise and information about the curriculum, instructional practices, and students' learning needs. They can draw upon additional resources and expertise if needed both inside and outside the organization.

◆ *Teacher leaders foster a collaborative learning environment.* Teachers work with colleagues to support mutual learning in areas that enhance student learning and teacher competence.

Other examples of teacher leadership include conducting action research,[29] initiating peer classroom observation,[30] and helping establish a collaborative school culture.[31] In these ways, teacher leadership can empower teachers to become closely involved with colleagues in decision making within the school, thus contributing to both school improvement and making teacher leadership an accepted part of school culture.

Identifying and Developing Teacher Leaders

Teacher leaders are individuals who are or have been teachers with significant instructional experience, are known to be excellent teachers, and hold their peers' respect.[32] Likewise, teachers attracted to leadership positions are achievement and learning oriented and willing to take risks and assume responsibility.[33] Through their classroom experiences, these teachers bring strong instructional, organizational, and interpersonal skills to their leadership roles. While transitioning to leadership responsibilities, these teachers learn about their school's culture, how to work effectively in the system, and how to influence their teaching peers.

Based on their continuing work with developing teacher leaders, Kazenmeyer and Moller (2001) suggested factors that indicate a teacher's readiness to assume teacher leadership roles and responsibilities.[34] These include excellent professional teaching skills, a clear and well-developed personal philosophy of education, location in a career stage that enables one to give to others, having an interest in adult development, and being in a personal life stage that allows one time and energy to assume a leadership position. These individuals have sensitivity and receptivity to others' thoughts and feelings, and demonstrate cognitive and affective flexibility.[35] They are also hardworking, are able to manage workload, and have strong organizational and administrative skills.[36]

Stages of Building Leadership Capacity

Building teachers' leadership capacity is a process. Lambert (2003) used the two dimensions—broad-based participation and skillful participation—to create a matrix that describes conditions in schools with different levels of leadership capacity. Figure 7–1 shows the four-quadrant matrix. Each set of descriptors addresses the formal leader's role, the information flow, defined staff roles, relationships among staff, norms, innovation in teaching and learning, and student achievement. Since the leadership capacity issues are complex, the matrix includes approximations that often overlap and intermingle.[37] Using the matrix as a reference, moving from quadrant 1 to quadrant 4, principals and teachers can assess the maturity of their school's teacher leadership practices and identify ways to institutionalize these into a sustainable school culture.

Accordingly schools with high leadership capacity exhibit the following five features:[38]

◆ Broad-based, skillful participation in the work of leadership
◆ Inquiry-based use of information to inform shared decisions and practice
◆ Roles and responsibilities that reflect broad involvement and collaboration
◆ Reflective practice and innovation as the norm
◆ High (and sustained) student achievement

Using the skillfulness and participation dimensions, Lambert's model describes a school's leadership capacity maturation through four quadrants. As schools develop leadership capacity in their teachers and staff, their practices reflect movement from low to high participation and skillfulness. Briefly, these quadrants are:

◆ *Quadrant 1: Low participation, low skillfulness.* Autocratic principal leadership; top-down information flow; regulatory and compliance-oriented information; teachers depend on the principal for answers and guidance, and the principal depends on teacher compliance to validate and reinforce his or her autocratic style; silent staff resistance (such as early afternoon departures, absenteeism, doctor appointments on faculty meeting days); weak to no supervision of instructional practices; instructional innovation and teacher learning are not priorities; no development of assessment or accountability systems to monitor student performance; short-term student gains not sustainable.
◆ *Quadrant 2: High participation, low skillfulness.* Laissez-faire and unpredictable leadership; fragmented, incoherent information, programs, and relationships; inconsistent school practices (such as a grading policy); weak supervision of instruction with poor teaching often unnoticed; inconsistent teaching quality and instructional

	Low degree of participation	High degree of participation
Low degree of skill	◆ Principal as autocratic manager ◆ Limited (one-way) communications; no shared vision ◆ Codependent, paternal/maternal relationships ◆ Rigidly defined roles ◆ Norms of compliance and blame; technical and superficial program coherence ◆ Little innovation in teaching and learning ◆ Student achievement poor or showing short-term improvement on standardized tests **1**	◆ Principal as laissez-faire manager ◆ Fragmented information that lacks coherence; programs that lack shared purpose ◆ Norms of individualism; no collective responsibility ◆ Undefined roles and responsibilities ◆ "Spotty" innovation; both excellent and poor classrooms ◆ Static overall student achievement (unless data are disaggregated) **2**
High degree of skill	**3** ◆ Principal and key teachers as purposeful leadership team ◆ Limited uses of school-wide data; information flow within designated leadership groups ◆ Polarized staff with pockets of strong resistance ◆ Efficient designated leader; others serving in traditional roles ◆ Strong innovation, reflection skills, and teaching excellence; weak program coherence ◆ Student achievement static or showing slight improvement	**4** ◆ Principal, teachers, parents, and students as skillful leaders ◆ Shared vision resulting in program coherence ◆ Inquiry-based use of data to inform decision and practice ◆ Broad involvement, collaboration, and collective responsibility reflected in roles and actions ◆ Reflective practice that leads consistently to innovation ◆ High or steadily improving student achievement

FIGURE 7–1

Leadership Capacity Matrix (Source: From Lambert, Linda. (2003). *Leadership capacity for lasting school improvement* (Figure 1.3, p. 13). Alexandria, VA: ASCD. © 2003 by ASCD. Reprinted with permission. Learn more about ASCD at www.ascd.org. *Building leadership capacity in schools* (p. 5). Alexandria, VA: Association for Supervision and Curriculum Development.)

innovation; unclear roles and responsibilities; weak or no development of assessment and accountability systems to monitor student progress; static overall student achievement; disaggregated data show few students are achieving well.

◆ *Quadrant 3: High skillfulness, low participation.* A small selected leadership team including activist teachers work with the principal and develop effective leadership skills; development of assessment and accountability systems to monitor student progress with use of available data to make informed school decisions; active resistance coexists with strong classroom innovation and excellence; moderate but inconsistent supervision of instruction; focus on student learning is not a school-wide norm; unclear roles and responsibilities for those not among the designated leaders; slight student achievement gains but not sustainable.

◆ *Quadrant 4: High skillfulness, high participation.* High leadership capacity; inclusive principal collaborates with teachers; majority of staff have mastered necessary leadership skills to influence the school's norms, roles, and responsibilities; well-developed assessment and accountability systems to monitor student progress; ongoing and effective principal and peer supervision of instruction; school climate with maximized time on quality instruction; school-wide inquiry generates and uncovers information that informs practice and shared decisions; information spirals keep all informed; reflection and shared meaning encouraged. Staff describes themselves as being parts of a professional community. Roles and responsibilities overlap; each person takes personal and collective responsibility for the leadership work. Student achievement is high, and few differences appear in achievement among different socioeconomic or gender groups.

Building leadership capacity in schools brings new patterns of interactions and participation as all individuals work in different ways. Teachers are viewed as sources of expertise rather than as implementers of others' ideas for improved practice. Likewise, parents are crucial stakeholders possessing knowledge and expertise about their children that are unavailable to anyone else and whose participation with the school can support teacher and student success.[39] Activity 7.2, "Applying the Leadership Capacity Matrix at the Two High Schools," (page 261) offers an occasion to apply this leadership matrix to the two case study schools.

Creating Opportunities for Leadership

After setting the cultural and emotional climates for nurturing teacher leadership, principals provide opportunities for teachers to use and mature their leadership skills. Schools offer many frameworks in which teachers can take on leadership roles. These include governance groups, instructional teams, learning communities, action research, and study groups. Similarly, principals help teachers practice and refine their leadership abilities through personal interactions including conversations, coaching, mentoring, consulting, networking, integrating new teachers into the organization, and other means.

Conversations. Conversations can begin and sustain teacher leadership. These may take the forms of coaching questions asked; ideas shared in one-on-one talks conducting data dialogues; exploring action research; engaging with parents and community members about mutual concerns for student safety, achievement, equity, diversity, and democracy; and holding ongoing discussions about long-range planning. These conversations have common factors: shared purpose, search for understanding, remembering and reflecting on beliefs and experiences, revealing ideas and information, and respectful listening.[40] Likewise, these processes evoke participants' values and experiences, and prompt increasingly skillful actions.

ACTIVITY 7.2   Applying the *Leadership Capacity Matrix* at the Two High Schools

Work in pairs or small groups, then discuss findings as a class:

1. Using the *Leadership Capacity Matrix*, review the seven situations that Mr. Jones and Mrs. Smith handled in the case study, and identify the quadrant into which you think each principal's leadership development approach falls. Name the behaviors that you can cite to support your decision.

Situation	Mr. Jones's Behaviors Quadrant (Q)	Mrs. Smith's Behaviors Quadrant (Q)
Resolving interpersonal conflict	Behaviors: Q:	Behaviors: Q:
Curriculum decision	Behaviors: Q:	Behaviors: Q:
Faculty meeting planning	Behaviors: Q:	Behaviors: Q:
Developing teacher leadership	Behaviors: Q:	Behaviors: Q:
Master schedule development	Behaviors: Q:	Behaviors: Q:
Parent conference	Behaviors: Q:	Behaviors: Q:
Student achievement data use	Behaviors: Q:	Behaviors: Q:

2. Looking at the quadrants' behaviors apparent for each school, how would you characterize the broad-based participation and skillful status of each faculty?
3. **Case Study Question 3:** What are the major differences in the ways Mr. Jones and Mrs. Smith handled the seven situations in terms of encouraging broad-based participation and skill development?
4. **Case Study Question 4:** From the teacher behaviors you notice in the case study, what is Mr. Jones's impact on developing teacher leadership?
5. **Case Study Question 5:** From the teacher behaviors you notice in the case study, what is Mrs. Smith's impact on developing teacher leadership?
6. **Case Study Question 6:** What is the impact of each principal's leadership on how the faculty works to enhance student achievement?
7. In which areas does each school have room to further develop its teachers' leadership capacities?
8. Which quadrant best describes the school capacity in which you are currently working—and why?
9. Discuss in pairs, then as a class: Does leadership style build capacity or does capacity determine the leaders' style? Give support for your answer.

For instance, instead of encouraging dependency, the principal can respond to a staff member's request for permission to do something with, "What do you recommend?" When the teacher silently waits for "the answer," the principal can respond, "Help me analyze and critique these ideas—Let's think it through together." When staff refuse to take on responsibilities "because that is the principal's job," the principal can use a faculty meeting to ask the staff to clarify expectations and clearly negotiate everyone's roles and responsibilities. Likewise, school leaders can provide time and space for people to struggle with challenging issues. They can admit to not having all the answers or making mistakes and ask teachers for their insights, suggestions, and participation to effectively address mutual concerns. In these ways, principals can use their authority to establish and nurture processes that improve the school's leadership capacity.

Coaching.   Teachers also develop leadership skills through coaching. Principals coach faculty into leadership by asking the questions that expand a teacher's (or staff's, parent's, student's, or community member's) focus from expressing oneself to facilitating others. Coaching questions which prompt teachers' thinking may include: What outcomes do you want your team to accomplish? What role will you play? What evidence will tell you that you have been successful?

Douglas Reeves (2009), education consultant and author, observed that the coaching literature defines coaching in two different ways. One version sees the coach as a "cross between a bar-stool buddy and a therapist"—a trusted ally to whom one can blow off steam. This coaching model concentrates on meeting short-term emotional needs rather than the performance needs of the school or district. In contrast, the second version of coaching centers exclusively on enhancing individual and organizational performance.[41] Appropriate for educators, it includes a focused exploration of a learning agenda, experimentation with new leadership strategies, generating and receiving feedback on effectiveness, and a relentless comparison of the present to the ideal state. In performance coaching for educators, the principal as coach is consistently available for support and practical guidance.

The research literature on coaching effectiveness is inconsistent, with most studies anecdotal rather than empirical, and with few empirical studies meeting standards of reliable methodology.[42]

Mentoring.   More broad and personal than coaching, mentoring is a personal/professional relationship directed at strengthening teachers' performance. The mentoring practice involves coaching and feedback, modeling, providing for leadership experiences, training, and participating in arenas outside the classroom and school. Mentoring teachers may involve helping teachers learn how to set priorities and run effective meetings as first steps toward increasing their confidence and taking on more responsibility. The mentoring process can help the mentee accurately define programs as well as consider and evaluate the potential moral and legal consequences of decision making, offer support and challenge, and facilitate a professional vision. Both principals and teacher leaders mentor others into leadership.

Most of the research on leadership development centers on preparing teachers to become principals rather than to become teacher leaders. Recent reviews of the mentoring literature conclude that there is little evidence of mentoring's and coaching's effectiveness for new leaders.[43] This absence may reflect weaknesses in the studies's designs and methodologies. Nonetheless, agreement exists that mentoring appears to offer significant benefits for leaders, including role socialization, reduced feelings of isolation, professional development, increased job satisfaction, improved leadership skills, and leadership-capacity building.[44] Mentoring is still viewed as a particularly helpful approach to leadership development.[45] If capacity building involves developing a community of practice in which steadily improving role performance is the ultimate goal, and if effective mentoring relationships can expand leadership skills for all participants, mentoring is one means that can potentially lead to successful school improvement.[46]

Consulting.   Consulting brings a skill set that has principals listening to staff, students, and parents, and helping them translate their concerns about student learning into actionable strategies. Principals cannot simply direct teachers to use "best practices." Rather, principals must combine active listening, problem solving, and support with a reasonable understanding of the pedagogy and curriculum. Research on teaching and learning is available through professional journals and associations, the Internet, and staff development. Rather than being the all knowing "expert," principals need to help others examine and reframe their own challenges and develop strategies for action. Developing effective consulting skills is a long-term process that requires much practice.

Networking.   Networking offers a still larger context for developing teacher leadership. In regional and national networks, teachers see themselves as part of the profession. Significant networking practices include:[47]

◆ Approaching every colleague as a valued contributor
◆ Viewing teachers as experts
◆ Creating forums for sharing, dialogue, and critique
◆ Transferring ownership of learning to the learners
◆ Situating learning in practice and relationships, providing multiple entry points into learning communities, and adopting an inquiry stance
◆ Sharing leadership
◆ Rethinking professional identity and linking it to professional community

Networking flourishes best in a social context when its practitioners have opportunities to learn, be in a community, and take on local-site leadership responsibilities. As with local, district, or regional learning communities, networking can provide the context in which teachers can expand their professional identities and skills.

New Teacher Induction.   The induction program helps new teachers begin their career in a culture that supports adult learning and teacher leadership. Acculturating fresh faculty to the school's vision, community of adult and young learners, and the various legitimate roles and responsibilities available for teachers helps the school uphold its teacher leadership culture. Supporting new teachers with a clear, ongoing induction process and appropriate mentors can foster leadership capacities in both newcomer and veteran educators. Mentors model the actions and behaviors that lead to quality instruction and teacher leadership, enacting reflective inquiry into classroom practice as well as school-based issues.

With a focus on teacher effectiveness and professional standards, new teachers emerge as leaders early in their careers.

Additional Practices.   More generally, principals' practices that build leadership capacity include offering intellectual stimulation, providing individualized support, presenting an appropriate model, and providing a strong, in-house professional development program.[48] In addition, studies have identified school practices that build teachers' leadership capacity; these include the principal's active support,[49] a collaborative school culture,[50] participatory decision making,[51] and mutual teacher support.[52] Notably, research has found that providing time for teacher leaders to meet, plan, and discuss issues is crucial to successful teacher leadership.[53]

Obstacles to Developing Teachers' Leadership Capacity

Teachers are not always able or willing to develop and use leadership skills. Factors that affect the development of teachers' leadership capacity include professional roles, school environment, and personal capacities.[54] The principal, too, might be a barrier to developing teachers' leadership capacity.

Professional Roles.   How principals, school colleagues, the wider professional community, and the society as a whole define the principals' and teachers' roles has an impact on the possibilities for leadership.

Developing collegial relationships in an environment that may previously have encouraged dependent ones is complicated. For principals, nurturing and facilitating colleagues' leadership capacities is more difficult than directing faculty what to do. For teachers in traditional school environments, asking permission, waiting to discover the principal's clues to correct behavior, expecting the principal to clarify goals and programs and to deliver praise and criticism, and remaining uninformed (and perhaps indifferent) to the school's overall direction are familiar and expected behaviors. Giving up the benevolent authority role to share leadership responsibilities with teachers may cause the principal considerable discomfort.

Likewise, until recently, teachers have been socialized to be private, to be followers, and to avoid accepting responsibilities outside the classroom.[55] Egalitarianism is an important teacher norm that encourages the view that teachers who accept leadership roles are stepping out of line. Teacher leadership conflicts with this norm, which can result in distance or conflict among teacher colleagues. Duke (1994) referred to this norm metaphorically as a "crab bucket culture" because when one is crabbing, one does not have to put a lid on the bucket because the crabs already caught will reach up and drag each other down should any attempt to climb out.[56]

Tensions sometimes develop between teachers who take on leadership roles and those who do not. Similarly, teachers sometimes experience role conflicts between their need for achievement and leadership and their need for affiliation and belonging with their teaching peers. High job satisfaction and a school culture that supports teacher collaboration tend to lessen this conflict, however.[57] When lead teachers and other faculty encourage classroom teachers to serve on school-wide committees and present staff development programs to colleagues, teachers are more likely to accept these leadership roles. Likewise, if the larger society views teachers as team leaders rather than as solitary practitioners, classroom teachers feel more comfortable taking on informal leadership assignments.

Developing teacher leaders requires both principals and teachers to become reflective, inquiring practitioners who can sustain real dialogue and seek outside feedback to foster self-awareness. These learning processes require well-honed skills in communication, group process facilitation, investigation, conflict mediation, and dialogue. These key skills may not yet be a focus of many professional preparation programs.

New norms more supportive of teachers sharing valued leadership functions are taking hold, however. These cultures encourage a school-wide focus on learning, an expectation for participation, and a view that teacher leaders are positive models for the teaching profession.

School Environment.   Organizational factors—organizational structure, culture, social capital, and political infrastructure—also affect teachers' willingness to accept informal leadership roles.

Organizational structures do not easily give way to support shared leadership and teacher collaboration. Despite being in the learning business, schools are "notoriously poor knowledge sharers."[58] Classical management theory conceives of clear lines separating management from employees. Teacher leadership blurs the lines between those who set goals, plan, control, and supervise and those who carry out these directives. In fact, traditional bureaucratic and physical structures (teaching schedules, room locations, lack of clerical resources to support leadership roles, lack of opportunities to work on leadership skills, for example) are designed to separate teachers and promote autonomy and isolation among them.[59] Schools' egg-crate arrangement of classrooms is more conducive to "parallel play" than collaborative growth. In order to support teacher leadership, it is necessary to replace such hierarchical structures with time, space, access to daily collaborative work focused on valued teaching practices, and participation on school improvement teams.

An organization's culture includes its values, beliefs, and normal ways of behaving that underpin how people function. According to Sergiovanni (2003), school culture is "the normative glue that holds a particular school together."[60] This culture affects the extent that teachers feel accepting leadership roles is appropriate and legitimate. Negotiated norms and standards of daily practice within departments, schools, and school districts greatly influence teachers' professional lives, opportunities, and relationships. Normatively, teachers do not have the habits of giving and receiving information about their effective instructional practices. Schools' traditional culture even discourages such sharing as "blowing your own horn." Likewise, when the school ethos defines leadership as a person who occupies a position of formal authority, teachers do not see themselves reflected in that image.

In contrast, when the school's culture views leadership as a broadly inclusive concept, teachers respond differently. Teachers can see themselves participating with colleagues in a learning network. Leadership for shared learning realizes the purpose that attracted teachers into the profession in the first place.[61] If, as some believe, information only becomes knowledge when it is socially processed through conversations and professional learning communities, a norm of contributing one's knowledge to others is the key to continuous growth for all.[62]

Accordingly, much research evidence points to the importance of shared organizational norms and values as necessary for teachers' collaborative practice. Teachers need trust among themselves before they can develop a professional learning community.[63] In fact, studies are mixed about the extent that teacher leadership flourishes in a collaborative environment. Some have found that teacher leadership thrives in collaborative environments.[64] In contrast, it is possible to have a collegial and open school culture in which teacher leadership does not flourish because the collegial norm does not necessarily extend to teachers as leaders but only to teachers as peers. The hierarchical relationship of teacher leader may violate the traditional professional norms of equality and independence.[65] As such, a collaborative school culture may be a necessary—but not sufficient—condition to promote teacher leadership.

Social capital is the degree of trust that exists between members and stakeholders. It reflects the extent and quality of networks between members and their external partners.[66] School contexts that support teacher leadership have a culture that embodies trust, collaboration, professional learning, and reciprocal accountability; a strong consensus about the important problems facing the organization; and available expertise to improve teaching and learning.[67] Trust determines whether colleagues can see each other exercising leadership as legitimate and acceptable. Trust in others generates solidarity, someone on whom they can rely. Reliance becomes a mutual obligation and reciprocity.[68] Unless teachers trust their colleagues to act fairly toward one another, and to support one another when their opportunity for leadership arrives, they cannot risk allowing a peer to accept additional leadership responsibilities. These critical cultural and interpersonal dimensions take time and nurturing to develop.

In addition, the school's unique political infrastructure or "management arrangements" affect the extent to which teachers can exercise leadership by influencing the space in which teachers' voices can legitimately be heard and decisions made. They establish patterns of communication and accountability within the organization. For instance, some schools hold faculty or grade level meetings as occasions for teachers to have open discussions of policy and school practices and make recommendations to the principal about how they wish to enact the policy at their school. At other schools, information only flows downward, from superintendent to principal to teacher. Here, faculty and grade level meetings are occasions to receive, not discuss, information.

Personal Capacities. To be effective in leadership roles, teachers need certain personal resources and abilities. Developing teachers depends on leaders' knowing schooling's "technical core"—what is required to improve the quality of teaching and learning, often called *instructional leadership*—and having the "people skills" to work successfully with others. Increasingly, this includes leaders' *emotional intelligence*—that is, high levels of interpersonal skill and emotional acuity.[69] Recent evidence suggests that emotional intelligence displayed through a leader's personal attention to an employee and more fully utilizing the employee's capacities increases the employee's enthusiasm and optimism, reduces frustration, transmits a sense of mission, and indirectly increases performance.[70]

Collaboration requires skill sets that many teachers and staff have not yet developed. Shared work not done skillfully can be unproductive. Members need to move beyond exchanging war stories, complaints, and tales of atypical students. Instead, colleagues need to develop a shared sense of purpose, communicate well (ask questions, listen, give and receive feedback), understand transition and change and how these affect people, mediate conflict, and recognize how adults learn. They need to create mutual trust as they listen to each other, pose questions, and look for answers together. Individuals learn these perspectives and skills through observation and guided practice, feedback, coaching, skill-focused dialogue (talking through strategies and approaches), and training.

In order for teachers to become leaders, they require the authority that comes from having a formal leadership role (such as lead teacher) or they need the desired technical or rational skills (such as preparing accurate, thorough, and timely reports; knowledgably disaggregating data; or speaking effectively in front of a group), professional skills (such as being respected for their teaching expertise by their colleagues), and moral authority (such as sharing the community's values, beliefs, and ideals).[71] Then too, teachers need the pedagogical, organizational, and community knowledge to deeply understand the educational issues at hand, to comprehend the right time and occasion to have input that influences practice, and to access community resources and networks that make their contributions widely and influentially supported.

Similarly, having situational understanding is the type of personal capacity that allows teachers to read situations, show emotional intelligence, and demonstrate sensitivity to others' responses. Lastly, interpersonal skills play a key part in determining the teacher's likelihood of success in having influence in the school. Teachers with strong "people skills" are more likely to have informal sway on their colleagues—and be effective in leadership roles—than are more insensitive or indifferent peers.

How teachers and others view their professional role, the school's environment, and their personal capacities all play key parts in setting the climate for permitting and developing teacher leadership.

The Principal as an Obstacle.   Many principals are obstacles to teachers' leadership aspirations. Principals have many reasons for guarding their authority. Apart from working long and hard to earn the school's leadership positions, sharing leadership with teachers is risky. Since principals are held responsible for what others do, many are hesitant to delegate responsibilities for important actions or decisions that might not be up to their standards. In addition, supporting teacher leaders requires much time for advising, encouraging, and "hand holding." Given the plethora of tasks to be completed effectively within quick deadlines, principals understandably (if shortsightedly) believe that it is more efficient to do the job themselves rather than setting up, meeting with, and managing a committee to do so.

Some principals discourage teacher leadership for personal reasons. One study found the weaker the principals' personality, the less likely they are to share leadership. Stronger, more confident principals are more likely to share leadership with others.[72]

Delineating Principal and Teacher Leadership Roles.   Despite sharing school leadership, the principal's leadership remains crucially important. Some responsibilities cannot—and should not—be delegated.

Crowther and colleagues (2002) have offered clear and complementary delineations between principal and teacher leadership roles.[73] They advance a concept of parallel leadership in which teachers assume primary responsibility for leading improvement in teaching and learning while principals assume primary responsibilities for strategic leadership, involving aligning resources to support teaching and learning improvements. In this model, principals:

- Link the work in schools to an inspiring image of a desired future.
- Generate an identity that promotes creation of cultural meaning.
- Align the organization's human, fiscal, and technical resources to foster holistic implementation of school-based initiatives.
- Distribute power and leadership so as to encourage teachers and community members to see themselves as important players in shaping the school's direction and values.
- Form and sustain external alliances and networks with community partners to allow schools to collaborate with other schools and the broader public.[74]

In this framework, principals remain catalysts for change, protectors of the vision, and leaders of inquiry—all of which require significant time and effort, especially at the start of capacity building. Principals craft, articulate, and continue the school's vision. They perform key functions that protect the school's goals and work, hire (and dismiss) teachers to protect the school's vision, and sometimes act as a buffer between the district and the school.

Likewise, principals in schools with shared leadership tend to display less of a role-based authority and engage more in framing questions and problems and providing space and time for inquiry to occur. Rather than tell others what to do, these principals ask questions, explore data, and involve faculty and the wider community in activities that can advance the school's interests. Principals in successfully reforming schools do not give up their responsibility. Instead, principals who expand and share leadership within the school view their colleagues as professional equals. They intentionally and steadily seek to include others in the work of change.

ACTIVITY 7.3   Leadership Development Practices at the Two High Schools

Discuss as a class:

1. In which of the case study situations did Mrs. Smith use the following leadership development practices? What did their effect seem to be on the teachers or community members?
   - Conversations
   - Coaching
   - Mentoring
   - Consulting
   - Networking
   - New teacher induction
2. How might Mr. Jones have used each of the above leadership development practices in his case study situations? What might have been the effect of using such practices on the teachers or community members for building their leadership capacities?
3. How might the obstacles to the development of school leadership capacity—namely, principals' roles, school environment, personal capacities, and the principal—influence principals' and teachers' expectations and behaviors?

Research on Building a School's Leadership Capacity

Substantial evidence collected in both school and nonschool organizations identifies the benefits of building leadership capacity. The empirical literature reveals numerous small-scale qualitative studies, case studies, and self-reporting methodologies that describe dimensions of teacher leadership practice, teacher leadership characteristics, and conditions that promote and challenge teacher leadership. The definitions of teacher leadership vary, and the range of teacher leadership roles is quite diverse. Studies are largely focused on teachers in formal leadership positions although informal leadership roles for teachers are increasingly popular. The few large-scale studies have been less able to demonstrate teacher leadership effects than to expose the dilemmas in trying to define teacher leadership in ways that make quantification possible and meaningful.[75]

Given these limitations, it is still possible to summarize findings. Research data show that increasing teachers' leadership capacity enhances their self-esteem, skills, motivation, commitment, and beliefs about their working environment even as it improves schools' quality.

Teachers' Affect and Motivation.   Research finds that empowering teachers to take on leadership roles enhances their self-esteem and work satisfaction. In turn, this leads to higher motivation, higher levels of performance, and possibly higher levels of retention in the profession.[76] Some studies have found a direct relationship between teacher leadership and motivation. Teacher leadership improves teachers' confidence in their own abilities and teaches them to motivate, lead, and encourage other adults.[77] Additionally having leadership roles increases teachers' knowledge and improves their attitude toward teaching (although the leadership role takes time away from the classroom).[78]

Smylie (1997) found evidence for positive affective outcomes for teachers taking on leadership roles that provided opportunities for professional learning and development as well as increasing teachers' influence over curricular, instructional, and administrative decisions.[79] Other findings suggest that the enhanced self-esteem and work satisfaction that stem from empowering teachers to take on leadership roles lead to higher levels of performance and possibly higher levels of retention in the teaching profession.[80] Studies have also found that involving teachers in school decision making leads to decreases in teacher absenteeism[81] and diminishes teacher alienation.[82]

Researchers have found connections between teachers' emotions, their leadership behaviors, and student learning. A recent synthesis of evidence about the emotions that shape teachers' motivations (levels of commitment, sense of efficacy, morale, job satisfaction, stress, and the like) and the impacts on their pupils' learning indicates strong effects of teachers' emotions on their practices, and strong effects of leadership practices on those emotions.[83] Such evidence suggests that principals make a greater direct contribution to staff capacities than to student achievement, as illustrated in Figure 7–2.

Impact on School Improvement.   Evidence from the literature also suggests that generating teacher leadership has positive effects on transforming schools as organizations and on helping reduce teacher alienation.[84] Teacher leadership has been found to far outweigh principal leadership effects before taking family educational culture's moderating impact

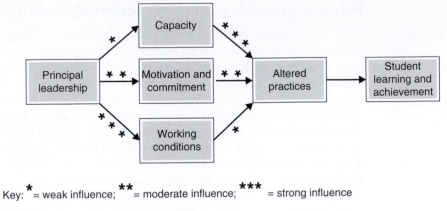

Key: *= weak influence; **= moderate influence; ***= strong influence

FIGURE 7–2
Effects of School Leadership on Teacher Capacity, Motivation, Commitment, and Beliefs About Working Conditions (Source: Adapted from "Seven strong claims about successful school leadership," by Leithwood, K., Harris, A., & Hopkins, D. *School Leadership and Management, 28*(1), p. 33, 2008, reprinted by permission of Taylor & Francis Group, http://www.informaworld.com.)

into account.[85] In schools where teachers share leadership with the principal, school improvement changes are better accepted and implemented as compared with schools without shared leadership.[86] In addition, teacher leadership has been found to be an important factor in improving the life chances of students in disadvantaged schools.[87] The message is clear: School improvement is more likely to occur when leadership is distributed and when teachers have a vested interest in leading school development.[88]

Conditions That Enhance or Hinder Teacher Leadership.   Research has identified conditions under which teacher leadership is more likely to occur. In an extensive review on teacher leadership, Smylie (1997) found that teachers were motivated to assume new leadership roles when they saw them connected to the classroom and their work with students or as a means to professional development.[89] They avoided roles that conflicted with the classroom or with their relationships with other teachers. Overall, teachers assuming leadership roles worked in partnership with other teachers, preferring a collaborative to a superior approach.

Conversely, when some teacher leaders find their new roles conflict with classroom teaching or create tensions with colleagues, stress and role ambiguity often result. How these leadership roles are structured and the extent of active support they receive from principals, colleagues, and district administrators affect their performance and outcomes.[90] Additionally, how teacher leaders are treated reflects how the school's students are treated. Teachers cannot create and sustain the conditions for the productive development of children if those conditions do not exist for teachers.[91]

Similarly, a study by Louis (1998) found a strong association between teachers' quality of work life and their commitment and sense of efficacy.[92] When the quality of work life was high, teachers' commitment resulted in behaviors and attitudes very much like teacher leaders. Seven criteria found to measure the teachers' quality of work life—similar to characteristics evident in school cultures that encourage teacher leadership—included:[93]

- ◆ Respect from relevant adults, such as the principal
- ◆ Participation in decision making, which increases teachers' influence
- ◆ Frequent and stimulating professional interaction among peers
- ◆ School structures and procedures that contribute to a high sense of efficacy by providing feedback on performance
- ◆ Opportunities to use existing skills and knowledge and to experiment and acquire new skills and knowledge
- ◆ Adequate resources to carry out the job and be effective
- ◆ Congruence between personal goals and the school's goals

Finally, Browne-Ferrigno and Muth (2004) found that immersing future school leaders in the authentic, job-embedded learning activities that produce real products used by the school where the work is conducted is a necessary part of learning how to become a school leader.[94]

Teachers' Perceptions of Their Schools.   Taking on school leadership roles positively influences teachers' perceptions of their school. Research supports the view that high school "bureaucracies" become "communities" only when teachers perceive governance regimes as legitimate, and legitimatization comes from teachers being actively involved in decision making.[95] Where teachers believe they are empowered in areas of importance to them, they are very positive about their school and the way it is organized and run. Areas of importance to teachers include being well informed and having collaborative, cooperative, and consultative decision making, especially about school goals.[96] In this way, teachers become a profession of learners who engage in inquiry, reflective practice, and continuous problem solving as they simultaneously build leadership capacity.[97]

Negative Impacts of Teacher Leadership.   Not all the reported effects of teacher leadership are positive. Teacher leaders are known to experience difficulty in switching roles between teacher and leader. Stress can result from the juggling that happens when these persons are simultaneously teaching and leading and from the varied, ambiguous, and sometimes all-consuming nature of their leadership work.[98] The shifting nature of their relationships with colleagues can also create difficulties.[99] Teachers in leadership roles may find their peer relationships become more hierarchical than horizontal. As a result, a once comfortable social relationship with colleagues changes to include implicit or explicit instructional, professional, and organizational expectations. All these adjustments violate egalitarian professional norms, creating a sense of greater distance from and occasionally a loss of valued relationships with colleagues. Tension among coworkers may grow.

Principals' Role in Building Teacher Leadership.   In their 2008 review of the leadership literature, Leithwood, Harris, and Hopkins found very little evidence that most school leaders build staff capacity in curriculum content knowledge, or that they do so directly and by themselves.[100] While school leaders make modest direct contributions to staff capacities, they have quite strong and positive influences on staff members' motivations, commitments, and beliefs concerning the supportiveness of their working conditions but unrelated to pupils' learning or achievement.[101] Again, Figure 7–2 illustrates this relationship. This study's findings have been replicated in the United States and England.[102]

Benefits of Distributed Leadership.   Research also finds that some patterns of leadership distribution are more effective than others. Investigations on a sample of 110 schools demonstrated relationships between the use of different patterns of leadership distribution and levels of value-added student achievement (illustrated in Figure 7-2). Schools with the highest levels of student achievement attributed this to relatively high levels of influence from all leadership sources (school teams, parents, and students). Conversely, schools with the lowest levels of student achievement attributed this to low levels of influence from all leadership sources.. Finally, principals were rated as having the greatest (positive and negative) influence in all schools.[103]

In the same study, the relationship between total leadership and teachers' capacity was much stronger than the relationship between the principal's leadership alone and teachers' capacity.[104] Most notably, the total leadership accounted for a statistically significant 27% of the variation in student achievement across schools. This direct evidence of distributed leadership's effects is a 2 to 3 times higher proportion of the explained variance than typically reported in studies of individual principals' effects.[105]

The benefits of distributed leadership are less directly evident in research on formal leadership succession, school improvement initiatives, processes used to successfully turn around low-performing schools, and the movement toward flatter organizational structures and team problem solving.[106]

This evidence is consistent with claims about the ineffectiveness of laissez-faire forms of leadership.[107] It also reflects earlier findings about power as a relatively unlimited organizational resource.[108] Principals experience no loss of power and influence when the power and influence of many others in the school increase.

ACTIVITY 7.4   The Impact of School Leadership Style on Faculty, Students, and Community in the Two High Schools

Case Study Question 7: What is the impact of Mr. Jones's leadership style on the faculty, students, and community?

Case Study Question 8: What is the impact of Mrs. Smith's leadership style on the faculty, students, and community?

Discuss in small groups then as a class:

1. Generalizing from the research and applying case study information, what would be your answers to these questions?
2. Given the differences in leadership style between the Alpha and Omega High Schools' principals with regard to building leadership capacity and the school environment that supports it, what obstacles does research suggest that Alpha High School might have to overcome to begin developing teachers' leadership capacity?

Criticism of Research on Teacher Leadership.   The research on teacher leadership offers little insight on the range of leadership patterns that actually exist in schools and, most important, the relative effects of these patterns on the quality of teaching, learning, and pupil achievement. Efforts to fill this gap represent the advancing edge of current leadership research.[109] One recent report on data from private sector organizations begins to support the claim that more coordinated patterns of leadership practice are associated with more beneficial organizational outcomes.[110] Comparable evidence is only beginning to become available about schools.

Criticism of teacher leadership also notes that it addresses only selected people rather than building the organization's capacity.[111] At an operational level, some critics highlight a lack of understanding about how mentoring relationships operate, and suggest that mentors can feel vulnerable, inexpert, exposed, and without the necessary skills.[112] Others outline some of the difficulties in mentoring leadership, including selecting mentors, the demands of working with high-level issues, and continuously having to reassess and refocus due to role complexity.[113]

In addition, teacher leadership depends, in part, on teachers working collaboratively and collegially with other educators and stakeholders. Most critiques of teacher collegiality in a variety of contexts have focused on implementation difficulties, particularly finding time for teachers to work together[114] and teachers' unfamiliarity with the collegial role.[115] Similarly, critics note, the big-city teachers, community representatives, and others often have hidden agendas that prevent them from working in the school's best interests.[116] These criticisms are relatively specific, technical, and managerial in nature.[117]

It is important to see developing teacher leadership capacity not as an end in itself. Rather, it is a leadership process for the principals and teachers that allows them to share power, responsibility, and accountability in ways which benefit the students and the school. Likewise, parents and community members should be involved in a limited way, as consumers and citizens, and not necessarily as policy makers.

LEADERSHIP AND ATTRIBUTION THEORY

Part of the challenge of building teachers' leadership capacity is helping teachers develop the skills and confidence to take on school leadership roles and responsibilities. Understanding how others define success or failure, interpret cause and effect, and gain greater control over their environment can aid principals as they help teachers reframe their experiences and build confidence in their own efficacy.

Attribution Theory of Motivation

Attribution theory is a general theory of social motivation that concerns how people explain the reasons why events in their lives occur.[118] Stimulated by Fritz Heider's (1958) early writings,[119] social and educational psychologists have become increasingly interested in the way people explain their own—and others'—successes and failures.

Beginnings of Attribution Theory.   Basically, Heider believed that people have an innate need to understand and control their environments. They develop causal explanations for events which influence their later behavior. Individuals infer key factors, or attributions, to explain outcomes of their own actions. Doing so gives the person a sense of control over his or her world that will affect later behavior.

Psychologist Harold Kelley contributed a final development to attribution theory by examining how individuals could use consistency, distinctiveness, and consensus to establish the validity of their perceptions.[120] Today, no one monolithic theory of attribution exists.[121]

Factors That Determine Causal Inferences. Causal inferences are complex and determined by many factors. The answer to why something happened will be influenced, for instance, by the person's past history of success and failure, social norms, or others' performance. More specifically, if the person has always failed at this sort of task in the past, then the current failure is likely to be attributed to the self. If others succeed when the person fails, again the failure is likely attributed to the self (rather than to the task). Personal feeling states as well as feedback from others affect which causal explanation is selected.

Figure 7–3 illustrates the attribution process. Although the premise that our beliefs about ourselves and others influence our behaviors is not new, attribution theory articulates how this process occurs and provides a basis for understanding and acting upon variables that motivate self and others.[122]

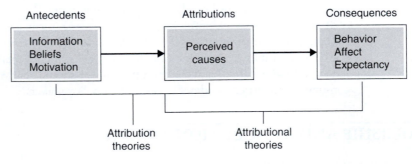

FIGURE 7–3
General Attribution Model (Source: Porter, L. W. Annual review of psychology. Volume 35, 1984. Copyright 1984 by Annual Reviews, Inc. Reproduced with permission of Annual Reviews, Inc. In the format Textbook via Copyright Clearance Center.)

Attribution Theory in Action. Perceived attributions or causes of behavior may influence managers' and employees' decisions and actions. For instance, principals must often observe teachers' performance and make related judgments. If the principal attributes a teacher's poor performance to a lack of effort, then the teacher may receive a poor performance appraisal rating or possibly be moved into intensive clinical supervision. Conversely, if a principal infers that a teacher's poor performance results from a lack of skill, the principal may assign the teacher to further professional development or provide coaching. Making an inaccurate judgment about the causes of poor performance can have negative repercussions for the individuals and the organization.

Attributions also may influence employee motivation. Teachers or staff who perceive the cause of their success to be outside of their control may be reluctant to attempt new tasks and may lose motivation to perform well in the workplace. In contrast, teachers and staff who attribute their success to themselves are more likely to have high motivation for work. Thus, understanding attributions that people make can have a robust effect on both employee performance and managerial effectiveness.

Skill Versus Chance.   Bernard Weiner, a cognitive psychologist and professor at the University of California at Los Angeles, and colleagues have extensively studied attribution theory.[123] They have concluded that the explanations that people make to explain success or failure can be analyzed in terms of three sets of characteristics:[124]

◆ *Locus: internal or external.* The cause of the success or failure may be *internal* or *external.* That is, we may succeed or fail because of factors that we believe originate within us (such as ability or effort) or in our environment (such as task difficulty or help from others).

◆ *Stability: stable or unstable.* The cause of the success or failure may be either *stable* or *unstable, long-lasting* or *short term.* Math aptitude, for instance, is a constant whereas a bad mood is likely temporary. The perceived duration of the causes influences the expectancy for success. If people believe cause is stable and enduring, then the outcome is likely to be the same if they perform the same behavior on another occasion. If it is unstable and temporary, the outcome is likely to be different on another occasion.

◆ *Control: controllable or uncontrollable.* The cause of the success or failure may be either *controllable* or *uncontrollable.* A controllable factor, such as effort, is one that we believe we can change if we choose to do so. An uncontrollable factor, such as luck and aptitude, is one that we do not believe we can easily change. People can control their internal factors through effort, for example, by working harder; but they cannot easily influence internal uncontrollable factors, such as their tendency to be introverted or extroverted. Likewise, an external factor can be controllable (if the lawn is overgrown, we can cut it) or uncontrollable (if it rains daily during the summer, the grass will grow more rapidly).

All three dimensions of causality affect a variety of common emotional experiences, including anger, gratitude, hopelessness, pride, and shame. The expectancy of success or failure—along with the emotions these expectations prompt—is assumed to guide motivated behavior.

Using these three variables, four attributions that influence personal motivation in education can be identified:

◆ *Ability.* A relatively *internal* and *stable* factor over which the person *does not exercise much direct control.*

◆ *Effort.* An *internal* and *unstable* factor over which the person *can exercise a great deal of control.*

◆ *Task difficulty.* An *external* and *stable* factor that is *largely beyond the person's control.*

◆ *Luck.* An *external* and *unstable* factor over which the person exercises *very little control.*[125]

The interaction of ability, effort, task difficulty, and luck will influence how the individual perceives the cause of outcomes and the motivation to act in similar situations in the future.

Locus, Stability, and Controllability. The causal properties of locus, stability, and control affect the two main determinants of motivation: expectancy and value. *Expectancy* refers to the subjective likelihood of future success, and *value* is often considered the emotional consequence of goal attainment or nonattainment.

The individual's sense of internal locus, stability, and controllability over his or her world are essential factors in explaining attributions; and they relate to feeling states or the value of achievement outcomes. Locus influences feelings of pride in accomplishment and self-esteem. Pride and increasing self-esteem require internal causality for success. As Weiner put it, "It has been said that all at the table can enjoy a great meal, but only the cook can experience pride."[126] Stability influences whether the same outcome can be expected. Controllability plus locus determines how a person feels after not achieving a goal. Attributing failure to insufficient effort, which is internal and controllable, may elicit guilt (or the desire to create ambiguity about the failure's cause), whereas ascribing failure to lack of aptitude, which is internal but uncontrollable, often prompts feelings of shame, embarrassment, and humiliation.[127]

Attribution and Self-image. A person's interests determine the types of causal explanations he or she is likely to conclude. Because attributions—or explanations of causality—affect self-esteem, social standing, sense of competence, and other factors, the search for causal explanations is not entirely objective.[128]

Attribution theory assumes that people are motivated to interpret their environment in ways that protect and enhance a positive self-image. A person's positive and successful behavior has the potential for enhancing self-esteem if the person was causally responsible for it. That is, they will *attribute* their successes or failures to factors that help them to feel as good as possible about themselves. Consistent with these assumptions, the research on attributions for success and failure shows that attributions for success are usually internal whereas attributions for failure are usually external.[129] In our culture, a general belief exists that success is internally caused, and effort is an internal cause of success. If, however, high effort appears with failure, the person must seek some explanation other than internal cause.[130]

For example, when principals successfully facilitate school improvement meetings, they are likely to attribute this success to their own efforts or abilities; when they fail, they will want to attribute their failure to factors over which they have no control, such as poor teacher or parent attitudes, holding the meeting after school when members are tired and want to go home, or bad luck.

Attributions are also an important part of how people present themselves to others. People are motivated to present themselves to others in a favorable manner. Interpretations of studies that consider this dimension have ambiguous findings. In social contexts, people may attribute their success to external factors in an attempt to appear modest or to internal factors in an attempt to present themselves as competent.[131]

Similarly, people are motivated to feel and appear as if they are in control of their environments, that they can satisfy their goals through their own efforts. Teachers may know they are competent inside their classrooms, but taking on responsibilities in unfamiliar arenas where they feel less in control makes them think twice. Teachers need to believe that the world in general is predictable and that their own strivings will not be blocked by chance or deliberate interferences from the physical or social environments. Research on this hypothesis finds that people tend to disparage others who are victims of negative events. Making the victim responsible (attributing causality) for the negative event—rather than considering systemic or situational flaws—allows observers to continue believing in a fair and orderly world (requiring no expectation of change or action on their part).[132]

Attribution Error.   Since attributions are inherently subjective, people make incorrect attributions every day because their causal explanations are often wrong. Fundamental attribution error is the tendency of a person to overestimate the influence of personal factors and underestimate the influence of situational factors when assessing someone else's behavior. In the workplace, this may mean that supervisors are more likely to assume that employees' poor performance is due to a lack of ability or effort rather than to task difficulty or luck (or any circumstantial or systemic factor).[133]

The nature of the attribution error is culturally determined. The fundamental attribution error of assigning personal responsibility for outcomes, while prominent in North America, is not as common across the rest of the world. The United States and Western European culture tends to value individualism (celebration of personal independence and individual achievement) whereas other cultures value collectivism (celebration of group success and collaboration). As a result, in other cultures, such as in India, the fundamental attribution error is that people assume that others are more influenced by situation than by personal factors. Thus, while one can assume this error to be present in American managers' or school leaders' perceptions, this may not be the case for managers or school leaders from other cultures. Nor may it be true for employees from other cultures.

Importantly, it is the underlying cognitive structure that represents the individual's beliefs about the nature of the attribution—rather than the specific attribution itself—which shapes the expectancies which motivate individuals.

ACTIVITY 7.5   Using Attribution Theory at the Two High Schools

Attribution theory is a general theory of social motivation that concerns how people explain the reasons why events in their lives occur. Discuss as a class:

1. How might attribution theory—particularly the factors of environment, ability, effort, task difficulty, and luck—be operating at Alpha and Omega High Schools? Give examples from the case study to support your answers.
2. How might the principals at each high school be contributing to a school climate that affects how teachers attribute, or perceive, the outcomes of events at their school—and their responses to accepting school leadership opportunities?

Research on Attribution Theory

Research on topics as varied as achievement motivation, parole decisions, smoking cessation, and helping behavior has suggested attribution theory's generalizability.[134] The research shows that attributions affect our feelings about past events and our expectations about future ones, our attitudes toward other persons, and our efforts to improve our desired outcomes.[135]

Limitations in Attribution Research.   The problems of researching people's attributions are highly complex.[136] Most people do not consciously think in terms of ability, effort, task difficulty, and luck as causes that explain their behaviors. This makes research difficult because investigators must make numerous assumptions about motives that they can only infer and not directly see. Even asking research participants for self-reports about their thinking requires them to speculate about internal dynamics that are largely unfamiliar to them and to use language and concepts with which they have little to no experience.

Methodological problems also affect attribution research. Investigators have tried to design studies that would measure attribution in a manner that preserved its naturalistic character and to induce people in laboratory settings to make natural attributions. Inter-rater reliability, generalizability of procedures for coding number and type of attributions people generate in lab settings, and the tendency of people to overvalue personal as opposed to environmental factors as behavioral causes (the so-called fundamental attribution error) also create major difficulties in studying attribution.[137]

Investigational problems aside, much of the attribution research holds interest for social, personality, cognitive, and experimental psychologists, and it also has practical relevance for school leaders.

Attribution and Achievement, Control, and Motivation.   Attribution theory is frequently applied in understanding achievement. It has been documented that perceptions of the causes of personal success or failure, such as ability or effort, give rise to emotions such as pride or guilt. These emotional reactions, in part, influence later behavior and achievement strivings.[138]

The effects of attributions upon achievement strivings were first investigated in relation to causation differences between skill and chance. When subjects were told that their success on a judgment task was due to skill, expectancy of future successes was higher than when success was due to chance. On the other hand, failure due to chance rather than skill yielded a higher expectancy of future success.[139] Weiner, Russell, and Lerman (1978) have presented the most systematic consideration of the affective consequences of achievement-related attributions.[140] Affects relevant to self-esteem depend on attributions made during performance. For instance, ability attributions following success lead to feelings of pride and competence whereas ability attributions after failure may result in feelings of incompetence.

Likewise, attribution theory has been investigated as a means to improve students' persistence and self-esteem after failure by attributing causation to lack of effort rather than lack of ability, task difficulty, or luck.[141] For instance, many youngsters are willing to shoot hoops for hours at the playground (even after missing many shots) but refuse to study academic content necessary to perform well in school. When they can understand the connection between their personal efforts and time invested in improving their basketball performance and their personal efforts and time invested in thoughtfully completing homework and mentally rehearsing information to prepare for school tests, their attributions may change along with new study behaviors. Higher effort—a factor within their control—improves ability and reduces task difficulty and luck as winning strategies in both arenas.

Research on attribution and motivation has relevant implications for school leaders. One of the more vigorous findings in social psychology is the tendency for individuals to accept more causal responsibility for their positive outcomes than for their negative outcomes.[142] By taking credit for good outcomes and denying blame for bad ones, an individual presumably enhances or protects his or her self-esteem. Scholars have proposed that self-enhancing attributions (i.e., congratulating oneself) for success are mediated by and serve to maintain relatively high levels of positive feelings about oneself whereas self-protective attributions (i.e., blaming others for failure) are mediated by and function to reduce high levels of negative feelings and threat toward self.[143] For example, a student who earns an A on a school essay prides herself on being smart. But when she receives a D on another essay, she blames her dog for eating her notes, her parents for not allowing her enough time to write a decent paper, or her teacher for being unfair. Additional studies appear to support this hypothesis.[144]

Similarly, individuals may express causal judgments designed to gain approval from others or otherwise control other people's responses. Studies have found that attributions may be used to defend or justify one's behavior or call into question a partner's behavior,[145] to avoid embarrassment, or to gain public approval.[146] Further studies have found that participants accepted more credit for success than failure when they did not expect a group of experts to evaluate their behavior but reversed this behavior when they did expect experts to evaluate them.[147] These results support the belief that wanting to "look good" (either competent or modest, respectively) in front of others influences how individuals attribute causes of events.

In turn, what people say about the causes of their own outcomes affects observers' evaluations of them. In one study, teachers were led to believe that they had been successful or unsuccessful in teaching a lesson to students. Teachers tended to take responsibility for student failure but attributed success to the student.[148] Because our society expects teachers to take responsibility for student learning, teachers in this study may have strategically selected attributions that matched normative requirements of the teachers' role in an attempt to create a positive public image.[149] In fact, subjects in another study judged the teachers who accepted responsibility for student learning—that is, who accepted responsibility for the failed lesson—more highly than teachers who denied responsibility for the failure.[150]

Some have argued that individuals like to think they have many choices about how to act. Since some attributions reduce the person's sense of control, the individual may behave in ways that make any search for the cause ambiguous (so as to not directly place blame on themselves).[151] For instance, a student unsure about how well he or she would score on the Graduate Record Exam (GRE) might "party" the night before the exam. Should he or she score poorly on the next morning's exam, the cause of failure would not be clear. Did lack of ability, lack of effort, too many difficult questions, poor time management, bad luck, or some other cause contribute to the low score? Research found that highly test-anxious students were more likely than low test-anxious students to create uncertainty about the causes of negative results and were more likely to report anxiety when it was presented as a viable explanation for poor test performance. When the anxious students could not create doubt about the cause of their unsuccessful results, they created some by reporting spending less effort on the test to explain their low scores.[152] These students protected their self-images by having other consider them lazy—something over which they have control—rather than think of them as dumb—an attribute over which they have none. The bulk of the research evidence supports the idea of a motivation—cognition interaction.[153]

Harvey and Weary (1984) concluded that the breadth of the attribution research supports the broad conception of attribution as a quest for meaning that may occur spontaneously and continuously in daily life.[154]

Using Attribution Theory to Build Teachers' Leadership Capacity

Principals can help teachers understand that leadership capacity can be learned, practiced, and applied to benefit educators, students, and the school community.

Many teachers do not feel confident or competent to take on school leadership roles. This may be a realistic self-assessment. When teachers lack prior leadership experiences, lack knowledge of critical school issues, do not have current and usable data about their own school's and students' performance on important measures, and require a clear sense of direction as to where their school is heading, they realistically foresee problems with accepting school leadership roles. Likely, they will conclude that they lack sufficient ability; the task is too complex, unclear, and overwhelming; and working collaboratively on school improvement endeavors is not worth the effort it would take to get up to speed.

When principals can help teachers focus and control the internal attributions (ability and effort) while reducing the teachers' concern about external attributions (task difficulty and luck), principals can help teachers build their leadership capacity.

Rather than see aptitude for leadership as fixed, unchanging, and uncontrollable, principals can help teachers understand that aptitude depends on having learning experiences to observe, practice, and eventually master certain critical interpersonal and technical skills. Teachers' own aptitudes and abilities can grow through focused learning, practice, feedback, and refinement in a safe and supportive environment. When principals provide professional development on major issues affecting their school and supply modeling, conversations, coaching, mentoring, and occasions for practicing skills in trustworthy settings to build teachers' listening, problem-solving, and group facilitation skills, teachers can learn how to act effectively as leaders in their own schools.

Therefore, teachers who have internal frames of reference, who perceive their ability and effort as factors over which they have control, and who experience a work environment that consistently reduces task difficulty and lessens reliance on luck are more likely candidates for school leadership. In contrast, teachers who continue to see their ability as stable and unchanging (even with additional learning), the environment as ambiguous or threatening, and task difficulty or reliance on luck ever present may lack the sense of control and motivation necessary to invest their effort in accepting new leadership roles.

Workplace learning promotes teachers' leadership capacity. Improvement depends on learning to do the right thing in the setting where they work. Learning in context addresses real problems with real solutions as they evolve in their own systems. In contrast to learning out of context at off-site workshops or conferences, learning in the place where teachers work has the greatest payoff because it is more specific and social. It is directly applied to the teachers' actual job and develops collective and shared knowledge and commitments. According to Fullan, "Learning in context is developing leadership and improving the system as you go."[155] Learning in context also increases sustainability because it improves the system in a way that establishes conditions which support continuous development. These conditions include opportunities to learn from others on the job, the daily nurturing of current and future leaders, the selective retention of good ideas and best practices, explicit monitoring of performance—and an evolving school culture which supports all these factors.

When principals provide sufficient vision, professional development, and leadership-enhancing activities that actively and sensitively support teachers' learning and taking on school leadership roles, teachers' understanding, skills, and confidence grow. An environment that teachers once perceived as external, stable, and uncontrollable may now be perceived as internal, changeable, and controllable. Over time, principal and teacher behaviors can shape the school culture to reinforce distributed leadership. When principals give teachers what they need to change their attitudes, skill sets, and behaviors, teachers can become leaders.

SUMMARY

Schools depend on leadership throughout the organization to shape productive futures through a process of self-renewal. In this context, principals are expected not only to head their schools but to build leadership capacity among faculty and staff. Substantial research supports this finding.

Theorists define *capacity building* as helping people to acquire skills and dispositions to learn new ways of thinking and acting. By helping teachers develop their instructional and leadership skills, schools increase their organizational capacity.

Developing teacher leadership benefits the organization. Teachers have experiences inside and outside the classroom that can significantly contribute to improved student achievement and enhanced work-life quality. Functioning in school leadership roles, teachers can shape their schools' goals and culture while retaining ties to their classrooms. The principal becomes "the leader of instructional leaders."

Building teachers' leadership capacity is a process. Two dimensions—broad-based participation and skillful participation—create a dynamic matrix that describes conditions in schools with different levels of leadership capacity.

After setting the cultural and emotional climate for nurturing teacher leadership, principals provide opportunities for actualizing teachers' leadership potential. Frameworks within schools for teachers to take on leadership roles include governance groups, instructional teams, learning communities, action research, and study groups. Similarly, principals help teachers practice and refine their leadership skills through practices including conversations, coaching, mentoring, consulting, networking, and integrating new teachers into the organization.

Factors that affect the development of teachers' leadership capacity include how educators define their professional roles, the school environment, and personal capacities.

Despite sharing school leadership, the principal's leadership remains crucially important. Some responsibilities cannot—and should not—be delegated.

Although methodological limitations in the research literature exist, research data show that increasing teachers' leadership capacity positively affects teachers, student achievement, and the school.

Attribution theory helps explain how others interpret success or failure, understand cause and effect, and gain greater control over their environment. People use the factors of locus, stability, and controllability—apparent in actual situations as the interaction of ability, effort, task difficulty, and luck—to identify variables that influenced outcomes and to shape their motivation for future action. Research shows that attributions affect our feelings about past events and our expectations about future ones, our attitudes toward other persons, and our efforts to improve desired outcomes.

Principals can use attribution theory to help build teachers' competence and confidence in their school leadership capabilities. When principals can help teachers perceive their school environment as internal, changeable, and controllable, teachers can develop their attitudes, skill sets, and behaviors, and become leaders.

Teachers' leadership capacity grows when principals provide sufficient vision, professional development, and leadership-enhancing activities that actively and appropriately support teachers as they learn and accept school leadership roles.

ENDNOTES

1. Leithwood, K., Harris, A., & Hopkins, D. (2008). Seven strong claims about successful school leadership. *School Leadership and Management, 28*(1), 27–42 (p. 27).
2. Barth, R. (2001). *The teacher leader.* Providence, RI: Rhode Island Foundation.
3. Slater, L. (2008). Pathways to building leadership capacity. *Educational Management Administration and Leadership, 36*(1), 55–69, p. 55.
4. Leithwood, K., & Riehl, C. (2003, January). *What we know about successful school leadership.* Philadelphia, PA: Laboratory for Student Success, Temple University. Retrieved from http://www.fuzzykritters.com/public_html/uploads/pdf/resource_20030811103226_What%20We%20Know.pdf
5. Barth, R. (1986). On sheep and goats and school reform. *Phi Delta Kappan, 68*(4), 293–296; Cuban. (1988). Op. cit.
6. Hallinger, P., & Murphy, K. (1986). The social context of effective schools. *American Journal of Education, 94*(3), 328–355.
7. Fullan, M. (2001). *Leading in a culture of change.* San Francisco, CA: Jossey-Bass; Hopkins, D., & Jackson, D. (2002). Building the capacity for leading and learning. In A. Harris, C. Day, M. Hadfield, D. Hopkins, A. Hargreaves, & C. Chapman (Eds.), *Effective leadership for school improvement* (pp. 84–105). London, United Kingdom: Routledge.
8. Day, D., Harris, A., & Hadfield, M. (2000). Grounding knowledge of schools in stakeholder realities: A multi-perspective study of effective school leaders. *School Leadership and Management, 21*(1), 19–42; Harris, A. (2002). *School improvement: What's in it for schools?* London, United Kingdom: Falmer.
9. Leithwood, K., & Jantzi, D. (1998). *Distributed leadership and student engagement in school.* Paper presented at the annual meeting of the American Educational Research Association, San Diego, CA.; Ogawa, R. T., & Bossert, S. T. (1995). Leadership as an organizational quality. *Educational Administration Quarterly, 31*(2), 224–243; Spillane, J. P., Halverson, R., & Diamond, B. (2001). Investigating school leadership practice: A distributed perspective. *Educational Researcher, 30*(3), 23–28.

10. Holden, G. (2002). *Towards a learning community: The role of teacher-led development in school improvement.* Paper presented at the CELSI British Council Leadership in Learning Conference, London, United Kingdom; Morrissey, M. (2000). *Professional learning communities: An ongoing exploration* (Unpublished paper). Southwest Educational Development Laboratory, Austin, TX.

11. Harris, A., & Lambert, L. (2003). *Building leadership capacity for school improvement.* London, United Kingdom: Open University Press.

12. Sergiovanni, T. J. (1992). Why we should see substitutes for leadership. *Educational Leadership, 49*(5), 41–45.

13. Harris, A. (2003a). Introduction: Challenging the orthodoxy of school leadership. Towards alternative theoretical perspectives. *School Leadership and Management, 23*(2), 125–128.

14. Hallinger, P. (2003). Op. cit.; Bass, B. (1985). *Leadership and performance beyond expectations.* New York, NY: Free Press; Bass, B. (1997). Does the transactional-transformational leadership paradigm transcend organizational and national boundaries? *American Psychologist, 52*(2), 130–138; Leithwood, K., & Jantzi, D. (2000). The effects of transformation leadership on student engagement with schools. *Journal of Educational Administration, 38*(2), 112–129; Silins, H., & Mulford, B. (2002). Leadership, restructuring, and organizational outcomes. In K. Leithwood, P. Hallinger, G. Furman-Brown, B. Mulford, P. Gronn, W. Riley, & K. Seashore Louis (Eds.), *Second international handbook of educational leadership and administration.* Dordrecht, The Netherlands: Kluwer Academic Press.

15. Harris, A. (2003b). Teacher leadership as distributed leadership: Heresy, fantasy, or possibility? *School Leadership and Management, 23*(3), 313–324.

16. Sessa, V. I. (2003). Creating leaderful organizations: How to bring out leadership in everyone. *Personnel Psychology, 56*(3), 762–765.

17. Frost, D., & Durrant, J. (2003). Teacher leadership: Rationale, strategy, and impact. *School Leadership and Management, 23*(2), 173–186.

18. Raelin, J. A. (2003). *Creating leaderful organizations: How to bring out leadership in everyone.* San Francisco, CA: Berrett-Koehler.

19. Lieberman, A. (2003). Foreword. In L. Lambert, *Leadership capacity for lasting school improvement* (p. vi). Alexandria, VA: Association for Supervision and Curriculum Development.

20. Lambert, L. (2003). Ibid., p. 2

21. Apple, M. W., & Beane, J. A. (1999). *Democratic schools: Lessons from the chalk face.* Buckingham, United Kingdom: Open University Press; Frost, D., & Durrant, J. (2003). Teacher leadership: Rationale, strategy, and impact. *School Leadership and Management, 23*(2), 173–186; Fullan. (2002). Op. cit.; Lambert. (1998). *Building leadership capacity in schools* (p. 3). Alexandria, VA: Association for Supervision and Curriculum Development.

22. Glickman, C. (1989). Has Sam and Samantha's time come at last? *Educational Leadership, 46*(8), 4–9 (p. 6).

23. For a thorough discussion on the varying ways of defining teacher leadership, see: York-Barr, J., & Duke, K. (2004). What do we know about teacher leadership? Findings from two decades of scholarship. *Review of Educational Research, 74*(3), 255–316.

24. Lambert, L. (1998). Op. cit.

25. Lambert. (1998). Ibid., p. 12.

26. Lambert. (1998). Ibid., pp. 3–4.

27. Katzenmeyer, M., & Moller, G. (2001). *Awakening the sleeping giant. Helping teachers develop as leaders* (2nd ed.). Thousand Oaks, CA: Corwin.

28. Day, D., & Harris, A. (2003). Teacher leadership, reflective practice, and school improvement. In *International handbook of educational administration* (pp. 724–749). Dordrecht, The Netherlands: Kluwer.

29. Ash, R. L., & Persall, R. M. (2000). The principal as chief learning officer: Developing teacher leaders. *NASSP Bulletin, 84*(616), 15–22.

30. Little, J. W. (2000). Assessing the prospects for teacher leadership. In *Jossey-Bass reader on teacher leadership* (pp. 390–419). Chicago, IL: Jossey-Bass.

31. Lieberman, A., Saxl, E. R., & Miles, M. B. (2000). Teacher leadership: Ideology and practice. In *Jossey-Bass reader on educational leadership* (pp. 339–345). Chicago, IL: Jossey-Bass.

32. York-Barr & Duke. (2004). Op. cit.

33. Wilson, M. (1993). The search for teacher leaders. *Educational Leadership, 50*(6), 24–27; Yarger, S. J., & Lee, O. (1994). The development

and sustenance of teacher leadership. In
D. R. Walling (Ed.), *Teachers as leaders: Perspectives on the professional development of teachers*
(pp. 223–237). Bloomington, IN: Phi Delta
Kappa Educational Foundation.

34. Katzenmeyer & Moller (2001). Op. cit.

35. Yarger & Lee. (1994). Op. cit.

36. Lieberman et al. (1988). Op. cit.; Wilson.
(1993). Op. cit.

37. Lambert. (2003). Op. cit., p. 13.

38. Lambert. (1998). Op. cit., pp. 16–17.

39. Leadership training for parents and students has
been found to be related to gains in student
achievement. See: Maxwell, L. A. (2009,
October 14). Community organizing. Organized
communities, stronger schools: A case study
series. *Education Week, 29*(7), 5.

40. Lambert. (2003). *School Leadership and
Management, 23*(4). Op. cit.

41. Reeves, D. A. (2009). *Leading change in your
school* (pp. 72–74). Alexandria, VA: ASCD.

42. Reeves. (2009). Ibid.

43. Hobson, A., & Sharp, C. (2005). Leadership
development: A systematic review of the
research evidence on mentoring new head
teachers. *School Leadership and Management,
25*(1), 25–43.

44. Browne-Ferrigno, T., & Muth, R. (2004). Leadership mentoring in clinical practice: Role socialization, professional development, and capacity
building. *Educational Administration Quarterly,
40*(4), 468–494; Fagan, M., & Walter, G. (1982).
Mentoring among teachers. *Journal of Educational
Research, 76*(2), 113–117; Scandura, T. A.,
Tejeda, M. J., Werther, W. B., & Landau, M. J.
(1996). Perspectives on mentoring. *Leadership
and Organizational Development Journal, 17*(3),
50–57; Stott, K., & Walker, A. (1992).
Developing school leaders through mentoring:
A Singapore perspective. *School Organization,
12*(2), 153–169.

45. Belasco, J. (2000). Foreword. In M. Goldsmith,
L. Lyons, & A. Freas (Eds.), *Coaching for leadership: How the world's greatest coaches help others
learn*. San Francisco, CA: Jossey Bass/Pfeiffer;
Hopson & Sharp. (2005). Op. cit.; Stead, V.
(2005). Mentoring: A model for leadership
development? *International Journal of Training
and Development, 9*(3), 170–184.

46. Barth, R. S. (1990). *Improving schools from within:
Teachers, parents, can make the difference*. San
Francisco, CA: Jossey-Bass; Hansen, J. M., &
Matthews, J. (2002). The power of more than
one. *Principal Leadership, 3*(2), 30–33;
Mullen, C. A., Gordon, S. P., Greenlee, B. J., &
Anderson, R. H. (2002). Capacities for school
leadership: Emerging trends in the literature.
International Journal of Educational Reform, 11(2),
158–198.

47. Lipton & Wellman. (2001). Op. cit., p. 7.

48. Leithwood, Louis, Anderson, & Wahlstrom.
(2004). Op. cit.; Marzano, R. J., Waters, T., &
McNulty, B. A. (2005). *School leadership that
works. From research to results*. Alexandria,
VA: ASCD.

49. Bredeson, P. V. (1995). Role change for principals
in restructured schools: Implications for teacher
preparation and teacher work. In M. O'Hair &
S. Odell (Eds.), *Educating teachers for leadership
and change* (pp. 25–45). Thousand Oaks, CA:
Corwin; Stone, M., Horejs, J., & Lomas, A.
(1997). *Commonalties and differences in teacher
leadership at the elementary, middle, and high school
levels*. Paper presented at the annual meeting of
the American Educational Research Association,
Chicago, IL.

50. Leithwood, K. (1992). The move towards transformational leadership. *Educational Leadership,
49*(5), 8–18; Yarger, S. J., & Lee. (1994). Op. cit.

51. Leithwood. (1992). Op. cit.

52. Wasley, P. D. (1991). *Teachers as leaders. The
rhetoric of reform and the realities of practice*.
New York, NY: Teachers College Press.

53. Ovando, M. (1994). *Effects of teacher leadership on
their teaching practices*. Paper presented at the
annual meeting of the University Council of
Educational Administration, Philadelphia, PA;
Seashore-Louis, K., Kruse, S., & Raywid, M.
(1996, May). Putting teachers at the center of
reform: Learning schools and professional
communities. *NASSP Bulletin, 80*(580), 10–21.

54. Frost, D., & Harris, A. (2003). Teacher leadership: Towards a research agenda. *Cambridge
Journal of Education, 33*(3), 479–498.

55. Lieberman, A., & Miller, L. (1999). *Teachers:
Transforming their world and their work*. New York,
NY: Teachers College Press; Little, J. W. (1988).
Assessing the prospects for teacher leadership. In

A. Lieberman (Ed.), *Building a professional culture in schools* (pp. 78–106). New York, NY: Teachers College Press; Moller, G., & Katzenmeyer, M. (1996). The promise of teacher leadership. *New Directions for School Leadership, 1*(1), 1–17.

56. Duke, D. L. (1994). Drift, detachment, and the need for teacher leadership. In D. R. Walling (Ed.), *Teachers as leaders: Perspectives on the professional development of teachers* (pp. 255–273). Bloomington, IN: Phi Delta Kappa Educational Foundation.

57. LeBlanc, P. R., & Skelton, M. M. (1997). Teacher leadership: The needs of teachers. *Action in Teacher Education, 19*(3), 32–48.

58. Fullan, M. (2002). The role of leadership in preparation of knowledge management in schools. *Teachers and Teaching, 8*(3/4), 409–419 (p. 409).

59. LeBlanc & Skelton (1997). Op. cit.; Moller & Katzenmeyer. (1996). Op. cit.; Ovando, M. N. (1996). Teacher leadership: Opportunities and challenges. *Planning and Changing, 27*(1/2), 30–44; Smylie, M. A., & Denny, J. W. (1990). Teacher leadership: Tensions and ambiguities in organizational perspective. *Educational Administration Quarterly, 26*(3), 235–259.

60. Sergiovanni, T. (2003). The lifeworld at the center: Values and action in educational leadership. In N. Bennett, M. Crawford, & M. Cartwright (Eds.), *Effective educational leadership* (pp. 14–24). London, United Kingdom: Paul Chapman, p. 14.

61. Lambert, L. (2003). Leadership redefined: An evocative context for teacher leadership. *School Leadership and Management, 23*(4), 421–430 (pp. 421–422).

62. Fullan. (2002). Ibid; Brown, J. S., & Duguid, P. (2000). *The social life of information.* Boston, MA: Harvard Business Books Press.

63. Longquist, M. P., & King, J. A. (1993). *Changing the tire on a moving bus: Barriers to the development of a professional community in a new teacher-led school.* Paper presented at the annual meeting of the American Educational Research Association, Atlanta, GA.

64. Caine, G., & Caine, R. N. (2000, May). The learning community as a foundation for developing teacher leaders. *NASSP Bulletin, 84*(616), 7–14.

65. Smylie, M. A. (1992). Teachers' reports of their interactions with teacher leaders concerning classroom instruction. *Elementary School Journal, 93*(1), 85–98.

66. Hargreaves, D. (2003). *From improvement to transformation.* Keynote lecture. International Congress for School Effectiveness and Improvement. Sydney, Australia.

67. Copeland, M. A. (2003). Leadership of inquiry: Building and sustaining capacity for school improvement. *Educational Evaluation and Policy Analysis, 25*(4), 375–395.

68. Gliddens, A. (1994). *Beyond left and right: The future of radical politics.* Oxford, United Kingdom: Polity Press.

69. Goleman, D., Boyatzis, R., & McKee, A. (2002). *Primal leadership: Realizing the power of emotional intelligence.* Boston, MA: Harvard Business School Press.

70. McColl-Kennedy, J. R., & Anderson, R. D. (2002). Impact of leadership style and emotions on subordinate performance. *Leadership Quarterly, 13*(5), 545–559.

71. Sergiovanni, T. (1992). *Moral leadership: Getting to the heart of school improvement.* San Francisco, CA: Jossey-Bass.

72. Barth. (2001). Op. cit.

73. Crowther, F., Kaagen, S. S., Ferguson, M., & Hann, L. (2002). *Developing teacher leaders: How teacher leadership enhances school success.* Thousand Oaks, CA: Corwin Press.

74. Crowther et al. (2002). Ibid.

75. York-Barr & Duke (2004). Op. cit. For a thorough discussion of the studies in this area, we recommend reading this article in its entirety.

76. Katzenmeyer & Moller. (2001). Op. cit.; Ovando, M. (1996). Teacher leadership: Opportunities and challenges. *Planning and Changing, 27*(1/2), 30–44.

77. Lieberman et al. (2000). Op. cit.

78. O'Connor, K., & Boles, K. (1992). *Assessing the needs of teacher leaders in Massachusetts.* Paper presented at the annual meeting of the American Educational Research Association, San Francisco, CA.

79. Smylie, M. A. (1997). Research on teacher leadership: Assessing the state of the art. In B. J. Biddle, T. L. Good, & I. F. Goodson (Eds.), *International handbook of teachers*

and teaching (pp. 521–592). Dordrecht, The Netherlands: Kluwer Academic Publishers, p. 574.

80. Katzenmeyer & Moller (2001). Op. cit. Ovando, M. (1996). Teacher leadership opportunities and challenges. *Planning and Changing, 27*(1/2), 30–44.

81. Rosenholz, S. (1989). *Teachers' workplace: The social organization of schools.* New York, NY: Teachers College Press; Stickler, J. L. (1988). Do teachers feel empowered? *Educational Leadership, 55*(7), 35–36.

82. Mujis & Harris. (2003). Op. cit.

83. Day et al. (2006). Op. cit.

84. Majis & Harris. (2003). Op. cit.

85. Leithwood, K., & Jantzi, D. (1998). *Distributed leadership and student engagement in school.* Paper presented at the annual meeting of the American Educational Research Association, San Diego, CA.

86. Davidson, B. M., & Taylor, D. L. (1999). *Examining principal succession and teacher leadership in school restructuring.* Paper presented at the annual meeting of the American Educational Research Association, Montreal, Quebec; Griffin, G. A. (1995). Influences of shared decision making on school and classroom activity: Conversations with five teachers. *Elementary School Journal, 96*(1), 29–45; Pechman, E. A., & King, J. A. (1993). *Obstacles to restructuring: Experience of six middle grade schools.* New York, NY: National Center for Restructuring Education, Schools, and Teaching; Weiss, C., & Cambone, J. (2000). Principals, shared decision making, and school reform. In *The Jossey-Bass reader on educational leadership* (pp. 339–345). Chicago, IL: Jossey-Bass.

87. Crowther, F., Hann, L., McMaster, J., & Fergurson, M. (2000). *Leadership for successful school revitalization: Lessons from recent Australian research.* Paper presented at the annual meeting of the American Educational Research Association, New Orleans, LA.

88. Gronn, P. (2000). Distributed properties: A new architecture for leadership. *Educational Management and Administration, 28*(3), 317–381.

89. Smylie. (1997). Op. cit.

90. Smylie. (1997). Op. cit.

91. Bishop, P., & Mulford, W. (1999). When will they ever learn? Another failure of centrally-imposed change. *School Leadership and Management, 19*(2), 179–187; Blase, J., & Blase, J. (2000). Implementation of shared governance for instructional improvement: Principals' perspectives. *Journal of Educational Administration, 37*(5), 476–500; Louis, K. S. (1998). Effects of teacher quality of work life in secondary schools on commitment and sense of efficacy. *School Effectiveness and School Improvement, 9*(1), 1–27; Sarason, S. (1990). *The predictable failure of educational reform.* San Francisco, CA: Jossey-Bass.

92. Louis. (1998). Op. cit.

93. Louis. (1998). Op. cit.

94. Brown-Ferrigno, T., & Muth, R. (2004). Leadership mentoring in clinical practice: Role socialization, professional development, and capacity building. *Educational Administration Quarterly, 40*(4), 468–494.

95. Vergugo, R., Greenberg, N., Henderson, R., Uribe, O., & Schneider, J. (1997). School governance regimes and teachers' job satisfaction: Bureaucracy, legitimacy, and community. *Educational Administration Quarterly, 33*(1), 38–66.

96. Churchill, R., & Williamson, J. (1999). Traditional attitudes and contemporary experiences: Teachers and educational change. *Asia-Pacific Journal of Teacher Education and Development, 2*(2), 43–51; Mulford, B., Hogan, D., & Lamb, S. (2002). Professionals' and lay persons' views of school councils in Tasmania. *Leading and Managing, 7*(2), 109–130.

97. Fullan, M. (1995, November). *Broadening the concept of teacher leadership.* Paper prepared for the National Staff Development Council, New Directions.

98. LeBlanc. & Skelton (1997). Op. cit.; Porter, A. C. (1987). Teacher collaboration: New partnership to attack old problems. *Phi Delta Kappan, 69*(2), 147–152; Ovando, M. N. (1996). Teacher leadership: Opportunities and challenges. *Planning and Changing, 27*(1/2), 30–44.

99. Cooper, B. S. (1993). When teachers run schools. In T. A. Astuto (Ed.), *When teachers lead* (pp. 25–42). University Park, PA: University Council for Educational Administration; Duke,

D. L. (1994). Drift, detachment, and the need for teacher leadership. In D. R. Walling (Ed.), *Teachers as leaders: Perspectives on the professional development of teachers* (pp. 255–273). Bloomington, IN: Phi Delta Kappa Educational Foundation; Little, J. W. (1988). Assessing the prospects for teacher leadership. In A. Lieberman (Ed.), *Building a professional culture in schools* (pp. 78–106). New York, NY: Teachers College Press; Smylie, M. A. (1992). Teachers' reports of their interactions with teacher leaders concerning classroom instruction. *Elementary School Journal, 93*(1), 85–98; Wasley, P. A. (1991). *Teachers who lead: The rhetoric of reform and the realities of practice.* New York, NY: Teachers College Press.

100. Leithwood, Harris, & Hopkins. (2008). Op. cit.

101. Leithwood, K., & Jantzi, D. (2006). Linking leadership to student learning: The contribution ofleader efficacy. *Educational Administration Quarterly, 43*(3), 425–446; Leithwood, Harris, & Hopkins. (2008). Op. cit.

102. Leithwood, K., & Mascall, B. (2008). Collective leadership effects on student achievement. *Educational Administration Quarterly, 44*(4), 529–561; Day, C., Stobart, G., Sammons, P., Kington, A., & Gu, Q. (2006). *Variations in teachers' work and lives and their effects on pupils: VITAE report* (DfES Research Report 743). London: Department for Education and Skills; Day, C., Sammons, P., Stobart, G., Kington, A., & Gu, Q. (2007). *Teachers matter: Variations in work, lives and effectiveness.* Milton Keynes, United Kingdom: Open University Press.

103. Mascall & Leithwood. (2006). Op. cit.; Leithwood, Harris, & Hopkins. (2008). Op. cit.

104. Leithwood, Harris, & Hopkins. (2008). Op. cit.

105. Leithwood, Harris, & Hopkins. (2008). Op. cit.

106. Leithwood, Harris, & Hopkins. (2008). Op. cit.

107. Bass, B. M. (1985). *Leadership and performance beyond expectations.* New York, NY: Free Press.

108. Malen, B. (1995). The micropolitics of education: Mapping the multiple dimensions of powerrelations in school polities. In J. Schribner & D. Layton (Eds.), *The study of educational politics.*New York, NY: Falmer Press.

109. Leithwood, Harris, & Hopkins. (2008). Op. cit.

110. Ensley, M. D., Hmieleski, K. M., & Pearce, C. L. (2006). The importance of vertical and shared leadership within new venture top management teams: Implications for the performance of startups. *Leadership Quarterly, 17*(3), 217–231.

111. Hartley, J., & Hinksman, B. (2003). *Leadership development: A systematic review of the literature.* A report for the NHS Leadership Centre, Warwick Business School.

112. Bullough, R. V., Jr., & Draper, R. J. (2004). Mentoring and the emotions. *Journal of Education for Teaching, 30*(3), 271–288.

113. Clutterbuck, D. (2004). *Everyone needs a mentor: Fostering talent in your organization* (4th ed.). London, United Kingdom: Chartered Institute of Personnel Development.

114. Bird, T., & Little, J. W. (1987). How schools organize the teaching occupation. *Elementary School Journal, 86*(4), 493–512; Bullough, R. V., Jr. (1987). Accommodation and tension: Teachers, teacher role, and the culture of teaching. In W. J. Smyth (Ed.), *Educating teachers: Changing the nature of knowledge* (pp. 183–194). London, United Kingdom: Falmer Press; Campbell, R. J. (1985). *Developing the primary curriculum.* London, United Kingdom: Holt, Rinehart, & Winston; Little, J. W. (1984). Seductive images and organization realities in professional development. *Teachers College Record, 86*(1), 84–102.

115. Campbell. (1985). Op. cit.; Campbell, R. J., & Southworth, G. (1990, April). *Rethinking collegiality: Teachers' views.* Paper presented at the annual meeting of the American Educational Research Association, Boston, MA; Copeland, M. A. (2001). The myth of the superprincipal. *Phi Delta Kappan, 82*(7), 528–533; Elmore, R. F. (2002). Hard questions about practice. *Educational Leadership, 59*(8), 22–25; Nias, J. (1987). Learning from difference: A collegial approach to change. In W. J. Smyth (Ed.), *Educating teachers: Changing the nature of pedagogical knowledge* (pp. 89–120). Lewes, United Kingdom: Falmer.

116. Glickman, D. (2006). Educational leadership: Failure to use our imagination. *Phi Delta Kappan, 87*(9), 689–690; Lindle, J. C., & Shrock, J. (1993). School based decision-making councils and the hiring process. *NASSP Bulletin, 77*(551), 71–76; Midgley, C., & Wood, S. (1993). Beyond site-based management. *Phi Delta Kappan, 75*(2), 245–249.

117. Hargreaves, A. (2000). Contrived collegiality: The micropolitics of teacher collaboration. In S. J. Ball (Ed.), *Sociology of education: Major themes* (pp. 1480–1503). London, United Kingdom: Routledge.

118. Wimer, S., & Kelley, H. H. (1982). An investigation of the dimensions of causal attribution. *Journal of Personality and Social Psychology, 43*(6), 1142–1162.

119. Heider, F. (1958). *The psychology of interpersonal relations.* New York, NY: Wiley.

120. Kelley, H. H. (1972). Attribution in social interaction. In E. E. Jones, H. H. Kanouse, R. E. Kelley, & R. E. Nisbett (Eds.), *Attribution: Perceiving the causes of behavior* (pp. 1–26). Morristown, NJ: General Learning Press.

121. Harvey, J. H., & Weary, G. (1984). Current issues in attribution theory and research. *Annual Review of Psychology, 35*(1), 427–459.

122. Jones, E. E. (1976). How do people perceive the causes of behavior? *American Scientist, 64*(3), 300–305; Kelley, H. H., & Michela, J. L. (1980). Attribution theory and research. *Annual Review of Psychology, 31*, 457–501; Martinko, M. J. (1995). The nature and function of attribution theory within the organizational sciences. In M. L. Martinko (Ed.), *Attribution theory: An organizational perspective* (pp. 7–16). Delray Beach, FL: St. Lucie Press; Weiner, B. (1987). The social psychology of emotion: Applications of a naïve psychology. *Journal of Social and Clinical Psychology, 5*(4), 405–419; Weiner, B. (2000). Intrapersonal and interpersonal theories of motivation from an attributional perspective. *Educational Psychology Review, 12*(1), 1–14.

123. Weiner, B. (1985). Attribution theory of achievement motivation and emotion. *Psychological Review, 92*(4), 548–573.; Weiner. (1995). Op. cit.; Weiner. (1996). Op. cit.; Weiner. (2000). Op. cit.; Jones, E. E., Kanouse, D. E., Kelley, H. H., Nisbett, R. E., Valins, S., & Weiner, B. (Eds.). (1972). *Attribution: Perceiving the causes of behavior.* Morristown, NJ: General Learning Press.

124. Weiner, B. (1985). Op. cit.; Weiner. (2000). Op. cit.

125. Weiner. (1985). Op. cit

126. Weiner. (2000). Op cit., p. 5.

127. Weiner. (2000). Op. cit.

128. Kelley, H. H., & Michela, J. L. (1980). Attribution theory and research. *Annual Review of Psychology, 31*(1), 457–501.

129. Miller, D. T., & Ross, M. (1975). Self-serving biases in the attribution of causality: Fact or fiction? *Psychological Bulletin, 82*, 213–225; Zuckerman, M. (1979). Attribution of success and failure revisited: The motivational bias is alive and well in attribution theory. *Journal of Personality, 47*(2), 245–287.

130. Deaux, K. (1976). Sex: A perspective on the attribution process. In J. H. Harvey, W. J. Ickes, & R. F. Kidd (Eds.), *New directions in attribution research* (pp. 335–352). Hillside, NJ: Erlbaum; Miller & Ross. (1975). Op. cit.

131. Kelley & Michela. (1980). Op. cit.

132. Kelley & Michela. (1980). Op. cit.

133. Thomson Gale. (2005–2006). Attribution theory. *Encyclopedia of Management.* Author. Retrieved from http://www.bookrags.com/research/attribution-theory-eom/

134. Weiner. (1985). Op. cit.

135. Kelley & Michela. (1980). Op. cit.

136. Wimer, S., & Kelley, H. H. (1982). An investigation of the dimensions of causal attribution. *Journal of Personality and Social Psychology, 43*(6), 1142–1162.

137. Harvey & Weary. (1984). Op. cit.

138. Weiner. (1985). Op. cit. Weiner, B. (1986). An *attributional theory of motivation and emotion.* New York, NY: Springer-Verlag.

139. Phares, E. J. (1957). Expectancy changes in chance and skill situations. *Journal of Abnormal Social Psychology, 54*(3), 339–342.

140. Weiner, B., Russell, D., & Lerman, D. (1978). Affective consequences of causal ascriptions. In J. H. Harvey, W. Ickes, & R. F. Kidd (Eds.), *New directions in attribution research* (Vol. 2, pp. 59–90). Hillside, NJ: Erlbaum; Weiner, B., Russell, D., & Lerman, D. (1979). The cognitive-emotional process in achievement-related contexts. *Journal of Personality and Social Psychology, 37*(7), 1211–1220.

141. Andrews, G. R., & Debus, R. L. (1978). Persistence and causal perception of failure: Modifying cognitive attributions. *Journal of Educational Psychology, 70*(2), 154–166; Dweck, C. S. (1975). The role of expectations and attributions in the alleviation of learned

helplessness. *Journal of Personality and Social Psychology, 31*(4), 674–685.

142. Greenwald, A. G. (1980). The totalitarian ego: Fabrication and revision of personal history. *American Psychology, 35*(7), 603–618.

143. Weary Bradley, G. (1978). Self-serving biases in the attribution process: A reexamination of the fact or fiction question. *Journal of Personality and Social Psychology, 36*(1), 56–71; Weary, G. (1980). Examination of affect and egotism as mediators of bias in causal attributions. *Journal of Personality and Social Psychology, 38*(2), 348–357.

144. Carver, C. S., DeGregorio, E., & Gilllis, R. (1980). Field-study evidence of an ego-defensive bias in attribution among two categories of observers. *Personality and Social Psychology Bulletin,* 6(1), 44–50; Greenberg, J., Pyszczynski, T., & Solomon, S. (1982). The self-serving attributional bias. Beyond self-presentation. *Journal of Experimental Social Psychology, 18*(1), 56–67; Lau, R. R., & Russell, D. (1980). Attributions in the sports pages. *Journal of Personality and Social Psychology, 39*(1), 29–38; Peterson, C. (1980). Attribution in the sports pages: An archival investigation of the covariation hypothesis. *Social Psychology Quarterly, 43*(1), 136–141; Smith, E. R., & Manard, B. B. (1980). Causal attributions and medical school admissions. *Personality and Social Psychology Bulletin,* 6(4), 644–650.

145. Orvis, B. R., Kelley, H. H., & Butter, D. (1976). Attributional conflicts in young couples. In J. H. Harvey, W. Ickes, & R. F. Kidd (Eds.), *New directions in attribution research* (Vol. 1, pp. 405–422). Hillsdale, NJ: Erlbaum.

146. Weary & Bradley. (1978). Op. cit.; Weary, G. (1979). Self-serving attributional biases: Perceptual or response distortions. *Journal of Personality and Social Psychology, 37*(8), 1418–1420.

147. Arkin, R. M., Appelman, A. J., & Bergur, J. M. (1980). Social anxiety, self-presentation, and the self-serving bias in causal attributions. *Journal of Personality and Social Psychology, 38*(1), 23–35; Weary, G. (1980). Examination of affect and egotism as mediators of bias in causal attribution. *Journal of Personality and Social Psychology, 38*(2), 348–357.

148. Ross, L., Bierbrauer, G., & Pally, S. (1974). Attribution of educational outcomes by professional and nonprofessional instructors. *Journal of Personality and Social Psychology, 29*(5), 609–618.

149. Tetlock, P. E. (1981). Explaining teacher explanations of pupil performance. A self-presentation interpretation. *Social Psychology Quarterly, 44*(3), 300–311.

150. Tetlock. (1981). Ibid.

151. Snyder, M. L., & Wicklund, R. A. (1981). Attribute ambiguity. In J. H. Harvey et al. (Eds.), *New directions in attribution research* (Vol. 1, pp. 197–221). Hillsdale, NJ: Erlbaum.

152. Smith, T. W., Snyder, C. R., & Handelsman, M. M. (1982). On the self-serving function of an academic wooden leg: Test anxiety as a self-handicapping strategy. *Journal of Personality and Social Psychology, 42*(2), 314–321.

153. Harvey & Weary. (1984). Op. cit.

154. Harvey & Weary. (1984). Op. cit.

155. Fullan. (2002). Op. cit., p. 417.

CHAPTER 8

Leadership, Conflict, Problem Solving, and Decision Making

Focus Questions

- How is decision making a key to understanding organizations?
- How can organizational conflict be functional as well as dysfunctional?
- In what ways is leadership a problem-solving process?
- What are the benefits and limits to rationality in decision making?
- What factors of leadership style, the situation, and the outcome contribute to shared decision making?
- How does groupthink contribute to our understanding of shared decision making?
- What does the research on shared decision making say about its effectiveness?

CASE STUDY: SHARED DECISION MAKING

At the April school board meeting, you are appointed principal of Dumont Middle School (DMS), a 1,200-student, middle-class, ethnically diverse school. The Dumont County Public Schools (DCPS) are an hour outside of one of the nation's largest cities. DMS is one of 34 schools in the county and one of five middle schools. You have been a teacher and middle school assistant principal in a neighboring progressive suburban area 40 minutes away from Dumont Middle School. You are eagerly anticipating your new appointment.

Dumont Middle School is an unusual mix of teacher and student demographics. Dr. Smith, the superintendent, has told you that there are some differences from your previous assignment to this one, but your decisions will be supported as changes need to be made. Dr. Smith provides you summary data concerning the school and asks to meet with you in a month or so when you have finished reviewing the data. As you are introduced to the central office staff, they greet you warmly and hold a reception for you to meet the school community. As you review the data by school and by school district preparing to meet with the superintendent, your notes reflect the following:

Student Demographic Data

% DMS	% DCPS	
66	34	Eligible for free or reduced-price lunch
58	30	African American students
32	59	Caucasian students
8	8	Latino students
2	2	Asian students
62	6	Missing more than 10 days of attendance
8	71	Missing 5–10 days of attendance
19	18	Missing 1–4 days of attendance
11	5	Perfect attendance
38	13	Suspended from school last year
64	29	Students in remedial classes
36	71	Students in honors classes

Teacher Demographic Data

% DMS	% DCPS	
43	80	Caucasian
50	16	African American
7	4	Latino
33	71	Greater than 10 years teaching at DCPS
13	22	5–10 years teaching at DCPS
54	7	Fewer than 5 years teaching at DCPS
18	34	Hold master's degrees
6	22	Hold degrees higher than master's degree

School Status

The school has not made adequate yearly progress (AYP) for the past 2 years. The state testing pass rate has remained constant for the last 6 years showing no improvement.

Notes to Self

It appears that more than 90% of the students and teachers in the honors classes are Caucasian. Approximately 130 students had perfect attendance last year—almost all Caucasian. More than 90% of the suspensions were to minority students. It appears that there are only two tracks: academic and remedial. This needs to change, but more data are needed before coming to a conclusion about what steps to take.

Case Study Continued

In May, you have your meeting with Dr. Smith. He asks if you have reviewed the school data, and you show him how you have disaggregated the summary data he gave you. Dr. Smith appears surprised by what you have found and asks how you plan to proceed with leading the school since your contract begins on July 1. You ask permission to have a survey sent to the school's teachers and parents. Dr. Smith suggests that the school PTA send out the survey to the parents, teachers, and school leadership council. He will forward the survey responses and any specific comments made on the survey to you. In mid-June, Dr. Smith calls and tells you that the survey data are in the mail to you, and he would like to meet with you again once you have had a chance to review the results and think about how you might like to proceed. The survey data show the following:

96%   Parent response rate
100%   Teacher response rate
100%   School leadership council response rate (department chairs, team leaders, assistant principals, and principal)

Parent Responses (Please respond to the following statements by your level of agreement, with 1 being low and 5 being high. 1 = strongly disagree; 2 = disagree; 3 = not certain; 4 = agree; 5 = strongly agree.)

1. Overall, I am pleased with the education my child is getting at DMS.
   1 (41%)   2 (19%)   3 (7%)   4 (11%)   5 (22%)
2. Race is not a problem at DMS.
   1 (44%)   2 (21%)   3 (2%)   4 (13%)   5 (20%)
3. Discipline is a problem at DMS.
   1 (43%)   2 (22%)   3 (1%)   4 (19%)   5 (15%)
4. I feel that my child's teachers care about all the children's progress in school.
   1 (39%)   2 (23%)   3 (11%)   4 (13%)   5 (14%)
5. My child's teacher communicates with me frequently about academic progress.
   1 (33%)   2 (20%)   3 (4%)   4 (30%)   5 (13%)

6. The principal's office communicates with me as needed regarding my child's progress.

     1 (29%)   2 (16%)   3 (33%)   4 (12%)   5 (10%)

7. Children from poor families are served as well as children from wealthier families at DMS.

     1 (54%)   2 (23%)   3 (6%)   4 (6%)   5 (11%)

8. Generally, better teachers are placed with higher achieving students.

     1 (32%)   2 (13%)   3 (1%)   4 (25%)   5 (29%)

9. Overall, I believe DMS is a safe place for my child.

     1 (31%)   2 (31%)   3 (16%)   4 (12%)   5 (10%)

10. DMS has high learning expectations for all students.

     1 (35%)   2 (25%)   3 (5%)   4 (25%)   5 (10%)

Comments

◆ "Both my children have had wonderful experiences at DMS's talented and gifted program. I could not be happier!"

◆ "DMS has two classes—the haves and have-nots. If you are a have, you get. If you are a have-not, you get nothing."

◆ "Safety is not an issue during the day, but I would not go to any of the night activities. That's where all the other students congregate."

◆ "My son's teachers really care about his progress. I am especially impressed by the honors algebra teacher. She really pushes my son to high levels of achievement and makes contact with me weekly."

◆ "I have never heard one teacher make a positive comment about my children even though Kevin is getting A grades in remedial math class."

Teacher Responses (Please respond to the following statements by your level of agreement, with 1 being low and 5 being high. 1 = strongly disagree; 2 = disagree; 3 = not certain; 4 = agree; 5 = strongly agree.)

1. Overall, I am pleased with the education DMS provides for its students.

     1 (26%)   2 (17%)   3 (14%)   4 (11%)   5 (32%)

2. Race is not a problem at DMS.

     1 (34%)   2 (21%)   3 (2%)   4 (23%)   5 (20%)

3. Discipline is a problem at DMS.

     1 (33%)   2 (12%)   3 (2%)   4 (28%)   5 (25%)

4. I feel that my students' parents know that I care about the children's progress in my classes.

     1 (11%)   2 (13%)   3 (23%)   4 (23%)   5 (30%)

5. I communicate with parents frequently about academic progress.

     1 (23%)   2 (20%)   3 (4%)   4 (30%)   5 (23%)

6. The principal's office communicates with parents as needed regarding student progress.

   1 (29%)   2 (36%)   3 (13%)   4 (12%)   5 (10%)

7. Children from poor families are served as well as children from wealthier families at DMS.

   1 (44%)   2 (13%)   3 (5%)   4 (21%)   5 (17%)

8. Generally, better teachers are placed with higher achieving students.

   1 (22%)   2 (23%)   3 (11%)   4 (20%)   5 (24%)

9. Overall, I believe DMS is a safe place for my students.

   1 (25%)   2 (21%)   3 (16%)   4 (18%)   5 (20%)

10. DMS has high learning expectations for all students.

   1 (35%)   2 (15%)   3 (5%)   4 (25%)   5 (20%)

Comments

- "DMS has changed so much in the 25 years I have been teaching here. Thank goodness I teach the honors classes or I'd leave in a heartbeat!"
- "It is really not fair how classes are assigned to us new teachers. We get all the remedial students and the behavior problems. The first year of teaching is hard enough without having all the trouble makers in our classes."
- "This is my third year of teaching, and I am working my butt off. Still, I get the remedial students. Some of the older teachers have been here for 20 years and really don't do much. How come they get the gravy teaching assignments?"
- "I like teaching at DMS. Here the students get to see that if you work hard, you can get into the good classes where you can really learn and excel."
- "I am not tenured yet, so I will not say anything except I am glad to have a job. I did not know how hard teaching would be and how unfair the seniority system is here."

Leadership Council Responses (Please respond to the following statements by your level of agreement, with 1 being low and 5 being high. 1 = strongly disagree; 2 = disagree; 3 = not certain; 4 = agree; 5 = strongly agree.)

1. Overall, I am pleased with the education students receive at DMS.

   1 (1%)   2 (9%)   3 (5%)   4 (35%)   5 (50%)

2. Race is not a problem at DMS.

   1 (5%)   2 (5%)   3 (5%)   4 (30%)   5 (55%)

3. Discipline is a problem at DMS.

   1 (5%)   2 (5%)   3 (5%)   4 (35%)   5 (50%)

4. I feel that all teachers care about all the children's progress in school.

   1 (10%)   2 (10%)   3 (10%)   4 (30%)   5 (40%)

5. Teachers communicate with parents frequently about academic progress.

   1 (70%)   2 (20%)   3 (0%)   4 (5%)   5 (5%)

6. The principal's office communicates with parents as needed regarding their children's progress.

   1 (29%)   2 (16%)   3 (33%)   4 (12%)   5 (10%)

7. Children from poor families are served as well as children from wealthier families at DMS.

   1 (10%)   2 (10%)   3 (10%)   4 (30%)   5 (40%)

8. Generally, better teachers are placed with higher achieving students.

   1 (15%)   2 (10%)   3 (15%)   4 (20%)   5 (40%)

9. Overall, I believe DMS is a safe place for students.

   1 (0%)   2 (0%)   3 (0%)   4 (10%)   5 (90%)

10. DMS has high learning expectations for all students.

    1 (5%)   2 (5%)   3 (5%)   4 (35%)   5 (50%)

Comments

◆ "DMS is a wonderful place to teach. The students work hard, and the parents are supportive. I could not ask for more."
◆ "The job of the school leadership council is to assist the principal in making decisions. The principal is wonderfully supportive of our recommendations. I think we have helped to make this a wonderful school."
◆ "This is my first year on the school leadership council after having taught here for 11 years. I have been teaching the honors classes and two sections of TAG (talented and gifted). I do remember my first 7 or 8 years teaching the remedial students. I am totally in the minority with this idea, but the poorer and lower academic ability kids may be getting the short end of the stick at DMS. On the other hand, if they work hard, they can move to the higher level classes with all the benefits that brings to them. It really is a microcosm of the free enterprise system."
◆ "Our school provides outstanding opportunities to students. I could not be more pleased with how everything operates at DMS."

After you have reviewed the survey results and comments, you make the following notations. It appears that parents' survey results show:

◆ There may be a split in the satisfaction level. Is there a group that is very happy with how the school works for them and their children?
◆ Overall, 60% of the parents are not pleased (1 or 2) while 33% are pleased (4 or 5). This is a rather large percentage of parents not pleased with the overall education provided at DMS.
◆ 65% feel that race is a problem; 33% don't. Are people living in two distinct worlds here?

- 65% feel that discipline is a problem; 33% don't. Ditto note from above.
- The majority of parents feel that teachers do not care about student progress. Ouch!
- Communication issues appear split.
- There may be some class issues as seen in questions 7 and 8. That might be indicated by many of the responses.
- Student safety may be a parent concern (62% responses of 1 or 2).
- High teacher expectations may be an issue. If there are not high expectations, little else will go on.

It appears that the teachers' survey results show:

- The same split in the overall satisfaction level appears with the faculty. I wonder if those who teach the upper level classes think the school is doing a good job. What about those who teach the lower achieving children?
- 55% feel race is a problem and 53% feel it is a problem. Again, it appears there are two different worlds.
- 45% feel discipline is not a problem while 43% feel it is. Again, ditto note above!
- 57% feel that poor children are not served well whereas 44% feel they are served well. I think we are on to something here. Parents and teachers are about equally split on this issue.
- 45% disagree that better teachers are placed with higher achieving students while 44% agree with that statement.
- Virtually all the rest of the statements are evenly split between agree and disagree.

It appears that the school leadership council survey results show:

- This group has a very high level of satisfaction with each of the statements. The results are not reflective of the parent or teacher survey results. Is this the group advising the principal on matters of importance?
- This group, for the most part, only sees positive aspects of the school. I would like to know a bit more about this group's makeup. Are they teaching the high-achieving students from wealthy families? Do they see the other part of the school that parents and teachers are mentioning?

As you meet with the superintendent, you point out your observations and questions. The school appears to be working much better for the brighter students than for the needier students. The parent and teacher survey and comments seem to back up that idea. The school leadership council, however, feels that all is going well. They may not be seeing the entire picture, and perhaps a change in membership is in order. You want DMS to be an effective school for all its students. That concept needs to be priority one.

Dr. Smith agrees with your initial observations and asks you some rather pointed questions about how you plan to deal with the conflict that will arise from your decisions. Specifically, he asks you the following questions:

Case Study Questions

1. What is your understanding of the major issues you will face in the decision-making process at DMS?
2. What are the specific changes you believe are most important?
3. How do you plan to make the changes that need to be made?
4. Where do you see the major sources of conflict as you proceed with changes?
5. What do you see as the differences between conflict resolution and conflict management in what you will be facing?
6. How would satisficing, optimizing, and simplifying affect your decisions?
7. How does groupthink contribute to poor problem solving and decision making?

INTRODUCTION

Like other organizations, schools exist to focus human activity around goals that can only be met cooperatively; organizational norms emphasize teamwork, harmony, and collaboration. Yet in reality, no group can be wholly harmonious.

Organizational conflict generates opportunities for decision making. Educational leaders must continually choose between independently and quickly addressing an issue and efficiently moving on to other business—or opening participation in decision making to relevant people in the organization to improve the decision's quality and gain employees' support for its implementation.

Herbert Simon (1997), the University of Chicago economist and management expert, wrote that management *is* decision making. "Decision-making processes hold the key to understanding organizations."[1] Deciding how to make decisions and who should be involved has become a critical component of leadership.

This chapter looks at conflict in organizations and how it prompts decision making. Rational decision making, shared decision making, and groupthink models will be explored along with the research supporting or challenging their effectiveness.

LEADERSHIP AND CONFLICT IN ORGANIZATIONS

Conflict is inevitable among humans. When two or more people seeking to attain their objectives come into contact with one another, tensions occur. Social interaction may be viewed as a process involving a struggle over claims to resources, power and status, beliefs, and other preferences. Conflict may arise from attempting to persuade the other to accept your preference, trying to secure the resource advantage, or, in extreme cases, trying to injure or eliminate one's opponents.[2]

Constant organizational change, however, does not mean businesses or schools are learning how to manage conflict more effectively. In fact, most organizational leaders try not so much to understand and productively deal with conflict but to find ways to reduce, avoid, or end it. As a result, organizations waste valuable resources as employees engage in dysfunctional conflict and miss opportunities to use functional conflict to improve their efficacy.

Defining Conflict

While the scientific literature has no consensus on its specific meaning,[3] *conflict* has traditionally been defined in terms of opposing, divergent interests involving incompatible activities. Conflict can be intrapersonal or interpersonal.

Conflict as Incompatibility.   M. Afzalur Rahim, business professor at Western Kentucky University and conflict management scholar, broadly defined conflict as an interactive process that appears in incompatibility, disagreement, or dissonance within or between social entities (i.e., individual, group, organization).[4] Conflict can relate to incompatible preferences, goals, and activities. Generally, conflict may occur when:[5]

- ◆ A party is required to engage in an activity that is incongruent with his or her needs or interests.
- ◆ A party holds behavioral preferences that, if satisfied, prevent another person from implementing his or her preferences.
- ◆ A party wants some mutually desirable but limited resource, such that not everyone's wants may be fully satisfied.
- ◆ A party possesses attitudes, values, skills, and goals that are influential in directing his or her behavior but are perceived to exclude the attitudes, values, skills, and goals held by others.
- ◆ Two parties have partially exclusive behavioral preferences regarding their joint actions.
- ◆ Two parties are interdependent in the performance of functions or activities.

Morton Deutsch, Columbia University professor emeritus who is widely regarded as the founder of modern conflict resolution theory and practice, defined conflict more narrowly. Deutsch observed that "a conflict exists whenever incompatible activities occur."[6] This incompatibility produces a dilemma: Individuals pursue incompatible, or seemingly incompatible, goals such that one side gains at the other's expense. Conflict may produce a classic, zero-sum, win–lose situation that is potentially harmful to organizational life. Everyone tries to avoid losing, and losers struggle to become winners. As a result, what begins as a substantive, seemingly objective disagreement regarding a task may quickly become personal and emotional. This affective involvement is a central quality of conflict in organizations.

Conflict as Intrapersonal or Interpersonal.   Conflict may occur within a single individual (intrapersonal conflict)—a common situation in which a person feels divided between wanting to achieve two incompatible goals. This leads to feelings of stress, to stress-related behaviors such as indecisiveness, and occasionally to physiological symptoms such as hypertension or ulcers. Conflict may also occur between persons or social units (interpersonal, intergroup, or international). Conflict in organizational life usually involves interpersonal conflict and intergroup conflict.

From the organization's perspective, leaders must learn to manage conflict so that hostility can be either avoided or minimized. When the conflict can be constructively handled in ways that solve the problem and prevent or minimize antagonism, the organization stands to benefit. In contrast, when the conflict is not handled properly, the results may be harmful for the organization.

Classical View of Organizational Conflict. Conflict has been a central focus of social psychologists and organizational theorists. In the mid 19th century, English naturalist Charles Darwin stressed "the competitive struggle for existence" and "the survival of the fittest." He believed that all nature is at war, one organism with another or with external nature. Also during the 19th century, the philosopher and revolutionary Karl Marx emphasized class struggle which fractured the whole society into directly antagonistic classes, bourgeoisie and proletariat. Similarly, Sigmund Freud, the founder of psychoanalysis, saw psychosocial development as a constant struggle between the infantile id and the socially determined superego.

The classical organizational theorists Henri Fayol (1916/1949), Luther Gulick and Lyndall Urwick (1937), Frederick Taylor (1911), and Max Weber (1929/1947) implicitly appreciated the difficulties conflict could inflict on organizations.[7] Strongly biased toward a smooth-functioning organization typified by harmony, unity, coordination, efficiency, and order, these early theorists intuitively assumed that conflict was bad for organizations. To their minds, discord harmed organizational efficiency and should be minimized. Accordingly, they recommended managerial structures—rules and procedures, hierarchy, lines of authority, and the like—to prevent organization members from engaging in disagreements. These classical theorists' management perspective presumed that accord, cooperation, and the absence of interpersonal friction were necessary conditions for achieving organizational success.

Contemporary View of Organizational Conflict. After World War II, conflict resolution as an area of scholarship and professional practice emerged as an academic discipline. Unlike the earlier perspectives, contemporaries view conflict as inevitable, endemic, and often legitimate. Individuals and groups are interdependent and constantly engaged in the dynamic process of defining and redefining the nature and extent of their involvement. Environments are constantly changing. As Chester Barnard, the American business executive and sociological theorist, noted, social patterns characterized by negotiating stress and conflict are "inherent in the conception of free will in a changing environment."[8] Any well-led organization will experience conflict. The leadership role requires gathering resources—people, money, time, facilities, and material—in order to achieve new goals. Given the finite resources available to schools, competing ideas for how to use the resources are inevitable. Today, we view conflict as a way of confronting reality and creating new solutions to difficult problems. When well managed, conflict brings life and energy into our relationships and strengthens our interdependence. Conflict can make organizations more innovative and productive. The main issue is not whether and to what degree the organizational conflict is present but how well leaders manage conflict within the organization. It has been said that when two persons in business always agree, one of them is unnecessary.[9]

Conflict is necessary for true involvement, empowerment, and democracy. By debating their varying viewpoints, people express their concerns and create solutions reflecting their varied perspectives. Through conflict, people can become united and committed. As Dean Tjosvold, professor and international management expert concluded, "Well-managed conflict is an investment in the future."[10]

Functional and Dysfunctional Outcomes.   Depending on how it is handled, conflict within organizations may have functional and dysfunctional outcomes. Several researchers have noted the positive consequences of conflict.[11] Organizations with little or no conflict may stagnate. In contrast, organizational conflict left uncontrolled may have damaging effects. The consensus among organizational theorists is that a moderate amount of conflict is necessary for attaining an optimal level of organizational effectiveness. The relationship between conflict and organizational effectiveness approximates an inverted-U function.[12] Picture an upside down letter U as representing the normal distribution. Too little conflict/stagnation is represented on the left side and too much conflict/uncontrollable change is represented on the right side. Each end point is associated with low organizational effectiveness. The "hump" in the middle of the inverted U-curve represents moderate conflict, the peak effectiveness level. It has been suggested that "conflict management can require intervention to reduce conflict if there is too much, or intervention to promote conflict if there is too little."[13]

In *The Functions of Social Conflict* (1956), Lewis Coser presented two opposing viewpoints about the outcome of conflict.[14] Realistically, he observed, conflict had productive as well as destructive potentials.

Functional outcomes of conflict include:[15]

◆ Stimulating innovation, creativity, and growth
◆ Improving organizational decision making
◆ Finding alternative solutions to problems
◆ Finding synergistic solutions to common problems
◆ Enhancing individual and group performance
◆ Affording individuals and groups occasions to search for new solutions
◆ Requiring individuals and groups to articulate and clarify their positions

Dysfunctional outcomes of conflict include:[16]

◆ Causing job stress, burnout, and dissatisfaction
◆ Reducing communication between individuals and groups
◆ Developing a climate of distrust and suspicion
◆ Damaging relationships
◆ Reducing job performance
◆ Increasing resistance to change
◆ Affecting organizational commitment and loyalty

Clearly, conflict has both positive and negative consequences. If an organization is to benefit from conflict, leaders must find ways to reduce its negative effects and enhance its positive effects. And, as discussed in an earlier chapter, organizational learning is a significant and essential construct for organizational health.[17] Managing conflict wisely therefore, is essential to promoting organizational fitness.

Conflict Resolution and Conflict Management

Conflict resolution is not the same as conflict management. *Conflict resolution* implies reducing, eliminating, or ending conflict. *Conflict management*, on the other hand, involves designing effective macro-level strategies to minimize the conflict's dysfunctions and enhance conflict's constructive functions in order to improve organizational learning and efficacy.[18] Rather than simply contain and end organizational discord, conflict management uses discord to construct a more flexible, resilient, and productive organization.

Some scholars see *conflict resolution* as containing both constructive (management) and destructive processes. Deutch, Coleman, and Marcus (2006) described their theory of conflict resolution as a constructive or destructive process.[19] Whether participants in a conflict have a cooperative or a competitive orientation toward solving the mutual problem is decisive in determining the conflict's course and outcome. The persons' character and experiences, social contexts, aspirations, social norms, desire for power and influence, and conflict orientations each play a role. A cooperative approach leads to a constructive process in which the two parties successfully solve the problem. A competitive approach leads to a process in which the two parties engage in a contest or struggle to determine winners and losers. Occasionally, both parties lose. Almost all conflicts are mixed-motive, containing both cooperative and competitive elements.

Regardless of the terms used, a cooperative or win-win orientation to resolving a conflict greatly facilitates finding a constructive solution. A competitive win-lose outlook hinders it. It is easier to develop and maintain a win-win attitude if one has social support for it from friends, colleagues, employers, the organizational culture, the media, and the larger community.

Reframing the Conflict.   The heart of cooperative conflict resolution is *reframing* the conflict—that is, placing a different perception around the conflict as if inserting a familiar photo into a different border to create a new appearance for the picture and fresh affective response in the viewer. Reframing the conflict as a mutual problem, for instance, identifies it as one that can be solved through joint cooperative efforts. Reframing helps to establish a cooperative orientation to the conflict—even if the conflicting parties' goals are initially perceived to be win-lose—and leads the parties to search for fair procedures to decide how they can both gain as they resolve the problem. Reformulating the situation as a joint problem to be solved cooperatively for a mutually satisfactory or win-win outcome inherently assumes that whatever the resolution, each party considers it acceptable and fair.

Norms of Cooperation.   Parties are more likely to successfully reframe their conflict into a mutual problem if they follow norms of cooperative behavior and if they have the skills that facilitate effective cooperation. These norms are similar to those for respectful, responsible, honest, empowering, and caring behaviors toward friends or fellow group members. These norms include:[20]

- ◆ Placing the disagreements into perspective by identifying common ground and common interests.
- ◆ When disagreement occurs, focusing on the issue and refraining from making personal attacks.
- ◆ Building on others' ideas and fully acknowledging their value.
- ◆ Emphasizing the positive in the other party and possible constructive resolution of the conflict. Limit and control expression of negative feelings so they are primarily directed at the other's violation of cooperative norms (if that occurs) or at the other's defeatism.
- ◆ Being responsive to the other's legitimate needs.
- ◆ Empowering the other to contribute effectively to the cooperative effort, soliciting the other's views, listening responsively, sharing information, and otherwise helping

the other party—when necessary—to be an active, effective participant in the cooperative problem-solving process.

◆ Being appropriately honest. Being dishonest or attempting to mislead or deceive violates cooperative norms. At the same time, it is not necessary to be unnecessarily or inappropriately truthful. Unless the relationship has been developed to a very high level of intimacy, expressing every suspicion, doubt, fear, and sense of weakness one has about oneself or the other (especially in a blunt, unrationalized, and unmodulated manner) is likely to harm the relationship.

◆ Remaining a moral, caring, and fair-minded person throughout the conflict and considering the other person as a member of one's moral community and entitled to care and justice.

Sticking to the issues and speaking respectfully is challenging but essential. In the heat of conflict, the tendency to violate the cooperative norms is understandable. Clearly, attacking the other person as "stubborn," "selfish," or "unreasonable" undermines the problem-solving process. Recognizing when this behavior begins and then stopping, apologizing, and explaining what made one angry enough to want to hurt the other helps refocus on constructive engagement. Likewise, recognizing that each party has "hot buttons" that, if pressed, are likely to generate strong emotions—and not activating them—will help the participants control their reactions. Preventing disruptive emotions during problem solving can only speed up movement toward a satisfactory resolution. Of course, while remaining calm and acting cooperatively is more easily said than done, it can be learned with practice and feedback.

Conflict and Organizational Performance

Whether a conflict is good or bad, functional or dysfunctional, depends on how it affects the organizational performance. In schools, conflict's functional or dysfunctional consequences appear in organizational health, adaptability, and stability.

Modern motivational theory clearly affirms that challenge, meaning, and the need to solve problems are important work characteristics that people find interesting, enjoyable, and rousing. Similarly, views of participatory leadership rest on the belief that many people in the organization have good ideas and essential information to contribute to making informed decisions. Constructively receiving divergent viewpoints often produces superior quality ideas. They provide different evidence, additional considerations, novel but relevant insights, and varied frames of reference. Disagreements may prompt the individual into considering factors previously overlooked and help create a more comprehensive view that synthesizes a wider array of elements into a more complex whole. Successfully managing conflict also improves organizational functioning by clarifying relationships, increasing cohesiveness, and enhancing problem-solving procedures.

Deutsch (1973) observed that conflict within a group frequently serves to revitalize existing norms or contributes to emergence of new ones. In this way, social conflict is a means for social norms to adjust to new conditions. A flexible society benefits from conflict because such behavior helps create and modify norms which allow it to continue under changed conditions. In contrast, rigid systems that suppress conflict smother a useful warning system, ironically increasing the danger of catastrophic societal breakdown.[21] Conflict in a group or organization can be viewed as the "canary in the coal mine," used as an early warning of impending danger.

By applying the concepts of conflict management, organizational leaders can minimize conflict's destructive potential and maximize its productive, creative, and useful possibilities to strengthen their organizational processes and outcomes.

ACTIVITY 8.1   Using Data to Identify Areas of Possible Conflict

Case Study Question 1: What is your understanding of the major issues you will face in the decision-making process at Dumont Middle School?

As you review the data that Dr. Smith has shared with you, discuss as a class:

1. What are the academic achievement issues?
2. What are the students' demographics and curricular issues?
3. What are the school climate issues?
4. What are the leadership issues?
5. What are the teacher issues?
6. What are the parent issues?
7. What are the communication issues?
8. What are the issues related to conflict management versus conflict resolution?
9. What are the expectation issues for students? What are the expectation issues for teachers?

Case Study Question 4: Where do you see the major sources of conflict as you proceed with changes?

10. What do you see as the major sources of conflict as you proceed with changes—and why?

ACTIVITY 8.2   Conflict Resolution and Conflict Management at Dumont Middle School

Case Study Question 5: What do you see as the differences between conflict resolution and conflict management in what you will be facing?

Conflict arises whenever incompatible activities occur so that one side gains at the other's expense in a win-lose situation. *Conflict resolution* implies reducing, eliminating, or avoiding conflict while *conflict management* involves designing effective strategies to minimize conflict's dysfunctions and enhance its constructive functions to improve organization learning and effectiveness. Discuss in pairs and then as a class:

1. From the Dumont Middle School data you have reviewed, did the former principal appear to be relying on conflict resolution or conflict management in his or her leadership style? What data can you use to support your conclusions?
2. If conflict can be understood as occurring when one side gains at the other's expense, what areas of conflict can you infer from reviewing the DMS data?
   ◆ How were the leadership council teachers gaining at others' expense?
   ◆ How were the experienced teachers gaining at new teachers' expense?
   ◆ How were affluent and high-achieving students gaining at lower socioeconomic students' and slower learning students' expense?
   ◆ How were affluent parents gaining at less affluent parents' expense?
   ◆ How can the new principal reframe the conflict as a mutual problem that requires joint cooperative efforts to solve so that all parties can gain?

ACTIVITY 8.3   Identifying Parties in Conflict

Conflict occurs when:

- A party holds behavioral preferences, which, if satisfied, prevents another person from implementing his or her preferences.
- A party wants some mutually desirable but limited resource, such that everyone's wants may not be fully satisfied.
- A party possesses attitudes, values, skills, and goals that are influential in directing his or her behavior but are perceived to exclude the attitudes, values, skills, and goals held by others.

As a class, answer the following about what you learned from the DMS data:

1. Who are the various parties engaged in conflict?
2. What are the behavioral preferences that seem to have the upper hand?
3. What are the mutually desirable but limited resources?
4. Who is the party with influential attitudes, values, skills, and goals that is perceived to exclude the attitudes, values, skills, and goals of others?

ACTIVITY 8.4   Reframing Conflict at Dumont Middle School

If **reframing** the conflict places a different perception around it and redefines it as a mutual problem that can be solved through joint cooperative efforts, how can the new principal reframe the conflict evident at Dumont Middle School to develop a cooperative orientation and shared goals among the key stakeholders?

PROBLEM SOLVING AND DECISION MAKING IN ORGANIZATIONS

Change and conflict are natural processes which create situations that require organizational members to solve problems. The ways in which leaders resolve dilemmas affect organizational effectiveness and capacity.

People in organizations make decisions to solve problems. Since circumstances, people, and organizations differ, no one right or best way for making effective decisions exists. The multiple benefits and hazards inherent in decision making make it a high-stakes and stressful process.

Many scholars and practitioners have added to our understanding of decision making in organizations. Chester Barnard, Robert Tannenbaum, and Warren H. Schmidt contributed broadly to our knowledge of leadership, shared decision making, and problem solving. Peter Drucker and Herbert Simon offered more nuanced views about rational decision making. Victor Vroom and colleagues' normative models presented shared decision making in complex detail. Other theorists have offered more descriptive decision-making models. Finally, the groupthink phenomenon illustrated how certain group interaction styles could have adverse effects on shared decision making and problem solving.

Chester I. Barnard and Problem Solving in Organizations

As a perceptive business practitioner, Chester I. Barnard is widely recognized for his path-breaking contributions to the field of organizational theory. Barnard developed a realistic description of organizational decision making as coordinated adaptation expressed in a "conscious, deliberate, purposeful" way.[22]

In the 1930s, Barnard concluded that most organizations fail. If they are to survive, organizations continually must adapt to fluctuating circumstances. This means that organizations must occasionally change their leadership, objectives and goals, work styles, methods and processes, structures, rules and regulations, and personnel. To stay alive, they must virtually become different organizations. Failure to innovate means stagnation. To stay in the same place in a rapidly changing world is to fall behind.[23]

Barnard noted that since organizational leaders can only tackle high-priority problems, the operational units must solve their own problems and manage conflict. To do this, organizations must shift from accumulating information to developing personal skills that can anticipate problems, mobilize resources in advance, devise appropriate solutions, adopt self-corrective measures, and assess results.

Barnard believed that leadership is a problem-solving process that depends on the interaction of three variables: the individual, the group of followers, and the conditions. Pragmatic leaders are responsible for the contingencies of organizational conditions. The process of leading includes setting goals, allocating resources, controlling and coordinating people and units, and developing incentives. The leadership challenge is to perform these functions under conditions of both organizational stability and change.

Barnard also advised that the ability of organizational leaders and members to solve problems requires several capacities:[24]

♦ The ability to recognize new problems that need new solutions rather than modifying old solutions
♦ The ability to reformulate problems in new terms so as to elicit new responses and initiatives
♦ The ability to deal with uncertainty and fluidity, and to absorb change, instability, and interdependence
♦ The ability to encourage error correction, initiative, and creativity and to learn from mistakes, experience, and uncertainty
♦ The ability to remain human and humane under stress

In addition, Barnard believed that problem-solving solutions can be either efficient or inefficient. Inefficient solutions create new problems whereas efficient solutions do not.

ACTIVITY 8.5   Problem-Solving Leadership

If, as Barnard said, leadership is a problem-solving process that depends on the interaction of the individual, the group, and the conditions, then how ready are you as a new school leader to take on the challenges at Dumont Middle School? Answer individually and share with a partner:

1. How can you as principal adjust the leadership process—including goal setting, resource allocation, control and coordination of people and units, and incentives—to effectively address the conflicts at DMS?

2. If effective leadership requires the capacities named in the following list, in which of these do you feel most confident? Which of these capacities do you wish to develop further? How will you identify where your teachers (especially those in the leadership team) are on these capacities? How could you help them develop such capacities?
   ◆ Ability to recognize new problems that require new solutions rather than modifications of old solutions
   ◆ Ability to reformulate problems in new terms so as to elicit new responses and initiatives
   ◆ Ability to deal with uncertainty and fluidity and to absorb change, instability, and interdependence
   ◆ Ability to learn from mistakes
   ◆ Ability to remain human and humane under stress

3. Which of these capacities do you think will be most essential to success working with DMS—and why?

The Problem-Solving Continuum of Leadership Behaviors

If leadership is a problem-solving process, it is one in which leaders and subordinates both hold stakes in the outcome. The various ways in which leaders and subordinates work together to solve problems impacts organizational functioning and productivity.

In 1958, University of California management professors Robert Tannenbaum and Warren H. Schmidt proposed that leadership could follow different patterns of problem-solving with subordinates.[25] Figure 8–1 illustrates the continuum of possible leadership behaviors available to organizational managers (in this context, the school principal), related to the degrees of the boss's authority and the subordinates' freedom in reaching decisions. On the figure's extreme left, the manager maintains a high degree of control. On the figure's extreme right, the manager gives up a high degree of control and confers greater attention to employees' interests, feelings, and perspectives. Authority and freedom each have their limitations, however.

Involving employees in problem solving entails risk. Tannenbaum and Schmidt believed that managers must expect their supervisors to hold them responsible for the quality of decisions made, even though operationally, the group may have made these decisions. As a result, the manager must be ready to accept whatever jeopardy is involved in delegating decision-making power to subordinates. When the leader is accountable, delegating is not a way of "passing the buck." Then too, the amount of freedom the boss gives to subordinates cannot be greater than the freedom that the superior has given the manager. It is also important that the group recognize what kind of leadership behavior the boss is using so members can clearly understand the limits on their decision-making input. The significance of the decisions to be made—not the number of the decisions permitted to the group members—is a more accurate index of their boss's confidence in them and in the amount of freedom granted for decision making.

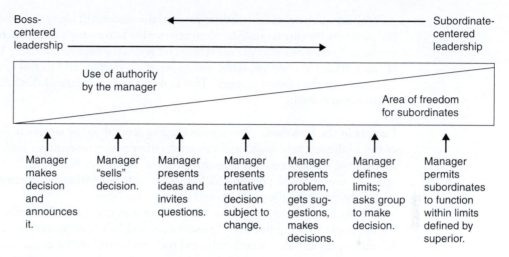

FIGURE 8–1

Problem-Solving Continuum of Leadership Behavior (Source: Reprinted by permission of Tannenbaum, R., & Schmidt, W. H. (1958). How to choose a leadership pattern. *Harvard Business Review*, (36)2. Copyright © 1958 by the Harvard Business School Publishing Corporation; all rights reserved.)

Factors in the Manager.   Tannenbaum and Schmidt identified factors in the manager, the subordinates, and the situation that influence a manager's action in decision making. The manager's internal value system, confidence in the subordinates, leadership inclinations, feelings of security in an uncertain situation, and other variables consciously or unconsciously influence the manager's behavior. When managers can understand how these factors affect their willingness to share decision making in certain situations, they can become more skilled in involving others.

Factors in the Subordinates.   Subordinates are influenced by many personality variables and expectations about how the boss should act in relation to the subordinates. Generally speaking, the manager can permit subordinates greater freedom when:[26]

- ◆ Subordinates have relatively high needs for independence. Some people desire more or less direction.
- ◆ Subordinates have a readiness to assume responsibility for decision making. Some see additional responsibility as a tribute to their ability. Others view it as "passing the buck."
- ◆ Subordinates have a relatively high tolerance for ambiguity. Some employees prefer to be given clear-cut directions. Others prefer a wider area of freedom.
- ◆ Subordinates are interested in the problem and believe it is important.
- ◆ Subordinates understand and identify with the organization's goals.
- ◆ Subordinates have the necessary knowledge and experience to deal with the problem.
- ◆ Subordinates have learned to expect to share in decision making. Those who expect to share in decision making resent the boss who makes all decisions autonomously whereas subordinates who expect the boss to display "strong leadership" may be upset by receiving the responsibility to share in decision making.

Without all the above conditions present, the leader will likely make fuller use of his or her authority because no realistic alternative exists to running a one-person show. Alternatively, in a climate of mutual confidence and respect, where subordinates have high levels of the relevant knowledge, skills, and experience, people tend to feel less threatened by changes from the normal practice. This makes a higher degree of flexibility in the whole relationship possible.

Factors in the Situation.   Leadership choices depend on the situation. Today, most leadership studies include situational variables, either as determinants of leader behavior or as moderating variables interacting with leaders' traits and behaviors.[27] Among the most crucial environmental pressures include those stemming from the organization, the work group, the nature of the problem, and the time pressures.

Like individuals, organizations have values and traditions that influence the behavior of people working in them. These values and behaviors are communicated through job descriptions, policy statements, and top executives' public comments. Some organizations prefer a dynamic, decisive, and persuasive "change agent" as its leader. Other organizations put more emphasis on the executive's people skills and human relations expertise. In addition, the size of the working units, their geographic distribution, and the degree of inter- and intraorganizational security required to attain company goals affect the amount of employee participation in decision making. The need to keep plans confidential may make it necessary for the boss to exercise more control than in less restricted situations. These factors may greatly affect the manager's ability to function flexibly on the continuum.

Effective groups can participate more fully in decision making. Well-established and functioning groups have developed cooperative habits that allow them to confront problems more successfully than a new group. Likewise, groups composed of members with similar backgrounds and interests will work together more quickly and easily than groups composed of people with dissimilar backgrounds because they are likely to have fewer communications problems. Finally, the members' degree of confidence in their group problem-solving ability is another key consideration. Variables including cohesiveness, permissiveness, mutual acceptance, and commonality of purpose will apply subtle but vital influences on the group's functioning.

In addition, the nature of the problem may determine the degree of authority that the leader should delegate. Subordinates will need to have the relevant background, content, and specialized knowledge to make informed decisions about the issue at hand. At times, however, the leader may have most of the contextual and factual data relevant to a given issue, making it easier for the leader to think it through and resolve it independently.

The pressure of time, although occasionally more imagined than actual, also influences the leader's decision about sharing decision making. The more the leader feels the need for an immediate decision, the more difficult it is to involve others. In organizations in a constant state of crisis, leaders are more likely to use a high degree of authority with relatively little delegation to subordinates. In contrast, when time pressure is less intense, it is easier to give subordinates a hand in decision making.

In any given instance, a range of factors influence leaders' tactical behavior in relation to subordinates. In each situation, leaders will ideally act in ways that make possible the successful attainment of their immediate goal within the limits available. In the long run, leaders may perceive many of the variables active in the immediate situation as factors over which they can gain some control. For instance, they can gain new insights or skills for themselves, provide training for individual subordinates, and offer participative experiences to the employee group. Nevertheless, the question "At which point along the continuum should I act?" remains an ongoing concern.

Tannenbaum and Schmidt concluded that leaders who want to build organizational capacity can shift their attention from completing the immediate assignment to seeking the following long-term objectives:[28]

- ◆ To raise their employees' motivation level
- ◆ To increase subordinates' readiness to accept change
- ◆ To improve the quality of all managerial decisions
- ◆ To develop teamwork and morale
- ◆ To further employees' individual development

As discussed in Chapter 7 on building leadership capacity, much research and experience supports the idea that giving employees opportunities for professional growth and leadership roles is associated with accomplishing these five purposes.

ACTIVITY 8.6   Identifying Factors in the Leader, the Subordinates, and the Situation for Facilitating Change

Case Study Question 2: What are the specific changes you believe are most important?

Case Study Question 3: How do you plan to make the changes you need to make?

Tannenbaum and Schmidt described factors in the individual leader, the subordinates, and the situation that affect the degree of control and freedom the leader exercises over decision making. In addition, a climate of mutual confidence and respect is necessary to share decision making effectively with subordinates. Discuss as a class:

1. At this point, what specific changes do you think are most important for Dumont Middle School?
2. In which sequence do you believe they need to be addressed? Prioritize the list developed in question 1.
3. What factors will influence how much you (as the new principal) involve teachers and the leadership team in accurate and effective problem identification and problem solving?
4. Which decisions should you make independently (in consultation with the superintendent), and which issues should be open for shared decision making with the leadership team?
5. Looking long term, what can you do to:
   - ◆ Raise teachers' motivation levels to permit them to rethink their present expectations for themselves and ALL their students?
   - ◆ Increase teachers' readiness to accept change?
   - ◆ Improve the quality of your decisions?
   - ◆ Advance teachers' individual development and increase organizational capacity?

LEADERSHIP AND RATIONAL DECISION MAKING

Organizational conflict produces opportunities for decision making. Conflict generates diverse viewpoints around organizational goals, processes, and practices, often producing new information. Organizations search for and evaluate information in order to make important decisions that help them adapt and grow. This choice should be made rationally, based on complete data about the organization's goals, feasible alternatives, likely outcomes, and the values of these outcomes to the organization.

In practice, however, making rational choices is often jumbled by the competing interests among organizational stakeholders, bargaining and negotiating between powerful groups and individuals, the limitations and idiosyncrasies of personal preference and the lack of information. Nonetheless, an organization must maintain an appearance of rational, reasoned behavior to keep internal trust and preserve external legitimacy. Organizational decision making is a complex, messy process yet an essential part of organizational life.

Both classical and contemporary organizational theorists have views about rationality—and its limits—in decision making.

The Classical Decision-Making Model

Classical decision theory assumes that decisions should be completely rational, using an optimizing strategy that seeks the best possible alternative to maximize the achievement of organizational goals and objectives. In this classical model, decision making is a process of sequential steps:

1. Identify the problem.
2. Establish goals and objectives.
3. Generate all possible alternatives.
4. Consider consequences of each alternative.
5. Evaluate each alternative in terms of the goals and objectives.
6. Select the best alternative, the one that maximizes the goals and objectives.
7. Implement and evaluate the decision.

Most scholars view this classical model as an unrealistic ideal. Decision makers rarely have access to all the relevant information, and generating all the possible alternatives and their outcomes is impossible. Likewise individuals lack the information-processing capacities, rationality, and knowledge (and time) that this normative model assumes. As a result, the classical decision-making model remains an exemplar of relevant factors in the decision-making process, however, rather than a practical guide.

Rationality and Decision Making

According to Simon, "Rationality is the set of skills or aptitudes we use to find courses of action that will lead to the accomplishment of our goals. Action is rational to the degree that it is well adapted to those goals. Decisions are rational to the extent that they lead to such action."[29] Theories of rational behavior may be normative or descriptive. They may prescribe how people or organizations should behave in order to achieve certain goals under certain conditions, or they may attempt to describe how people in organizations actually behave.[30]

Our culture believes in rationality. Greek philosophers viewed rationality as an important aspect of the reasoning process. One constructs a proof by formally or pragmatically reasoning from premises. These ideas form the assumptions about how we ought to make decisions. Later, rational thinking supported the science that led to the Industrial Revolution, the Enlightenment's ideas about human reason and freedom which gave birth to our nation, and the ever-advancing infusion of technology into all aspects of our lives.

Frederick Taylor's scientific management and Max Weber's bureaucratic organization adapted scientific methods and principles to industry and organizations, creating a science of management that could be applied to everyday organizational problems. Taylor's view of workers as inherently lazy and incapable of exercising judgment and discretion has gradually evolved into a management view that stresses human capability and the need to move from management control to employee commitment.

During the first half of the 20th century, the concept of management as a science grew steadily. World War II's "operations research" stimulated management science's increased development as a way to win the war: creating and applying mathematical modeling to solve complex problems (such as how to reduce the loss of shipping from submarine attacks or how to increase the accuracy of aerial bombing). After the war, confidence in science and technology continued to expand, and science's logical methods grew in acceptance and prestige. By the late 1970s, after the United States had rocketed a man to the moon, people confidently confronted new problems with, "If we can place a man on the moon, why can't we solve this problem?" Focusing on effective problem solving and successful outcomes, people assumed that no challenges were beyond our capacity to resolve.

Rationality, however, has its limits. When rationality is associated solely with reasoning processes and not simply with its products, constraints on human reasoning become apparent. Humans have reasons for what they do, and these may not be the best or most consistent. The French philosopher Voltaire, in his *Dictionnaire Philosophique* (1746), proclaimed that "the best is the enemy of the good."[31] If one is too focused on attaining the optimum, getting an acceptable result is not likely.

Until the late 20th century, classical economists were using a theory of utility maximization, ignoring the decision-making process, and treating decision making mathematically. Peter Drucker and Herbert Simon expanded the definition and practice of rationality to include the uncertainty inherent in real-world thinking.

Peter Drucker: Essential Steps in Effective Decision Making

Peter Drucker, an internationally recognized organizational scholar, believed that effective executives try to make a few important decisions at the highest level of conceptual understanding. They try to find the constants in a situation, to think through what is strategic and generic, and to understand the underlying realities that the decision must satisfy. In fact, Drucker concluded that effective decision makers consider expertise in manipulating a great many variables a symptom of "sloppy thinking."[32]

Drucker saw every decision as a risk-taking judgment. The elements in the classic decision-making model do not, by themselves, "make" the decisions. Instead, Drucker saw them as necessary stepping stones in the effective decision-making process, which include:[33]

1. *Classifying the problem.* Is it generic or truly exceptional? Is it routine or is it the first appearance of a new type of problem for which no rule has yet been developed? Generic problems can be solved by applying the rules, policies, or principles. Exceptions must be handled as they appear. Common mistakes by decision makers are to treat generic situations as if they were unique, and unique events as if they were a new example of an old problem.

2. *Defining the problem.* What are we dealing with? Errors occur here when decision makers select the plausible but incomplete definition of the problem.[34]

3. *Specifying the answer to the problem.* What are the "boundary" conditions? What are the goals and objectives—the minimum criteria—that the decision has to accomplish? This is decision making's most difficult step.

4. *Deciding what is "right" rather than what is acceptable, in order to meet the boundary conditions.* What will fully satisfy the specifications *before* attention is given to the compromises, adaptations, and concessions needed to make the decision acceptable? Compromise is always necessary in the end, but the decision maker must be able to distinguish the right compromise from the wrong compromise.[35]

5. *Building the action to carry it out into the decision.* What does the action commitment have to be? Who has to know about it? What does the action have to be so that the people who have to do it *can* do it? This is the most time-consuming step in the decision-making process. Moreover, unless a decision includes specific steps for someone's work and responsibility, it is not a decision but only a good intention. And the people to whom the action is assigned must have the capacity (knowledge, behaviors, habits, attitudes) and resources to carry it out.

6. *Testing the validity and effectiveness of the decision against the actual course of events.* How is the decision being implemented? Are the assumptions on which it is based appropriate or obsolete? Gaining and using feedback is an essential component of decision making. Information monitoring and feedback have to be built into the decision to provide continuous testing of the decision's expectations against actual events. This usually means looking at how a decision is being implemented and the results of these actions for oneself rather than relying totally on others' reports.

Drucker believed that the executive's *specific* task is to make important decisions that have a significant and positive impact on the entire organization. Effective leaders make decisions as a systematic process with clearly defined elements and in a distinct series of steps. While appreciating many limitations on making good decisions, Drucker's approach brought a practical shrewdness to the decision-making process.

ACTIVITY 8.7   Applying Drucker's Six Steps in Decision Making

Peter Drucker saw every decision as a risk-taking judgment. To Drucker, an executive's specific task is to make important decisions that have significance and a positive impact on the entire organization.

Using Drucker's six steps, think through the situation at Dumont Middle School and answer the questions posed in each step:

1. Classifying the problem—For DMS, is this problem generic or exceptional?
2. Defining the problem—How would you define the problem plausibly and completely?
3. Specifying the answer to the problem—What are the minimum conditions that the decisions must accomplish?
4. Deciding what is "right" rather than what is acceptable. What is the best (optimal-solution to the problem before having to compromise, adapt, and concede to make the decision acceptable?
5. Building the action to carry it out into the decision—What does the action have to be, and who has to know about it? Do the people to whom the action is assigned have the capacity (knowledge, behaviors, habits, attitudes) and resources to carry it out? If not, then what?
6. Testing the validity and effectiveness of the decision against actual events—How will information monitoring and feedback be built into the decisions to provide continuous testing of the decision's expectations against actual events?

Herbert Simon: Bounded Rationality in Decision Making

Herbert Simon, a 1978 Nobel Prize–winning economist and Carnegie Mellon psychology professor, believed that a decision is not a single event but the product of a complex social process generally extending over a long period of time.[36] What set Simon apart from other economists and social scientists was his early interest in not only *what* decisions are made but also *how* they are made—and his detailed articulation of rationality's limits in the decision-making process.

Limits on Rationality in Decision Making.   Trained as an economist, Simon was an endlessly curious social scientist, involved in many aspects of understanding human behavior. As an economist, Simon saw decision making as rational behavior that was evident in choices (outcomes). Yet as a psychologist, he recognized the rational and irrational aspects in decision-making processes.[37] He understood that the real world is characterized by ambiguity and uncertainty. Everyone has reasons (motives) for what they do. Organizations' goals, technologies, and environments are highly complex. Even the best models are only simplifications.

Questioning old assumptions about rationality in decision making, Simon came to believe that people's reasoning is fallible. A gap exists between theory and practice. Because of the great number of options and an unlimited amount of information, an individual cannot reach any high degree of rationality. When they evaluate options, people conduct a limited search along familiar and well-traveled routes, typically selecting the first satisfactory alternative that appears.

Exploring the borders between economics and psychology, Simon suggested that decision making in organizations is constrained by the principle of *bounded rationality*. He noted, "

> The capacity of the human mind for formulating and solving complex problems is very small compared with the size of the problems whose solution is required for objectively rational behavior in the real world—or even for a reasonable approximation to such objective rationality. (p. 198)[38]

Bounded rationality, then, is adaptive behavior within the constraints that Simon saw as imposed by three categories: the person's mental skills, habits, and reflexes; the extent of the knowledge and information possessed; and the values or conceptions of purpose which may diverge from organizational goals.[39]

The persons themselves as information processors have limiting characteristics—perceptions, experiences, memories, knowledge, skills, aspirations, competing goals—to which they must adapt. People's subjective perceptions act as filters to actively exclude information from their consideration. They have simple or complex goals and values which may be consistent or contradictory and depend on premises and assumptions which may not be true. Even facts may be real or supposed and rest on certain assumptions. The information about the issue and the alternatives may be incomplete. The instruments that collect data are assumed to be accurate and represent the complete universe of relevant information. Inferences may be valid or spurious. Risk and uncertainty also affect rationality in decision making.[40]

External limits to rationality also exist. Environments impose limitations of information, time, and processes to which people working must rationally adapt.

As a result, rational behavior in the real world is as much determined by people's inner mental environments and processes as by the outer environments on which they act and which, in turn, act on them.[41] The key to organizational effectiveness, then, is overcoming each member's "bounded rationality." Given this context, Simon concluded, "The resemblance of decision-making to logical reasoning is only metaphorical . . ."[42]

Satisficing, Optimizing, and Simplifying.   Most psychological theories posit that the motive to act stems from physical, cognitive, or emotional drives; when the drives are satisfied, the action ends. The conditions for fulfilling a drive are often subjective. A person's values, goals, and aspirations adjust what satisfies the person. Unlike economic theory's ideal of maximizing or optimizing, Simon believed that people's adaptive behavior in learning and choice situations falls far short.

Satisficing and *optimizing* are labels Simon assigned to two broad approaches to rational behavior in situations where complexity and uncertainty make full rationality impossible.[43] *Satisficing* means seeking an acceptable, good enough—as opposed to optimal—solution. A course of action is satisfactory if it is practical and exceeds some minimally acceptable threshold. This solution-seeking behavior reflects the participants' training, experience, and goals. Satisficing also means attending to problems sequentially rather than simultaneously and repeating standard solutions.

In contrast, *optimizing* describes the classic decision-making model: a process that involves considering all potential alternatives and relevant factors, balancing the detrimental impacts of each alternative against its benefits, and choosing the alternative that maximizes some measure of the individual's preference. In comparing the two approaches, optimizing complex decisions requires collecting and processing vast amounts of information, which individuals generally have neither the time to collect and analyze nor the capability to perform all the needed comparisons required. Instead, people simplify the cognitive task and satisfice, considering alternatives until they identify one that meets the present level of satisfaction, even if it may not be the best available option. Although iron-clad formal distinctions between optimizing and satisficing are difficult to draw, the practical differences can be great.

Next, the organization or organizational actor *simplifies* the decision process, following routines and learned "rules of thumb" to avoid uncertainty and to reduce complexity. For instance, the organization develops action repertoires using *performance programs* to handle recurring situations. These programs determine what paths to take and which to ignore, with the search ending when a satisfactory solution has been found (almost always long before all alternatives have been examined). By restricting the range of situations and alternatives available, performance programs greatly reduce decision making's cognitive and informational requirements. For example, a ringing bell in a fire station, a bank customer appearing at the teller's window, an automobile chassis parking in front of a garage mechanic, or an unfamiliar parent standing with a child at the counter in a school's main office initiate a predefined series of actions to solve the problem.

Controlling Decision Premises. Given the overwhelming array of factors affecting decision making in organizations, Simon suggested that the organization influences its members' behaviors by controlling the decision premises–or assumptions–upon which decisions are made, rather than controlling the actual decisions themselves.[44] One of leadership's tasks is to design the work environment so individuals will approach as close as practically possible to rationality, in terms of the organization's goals, for their decisions.

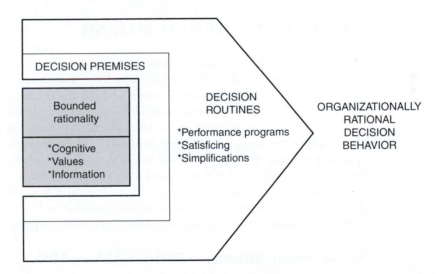

FIGURE 8–2
Organizations as Decision-Making Systems (Source: Reprinted from Choo, C. W. (1996). The knowing organization: How organizations use information to construct meaning. *International Journal of Information Management, 16*(5), p. 332. Copyright 1996, with permission from Elsevier.)

Figure 8–2 illustrates the key features of rational decision making in organizations. While organizations seek rational behavior in the actions that contribute to their goals and objectives, individual members' behaviors are constrained by their cognitive capacities, values, and available information. Designing decision premises and decision routines that guide or control individual decision behavior creates ways to bridge the gap between organizational rationality and the individual's bounded rationality. This is a linear, input–output model that focuses on the information flow in the organization's decision-making process.

ACTIVITY 8.8   Satisficing, Optimizing, and Simplifying Decision Making

Case Study Question 6: How would satisficing, optimizing, and simplifying affect your decisions?

Interested in what and how decisions are made, Herbert Simon detailed the limits of rationality in the decision-making process. **Bounded rationality** is adaptive behavior that considers the internal and external constraints on decision making. Using Simon's ideas, as a class:

1. Identify the internal constraints in the principal and the Dumont Middle School teachers (and leadership team) that will limit their rationality in decision making.
2. Identify the external constraints that will limit rationality in decision making.
3. How will **satisficing**, **optimizing**, and **simplifying** likely come into play as the principal and teachers work on problem solving at DMS?
4. What might satisficing, optimizing, and simplifying look like in practice—so the principal can recognize each when he or she sees or hears it?
5. Where might satisficing, optimizing, and simplifying benefit—or detract from—the best solutions to the problems at DMS?

LEADERSHIP AND SHARED DECISION MAKING

During the early 20th century, successful organizational leaders expected to use their intelligence, imagination, initiative, and capacity to make rapid (and usually wise) decisions and to inspire subordinates to accept and put the decisions into practice. People tended to think of the world as being divided into leaders and followers.

Gradually, the concept of group dynamics emerged, focusing on group members rather than solely on the group leader. Research underscored the importance of employee participation in decision making.[45] Evidence began to challenge the efficacy of highly directive leadership. Motivating employees gained increased attention.

Scholars and practitioners including Victor Vroom, Edwin Bridges, Wayne Hoy and John Tarter, and others studied shared decision making and developed an assortment of normative and descriptive models to illustrate and guide the process.

Victor Vroom: Situational Decision-Making Model

After several decades of studying participation in decision making, Victor Vroom, a Yale University management professor and consultant, and his colleagues concluded that different situations require different types of participatory leadership.[46] Vroom and colleagues have attempted to model the decision-making interactions between leadership style, situation, and outcome effectiveness. Their approach considers the effective leader as one who is capable of analyzing the context and choosing from the various styles the one that is most appropriate for that situation.

The Vroom-Yetton-Jago model (Figure 8–3) is a complex decision-making tree that enables a leader to examine a situation and determine which style or level of involvement to engage. By matching the decision-making process to the situation at hand, the model seeks to guide leaders about whether they should make a decision alone or involve a group, and to what extent the group should be involved.

Effective decision making requires many sequential steps and assessments. First, Vroom identified five leadership styles along a continuum ranging from highly autocratic through consultative to group based, as seen in Table 8–1.[47]

TABLE 8–1
Decision-Making Styles

Decision-Making Style	Description
Autocratic I (AI)	Leader solves the problem alone using information that is readily available to him or her.
Autocratic II (AII)	Leader obtains additional information from group members, then makes decision alone. Group members may or may not be informed.
Consultative I (CI)	Leader shares problem with group members individually, and asks for information and evaluation. Group members do not meet collectively, and leader makes decision alone.
Consultative II (CII)	Leader shares problem with group members collectively, but makes decision alone.
Group II (GII)	Leader meets with group to discuss situation. Leader focuses and directs discussion, but does not impose will. Group makes final decision.

Source: Adapted from Vroom, V. H. & Jago, A. G., *New Leadership: Managing Participation in Organizations*, Table "Decision Making Styles," © 1988 Pearson Education, Inc. Reproduced by permission of Pearson Education, Inc.

Next, the leader must clearly address the following seven contextual factors about decision importance, commitment, expertise, and decision acceptance in order to determine the followers' level of involvement in decision making.[48]

♦ *Decision significance:* Importance of the decision to the project's or organization's success.
♦ *Importance of commitment:* Importance of the team members' commitment to the decision.
♦ *Leader's expertise:* Leader's knowledge or expertise in relation to this problem.
♦ *Likelihood of commitment:* Likelihood that the team would commit itself to a decision that the leader might make independently.
♦ *Group support for objectives:* Degree to which the team supports the organization's objectives at stake in the problem.
♦ *Group expertise:* Team members' knowledge or expertise in relation to this problem.
♦ *Team competence:* Team members' ability to work together in solving problems.

Answering whether these factors are present gives leaders guidance about the nature of the problem, decision, and consequences. Knowing this will help the leader decide how much involvement others should have in making the decision.[49]

Finally, using the decision tree in Figure 8–3, the leader begins at the far left by stating the problem and asks questions related to the attribute quality response (QR) ("How important is the technical quality of the decision?"). The leader's answer ("high" or "low") leads to a node signifying the next question. The process continues until encountering an endpoint that determines the recommended degree of subordinate involvement. The numbers across the decision tree's top indicate the sequence in which decision makers ask and answer questions during the process of determining the extent of autocratic or participatory involvement. This is a very autocratic decision tree in that it places no value on the long-range outcome of team development.[50]

As graphically depicted in Figure 8–3, conflict and goal congruence interact to create a variety of patterns and combinations for making decisions, especially in complex situations.

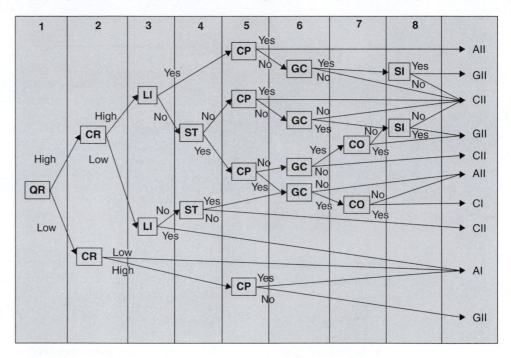

FIGURE 8–3

Time-Driven Vroom-Yetton-Jago Decision Model (Source: Adapted from Vroom, V. H. (2001). Two decades of research on participation: Beyond buzz words and management fads. In J. S. Osland, D. A. Kolb, & I. M. Rubin (Eds.), *The organizational behavior reader* (pp. 429–436). Upper Saddle River, NJ: Prentice Hall (p. 433).)

Abbreviation codes: **QR** = quality requirement; **CR** = subordinate commitment to the decision; **LI** = leader's information to make high-quality decision independently; **ST** = problem structure (degree it is defined, clear, organized, time limited, lends itself to solution); **CP** = commitment probability of subordinates to decision if leader makes it independently; **GC** = goal congruence of subordinates with organizational goals attained in solving the problem; **CO** = likelihood of subordinate conflict over preferred solutions; **SI** = likeliness that subordinates have sufficient information to make a high-quality decision.

Research on the Vroom-Yetton-Jago Model. Consultation with followers in making decisions is one form of participative leadership, and studies provide evidence that consultation is a distinct and meaningful form of leadership behavior.[51] Its effectiveness, however, may depend on situational aspects such as the type of task, the distribution of relevant information, and the followers' values.[52]

The Vroom-Yetton-Jago model has stimulated much research on leadership style,[53] decision-making style,[54] decision quality and acceptability,[55] individuals' views on leaders' effectiveness,[56] and subordinate productivity and job satisfaction.[57] Studies document that leaders use complex decision rules that respond to varying combinations of situational dimensions.[58] Several studies confirm the model's validity in its ability to identify the relative efficacy of various decision processes.[59] Research on the model's earlier (Vroom-Yetton) version found that leaders who used decision-making styles that agree with the model had more productive subordinates, and the subordinates were more satisfied with some aspects of their jobs (work itself and their coworkers).[60] In addition, studies using the model found that about 3 times as much variance in leadership style could be attributed to the situation than to a generalized disposition.[61] These models' computational complexity, however, makes their use for practical decision making questionable—except perhaps in preplanning.[62]

In addition, methodological problems limit the findings' generalizability. Many studies on these models use hypothetical situations rather than observations of actual behaviors.[63] Others employ sampling of work input (percentage of time devoted to productive work activities) rather than output—missing employees' "busy work" and, as a result, possibly overstating worker productivity. Also, many studies with these models use self-reports, introducing many possible perception errors. For instance, most leaders report using a more democratic style than their followers and others perceive.[64] Evaluating the impact of perception errors is difficult. Then too, many studies occur short term rather than over time, making concurrent validity debatable, while raising concerns about possible Hawthorne effects from the novelty of being studied. It is important to remember that the Vroom-Yetton-Jago model focuses only on one aspect of leadership—decision making—telling little about how and why a leader perceives the problem and subordinate reactions.

ACTIVITY 8.9   Using Vroom's Decision Model

Situational variables affect organizational decision making. When deciding on the amount of group participation in decision making, leaders use complex decision rules that respond to the situational context.

1. Considering the data received as the new DMS principal, work with a partner to answer "high" or "low" to each of Victor Vroom's seven contextual factors that affect decision making. Give your rationale for each answer. Discuss partners' responses as a class.
   ◆ Significance of the decision for the school's success
   ◆ Importance of group members' (teachers, parents) commitment to decisions
   ◆ Leader's expertise regarding the problem
   ◆ Likelihood of group members' commitment to leader-made decisions
   ◆ Group members' support for the objectives
   ◆ Group expertise regarding this problem
   ◆ Team competence to work together in solving problems
2. If the situation remains as is (without professional development or other interventions to increase the teachers' information and decision-making capacity), which DMS decisions would be appropriate for group participation and which should be the sole preserve of the principal (in consultation with the superintendent)? Which decisions should have leadership team participation? Which decisions should have direct teacher participation?
3. What would be appropriate roles for teacher participation in decision making after receiving relevant information and professional development?
4. Do you think the new principal should use Vroom and colleagues' decision tree (Figure 8–3) when making decisions about changes at DMS? Explain your answer.

Edwin Bridges: Shared Decision Making in Schools

While the Vroom-Yetton-Jago model offers an intellectually precise normative structure, school leaders need a rational but more realistic paradigm for understanding and involving faculty and staff in the decision-making process.

Subordinates may or may not care about whether they participate in particular organizational decisions. As Barnard explained, there is a **zone of indifference** in individuals within which they accept orders without consciously questioning their authority.[65] More positively, Simon called this the **zone of acceptance**.[66] The literature uses the terms interchangeably. The subordinates' zone of acceptance is critical in deciding under what conditions to involve or not involve subordinates in decision making.

Drawing on the work of Barnard (1938),[67] Simon (1947),[68] and Chase (1951),[69] Edwin M. Bridges (1967), Stanford University education professor, studied teachers' role in school decision making and recognized that they have a "zone of indifference" within which an administrator's decisions will be accepted without question. He proposed two ideas about shared decision making:[70]

1. As the principal involves teachers in making decisions located in their zone of indifference, participation will be less effective.
2. As the principal involves teachers in making decisions clearly located outside their zone of indifference, participation will be more effective.

The principal's challenge is determining which decisions fall inside and which fall outside the zone. Bridges suggested two tests to answer this question:

◆ *The test of relevance:* Do the subordinates have a personal stake in the decision outcomes? For teachers, relevant decisions are those that primarily deal with classroom affairs, such as teaching methods, curriculum, assessment techniques for evaluating pupil progress, and handling student disturbances. If yes, then their participation should be high.

◆ *The test of expertise:* Do subordinates have the expertise to make a useful contribution to the decision? For a teacher to be interested in participation, he or she must not only have some stake in the outcome but be capable of contributing to the decisions affecting the outcome. For instance, a foreign language teacher would want to be involved in prescribing the functions of a foreign language laboratory but would be willing to allow an electronics engineer to decide the technical specifications. If both of these conditions are met to at least a minimum extent, teacher participation is recommended.

In a related decision, the principal must also decide at what phase in the decision-making process teachers will be included and what their roles will be. This choice will establish the amount of freedom that the teachers have in the decision-making process. Bridges deconstructed the principals' decision-making process into small components and analyzed the leaders' considerations and concerns at each step:[71]

◆ *Problem-defining stage:* The principal specifies the objectives to be attained, gathers relevant information, pinpoints perceived barriers to attainment, and decides whether—and how—to involve teachers.

◆ *Identify relevant action alternatives:* The principal develops a list of action alternatives autonomously or with teacher input.

◆ *Predict the consequences related to each alternative considered:* The principal decides whether to involve teachers in predicting consequences of alternatives.

◆ *Choose from among the alternatives:* The principal weighs alternatives and consequences and selects the most appropriate course of action, or may involve teachers to recommend which alternative they prefer.

Bridges reckoned that if the decision to be made is clearly outside the teachers' zone of indifference, the principal should allow the teachers maximum freedom to participate in all phases of the decision-making process—as long as they do not exceed the limits of freedom granted to the principal (that is, make decisions beyond the principal's authority to carry out). If the decision falls within the teachers' zone of indifference, the principal might ask teachers to suggest alternative courses of action and their consequences, but reserve the final choice of action for him- or herself. Regardless, it is important to make very clear to the teachers the boundaries of their authority and the area of freedom in which they can operate.

Bridges also described how principals leading school problem-solving groups can facilitate the group's functioning. These leadership behaviors can ensure that those in the minority have the opportunity to fully state their position and supply facts to support their views, help members see similarities and advantages in varying positions so as to move the group toward consensus, and help group members focus their thoughts on the same aspect of the problem at the same time.

ACTIVITY 8.10   Determining Teachers' Zone of Indifference

Subordinates care more about having input to certain organizational decisions than others. Edwin Bridges proposed that decisions that fall outside employees' zone of indifference should be tested for relevance and expertise to help leaders determine the extent to which they should involve subordinates in organizational decision making.

First in pairs, then as a class, answer the following questions about the DMS faculty:

1. Which decisions about DMS will fall **outside their zone of indifference**?
2. Which decisions meet the teachers' **test of relevance**?
3. Which decisions meet the teachers' **test of expertise**?
4. What clear boundaries should the principal set and communicate about teacher authority and input for the coming school improvement decisions?

At which phases of decision making should the principal invite teacher participation (and if so, which teachers?), and why?

◆ At the problem-defining stage?
◆ As the leader identifies relevant action alternatives?
◆ To predict consequences to each alternative?
◆ To choose from among alternative strategies?

Wayne Hoy and John Tarter: Situation and Subordinate Model

Wayne Hoy, professor at Ohio State University, and John C. Tarter, professor at the University of Alabama, have built upon Bridges's ideas concerning shared decision making in schools. Considering the degree to which participation in decision making matters to subordinates, Hoy and Tarter present a relatively user-friendly model.

Figure 8–4 depicts Hoy and Tarter's descriptive model to help decision makers consider involving employees in shared decision making. When subordinates have both expertise and a personal stake in the outcomes, then the decision is outside their zone of acceptance, and they should be involved in decision making. In contrast, if the subordinates have neither expertise nor a personal stake, then the decision is inside the zone, and they need not be included in decision making. Hoy and Tarter recognized that marginal conditions exist, each with different constraints, however. When subordinates have expertise but not personal stake—or have a personal stake but no specific expertise—the conditions become more problematic. To address these constraint conditions, Hoy and Tarter (1995) proposed two more ideas:[72]

◆ As subordinates are involved in making decisions for which they have marginal expertise, their participation will be marginally effective.
◆ As subordinates are involved in making decisions for which they have marginal interest, their participation will be marginally effective.

Hoy and Tarter have combined this logic into a decision-making model (Figure 8–4) that considers employees' zone of acceptance in light of their expertise and personal stake in the decision's outcome.

		Do subordinates have a personal stake?	
		Yes	**No**
Do subordinates have expertise?	**Yes**	**Outside zone of acceptance** (Probably include)	**Marginal with expertise** (Occasionally include)
	No	**Marginal with relevance** (Occasionally include)	**Inside zone of acceptance** (Definitely exclude)

FIGURE 8–4
The Zone of Acceptance and Involvement (Source: Hoy, W. K., & Miskel, C. G. (2008). *Educational administration. Theory, research, and practice* (8th ed., p. 365). Boston, MA: McGraw-Hill. Used with permission.)

In their attempts to make their model more practitioner-friendly, Hoy and Tarter considered the issue of trust when deciding on employees' level of decision-making participation. Subordinates whose personal goals conflict with organizational ones may not keep the organization's best interests in mind when making decisions. Hoy classified situations related to trust into five different alternatives.[73] They are illustrated in Figure 8–5.

- *Democratic situation:* If the decision is outside the zone of acceptance and if the subordinates can be trusted to make decisions in the organization's best interests, then their participation should be extensive. The only issue is whether the decision should be made by consensus or majority rule.
- *Conflictual situation:* If the decisions are outside the zone and the leader has little trust in the subordinates, participation should be restricted. Otherwise, the employees may not move in directions consistent with the organization's overall well-being.
- *Stakeholder situation:* If subordinates have a personal stake in the issue but little expertise, participation should be limited and only occasional. This limited and occasional involvement, however, may lead to frustration and possible hostility if teachers perceive the experience as a formality, an empty exercise to make it appear as if teachers have influence while, in fact, the decisions have already been made.[74] Yet, it may be useful to involve teachers in a limited way to have open communications, to educate subordinates, and to gain their support for the decision.
- *Expert situation:* If subordinates have no personal stake take in the outcomes but do have the knowledge to make a useful contribution, they should only be involved occasionally. While employee input may increase the quality of the decision, subordinates are likely to become alienated and tell themselves, "This is what administrators get paid for."
- *Noncollaborative situation:* If the decision issue is not relevant to subordinates and they have no expertise, then the decision falls within their zone of acceptance and involvement should be avoided. In this type of situation, participation is likely to produce resentment because subordinates are typically not interested.

Once the leader has decided to include subordinates to participate in decision making, the next question involves how the process should move ahead. Hoy and Tarter (2003) suggested five decision-making structures, also illustrated in Figure 8–5.[75]

- *Group consensus:* The administrator involves participants in the decision making and then the group decides. All group members share equally as they generate and evaluate a decision, but a decision can only be made with total consensus.
- *Group majority:* The administrator involves participants in the decision making and then the group decides by majority rule.
- *Group advisory:* The administrator solicits the group members' opinions, discusses the implications of group suggestions, and then makes a decision that may or may not reflect subordinates' wishes.
- *Individual advisory:* The administrator consults individually with subordinates who have expertise to inform the decisions and then makes a decision that may or may not reflect their opinions.
- *Unilateral decisions:* The administrator makes the decisions without consulting or involving subordinates in the decision.

Next, Hoy presented the administrator's role in shared decision making as the model's last component and defined five leadership roles. Table 8–2 summarizes these roles, their functions, and their aims, and they appear again in Figure 8–5.

TABLE 8–2
Administrative Roles for Shared Decision Making

Role	Function	Aim
Integrator	Integrates divergent positions	To gain consensus
Parliamentarian	Promotes open discussion	To support reflective group deliberation
Educator	Explains and discusses issues	To seek acceptance of decision
Solicitor	Solicits advice	To improve quality of decision
Director	Makes unilateral decisions	To achieve efficiency

Source: Adapted from Hoy, W. K., & Miskel, C. G. (2008). *Educational administration. Theory research, and practice* (8th ed., p. 368). Boston, MA: McGraw-Hill. Used with permission.

Finally, Hoy integrated these various factors—relevance to subordinate, expertise of subordinate, and trust of subordinate—plus the decision-making structures and the administrative roles for shared decision making into a coherent model of shared decision making (Figure 8–5). The model suggests that administrators make direct unilateral decisions when the issue is within the subordinates' zone of acceptance.

ACTIVITY 8.11   Using the Zone of Acceptance to Determine Who Participates in Decision Making

Hoy and Tarter provide a decision-making model that considers employees' zone of acceptance in light of their expertise and personal stake in the decision's outcome as well as the leader's trust that the employees' personal goals will not conflict with the organization's best interests. Discuss as a class:

1. Considering the trust issue, which situation do you think currently exists at Dumont Middle School? Explain your reasons for this conclusion.
   ◆ Democratic situation
   ◆ Conflict situation
   ◆ Stakeholder situation
   ◆ Expert situation
   ◆ Noncollaborative situation
2. Use Figure 8–5 as if you were the new DMS principal trying to decide upon the degree and type of teacher involvement in making decisions about going forward. Start with determining your teachers' relevance, expertise, and trust, and continue with each step (situation, involvement, decision-making structure, and principal's role). Do you agree or disagree with the process and its recommendations? In your opinion, to what extent does this model clarify or confuse the situation for the new principal—and how?

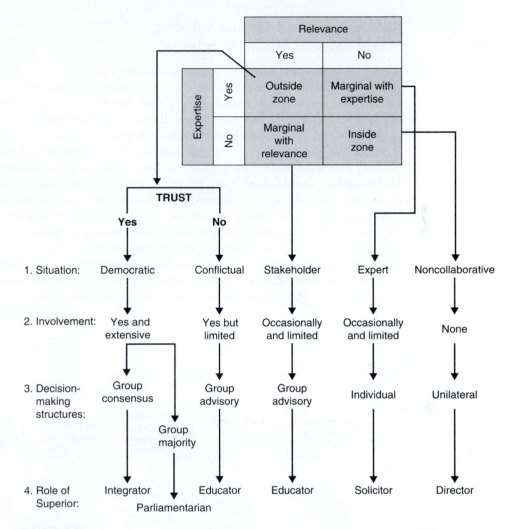

FIGURE 8–5
Decision Situation and Subordinate Involvement (Source: Adapted from Hoy, W. K., & Miskel, C. G. (2008). *Educational administration. Theory research, and practice* (8th ed., p. 370). Boston, MA: McGraw-Hill. Used with permission.)

Hoy reminds us that this shared decision-making model is not a panacea or substitute for sensitive and thoughtful leadership action. It simply offers guidelines for determining when and how teachers and principals should be involved in joint decision making. The decision quality and the subordinates' acceptance and commitment to implement it determine the decision's effectiveness.

Robert Owens and Thomas Valesky: Shared Decision Making in Schools

School leadership professors Robert Owens of Hofstra University and Thomas Valesky of Florida Gulf Coast University offered a decision-making model that permits people involved in organizational decision making to know *how* they are to participate by identifying their role, functions, and when they will take part. Their model also articulated the orderly steps of the organizational decision-making process as it moves toward a selection.[76]

Figure 8–6 illustrates their proposed decision-making paradigm which shows Edwin Bridges's four steps usually involved in reaching a decision: (1) defining the problem, (2) identifying possible alternatives, (3) predicting the consequences of each reasonable alternative, and (4) choosing the alternative to follow.[77] The figure shows these along a *time* dimension. In practice, school leaders and teachers may use a different series of steps, perhaps with different labels. Along the *behavior* dimension, a choice must be made about who will perform each necessary decision-making function. Here broken lines indicate action choices that the administrator can select to involve the staff at any one step or at all of them, or not to involve them at all. In reality, depending on the circumstance, the leader can handle every phase of the process alone or can engage any combination of participants.

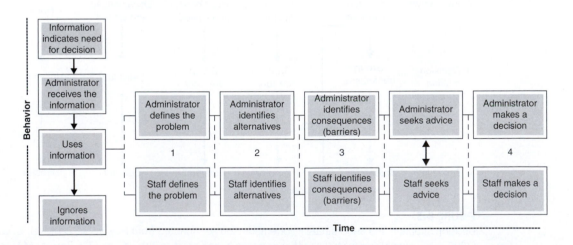

FIGURE 8–6

Paradigm for Shared Decision Making in Schools (Source: Adapted from Owens & Valesky, *Organizational Behavior in Education*, Figure 9–3, "A paradigm for shared decision making in the school," p. 329, © 2007 by Pearson Education, Inc. Reproduced by permission of Pearson Education, Inc.)

Irving Janis and Leon Mann: A Psychological Perspective

Both the situation and the decision-making process are often stressful. Conflicting values, fear of failure, worry about unknown consequences, concern about making a public fool of oneself, and losing self-esteem if the decision fails all create anxiety. People handle psychological tension in different ways as they make decisions. Recognizing these realities, Yale research psychologist Irving Janis and University of Melbourne research professor Leon Mann (1977) viewed decision making from a psychological perspective.[78]

Their model answers the following two questions:

◆ Under what conditions does stress have unfavorable effects on the quality of decision making?
◆ Under what conditions will individuals use sound decision-making procedures to avoid choices that they would quickly regret?

Errors in decision making result from many causes, including poor analysis, bias, impulsiveness, time constraints, and organizational policies. Yet other errors stem from individuals' efforts to overcome stress by using defense mechanisms. These include ignoring information about risks, accepting the most popular course of action, procrastinating and avoiding making a decision. Other persons become hypervigilant, anxiously searching for a solution, vacillating between alternatives, and then impulsively grabbing a hastily contrived solution that promises immediate relief from pressure but no assurance of solving the problem. All of these behaviors are dysfunctional.

Janis and Mann concluded that better decisions come from vigilant decision makers, those who carefully search for relevant information, assimilate it in an unbiased manner, and then evaluate the alternatives before making a reflective choice. Even watchful decision makers can make mistakes when they take "cognitive shortcuts,"[79] however.

Accordingly, Janis and Mann developed a model to foster vigilance in decision making.[80] When confronted with a decision, typical decision makers consciously or unconsciously consider the following issues:

◆ *Question 1: Are the risks serious if I don't change?* If the answer is no, then change is unlikely. If the answer is yes, then a second question is asked.
◆ *Question 2: Are the risks serious if I do change?* If the anticipated losses of changing are minimal, then the risks are not serious and the decision maker is predicted to uncritically accept the first reasonable alternative. If the answer to the second question is yes, then stress builds because serious risks exist in both changing and not changing. The anxiety usually prompts another question.
◆ *Question 3: Is it realistic to hope to find a better solution?* If the decision maker believes there is no realistic hope of finding a better solution, then the result is a state of defensive avoidance. In order to escape from the conflict and reduce the stress, the individual avoids making the decision by either "passing the buck" or rationalizing the current situation. If, however, hope exists for a better solution, another question emerges.
◆ *Question 4: Is there sufficient time to search and deliberate?* If the answer is no, then a state of hypervigilance may occur. The individual panics and seizes upon a quickly contrived solution that promises immediate relief. If time is available, the decision maker is more likely to engage in vigilant information processes to enhance the decision making through careful search, appraisal, and contingency planning.

Figure 8–7 illustrates the path to vigilant decision making.

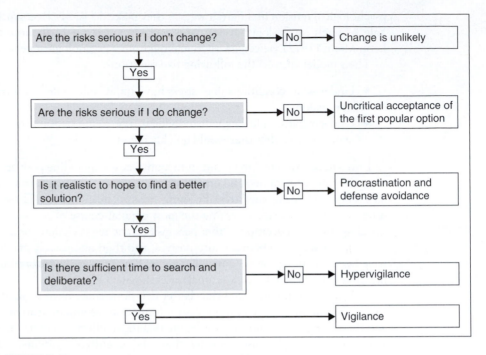

FIGURE 8–7

The Path to Vigilance in Decision Making (Source: Janis, I. L., & Mann, L. (1977). *Decision making: A psychological analysis of conflict, choice, and commitment.* New York, NY: Free Press, a division of Simon & Schuster, Inc. As cited in W. K. Hoy & C. G. Miskel. (2008). *Educational administration. Theory, research, and practice* (p. 347). Boston, MA: McGraw-Hill. All rights reserved.)

The decision maker seeks caution, but labor, time, and stress often operate against it. Knowing the dangers to anticipate in pressure-filled decision situations can help prevent decision-making errors. Aware decision making usually requires risk taking, determination, and finding or making time to engage in reflection and contingency planning.

ACTIVITY 8.12   How Stress Negatively Impacts Decision Making

Decision making is psychologically stressful. Irving Janis and Leon Mann identified the situational conditions and individual factors under which stress produces either favorable or unfavorable outcomes. Answer in pairs before discussing as a class:

1. Describe situations in which individuals under stress might use the following dysfunctional behaviors in the decision-making process:
    ◆ Ignoring information about risks
    ◆ Accepting the most popular course of action
    ◆ Procrastinating and avoiding
    ◆ Vacillating between alternatives and impulsively choosing a hastily contrived solution that promises immediate relief from stress but no assurance of solving the problem
2. How do **you** deal with stress in decision-making situations?
3. How might Janis and Mann's model reduce dysfunctional behavior in decision-making situations?

LEADERSHIP AND GROUPTHINK

For the last few decades, the groupthink phenomenon has become a mainstream concept. Groupthink has been blamed for such decision-making fiascoes as the 1960s Bay of Pigs invasion, the escalation of the Vietnam conflict, the 1986 NASA *Challenger* disaster, and the 2003 U.S. invasion of Iraq as well as for flawed group problem solving in business and organizations. Groupthink is popularly considered to be a defective process that should be guarded against. In fact, the term *groupthink* was chosen for its clearly Orwellian connotation, similar to *doublethink* and *crimethink*.[81]

Defining Groupthink

Groupthink is a term coined by Irving L. Janis (1972), who was a Yale research psychologist and professor emeritus at University of California, Berkeley. Groupthink describes deterioration in groups' decision-making efficiency as a function of the leader's style, the level of group cohesiveness, and certain group norms.[82] It is "a mode of thinking that people engage in when they are deeply involved in a cohesive in-group, when the members' strivings for unanimity override their motivation to realistically appraise alternative course of action."[83] A group suffering from groupthink tends to arrive at a decision before realistically appraising all available courses of action, thus making a poor decision.

Groupthink is not simply a group making a bad decision, however. Groupthink can sometimes produce good decisions just as high-quality decision-making procedures can occasionally produce bad decisions.

Irving Janis, Leon Mann, and Groupthink

Janis and Mann (1977) posited that thinking about vital, affect-laden issues generally results in "hot" cognitions, in contrast to the "cold" cognitions of routine problem solving. Such hot cognitions can lead to errors when scanning alternatives in stressful situations, characterized by lack of vigilant search, distorted meanings of warning messages, selective inattention and forgetting, and rationalizing. Groupthink is viewed as the group counterpart of defensive avoidance.[84]

Janis and Mann made an exhaustive ex post facto analysis of written records and interviews with top-level government and military persons involved in several weighty decisions with potentially grave national consequences.[85] The governmental decisions made under high-pressure conditions resulted in either major debacles or complete successes. As a result, the term *groupthink* has been used to understand high-stakes and high-pressure group decision making.

Antecedents of Groupthink.   Janis suggested that factors including leadership behavior, group cohesiveness, and the influence of group norms on group decision making interact in a special way in any group faced with making urgent, crisis-laden decisions. He concluded that groupthink is likely to occur when the following circumstances (antecedents) are present:[86]

- ◆ A decision-making group is faced with a crisis situation involving threat from an outside agent.

- ◆ The group forms a cohesive unit; they have esprit de corps and work together on a continuing basis. A moderate to high level of group cohesion—or attractiveness of the group to its members—is a necessary but not sufficient condition for groupthink.
- ◆ Under the leader's direction, the group adheres to an unspoken norm that apparent, group unanimity should not be broken.
- ◆ The leader promotes a favored solution to the problem.

Psychologically, Janis saw these conditions as increasing group members' needs for agreement to create a social reality that could replace the uncertainty and threat of failure associated with responsibility for making a difficult decision. Additionally, internal stress antecedents come from temporary low self-esteem due to members' recent failures, perceptions that the task is too difficult to accomplish, and the perception that a morally correct alternative does not exist.

Later, Janis refined his views about groupthink antecedents, categorizing them either as situational structural faults or as provocative situational contexts. Both structural (a leader who reveals a favored policy alternative early in the discussion and the absence of systematic procedures for generating and evaluating alternatives, group homogeneity in social background and ideology, and group insulation from outside information) and situational conditions (time of crisis or stress in reaction to an external threat, a complex and difficult problem, and recent group failure in a prior decision's outcome) contribute to the degree of stress experienced, and both contribute to the covert desire to reach a premature consensus.

Symptoms of Groupthink. Janis proposed that groupthink has eight identifiable symptoms, representing ways that group members try to reduce the anxiety associated with decision making and protect their self-esteems. Categorizing them into three types, symptoms include:[87]

- ◆ *Type I symptoms: Overestimating the group.* Group members share the illusion that the group is invulnerable and the unquestioned belief that the group's cause is just.
- ◆ *Type II symptoms: Close-mindedness.* Group members collectively rationalize away information that is inconsistent with their preferred position and stereotype enemies as weak or stupid, leading them to underestimate the opposing forces' capabilities. They do not discuss the positive and negative aspects of alternative courses of action. They believe their own action is inherently righteous and moral.
- ◆ *Type III symptoms: Pressure toward uniformity.* Members tend to censor their own misgivings about the group's position, contributing to a shared illusion that the group unanimously accepts the majority position. Seeing itself as invulnerable to outside attack, the group engages in excessive risk taking and nonreality thinking. The group also puts direct pressure on any member who expresses a dissenting view. Finally, members may act as "mindguards" to protect the group from outside information that could threaten the members' confidence in the correctness of the group's position.

When most or all of the groupthink symptoms are present, the group's decision-making process is likely to be seriously flawed.

Defects of Groupthink.   In addition, Janis believed that groupthink results in a range of consequences that interfere with effective group decision making:[88]

♦ The group limits its discussion to only a few alternatives.
♦ After a course of action is initially selected, members ignore new information concerning its risks and drawbacks.
♦ Group members avoid information concerning the benefits of rejected alternatives.
♦ Members make little attempt to use experts to obtain more precise information.
♦ Members fail to consider what may go wrong and do not develop contingency plans.

The end result of this causal chain is a greater probability that a poor-quality decision will be made.

Preventing Groupthink.   Finally, Janis suggested methods to prevent or minimize groupthink's dysfunctional consequences:[89]

♦ The group leader should encourage all group members to air their doubts and objectives.
♦ The group leader should adopt an impartial stance rather than initially state his or her preferences.
♦ Group members should be encouraged to discuss the group's deliberations with trusted associates and report their reactions back to the group.
♦ Outside experts should be invited to meetings and encouraged to challenge members' views.
♦ When a competitor is involved, time should be devoted to assessing the warning signs from the competitor and alternative scenarios of the competitor's intentions.
♦ When considering alternatives, the group should occasionally split into subgroups to meet separately.
♦ The group should hold a "second chance" meeting after reaching a preliminary consensus on a preferred alternative.
♦ The group should consider using dissonance-inducing group processes, such as asking and answering "Devil's advocate"-type questions.

A graphic model of Janis and Mann's groupthink process appears in Figure 8–8.

ACTIVITY 8.13   Groupthink and Poor Problem Solving

Case Study Question 7. How does groupthink contribute to poor problem solving and decision making?

Groupthink describes the decrease in groups' decision-making efficiency as a function of the leader's style, the level of group cohesiveness, and certain group norms. Discuss as a class:

1. Give examples of what groupthink might look and sound like in schools.
2. Give examples of what school leaders can do to prevent or minimize the harmful effects of groupthink in schools.

ANTECEDENTS

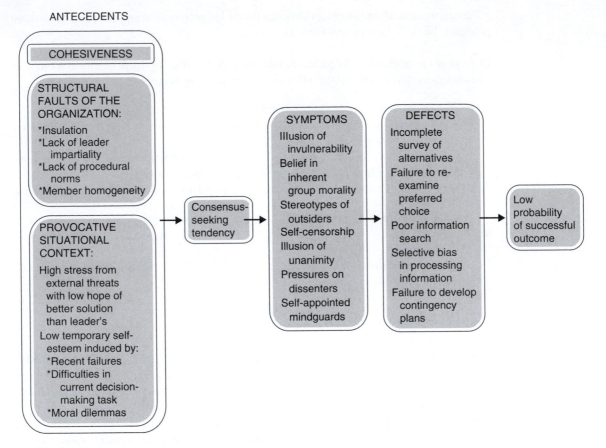

FIGURE 8–8

Groupthink Antecedents, Symptoms, and Defects (Source: Adapted from Janis, I. L., & Mann, L. (1977). *Decision making: A psychological analysis of conflict, choice, and commitment* (p. 132). New York, NY: Free Press.)

RESEARCH ON SHARED DECISION MAKING

Across many decades of research, investigators concur that group decision making usually falls short of its reasonable potential productivity.[90] More recent research finds that situational and procedural contexts that differentially affect members' motivation and resource coordination influence decision process gains and losses.[91]

Critics also claim that small-group research oversimplifies an obviously complex set of interactions. Most of the work on small-group decision making has tended to focus on linear, before-and-after type relationships with manipulations of independent variables (such as group size or task type) causing changes in dependent variables (such as group choice). This approach focuses on one or few variables while ignoring almost all others. As laboratories only simulate portions of the group decision-making process, these studies cannot draw firm conclusions or generalize to more varied (and more realistic) situations.[92]

Group Decision Making

For our purposes, we will focus narrowly on group decision-making research. Groups are routinely expected to perform under highly stressful conditions, and research finds the effects of increasing stress (e.g., time pressure, poor work environments, and multifaceted tasks) are complex. Stress tends to both increase and decrease performance quality, to narrow attention to more vital task features, and to prompt more simplified information processing.[93] Within certain limits, groups seem able to adapt to higher levels of stress.[94] But if the stress grows sufficiently high, group performance will eventually be degraded.[95] The impact of stress on group performance, therefore, varies with the specific circumstances (time pressure and the group members' perceptions about the initial task difficulty).[96] Groups under stress exhibit a stronger desire for uniformity of options/preferences. They are motivated to exert pressure on group members to accept that position, to reject those who deviate from that position, and to reach closure (have a definite, unambiguous solution).[97] In short, stressful conditions surrounding group decision making result in a "closing of the group mind"—an aversion to unpopular options and an acceptance of autocratic leadership and existing group norms.

Similarly, empirical studies on group decision making during the 1990s found that groups are less-than-optimal users of information and often ignore information that is not widely shared among the members.[98]

Groupthink

Considering the high interest in the groupthink concept, scarce research examines its propositions, and the model has not received consistent empirical support.[99] Plus, it appears that both good and poor decision outcomes can occur because of—or in spite of—many of the conditions hypothesized to trigger groupthink.[100]

Groupthink research suffers from serious methodological and theoretical problems. Frequently, it consists of content analysis of decision makers' public statements, case analyses, correlational studies of archival records, and empirical analyses of laboratory tests of various aspects of Janis's framework.[101] Although the first three may have ecological validity, their small and relatively restricted samples limit their interpretations and generalizability.[102] Experimental studies of groupthink have considered only a small portion or various combinations of the model's antecedents, often without a cohesive group, and in situations unlike Janis's. They also deal with student samples and hypothetical or simulated short-term decisions, creating potential problems for external validity.[103] The ability to generalize from such situations is questionable. While laboratory experiments manipulating structural or situational conditions can provide useful evidence about the group dynamics contributing to groupthink, they still do not approach the reality of assessing group behavior in more naturalistic settings. Others point to deficiencies in the theory itself, calling it incomplete, and offer both cautions and recommendations.[104]

Whatever its actual validity, the groupthink phenomenon has been accepted more because of its intuitive appeal than because of solid evidence. Although the model is relevant, it is incomplete. Even with validity concerns, the groupthink models have proved to be extremely valuable by stimulating research on group dysfunctions and have encouraged viewing outcomes in problem-solving terms. They have shown how the decision process may be relevant to a wide range of situations. They provide connections to other professional literature, such as stress and vigilance, and have identified potentially important variables in group problem solving. Groupthink models have also provided a fertile base for further development and testing.[105]

Probably groupthink theory's main contribution is the provocative research that it has generated, showing that constructs typically seen as positive aspects of groups—cohesiveness and collective efficacy, for example—do not invariably lead to improved group outcomes.[106]

Shared Decision Making in Schools

Briefly, studies of shared decision making in schools tend to be case studies occurring in a particular setting. Factors that enhanced shared decision making include members' confidence in themselves and in one another; needed resources provided at critical points (especially meeting time for face-to-face talk); the adoption of democratic rules and procedures (especially those that provided open access for members to set agenda items, initiate discussions, and set attendance expectations); early, concrete accomplishment; and the principal's support (encouraged active membership participation, provided essential resources, provided training in group decision making, and supplied the information necessary to make informed decisions about the issues under discussion).[107]

In contrast, factors that constrained the group decision-making process included inadequate time, lack of enthusiasm for democratic reform (teachers' role in decision making), teachers' lack of experience in debating issues in an open forum (had difficulty presenting policy arguments without resorting to personal attacks), and the school community's distrust of the district administration.[108]

Leadership and Limitations to Group Problem Solving

Group processes are seldom purely rational. The desire to simplify organizational decision making and make it more rational has generated many decision-making models. Each model attempts to highlight the order and logic of organizational life.

Principals are rarely observed using such models in their work or spending significant time in reflective thinking. Recent research has concluded that educational organizations and administrative work are far more complex than had been formerly believed, and that school leaders think about decision making differently than scholars and researchers. Problems in the real world rarely present themselves in neat sequences or one at a time. Many organizational problems are ill-defined and not well understood at the time decisions must be made. School leaders typically face ambiguous circumstances in which several events are occurring simultaneously, goals and values may conflict, many "right answers" may be possible, and time for decision making is always less than one would wish it to be.

Given this uncertainty and ambiguity, the trend in educational decision making has been to invite teachers and others to participate more fully in making important decisions. Primarily, this is to improve the decision quality by eliciting the knowledge and expertise of key people closest to the action. Likewise, empowering teachers and others through decision making participation tends to address these employees' intrinsic motivational needs and strengthen the growth of positive organizational culture. Contemporary school leaders understand that they gain power by sharing it with others because collaborative efforts frequently increase the group's effectiveness.[109]

Successful leaders are insightful and flexible. They are sharply aware of those forces most relevant to behavior at any given time. They have accurate self-awareness, a keen understanding of the individuals and groups with whom they are working and their readiness for growth, and a deep understanding of the organization and the broader social environment within which they operate. They recognize that group members often respond to situational, personal, and psychological presses that may not lead to the most successful problem solving. And successful leaders can behave appropriately in light of these varied perceptions—direct when being direct is required, and permitting participative freedom when involving group members in decision making is called for. Effective leaders maintain a high rate of accurately assessing the forces that determine the most appropriate behavior at any given time and are able to act accordingly. Learning how to become such a leader takes time, information, practice, feedback, and reflection.

SUMMARY

Conflict—or incompatibility of preferences, goals, and activities—is inevitable among humans. Conflict may be intrapersonal or interpersonal.

Classical organizational theorists appreciated the difficulties conflict could inflict on organizations, and they promoted managerial structures to prevent or minimize it. In contrast, contemporary theorists view conflict as inevitable, endemic, and often a legitimate way to confront reality and create new solutions to difficult problems. Depending on how it is handled, conflict within organizations may have functional and dysfunctional outcomes.

Whether a conflict is good or bad, functional or dysfunctional, depends on how it affects the organizational performance *Conflict resolution* implies reducing, eliminating, or ending conflict. *Conflict management* involves designing effective macro-level strategies to minimize the conflict's dysfunctions and enhance its constructive functions to improve organizational learning and effectiveness. Some scholars see conflict resolution as containing both constructive and destructive processes. The heart of cooperative conflict resolution is *reframing* the conflict as a mutual problem to be resolved cooperatively for a mutually satisfying outcome.

People in organizations make decisions to solve problems. Since circumstances, people, and organizations differ, no one right or best way exists for making effective decisions. Decision making's multiple inherent benefits and hazards make it a high-stakes and stressful process.

Barnard saw leadership as a problem-solving process that depends on the interaction of three variables: the individual, the group of followers, and the conditions. Tannenbaum and Schmidt proposed that leadership for shared decision making follows a continuum of different problem-solving patterns. Factors in the leader, the subordinates, and the situation all play roles in affecting shared decision making's effectiveness.

Classical decision theory assumes that decisions should be completely rational, using an optimizing strategy that seeks the best possible alternative to maximize the achievement of organizational goals and objectives. However, rational choice making is often jumbled by the competing interests among organizational stakeholders, individual limitations and idiosyncrasies, and lack of critical information.

Drucker articulated effective decision makers' thinking as they seek the highest level of conceptual understanding while bringing a practical shrewdness to the process. Simon suggested that decision making in organizations is constrained by the principle of *bounded rationality*, and that people *satisfice* rather than *optimize* and simplify the decision process with routes and "rules of thumb" to reduce its complexity.

Believing that circumstances influence decision-making participation, Vroom and colleagues attempted to model the decision-making interactions between leadership style, the situation, and effectiveness outcomes. Their approach considers the effective leader as one who is capable of analyzing the context and choosing from the various styles the one that is most appropriate for that situation. Substantial research supports aspects of their model, but it is impractical for daily use.

Other theorists have proposed alternative ways to accomplish shared decision making. Bridges used the "zone of indifference" theory and tests of relevance and expertise to help principals decide when and how to use subordinates in shared decision making. Hoy and Tarter extended Bridges's ideas with a decision-making model that includes trust, decision-making structures, and principals' leadership roles. Likewise, Owens and Valesky suggested a model for how and when people are to participate in shared decision making.

Janis and Mann offered a psychological perspective on stress in decision making and the consequences of decision outcomes. Janis and Mann also studied groupthink, the deterioration in groups' decision-making efficiency as a function of the leader's style, the level of group cohesiveness, and certain group norms.

Research on shared decision making is subject to many methodological limitations that restrict their findings' generalizability. Research data suggest that shared decision making has both good and poor decision outcomes, both frequently explained by situational and procedural variables that differentially affect members' motivation and resources.

ENDNOTES

1. Simon, H. A. (1997). *Administrative behavior: A study of decision-making processes in administrative organizations* (4th ed., pp. ix–x). New York, NY: Simon & Schuster, Free Press.

2. Bisno, H. (1988). *Managing conflict* (pp. 13–14). Newbury Park, CA: Sage. Conflict is such an important organizational phenomenon that a content analysis of organizational behavior courses for a master of business administration found that conflict was the fifth most mentioned among 65 topics. See: Rahim, M. A. (1981). Organizational behavior courses for graduate students in business administration: Views from the tower and battlefield. *Psychological Reports, 49,* 583–592.

3. Thomas, K. (1976). Conflict and conflict management. In M. D. Dunnette (Ed.), *Handbook of industrial and organizational psychology* (pp. 889–935). Chicago, IL: Rand McNally & Company, p. 890.

4. Rahim, M. A. (2001). *Managing conflict in organizations* (3rd ed.). Westport, CT: Quorum Books;

Rahim, M. A. (2002). Towards a theory of managing organizational conflict. *International Journal of Conflict Management, 13*(3), 206–235.

5. Rahim. (2002). Ibid., p. 207.

6. Deutsch, M. (1973). *The resolution of conflict: Constructive and destructive processes* (p. 10). New Haven, CT: Yale University Press.

7. Fayol, H. (1949). *General and industrial management* (C. Stors, Trans.). London, United Kingdom: Pitman (originally published in 1916); Gulick, L. H., & Urwick, L. (Eds.). (1937). *Papers on the science of administration.* New York, NY: Institute of Public Administration, Columbia University; Taylor, F. W. (1911). *The principles of scientific management.* New York, NY: Harper & Row; Weber, M. (1947). *The theory of social and economic organization* (A.M. Hendeson & T. Persons, Trans.). New York, NY: Oxford University Press.

8. Barnard, C. I. (1938). *The functions of the executive* (p. 36). Cambridge, MA: Harvard University Press.

9. Wrigley, W., as cited in Tjosvold, D. (1997). Conflict within interdependence: Its value for productivity and individuality. In C. deDreu & E. van deVliert (Eds.), *Using conflict in organizations* (p. 23). Thousand Oaks, CA: Sage.

10. Tjosvold, D. (1997). Conflict within interdependence: Its value for productivity and individuality. In C. deDreu & E. van deVliert (Eds.), *Using conflict in organizations* (pp. 23–37). Thousand Oaks, CA: Sage, p. 23.

11. Cosier, R. A., & Dalton, D. R. (1990). Positive effects of conflict: A field assessment. *International Journal of Conflict Management, 1*(1), 81–92; Janis, I. J. (1972). *Victims of groupthink.* Boston, MA: Houghton Mifflin; Wilson, J. A., & Jerrell, S. L. (1981). Conflict: Malignant, beneficial, or benign? In J. A. Wilson (Ed.), *New directions for higher education: Management science applications in academic administration* (pp. 105–123). San Francisco, CA: Jossey-Bass; Rahim, Garrett, & Buntzman. (1992). Op. cit.

12. Rahim, M. A., & Bonoma, T. V. (1979). Managing organizational conflict: A model for diagnosis and intervention. *Psychological Reports, 44*(3, Pt. 2), 1323–1344.

13. Brown, L. D. (1983). *Managing conflict at organizational interfaces* (p. 9). Reading, MA: Addison-Wesley.

14. Coser, L. (1956). *The functions of social conflict.* New York, NY: Free Press.

15. Rahim. (2001). Op. cit., p. 7.

16. Rahim. (2001). Op. cit., p. 7.

17. Argyris, C., & Schon, D. (1996). *Organizational learning—II.* Reading, MA: Addison-Wesley; Schein, E. H. (1993). How can organizations learn faster? The challenge of entering the green room. *Sloan Management Review, 35*(2), 85–92; Senge, P. M. (1990). *The fifth discipline: The art and practice of the learning organization.* New York, NY: Doubleday; Luthans, F., Rubach, M. J., & Marsnik, P. (1995). Going beyond total quality: The characteristics, techniques, and measures of learning organizations. *International Journal of Organizational Analysis, 3*(1), 24–44.

18. Rahim, M. A., Garrett, J. E., & Buntzman, G. F. (1992). Ethics of managing interpersonal conflict in organizations. *Journal of Business Ethics, 11*(5/6), 423–432.

19. Deutsch, M., Coleman, P. T., & Marcus, E. C. (2006). *The handbook of conflict resolution* (pp. 23–33). New York, NY: Wiley.

20. Deutsch, Coleman, & Marcus. (2006). Ibid., pp. 34–35.

21. Deutsch, M. (1973). *The resolution of conflict: Constructive and destructive processes* (p. 9). New Haven, CT: Yale University Press.

22. Barnard, C. (1938). *The functions of the executive* (p. 9). Cambridge, MA: Harvard University Press Williamson, O. E. (1995). Chester Barnard and the incipient science of organization. In O. E. Williamson (Ed.), *Organization theory: From Chester Barnard to the present and beyond* (pp. 172–206). New York, NY: Oxford University Press. In Chapter 2, we discussed Barnard's insights into the importance of informal organization in relation to the Westinghouse Hawthorne studies.

23. Barnard. (1938). Ibid., p. 5.

24. Barnard. (1938). Op. cit.

25. Tannenbaum, R., & Schmidt, W. H. (1958). How to choose a leadership pattern. *Harvard Business Review, 36*(2), 95–101.

26. Tannenbaum & Schmidt. (1958). Ibid.

27. Vroom, V. H., & Jago, A. G. (2007). The role of the situation in leadership. *American Psychologist, 62*(1), 17–24.
28. Tannenbaum & Schmidt. (1958). Ibid.
29. Simon, H. A. (1993). Decision making: Rational, nonrational, and irrational. *Educational Administration Quarterly, 29*(3), 393.
30. Simon, H. A. (2001). Theories of bounded rationality. In P. E. Earl (Ed.), *The legacy of Herbert Simon in economic analysis* (Vol. 1, pp. 51–66). Northampton, MA: Edward Elgar.
31. Voltaire, F. M. A. (1746). *Dictionnaire philosophique* (Paris, Garnier, 1973).
32. Drucker, P. F. (2008). *Classic Drucker. Essential wisdom of Peter Drucker from the pages of* Harvard Business Review. Boston, MA: Harvard Business Review Publishing.
33. Drucker. (2008). Ibid., p. 36.
34. For example, he noted that the problem with the American automobile industry was not "safety"—accidents were going to happen regardless of the engineering quality—but that cars would have to be made safe even when used incorrectly. Decision makers had to repeatedly check their problem definition against all available facts and observations and toss away the definition the moment it failed to include any of them. See: Drucker. (2008). Op. cit., p. 40.
35. Drucker pointed out two different types of rational compromises: "Half a loaf is better than no bread" (get what you can—don't let excellent be the enemy of the good) and the wise biblical decision that "Half a baby is worse than no baby" (set reasonable limits for solutions). See: Drucker. (2008). Op. cit., pp. 42–43.
36. Simon, H. A. (1965). Administrative decision making. *Public Administration Review, 25*(1), 31–37; Simon, H. A. (1993). Decision making: Rational, nonrational, and irrational. *Educational Administration Quarterly, 29*(3), 392–411.
37. Simon, H. A. (1986). Rationality in psychology and economics. *Journal of Business, 59*(4), S209–S224.
38. Simon, H. A. (1957). *Models of man: Social and rational.* New York, NY: John Wiley.
39. Simon, H. A. (1985). Human nature in politics: The dialogue of psychology with political science. *American Political Science Review, 79*(2), 293–304; Simon, H. A. (1976). *Administrative*

behavior: A study of decision-making processes in administrative organizations* (3rd ed.). New York, NY: Free Press.
40. Simon, H. A. (1956). Rational choice and the structure of the environment. *Psychological Review, 63*(2), 129–138.
41. Simon, H. A. (2000). Bounded rationality in social science: Today and tomorrow. *Mind and Society, 1*(1), 25–39.
42. Simon, H. A. (1959). Theories of decision making in economics and behavioral science. *American Economic Review, 49*(3), 273.
43. Simon, H. A. (1995). A behavioral model of rational choice. *Quarterly Journal of Economics, 69*, 99. Reprinted from Simon, H. A. (1982). *Models of bounded rationality. Volume 2: Behavioral economics and business organizations.* Cambridge, MA: MIT Press.
44. Simon. (1976). Op. cit.
45. Chapter 7 on building leadership capacity presents these research findings.
46. Vroom, V. H., & Yetton, P. W. (1973). *Leadership and decision-making.* Pittsburgh, PA: University of Pittsburgh Press; Vroom, V. H., & Jago, A. G. (1988). *The new leadership: Managing participation in organizations.* Englewood Cliffs, NJ: Prentice Hall; Vroom, V. H., & Jago, A. G. (1995). Situation effects and levels of analysis in the study of leader participation. *Leadership Quarterly, 6*(2), 169–181; Vroom, V. H., & Jago, A. G. (2007). The role of the situation in leadership. *American Psychologist, 62*(1), 17–24; Vroom, V. H. (2000). Leadership and the decision-making process. *Organizational Dynamics, 28*(4), 82–94.
47. Vroom, V. H. (2001). Two decades of research on participation: Beyond buzz words and management fads. In J. S. Osland, D. A. Kolb, & O. M. Rubin (Eds.), *The organizational behavior reader* (pp. 429–436). Upper Saddle River, NJ: Prentice Hall, p. 433.
48. Vroom (2000). Op. cit., p. 89.
49. Vroom & Jago. (1988). Op. cit.
50. Vroom. (2001). Op. cit., p. 430.
51. Yukl, G., Gordon, A., & Taber, T. (2002). A hierarchical taxonomy of leadership behavior: Integrating a half century of research. *Journal of Leadership and Organizational Studies, 9*(1), 15–32. See the Yukl article for exact citations of studies investigating various aspects of leadership.

52. Vroom & Yetton. (1973). Op. cit.; Yukl, G. (2002). *Leadership in organizations* (5th ed.). Upper Saddle River, NJ: Prentice Hall.

53. Jago, A. G. (1978). A test of spuriousness in descriptive models of participative leader behavior. *Journal of Applied Psychology, 63*(3), 383–387.

54. Jago, A. G., & Scammell, R. W. (1982). Decision-making styles of MJIS managers: A comparative evaluation. *Information and Management, 5*(1), 19–29.

55. Vroom, V. H., & Jago, A. G. (1974). Decision making as a social process: Normative and descriptive models of leader behavior. *Decision Science, 5*(4), 743–769; Vroom, V. H., & Jago, A. G. (1978). On the validity of the Vroom-Yetton model. *Journal of Applied Psychology, 63*(2), 151–162.

56. Heilman, M. E., Cage, J. H., Hornstein, H. A., & Herschlag, J. K. (1984). Reactions to prescribed leader behavior as a function of role perspective: The case of the Vroom-Yetton model. *Journal of Applied Psychology, 69*, 50–60.

57. Margerison, D., & Glube, R. (1979). Leadership decision-making: An empirical test of the Vroom and Yetton model. *Journal of Management Studies, 16*(1), 45–55; Paul, R. J., & Ebadi, Y. M. (1989). Leadership decision making in a service organization: A field test of the Vroom-Yetton model. *Journal of Occupational Psychology, 62*(1), 201–211. In 2004, Goethals and colleagues noted that Jago has compiled a list of 150 studies in scientific journals and over 40 doctoral dissertations dealing directly with these related models. See: Goethals, G. R., Sorenson, G. J., & Burns, J. M. (2004). *Encyclopedia of leadership, Volume 1.* Thousand Oaks, CA: Sage.

58. Jago, A. G. (1978). Configural cue utilization in implicit models of leader behavior. *Organizational Behavior and Human Performance, 22*, 474–496.

59. Brown, F. W., & Finsteun, K. (1993). The use of participative decision making: A consideration of the Vroom-Yetton and Vroom-Jago normative models. *Journal of Behavioral Decision Making, 6*(3), 207–209; Field, R. H. G. (1998). Testing the incremental validity of the Vroom-Jago vs Vroom-Yetton models of participation in decision making. *Journal of Behavioral Decision Making, 11*(4), 251–261.

60. Paul, R. J., & Ebadi, Y. M. (1989). Leadership decision making in a service organization: A field test of the Vroom-Yetton model. *Journal of Occupational Psychology, 62*(1), 201–211.

61. Sternberg, R. J., & Vroom, V. (2002). The person vs. the situation in leadership. *Leadership Quarterly, 13*(3), 301–323.

62. Tjosvold, D., Wedley, W. C., & Field, R. H. G. (1986). Constructive controversy, the Vroom-Yetton model and managerial decision making. *Journal of Occupational Behavior, 7*(2), 125–138.

63. Vroom & Jago. (2007). Op. cit.

64. Paul & Ebadi. (1989). Op. cit.

65. Barnard. (1938). Op. cit., p. 167.

66. Simon, H. A. (1947). *Administrative behavior.* New York, NY: MacMillan.

67. Barnard. (1938). Op. cit.

68. Simon. (1947). Op. cit.

69. Chase, R. S. (1951). Factors for satisfaction in teaching. *Phi Delta Kappan, 33*(2), 127–132.

70. Bridges, E. M. (1967). A model for shared decision making in the school principalship. *Educational Administration Quarterly, 3*(1), 49–61.

71. Bridges. (1967). Ibid.

72. Hoy, W. K., & Tarter, C. J. (1995). *Administrators solving the problems of practice: Decision making concepts, cases, and consequences.* Boston, MA: Allyn & Bacon.

73. Hoy & Miskel (2008). Op. cit. pp. 366–367.

74. Duke, D. L., Showers, B. K., & Imber, M. (1980). Teachers and shared decision making: The costs and benefits of involvement. *Educational Administration Quarterly, 16*(1), 93–106.

75. Hoy, W. K., & Tarter, C. J. (2003). *Administrators solving the problems of practice: Decision-making concepts, cases and consequences.* Boston, MA: Allyn & Bacon.

76. Owens, R. G., & Valesky, T. C. (2007). *Organizational behavior in education. Adaptive leadership and school reform* (9th ed., pp. 326–329). Boston, MA: Pearson/Allyn & Bacon.

77. Bridges, E. M. (1967, Winter). A model for shared decision making in the school principalship. *Educational Administration Quarterly, 3*(1), 52–59.

78. Janis, I. L. (1985). Sources of error in strategic decision making. In J. M. Pennings (Ed.), *Organizational strategy and change* (pp. 157–197). San Francisco, CA: Jossey-Bass.; Janis, I. L., & Mann, L. (1977). *Decision making: A psychological* *analysis of conflict, choice, and commitment.* New York, NY: Free Press.

79. "Cognitive shortcuts" include overestimating the likelihood that events can be easily imagined, overvaluing information about representativeness, relying on too small samples, and failing to discount biased information. See: Tyversky, A., & Kahneman, D. (1973). Availability: Heuristic for judging frequency and probability. *Cognitive Psychology, 5*(2), 207–232; Nisbet, R. E., & Ross, L. (1980). *Human interferences: Strategies and shortcomings in social judgments.* Englewood Cliffs, NJ: Prentice Hall; Janis. (1985). Op. cit.

80. Janis & Mann. (1977). Op. cit.

81. Aldag, R. J., & Fuller, S. R. (1993). Beyond fiasco: A reappraisal of the groupthink phenomenon and a new model. *Psychological Bulletin, 113*(3), 533–552; Janis. (1982). Op. cit., p. 9. George Orwell wrote *Nineteen Eighty-Four* (1949), a prophetic vision of the results of totalitarianism in which he introduced the terms "Big Brother," "doublethink," and "thought police."

82. Janis, I. (1972). *Victims of groupthink.* Boston, MA: Houghton Mifflin; Janis, I. (1982). *Victims of groupthink* (2nd ed.). Boston, MA: Houghton Mifflin.

83. Janis. (1982). Op. cit., p. 9.

84. Janis, I. L., & Mann, L. (1977). *Decision making: A psychological analysis of conflict, choice, and commitment.* New York, NY: Free Press.

85. Janis studied historical records and interviews related to the Cuban Bay of Pigs invasion and the escalation of the Vietnam War.

86. Janis, I. L. (1972). *Groupthink.* Boston, MA: Houghton Mifflin.

87. Ahlfinger, N. R., & Esser, J. K. (2001). Testing the groupthink model: Effects of promotional leadership and conformity predisposition. *Social Behavior and Personality. An International Journal, 29*(1), 31–41.

88. Janis. (1972). Op. cit.; Janis. (1982). Op. cit.; Janis, I. L. (1989). *Crucial decisions: Leadership in policymaking and crisis management.* New York, NY: Free Press.

89. Janis. (1972). Op. cit.; Janis. (1982). Op. cit.; Janis. (1989). Ibid.

90. Steiner, I. D. (1972). *Group process and productivity.* New York, NY: Academic; Hill, G. W. (1972). Group versus individual performance:

Are N+1 heads better than one? *Psychological Bulletin, 91*(3), 517–539.

91. Kerr, N. V., & Tindale, R. S. (2004). Group performance and decision making. *Annual Review of Psychology, 55*(1), 623–655. For a more complete discussion of the research on group decision making, see Kerr & Tindale.

92. Kerr & Tindale. (2004). Ibid.

93. Kaplan, M. F., Wanshula, L. T., & Zanna, M. P. (1993). Time pressure and information integration in social judgment: The effect of need for structure. In O. Svenson & J. Maule (Eds.), *Time pressure and stress in human judgement and decision making* (pp. 255–267). New York, NY: Plenum; Karau, S. J., & Kelly, J. R. (1992). The effects of time scarcity and time abundance on group performance quality and interaction process. *Journal of Experimental Social Psychology, 28*(6), 542–571; Brown, T. M., & Miller, C. E. (2000). Communication networks in task-performing groups: Effects of task complexity, time pressure, and interpersonal dominance. *Small Group Research, 31*(2), 131–157; DeGrada, E., Kruglanski, A. W., Mannetti, L., & Pierro, A. (1999). Motivated cognition and group interaction: Need for closure affects the contents and processes of collective negotiations. *Journal of Experimental Social Psychology, 35*(4), 346–365.

94. Brown & Miller. (2000). Op. cit.; Hollenbeck, J. R., Sego, D. J., Ilgen, D. R., Major, D. A., Dehlund, J., & Phillips, J. (1997). Team judgment-making accuracy under difficult conditions: Construct validation of potential manipulations using the TIDE 2 simulation. In T. Brannick, E. Salas, & C. Prince (Eds.), *Team performance assessment and measurement: Theory, methods, and applications* (pp. 111–136). Mahwah, NJ: Erlbaum; Volpe, C. E., Cannon-Bowers, J. A., Salas, E., & Spector, P. E. (1996). The impact of cross-training on team functioning: An empirical investigation. *Human Factors, 38*(1), 152–172.

95. Adelman, L., Miller, S. L., Hendeson, D., & Schloelles, M. (2003). Using Brunswikian theory and a longitudinal design to study how hierarchical teams adapt to increasing levels of time pressure. *Acta Psychologica, 112*(2), 181–206; Entin, E. E., & Serfaty, D. (1999). Adaptive team coordination. *Human Factors, 41*(2), 312–325;

Urban, J. M., Weaver, J. L., Bowers, C. A., & Rhodenizer, L. (1996). Effects of workload and structure on team processes and performance: Implications for complex team decision making. *Human Factors, 38*(2), 300–310.

96. Kerr & Tindale. (2004). Op. cit.

97. Kruglanski, A. W., Shah, J. Y., Pierro, A., Mannetti, L., Livil, S., & Kosic, A. (2002). *The closing of the "group mind" and the emergence of group-centrism.* Paper presented at the Society for Experimental Social Psychology, Columbus, OH; Kruglanski, A. W., Webster, D. M., & Klem, A. (1993). Motivated resistance and openness to persuasion in the presence or absence of prior information. *Journal of Personality and Social Psychology, 65*(5), 861–876.

98. Stasser, G., & Titus, W. (1985). Pooling of unshared information in group decision making: Biased information sampling during discussion. *Journal of Personality and Social Psychology, 48*(6), 1467–1478.

99. Aldag, R. J., & Fuller, S. R. (1993). Beyond fiasco: A reappraisal of the group think phenomenon and a new model of group decision processes. *Psychological Bulletin, 113*(3), 533–552; Kerr & Tindale. (2004). Op. cit.

100. Kerr & Tindale. (2004). Op. cit. See Kerr & Tindale for the specific studies addressing groupthink.

101. For a fuller discussion of the research on groupthink, see Neck & Moorhead. (1995). Op. cit.; and McCauley, C. (1989). The nature of social influence in groupthink: Compliance and internalization. *Journal of Personality and Social Psychology, 57*(2), 250–260.

102. Tetlock, P. E. (1979). Identifying victims of groupthink from public statements of decision makers. *Journal of Personality and Social Psychology, 37*(8), 1314–1324; Aldag & Fuller. (1993). Op. cit.

103. Aldag & Fuller. (1993). Op. cit.

104. Longely, J., & Pruitt, D. G. (1980). Groupthink: A critique of Janis' theory. In L. Wheeler (Ed.), *Review of personality and social psychology* (pp. 507–513). Newbury Park, CA: Sage; Whyte, G. (1989). Groupthink reconsidered. *Academy of Management Review, 14*(1), 40–56; Hart, P. (1991). Irving L. Janis' victims of groupthink. *Political Psychology, 12*(2), 247–278; Whyte, G. (1989). Groupthink reconsidered. *Academy of Management Review, 14*(1), 40–56.

105. Aldag & Fuller. (1993). Op. cit.

106. Mullen, B., Anthony, T., Salas, E., & Driskell, J. W. (1994). Group cohesiveness and quality of decision making. *Small Group Research, 25*(2), 189–204; Whyte, G. (1998). Recasting Janis's groupthink model: The key role of collective efficacy in decision fiascoes. *Organizational Behavior: Human Decision Process, 73*(2/3), 185–209.

107. Weiss, C. H., Camboine, J., & Wyeth, A. (1992). Trouble in paradise: Teacher conflicts and shared decision making. *Educational Administration Quarterly, 28*(3), 350–367; Johnson, M. J., & Pajares, F. (1996). When shared decision making works: A 3-year longitudinal study. *American Educational Research Journal, 33*(3), 599–627.

108. Johnson & Pajares. (1996). Op. cit.

109. This issue and the supporting research has been discussed in Chapter 7.

CHAPTER 9

Leadership and Resource Allocation

Focus Questions

- ◆ In what ways is resource allocation a political, ethical, fiscal, and social process?
- ◆ How do the concepts of equity, equality, and adequacy affect the resource allocation process?
- ◆ What is learning-focused resource allocation, and how does it affect resource assignments?
- ◆ What fiscal, people, and time resources are available to schools, and what constraints operate on each?
- ◆ What are the research findings on resource allocation (fiscal, people, time) and student achievement?
- ◆ What enduring dilemmas remain as factors in resource allocation decisions?

CASE STUDY: BUDGETING AT MANHASSET HIGH SCHOOL

Three years ago, Allan Todd was appointed assistant principal of the 2,000-student Manhasset High School, an organization with a very traditional, top-down leadership structure. He came to Manhasset from a Chicago school district that had a more progressive leadership. Allan had served as the principal of the local Chicago area high school for 5 years. He left when his Chicago superintendent announced he was leaving to become superintendent of Manhasset Public Schools and asked Allan to come with him to the new school system.

The principal at Manhasset was retiring at the end of the school year. On April 15, he announced that Allan had been tapped to take the school's leadership role. It was widely reported that the principal was forced to retire after the high school had not made adequate yearly progress (AYP) for the past 3 years, even though the overall test scores were good. Allan recognized the high level of ability and willingness that existed in Manhasset High School's staff and thought it underused. The teachers cared about all students' achievement, and they had ideas about how to meet student needs more effectively than the prior administration had allowed. The teachers wanted to take on leadership roles to help advise the principal on the school's instructional, financial, and logistic aspects.

The week after Allan's appointment was made public, he held a faculty meeting with the Manhasset High School staff to announce he was soliciting ideas to help make their school a more effective place for learning and teaching. He told the staff that he wanted to maximize the resources available to fulfill the school mission, including people, money, time, and space. He would be willing to entertain any improvement suggestions regarding those four areas. He wanted to make the school operation as transparent as possible.

Allan told the staff that two principles would guide all the Manhasset decisions. The first principle was that there must be equality of educational opportunity for all students. The second principle was that resources had to be distributed equitably for students. Department meetings should now revolve around instructional and management ideas to improve student learning and offering suggestions for resource allocation to accomplish those goals. Allan announced that the department chairs would meet twice each month to discuss ideas and progress in improving education at Manhasset High School. A copy of the school budget was sent electronically to each staff member.

The staff left the faculty meeting thinking that the school was moving in the right direction. Department meetings became lively discussion forums for making the school a better place. Quickly, however, there arose a difference about what a "better place" meant to everyone. This was reflected in the advanced placement (AP) and international baccalaureate (IB) teachers wanting more resources (smaller class size from 15 to 12 students). Teachers in classes with less able students also wanted class size reduced from 25 to 20. Conflicts began to emerge within and among departments.

The department chairs met with Allan in May before school ended. The English department chair recommended that AP and IB class size be reduced from 15 students per class to 12 students. Allan asked the department chair if that suggestion was an equitable distribution of resources when some classes had more than 30 students per class. The English department chair withdrew his request.

The social studies department chair questioned the funds for substitute teachers. With 2,000 students and 160 faculty members, the $85,500 allocated for substitutes seemed high. Allan explained that the faculty had a 3% absentee rate, equating to five substitute teachers a day for each of the 180 school days. The standard rate for subs was $95 per day. That is how the figure was derived. The chair then stated that the school was on a traditional seven-period day where teachers had five class assignments, a planning period, and a duty period. The chair then asked if the faculty could use the duty period to cover for absent colleagues and retain the substitute monies for professional development. Other chairs disagreed with this proposal, saying it would put extra work on already burdened teachers. Allan then stated he would be willing to allocate all saved substitute monies for professional development for those teachers who participated in the proposal.

At the next department chair meeting, Allan reviewed the school improvement plan and its mission statement with the staff. He also distributed the latest summary state test data to the chairs. It looked as follows:

Subject	*Manhasset High School Overall Pass Rate Percentages (with variance noted in parentheses)*							
	Over-all	Special Ed.	LEP	All Minority	African American	Latino	Asian	White
English	83	52 (−31)	67 (−16)	70 (−13)	67 (−16)	65 (−18)	99 (+16)	96 (+13)
History	81	67 (−14)	79 (−2)	71 (−10)	72 (−9)	70 (−11)	98 (+17)	93 (+12)
Math	80	75 (−5)	79 (−1)	63 (−17)	70 (−10)	71 (−9)	99 (+19)	92 (+12)
Science	82	49 (−33)	65 (−17)	74 (−8)	67 (−15)	64 (−18)	99 (+17)	94 (+12)

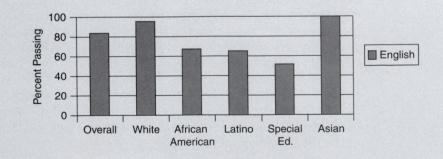

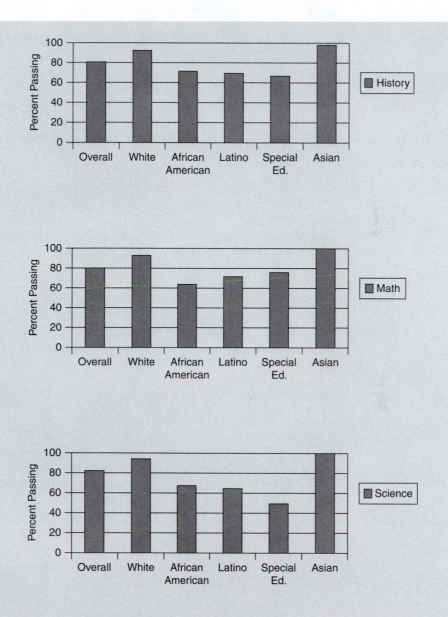

Allan asked the department chairs to review the test data in detail with their faculty members and address the question of achievement gaps. Which teachers are working with the neediest students, and which teachers are working with the most capable students? Are the resources equitably being matched with the student needs? Do the neediest students have equality of opportunity to learn?

The next department chair meeting was somewhat somber. The chairs had an encounter with cognitive dissonance and felt uncomfortable. The "best" (most experienced, most effective) teachers were working with the most capable students. The newest teachers were working with the neediest students. The faculty realized that the "best" students had been getting the best resources while the rest got what was left. The group recognized that students at Manhasset High School did not have equal educational opportunity. Allan then asked the group to consider how they could fix the situation.

Over the next 3 years, Manhasset High School's test scores increased and the achievement gaps all but disappeared. Last year, the school hired only three substitutes the entire year. The school had entered into a sustained professional development agreement with a local university with part of the saved substitute funds. Teaching assignments were changed; class size increased for IB and AP classes and decreased in other areas. The school hired a block scheduling consultant to work with them about the pros and cons of moving to a block schedule. After a year of research, the faculty voted 158 to 2 for proceeding to the block schedule. They also decided that they needed one full year of professional development activities prior to implementing the move to prepare them for the instructional changes needed to successfully implement the program. The Manhasset High School PTA Executive Committee, which had revitalized over the previous 2 years, voted unanimously to endorse the move to block scheduling.

Case Study Questions

1. What resources did Allan have available to allocate?
2. Why is it difficult to reallocate teaching resources to the "needy" students?
3. From looking at the test score gaps, who were the students needing additional instructional resources? What subject would you have examined first? Why?
4. How would you have handled this situation if the faculty had not had a high level of ability and willingness?

INTRODUCTION

School leaders at all levels are responsible for effectively managing the organization's operations and resources for a safe, efficient, and effective learning environment. They do this in part, by making decisions about how to successfully leverage and distribute human, fiscal, structural, and technological resources to support teaching and learning as well as to protect the welfare and safety of students and staff. As stewards of their communities' most valuable resources (children and tax dollars), school leaders must understand both the organization's values and priorities and their students' learning needs so they can make informed decisions about how best to allocate available resources.

Understanding their student population and issues related to equity of resource allocations, understanding their schools' and stakeholders' beliefs and values, knowing the various resource streams and their constraints, and rethinking familiar practices can generate resources and opportunities to support greater student learning. In addition, current research suggests areas where fiscal investments pay the greatest gains in student achievement. Understanding where to get the "biggest academic bang for the buck" and working with stakeholders to wisely and fairly direct available resources is an increasingly critical leadership responsibility.

WHAT IS RESOURCE ALLOCATION?

Making resource allocation decisions is among school leaders' most challenging tasks. When everyone's goal is improved student learning, however, resource allocation decisions remain difficult, but the choices often become clearer. Knowing how to distribute resources wisely can lead to long-term goal accomplishment.

Defining Resource Allocation

Resource allocation is the distribution of assets—usually financial—among competing groups of people or programs.[1] Because a society's reserves are in limited supply while human desires are usually unlimited, and because any given resource can have many alternative uses, resource allocation becomes the focus of competing agendas.

All organizations, including schools, operate with financial, human, and structural (time and space) resources. The extent to which those resources are appropriately assigned, ably managed, closely monitored, and accurately evaluated contributes to the school and principal's overall success. To make the most effective and productive use of the school's available or securable assets, principals must think shrewdly about the funds, people, time, classroom areas, and material at hand. Likewise, how school leaders apportion resources must reflect the schools' articulated purposes.

Levels of Resource Decision Making

Since competing interests vie for limited reserves, resource allocation is a political, ethical, fiscal, and social process. Governments make two broad types of resource decisions: the total size of the overall budget they will give to schools ("the size of the cake") and how that amount is to be allotted to schools ("how the cake is cut").[2] Operating within the varied fiscal, legal, and ethical restrictions placed on how the funds can be used, district and school-level decisions often employ political and social processes to manage these resources.

At the State Level.   At the state level, governors must weigh competing societal interests in their decision making about how to apportion state revenues. Governors must first decide how to distribute resources for education over other competing public needs, such as health care, law enforcement, transportation, or museums. Next, they must decide how to apportion resources within the education sector. How much, for instance, should be directed toward preschool programs, how much for K–12 education, and how much for higher education? Political, ethical, fiscal, and social factors and governors' own values and priorities all play crucial roles in formulating these decisions.

At the District Level. Although district level educators are generally concerned about overall resource amounts for their schools, they have little control over the "size of the cake" decisions. According to educational leadership professors John Hoyle, Fenwick English, and Betty Steffy, "Today's reality is that the public schools must stand in line with the other public institutions and plead for their share of the tax revenue."[3] This assertion has never been more true. District superintendents do, however, have considerable authority over how to deploy the allocated resources at the school level.

At the School Level. Accountability for managing the school's resources rests with the principal. Because principals function in an environment of high expectations and accountability, they participate in decision making that includes a greater assortment of stakeholders than previously experienced by school leaders in our society.

The community and profession expect principals to share resource allocation decisions with the school's stakeholders. Site-based decision making by the principals participating with school improvement teams, site councils, and leadership teams reflects a move from a centralized to a decentralized leadership process. Decisions are made by those closest to their implementation and by those with a vested interest in the outcomes. Principals are expected to knowledgeably and accurately demonstrate that they have used the resources entrusted to them to benefit teaching and learning and that they will be able to credibly express the need for additional assets.

Today's school leaders are also expected to build the staff's capacity to pursue funding sources, analyze relevant financial data, and manage money. This requires developing relationships with community organizations and individuals who may have the wherewithal to support school improvement and assessing whether the services or resources that partnerships provide are appropriately being used in line with the school's vision. The school leadership team should view building partnerships and searching for new funding sources as a continuous, long-term process to ensure that they have sufficient means to sustain improvement efforts.

EQUITY, ADEQUACY, LEADERSHIP, AND RESOURCE ALLOCATION

Principals make resource allocation decisions within a larger social, ethical, and fiscal context. Most of us believe in equal treatment for individuals, yet students come to school with different learning needs. When school leaders make decisions about assigning resources, they must first collect and analyze data relevant to their unique educational environment and student achievement. They must consider their students' learning needs as well as the fiscal, people, and structural resources necessary to keep all students and staff safe and to bring all students to high achievement. With today's students reflecting wide diversity in their families' economic assets and prior educational experiences, issues of equity and adequacy become essential concerns in allocating resources.

Equity, Equality, and Adequacy

In a school funding context, the terms *equity* and *equality* sound alike but their meanings are quite different. *Equity* is providing the services students actually need whereas *equality* is providing the same services for all students regardless of the students' or locality's needs. Equity can be defined as a fairness issue for both students and taxpayers. The difference between equity and equality explains why equity, much more than equality, is a basic tenet of our school finance system.[4]

Adequacy is another money issue affecting fairness in school funding. *Adequacy* involves providing sufficient resources to accomplish the job of educating our children. A workable definition would be providing enough funds to teach the average student to state standards, and then to identify how much each district/school requires to teach children with special needs—children with learning disabilities, children from poverty and educationally limited backgrounds, and children without English proficiency—to the same high and rigorous achievement standards.[5] How much funding is adequate? As a fiscal concept, adequacy is value driven with people defining it subjectively according to their own priorities and opinions. Attempts have been made to quantify how much a state or school district needs to spend for its students, but the actual figures remain unclear.

Increasingly, courts have recognized that public school funding practices are inequitable. School funding systems that rely too heavily on local property taxes have been deemed unconstitutional, denying certain students equal protection under the law. Nonetheless, wide and growing gaps in education quality appear between more-affluent school districts and less-affluent ones. Research shows that, depending on their location, some school districts receive 8 *times* as much per-pupil funding as others.[6] This translates into differences in such areas as teacher quality, class size, facilities upkeep, professional development, available technology, and other factors that can affect student outcomes and, ultimately, students' life chances.

As a result, the states try to offset these local wealth differences with their funding formulas. Deborah Verstegen, an education finance scholar, reported, "There have been no new approaches developed or used to distribute state aid to school systems since the 1920s and 1930s."[7] In those days, fewer than one third of the eligible population attended high school, and even fewer graduated.[8] In 2007, 96.4% of students ages 14 to 17 were enrolled in school.[9]

School funding adequacy has been actively litigated. Since 1995, several school funding court cases have produced major changes in state education policy around the United States. School finance litigation has forced states to not only alter the way they fund schools but also improve and update their states' assessment and accountability systems.

In reviewing the educational adequacy litigation, four goals consistently appear: (1) prepare students to be citizens and economic participants in a democratic society, (2) relate to contemporary, not archaic educational needs, (3) anchor educational standards to more than a minimal level, and (4) focus on providing opportunity rather than outcome.[10]

As of February 2011, at least 46 states have been involved in some form of K–12 school finance litigation.[11] These court challenges address the state's role in ensuring equitable spending among districts, providing suitable school facilities, and directing adequate funds to programs designed for special education and at-risk students. Plaintiffs have won

20 of 28 adequacy cases since 1989. When used wisely, the money awarded in these cases has repeatedly translated into more resources for poorer districts and improved results for schools and students.[12]

Example of Fiscal Inequity. Consider the scenario in Table 9–1. Two relatively similar school systems have approximately the same amount of money coming to them from the federal, state, and local governments—$10,600 per student. The two systems have roughly the same capacity to fund education, as seen from the average family income, and both have the same number of students to educate.

TABLE 9–1
Equality Versus Equity Example

School System	Average Family Income	Federal Revenue	State Revenue	Local Revenue	% Eligible for Special Education
A	$65,000	$1,050	$3,550	$6,000	3%
B	$65,100	$1,100	$3,450	$6,050	18%

Source: Owings & Kaplan.

Both school systems draw from upper-middle-class neighborhoods where parents expect their children to go to college. In school system A, 3% of the students have been identified as eligible for special education services—far below the national average. In school system B, 18% or 6 times as many students have been identified as eligible to receive special education services—higher than the national average.

If we look solely at the issue of equality, both school systems have the funds they need: $10,600 per pupil. If we look at the equity issue, however, the students' needs in school system B are greater than those in school system A. School system B must spend more money to meet the identified learning needs than does school system A. Equal funding for these systems may seem fair, until we consider the students' needs. Because of the varying student needs and their associated costs, treating these two systems equally on a financial basis would not be fair or equitable.

An analogy may be instructive. Imagine visiting a physician who treats all patients equally. Each patient gets the same treatment at the same cost. It sounds ridiculous, because we expect to be treated on the basis of our differing health conditions. We expect the care for a common cold to be different than the care for Stage 2 cancer, and we realize that the chemotherapy and radiation needed to shrink tumors costs more than the facial tissues and over-the-counter remedies used to treat one week's sniffles and coughs. We want and expect to receive the medical care we require. The same is true in education. While we should have an equal opportunity for a good education, students require different services depending on their unique situations.

Although education is expensive, providing poor and inadequate education for large numbers of students may be even more costly. Inadequately educated students bring steep public and social consequences. Money matters when it comes to student achievement. Many studies confirm this relationship.[13] The more money targeted appropriately on student learning, the more students learn.

Although principals do not have control over their student body's demographics, educators do have influence over the instructional strategies and interventions directed toward helping diverse students achieve to high levels. As moral stewards, principals are responsible for ensuring a system of accountability for every student's academic success. Awareness of the need to make equitable and adequate—not merely equal—resource decisions brings an attuned perspective and set of ethical values into the resource allocation process.

ACTIVITY 9.1   Allocating Resources at Manhasset High School

Case Study Question 1: What resources did Allan have available to allocate? Discuss as a class:

1. From the case study, list the potential resources that were available at Manhasset High School in the following categories:
   ◆ Fiscal:
   ◆ People:
   ◆ Time:
   ◆ Space:
   ◆ Other:
2. Describe the equality, equity, and adequacy issues that Manhasset High School might be facing, and provide evidence of these possible concerns.
3. How do the political, social, legal, and ethical factors come into play in deciding how to allocate Manhasset High School's resources?

Case Study Question 4: How would you have handled this situation if the faculty had NOT had a high level of ability and willingness?

LEADERSHIP, STAKEHOLDERS, AND RESOURCE ALLOCATION

Critical to resource allocation's success is the way in which the school leader chooses to share the information with the stakeholders, the specific knowledge and data communicated, and the leader's expertise in helping the stakeholder groups effectively use the facts and context details to make appropriate resource allocation decisions for the school. The leader's philosophy and beliefs, student needs, and various resource allocation factors play essential roles in this process.

Philosophy, Beliefs, and Resource Allocation

Like others, principals bring past experiences, beliefs, and values to the workplace that impact their decisions and actions. The principal who believes that people want to be part of something larger than themselves and contribute to developing a school program or practice that makes an important difference to students and the community will provide teachers with increased involvement in decision making.

Involving Stakeholders.   Successful principals know that they and their teachers cannot educate students by themselves. They need the community's interest and support—both social and financial. This backing is more likely when a strong relationship exists between the school and the community, both with families and caregivers as well as with businesses and nonparent residents. To fortify school-community relationships, successful schools help area members understand their goals and programs and point out how investing in the school can assist businesses and local organizations accomplish their own missions. Schools also help businesses understand that education is a critical part of the area's economic vitality: generating skillful employees, informed customers, and responsible neighbors. In this way, contributing resources to school improvement is a farsighted investment, rather than a donation.

In addition, successful schools develop partnerships when they find ways to connect their students directly with the community. For example, they create occasions for students to participate in service learning projects that benefit the public and encourage district members to attend student-centered activities such as concerts, plays, and athletic events. When the local residents and businesses view the school as integral to their social and economic fabric, they are more likely to offer financial and other supports.

The principal may conceptualize an information network within the local school community and identify by name the groups represented. This information network reflects the stakeholder groups concerned with the school's allocation of resources. As illustrated in Figure 9–1, these stakeholders have the greatest degree of personal interest and welfare in the school's overall success and should be involved in the school's decision-making process.

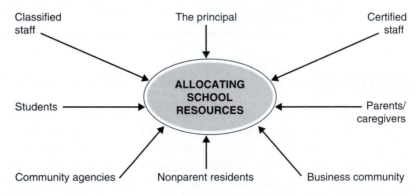

FIGURE 9–1
Stakeholder Groups Concerned with Allocation of School Resources (Source: Adapted from Norton, M. S., & Kelly, L. K. (1997). *Resource allocation: Managing money and people* (pp. 5, 10). Larchmont, NY: Eye on Education.)

School leaders must remember that public schools are civic institutions. As such, community members have a right to access certain records and information, including financial data. The principal serves as a resource person, providing or clarifying specifics, assisting in facilitating group discussion and decision making, advocating for meaningful involvement of stakeholder groups, and helping carry out the group's wishes and decisions. The leader who shares and discusses available facts with interested community groups and individuals in the planning process will create and sustain a much different school climate than the principal who chooses to withhold such details.

Learning-Focused Resource Allocation

Ideally, learning-focused leadership aspires to a more vigorous allocation process that offers varied ways to direct resources at learning improvement priorities. Figure 9–2 represents a theory of action shared by leaders or leadership team members that prioritizes specific teaching and learning improvement goals and articulates a set of strategic actions that make the goal achievement more likely. The process places greater emphasis on evidence than on opinion. By collecting and analyzing information about the students' learning needs, current programs, emerging trends and initiatives, and the effects of previous investments on student and school outcomes, leaders seek more fully informed ways of developing and appraising allocation options. While attempting to balance a number of competing interests, this process gives voice to a strong set of otherwise silent considerations about teaching and learning. In this model, the leader's initial responsibility is to structure and guide the decision-making process so that the focus on learning, the strategies for addressing it, and the evidence that informs decisions may be fully presented and heard.[14]

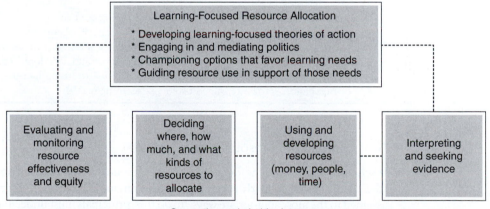

FIGURE 9–2
Learning-Focused Resource Allocation (Source: From Plecki, M. L., Alejano, C. R., Knapp, M. S., & Lockmiller, C. R. (2006, October). *Allocating resources and creating incentives to improve teaching and learning* (p. 15). Seattle: University of Washington. Retrieved from http://www .wallacefoundation.org/wallace/2AllocatingResourcesandCreating.pdf. Used with permission.)

During this resource allocation process, school leaders keep the activities focused on learning improvement. They engage in multiple perspectives and invite competing interests, especially those that place value on increasing student and teacher learning. The school leaders manage the deliberations so that learning priorities and equity remain central to decision making. The leader and team continually assess resource allocation's equity and effectiveness, identify and secure relevant resources for further improvement priorities (within constraints), and distribute these resources according to identified needs. Throughout, leaders promote the instructional plan's continuous and sustainable improvement. If feedback loops and a culture of data-informed decision making become well established, an allocation cycle may appear.

ACTIVITY 9.2   Making Learning-focused Resource Allocation Decisions

Case Study Question 2: Why is it difficult to reallocate teaching resources to "needy" students? Discuss as a class:

1. Explain the fiscal, ethical, legal, political, and social factors that make it difficult to reallocate teaching resources to the "needy" students.
2. Figure 9–2 presents a model for learning-focused resource allocation. In the case study, how did Allan accomplish the following tasks?
   ◆ Become aware of the multiple perspectives and competing interests in his faculty.
   ◆ Provide and interpret data about the learning needs present in Manhasset High School.
   ◆ Champion options that favor students' learning needs.
   ◆ Guide resources in support of these learning needs.
   ◆ Use and develop resources (money, people, time) to address students' and teachers' learning needs.
   ◆ Evaluate and monitor that resources are being used effectively and equitably.
   ◆ Develop feedback loops and a data-supporting school culture.
3. To what extent is this learning-focused resource allocation model in practice in the school where you currently teach? What evidence and anecdotes support your conclusion? What factors could your leadership team use to strengthen their resource allocation practices to better support students' learning needs?

Key Elements of Resource Allocation

If schools are to know the range of available resources, they must periodically inventory them. This means regularly reviewing whether financial, human, and structural assets are assigned in the most appropriate ways. To do this, principals must understand the school and district's mission, goals, and objectives; identify their vision for the school and their own educational values; know the student population's specific learning needs; and recognize the assorted constraints and competing interests that impact resource allocation.

School and District Mission, Goals, and Objectives.   Planning how to use funds available to the school principal begins by understanding the school's mission, goals, and objectives as developed by the school personnel and other key stakeholders. School leaders must be able to translate the school's goals and objectives into appropriate resource demands that will enable the school and staff to accomplish them. School leaders work collaboratively with school planning groups to identify specific strategies or interventions needed to meet these desired outcomes.

Alongside identified strategies and interventions, the principal and leadership team identify related needs in supplies, equipment, materials, and staffing. This information frequently appears in the school's improvement plan. Key allocation issues for schools wanting to improve teaching and learning include:[15]

◆ *Targeting achievement gaps.* Making resource-related decisions that seek to close achievement gaps creates good possibilities for enhancing the equity of educational outcomes. This may mean evaluating the equitable allotment of experienced and skilled teaching staff to schools (and classrooms) with high percentages of students of color, students from disadvantaged backgrounds, or students for whom English is not their first language.

◆ *Organizing schools and districts to align resources with learning improvement agendas.* Apportioning resources effectively requires structuring time, reviewing the nature and assignment of staff, and assessing instructional programs so they collectively emphasize the school's learning improvement priorities. Correctly aligning resources with learning improvement means rethinking school schedules, considering how teachers are organized into teams and subject departments, and addressing contractual issues.

◆ *Managing the politics of learning-focused leadership.* Mediating the political pressures associated with learning-focused resource decision making includes redistributing the authority to act. This requires being ready to challenge existing interests at all levels of the educational system because of competing demands for resources by persons inside and outside the school.

◆ *Developing human capital.* Providing supports, incentives, and opportunities for learning builds faculty motivation and expertise which can lead to higher performance. At least three quarters of schools' fiscal resources are spent on people. Developing and nurturing capacities of principals and teachers can increase their knowledge and skills, connect them with learning improvement priorities, and inspire their interest in pursuing improvement goals in particular settings.

During the school improvement planning process, the principal provides the planning groups with the information regarding allocation of the school's resources. Using these data, the groups identify additional resources needed and compare those amounts with what the school has been assigned. Areas of discrepancy—high needs but low resources—become targets for identifying and securing additional assets.

Vision and Principals' Role.   Every effective principal has a vision of the school in which he or she works. That vision often includes expectations concerning (1) student success, (2) the overall climate or school environment, (3) the decision-making processes, and (4) the ways in which the leader envisions individuals and groups interacting together. This educational vision as well as the principal's personal philosophy and belief system about the ways in which key school and community persons participate in the decision-making process influence the school climate, the level of staff collegiality, and their commitment to achieve the school's mission and goals.

As the school leader, the principal has—or is responsible for obtaining—the information about the school necessary for decision making. These data come from an array of sources: the central office, in-house data collection and analysis, local newspapers, staff, students, parents, and other school administrators. The information may be accurate or inaccurate, favorable or unfavorable, positive or negative, realistic or unrealistic. Typically, the superintendent notifies the principal about the school's total dollar allocation. Often, this is a block allotment that includes the funds needed to operate the entire school for one year. Those funds can be used for personnel, transportation, food services, maintenance, supplies, furniture, and equipment.

Principals must decide on a conceptual model for sharing data. They must determine what information they have and decide what and how much information to share, with whom, and what mechanisms will be used to share it. How the principal answers these questions and translates those answers into action will send important messages to the staff and community groups. For example, principals who choose to involve others in the decision-making process and provide them with all relevant data will more likely create a climate of trust and openness that encourages others to behave similarly. Next, principals must identify a representative list of individuals, groups, or agencies within each stakeholder unit from the entire school community who will participate in the resource allocation process.

Educational Values. The principal's personal beliefs and values about shared decision making are not the only ones in play during the resource allocation process. Educational values provide direction and priorities to how resources might be assigned and shared. These values may include academic considerations, fairness, equity for various student populations, transparency, accountability, and long-term organizational goals. A good resource allocation process allows the institution to achieve a proper balance between its intrinsic values (educators' academic vision and mission, their beliefs and goals, societal expectations for certain outcomes) and those of its clients (students, parents, community, and local businesses).

Additional competing principles affecting resource allocation come from the diverse values that exist within any organization. Different teachers and departments advocate for their own priorities, materials, and advantages, often as a result of good-faith ideas of what they think is important—as well as their own self-interest—rather than what the principal, the superintendent, or the school board thinks is most important to reach institutional goals.

Student Needs. The type of students the school serves influences the amount of resources needed and how these should be directed. Student demographics including whether the school is elementary, middle, or high school; the student body size and its racial and ethnic composition; percent of students receiving free and reduced-price lunches; percent of students receiving special education services; percent of students speaking English as a second language; and percent of homeless students all have an impact on the amounts and types of educational supports needed for all students to succeed in a high-challenge curriculum.

Likewise, indications of how well students are achieving by using a variety of measures, including teacher tests; report cards; standardized test scores for reading, math, and other content; attendance rates; and discipline records—all disaggregated by grade, gender, race or ethnicity, and socioeconomic group—provide essential data about resources needed for school success. Targeting resources toward problem areas becomes a critical part of a school's goal to boost student learning and achievement.

ACTIVITY 9.3   Using School Data to Target Resource Needs

Case Study Question 3: From the test score gaps, who are the students needing additional instructional resources? Discuss in pairs and then as a class:

1. From the test data, which students appear to be in need of targeted instructional resources?
2. What subject would you have examined first, and why?
3. In what ways did the new principal address—or fail to fully address—the following key allocation issues?
   ◆ Targeting achievement gaps
   ◆ Organizing schools and districts to align resources with learning improvement agendas
   ◆ Managing the politics of learning-focused leadership
   ◆ Developing human capital

Constraints on Resource Allocations.   State, district, and school policies and practices impose limits on how school leaders can allocate resources. State policies either allow flexibility or check the superintendents' and principals' discretion over budgets, about how to arrange school schedules and days, and around issues including teacher certification, employment, and termination of district and school staff.

At the district level, the school board's leadership provides policy guidance for the district's resource allocations. The board works with the superintendent to determine school and central office budget allocations. Additionally, school leaders create district policies and practices that support and limit effective resource allocation. These policies and practices include hiring and assigning teachers to schools, providing professional development to improve teaching, supporting schools' instructional improvements according to the schools' needs, and supplying additional teaching and learning assets for students needing extra tutoring, more time for learning in class, and additional in-depth lessons in difficult subjects.

At the school level, principal leadership is essential to appropriate resource allocation. While abiding by federal, state, and district guidelines, principals are responsible for deciding how schools organize time into instructional classroom periods and common planning. Principals decide the most effective use of space to support student learning and teacher collaboration. Principals assign teachers to specific courses and specific students, making staffing changes as necessary to fit the teachers' knowledge and skills to the students' learning needs.

Competing interests also constrain resource allocation. Given the considerable variations in schools' needs, capacities, and learning challenges in their environment, leaders can expect conflicting expectations, tensions, and barriers impeding their ability to think creatively and act strategically about how to organize and allocate limited resources.

Determining priorities is always a critical issue in developing school budgets. Reaching consensus with stakeholders about the most important resource allocation targets is difficult and highly political. Despite the incentive of adopting an incremental approach to ease competing tensions—by increasing all prior budgets by a given percentage, for example—the realities of reduced monies available, emerging instructional practices, new technologies, and students' needs make discussions about "who gets more and who gets less (or nothing)?" inevitable. The school context, the variations in any particular improvement strategy, the motivations present in the leadership team and faculty, and the need to adapt strategies to fit specific circumstances and limited funds all interact with the resources available to address learning improvement goals.

Amid these competing realities, principals and their school improvement teams can look for possible ways to reallocate available school resources in financial, human, and structural areas. Advocating for resource allocation possibilities is more than challenging a bureaucracy. It requires confronting a mind-set and possibly reshaping a school's culture. While "these barriers can loom large, . . . the biggest constraint may be the lack of vision about the concrete changes in school organization that can create a more professional organization and improve student achievement."[16]

Types of Resources

Basically, school leaders have three categories of resources: fiscal, human, and structural. Fiscal resources typically become available in annual cycles and determine both the amount of money available and the purposes for which it will be used. No one level of the education system has complete control of the flow, distribution, and expenditure of funds. Human capital (people) is hired with the allocated funds to do the education system's work. They bring different levels of motivation and expertise developed during years of training and experience. Structural resources (especially time use) apportion hours within the day and across the year in specific rooms and spaces to maximize the time spent on quality instruction with people assigned to tasks within time blocks to accomplish certain goals. These resources are intimately linked together, each affecting the others, and depending on the others to achieve their intended purposes.[17]

Educational leaders can critically examine the equity, efficiency, and effectiveness of existing resource allocation policies and practices and make decisions regarding ways that resources might be more productively assigned.

Money Resources. Leaders are increasingly pressed to obtain more revenue to expand school programs, obtain essential instructional materials and technologies, finance necessary professional development, and compete for students and resources with private and charter schools. School funding formulas and school finance laws are highly complex topics, and it is not within this chapter's scope to discuss them here.[18] Nevertheless, principals must be able to conceptualize the broader range of school district funding and comprehend how school funding flows from district funding.

Allocated and sought funds. Primarily, schools receive financial resources in two different ways. The first sources are those funds provided annually by or through the school district. The initial allocation of these funds depends mainly on factors such as student enrollment; the students' socioeconomic levels; their ethnic and racial balance; sudden growth or declining enrollments; special needs students; and other factors related to student need that the district, the school, or the state determines to be important. For instance, schools facing rapid student growth may receive increased funding that allows the school to hire additional staff or increase its purchasing power. Schools may also receive extra funds to be used for free or reduced-price lunches as well as for student transportation to and from school.

The second funding source is from the school leader's initiative in seeking outside monies. This is accomplished by presenting the students' needs, the school's needs, or the leader's vision of what the additional finances would accomplish. These types of funds are typically sought from school/business partnerships, state or federal grants, or private foundations.

Regardless of how the funds are secured, their source and allocation purpose often dictate how these monies can be used. Schools have varying authority to allocate financial resources. These range from complete to little, depending upon the authority granted by the school district to the school's site-based decision-making team. Despite the degree of decentralized decision making, certain factors curb the availability of monies or dictate the areas in which they may or may not be spent. These limitations come from federal and state grants, employee agreements or contracts, case law, state and federal statute, organizational restrictions, and the schools' or districts' mission, goals, and objectives.

The effective school leader must know the permissible ways to spend the various funds allocated to the school. To ensure allowable expenditures, the principal should develop a system or model to provide a picture of where and how the financial resources can appropriately be used to accomplish the school's goals and objectives. Figure 9–3 suggests a model that the principal can use to conceptualize the factors that affect resource utilization.

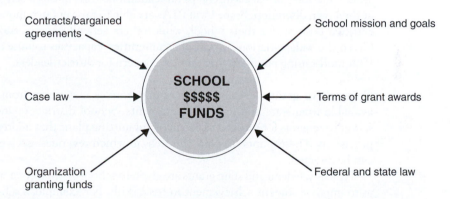

FIGURE 9–3
Forces Affecting the Utilization of School Funds (Source: Adapted from Norton, M. S., & Kelly, L. K. (1997). *Resource allocation: Managing money and people* (p. 28). Larchmont, NY: Eye on Education.)

Local and nonlocal funds. Funding sources are classified as either *local* or *nonlocal*. Local funds are generated by local (city, county, or state) taxation. Nonlocal funds are those received from the federal government. Nonlocal funds typically are allocated to districts and schools on the basis of a predetermined formula that considers such factors as the percentage of the student body receiving free or reduced-price lunches, a proxy for low family income. These entitlement funds remain available to schools as long as the providing legislation remains in force and the related monies are earmarked and distributed.

Nongovernmental funds.   Nongovernmental funding—from school-based fund-raising (often through the PTA), school business partnerships, not-for-profit organizations, and educational philanthropies—presents school leaders with important opportunities as well as potential constraints. Increasingly, district and school leaders are looking toward non-governmental revenue sources to provide extra learning opportunities for students and staff. Given chronic funding shortages, school leaders are under pressure to become more entrepreneurial and proactive in seeking financial support.

School-business partnerships and philanthropic aid to schools present leaders with a related set of allocation issues. While providing more flexible funding tied to specific local needs, they also have their own set of reporting requirements and political expectations for educational leaders to address and manage. In combination with each other or with existing school and district initiatives, school-business partnerships and philanthropic funding raise potentially competing sets of priorities for leaders' time and attention, the possibility of incoherence, and perhaps mixed messages for students. In some districts, school leaders may give up opportunities to bring in major new funding—even turning down millions of dollars—because these sources would distract from the learning improvement priorities to which the district has made long-term commitments.[19]

Nongovernmental funding also raises equity issues, since schools have differential access to such sources. For example, PTA fund-raising through formal fund-raising vendors, school auctions, or bake sales helps raise additional revenues for schools that can be used at their own discretion. Some local PTAs are able to raise enough money to hire a full-time certified position for their school, while others generate barely enough to break even. Given the wide variations in school communities' capacities to raise additional resources, PTA fund-raising poses another fairness concern for district leaders.

Competitive grants.   Additional funding reserves may come from competitive grants available from state and federal governments. School districts or individual schools respond to requests for proposals (RFPs) by submitting plans that address the specific fund's provisions. These grants stipulate the areas in which revenues received through the grant can be directed.

Typically, federal and state grants are given to school districts for a specific purpose, such as to improve student achievement in basic skills. For example, a school or district might be awarded a competitive grant that provides specifically for hiring additional staff to coordinate and provide training to teachers, hiring instructional aides and purchasing supplies needed for training, or acquiring instructional equipment to be used as part of the training. Recently, "Race-to-the-Top" federal grants have used financial incentives to initiate educational reforms, awarding monies to states whose schools develop processes to improve teacher and principal evaluation systems, link educator evaluation with student achievement, and remove legislative "caps" on charter schools, for example. Typically, grants have criteria that restrict how their funds can be spent, and schools are legally accountable for spending the monies in these ways.

Funds received through competitive grants are usually available only for the grant duration or funding period, typically 1 year from the date of award, but monies may be available as long as 3 to 5 years. These resources are typically referred to as "soft" monies because the funding usually ends at the grant's termination period unless legislation renews the program. In that event, schools or districts may reapply.

Foundation funds.   Foundations and philanthropic organizations are often interested in particular types of projects or programs. They give money to schools or community groups that have programs that enhance or address those interests. As with competitive grants awarded by the federal government, foundation and philanthropic grants are competitive and are offered annually. Also similar to competitive grants, foundations set criteria for how their monies are allowed to be spent, and receiving organizations are accountable for spending these resources as designed and approved.

A recent innovation is for school districts to begin their own nonprofit educational foundations to aid schools with extra funding and community service support. Education foundations are privately operated, nonprofit organizations established to assist public schools. They qualify as charitable organizations. A public school foundation is designed to augment, supplement, or complement programs and activities that the school district currently provides. As of 2001, the United States had over 6,500 school foundations in 14,500 school districts,[20] each with its own board of directors and its own paid and/or volunteer staff. Most school foundations operate as independent entities, with no formal, legal relationship to the school district. Foundations' bylaws can specify whether the school board will participate in voting.

Educational foundations focus on three main activities: raising, handling, and redirecting money. Fund-raising pursuits might include art projects, athletic events, auctions for students' services, book and craft fairs, Christmas cards, calendars, yearbooks, and school symbols. Funds can be used for such purposes as grants to teachers and projects, scholarships, sabbaticals, and staff development. Initial funding sources include corporate aid projects and endowments, and the foundation must account for the use of funds. An annual audit assesses the way the funds were received and distributed. The school or the district affiliated with the foundation presents quarterly reports for the funds received. Such accountability helps the school, district, and foundation gain credibility with the donors and the community.

School–business partnership funds.   When the principal can generate sufficient local business interest, school–business partnerships provide funds for schools. Frequently, the request is for a cash donation to the school to be used for the specific purpose outlined in the principal's request. Sometimes, the organization may give schools a block grant that can be used as the school chooses, with no limitations on how monies are spent other than the program must be something for students. Principals may have a more direct influence on using resources developed through such business partnerships since the resources or services are provided to meet a specific need presented by the school.

Student activity funds.   Generated through the student activity program, student activity funds include gate receipts from athletic events and fine arts productions, revenues from club sales or projects, yearbook and class ring sales, or sales from the soft drink or fruit machines. Depending on the district policy, all or part of the student activity funds may be available to the building principal for use at the school. Many school districts require these funds to be used for students.

Facility rental funds.   Funds generated by rental of school buildings or facilities to outside organizations such as churches, local civic organizations, and service clubs provide another revenue source for principals. Again, depending on the school district policy, all or part of the facility rental funds may be available for use at the school.

Constraints on Money Resources. The fiscal context exerts significant restrictions on money resources available to school leaders. Both the school and district's financial health, and state and political conditions, contribute to this milieu. The fiscal context also includes school district budget practices, the previous year's financial decisions, the fixed or unanticipatable costs associated with the physical plant (building maintenance) or human resources (such as health care benefits), accountability demands for specific funds and system performance, labor agreement stipulations and the relationships between the school district and the education association, and conflicting expectations of parents and the general public. Each of these factors limits leadership actions and bars certain resource-related decisions that might be desirable in a learning-focused approach.

Costs are only one kind of resource allocation constraint. Various policies regulate what is available for leaders to allocate, how those resources can be used, and how to account for their use. For instance, policies govern how public education and school districts can generate revenues. The multiple layers of government and the overlapping authorities for making decisions about education may send mixed messages about how national, state, or local funds can be used, which may or may not coincide with actual local learning improvement priorities. Finally a focus on accountability directs leaders' attention to investments that appear to align most closely with how their schools will be judged.

Each of these conditions not only limits a leader's range of options or discretion in assigning resources but also contributes to multiple and often conflicting expectations among parents and the public about what schools should provide and how they should provide it. The result is complicated political territory in which learning-focused leaders must proceed carefully and strategically while taking these many factors into consideration.

Schools that have authority over their budgets are in a better position to sustain school improvement efforts because they can direct money to support priority goals and programs. If a school does not have adequate budget authority, it may need to seek funding outside the district or form partnerships to support its priority reform efforts.

To use financial resources wisely, schools should understand guidelines for combining various funding streams. Specifically, schools should be familiar with federal regulations that allow funds to be combined to support school improvement. For instance, schools might use their Title I and Title II funds to support professional development activities that increase teachers' knowledge and use of research-based practices for teaching reading. Combining funds is a good strategy for sustaining improvements because it allows money targeted for special programs to be redirected to support the school's overall academic priorities.

When discussing how resources can best be used at the school level, school leaders must know the limitations placed on the use of funds and what possibilities exist to use the funds creatively. Because states, school districts, and schools vary in many aspects of school finance and in their particular goals and objectives, the principal must carefully analyze the available resources, their sources and purposes, and how they might be used in light of the local situation. It is essential to become familiar with statutory limitations or mandates, district policies or procedures, and the language of any federal grants or organizational awards that affect funds usage.

People Resources.   People are among schools' most essential and expensive resources. Teachers are the adults who directly affect student learning. Teachers, teaching assistants, curriculum support personnel in the schools, and anyone directly related to teaching make up 53% of the average school district's budget.[21] Employee agreements or contracts dictate their salaries and fixed benefits. Likewise, the bargaining agreements between the various employee organizations often dictate how teachers may be used.

For example, the central office may allocate a specific number of teachers to the school based upon a projected number of students, using a negotiated pupil-to-teacher ratio in a variety of instructional or programmatic situations. Classroom size, the number of laboratory stations, or the amount of instructional equipment may determine the number of students and, in turn, the number of teachers required in a given classroom or program. The school leader must be aware of the specific staffing demands that the employee contract or agreement mandates and then determine how much if any salary funds remain that might be used at the leader's discretion.

Despite the assorted restrictions, schools may still have several options to reallocate these human resources to better support student learning. It might be possible to rethink the use of existing instructional resources—especially teachers, who are schools' most important and costly resource.

Table 9–2 divides school staff into six categories, with possible limitations on their use, their funding sources, and possible flexibility for resource allocation noted.[22]

As mentioned, some funding sources allow some flexibility in how the monies are used. In 1995, Title I legislation was changed to allow these funds to be applied to school-wide programs if a school's student population is at least 50% low income. As a result, Title I is one area over which schools have the most fiscal discretion. Similarly, special education dollars that come from local, state, and federal sources may be used to hire special education teachers with dual certification in learning disabilities and regular education to work in an inclusion model, effectively reducing class size and permitting more individual assistance for all pupils.[23] Likewise, the school may hire teachers with dual certification in English as a second language (ESL) and regular education, allowing the school to substitute one regular classroom and one ESL pullout classroom into two smaller sized regular classrooms where ESL students actually receive more rigorous, intensive, and individualized language arts instruction.

Not all people resources are contractual, however. Frequently, community members offer expertise or perspectives that can enrich the educators' views about school improvement issues. For example, bankers know of fiscal resources available for student incentives while architects and engineers can help with curriculum development, such as integrating AP physics and calculus on how to best develop real-world projects. The police chief or sheriff can provide useful suggestions about lighting the building properly to reduce vandalism and theft. Juvenile justice personnel can advise educators on how to work with the juvenile justice system and how educators can support rather than punish disruptive students. The chamber of commerce can help provide internships for students' career development and community service projects. Similarly, community members from different ethnic groups can provide a deeper understanding, appreciation, and use of the community's diverse cultural, social, and intellectual assets to make classroom learning more personally relevant, meaningful, and motivating for all students.

TABLE 9–2
School Staff Resource Possibilities and Limitations

School Staff and Possible Limitations	Funding Sources	Resource Allocation Possibilities
Classroom teachers: Teachers of the core curriculum. Teachers' contracts specify their salaries and fringe benefits. *Possible limitations:* Contracts, case law, and statutory law may dictate how or when a school may use its teachers.	*Funding:* Mainly from state and local equalization aid dollars.	*Limited possibilities:* These dollars may arrive as a lump sum to be spent as the school sees fit or may come with district directives either specifying or strongly suggesting how these monies should be spent.
Regular education specialists: Teachers of subjects outside the core curriculum, such as art, music, physical education, and library, who also provide planning and preparation time for classroom teachers. *Possible limitations:* Contracts, federal statute and state law, and case law may dictate how or when a school may use its teachers.	*Funding:* Mainly from state and local equalization aid dollars, as with classroom teachers.	*Limited possibilities:* These dollars may arrive as a lump sum to be spent as the school sees fit or may come with district directives either specifying or strongly suggesting how these monies should be spent.
Categorical program specialists: Teachers outside the regular education classroom whose salaries are paid largely by categorical program dollars, including special education, compensatory education (Title I), bilingual/ESL, and other programs for special needs students. *Possible limitations:* Legislative mandates on using teachers and monies.	*Funding:* Three funding sources: compensatory education funding (federal Title I) for remedial and resource assistance to low-income students, special education funding, and ESL funding.	*Greater possibilities:* Title I, special education funds, and ESL funds allow some flexibility in how schools use them.
Pupil support specialists: Professional staff who provide mainly nonacademic support services to students outside the regular education classroom, such as school counselors, psychologists, and nurses. *Possible limitations:* Contracts, case law, and statutory law may dictate how or when a school can use its pupil support specialists.	*Funding:* Most positions are funded with local dollars and are a small share of the school budget.	*Limited possibilities:* Schools may choose to reallocate money from a half-time nurse to a half-time Reading Recovery teacher, and schools implementing Success for All, which has a family liaison position as part of its design, can use pupil support positions already on staff to cover those functions.
Aides: Paraprofessional staff who provide either instructional support (including working one on one with children within the regular classroom and in resource rooms) or noninstructional support (including clerical tasks and supervising the cafeteria or playground). *Possible limitations:* Case and statutory law may dictate how or when a school can use its noncertified employees.	*Funding:* Same as classroom teachers.	*Possibilities:* Flexibility in assignment and responsibilities may exist if funded by a categorical program.
Other: Any other staff employed by the school, including clerical, cafeteria, and custodial workers. *Possible limitations:* Case law, the Fair Labor Standards Act, and statutory law may dictate how or when a school can use its noncertified employees.	*Funding:* Same as classroom teachers.	*Limited possibilities:* Clerical and custodial position funds do not comprise a large portion of the school budget, but they are a potential area for resource allocation, especially if fully computerized budgeting is a reality in the school.

Source: Based on from Odden, A., & Archibald, S. (2000, Spring). Reallocating resources to support higher student achievement: An empirical look at five sites. *Journal of Education Finance, 25*(4), 545–564. Used by permission.

Time Resources.   School structures tend to include "rule of thumb" practices that mask possibilities for resource reallocations. Most of these relate to time (and space requirements) and how the schools integrate it into the school day to accomplish various functions. Emerging instructional leadership practices focus on at least these areas: reallocating and rearranging time for instruction, making time for teachers' collaboration and professional development, expanding time to improve students' learning, and guiding time use to a learning agenda.[24]

Reallocating and rearranging time for instruction and other interactions with students.   This includes strategies to reallocate or refocus instructional time including block scheduling, literacy blocks, team teaching, and interdisciplinary teaching.

◆ *Ending "pullouts."* One example of reallocating time and space is by ending pullout programs. These are educational activities outside the regular classroom with student populations in categorical programs such as special education, Title I compensatory education, bilingual education, and remedial or gifted education. Most of these programs operate under federal, state, or district regulations and sometimes collective bargaining agreements that prescribe how to use teachers and how to group students. Pullout programs are extremely costly, they segregate students in sometimes stigmatizing ways, and their fragmentation and lack of connection to the students' classroom experiences often leads to ineffective services and poor learning outcomes.[25] Funds and other resources that would normally support pullout programs can be used to reduce adult-to-student ratios by adding staff to the regular classrooms or by hiring more full-time regular classroom teachers. Schools rethinking resources might consider how remedial, special education, Title I, and bilingual education resources could work together in an integrated plan (in accordance with IEPs) to benefit all students in "regular education" settings with additional supports.

◆ *Rescheduling high schools.* Time and space are particularly wasted resources in high schools. High school academic tracking, schedules with many short periods (45–50 minutes long), and teacher and subject specialization compound the problems. Five classes of 25 to 30 students each give most secondary teachers student loads of 125 to 150 students per day (or every 2 days for four alternating classes). Schools can reduce teaching loads without dramatically increasing costs by reducing the number of different groups teachers teach. Methods of "creating" this time include alternating days of courses, having fewer courses per semester/trimester, or allotting more time to core academics than to elective classes. Extra time can also be gained by combining traditionally separate subject areas (such as English and history, math and science), lengthening the class durations (from 45 to 90 minutes in a four-course day), or having small groups of students work intensively with teachers in a smaller number of subjects.

Research suggests that allocating longer and varied blocks of time to a given subject area can enhance student achievement by allowing for more flexibility in instructional approaches.[26] Managing time in ways that support the school's goals for the long term is an important task that may require new ways of thinking about schedules and about where and in what formats the most effective learning can take place.

Making time for collaboration and professional learning related to learning improvement goals.   Although most school time is spent working directly with students, educators need time to pursue skill development and conduct collaborative planning and learning that will allow them to do a better job of instructing students and meeting diverse needs in the classroom.

◆ *Rescheduling noninstructional time.* Most schools currently provide teachers with short periods of time free from instructional duties while other classroom teachers instruct their students. For instance, elementary teachers may have a 34-minute duty-free period daily while their students attend art, physical education, or music classes. Secondary teachers may teach five of seven instructional periods during the day, using one period for planning and the other for a duty assignment (lunchroom, study hall, monitoring hallways) while their students are taking other courses. These short blocks of individual noninstructional time do not allow much opportunity for substantive planning or collaboration.

Alternatively, a restructured schedule could mean arranging teachers' planning periods in conjunction with noninstructional time (e.g., adjacent to lunch or before or after school) or creating early-release days. Students' schedules can be adjusted to provide time for teacher learning. For instance, a certain time of the day or day of the week can be designated for students to volunteer in the community, take college courses, or conduct study or peer-tutoring sessions. Allocating time for collaborative planning and professional development energizes staff around shared goals for improvement and prevents situations in which teachers are donating large amounts of their personal time to school reform efforts.

◆ *Rethinking workday requirements and job descriptions.* Similarly, inflexible teacher workday requirements and job descriptions provide a focus for rethinking resource allocations. Most teacher contracts specify the required hours of work, starting and ending times, and how teachers can be assigned throughout the day. This limits the use of teachers as resources, making it difficult to stagger starting times to make the best use of staff time or to meet student needs more fully. The contract may also require that planning time be spread out over the day, making it difficult to combine instruction-free periods to create longer shared blocks of time. Other contract specifics may forbid hiring of part-time teachers if they substitute for potential full-time positions, making it difficult for schools to provide affordable coverage for teachers' noninstructional time. Rethinking and renegotiating these rules to better support teachers and students may benefit both groups.

Expanding time available for learning improvement activities.   Three time-related resource allocation strategies expand the amount of time for students who fall short of meeting academic standards: tutoring, an extended day, and summer school programs.

◆ *Tutoring.* Individual one-on-one tutoring has been shown to be a very effective form of instruction. Unlike classroom teaching, tutors have the opportunity to pursue a given topic or problem until the students have mastered it. As a result, one-on-one tutored students gain greater understanding, are more motivated, and work faster.[27] Studies have found that the average student in a tutoring situation achieves a performance gain ranging from 0.4 to 2.3 standard deviations above the average student in a traditional transmission-based classroom.[28] An added bonus: tutors also gain greater mastery in the subject matter that they tutor.[29] Tutoring has been found to be effective despite the fact that tutors often do not have formal training in tutoring skills although they do have mastery of the content knowledge.[30]

◆ *Extended day*. Extended-day learning strategies have been found to be effective in increasing elementary grade students' reading and math achievement among at-risk students.[31] Research results on preschool, Head Start, and full-day kindergarten (as compared with half-day) are mixed. Several studies show immediate strong language and IQ effects which become undetectable by second and third grades[32] while other studies find positive long-term effects including high school graduation, reduced delinquency,[33] and reduced special education referrals.[34] Extended time using tutoring or computer-assisted teaching as a supplement to classroom instruction shows evidence of effectiveness.[35] Some suggest that an extra 35 days would be needed to produce a noticeable change in student achievement however.[36] It is important to note that the increased time in school—or a longer school year—will not automatically increase student achievement unless students receive effective instructional delivery.

◆ *Summer school*. Summer programs are an effective intervention for academic remediation, enrichment, or acceleration. One research meta-analysis found that summer learning loss equals at least 1 month of instruction as measured by grade level equivalents on standardized test scores, especially for math facts and spelling.[37] Disadvantaged children show the greatest losses. Another meta-analysis found that summer programs focusing on remedial, accelerated, or enriched learning have a positive impact on the participants' knowledge and skills. Students from middle-class homes showed larger positive effects than students from disadvantaged homes.[38] For remedial programs, larger effects occur when the program is relatively small and uses individualized instruction. Requiring parent involvement also appears related to more effective outcomes. While students in all grades benefit from remedial summer school, students in the earliest grades and in secondary school may benefit the most.[39]

Guiding the use of restructured time toward a learning improvement agenda.   While the amount of time educators can spend working is endless, there is no guarantee that time allotted for professional development, collaboration, or block scheduling will be used effectively.

◆ *Focus on learning*. Time is a necessary but not sufficient condition for increased student learning. Leaders must have various tools to guide and direct how time is used and to motivate participants to use time in these ways. Leadership that *shows*, rather than *tells*, staff what to do with their time and then supports and reinforces those activities on an ongoing basis is more likely to advance learning improvement goals.

Challenging Assumptions and Practices

Schools' assumptions and practices sometimes waste money, people, and time resources. Schools expect students to move through school in even, uniform rates, and formula-driven student assignments systematically disperse students to classrooms by age, subject, and program.

These actions are costly because the uneven allocation of teachers over grades, small programs, and low-enrollment subjects contributes to unplanned differences in class sizes that do not reflect sound educational strategies. For instance, if a school district caps class enrollment at 28 students and requires a new teacher be added for the 29th student, class size averages can fall dramatically from 28 to 14.5 students per teacher if there are two teachers per grade. The more separate programs and subjects a school has and the more age grading or tracking constraints, the more unplanned and costly variations in resource allocations occur. These student assignment practices merit rethinking to see whether multiage or multiability grouping, or matching instructional resources and strategies to students' needs rather than to standard classifications, can be more effective uses for both students and teacher time.

Changing school organizations to better fit an instructional vision will require schools to confront tradition and an array of state, district, and union policies and practices. Waivers from meeting regulations may need to be sought. Many high-performing schools successfully confront traditional structures and gain valuable resource allocation opportunities that benefit their teachers and students.

Reallocating Teaching and Time Resources

Flexibly and realistically thinking about reallocating teaching and time resources can lead to student achievement gains. In a study of high-performing schools, Miles and Darling-Hammond (1998) found that the school leadership successfully reallocated the structural resources of teaching assignments and time to improve student achievement by using the following six principles:[40]

◆ Reducing specialized programs to provide more individual time for all in heterogeneous groups;
◆ Providing more flexible student grouping;
◆ Creating structures that offer more personalized environments;
◆ Providing longer and varied blocks of instructional time;
◆ Scheduling more common planning time for staff; and
◆ Creatively defining staff rules and work schedules.

Schools might also consider assigning staff in ways that limit class size in particular target areas. For instance, if literacy is a high priority for school improvement efforts, the number of students per reading group or in other literacy activities could be reduced while maintaining larger grouping in other subjects, such as physical education. Larger classes in those areas usually allow one specialist teacher to cover preparation time for several regular teachers.

Making these changes can create opportunities for realigning teaching resources to school goals. Table 9–3 shows what schools stand to gain by implementing these resource allocation principles and identifies how schools can assess their impact. Altering one practice alone, however, may not free enough resources to significantly change the possibilities for student or teacher learning.

What Effective Resource Allocation Looks Like

Effecting and maintaining successful school programs requires having access to adequate resources directed properly. Table 9–4 illustrates a continuum of how schools can apply more or less effective strategies to assess the adequacy of their resource allocation process.

TABLE 9–3
Expected Impact on Resources of Staff Allocation Changes

Resource Allocation Principles	Expected Impact on Resources	School Measure
Reduction of specialized programs to create more individual time for all students	Smaller sized regular education instructional groups	Students per teacher
	More even distribution of resources between regular and special program students	Average size of regular education instructional groups
		Percentage teachers in regular instructional groups
More flexible student grouping by school professionals	Smaller instructional groups in focus areas	Percentage students in target regular education size groups
	Less unplanned variation in class sizes	Average size of group in focus area
Structures to support more teacher-student relationships	Lower teacher student loads	Teacher student loads per day
	More adults involved in instruction	Percentage adult instructors/advisors
	Smaller teams of teachers and students	Size of teacher/student clusters
	Multiyear relationships between students and teachers	Length of student/teacher relationship
Longer and more varied blocks of instructional time	Longer instructional periods for academic subjects	Average length of instructional period for academic subjects
More common planning time	More minutes of common planning	Common planning minutes/week
	Longer periods of time for planning	Length of longest planning period
Creative definition of staffing roles and workday	Use of part-time or contract staff	Job descriptions
	Use of interns or paraprofessionals for instruction	School schedules
	Staggered work schedules	

Source: Adapted from Miles, K., & Darling-Hammond, L., "Rethinking the allocation of teaching resources: Some lessons from high-performing schools," *Educational Evaluation and Policy Analysis, 20*(1), p. 15, copyright © 1998. Reprinted by Permission of SAGE Publications.

Allocating Resources Fairly and Wisely

Once schools receive adequate resources, their job is to spend them on the most effective educational strategies. This does not always happen. Education finance professor Allan Odden and his colleagues have studied how school districts use their education dollars. Their findings: While a considerable national investment in public education occurred during the late 20th and early 21st centuries, the funds have been distributed unfairly and used ineffectively.[41]

Contrary to popular belief, the data also show that administration and teacher salary costs are not to blame for education dollars' low productivity. Instead, Odden and colleagues pointed to poor resource allocation decisions for education funds' low impact on student achievement: faulty resource distribution, unimaginative use of money, a bureaucratic approach to spending, failure to focus on results, concentration on services rather than outcomes, and other practices that drive up costs without improving student achievement.[42]

First legislators and then administrators distribute their educational funds unequally across states, districts, schools, and students, sometimes varying as much as three to one

TABLE 9–4
Resource Allocation Continuum

Least Effective	Somewhat Effective	Most Effective
Money Resources		
The school makes some decisions about how to allocate funds in support of school improvement goals. Staff members seek new sources of funding or other support only as necessary.	The school has control over a portion of its budget. The school combines and directs some funds from different sources in support of the school's goals. Staff members regularly seek new funding sources and other support to supplement existing resources.	The school has control over most of its budget. To the extent possible, all funds from different sources are combined and directed in support of the school's goals. Staff members actively and systematically seek new funding sources and partnerships with businesses and community organizations. The school regularly reviews and evaluates resources, including current partnerships to ensure that they are used efficiently.
People Resources		
Staff positions are a mix of academic, noninstructional, and specialized positions, which may not efficiently support school improvement goals and priorities.	The majority of staff positions are focused on full-time instruction and areas that fall under the school's academic goals and priorities. The district invests in leadership development. The district develops alternative compensation systems and incentive, merit/performance pay. Greater school discretion in hiring. Expanded systems of novice teacher support. The school redirects teachers' work with special needs students.	The district reallocates staff to schools to address inequities. All staff positions are focused on full-time instruction and areas that fall under the school's academic goals and priorities. Greater use of accomplished National Board of Professional Teaching Standards (NBPTS) teachers. Adult-to-student ratios may change depending on the specific academic area and related goals. Retention strategies are designed to minimize staff turnover.
Time Resources		
Common planning or professional development events are not part of school scheduling. They rarely take place during the school day.	School schedules are arranged to provide some job-embedded time for common planning and professional development.	Restructuring school schedules provides appropriate time for job-embedded common planning and professional development. Restructuring the school day (e.g., block scheduling, team time blocks) and varying class length provides students with more time for meaningful instruction in core academics.

Source: From Sustaining School Improvement Resource Allocation, www.mcrel.org. Reprinted by permission of Mid-Continent Research for Education in Learning (McREL).

across states, and even greater across districts within states[43] and substantially across schools within districts.[44] In addition, mechanisms for disbursing education dollars often provide more money to socioeconomically advantaged and higher achieving areas.[45]

Next, districts and schools often use education dollars unproductively, not in ways that directly raise student achievement. Using increased revenues to hire more teachers to reduce class size or provide more out-of-classroom services does not substantially boost student achievement.[46] Those monies used to increase teachers' salaries have not been used strategically to enhance teacher professional expertise.[47] And those funds used to expand services for special education students show little evidence of having boosted learning.[48] Similarly, states undergoing school finance reform showed relatively few dollars assigned to improve the regular school program, choosing instead to construct and improve facilities, buy books and supplies, and fund health and social services before addressing central educational issues.[49]

Odden and others have identified additional unproductive uses of school funds, including spending on a bureaucratic array of noninstructional professionals who do not teach academic subjects,[50] not using clear and high goals and standards to drive student achievement, not using test feedback to improve teaching and learning,[51] directing monies toward related services (such as student nutrition or parent involvement) rather than at direct education services,[52] and further expensive practices such as spending for adding new staff for each new categorical program, reducing teacher loads, or lowering class sizes.[53]

Well-targeted fiscal investments in teaching and learning can make a measurable difference, however. Although research on the relationship between spending and student achievement is often mixed and occasionally contradictory, several observers have noted that such gains are unlikely to be achieved without purposeful links between school practices and classroom activities.[54] Laine, Greenwald, and Hedges (1996) concluded that "school resources are systematically related to student achievement and that these relations are large enough to be educationally important" (p. 57).[55] Likewise, Verstegen and King's (1998) meta-analysis of 35 years of data found that teacher characteristics, class size, and classroom resources all positively influence student achievement,[56] while Smith (2004),[57] Archibald (2006),[58] and Grubb (2006) have concluded that increased spending in instructional areas appears to positively affect student achievement.[59]

Likewise, research has identified positive impacts on student achievement from spending in areas including increased course taking in rigorous academic subjects,[60] high-level academic instruction for all students and minimizing the amount of time students spend in lower level classes or electives,[61] organization and management (distributive decision making and shared responsibility with facilitative principal leadership), improving high-poverty schools, changing state school finance structures, restructuring teacher compensation (from a single salary scale based on experience and educational units to direct professional measures of teachers' knowledge and skill and to the norms and goals of standards-driven education reform),[62] and providing effective professional development.[63]

Together, these varied findings suggest that improved fiscal management of current resources, rather than increased funding, is necessary to improve student achievement.[64]

Fair and wise resource allocation and classroom-specific expenditures can positively affect educational outcomes. Also, these data imply that by and large, school administrators and teachers do not know how to appropriately target and use school funds to increase student learning.

ACTIVITY 9.4   Making Wise Resource Allocation Decisions to Improve Student Learning and Achievement

1. What school improvement strategies using fiscal, people, and time resources might Allan and his leadership team consider to improve teaching and learning for Manhasset High School's neediest students?
2. Which strategies appear to have the best research support for their effectiveness?
3. Which of these strategies probably require securing central office permission?
4. How do these additional resource allocation strategies address the four key allocation issues (targeting achievement gaps, organizing schools and districts to align resources with learning improvement agendas, managing the politics of learning-focused leadership, and developing human capital)?
5. Where does each of these strategies fall on Table 9–4: Resource Allocation Continuum?

RESEARCH SUPPORTING RESOURCE ALLOCATION THAT IMPACTS STUDENT ACHIEVEMENT[65]

Shrewdly directed money matters when it comes to education. Principals and school improvement teams want to allocate their resources fairly and wisely to those areas that research and best practice support as having measurable payoffs for student achievement. Investments in the following critical areas lead to student learning gains:

- Teacher quality
- Teacher salaries
- Reduced class size[66]
- School size
- Professional development
- School facilities

Teacher Quality

Educational research shows widespread agreement that the quality and effectiveness of the classroom teacher makes a measurable difference in student learning outcomes. Research continues to confirm that the classroom teacher—in preparation, personal characteristics, and instructional practices—is the most important school factor in predicting student achievement.

We know what constitutes good teaching, and we know that good teaching can matter more than students' family backgrounds and economic status in terms of student achievement. Linda Darling-Hammond, Stanford University education professor, observed that teacher quality variables such as full certification and completing a major in the teaching field are more important to student outcomes in reading and math than are student demographic variables such as poverty, minority status, and language background.[67]

Specifically, Darling-Hammond (2000) identified the following teacher quality factors related to student achievement:[68]

◆ Verbal ability
◆ Content knowledge
◆ Education methods coursework related to their discipline
◆ Licensing exam scores that measure basic skills and teaching knowledge
◆ Skillful teaching behaviors
◆ Ongoing professional development
◆ Enthusiasm for teaching
◆ Flexibility, creativity, and adaptability
◆ Teaching experience
◆ Asking higher order questions (application, analysis, synthesis, evaluation as opposed to recognition and recall questions) and probing student responses

Principals and interview teams should look for these personal and classroom skills when conducting their teacher candidate interviews, reviewing position applicants' portfolios, and observing their demonstration lessons.

Teaching Effectiveness and Student Achievement.   Conventional wisdom has long held that family backgrounds and economic status are the primary and largely exclusive determiners of students' learning. In the 20th century's last decade, researchers found that aside from a well-articulated curriculum and a safe and orderly environment, the individual teacher is the single most influential school factor in students' achievement—an effect relatively independent of anything else that occurs in the school. Consistently working with highly effective teachers can overcome the academic limitations placed on students by their family backgrounds. Hanushek (1992) found that all things being equal, a student with a very high-quality teacher will achieve a learning gain of 1.5 grade level equivalents, while a student with a low-quality teacher achieves a gain of only 0.5 grade level equivalents. A teacher's effectiveness can make the difference of a full year's learning growth.[69] In fact, educators and policy makers widely agree that a clear predictive relationship exists between teachers' basic skills, especially verbal ability, and student achievement.[70]

Researchers William Sanders and colleagues in Tennessee and William Webster and colleagues in Texas provided data from two different states that strongly affirm this. Working separately, they determined that 3 consecutive years with effective versus ineffective teachers can make students' achievement appear to be either gifted or remedial, respectively.[71] The cumulative impact over 3 years of effective elementary teachers is estimated to produce (on a 100-point scale) a 35-point difference in reading and more than a 50-point difference in math on standardized tests.[72]

Sanders and colleagues observed that the individual classroom teacher is the essential factor in whether and how much students learn.[73] After analyzing the achievement scores of more than 100,000 students across hundreds of schools, they concluded that more could be done to improve education by improving teachers' effectiveness than by any other single factor.

In addition, effective teachers appeared to be successful with students of all achievement levels, regardless of the degree of heterogeneity in their classrooms. On the other hand, if the teacher is ineffective, students working with that teacher will show inadequate academic progress, regardless of how similar or different they are in their academic achievement.[74] What their teachers know and do can be more important influences on student achievement than family characteristics and ethnicity.

One noteworthy 2004 study looked at teacher effectiveness in K–3 elementary school grades. The 4-year experimental study randomly assigned students to classes controlled for students' previous achievement, socioeconomic status, ethnicity, gender, class size, and whether an aide was present in class. As illustrated in Table 9–5, investigators found that students who have a teacher at the 75th percentile of pedagogical competence (an effective teacher) will outgain students who have a teacher at the 25th percentile (not so effective teacher) by 14 percentile points in reading and 18 percentile points in mathematics. Similarly, students who have a 90th percentile teacher (a very effective teacher) will outgain students who have a 50th percentile teacher (an average teacher) by 13 percentile points in reading and 18 percentile points in mathematics.[75] The more effective the teacher, the more the students' learning and measured achievement increases.

TABLE 9–5
Teacher Effectiveness and Student Achievement Comparisons

Student Achievement	Teacher Effectiveness			
	25th Percentile (Not effective)	75th Percentile (Effective)	50th Percentile (Average)	90th Percentile (Very effective)
Reading achievement	—	+14 percentile points	—	+13 percentile points
Mathematics achievement	—	+18 percentile points	—	+18 percentile points

Source: Based on: Nye, B., Konstantopoulos, S., & Hedges, L. V. (2004). How large are teacher effects? *Educational Evaluation and Policy Analysis, 26*(3), 237–257.

Teachers who learn and practice sound instructional techniques can affect students' measured achievement. A 1996 National Assessment of Educational Progress (NAEP) study found that students of teachers who conducted hands-on learning activities outperformed their peers by more than 70% of a grade level in math and 40% of a grade level in science. In addition, students whose teachers had strong content knowledge and who had learned the professional skills needed to work with pupils from different cultures or with special needs tested more than one full grade level above their peers. Students whose math teachers stressed critical thinking skills, such as writing about math, scored 39% of a grade level higher. What is more, "the aspects of teaching quality measured have an impact seven to 10 times as great as that of class size" in affecting student achievement.[76]

Educators and policy makers also agree that teachers' content knowledge affects student achievement. On the 1996 NAEP, students whose teachers had college majors or minors in the subjects they taught—especially in secondary math and science—outperformed students whose teachers lacked this content knowledge by about 40% of a grade level in each subject.[77] Similarly, evidence suggests that teacher content knowledge in English and social studies may be no less important.[78]

Teacher Preparation and Student Achievement.   Credible research shows that teachers' instructional preparation increases student achievement. Darling-Hammond (2000) found teacher preparation to be a stronger correlate of student achievement than class size, overall spending, or teacher salaries and accounts for 40% to 60% of the total achievement differences after considering students' ethnicity and family wealth.[79]

Sometimes, teacher education coursework is more important than extra subject matter classes in advancing students' math and science achievement.[80] Nonetheless, education classes do have a point of diminishing returns. Several studies have concluded that teachers with advanced subject matter degrees, rather than advanced education degrees, have students who perform better in math and reading. This is especially true after elementary school as students need a deeper and more complex understanding of increasingly complex content.[81]

Professional preparation includes classroom management skills. Teachers who cannot effectively manage their classrooms have students who learn less than their peers. Research suggests that teachers who lack classroom management skills, regardless of how much content they know, cannot create a classroom environment that supports student learning. A study of the impact of teachers' different disciplinary practices on student achievement found that student classroom disorder results in lower achievement.[82]

Teacher Quality and Equity.   Effective teachers are not evenly distributed across schools. Too often, schools serving children in poverty have lower teacher retention, less experienced staff, and higher percentages of teachers who lack the preparation and expertise necessary for their teaching assignment.[83] Leaders at state, district, and school levels struggle with ways to reduce these inequities so that all students have the teachers they need and all schools are productive learning environments that support high-quality teachers and teaching.

Some of the emerging strategies to remedy these disparities include alterations to teacher compensation systems that reward performance or provide differential pay for particular knowledge and skill sets or for working in high-challenge schools.[84] Other ideas include reorganizing time in the school day for teachers to collaborate and participate in professional learning and reallocating staffing to accomplish particular improvement strategies, such as reducing class size in targeted grades or subject areas.[85] Each of these emerging strategies involves making decisions about how to allocate money, people, and time.

Teacher Quality and Certification.   Teacher quality standards are extremely complex, reflecting "the wide range of knowledge, skills, abilities, and dispositions that contemporary educators believe competent teachers must possess and demonstrate in the classroom."[86] While researchers tend to agree that teacher quality is an important factor influencing student outcomes, disagreement exists about the relationship between specific teacher credentials (such as experience, degree level, and certification status) and characteristics (such as age, race, and ethnicity) and teacher effectiveness. This topic is effectively discussed elsewhere.[87]

Nevertheless, the recent studies on teacher certification and student achievement are bringing a fuller understanding closer. Overall, the teacher certification evidence suggests that existing credentialing systems do not distinguish very well between effective and ineffective teachers. Wide variation in teacher effectiveness exists within each certification type, with effective teachers coming from both traditional and nontraditional certification routes (including New York City Teaching Fellows, Teach for America, and Troops to Teachers).[88]

Additionally, research has found that teacher experience, rather than type of certification, tends to make a difference in increasing student achievement. Many studies document the improvement of student achievement with increases in teacher experience during the first 3 to 5 years in the classroom with virtually no additional gains for experience beyond the first 5 years.[89]

Limitations in the Research. As with all research, methodological weaknesses suggest caution in interpreting the data. Teachers are not randomly assigned to classes within schools. The most experienced, credentialed, and respected teachers usually receive assignments to upper level and advanced courses. School culture, parents, and students expect mature educators with advanced degrees and considerable classroom experience to teach these high-status, intellectually rigorous classes. Likewise, students cannot ethically be transferred from one teacher's classroom to another simply to provide the random conditions needed for an empirical study. Then too, some teacher quality studies use highly sophisticated "value-added" statistical models that estimate student gains and contribute their own technical limitations. Therefore, while recognizing the methodology weaknesses in the research findings is important, the reality that excellent teaching practices can make a tremendous difference in student learning deserves serious attention.

In sum, the data supporting the impact of effective teaching practices on student achievement are credible and substantial. Both evidence and experience show that effective teaching requires content knowledge and a set of professional practices different from but connected to the content taught. While the content knowledge is unarguably essential, knowing *how* to teach content makes a measurable impact on student achievement, and that may come from several years of successful teaching experience regardless of the path to certification.

Teacher Salaries

The issues of teacher salaries, teacher quality, and student achievement are connected. The more experienced teachers tend to generate more student learning. It is difficult, however, to link empirical evidence of increased teacher effectiveness with higher teacher salaries because traditionally, most school districts have salary schedules based on years of experience and earned academic degrees rather than on student achievement.

In addition, children in the highest poverty schools are assigned to lower salaried novice teachers almost twice as often as students in low-poverty schools.[90] Until 2002's No Child

Left Behind law required teachers to have bachelor's degrees in the subjects they were teaching, poor and minority students were more likely to have out-of-field teachers without majors or minors in the subjects they taught than were students in low-poverty schools.[91] It can be argued that, in part, low urban students' test scores may reflect their teachers' instructional inexperience because the schools lack the funds and other resources to attract more experienced, higher paid, and more effective educators.[92] And, as already discussed, research consistently affirms the relationship between teacher quality factors and student achievement.

Can increased teacher salaries make a difference in increased student achievement? Perhaps. It is logical to assume that increased salaries will expand the potential teacher applicant pool. A basic capitalistic and free market economy tenet is that higher wages attract more individuals seeking those jobs. If teachers' salaries increase, a larger applicant pool will seek teaching careers. An expanded applicant pool will include more individuals with higher levels of identified teacher quality factors. Indeed, the Teaching Commission, a nonprofit group formed in 2003 to improve teaching, has recommended raising base salaries to make teachers' pay more competitive and attract higher quality teachers.[93] More recently, the National Board for Professional Teaching Standards developed financial and other professional incentives to encourage their board-certified teachers to work in low-performing, urban schools.[94]

Class Size

Pupil-to-teacher ratios have dropped substantially over the past century. The pupil-to-teacher ratio declined from 35:1 in 1890, to 28:1 in 1940, to 24.9:1 in 1960, to 20.5:1 in 1970, to 15.4:1 in 1990[95] and increased slightly to 16.4: in 2000-2001, then declined to 15.7:1 in 2007-2008.[96] The ratios were higher or lower, depending on the grade level and school size. Reasons for this overall reduction include hiring more teachers to serve increasingly diverse students as a result of court-mandated desegregation,[97] the rising enrollments of special needs students who require teachers with specialized training and a smaller student-to-teacher ratio,[98] and recognizing that better learning occurs in classes with fewer than 30 to 40 students.[99] In addition, the pupil-to-staff ratios dropped as schools attempted to add a modest amount of time for teachers to collaborate with colleagues and to obtain professional development during the school day.[100]

The impact of class size has been studied for many years. Tennessee's successfully designed and managed experiments of class size reduction in primary grades showed positive results. The student-to-teacher achievement ratio, or STAR program, involved more than 12,000 students over 4 years. This highly controlled longitudinal study indicated that attending small classes for 3 consecutive years in grades K–3 is associated with sustained academic benefits in all school subjects through grade 8.[101] A California study had similar results.[102]

A review and synthesis of more than 100 class-size studies suggest that the most positive effect of small classes appears in kindergarten to third grade for mathematics and reading.[103] Researchers widely believe that student achievement increases as class size reduces from 30 to 16 students.[104] Although shrinking the number of students in a class can lead to higher test scores overall, it might not necessarily reduce the achievement gaps that exist between students in a given classroom.[105]

In reducing class size, it is essential to remember teacher effectiveness. Reducing class size without simultaneously improving the quality and effectiveness of what teachers do in the classroom to help all students learn to high levels is both expensive and unproductive. Even those who disagree over the research's implications agree that more scientific studies on class size are necessary.[106]

School Size

School size has a measurable impact on student outcomes. In 1987, after reviewing several studies, two researchers concluded that high schools should have no more than 250 students. Larger enrollments focused too much administrators' attention on control and order, harming the school climate. Additionally, the larger school population increased members' feelings of anonymity, making it more difficult to build a sense of community among students, teachers, and parents.[107] For instance, a 1994 study of 34 large New York City high schools found that when students are organized into "houses" of approximately 250 students, attendance improves, student responsiveness in school increases, and grades go up.[108]

Likewise, research has suggested that small and moderate size high schools foster more positive social and academic environments than large high schools. This is especially true for economically disadvantaged students.[109] Other research suggested that students in very small high schools learn less than students in moderate size (600–900 students) high schools. Learning also drops as schools grow in size. Achievement decreases considerably in high schools with more than 2,100 students.[110] This may be explained, in part, by the larger teacher-to-student ratio in high schools of 1,500 or more, which reported 18.2:1 as compared with a 12.0:1 ratio in secondary schools under 300 students. [111]

In contrast, another study observed that smaller is not automatically better when it comes to increasing student achievement. A 2008 federal study of high schools receiving grants to support forming smaller student learning communities found that when the proportion of students being promoted from 9th grade to 10th grade increases, extracurricular participation rises, and the rate of violent incidents declines. The evaluation, however, detected "no significant trends" in achievement on college entrance exams.[112] A similar study in Chicago concluded that while smaller schools have a more collegial, trusting, and innovative environment, this does not necessarily translate into instructional and curricular reform.[113]

Community affluence plays a role in school effectiveness, too. Studies show that more affluent communities have effective student learning even with larger schools, while schools in low socioeconomic neighborhoods or schools with high concentrations of minority students needed smaller schools to provide the most learning opportunities for their students.[114]

Similarly, a 2002 study by Ohio researchers for the Rural School and Community Trust found in a seven-state study that smaller schools reduce the harmful effects of poverty on student achievement. Smaller schools also help students from less affluent communities narrow the academic achievement gap between themselves and students from wealthier communities.[115]

Cost-effectiveness is another consideration of school size. A 2000 study of more than 140 schools and 50,000 students in the New York City Public Schools found that small academic high schools have budgets per graduate similar to those of large high schools (greater than 2,000 students). Smaller high schools have smaller dropout rates. Although smaller schools are more expensive to operate on a *per-pupil* basis, smaller schools can be more efficient when measured on a *cost-per-graduate* basis. Cost effectiveness is a relative term. Researchers concluded that both small and large schools are cost-effective when looking at graduates as the outcome.[116] Considering that high school dropouts also bring substantial costs, including lower earnings, higher unemployment rates, greater reliance on welfare, and increased incarceration rates, small schools seem more cost-effective.[117]

An Education Commission of the States (ECS) report details the benefits of reduced school size and draws five conclusions:[118]

◆ Under the right conditions, as schools get smaller, they produce stronger student performance as measured by attendance rates, test scores, extracurricular activity participation, and graduation rates.
◆ Smaller schools appear to promote greater levels of parent participation and satisfaction, and increase parent-teacher communications.
◆ Teachers in small schools generally feel they are in a better position to make a genuine difference in student learning than do teachers in larger schools.
◆ There appears to be a particularly strong correlation between smaller school size and improved performance among poor students in urban school districts. Smaller schools can help narrow the achievement gap between White/middle-class/affluent students and ethnic minority and poor students.
◆ Smaller schools provide a safer learning environment for students.

Sometimes, larger schools create smaller schools by implementing the school-within-a-school concept. This approach may be a way to achieve the smaller school benefits without having to actually build expensive new school facilities. Schools that personalize the learning environment for students can increase their engagement and academic achievement.

When considering the best school size to produce student achievement, school boards must consider the nature of their student body and decide whether they, as a community, prefer to pay now or pay later.

Professional Development

Once employed, principals can use professional development to develop and retain high-quality teachers. New teachers can get better, marginal teachers can improve, and successful teachers can strengthen their expertise through high-quality, ongoing professional development programs.

Characteristics of Quality Professional Development. National professional development standards define effective teacher learning as a comprehensive system of consistent and sustained activities directly related to teachers' actual classroom responsibilities. This high-quality professional development is driven by data concerning what teachers' own students need to know and be able to do. It involves teachers working and learning together in collegial conversations about their actual students' work and then designing and practicing strategies to improve their own classroom behaviors and student learning. Instead of calendar days set aside for staff development events, professional development involves just-in-time learning that occurs during the regular workday. Teacher learning in this manner benefits both educators and students.[119]

To be successful, professional development programs must include four components—theory, demonstration, practice, and feedback.[120]

- *Theory.* Teachers need to understand how this new information fits with their professional knowledge and connects to their beliefs about teaching and learning.
- *Demonstration.* Teachers need to watch an expert enact the instructional practice in question. Teachers need to see and hear what it looks and sounds like so they have a visual and auditory model upon which to draw as they practice the technique themselves.
- *Practice.* Teachers need opportunities to try out the new approach using role play or visualization in their own classrooms.
- *Feedback.* Teachers need clear and accurate feedback on how well they accomplished their goal. Did they do everything they planned to do? How did the students respond during the activity? What does assessment of student learning show they gained? Collecting feedback from caring and informed colleagues, thinking about how to use it, and making adjustments before the next attempt can bring the new practice slowly into the classroom.

When principals can design and plan for professional development according to national standards, they provide teachers with a successful way to continue learning and increasing their own effectiveness on the job.

Research on Professional Development.   A growing body of research shows that improving teacher knowledge and skills are essential to raising student performance. Since students spend most of their school hours either interacting with teachers or working under teachers' direction, what teachers know and can do directly affects the quality of student learning. For example, Eric Hanushek, professor at Stanford University, estimates that "the difference between a good teacher and a bad teacher can be a full level of achievement in a single year."[121] The National School Boards Foundation calls investment in teacher learning, "the primary policy lever that school boards have to raise student achievement."[122]

Working with teachers already on staff helps them become more effective immediately. In one 2003–2008 study, failing schools in Chattanooga, Tennessee, increased students' academic progress with the same teachers by using a variety of professional development activities to increase teacher effectiveness.[123] Studies of NAEP data indicated that professional development activities in cultural diversity, teaching techniques for addressing the needs of students with limited English proficiency and teaching students identified with special education needs are all linked to higher student achievement in math.[124] Sustained participation in professional development activities tied to state standards and curriculum improves teachers' instructional practices with the content and raises their students' achievement as compared to students whose teachers did not have this training.[125]

Well-designed professional development leads to enhanced teaching practices and increased student achievement.[126] One clear caution to principals: Having a motivational speaker at the beginning of the school year should not be confused with professional development.

Facilities

More money spent on school maintenance means a better upheld, repaired, and attractive building—and higher student achievement. One noteworthy study found a 5- to 17-point difference in standardized test scores for students in well-maintained buildings (with comfortable room and hall temperature, satisfactory lighting, appropriate noise levels, good roofs, and sufficient space) as compared with those students in poor facilities (poorly maintained, too cold or hot rooms, inadequate lighting, high noise levels, leaky roofs, overcrowding), controlling for the students' socioeconomic status.[127]

An earlier study determined that if a school district were to improve its schools' conditions from poor to excellent, student achievement scores would increase an average of 10.9 percentile points. Working in "sick" buildings creates serious health issues for students and staff, directly affecting attendance rates and teachers' capacity to effectively instruct students. A reduced instructional investment in classrooms may be a source of student and teacher detachment, disengagement, and absences.[128]

ACTIVITY 9.5   Applying Research Findings to School Improvement Resource Allocations

After identifying possible school improvement strategies using fiscal, human, and time resources in Activity 9.4, use the research findings from the section you just read to refine your strategies. Discuss in pairs and then as a class:

1. Which strategies still deserve serious consideration?
2. Which strategies lack the research support to make them viable options (and should be dropped or reworked to make them realistic)?
3. Which new strategies might be suggested that have research support and maximize fiscal, people, and time resources?

Continuing Dilemmas

After considering beliefs about shared decision making, educational values, students' needs, funding sources, appropriate resource allocations, and research findings on practices that increase student achievement, fundamental dilemmas remain. Long-term resource allocation decisions include resolving the following questions:

◆ *Securing more resources or making more efficient uses of existing resources?* Resources are always scarce, but it is important to ask how efficiently schools are using current resources. Since providing evidence of undisputable payoffs on investments is difficult, resources are increasingly scarce, and the public is suspicious of increased public education costs, good stewardship requires serious attention to ensuring that current funds are being used most appropriately and to measurable positive effect.

◆ *Staying the course or continuing to experiment?* Impatience and the impulse to try something new is ever-present when discussing resource uses. Resource investments of dollars, people, and time often show their benefits only in the long term. It takes years to educate a child, and it takes years to create and sustain strong educational programs and meaningful learning improvements, especially in large complex school systems. In contrast, continuity may also reflect inertia or the desire not to upset an existing status quo. Whatever the reason, the timeline of resource decision making is likely to bring repeated occasions to change course before the evidence is in, and expressions of both sides of this debate are likely.

◆ *Acting on available evidence or developing better evidence?* Resource allocations occur on timelines. Frequently, not enough good data are available on the questions at hand to make a well-informed judgment. Leaders tend to ask for more and better data and to resist making premature decisions until more convincing evidence exists. But the call for more data may not easily reconcile with the lack of a fully developed knowledge base about the connections between investments and results; the cost of creating better data sources, which diverts resources from the original purposes; and data's inherent ambiguity, which requires much interpretation. For these reasons, ambiguity will remain part of the resource allocation process.

Resource allocation in education does not take place in a vacuum. Instead, it often creates a context that creates opportunities for effective leadership. When effective leaders know how to share decision making and use data strategically to inform resource allocation decisions with insights about their resources' productivity, efficiency, and equity, they give their stakeholders the means to make informed decisions which can have a positive impact on student achievement.

SUMMARY

Resource allocation refers to apportioning productive assets among different uses. Because a society's resources are limited while human desires are often unlimited, and because any given resource can have many alternative uses, resource allocation becomes the focus of competing agendas. Principals are expected to knowledgeably and accurately demonstrate that they have used the resources entrusted to them in ways that benefit teaching and learning, and they must be able to credibly express the need for additional assets.

Governments broadly decide the total size of the overall budget that schools receive and how that amount is to be allotted. Given the variety of restrictions on how the funds can be used, decisions at the district and school level address managing and directing these resources. Resource allocation is a political, ethical, fiscal, and social process.

Equity is providing the services students actually need whereas *equality* is providing the same services for all students regardless of the students' or locality's needs. *Adequacy* involves providing sufficient resources to accomplish the job of educating our children. As a fiscal concept, adequacy is value driven, with the actual dollar amount a state or district needs to spend for its students undetermined. School finance litigation has forced states to become more equitable in how they fund schools.

In resource allocation, the principal's initial responsibility is to structure and guide the process with the focus on learning, strategies for addressing it, and the evidence that informs decisions. Resource allocation's equity and effectiveness are continually assessed, relevant resources for further improvement priorities are identified and secured, and these resources are distributed according to need. Principals must understand the school and district's mission, goals, and objectives; identify their vision for the school and their own educational values; know their student population's specific learning needs; and recognize the assorted constraints and competing interests that affect resource allocation.

Basically, school leaders work with three categories of resources: fiscal, human, and structural. These resources are intimately linked. Monetary resources include local and nonlocal funds, governmental and nongovernmental funds, competitive grants, foundations, school-business partnerships, student activities, and facility rentals. Each comes with its own opportunities and constraints.

People are among the schools' most critical and costly resources. By thinking flexibly, principals can help their schools reallocate these human resources to better support student and teacher learning and achievement.

Research suggests that increased spending in instructional areas positively affects student achievement. Improved fiscal management of current resources, rather than increased funding, is necessary to increase student learning. Investments in teacher quality and effectiveness, teacher salaries, reduced class size, professional development, and school facilities lead to increased student learning.

ENDNOTES

1. University of Minnesota. (n.d.). *Definition: What is resource allocation?* Retrieved from http://www.ahc.umn.edu/bioethics/prod/groups/ahc/@pub/@ahc/documents/asset/ahc_75702.pdf

2. Caldwell, B. J. (1998). Strategic leadership, resource management, and effective school reform. *Journal of Educational Administration, 36*(5), 445–461.

3. Hoyle, English, & Steffy. (1990). Op. cit., p. 49.

4. Owings, W., & Kaplan, L. (2006). *American public school finance* (p. 146). Belmont, CA: Thomson Wadsworth.

5. Odden, A., & Picus, L. (2004). *School finance: A policy perspective* (3rd ed., p. 25). New York, NY: McGraw-Hill.

6. Verstegen, D. A. (2002, October). The new finance. *American School Board Journal, 189*(10), 24–26. Retrieved from http://www.asbj.com/schoolspending/resources1002verstegen.html

7. Verstegen, D. (2002, Winter). Financing the new adequacy: Towards new models of state education finance systems that support standards based reform. *Journal of Education Finance, 27,* 749–782.

8. Owings & Kaplan. (2006). Op. cit.

9. National Center for Education Statistics. (2009). *Table A-1-1. Percentage of the population ages 3–34 enrolled in school, by age group: October 1970–2007.* Washington, DC: U.S. Department of Education, Institute of Education Sciences. Retrieved from http://nces.ed.gov/programs/coe/2009/section1/table-ope-1.asp

10. Rebell, M. A. (2002). Education adequacy, democracy, and the courts. In T. Ready, C. Edley, & C. E. Snow (Eds.), *Achieving high educational standards for all: Conference summary* (pp. 218–268). Washington, DC: National Academy Press.

11. Dinan, J. (2009). School finance litigation: The third wave recedes. In J. M. Dunn & M. R, West, (Eds.), *From schoolhouse to courthouse: The judiciary's role in American education* (pp. 96–120). Washington, D.C.: The Brookings Institution.

12. Rebell, M. (2008, February). Equal opportunity and the courts. *Phi Delta Kappan, 89* (6), 432–439.

13. Baker, K. (1991). Yes. Throw money at the schools. *Phi Delta Kappan, 72*(8), 628–631; Hedges, L. V., Laine, R. D., & Greenwald, R. (1994). Does money matter: A meta analysis of studies of the effects of differential school inputs on student outcomes. *Educational Researcher, 23*(3), 5–14; Verstegen, D., & King, R. (1998). The relationship between school spending and student achievement: A review and analysis of 35 years of production function research. *Journal of Education Finance, 24*(2), 243–262; Cooper, B., et al. (1994, Fall). Making money matter in education: A micro-financial model for determining school-level allocations, efficiency, and productivity. *Journal of Education Finance, 20*, 66–87; Fortune, J., & O'Neil, J. (1994). Production function analyses and the study of educational funding equity: A methodological critique. *Journal of Education Finance, 20*, 21–46; Verstegen, D. (1994). Efficiency and equity in the provision and reform of American schooling. *Journal of Education Finance, 20*, 107–131.

14. Plecki, M. L., Alejano, C. R., Knapp, M. S., & Lockmiller, C. R. (2006, October). *Allocating resources and creating incentives to improve teaching and learning* (p. 15). Seattle: University of Washington. Retrieved from http://www .wallacefoundation.org/wallace/2Allocating ResourcesandCreating.pdf

15. Plecki, et al. (2006, October). Ibid.

16. Miles, K., & Darling-Hammond, L. (1998). Rethinking reallocation of teaching resources: Some lessons from high-performing schools. *Educational Evaluation and Policy Analysis, 20*(1), 9–19. (p. 27).

17. Plecki, et al. (2006). Op. cit.

18. For a complete and readable discussion of school finance, see: Owings, W. A., & Kaplan, L. S. (2012). *American public school finance*. 2nd edition. Belmont, CA: Wadsworth/Cengage.

19. McLaughlin, M. W., & Talbert, J. E. (2002). *Reforming districts: How districts support school reform*. Seattle: Center for the Study of Teaching and Policy, University of Washington. Retrieved from http://depts.washington.edu/ctpmail/Reports .html#Reforming

20. McCormick, D.H., Bauer. D.G., & Ferguson, D.E. (2001). *Creating foundations for American schools*. Gaithersburg, MA: Aspen Publishers. The number of foundations is difficult to obtain. According to Jim Collogan, Executive Director of the National School Foundation Association (June 7, 2011), IRS compliance issues have complicated reporting data. For more information on Education Foundations go to www.schoolfoundations.org.

21. Kaplan, L. S., & Owings, W. A. (2010). *American education: Building a common foundation* (p. 319). Belmont, CA: Wadsworth/Cengage Learning. Adapted from Snyder, T. D., Dillow, S. A., & Hoffman, C. M. (2009). *Digest of education statistics 2008* (NCES 2009-020). National Center for Education Statistics, Institute of Education Sciences, U.S. Department of Education, Washington, DC: U.S. Government Printing Office, Table 183, p. 263.

22. Odden, A., & Archibald, S. (2000, Spring). Reallocating resources to support higher student achievement: An empirical look at five sites. *Journal of Education Finance, 25*(4), 545–564.

23. Other dual certification in special education and remedial reading, for instance, can provide an allowable infusion of special education dollars into the regular education classroom. This practice requires special education students to have changes in their individual education plans (IEPs) to reflect the new methods by which they are being served.

24. Plecki et. al. (2006). Op. cit.

25. Commission on Chapter 1. (1992). *High performance schools: No exceptions, no excuses*. Washington, DC: Author; Soo Hoo, S. (1990). School renewal: Taking responsibility for providing an education of value. In J. L. Goodlad & P. Keating (Eds.), *Access to knowledge: An agenda for our nation's schools* (pp. 205–222). New York, NY: Collete Entrance Examination Board.

26. Gottfredson, G. D., & Diager, D. C. (1979). *Disruption in 600 schools*. Baltimore, MD: Johns Hopkins University, Center for Social Organization of Schools; Lee, V. E., Bryk, A., & Smith, J. B. (1993). The organization of effective secondary schools. In L. Darling-Hammond (Ed.), *Review of research in education* (Vol. 19, pp. 171–267). Washington, DC: American Education Research Association; Lee, V. E., & Smith, J. B. (1994).

High school restructuring and student achievement: A new study finds strong links. *Issues in Restructuring Schools, 7*(1), 1–5, 16; Lee, V. E., & Smith, J. B. (1997). High school size: Which high school works best and for whom? *Educational Evaluation and Policy Analysis, 19*(3), 205–227; Lee, V. E., & Smith, J. B. (1995). *Effects of high school restricting and size on gains in achievement and engagement for early secondary school students*. Madison: Wisconsin Center for Education Research, University of Wisconsin.

27. Slavin, R. E. (1987). Making Chapter 1 make a difference. *Phi Delta Kappan, 69*(2), 110–119.

28. Bloom, B. S. (1984). The 2 sigma problem: The search for methods of group instruction as effective as one-to-one tutoring. *Educational Researcher, 13*(6), 4–16; Cohen, P. A., Kulik, J. A., & Kulik, C. L. C. (1982). Educational outcomes of tutoring: A meta-analysis of findings. *American Educational Research Journal, 19*(2), 237–248.

29. Cohen et al. (1982). Op. cit.; Juel, C. (1991). Cross-age tutoring between student athletes and at-risk children. *Reading Teacher, 45*(3), 178–186.

30. Fantuzzo, J. W., King, J. A., & Heller, L. A. (1992). Effects of reciprocal peer tutoring on mathematics and school adjustment: A component analysis. *Journal of Educational Psychology, 84*(3), 331–339; Rogoff, B. (1990). *Apprenticeship in thinking: Cognitive development in social context*. New York, NY: Oxford Press.

31. Slavin, R. E., & Madden, N. A. (1989). What works for students at risk: A research synthesis. *Educational Leadership, 26*(5), 4–13. Slavin defines "at-risk" students as those who experience low achievement, grade retention, behavior problems, poor attendance, low socioeconomic status, and attendance at schools with large numbers of poor students.

32. Karweit, N. I. (1989). Preschool programs for students at risk of school failure. In R. E. Slavin, N. I. Karweit, & N. A. Madden (Eds.), *Effective programs for students at risk*. Needham Heights, MA: Allyn & Bacon; McKey, R. L., Condelli, H. l., Ganson, B., Barrett, C., McConkey, C., & Plantz, M. (1985). *The impact of Head Start on children, families, and communities*. Washington, DC: CSK.

33. Berrueta-Clement, J. R., Schweinhart, W. S., Barnett, A. S., & Weikart, D. P. (1984). *Changed lives*. Ypsilanti, MI: High/Score.

34. Slavin & Madden. (1989). Op. cit.

35. Slavin & Madden. (1989). Op. cit.

36. Hazelton, J. E., Blakely, C., & Denton, J. (1992). *Cost effectiveness of alternative year schooling*. Austin: University of Texas, Educational Economic Policy Center.

37. Cooper, H. (2003, May). Summer learning loss: The problem and some solutions. *ERIC Digest*. Champaign, IL: ERIC Clearinghouse on Elementary and Early Childhood Education. (EDO-PS-0305) Retrieved from http://www.ceclf.edu.on.ca/ceclfce/desuet/_pdf/1-6/calendrier/cooper03.pdf; On average, children's test scores were at least one month lower when they returned to school in the fall than scores were when they left in the spring.

38. Cooper, H., Charlton, K., Valentine, J. C., & Muhlenbruck, L. (2000). Making the most of summer school: A meta-analytic and narrative review. *Monographs of the Society for Research in Child Development, 65*(1), 1–118.

39. Cooper et al. (2000). Ibid.

40. Miles & Darling-Hammond. (1998). Op. cit.

41. Odden, A., & Clune, W. (1995). Improving educational productivity and school finance. *Educational Researcher, 24*(9), 6–10, 22; Odden, A., Monk, D., Nakib, Y., & Picus, L. (1995). The story of the education dollar: No academy awards and no fiscal smoking gun. *Phi Delta Kappan, 77*(2), 161–168.

42. Odden & Clune. (1995). Ibid.

43. Hertert, L., Busch, C., & Odden, A. (1994). School financing inequities among the states: The problem from a national perspective. *Journal of Education Finance, 19*(3), 231–255.

44. Cooper, B. (1993, March). *School-site cost allocations: Testing a microfinancial model in 23 districts in ten states*. Paper presented at the annual meeting of the American Education Finance Association, Albuquerque, NM; Hertert, L. (1993). *Resource allocation patterns in public education: An analysis of school level equity in California* (Unpublished doctoral dissertation). University of Southern California.

45. Alexander, K., & Salmon, R. (1995). *American school finance*. Boston, MA: Allyn & Bacon; Owings & Kaplan (2006). Op. cit.

Hightower, A. M. (2009, January 8). Securing progress, striving to improve. In *Quality Counts 2009. Education Week, 28*(17), 44–47; Wiener, Ross, & Eli Pristoop. (2006). *How states short-change the districts that need the most help.* The Education Trust, Funding Gaps 2006 Report.

46. Arlington, R. L., & Johnston, P. (1989). Coordination, collaboration and consistency: The redesign of compensatory and special education interventions. In R. E. Slavin, N. L. Karweit, & N. A. Madden (Eds.), *Effective programs for students at risk* (pp. 320–354). Boston, MA: Allyn & Bacon; Odden, A. (1990). Class size and student achievement: Research based policy alternatives. *Educational Evaluation and Policy Analysis, 12,* 213–227; Slavin, R. E., Karweit, N., & Madden, N. (Eds.). (1989). *Effective programs for students at risk.* Needham Heights, MA: Allyn & Bacon.

47. Lankford, H., & Wyckoff, J. (1995). Where has the money gone? An analysis of school spending in New York. *Educational Evaluation and Policy Analysis, 17,* 195–218.

48. Independent Review Panel. (1993). *Reinventing Chapter 1: The current Chapter 1 program and new directions.* Washington, DC: U.S. Department of Education.

49. Adams, J. O. (1994). Spending school reform dollars in Kentucky: Familiar patterns and new programs, but is this reform? *Educational Evaluation and Policy Analysis, 16,* 375–390; Firestone, W. A., Goertz, M. E., Nagle, B., & Smelkinson, M. F. (1994). Where did the $800 million go? The first year of New Jersey's Quality Education Act. *Educational Evaluation and Policy Analysis, 16,* 359–373.

50. Odden, A., Monk, D., Nakib, Y., & Picus, L. (1995). The story of the educational dollar: No fiscal Academy Awards and no fiscal smoking guns. *Phi Delta Kappan, 77*(2),161–168.

51. Ravitch, D. (1995). *National standards in American education.* Washington, DC: Brookings Institution.

52. Barnett, S. (1994). Obstacles and opportunities: Some simple economics of school finance reform. *Educational Policy, 8*(4),436-452.

53. Odden, A., & Massy, W. (1993). *Education funding for schools and universities: Improving productivity and equity.* Madison: University of Wisconsin, Madison, Wisconsin Center for Education Research, Consortium for Policy Research in Education—The Finance Center.

54. Blloch, A., & Thomas, H. (1997). *The impact of local management in schools: Final report.* Birmingham, United Kingdom: University of Birmingham and National Association of Head Teachers; Hanushek, E. A. (1996). Outcomes, costs, and incentives in schools. In E. A. Hanushek & D. W. Jorgensen (Eds.). *Improving America's schools: The role of incentives* (pp. 29–52). Washington, DC: National Academy Press; Hanushek, E. A. (1997). Assessing the effects of school resources on student performance: An update. *Educational Evaluation and Policy Analysis, 19*(2), 141–164; Levacic, R. (1995). *Local management of schools: Analysis and practice.* Buckingham, United Kingdom: Open University Press.

55. Laine, R., Greenwald, R., & Hedges, L. V. (1996). Money does matter. In L. Picus & J. W. Wattenbarger (Eds.), *Where does the money go?* (pp. 44–70). Thousand Oaks, CA: Corwin Press.

56. Verstegen, D., & King, R. A. (1998). The relationship between school spending and student achievement: A review and analysis of 35 years of production function research. *Journal of Education Finance, 24,* 243–262.

57. Smith, M. (2004). How the apportionment of district money is associated with differences in the grade 8 mathematics and reading achievement scores for Minnesota students. *Journal of Education Finance, 29,* 299–314.

58. Archibald, S. (2006). Narrowing in on educational resources that *do* affect student achievement. *Peabody Journal of Education, 81*(4), 23–42.

59. Grubb, W. N. (2006). When money might matter: Using NEL88 to examine the weak effects of school funding. *Journal of Education Finance, 31*(4), 360–378.

60. Odden & Clune. (1995). Op. cit.

61. Lee, V., & Smith, J. (1997). High school size: Which works best, and for whom? *Educational Evaluation and Policy Analysis, 19*(3), 205–228; Raywid, M. A. (1997/1998). Synthesis of research: Small schools: A reform that works. *Educational Leadership, 55*(4), 34–39.

62. Odden & Clune. (1995). Op. cit.; Odden, A., & Clune, W. (1998). School finance systems: Aging structures in need of renovation. *Educational Evaluation and Policy Analysis, 20*(3), 157–177; Lawler, E. E. (1990). *Strategic pay: Aligning*

organizational strategies and pay systems. San Francisco, CA: Jossey-Bass; Bond, L., Smith, T., Baker, W. K., & Hattie, J. A. (2000, September). *Validation study: A distinction that matters.* University of North Carolina at Greensboro: Center for Educational Research and Evaluation; Lustick, D., & Sykes, G. (2006, February 23). National board certification as professional development: What are teachers learning? *Education Policy Analysis Archives, 14*(5), 1–43. Retrieved from http://epaa.asu.edu/epaa/v14n5

63. Garet, M. S., Porter, A., Desimone, L., Birman, B., & Yoon, K. (2001). What makes professional development effective? Results from a national sample of teachers. *American Educational Research Journal, 38*(4), 915–945; Odden, A., Archibald, S., Fermanich, M., & Galligher, A. (2003). Defining school level expenditures that reflect educational strategies. *Journal of Education Finance, 28*(3), 323–356.

64. Odden, A., & Archibald, S. (2000). Reallocating resources to support higher student achievement: An empirical look at five sites. *Journal of Education Finance, 25*(4), 545–564.

65. For a more complete overview of spending for student achievement, see Owings, W. A., & Kaplan, L. S. (2012). *American public school finance* 2nd edition. Belmont, CA: Thomson Wadsworth.

66. At certain grade levels and when combined with effective teaching.

67. Darling-Hammond, L. (2000). Teacher quality and student achievement: A review of state policy evidence. *Education Policy Analysis Archives, 8*(1).

68. Darling-Hammond. (2000). Ibid.

69. Hanushek, E. A. (1992). The trade-off between child quantity and quality. *Journal of Political Economy, 100*(1), 84–117.

70. Walsh, K. (2001). *Teacher certification reconsidered: Stumbling for quality.* Baltimore, MD: Abell Foundation; Darling-Hammond, L. (2000, January 1). Teacher quality and student achievement: A review of state policy evidence. *Educational Policy Analysis Archives, 8*(1). Retrieved from http://epaa.asu.edu/epaa/v8n1; Haycock. (1998). Op. cit.; Whitehurst, G. J. (2002, March). *Scientifically based research on teacher quality: Research on teacher preparation and professional development.* Paper presented at White House Conference on Preparing Tomorrow's Teachers. Retrieved from http://www.ed.gov/inits/preparingteachers conference/whitehurst.html

71. Sanders, W. L., & Horn, S. P. (1995). Educational assessment reassessed: The usefulness of standardized and alternative measures of student achievement as indicators for the assessment of educational outcomes. *Education Policy Analysis Archives, 3*(6), 1–15. Retrieved from http://epaa.asu.edu/epaa/v3n6.html; Sanders, W. L., & Rivers, J. C. (1996, November). *Cumulative and residual effects of teachers on future student academic achievement.* Knoxville: University of Tennessee Value-Added Research and Assessment Center; Webster, W. J., & Mendro, R. L. (1997). The Dallas value-added accountability system. In J. Millman (Ed.), *Grading teachers, grading schools. Is student achievement a valid evaluation measure?* (pp. 81–99). Thousand Oaks, CA: Corwin Press; Webster, W. J., Mendro, R. L., Orsak, T. H., & Weerasinghe, D. (1998a). *An application of hierarchical linear modeling to the estimation of school and teacher effect.* Dallas, TX: Dallas Independent School District. Retrieved from http://www.dallasisd.org/depts/inst_research/aer98ww2/aer98ww2.htm; Webster, W. J., Mendro, R. L., Orsak, T. H., & Weerasinghe, D. (1998b). *An application of hierarchical linear modeling to the estimation of school and teacher effects. Relevant results.* Dallas, TX: Dallas Independent School District. Retrieved from http://www.dallasisd.org/depts/inst_research/aer98ww2/aer98ww2.htm

72. Sanders & Rivers. (1996). Op. cit.

73. Sanders, W., & Horn, S. P. (1994). The Tennessee value-added assessment system (TVAAS): Mixed-model methodology in educational assessment. *Journal of Personnel Evaluation in Education, 8,* 299–311; Wright, S. P., Horn, S. P., & Sanders, W. L. (1997). Teacher & classroom context effects on student achievement: Implications for teacher evaluation. *Journal of Personnel Evaluation in Education, 11,* 57–67.

74. Wright et al. (1997). Ibid. p. 63.

75. Nye, B., Konstantopoulos, S., & Hedges, L. V. (2004). How large are teacher effects? *Educational Evaluation and Policy Analysis, 26*(3), 237–257; Marzano, R. (2007).*The art and science of teaching. A comprehensive framework for effective instruction*

(pp. 2–3). Alexandria, VA: Association for Supervision and Curriculum Development.

76. Wenglinsky, H. (2000). *How teaching matters. Bringing the classroom back into discussions of teacher quality* (p. 31). Princeton, NJ: Milken Family Foundation and Educational Testing Service.

77. Blair, J. (2000, October 5). ETS study links effective teaching methods to test-score gains. *Education Week, 20*(8), 24–25; Goldhaber, D. D., & Brewer, D. J. (2000, Summer). Does teacher certification matter? High school teacher certification status and student achievement. *Educational Evaluation and Policy Analysis, 22*(2), 129–145; Wenglinsky, H. (2000, October). *How teaching matters: Bringing the classroom back into discussions of teacher quality.* Princeton, NJ: Milken Family Foundation and Educational Testing Service.

78. Haycock, K. (1998, Summer). Good teaching matters . . . A lot. *Thinking K–16, 3,* 3–14.

79. Darling-Hammond. (2000). Op. cit., p. 27.

80. Monk, D., & King, J. A. (1994). Multi-level teacher resource effects in pupil performance in secondary mathematics and science: The case of teacher subject-matter preparation. In R. G. Ehrenberg (Ed.), *Choices and consequences: Contemporary policy issues in education* (pp. 29–58). Ithaca, NY: ILR Press.

81. Johnson, K. A. (2000, September). The effects of advanced teacher training in education of student achievement. *Report of the Heritage Center for Data Analysis,* No. 00-09, pp. 1–17; Greenwald, R., Hedges, L. V., & Laine, R. D. (1996). The effect of school resources on student achievement. *Review of Educational Research, 66*(3), 361–396.

82. Barton, P. E., Coley, R., & Wenglinsky, H. (1998). *Order in the classroom: Violence, discipline, and student achievement.* Princeton, NJ: Educational Testing Service.

83. Owings, W. A. & Kaplan, L. S. (2010). The alpha and omega syndrome: Is intra-district funding the next ripeness factor? *Journal of Education Finance, 36*(2), 162–185; Ingersoll, R. (2002). *Out-of-field teaching, educational inequality, and the organization of schools: An exploratory analysis.* Seattle: Center for the Study of Teaching and Policy, University of Washington. Retrieved from http://www.cpre.org/images/stories/cpre_pdfs/OutOfField-RI-01-2002.pdf; Boyd, D., Lankford, H., Loeb, S., & Wyckoff, J. (2000).

Understanding teacher labor markets: Implications for educational equity. In M. L. Plecki & D. H. Monk (Eds.), *School finance and teacher quality: Exploring the connections* (pp. 55–84). Larchmont, NY: Eye on Education.

84. Milanowski, A. (2003, January 29). The varieties of knowledge and skill-based pay design: A comparison of seven new pay systems for K–12 teachers. *Education Policy Analysis Archives, 11*(4). Retrieved from http://epaa.asu.edu/spaa/v11n4/

85. Odden & Archibald. (2000). Op. cit.

86. Mitchell, K. J., Robinson, D. Z., Plake, B. S., & Knowles, K. T. (2001). (Eds.).*Testing teacher candidates: The role of licensure tests in improving teacher quality* (p. 31). Washington, DC: National Academy Press.

87. Darling-Hammond, L. (2000, January 1). Teacher quality and student achievement: A review of state policy evidence. *Education Policy Analysis Archives, 8,* 1. Retrieved from http://www.epaa.asu.edu/epaa/v8n1; Darling-Hammond, L., Berry, B., & Thoreson, A. (2001). Does teacher certification matter? Evaluating the evidence. *Educational Evaluation and Policy Analysis, 23*(1), 57–77; Darling-Hammond, L., & Sykes, G. (2003). Wanted: A national teacher supply policy for education: The right way to meet the "highly qualified teacher" challenge. *Educational Policy Analysis and Archives, 11* (33). Retrieved from http://epaa.asu.edu/epaa/v11n33; Decker, P. T., Mayer, D. P., & Glazerman, S. (2004). *The effects of Teach for America on students: Findings from a national evaluation.* Princeton, NJ: Mathematica Policy Research. Retrieved from http://www.mathematica-mpr.com/publications/pdf/teach.pdf; Laczko-Kerr, I., & Berliner, D. C. (2002). The effectiveness of "Teach for America" and other under-certified teachers on student academic achievement: A case of harmful public policy. *Education Policy Analysis Archives, 10*(37). Retrieved from http://epaa.asu.edu/epaa/v10n37/; Legler, R. (2002). *Alternative certification: A review of theory and research.* Naperville, IL: Education Policy, Learning Points Associates, North Central Regional Education Laboratory. Retrieved from http://www.ncrel.org/policy/pubs/html/altcert/bg:htm; Podgursky, M. (2003, October). *Improving academic performance in U.S. public schools: Why teacher licensing is (almost)*

irrelevant. Paper presented at the Teacher Preparation and Quality: New Directions in Policy and Research Conference, Washington, DC.

88. Boyd, D., Grossman, P., Lankford, H., Loeb, S., & Wyckoff, J. (2005). How changes in entry re-quirements alter teacher workforce and affect student achievement. *Education Finance and Policy, 1*(2), 176–216; Gordon, R., Kane, T. J., & Staiger, D. O. (2006). *Identifying effective teachers using performance on the job.* Washington, DC: Brookings Institution, Hamilton Project. Retrieved from http://www.brookings.edu/views/ papers/200604Hamilton_1.pdf; Kane, T. J., Rockoff, J. E., & Staiger, D. O. (2006). *What does certification tell us about teacher effectiveness? Evidence from New York City.* Cambridge, MA: Harvard Graduate School of Education. Retrieved from http://www.gse.harvard.edu/news/features/ kane/nycfellowsmarch2006.pdf; Nunnery, J. A., Kaplan, L. S., Owings, W. A., & Pribish, S. (2009, December). The effects of troops to teachers on student achievement: One state's study. *National Association of Secondary School Principals' Bulletin, 93*(4), 249–272.

89. Boyd et al. (2005). Op. cit.; Gordon et al. (2006). Op. cit.; Darling-Hammond, L. (2001). Teacher quality and student achievement: A review of state policy evidence. *Education Policy Analysis Archives, 8*(1). Retrieved from http://epaa.asu.edu/ epaa/v8n1/; Rivkin, S. G., Hanushek, E. A., & Kain, J. F. (2005). Teachers, schools and academic achievement. *Econometric, 73*(2), 417–458; Rock-off, J. E. (2004). The impact of individual teach-ers on student achievement: Evidence from panel data. *American Economic Review, 94*(2), 247–252; Sanders, W. L., & Horn, S. P. (1995). Educational assessment reassessed: The usefulness of standard-ized and alternative measures of student achieve-ment as indicators for the assessment of educational outcomes. *Education Policy Analysis Archives, 3*(6), 1–15. Retrieved from http://epaa .asu.edu/epaa/v3n6.html; Sanders, W. L., & Rivers, J. C. (1996). *Cumulative and residual effects of teachers on future student academic achievement.* Knoxville: University of Tennessee Value-Added Research and Assessment Center.

90. "Novice" in this case refers to teachers with 3 years or less experience. National Center for Education Statistics. (2000, December). *Monitoring quality: An indicators report.* As cited in Peske, H. G., & Haycock, K. (2006). *Teaching inequality: How poor and minority students are shortchanged on teacher quality.* Washington, DC: Education Trust.

91. Jerald, C. D. (2002). *All talk, no action: Putting an end to out-of-field teaching.* Washington, DC: Education Trust.

92. Kaplan & Owings. (2010). Op. cit. (pp. 336–372).

93. See http://www.cnn.com/2004/EDUCATION/01/ 14/teacher.salaries.ap/

94. National Board for Professional Teaching Stan-dards. (2009). *Diversity initiatives.* Arlington, VA: Author. Retrieved from http://www.nbpts.org/ resources/diversity_initiatives; National Board for Professional Teaching Standards. (2009). *Profiles in excellence: Chicago, Illinois. Leveraging national board certification in a district-wide human capital initiative.* Arlington, VA: Author. Retrieved from http://www.nbpts.org/about_us/news_media/ press_releases?ID=529

95. Hanushek, E. A., & Rivkin, S. G. (1997). Under-standing the twentieth century's growth in U.S. school spending. *Journal of Human Resources, 32*(1), 35–68.

96. National Center for Education Statistics. (2010). Contexts of elementary and secondary education. Indicator 31 (2010).Tables. A-31-1. Student/teacher ratios in public elementary and secondary schools. Washington, D.C.: Author, U.S. Department of Education, Institute of Education Sciences. Retrieved from: http://nces .ed.gov/programs/coe/2010/section4/table-qpt-1.asp

97. For example, many formerly all–African American schools had much higher students-to-teachers ratios than found in local White schools. With desegregation, schools had to hire more teachers to reduce class sizes to more acceptable teacher/student levels and increase African American teachers' salaries to those comparable to what White teachers were earning.

98. Hanushek, E. A., & Rivkin, S. G. (1997). Under-standing the twentieth century's growth in U.S. school spending. *Journal of Human Resources, 32*(1), 35–68.

99. Hanushek & Rivkin. (1997). Ibid., p. 41.

100. Miles, K. H. (1997a). *Spending more at the edges: Understanding the growth in public school spending from 1967 to 1991.* Ann Arbor, MI: UMI Press; Miles, K. H. (1997b). Finding the dollars to pay for 21st century schools: Taking advantage of the times. *School Business Affairs, 63*(6), 38–42; Rothstein, R. (with K. H. Miles). (1995). *Where's the money gone?* Washington, DC: Economic Policy Institute.

101. Nye, B., Hodges, L. V., & Konstantopoulos, S. (2000, Spring). The effects of small class size on academic achievement: The results of the Tennessee class size experiment. *American Educational Research Journal, 37,* 123–151.

102. Stecher, B., Bornstedt, G., Dirst, M., McRobbie, J., & Williams, T. (2001, June). Class size reduction in California: A story of hope, promise, and unintended consequences. *Phi Delta Kappan, 82,* 670–674.

103. Robinson, G. (1990, April). Synthesis of research on the effects of class size. *Educational Leadership, 47*(7), 80–90.

104. Addonizio, M., & Phelps, J. (2000, Fall). Class size and student performance: A framework for policy analysis. *Journal of Education Finance, 26,* 135–156.

105. Konstantopoulis, S. (2008, March). Do small classes reduce the achievement gap between low and high achievers? Evidence from Project STAR. *Elementary School Journal, 108*(4), 275–292.

106. Jacobson, L. (2008, February 27). Class-size reductions seen of limited help on achievement gap. *Education Week, 27*(25), 9.

107. Gregory, T. B., & Smith, G. R. (1987, January). *High schools as communities: The small school reconsidered.* Bloomington, IN: Phi Delta Kappa; Sousa, R., & Skandera, H. (2001, Summer). Why bigger isn't better. *Hoover Digest, 3.* Palo Alto, CA: Stanford University.

108. Eichenstein, R., et al. (1994). *Project Achieve, part I: Qualitative findings, 1993–94.* Brooklyn, NY: New York City Board of Education.

109. Gerwitz, C. (2006, August 9). Chicago's small schools see gains, but not on tests. *Education Week, 25*(44), 5, 18.

110. Lee, V. E., & Smith, J. B. (1997, Autumn). High school size: Which works best and for whom? *Educational Evaluation and Policy Analysis, 19*(3), 205–227.

111. National Center for Education Statistics. (2010). Op. cit.

112. Hoff, D. J. (2008, May 21). Study of small high schools yields little on achievement. *Education Week, 27*(38), 10. For a thorough discussion of the effects of small school size on student achievement, see Chapter 9, "School Governance and Structure."

113. Gerwitz. (2006). Op. cit.

114. Lee & Smith. (1997). Op. cit.; Also see: *Size of high schools.* National Center for Education Statistics. Retrieved from http://www.nces.gov/programs/coe/2003/section4/indicator30.asp

115. Johnson, J. D., Howley, C. B., & Howley, A. A. (2002). *Size, excellence, and equity: A report on Arkansas schools and districts.* Athens: Ohio University College of Education, Educational Studies Department; Jimerson, L. (2006, September). *The hobbit effect: Why small schools work.* Arlington, VA: Rural School and Community Trust. States in the study included Alaska, California, Georgia, Montana, Ohio, Texas, and West Virginia.

116. Stiefel, L., Berne, R., Iatarola, P., & Fruchter, N. (2000, Spring). High schools size: Effects on budgets and performance in New York City. *Educational Evaluation and Policy Analysis, 22*(1), 27–39, at 36–37.

117. Lawrence, B. K., Bingler, S., Diamond, B. M., Hill, B., Hoffman, J. L., Howley, C. B., Mitchell, S., Rudolph, D., & Washor, E. (2002). *Dollars & sense. The cost effectiveness of small schools.* Cincinnati, OH: Knowledge Works Foundation. Retrieved from http://www.earlycolleges.org/Downloads/reslib79.pdf

118. *School size.* Denver, CO: Education Commission of the States. Retrieved from http://www.ecs.org/html/issue.asp?print=true&issueID=105&subIssueOD=0

119. Roy, P. (2004, September). Move beyond workshops with NSDC standards. *Results.* National Staff Development Council. Retrieved from http://www.nsdc.org/library/publications/results/res9-04roy.cfm

120. Showers, B., Joyce, B. R., & Bennett, B. (1987, February). Synthesis of research on staff development: A framework for future study and a state of the art analysis. *Educational Leadership, 45*(3), 77–87.

121. Haycock, K. (1998, Summer). Good teaching matters . . . a lot. *Thinking K–16, 4.* Washington, DC: Education Trust.

122. National School Boards Foundation. (1999). *Leadership matters: Transforming urban school boards.* Alexandria, VA: Author.

123. Keller, B. (2008, April 9). Failing schools showed progress with most of the same teachers. *Education Week, 27*(32), 8. Professional development in these schools included adding teacher coaches, reading specialists, reorienting administrators to instruction, beefing up student data and helping teachers make better use of it in their classrooms, and using bonuses for raising test scores and other rewards that the teachers' work was valued.

124. Blair, J. (2000, October). ETS study links effective teaching methods to test-score gains. *Education Week, 25,* 24–25.

125. Cohen, D. K., & Hill, H. C. (1998). *Instructional policy and classroom performance: The mathematics reform in California.* Philadelphia, PA: Consortium for Policy Research in Education; Alexander, D., Heaviside, S., & Farris, E. (1998). U.S. Department of Education, National Center for Education Statistics, Fast Response Survey System. *Status of education reform in public elementary and secondary schools: Teachers' perspectives* (NCES 1999-045). Washington, DC: U.S. Government Printing Office; Choy, S. P., & Xianglei, C. (1998). U.S. Department of Education, National Center for Education Statistics. *Toward better teaching: Professional development in 1993–94* (NCES 98-230). Washington, DC: U.S. Government Printing Office.

126. Hirsh, E., Koppcih, E., & Knapp, M. S. (1998, December). *What states are doing to improve the quality of teaching: A brief review of current patterns and trends.* Seattle, WA: Center for the Study of Teaching and Policy.

127. Earthman, G. (2002). School facility conditions and student academic achievement. *William Watch Series: Investigating the Claims of Williams v. State of California.* Los Angeles: UCLA Institute for Democracy, Education, and Access.

128. Bernier, M. (1993, April). Building conditions, parental involvement, and student achievement in the District of Columbia public school system. *Urban Education, 28*(1), 6–29.

CHAPTER 10

Formative and Summative Evaluation Issues in Leadership

Focus Questions

◆ How do effective evaluation practices serve both accountability and professional growth purposes?

◆ What evaluation characteristics and practices increase their validity and reliability, and support a balance between meeting individuals' needs and organizational expectations?

◆ How do the Interstate School Leaders Licensure Consortium (ISLLC) standards and the National Board Certification for Principals contribute to developing and evaluating principals as instructional leaders?

◆ What contemporary teacher evaluation practices better reflect the teaching factors that matter most to student achievement?

◆ How can the research findings for teacher evaluation help principals improve teacher evaluation practices and outcomes?

◆ How can principals create school cultures to positively affect teacher and administrator evaluation and professional growth practices?

CASE STUDY: TEACHER EVALUATION STORY

Don Duke was appointed the founding principal of the new 450-student Carter Grove Elementary School. Don brought along his former assistant principal, Jim Strong, to work with him. Don had told Jim that he would be retiring in 5 years, and if Jim continued to do a good job as the assistant principal, Don would recommend him for the principalship upon retirement. Jim loved working with Don, his mentor over the past 7 years. Jim had been known to take shortcuts at times when he considered himself rushed and in a difficult political situation.

Jim had been given the responsibility to observe and evaluate the 16 classroom teachers in grades K through 3. The principal took responsibility for observing and evaluating the six classroom teachers in grades 4 and 5 and for all the special areas of music, PE, art, and special education.

Don and Jim agreed that nontenured teachers would be observed four times during the school year. A preconference would be held before the observation, and the administrator would meet with the teacher following the observation to discuss how the lesson went. For the nontenured teachers, they agreed that the first three observations would be formative in nature. The final observation would be summative based on the district's benchmarks.

At the first faculty meeting, Don announced the observation and evaluation assignments to the faculty. The nontenured teachers stayed after the faculty meeting to review observation and evaluation procedures with Don and Jim. Don explained the formative and summative assessments. The formative would be used to help the newer teachers grow as professionals. For these formative assessments, either Don or Jim would act as the "guide on their side" giving suggestions to improve instruction and mentoring their professional growth. The formative assessments would not be used to judge their teaching or to make employment decisions. That would be the role of the yearly summative assessment using the teacher evaluation benchmark system (TEBS), the school district's formal model for evaluating teacher performance as unsatisfactory, satisfactory, or meritorious.

The nontenured teachers left the meeting with positive feelings about the formative assessment process—they would be free to share their weaknesses and questions about how to improve their instructional skills. Like everyone, however, they were a bit concerned about the summative part of the assessment, but the hectic pace of starting the new (and perhaps, their first) school year put classroom visits out of their minds for the time being.

Linda Branch was a first-year second-grade teacher assigned to Jim, the assistant principal. In each of the first three formative visits, Linda had felt comfortable sharing her concerns and asking questions about the curriculum and how to manage the more unruly students. She did have some classroom management issues the first month of school as students came into the classroom at the beginning of the day, after lunch, and after PE, music, or art. Jim shared with her that all new teachers have control issues at the start. He suggested having an assignment on the board for students to complete as they come into the room and collecting it for a quiz grade on a random basis. This way the students would have a task when they entered the room, and they did not know when it might be collected and graded. It would structure the students' time more effectively.

Jim had also given Linda good advice about content and classroom management skills. Linda had a tendency to call on the first student who raised a hand. Jim explained that this did not allow time for all the students to think through the question and mentally retrieve the information. He explained how important it was to allow for wait time so all students have a chance to recall the information and rehearse it in their minds.

Linda also had a tendency to call on students in the first row and down the middle of the classroom—the "Golden T," as it is known. Jim gave her tips on how to avoid this and to call on students seated in various locations around the room. Finally, Linda often repeated the students' correct answer. Jim explained how that tends to make students discount what other students say and listen only to the teacher. He explained the idea of horizontal and vertical communication in the classroom and how beneficial vertical communication among students can be.

Linda's summative evaluation was scheduled for mid-March. Linda and Jim sat down for the preconference meeting 2 days before the summative visit. Linda had all the necessary documentation ready for Jim, and she felt prepared for a very good lesson. After the observation, Jim gave Linda a big smile and a "thumbs up" sign as he left her classroom. After school, Jim and Linda reviewed the observation notes Jim had written. The lesson had gone well. Jim noted that all the district benchmarks had rated as "satisfactory" which was rather remarkable for a first-year teacher. Linda left feeling elated that her year had gone well, she was growing as a professional, and she was moving toward achieving tenure. Jim said he would have the completed official summative form in her mailbox by Friday afternoon.

On Friday afternoon, the summative evaluation form was in Linda's mailbox. When Linda read the summative evaluation, she became angry and felt betrayed. She saw that Jim was alone in his office and went in to talk with him. She asked why the formative information was mentioned in her summative evaluation. Jim said that he was only providing context for the summative comments showing how far she had progressed. Besides, he said, the evaluation was good—better than most. Linda left without saying goodbye.

Summative Evaluation Sheet 1 (for pre-tenure teachers)

Name: Linda Branch

School: Carter Grove Elementary School

Assignment: 2nd Grade

Evaluator: Jim Strong

Pre-Tenure Teacher Benchmarks			
#1—Curriculum Knowledge: **Met**	#2—Classroom Management: **Met**	#3—Lesson Content: **Met**	#4—Questioning Techniques: **Met**
#5—Student Engagement: **Met**	#6—Use of Time: **Met**	#7—Student Rapport: **Met**	Overall Rating: **Satisfactory**

Narrative: Linda Branch is completing her first year of teaching at Carter Grove Elementary School. The summative evaluation comes from the classroom observation held on March 15 of this school year. Mrs. Branch successfully addressed each of the district's seven benchmarks in the lesson. Each of the seven benchmarks is addressed below.

#1—Curriculum Knowledge: Mrs. Branch is progressing well in this benchmark. Like any new teacher, she struggled at the start of the year, not understanding how our curriculum guides and testing protocol worked, but that has all been overcome.

#2—Classroom Management: Mrs. Branch started the year with great difficulty in this area. Her students entered the room in a very unruly and unsafe manner. After several meetings and implementing suggestions I offered, this benchmark is now satisfactory.

#3—Lesson Content: This benchmark was met well. The preconference meeting reviewed what content had been covered, how the lesson fit in with prior learning, and what objectives the lesson would lead to in the overall unit of instruction.

#4—Questioning Techniques: In this observation, questioning techniques were performed quite well. In the past, however, Mrs. Branch has demonstrated a tendency to repeat student answers and not to allow sufficient "wait time" for student responses. Mrs. Branch should continue to monitor for these practices.

#5—Student Engagement: As in the benchmark above, Mrs. Branch has improved greatly in this area since the start of the year. Earlier she had a tendency to only call on students in the front of the room and in the center row of the room. This led to many students not being engaged in the classroom activities. This lesson showed no indication of this past practice.

#6—Use of Time: Benchmark #6 is no longer a problem as was demonstrated in the lesson. By structuring students' time productively using drills and assignments on the board when students enter the room, time is better used and disciplinary problems do not detract from instructional time.

#7—Student Rapport: The lesson demonstrated that this benchmark had been met. As with most of the district benchmarks, Mrs. Branch has made considerable progress in this area. Once the classroom management, curriculum knowledge, questioning techniques, and student engagement issues were resolved, student rapport improved to a satisfactory level.

Recommendation: It is recommended that Mrs. Branch return to teach second grade at Carter Grove Elementary School. She is making satisfactory progress.

Case Study Questions

1. Why was Linda upset?
2. Was Jim correct to include incidents from the formative assessments in the summative evaluation?
3. How should this situation have been handled?

INTRODUCTION

Improving educators' performance has become a central focus in education reform. Over the past 40 years, research has shown that both instructional leadership and teacher quality are related to student achievement. Principals' and teachers' qualifications, competence, and functioning are critically important to schools' success. The public interest is no less at risk from incompetent school principals or teachers than from incompetent doctors, lawyers, or engineers. Accordingly, it is important to clearly define and assess what effective instructional leaders and teachers are expected to do so schools can use hiring, professional development, and employee evaluations to augment their educators' effectiveness, increase student achievement, and protect the public from inferior practitioners.

School districts evaluate principals and teachers for several purposes. Formative purposes address professional development, identifying ways to improve the principal's and teachers' skills, attitudes, knowledge, and behaviors that advance the school's goals. Summative purposes deal with accountability: Is the principal or teacher doing an adequate and effective job of raising student achievement and successfully meeting the other role responsibilities? Formative and summative evaluation aims are connected.

Educator evaluation holds promise for furthering the school improvement agenda. Evaluation practices, however, bring complex technical, legal, and ethical issues surrounding their design, implementation, interpretation, and use. Considering these concerns and exploring best practices in these domains can help educators develop informed views about how to approach and conduct professional evaluations.

A CONCEPTUAL FRAMEWORK FOR EDUCATIONAL EVALUATION

Most people do not enjoy being evaluated, principals and teachers included. Nevertheless, in complex organizations like schools, evaluating human performance is arguably an activity essential to both the organization's and society's well-being.

Improving principal and teacher performance has been a significant part of educational reform. Principals' increased responsibilities for instructional leadership, site-based management, and shared decision making have provided a powerful impetus for carefully analyzing principals' roles, knowledge, duties, and leadership effectiveness. Parents, teachers, citizens, superintendents, and school board members want assurances that public money is being spent wisely and that children are learning in schools led by competent principals and taught by competent teachers. Better evaluation systems, the thinking goes, will motivate personnel to consistently higher levels of functioning and lead to improved school outcomes.

Defining Personnel Evaluation

Evaluation is the process of defining, obtaining, providing, and applying descriptive and judgmental information about the merit and worth of some object's goals, design, implementation, and outcomes. Educator evaluation systems serve a range of purposes, including:[1]

◆ Screen out unqualified persons from certification and selection processes
◆ Aid institutions in terminating incompetent or unproductive personnel
◆ Provide constructive feedback to individual educators
◆ Provide direction for staff development practices
◆ Recognize and help reinforce outstanding service
◆ Provide evidence that will withstand professional and judicial scrutiny
◆ Unify teachers and administrators in their collective efforts to educate students

Evaluation information is used to guide improvement decisions, provide accountability reports, inform institutional choices, and improve understanding of the phenomena involved.[2] Information collected can be descriptive and judgmental, quantitative and qualitative. Similarly, evaluations may be formative (when they collect data for improvement) and summative (when they look back on completed activities or performances and recap their meanings for accountability). In these ways, evaluations can provide data on the evaluatee's merit (quality) and worth (cost and effectiveness in benefiting the clients or organization).

Formative and summative evaluations cannot be seen as two separate categories. Evaluations form a continuum from being purely summative (the traditional type that stresses personnel decisions) to being formative (aimed at professional growth).

When it comes to making accountability or growth decisions about employees, *measurement, evaluation,* and *assessment* have different meanings. *Measurement* refers to the process of quantifying the aspects of some physical object. Measurement typically involves using a standard instrument—such as rules, scales, or thermometers—to determine how big, tall, heavy, fat, hot, cold, or fast something actually is. *Assessment* is the process of collecting information to describe or better understand an issue. *Evaluation* refers to the comparison of data to a standard or to defined criteria for the purpose of judging worth or quality.[3] In the present context, school districts gather data (measured and assessed) about the educator's performance with reference to the job description and expected outcomes so the institution's agents can determine (evaluate) the employee's value to the organization. Outcomes of evaluation decisions have implications for the employee's continued employment and professional growth.

Personnel evaluation can be conceived as a three-phase process involving (1) determining the desired competencies, (2) describing the desired competencies of performance, and (3) making judgments or decisions based on the closeness of fit between the desired and described competencies.[4] Ideally, standards of acceptable performance should be established for each of the desired competencies. These standards may be adjusted to suit the school's particular circumstances or the principal's or teachers' experiences. Discrepancies between standards and actual performance require specific attention. The gap may reflect either the individual's unacceptable performance or a weakness in the standards used to describe acceptable performance. Therefore, the evaluation decision can provide feedback to either performance (the actual) or standards (the ideal).

Accountability and Professional Growth

Two of the most frequently cited purposes of personnel evaluation are accountability and professional growth. These two purposes are often described as incompatible, repeatedly resulting in a focus on one to the virtual exclusion of the other. To be productive, personnel systems must remedy this imbalance and address each dimension fairly.

Accountability reflects the need to determine an individual's professional competence to ensure that services delivered are safe and effective. Individual principals' and teachers' performances need to be assessed to determine whether they are meeting predetermined expectations. Typically, this perspective is summative in nature. By contrast, performance improvement reflects the organization's and individuals' need for professional growth and development; this perspective has traditionally been considered as formative.

In reality, evaluations for summative accountability and formative professional development, are continuous and interactive processes. In fact, evaluation systems that reflect both accountability and personal growth goals are not only desirable but also necessary if the evaluation is to constructively serve both the individual evaluatees and the larger community.

If an evaluation system is to serve multiple purposes, a rational link must exist between them. According to McGreal (1988), a single evaluation system can successfully meet multiple evaluation purposes when the system is viewed as one component of a larger mission—advancing the organization's goals.[5] Combining institutional and individual development goals has its tensions, but an effective evaluation system needs both.[6] Performance improvement and accountability are mutually supportive, rather than competing interests—both essential for improving educational service delivery and generating acceptable outcomes.

Principals and Tenure

Summative decisions about employment or granting tenure have the most serious consequences. The accountability movement has produced major changes in administrator tenure policies. Principals and assistant principals do not always have tenure rights as administrators.

State law, case law, contract law, and school board policies determine whether principals may or may not have tenure's legal protections as principals.[7] Their continuing contract property rights may relate only to their tenure as teachers (*if* the principal has already earned tenure as a teacher in that school district). In this context, negative summative evaluations may mean return to a teaching position, assignment to a lesser administrative position, or loss of employment. In contrast, when teachers hold tenure and a continuing contract with the school district, evaluations are usually aimed at improving instruction. They may involve providing constructive feedback about performance or suggestions for change in a teacher's practice or preparation. If, however, the tenured teacher is not performing satisfactorily, the teacher may be given a written plan with intensive remediation assistance and the goal to either measurably improve or risk dismissal.

Many states that ended principal tenure allowed then-current administrators to retain their tenure status. In other states, the combination of contract laws and court rulings helps protect principals from arbitrary personnel actions. Many states with collective bargaining agreements for principals have adopted performance-based contract language without tenure protection. Principals must acquaint themselves with relevant contract law before entering negotiations for appointment, including state laws, school board policies, and case law. Administrators must also be prepared to negotiate specific working conditions and evaluation criteria reflecting the degree to which the districts provide resources required for success.[8]

The absence of principal tenure has serious implications for school effectiveness. First, a growing body of evidence demonstrates that principals have an important impact on schools, teachers, and student achievement.[9] Second, principal retention and teacher retention are closely linked. Schools with high levels of principal retention tend to have higher levels of teacher retention.[10] Plus, a small body of research has shown that low teacher retention can have serious negative financial and educational impacts on schools.[11] Third, any school reform effort relies on principals' efforts to create a common school vision that focuses on implementing the reform effort over multiple years. Creating such visions and thoughtfully integrating reform efforts into the school culture takes a sustained effort—possibly 5 years to fully implement a large-scale endeavor.[12] Finally, as with teacher turnover, principal turnover is costly. Not only does a school district have to spend resources on recruiting, hiring, and training a new principal, but high principal turnover also increases the district's losses of its investment in building the principal's capacity and the associated lower student achievement associated with ineffective principal leadership.[13]

Serving the Organization and the Individual

Evaluation serves both the individual's and the organization's needs for quality assurance (accountability) and growth. Table 10–1 illustrates the relationship among these dimensions. For the individual, decisions about professional improvement are formative information (identify areas for professional growth) whereas decisions about accountability are summative (e.g., whether the principal continues as principal or whether the teacher receives a contract extension, tenure, or dismissal). For the organization, information about change for the better leads to school improvement decisions while data about accountability leads to conclusions about school status (such as certification or adequate yearly progress).

TABLE 10–1

Basic Purposes of Educator Evaluation

Purpose	Individual	Organizational
Improvement (formative information)	Individual staff development	School improvement
Accountability (summative information)	Individual personnel (job status) decisions	School status (e.g., certification, accreditation) decisions

Source: Adapted from Darling-Hammond, L., Wise, A. E., & Pease, S. R., "Teacher evaluation in the organizational context: A review of the literature," *Review of Educational Research, 53*(3), p. 302, copyright © 1983. Reprinted by Permission of SAGE Publications.

In general, principal and teacher evaluation for accountability purposes must be capable of yielding reasonably objective, standardized, and externally defensible data about principal and teacher performance. In contrast, evaluation useful for improvement objectives must yield rich, descriptive information that highlights sources of difficulty as well as viable avenues for upgrading knowledge, skills, or practices. Educator evaluation methods designed to inform organizational decisions must be administered hierarchically and controlled to ensure credibility and uniformity across work settings. All principals in a school district must use the same formative and summative evaluation practices with all their teachers if results are to be perceived as fair and believable.

Likewise, evaluation methods intended to support making decision about individuals must consider the context in which individual performance occurs to ensure enough appropriate data. Evaluating a principal requires, for instance, the superintendent to review such data as the school's grade levels and total student enrollment, the student and teacher demographic information, several years' worth of disaggregated student achievement and school climate statistics (such as the dropout rate, discipline referrals, percentage of diplomas conferred), plus school improvement plans in order to make a fair and credible judgment about the principal's effectiveness.

Although formative and summative evaluation purposes and approaches are not necessarily mutually exclusive, an emphasis on one may tend to limit the pursuit of the other. Therefore, it is important to consider which techniques best support the desired ends if educator evaluation goals and process are to be congruent. Scholars have concluded that the typically low levels of reliability, generalizability, and validity attributed to traditional principal or teacher evaluation methods suggest that one-way approaches for assessing educator effectiveness are unlikely to capture enough information about principal or teacher attributes to completely satisfy any of the evaluation purposes.[14] Rather, multiple methods for evaluating principals and teachers can and should be employed.

Principals' Role Conflict.   Principals have responsibilities for both supervising and evaluating teachers. While *evaluation* refers to the administrative task of judging the effectiveness of teaching, often to determine the teacher's future employment status, *supervision* refers to a developmental process that includes efforts designed to improve the individual teacher's instructional behaviors. Evaluating involves judging; supervising involves coaching.

Although some argue that the two roles are irreconcilable,[15] contemporary practice and statutory requirements in many states oblige principals to assume both roles, regardless of the inherent conflict between evaluating and coaching behaviors.[16] Principals must rely on their people skills, their communication skills, and their professional ethics to successfully navigate these two roles.

ACTIVITY 10.1   Potential Areas of Confusion Between Formative and Summative Evaluation

Case Study Question 1: Why was Linda upset?

Accountability and professional development, and summative and formative evaluations, are continuous and interactive processes. Educational evaluation can encompass both purposes. In fact, evaluation systems that reflect both accountability and personal growth goals are not only desirable but also necessary if the evaluation is to constructively serve both the individual evaluatees and the larger community. Discuss as a class:

1. Given the close and interactive relationship between formative and summative evaluations—between the need for both professional growth and accountability—where are the areas of possible confusion and potential conflict for both Linda and Jim?
2. As assistant principal, what might Jim do from the first day of the school year to prevent teachers'—or his own—confusion about the role of formative evaluation data in a summative evaluation report and his own roles as a coach and evaluator?

Issues in Evaluating Educational Personnel

Educators' evaluation practices come with serious limitations. These include conceptual, methodological, and practical concerns: using simplistic and inaccurate approaches, balancing individual and institutional demands, navigating the political dynamics, and resolving ethical issues. To the extent possible, we will first consider the issues common to principal and teacher evaluation systems before looking at the unique aspects of each.

Simplistic and Inaccurate Approaches.   Evaluation methods that depend on test scores, job descriptions, personal qualities, or research-based "best practices" carry their own shortcomings. Results-based evaluations focus primarily on desired outcomes—usually easily measured test scores—and the degree to which the principal (working through teachers and the learning climate) or the teachers have been able to achieve these. But it is invalid and unhelpful to infer progress when comparing test scores from two different years of student cohorts—such as comparing this year's fifth graders with last year's fifth graders.[17] Additionally, while valid job descriptions focus on what principals are expected to do in their role, these descriptions must go beyond the generic and account for local context and individual school priorities if determining a gap between actual and expected performance is to be meaningful.[18]

Likewise, assessing the principal's personal qualities—such as leadership, knowledge of curriculum and instruction, time management, and interpersonal expertise—considered most likely to affect the school's academic quality or overall effectiveness, tends to artificially separate performance from the context in which it occurs. Then too, even the best practices approach requires an evaluation protocol that accurately and completely identifies the desired behaviors and provides sufficient evaluator training to permit valid and reliable results when different observers are providing data.

Given these very real concerns, research finds that principal evaluation has been less than clear, systematic, or purposeful. Questionnaires, checklists, interviews, observation scales, videotaping, time sampling, and critical incidents reports all attempt to measure principals' performance, but these instruments and procedures measure only behavior's frequency rather than its potency or quality.[19] Little empirical support exists for any of these practices.[20] Yet despite their weaknesses, these approaches are still used to collect data for principals' formal assessments.

If the overall purpose of educator evaluation is to provide data for making sound decisions and increasing organizational effectiveness, then evaluation procedures should match this intent. But largely, they do not. Several reasons explain why. Many districts use evaluation methods not designed to strengthen principal performance, but to satisfy accountability requirements that require principal evaluation.[21] Also, finding appropriate means to evaluate principals is difficult because the job is not easily described or characterized, the principal's work varies markedly, and different stakeholders hold varying expectations for principals' behavior.[22] In addition, principals often act in ways that may be judged appropriate or inappropriate depending on the situational context.[23]

As a result, Drake and Roe (1999) concluded, "In too many instances, principals have reported that their evaluations are superficial, nonexistent (in a formal sense), or based on informal feedback to the superintendent and/or board members."[24]

Ideally, principal and teacher evaluation should obtain information about performance in each of the desired role-related domains, recognize the local milieu and its cultural and contextual variables, have flexibility for different role perceptions, be multidimensional, and use various data sources.[25] This is a highly complex assignment and well beyond the scope of most local principal or teacher evaluation protocols.

Balancing Individual and Institutional Demands.   Healthy organizations support a dynamic relationship between the individual and the institution. What is assumed to be good for the organization is assumed to be good for the individual. Getzels and Guba's (1957) classic model of social behavior and the administrative process observed that since the social system's roles and expectations will be implemented by flesh-and-blood people with unmet needs, the organization must consider their personalities and dispositions.[26] This orientation enhances both the individual's and the institution's ability to achieve mutually desired goals and results in a satisfying organizational climate. The greater the fit between job characteristics and the individual's self-characterization, and between work requirements and the requirements of other personal roles, the higher the individual's satisfaction. Balancing individual needs with institutional expectations is vital for promoting productive and fulfilling work environments.

Providing this balance becomes easier when clear school or system-wide purposes anchor all organizational action, including personnel evaluation. If the school district's overriding purpose is to support the success of every student, then the evaluation system should reflect this perspective.[27] When individual and institutional goals are intertwined—when assessing principals' and teachers' effectiveness is seen as a means to support the success of every student—then an effective evaluation system can meet both accountability and professional growth/organizational improvement goals.

Likewise, an evaluation system that emphasizes professional growth rather than minimal competence offers greater potential for systematically enhancing the organization and moving it toward accomplishing its stated goals. Professional growth promotes organizational learning. If, however, performance evaluation systems are to support professional growth, both organizational barriers (such as incompatibility of individual and institutional needs) and personal barriers (such as disillusionment, distrust, stress, and fear of failure) must be removed.[28]

A properly designed and implemented personnel evaluation system supports a balanced relationship between institution and individual. It is a partnership between the organization and employees—a social process that results in a participatory approach to evaluation. Such a process creates a relevant, mutually beneficial personnel evaluation system.

Political Dynamics.   Schools are often seen as miniature political systems, "nested in multi-level governmental structure, charged with salient public service responsibilities and depending on diverse constituencies."[29] As American society becomes more complex and diverse, more people expect more of schools. School leadership becomes political work as leaders create "defensible guidelines for actions out of competing, values-based interests."[30]

Politics may be defined as "the study of influence," or "the exercise or use of power to achieve one's ends."[31] Power represents the potential ability to influence behavior, to change the course of events, and to get people to do things that they would otherwise not do. Such influence is central to all aspects of the development, adoption, and implementation of a personnel evaluation system in education.[32] In complex organizations like schools, political behavior thrives on conflict, disorder, ambiguity, and a lack of common purposes or goals.[33] Political activities often create winners and losers and compromise at the expense of quality.

In contrast, a more benign view of politics sees it as a natural and healthy process through which people and organizations resolve value conflicts; sort through competing interests and needs; and establish goals, priorities, and personal influence. In these settings, politics is the process by which things get done.[34]

Evaluations involve values, and values are open to competing expectations. Virtually every school district evaluates its employees, certified and classified, alike. Principal and teacher evaluations embody the school community's values and expectations regarding school leadership, teaching, and learning. Opposing expectations about what is good practice require educating and gaining political support from varied stakeholders.

Ideally, these personnel evaluation systems would be based solely on employee merit and performance, encourage improved practice, and remove those persons whose performance is marginal or unsatisfactory. Fairness, objectivity, and rationality would be emphasized. In many instances, however, this is not what happens. Personnel evaluation as a purely rational and objective process rarely exists. The extent to which performance evaluations may be tainted by political factors, however, varies greatly within schools and between schools and school districts. Given this reality, developing and conducting fair, objective, valid, and reliable performance evaluations becomes essential to protect effective educators.

Developing a *professional* evaluation system, therefore, requires school leadership to integrate keen technical and political skills during the evaluation program's development and implementation. Principal and teacher participation in designing the evaluation program enhances the final product because it allows the political processes of expression, discussion of opposing views, and bargaining to occur before people must work with the policy decision. Although a political compromise usually does not resolve all opposing views, involvement in the political process itself offers a forum for both information exchange and persuasion. At the very least, it makes the issues' complexities more understandable and appreciated. Also, given evaluation's high stakes, both principals and teachers must develop a sense of ownership in the final product and commitment to its success. Teacher–administrator collaboration is a means for developing and keeping trust and mutuality in the evaluation process and for building productive supervisory relationships.[35] Their active involvement encourages participants to understand and accept the system's validity, mechanics, and clear and consistent rationale—three essentials in producing a credible, feasible, and meaningful evaluation system.[36] In short, for a professional evaluation system to be effective, it must be both technically and politically viable.

Linking personnel performance with the organization's mission is another way to reduce political concerns in evaluation. If the evaluation system enhances the principals' and teachers' ability to grow professionally and improves their leadership and classroom performance, the data collected for the evaluation process support the mission. When the links between evaluation and mission become obvious, arbitrary political influences are less likely to intrude, and the school is more likely to be a better place for working and learning.

Being politically astute does not require capitulating to stakeholder views. Although principals must gain the support of teachers, parents, community members, and supervisors, school leaders do not have to concentrate on being well liked or overly accommodating. Effective principals use discretion in communicating with others. They understand that it is very difficult, if not impossible, to please all school constituents all the time. Instead, principals must be lucid communicators, fair and even-tempered in dealing with people and issues, and consistent in how they enact their basic philosophical convictions and beliefs about education in their day-to-day school management. Since disagreements become worse without positive relationships, it makes sense for principals to build strong associations with teachers, students, and parents to reduce the intensity of possible future conflicts. Establishing positive connections with influential groups like the PTA, boosters' clubs, and employees' unions not only builds trust and support but also helps offset the occasional "squeaky wheel's" harmful effects on superintendent and school board perceptions about a principal's competence.

Ethical Concerns.   Accurately evaluating educators raises several ethical concerns. Improper considerations may be made to appear legitimate. What counts as an acceptable level of worth depends on the context. For instance, when the supply pool for hiring outstanding principals is very low, a school district may hire or keep less-than-effective principals. What is "acceptable" varies with the circumstances. Similarly, a competent principal with unpopular political views may cost a school substantial community support in terms of goodwill and resources. Thinking simplistically about worth—possibly replacing an adequate principal with an outstanding principal—brings potential ethical and legal consequences. Principals and teachers are individuals with legal rights upon which their supervisors cannot infringe.

Invalid personnel evaluation methods have hidden costs to children, to taxpayers and society, and to the individuals involved. A false positive error occurs when a decision is wrongly made in favor of the evaluatee; a false negative error refers to an unfavorable action that was incorrect. Collectively, in one high school principal's career, the effect of incorrect advice and counseling, incorrect selection, and incorrect promotion and retention of faculty and staff will add up to a very large adverse effect on 20,000 students' education.[37]

Similar ethical issues affect teachers. On many occasions, the teacher evaluation model is invalid, and the teacher will be given incorrect advice about improvement. Similarly, good teachers are passed over for a job or for promotion in favor of less good teachers (false negative error), and bad teachers are retained who should have been let go (false positive error). Often, teachers are misdirected on the basis of formative evaluations so they waste much time changing themselves in ways that do not lead to improvement—and in some cases may lead to weakening their teaching skills (false negative). Or teachers are told they do not need to improve, while in fact they need a great deal of improvement (false positive). The total costs include wasted time and a reduced sense of accomplishment because the "improvements" do not work (and students continue to receive bad teaching mistakenly thought to be good).

Ethically, legally, and practically, validity and reliability are extremely important qualities for evaluation instruments and processes. Ethical evaluation system practices that increase validity and reliability include the following:[38]

♦ *Specificity of acceptable performance that permits structured, objective, and low-inference observations*. For example, if principals are expected to "create and implement school improvement plans to achieve goals," the evaluator would look for evidence of annually (or biannually) updated school improvement plans and collected school data used to identify and assess progress toward meeting these goals. Such details would increase interrater reliability. Unambiguous rubrics accompany this specificity and reduce prejudice and arbitrariness in evaluation practices. Designing performance expectations specific enough to be structured and objective but not too simplistic to be meaningful is a notable goal.

♦ *Complete criteria that describe the professional responsibilities*. For principals, this includes activities for instructional leadership, facility management, efficient resource allocation, and community involvement. For teachers, this includes activities inside and outside the classroom (marking and returning students' papers, working with parents, serving on committees, and planning) and less visible activities (in-depth knowledge of the subject, knowledge of assessment, and fairness to all students). Developing a complete set of competencies is very challenging.

♦ *Relevant criteria for the position*. Qualities on which the individual will be evaluated should be closely related to the position held. For instance, leadership potential, sociability, or students' raw achievement scores from standardized tests (without accounting for students' prior achievement, academic ability, and maturation rate) have no justification in evaluating teaching.

♦ *Adequate sampling*. A high school teacher has around 1,000 class sessions a year; an elementary teacher has many potential observation opportunities. Most teachers will have good days and bad days, for no particular reason or for a variety of reasons. A reasonable sample size might be a 4% to 5% sample (i.e., 40 to 50 visits). In practice, however, most teacher evaluations are based on one to four classroom visits. This may or may not be sufficient. Adequate sampling for principals is even more complicated. They perform more varied roles in a greater variety of settings than teachers do. What defines adequate sampling for principals has not yet been determined.

♦ *Typical sampling*. The evaluator's presence in the classroom is a nontypical sample. The principal's attendance during instruction changes the classroom environment—for better or worse. The same dynamic is likely true for a supervisor observing a principal in action. The very presence of the observer makes the sample atypical.

♦ *Properly weighing evaluation variables*. Certain evaluation components are worth more than others in the overall assessment of principal or teacher effectiveness. Sound evaluation criteria specify their relative importance. If a criterion is necessary, to some degree, a minimum score must be specified for it—qualitatively or quantitatively. Improperly weighting or having no specific weighting for criteria of merit makes the eventual synthesis into an overall evaluative conclusion highly arbitrary and subject to bias.

◆ *Using non-manipulable measures.* Evaluation criteria and artifacts to be used as evidence should be those that the employee cannot willingly distort or manipulate. For example, teacher grades for student achievement contain much teacher bias. Likewise, certain standardized tests are susceptible to teacher coaching and teaching to the test.

Additional Characteristics of High-Quality Performance Evaluation Systems

High-quality personnel evaluation systems contain certain concepts and criteria that balance the individuals' and organizations' needs. In addition to the ethical considerations already discussed, a balanced performance evaluation system also includes mutually-shared goals, effectively communicated evaluation expectations, an appropriate evaluation climate, two-way communication, technical rationality, and use of multiple data sources.[39]

◆ *Mutually-shared goals.* Reciprocity in the workplace respects both the organization's production orientation and the individual employee's personal and professional needs. Unless a rational relationship exists between institutional and individual purposes, the institution's efforts are likely to be ineffective or dysfunctional. The individual's and organization's belief systems must be compatible, with both tied to the organization's mission.

◆ *Fair, consistent, communicated evaluation expectations.* Personnel evaluation systems should practice effective communications in every aspect of the process, public (public relations) and private (interpersonal). Publicly, school employees and the general public have the right to know about institutional goals, how evaluation relates to these goals, how job descriptions and duties are developed, standards of acceptable performance, guidelines and safeguards in the evaluation system, and the evaluation timeline. In contrast, ongoing, two-way communication between evaluator and evaluatee must be more personal and private. Good communication in this area will include cooperative development of an evaluation plan, provide systematic opportunity for individual skill enhancement and improved performance, increase the likelihood of behavior changes, allow the employee to express expectations for his or her own growth;, identify ways to reach higher standards and correct significant gaps between actual and desired performance, and establish a checks and balances system for the evaluation process. In addition, this communication will be clear, meaningful, and relevant to the individual's and organization's goals.

◆ *Climate for quality evaluation.* An environment that fosters mutual trust and cooperation between evaluator and evaluatee holds the greatest potential for benefiting both parties. This requires consideration—fair and humane treatment among employers and employees—along with consistent empathy, honesty, and esteem in personal relationships. On the other hand, when employees are not measuring up to reasonable performance expectations, and when improvement through remediation (i.e., *clinical supervision*—intensive, structured efforts to improve performance) does not fix the problem, it may become necessary to make negative personnel decisions based on those evaluation results. Ultimately, the students' best interests must be protected.

◆ *Technical rationality.* While a conceptually sound and technically correct personnel evaluation system will not guarantee effective evaluations, a technically flawed and irrational system will ensure failure. *Technical rationality*—the ability of an evaluation system to meet established standards and guidelines—promotes the likelihood of achieving desirable outcomes that effectively serve students and society, establishes evaluation practices free from unnecessary threat or demoralizing characteristics, and facilitates planning for sound professional development. In addition, a technically rational evaluation system will meet standards of propriety (legally and ethically acceptable), utility (useful, informative, timely, and influential), feasibility (efficient, viable in the organizational context, and relatively easy to use), and accuracy (valid and reliable).[40] Proper use of the standards can provide assurances of quality control to stakeholders and can support improvement in the overall personnel evaluation process.[41]

◆ *Using multiple data sources.* An effective personnel performance evaluation system will emphasize multifaceted assessment techniques to document job performance. For any professional, multiple information sources increase an evaluation's validity. These data should be gathered throughout the year by regularly scheduled and unscheduled visits as well as by means other than direct formal observation. Although formal observation can be a significant data source, it is too frequently the only data source.[42] Additional performance data can come from ongoing anecdotal and informal performance observations, questioning (interviews with students, parents, teachers, peers, and self-assessment), artifact analysis (from performance logs, service records, school improvement data, lesson plans, and portfolios), and direct analysis of student performances, products, and achievement. Quantitative data that reflect the effects of principal decision making and leadership behaviors also inform this viewpoint. These sources provide the evaluator and evaluatee with a more complete, realistic, detailed, objective, valid, and reliable picture of actual job performance and provide a platform upon which to develop realistic improvement plans.

Given the political and ethical concerns that affect professional evaluations, educators can take the following pragmatic suggestions to enhance the process's fairness:

◆ *Maintain a file of important documents.* The principal should maintain a file of important documents such as the school's accomplishments, evidence of student achievement, positive data about dropouts and discipline, and a record of notable leadership activities and professional development accomplishments. These can verify and communicate the range and quality of the principal's job performance. Also essential to keep in this file are copies of all positive correspondence received from students, teachers, parents, community members, and other administrators. Likewise, teachers can keep copies of their students' achievement, an account of their leadership activities inside and outside the school, and evidence of positive correspondence from students, parents, community members, and administrators. Copies of such documents and other verifications of job effectiveness should be provided to evaluators throughout the year as data to refute arbitrary and capricious attempts to discredit the principal's or teacher's professional competence.

◆ *Take an active role in the evaluation process.* Principals and teachers must be fully aware of the criteria or processes used in their evaluations and make an effort to help shape both the evaluation process and job performance goals and objectives. Principals and teachers should ensure that important on-the-job decisions and behaviors align with the evaluation criteria and goals established with the supervisor.

◆ *Serve the public well.* Consistently dissatisfied teachers, parents, or community members generally result in brief principal tenures. Principals and teachers must maintain positive relationships with other people and develop their school stakeholders' trust and support. They must present themselves as caring, open, honest, forthright, and balanced in their efforts to address others' needs and concerns. And they must do a consistent and verifiably good job of meeting their responsibilities to their students.

ACTIVITY 10.2   Appropriate Data for Formative Assessments

Case Study Question 2: Was Jim correct to include incidents from the formative assessments in the summative evaluation? Discuss this as a class activity.

Case Study Question 3: How should this situation have been handled?

An evaluation system that emphasizes professional growth depends on removing organizational and personal barriers, including incompatibility of organizational and personal goals, personal disillusionment, distrust, stress, and fear of failure. A properly designed and implemented personnel evaluation system supports a balanced relationship—a partnership, a social process—between the institution and the individual. Discuss in pairs and then as a class:

1. How does the way Jim (the assistant principal) handled this situation jeopardize the ability of the school district's evaluation system to promote teachers' professional growth and improve teaching and learning?

2. In what ways is Jim mishandling the political aspects of teacher evaluation? What might he do now with an upset teacher to restore trust and develop a sense of mutual ownership in the final evaluation product?

3. Given what the case study tells you about the school district's evaluation system and the summative evaluation sheet, how does the system address the ethical issues of specificity, complete and relevant criteria, adequate and typical sampling, and proper weight? What might be an ethical way for Jim to handle this situation?

4. High-quality personnel evaluation systems include mutuality of goals, effective two-way communication, an appropriate evaluation climate, technical rationality, and use of multiple data sources. How well does the evaluation system described in this case study address each of these factors? What would have to happen to improve this system's quality?

PRINCIPAL FORMATIVE AND SUMMATIVE EVALUATION

Societal shifts and school reform efforts have made the principal's role more demanding. Expectations for principals' performance have increased. Using relevant metaphors, Beck and Murphy (1993) have described major changes in principals' role expectations: values broker (1920s), scientific manager (1930s), democratic leader (1940s), theory-guided administrator (1950s), bureaucratic executive (1960s), humanistic facilitator (1970s), and instructional leader (1980s to the present).[43] The 1990s' school restructuring reforms further identified the principal as a transformational leader who must be involved in school problem finding and problem solving, shared decision making, decentralized leadership, and systemic change.[44]

Chapter 1 considered the principal as an instructional leader whose responsibilities have an indirect but measurable impact on student achievement. Identifying the relevant performance expectations for principals' personnel evaluations, however, has proven more difficult.

Research on Principal Evaluation Practices

The systematic study of principal evaluation has been slow to develop. During the 1970s and 1980s, the increased research on school effectiveness advanced the use of achievement data to evaluate schools' instructional efforts. This research suggested that improved student outcomes could be attained through strategic school organization and strong principal leadership.[45] The demands for improved quality of educational outcomes are policy decisions directed at holding district administrators and principals accountable for schools' academic performance.

Despite the policy interest in evaluating principals' effectiveness, several investigators have decried the lack of research on actual principal evaluation practices.[46] In a comprehensive review of the literature to 1990, Ginsberg and Berry found a wide array of procedures reported but little systematic research to support one approach over another. Most commonly, principals were assessed by preset performance standards using behavioral criteria that applied observational rating scales.[47] Preset standards, however, have limitations. They ignore the situational nature and varied job expectations, use low inference criteria that can be observed, and thus present an oversimplified picture of the dynamic nature and complex tasks that are principals' work.[48]

Conceptual and Methodological Problems.   Establishing effective principal evaluation methods has significant conceptual and methodological problems.[49] In spite of the general consensus that principals' behaviors affect student achievement, the varying conceptualizations and applications of educational leadership and the differing methodologies used to examine leadership's effects on student achievement make principal leadership difficult to measure or evaluate.

Over the years, educational leadership has been understood and operationalized in different ways: as an administrator emphasizing stability and efficiency or as a leader stressing adaptive change and getting people to agree about what needs to be accomplished. Many theorists define the principalship in terms of general job tasks and responsibilities, while others label it in terms of administrative functions or behavioral competencies.[50] Constructs such as school climate, high expectations, coordination and organization, and even instructional leadership are difficult to translate into discrete, observable behaviors and do not easily lend themselves to observation and measurement for evaluation purposes. This lack of conceptual congruence and clarity requires empirical caution when studying school leadership regardless of statistical models or other methodology, because *school leadership* may not mean the same thing in all studies.

Additionally, traditional principal evaluation measures have been unreliable, of questionable validity, and incomplete. Evaluation instruments have included lists of behavioral objectives, principal characteristics, competencies, and performance standards. These tend to be descriptive and perceptually based, relying on teacher, parent, or district administrator surveys. Demonstrated competence, compliance, or completion of discrete tasks constitutes "excellent" (but often decontextualized) performance. Also, these criteria ignore the question of what educational goals the principal's impact achieved.

Some scholars see this checklist approach as promoting a "fudge factor"[51] that allows power and influence to affect the evaluation results more strongly than do criteria related to schools' performance or outcomes. As a result, principal evaluation systems break down even when they are state-wide and carefully monitored. Inconsistencies develop because of the differences between the nature of principals' work and the nature of the evaluation decoupled from context. These inconsistencies result in conflict and ambiguity.[52]

Likewise, researchers generally concur that principal leadership's effects are indirect if not difficult to measure.[53] Sometimes, the principal's effects on student achievement are interactive, with school leaders adapting to the organization in which they work, changing their own thinking and behavior over time.[54] Many studies focus on a narrow sample of schools—for example, urban elementary schools in large districts or outliers. This approach precludes the systematic study of how a wide spectrum of organizational conditions influence principal leadership and other school processes or produce larger effects than might be observed in more "average" school conditions.[55] Few studies link principal attributes directly to student achievement. Some that do have methodological weaknesses.[56] According to Hallinger and Heck (1998), studies in which indirect effect models are used show a greater impact of school leadership on student performance than do studies employing direct models.[57]

The sheer complexity of the principal's role within the school organization makes determining cause and effect difficult. Despite some encouraging findings about the principal's central role in promoting school effectiveness, the specific manner in which principals as school leaders may contribute to the precise linkages between school context, school variables, and student achievement outcomes is less clear. Creating a personalized and motivating learning environment for students may look different in separate schools. How the individual principal behaves may depend on personal values and beliefs as well as organizational and political factors associated with the school and community context (district size, level of schooling, students' socioeconomic status, pressures from district and community, access to knowledge, staff characteristics). As a result, empirical validating of the causal relationship among a complex set of variables comprising the school's cultural milieu remains vague.[58]

The need for accountability—practical and empirical—calls for the development of a principal evaluation protocol that is easy to use; brings consensus, clarity, validity, and reliability about the principal's role to the appraisal process; and serves both formative and summative ends. Heck and Marcoulides (1992) concluded that this endeavor must begin with a strong dose of humility, acknowledging that no one universal paradigm or theory for examining the complexity of school leader behavior will be valid in all contexts. At the same time, it seems reasonable that at a minimum, some relatively generic and finite set of leadership activities is required to manage institutions, and effective leadership may be the result of principals' abilities to fine-tune their actions to their particular settings' needs and realities. Since focusing on principals' behavior related to goal attainment is easier to operationalize and measure than principals' attitudes or cognitive strategies, it becomes a useful basis for developing principal assessments.[59] We will now consider several performance evaluation advances that move principal appraisal toward these ends.

The Personnel Evaluation Standards

Like other professional fields, educator evaluation requires standards to guide professional practice, hold practitioners accountable, and provide goals for upgrading the profession's services. Sponsored by the Joint Committee (which includes 16 professional education organizations) and first published in 1988 (updated in 2008), the *Personnel Evaluation Standards*[60] provides comprehensive sets of benchmarks and practical guidelines for educator evaluation that highlights the evaluatee's welfare. Focusing on processes, not content, the standards seek to ensure that any evaluation system possesses the following four attributes:[61]

◆ *Propriety.* The evaluation system protects the rights of persons affected by it, including students.
◆ *Utility.* Evaluations are informative, timely and influential, focused on predetermined uses, and conducted by people with expertise and credibility.
◆ *Feasibility.* The system is efficient, easy to use, adequately funded, and politically viable.
◆ *Accuracy.* Evaluations produce information that is dependable and technically defensible, with conclusions logically supported with data.

Rather than promote specific evaluation systems, the standards were designed to ensure that whatever system is in place provides ethical, legal, useful, feasible, accurate, and reliable procedures most likely to generate the desired results. While not complete in their context or policy scope, the standards serve as a relevant touchstone for developing successful principal and teacher evaluation systems.

ISLLC Standards and Principal Assessment

As discussed in Chapter 1, the Interstate School Leaders Licensure Consortium (ISLLC) produced the *ISLLC Standards for School Leaders* in 1996 (updated in 2008).[62] Not meant to be all-inclusive, these six research-based policy standards focus on indicators of traits, functions of work, and responsibilities that districts expect of their school leaders in order to raise student achievement. They are intended for use in principal preparation, licensing, hiring, induction, and professional development that span principals' career. At least 43 states are using the ISLLC Standards for School Leaders in their entirety or as a template for developing their own standards.[63] The 2008 ISLLC revision reflects the updated research base available since the original standards appeared.

The Chapter 10 Appendix at the end of the chapter includes a Principal Quality Rubric (PQR) based on ISLLC standards which this book's authors developed for use in principal professional growth and principal effectiveness assessment. Rated high in construct validity by a panel of 10 nationally-recognized educators involved with the ISLLC Standards' development or refinement, the PQR has been used in national studies,[64] unpublished research, and as a metric to help students in educational leadership assess their own professional skills and monitor their growth. It offers readers the opportunity to see how specific principal behaviors rate on four level of capacity according to professionally-validated standards.

Likewise, the National Council for the Accreditation of Teacher Education (NCATE) has scaffolded the ISLLC standards into their accreditation process for educational administration programs.[65] Presently, all NCATE-accredited principal preparation programs in the United States have adopted the ISLLC standards.[66]

By 2002, the Educational Testing Service (ETS) had developed the complementary School Leaders Licensure Assessment (SLLA) to assess beginning principal candidates. In 2009, the SLLA became a 4-hour test with 7 constructed-response essay questions and 100 multiple-choice questions. Each essay question focuses on a specific content area related to the standards addressed in ISLLC 2008 and calls for written answers based on scenarios and a set of documents that an educational leader may encounter. In answering the questions, candidates must analyze situations and data, propose appropriate courses of action, and provide rationales for their proposals. According to the ETS website, 18 states the District of Columbia, and the U.S. Virgin Islands use the SLLA to grant a credential to become a K–12 school administrator.

Instruments to Assess Principals' Effectiveness

The lack of valid and reliable measures for empirically exploring the principal's role limits successful studies of principals' impact on student learning. Prior to 1980, neither coherent models nor validated instruments were available for studying instructional leadership.[67] As of 2008, there were no school leadership assessment instruments in use in the United States that had undergone rigorous psychometric development or yield both norm- and standard-referenced scores.[68] Despite this, virtually all school districts in the United States continue to assess and evaluate principals, mostly using "homegrown" evaluation tools.

As discussed earlier, locally available principal assessment instruments have questionable usefulness in appraising principals' instructional leadership skills. One 2007 study of 66 principal assessment instruments concluded that not all those currently in use focus on learning-centered instructional leadership or show consensus about what should be assessed; over half of these report relying on the ISLLC standards or a variation of them. Only about two thirds of the instruments monitored curriculum, quality instruction, culture of learning, or professional behavior.[69]

Recognizing the growing need for school districts to have as much information as possible to make high-stakes decisions about whom they hire as principals and how or whether they should invest in their improvement, a 2009 study examined principal evaluation instruments to determine which method was best suited for judging school leaders' effectiveness. Learning Points Associates, a nonprofit educational consulting firm, reviewed eight principal performance instruments in use by school districts that were expressly intended for assessment purposes, were publicly available for purchase, and had been psychometrically tested for validity and reliability. Researchers concluded that the Vanderbilt Assessment of Leadership in Education (VAL-ED) rated the best among the instruments for validity and reliability.[70]

The newly developed VAL-ED is a set of evidence-based rating scales aligned with ISLLC standards with clear focus on school principals' learning-centered leadership behaviors known to directly influence teachers' performance and students' learning.[71] The 360-degree survey is taken by teachers, principals, and administrators to provide comprehensive and constructive feedback to the principal. Each individual rates the principal's performance on 72 behaviors, from 1 for "ineffective" to 5 for "outstandingly effective," after first being asked to consider the sources of evidence on which the rating is based, such as personal observations or school documents. For example, a typical item might ask, "How effective is the principal at ensuring the school evaluates the rigor of the curriculum?"[72] The results of the survey are designed to help the principal become a better school leader.

Although it may be an improvement over currently available principal evaluation protocols, VAL-ED has its limitations. These include its near complete reliance on participants' perceptions of principals' leadership behaviors without consideration of student learning gains, customer satisfaction, or actual presence of the core components in the school building such as a rigorous curriculum, high-quality instruction, or the value added to student achievement.[73]

National Board Certification for Principals

To create a consistently reliable process to develop, recognize, and retain effective principals, the National Board for Professional Teaching Standards (NBPTS) has completed work to develop National Board Certification for Principals. These standards define and validate what skills and characteristics school leaders need to be effective. The effort reflects a broad national consensus around standards for principals. The voluntary principal certification program was expected to become operational in 2011.[74]

The NBPTS program for principals is intended for practitioners with at least a few years of experience who can prove a high level of accomplishment. Designed to be rigorous and thorough, the certification program is expected to be used as a professional development tool and to recognize outstanding achievements. Some suggest that the certificate might be used in lieu of requiring principals to obtain doctor of education degrees or take the place of an individual state's licensing requirements.[75]

Research supports the belief that the most accomplished principals create a school-based learning community that involves teachers, students, parents, and the wider public. The Core Propositions for Accomplished Educational Leaders, adopted by NBPTS in 2009, identify the essentials of what skilled educational leaders should know and do at a consistently high level. As illustrated in Figure 10–1, these core propositions form the foundation upon which the educational leaders' certification is built.[76]

More specifically, the National Board Core Propositions for Accomplished Educational Leaders denote certain skills, applications, and dispositions that outstanding school leaders display in their daily performances:[77]

◆ *Skills*
   1. *Leadership:* Accomplished educational leaders continuously cultivate their understanding of leadership and change process to meet high levels of performance.

FIGURE 10–1
Core Propositions for Accomplished Educational Leaders
(Source: National Board for Professional Teaching
Standards. (2009). *National Board Certification for
Principals: Redefining educational leadership for the
21st century*. Arlington, VA: Author. Retrieved from
http://www.nbpts.org/products_and_services/
national_board_certifica. Reprinted with permission
from the National Board for Professional Teaching
Standards, www.nbpts.org. All rights reserved.)

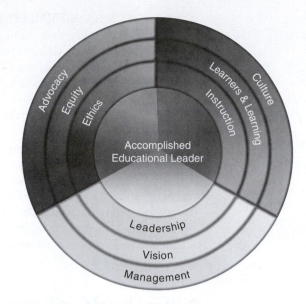

2. *Vision:* Accomplished educational leaders have a clear vision and inspire and
engage stakeholders in developing and realizing the mission.
3. *Management:* Accomplished educational leaders manage and leverage systems
and processes to achieve desired results.
◆ *Applications*
4. *Culture:* Accomplished educational leaders act with a sense of urgency to foster
a cohesive culture of learning.
5. *Learners and learning:* Accomplished educational leaders are committed to
student and adult learners and to their development.
6. *Instruction:* Accomplished educational leaders drive, facilitate, and monitor the
teaching and learning process.
◆ *Dispositions*
7. *Ethics:* Accomplished educational leaders model professional, ethical behavior
and expect it from others.
8. *Equity:* Accomplished educational leaders ensure equitable learning opportunities and high expectations for all.
9. *Advocacy:* Accomplished educational leaders advocate on behalf of their
schools, communities, and profession.

While these core propositions describe general areas of principal leadership, they have
yet to elaborate the clearly defined performances that can guide principal development
and evaluation. Accordingly, the high-level principal certification assessment remains a
work in progress. When the program is ready, principals seeking this certification will be
expected to show evidence that they are successfully raising achievement and to answer
tough questions about their work. The certification process will take place over an
extended period of time, and each candidate's assessment will be peer evaluated.

ACTIVITY 10.3   Challenges in Evaluating Principals

A variety of conceptual and methodological factors—plus the sheer complexity of the principal's role—makes principal evaluation a very difficult task. Discuss as a class:

1. Why have contemporary and evolving principal evaluation methods focused on behaviors related to goal attainment rather than on principals' attitudes, personality characteristics, or cognitive strategies?
2. The Personnel Evaluation Standards (1988, 2008) guide professional practice in personnel evaluation by using four attributes: propriety, utility, feasibility, and accuracy. In the case study, how well does the evaluation process used by Jim address these four qualities? How well does the principal or teacher evaluation system in your own school district address these four qualities?

As of 2008, no school leadership assessment instruments used in the United States had undergone rigorous psychometric development or yielded both norm and standard-referenced scores. Most school districts use "homegrown" principal evaluation instruments of questionable usefulness in appraising principals' instructional leadership skills. Discuss in pairs and then discuss as a class:

3. Does your school district's principal evaluation system use ISLLC standards as its basis?
4. Does your school district's principal evaluation system currently use a checklist of decontextualized principal behaviors or personal characteristics?
5. Does your state require principal candidates to pass the SLLA before they can be licensed/credentialed for K–12 administration?
6. Does your state principal certification process identify at least two levels of principals' competence, equivalent to basic/proficient and advanced performance levels?
7. Does your state or school district plan to use, or partially use, the voluntary National Board Certification for Principals credential as a professional development tool and to recognize outstanding principals' achievement?

TEACHER FORMATIVE AND SUMMATIVE EVALUATION

As with principals, teacher evaluation has become a fundamental aspect of school improvement. Policy makers, community members, and educational leaders agree that any significant improvement in schools and student learning must have the teacher as its centerpiece.[78] Just as a rational connection exists between school improvement and teacher performance, a necessary and rational connection also exists between teacher improvement and teacher evaluation.

The push for teacher quality developed from the modern school reform movement. Starting with the 1983 publication of *A Nation at Risk*,[79] and continuing to this day, attention has focused on the role of challenging academic standards for students and the use of high-stakes assessments of those standards. The 1996 publication of *What Matters Most: Teaching for America's Future*[80] further advanced these efforts by propelling the concept of teacher quality to the policy agenda forefront. Educators and policy makers alike recognize what shrewd parents have always known: The quality of individual teachers matters, and teacher evaluation requirements could support and enhance teacher quality.[81]

A Brief History of Teacher Evaluation

Teacher evaluation has been through many trends and cycles. Changes in teachers' roles, values and beliefs about effective teaching and teacher responsibilities, perceptions of how students learn best, societal demographics, and teaching contexts have all impacted teacher evaluation.[82] In short, the focus of teacher evaluation reflects the views held at any given point in time about effective pedagogy and student learning.

At the turn of the 20th century, teacher evaluation was essentially defined from a moralistic and ethical perspective. Good teachers were outstanding members of the community, assumed to hold high moral and ethical standards, to have basic reading skills (preferably at the high school level), and to be excellent role models for students. Most were single women with only minimal education (completing grade 9). Thus, teachers were largely evaluated on their personal characteristics rather than appraisals informed by knowledge about effective teaching and learning.

During the 1920s through the 1940s, emerging psychological theories focused on good teachers' personal characteristics. By the late 1940s, the knowledge base related to teacher evaluation began to appear. The 1950s and 1960s saw increased efforts among educational researchers to identify effective teaching methods, looking at linkages between observable teaching practices (behaviors) and a variety of student outcomes (grades and test results). Many classroom-based observation checklist systems were developed, most grounded in psychology and education behaviorism.

During the 1970s, studies attempting to demonstrate connections between various teaching practices and student outcomes continued to multiply. The 1980s renewed calls for educational reforms, teacher evaluation became a centerpiece of educational accountability, and the knowledge base related to teacher evaluation expanded and grew more sophisticated.[83] By 2010, over three decades of research on teaching had established a knowledge base to design new teacher evaluation systems around sets of criteria that had been reasonably well linked to desired student outcomes.[84]

Today, teacher evaluation for accountability, professional development, and school improvement continues at the forefront of school reform. At the same time, a variety of new conceptual and methodological developments in teacher evaluation have moved primary attention from teacher behavior and teacher performance (inputs) to the assessment and evaluation of teaching and learning (outcomes). These new approaches have greater potential for strengthening teaching, enhancing student learning, and improving schools than traditional evaluation systems.

The Clinical Supervision Process

In part, teacher evaluation depends on collecting and effectively using information about teachers' classroom practices and student outcomes. Clinical supervision is the best known and most widely used structure for working directly with classroom teachers to improve student learning, establish teacher competence, and provide data to support professional growth. A collegial and reflective approach, it has the potential to facilitate teachers' development through changes in their classroom behavior.

Traditionally, clinical supervision involves a teacher working with a supervisor, such as an assistant principal, department head, or principal. In the last quarter century, however, many policy makers, scholars, and practitioners have encouraged teaching peers to use clinical supervision as a means to promote professional development.[85]

Several models of clinical supervision exist, each including a number of phases. In general, these steps include planning the lesson, establishing the observation's focus through negotiation between the teacher and the supervisor, conducting a focused observation period, analyzing and providing feedback during a conference, and developing plans for changing some part of the teacher's practice.[86] This cycle repeats several times during the school year, depending on the teacher's employment status and teaching effectiveness. The more inexperienced or ineffective the teacher, the more frequent the series of clinical supervision activities.

Clinical supervision's usefulness depends on a variety of factors. First, the process assumes a professional working relationship between the teacher and the supervisor, characterized by a high degree of mutual trust. Additional variables include the quality of the supervisor's observational and feedback skills; the amount of valid and reliable data about the teacher's abilities, strengths, and weaknesses that the classroom observation can provide; varied data about student achievement; the reasonableness of the improvement suggestions; and the willingness and capacity of the teacher to accept and successfully modify his or her existing teaching pattern.[87] Finally, clinical supervision requires sufficient time and personnel because the process is labor intensive and time consuming.

Concerns with Traditional Teacher Evaluation Practices

Collecting, analyzing, and interpreting real-time data during clinical supervision rests on having identifiable, consensually validated standards of practice by which to compare and assess teachers' performances. Over the last century, state and school districts' attempts to scale up and structure teacher evaluation practices to promote teacher accountability and improved instruction have found few highly regarded models upon which to draw. Few districts have attempted to go beyond evaluation's typical function—ensuring that teachers meet a basic level of competence—to connect their systems to professional development, teacher promotion, and compensation.[88]

Among other criticisms, traditional teacher evaluation systems are discredited for lack of district or school level commitment, criteria based on narrow conceptions of teaching, inadequate feedback, and perceived subjectivity.[89] Teacher evaluation systems have also been accused of suffering from grade inflation in which evaluators deem nearly all tenured teachers "above average."[90] In 2009 surveys, found the great majority (73%) of teachers responded that their evaluations failed to identify an area for professional growth, and only 43% said their evaluations helped them improve. Nor do evaluation systems help identify and remove ineffective teachers.[91]

In contrast, current research on teaching and standards-based teacher evaluation reforms attempt to avoid these problems by anchoring evaluation systems in new teaching standards that represent a shared understanding of instruction.[92] Both streams are enhancing formative and summative teacher evaluation processes, providing more valid, reliable, and meaningful data for making decisions about accountability and professional development.

Current Research and Teacher Evaluation Practices

Teaching is a highly complex activity, affected by situational or contextual influences. Teaching can be characterized by its multidimensionality (different students, diverse reactions, activities, and interruptions), simultaneity (many things happening at the same time), immediacy (the teacher has little time to think), unpredictability (it is impossible to predict what will occur with certainty, so it is difficult to decide unequivocally), and dependency on time (activities, decisions, or events have consequences for following situations).[93] These qualities depict a complicated endeavor. Any effective teacher evaluation protocol and process will need to reflect this complexity.

Research consensus exists regarding the relationship between teaching quality and student achievement.[94] To better reflect teaching's complexity and the factors that matter most in educational practice, research on teaching and assessing teachers since the 1980s has focused on context and scientifically grounded indicators that identify teaching effectiveness[95] and emphasize teachers' thought processes[96] and practical knowledge.[97]

These newer teacher evaluation processes include:

◆ Contemporary conceptions of learning, and how these are connected to teaching practices
◆ The uniqueness of each teaching and learning context
◆ The importance of reflective practice and collegial sharing to teacher understanding, evaluation, and growth
◆ The expectation for greater command of knowledge of the subject matter taught
◆ The potential of teacher self-assessment for growth in teaching
◆ Large-scale research studies clearly documenting important connections between student achievement, school effectiveness, and quality teaching[98]
◆ Professional standards for developing and implementing new teacher evaluation systems[99]
◆ The importance in teaching and learning of developing higher order thinking skills
◆ Social-cognitive theory and self-efficacy beliefs research[100]
◆ Standards-based approaches to evaluation for national certification reflected in the work of the National Board for Professional Teaching Standards
◆ A variety of other knowledge bases

As a result, comprehensive, learner-centered, classroom-based assessment systems designed to provide information useful for improving teaching and learning are becoming available. These represent an integrated set of teaching and learning concepts, extending from comprehensive planning and reflective practice to the active engagement and involvement of learners in developing higher order thinking skills.

In addition, research conducted on teacher evaluation practices has identified features that improve the process. Specifically, findings on teachers' perceptions of feedback, enabling conditions, and fairness point to factors that principals can use to strengthen their teacher evaluation practices.

Feedback.   Teacher evaluation systems can be accepted or rejected by whether teachers come to view such systems as reliable and fair. Research suggests that perceptions of feedback[101] and fairness[102] are associated with teachers' evaluation acceptance and success.

Feedback is a central aspect of evaluation. Quality feedback is timely and frequent, credible, and useful. Attributes of feedback—including perceived evaluator credibility and trustworthiness, quality of ideas, depth of information, persuasiveness of rationale for suggested changes, usefulness of suggestions, and perceived relationship with the evaluator—have been identified as having the highest correlation with teachers' perceptions of evaluation quality.[103]

Timeliness, specificity, credibility, and intent are important feedback dimensions.[104] Regardless of the system used, feedback should be provided after data gathering, typically within a week of classroom observations and frequently enough for teachers to use it. When feedback is specifically tied to evidence and agreed upon criteria, the opportunity for teacher reflection and improvement are enhanced.[105]

Credibility includes evaluator trust, intent, confidentiality, and expertise.[106] While specific feedback from knowledgeable and trusted observers can help facilitate growth, evaluator credibility requires that they are adequately trained using the standards, rubrics, and multiple data sources so they can formulate performance-focused and reliable judgments about teacher performance. They must also have adequate knowledge of the subject matter content and student development.

Utility of feedback relates to whether feedback is based on the school district's conception of teaching, and whether it is specific, delivered constructively, and tied to growth recommendations. Finally, teachers must be able to reflect on the feedback so they can integrate it into their performance.

Enabling Conditions.   Feedback alone is not enough to stimulate instructional change. If teachers are to be accountable for growth to standards, conditions or opportunities must be present that enable them to apply feedback to their instructional practices. Teachers and evaluators must have access to the resources such as training and time to conduct evaluation activities, to reflect and act on feedback, and to document progress. Enabling conditions related to the organizational culture (such as acceptance of risk taking, collaborative professional learning, and problem solving) and structure (such as classroom contexts) may also impact feedback.

Perceptions of Fairness.   Likewise, perceptions of fairness influence employee satisfaction with performance appraisal, attitudes about evaluation acceptance, motivation to improve, trust in supervisors, organizational commitment, and legal defensibility in evaluation decisions.[107] Three central aspects of fairness are procedural fairness, interpersonal fairness, and outcome fairness.[108] Procedural fairness can be encouraged by giving employees opportunities to participate in decisions, providing consistency in all evaluation processes, ensuring that appraisals and feedback are job related and unbiased, and providing a formal channel for employees to appeal evaluation decisions. Interpersonal fairness is established by keeping employees informed, offering timely and informative feedback, and treating employees with courtesy, respect, and trust. Outcome fairness is gained by providing outcomes that are expected (that is, no surprises), and maintaining and communicating a formally structured incentive system.

Figure 10–2 provides a conceptual model that organizes the data relating to the nature and quality of feedback, conditions enabling its use, perceived fairness in evaluations, and teachers' use of feedback. The model begins with the premises that teaching practice, explicit standards, detailed performance rubrics, and adequate evaluator training using the standards, rubrics, and multiple data sources are essential features of teacher evaluation.

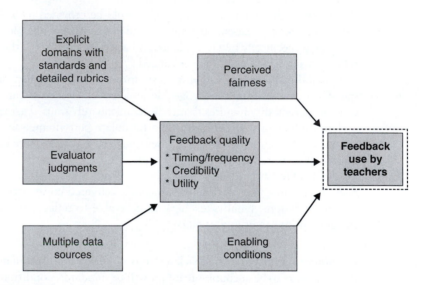

FIGURE 10–2

A Conceptual Model of Feedback in Standards-Based Teacher Evaluation (Source: *Journal of Personnel Evaluation in Education, 16*(4), 2002, p. 246, "Analysis of feedback, enabling conditions and fairness perceptions of teachers in three school districts with new standards-based evaluation systems," Kimball, S. M. Reprinted with kind permission from Springer Science+Business Media B.V.)

ACTIVITY 10.4   Factors Affecting the Usefulness of Clinical Supervision

Clinical supervision's usefulness depends on a professional working relationship between a teacher and a supervisor characterized by a high degree of trust; the quality of the supervisor's observation and feedback skills; the amount of valid and reliable data collected about the teacher's skills, strengths, and weaknesses; the reasonableness of the suggestions for improvement; and the teacher's capacity to successfully modify his or her existing teaching.

Discuss as a class:

1. In the case study, which aspects of the clinical supervision model are working effectively for Assistant Principal Jim and Mrs. Branch?
2. Which aspects are not working effectively? In what areas of professional growth does Jim need additional work?

ACTIVITY 10.5   Factors That Improve Teacher Evaluation Practices

Research of teacher evaluation practices has identified features that improve the process. These include feedback (quality of ideas, timeliness, credibility, and usefulness), enabling conditions, and perception of fairness. Discuss as a class:

1. How well is Jim addressing the issues of feedback, enabling conditions, and perception of fairness in his approach to evaluating Mrs. Branch?
2. What would Jim have to do—or have done differently—to improve his achievement of these essential teacher evaluation conditions?

Standards-Based Teacher Evaluation

At its core, standards-based evaluation uses rubrics to elaborate a vision of teaching with broad domains of practice, comprehensive principles, and detailed criteria for effective behaviors. Derived from research and theory on instruction, these standards are intended to be public and consensus based, and provide clear performance expectations. Combined with multiple data sources, standards and rubrics strengthen both objectivity and feedback and can generate a common dialogue about instruction.

Increasingly, school districts are looking to teaching standards and scaffolding that provide descriptions of instructional performance with increasing levels of competence. The Personnel Evaluation Standards (described earlier), the *Framework for Teaching*, and the National Board for Professional Teaching Standards offer principals (as supervisors and evaluators) and teachers (as clients and professionals) clear and researcher-supported models for teachers' performance appraisal.

A Framework for Teaching.   A notable development in standards-based teacher evaluation is the growing use of *Enhancing Professional Practice: A Framework for Teaching* (Danielson, 1996, 2002, 2007).[109] Designed using research on teacher effects, consultation with expert practitioners and researchers, job analysis studies, and an examination of state licensure systems, the model provides clear and detailed descriptions of what beginning through advanced teachers should know and be able to do. Constructed for formative and summative purposes, its clear descriptors of teaching behaviors across a range of instructional domains at four levels of competence (unsatisfactory, basic, proficient, and distinguished) help teachers and principals understand the performance targets (see Table 10–2). They also support evaluators' ability to help teachers identify where they need to improve. Using explicit standards, multiple data sources, and detailed rubrics, the *Framework* guides teachers' professional development as it helps observers evaluate teachers' performance at different career stages and ability levels.

The *Framework's* standards represent four teaching practice domains, further defined by 22 components of teaching and 66 elements. The domains are (1) planning and preparation, (2) the classroom environment, (3) instruction, and (4) professional responsibilities. The planning and preparation domain relates to how teachers organize the content for student learning, and how student learning is assessed. The classroom environment domain intends to measure teachers' abilities to structure and manage a physical and interpersonal climate that supports a community of learners. The instructional domain intends to assess the actual engagement of teachers and students with the content of instruction. The professional responsibility domain includes teacher behaviors within and outside the classroom, including the use of professional reflection and participation in professional activities.

The *Framework for Teaching* standards are not content specific by subject matter or grade level. Instead, the standards present a generic list of teaching and learning behaviors applicable to different grade levels and content areas. Evidence can document all criteria and allow teachers to demonstrate high performance through examples that they choose, including teacher-developed portfolios based on a professional development plan, supervisor or peer observations, teacher-evaluator conferences, and other interactions.

As illustrated in Table 10–2, each teaching element is described by behavioral indicators at four performance levels. Using evidence gathered from observations and other data sources, observers and teachers (conducting a self-assessment) can use the rubric to rate performance levels on each element. Teachers performing at the unsatisfactory level for an element do not meet the minimum performance expectations. Those at the basic level appear to understand the teaching concept contained in the element but implement the concept inconsistently or unsuccessfully. Teachers at the proficient level clearly understand the element's concept and implement it well. Finally, those performing at the distinguished level are highly accomplished teachers who master the element.[110]

TABLE 10–2
Demonstrating Knowledge of Content and Pedagogy

| Element | Level of Performance | | | |
	Unsatisfactory	Basic	Proficient	Distinguished
Knowledge of the content and the structure of the discipline.	In planning and practice, teacher makes content errors or does not correct errors made by students.	Teacher is familiar with the important concepts in the discipline but may display lack of awareness of how these concepts relate to one another.	Teacher displays solid knowledge of the important concepts in the discipline and how these relate to one another.	Teacher displays extensive knowledge of the important concepts in the discipline and how these relate both to one another and to other disciplines.

Source: From *Enhancing Professional Practice: A Framework for Teaching* (Table 10.3, p. 47), by Charlotte Danielson, Alexandria, VA: ASCD. © 2007 by ASCD. Reprinted with permission. Learn more about ASCD at www.ascd.org.

The *Framework* has been adapted and used for low-stakes formative purposes such as preparing new teachers, recruiting and hiring new teachers, mentoring new teachers, and providing professional guidance and growth for mature teachers.[111] It is also used for high-stakes summative purposes such as making employment and tenure decisions.[112]

Using these rubrics can help principals give teachers clearly articulated performance standards and the explicit feedback necessary for improved classroom practices. Unlike teacher evaluation protocols that allow principals to misrepresent teachers' general status with an overall "satisfactory" rating, evaluations using these rubrics provide specificity about how well teachers are meeting discrete performance standards. Such high-quality feedback is more likely to motivate teacher improvement or spur a good teacher on to excellence.[113]

Research on the* Framework *and Teacher Evaluation. Because the *Framework* model has a solid research base and is transparently tied to actual teaching practices, many U.S. school districts are currently using it for teachers' supervision, evaluation, and professional development.[114] Research supports the findings that teachers' ratings on this rubric are positively and significantly related to improved student achievement.[115] Several of these studies find that teachers and administrators accept the *Framework*'s uses.[116] Similarly, studies suggest that school leader evaluations of teachers with this approach may be valid measures of teaching effectiveness and provide certain justification for including evaluation ratings when making important decisions.[117]

Limitations of Teaching Standards for Evaluations. As with other evaluation approaches, standards-based evaluation models bring certain limitations. A general complaint is that using teaching standards to evaluate teachers reduces teaching's complexity to a simplistic level[118] and invites the socially constructed practice of teaching to a certain viewpoint about "correct" instruction.[119] Maintaining high interrater reliability is another challenging issue—whether several successive observers will make equally accurate judgments of teachers based on the performance standards.[120] For example, Kimball and Milanowski (2009) found considerable variation among evaluators in the relationship between their *Framework* ratings of teachers and student achievement in the classrooms of teachers they evaluated.[121] Differences in validity across principals are clearly problematic for teacher fairness and for using the evaluation data in high-stakes decisions. Training a cadre of evaluators—typically principals and assistant principals—to take part in high-quality observations is costly and time-consuming, especially when evaluations take place every year.[122] Factors including evaluator motivation, skill, and evaluation context also affect the relationship between teacher ratings and their actual performance.[123] The *Framework* teacher evaluation system also adds to the administrator and teacher workload.[124]

Broadly speaking, standards-based evaluation tools offer an effective vehicle for formative and summative uses if they can overcome the limitations of narrow implementation, focus on basic skills and lack of attention to instructional context,[125] and if they can consider the subject matter[126] and differentiate between varied teacher performance levels.

National Board for Professional Teaching Standards. While certain standards-based evaluation models are appropriate for beginning and maturing educators, other models are more suited for experienced master teachers. Professionalism requires continuously developing teachers' expertise to increase effectiveness with all students. The National Board for Professional Teaching Standards (NBPTS), established in 1987, operates a voluntary national system to assess and certify high-quality teaching. NBPTS sets high standards for what very effective teachers know and do. Their goal is to improve the teaching profession and positively affect student learning. As of June 2008, nearly 64,000 teachers had earned their National Board Certification (NBC) in 24 fields.[127] Approximately 41% of board certified teachers teach in high-needs schools.[128] In short, NBPTS spells out and recognizes the professional teaching expectations for highly effective teachers.

The 10-month certification process connects teaching and student learning by having applicants demonstrate knowledge of their subject matter and pedagogy, manage and monitor student learning, systematically think about classroom practice and learn from experience, and participate in learning communities. With widespread national professional support from major education associations, governors, state legislators, and school boards,[129] virtually every state and more than 25% of all school districts offer financial rewards or incentives for teachers seeking National Board Certification.[130] The Progressive Policy Institute estimates that states and districts are spending over $100 million per year on assessment fees ($2,500 per teacher) and salary supplements for teachers who earn the certificate.[131]

Five Core Propositions.   The National Board Standards define in five core propositions what effective teachers should know and be able to do if they are to successfully enhance student learning and demonstrate a high level of knowledge, skills, abilities, and commitments. Understanding these expectations can help principals and teachers comprehend what accomplished, highly effective teaching looks like. These propositions can also help teachers grow to meet high standards of professional practice. Briefly, these are:[132]

1. *Teachers are committed to students and their learning.* Accomplished teachers—that is, Nationally Board Certified teachers (NBCTs)—are dedicated to making knowledge accessible to all students and act on the belief that all students can learn. They treat students equitably, recognize individual differences, and account for those differences in their practice. Accomplished teachers understand how students develop and learn and incorporate prevailing theories of cognition and intelligence in their practice. They are also concerned with the development of character and civic responsibility.

2. *Teachers know the subjects they teach and how to teach those subjects to students.* NBCTs have mastery over the subjects they teach. They have a deep understanding of the subject's history, structure, and real-world applications. They have skill and experience in teaching it, and they are very familiar with the skills, gaps, and preconceptions students may bring to the subject. While faithfully upholding the value of disciplinary knowledge, they also develop their students' critical and analytical capacities. They are able to use diverse instructional strategies to teach for understanding.

3. *Teachers are responsible for managing and monitoring student learning.* NBCTs deliver effective instruction. They move fluently through a range of instructional techniques, keeping students motivated, engaged, and focused. They know how to engage students to ensure a disciplined learning environment, and how to organize instruction to meet instructional goals. They know how to assess individual and class progress using multiple measures and can clearly explain student performance to parents.

4. *Teachers think systematically about their practice and learn from experience.* NBCTs model what it means to be an educated person—they read, they question, they create, and they are willing to try new things. They are familiar with learning theories and instructional strategies and stay abreast of current issues in American education. They critically examine their practice on a regular basis to deepen knowledge, expand their repertoire of skills, and incorporate new findings into their practice. Accomplished teachers' decisions are grounded not only in the literature, but also in their experience.

5. *Teachers are members of learning communities.* NBCTs collaborate with others to improve student learning. They are leaders and actively know how to seek and build partnerships with community groups and businesses. They work with other professionals on instructional policy, curriculum development, and staff development. They know how to work collaboratively with parents to engage them productively in school's work.

Extending these five core propositions into various academic disciplines, the National Board has also created standards for 25 certificate areas, including art, English language arts, exceptional needs mathematics, music, science, social studies, history, health education, counseling, specialist, and generalist. Committees of educators including classroom teachers, child development experts, teacher educators, and professionals from relevant disciplines collaborated to develop these certifications. These specialized credentials identify specific knowledge, skills, and attitudes that support accomplished practices in their respective disciplines.[133]

The NBPTS certificate was not intended to replace state licensing of teachers, since the certificate is a professional credential, not a license to teach. However, many states have opted to allow the NBPTS certificate to substitute for the state license.[134]

Research on NBPTS Teachers. The NBPTS has been under increasing pressure to demonstrate that the millions of state and district dollars spent on bonuses for nationally certified teachers actually buy the likelihood of greater student learning.[135] NBPTS noted that at least 150 research studies have examined its effectiveness and more than 75% have found a positive impact on teacher performance, student learning, engagement, and achievement.[136]

Studies about the influence of National Board Certification on student achievement are mixed, but generally positive. Sample sizes tend to be small, limiting the ability to generalize conclusions. Research is consistently upbeat about NBC's effect on teachers' instructional practices, professional development, and student achievement.[137] On the other hand, two major studies using large student samples concluded that students did not show statistically significant academic gains from working with these teachers.[138]

Apart from the mixed findings on student achievement, NBPTS certification provides a valid, reliable, and highly respected assessment and credentialing system to recognize accomplished teachers. It offers the teaching profession a way to create stages to an otherwise "unstaged" profession—while keeping excellent teachers teaching.

ACTIVITY 10.6   Using a Standards-Based Teacher Evaluation Model

Discuss as a class:

1. As assistant principal, how might Jim use a standards-based teacher evaluation system and National Board for Professional Teaching Standards certification to help Mrs. Branch and more experienced teachers continue their professional growth?
2. What practices might Jim suggest to the principal and the school improvement team to help teachers at all career stages support and advance their professional growth?

A Model of the Formative and Summative Evaluation Process

Formative and summative evaluations are opposite but related sides of an evaluation continuum that produces organizational accountability and improvement and individual professional growth. As a career, teaching has a distinct life cycle. The job is complicated, and skillful practice takes time to develop. Novice teachers, experienced tenured teachers, and teachers needing intensive assistance to remedy unsatisfactory performance each require separate levels of supervision and support.

Figure 10–3 illustrates a basic integrated supervision model in actual use. It is differentiated to address both accountability and improvement.[139] Typically, teachers new to the profession are considered to be probationary, are employed on annual contracts, and participate in a 3-year summative evaluation cycle that culminates in either the teacher receiving a continuing contract (tenure) for the fourth year or dismissal.

Experienced teachers who work on continuing contracts proceed annually on one of three tracks: formative evaluation, summative evaluation, or improvement plan. All continuing contract teachers performing satisfactorily or higher participate in a 4-year evaluation cycle, with 3 years focused on formative evaluation (professional growth) and the fourth year on summative assessment (accountability). However, in the event that a continuing contract status teacher's performance is less than satisfactory according to any stated performance expectation, the principal and the teacher collaboratively develop an improvement plan or plan of action. The dates in Figure 10–3 provide an approximate school and human resources timeline for action that accommodates the legal issues surrounding issuing a contract.

In addition, this model places formative cycle teachers into support groups consisting of similar teachers in the formative assessment that year. Collegial groups offer professional and moral support to one another throughout the year, and they occasionally participate in collaborative activities to enhance all members' professional practices.

Teacher Contracts and Teacher Rights

The bottom line for teacher evaluation is accountability and organizational quality control. Teachers who receive unsatisfactory evaluations and who do not improve their practice while under a plan of action can have their contracts recommended for termination. While it is not this chapter's intent to discuss education employment law, a brief look helps us understand teacher evaluation in a more complete context.

Teachers' contracts are legal documents that provide teachers certain protections and assign hiring organizations certain obligations. Any teacher who earns tenure (continuing contract status) also acquires a *property right* or a legitimate claim to the teaching position. Tenure does not guarantee continued employment, but it does ensure that certified school personnel may not be arbitrarily removed from their employment positions without due process of law.[140] *Due process* usually consists of a formal hearing, the presentation of sufficient evidence to meet statutory requirements, and the teacher's right to have a lawyer present to help represent the teacher's interests and present evidence to support the teacher's position.

Once a property right is acquired, the teacher may be dismissed only for cause: incompetency, insubordination,[141] immorality, unprofessional conduct,[142] or other behaviors as noted in state statutes. Courts define *incompetency* as inadequate knowledge of the subject matter, inability or unwillingness to teach the curricula, failure to work effectively with

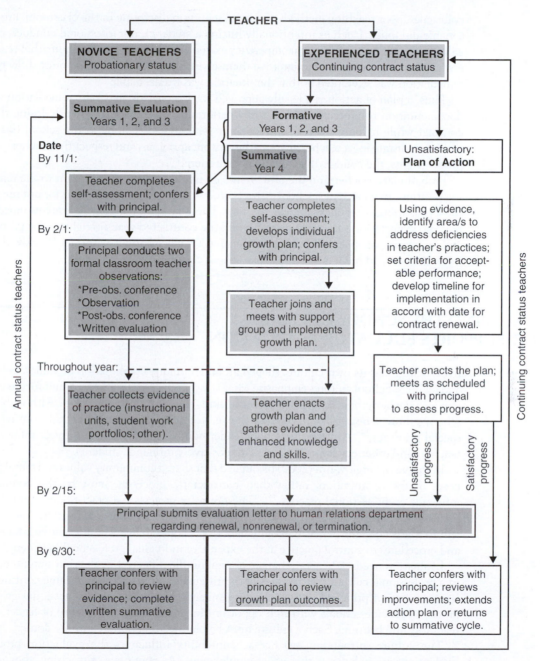

TEACHER

NOVICE TEACHERS
Probationary status

EXPERIENCED TEACHERS
Continuing contract status

Summative Evaluation
Years 1, 2, and 3

Formative
Years 1, 2, and 3

Summative
Year 4

Unsatisfactory:
Plan of Action

Date
By 11/1:

Teacher completes
self-assessment; confers
with principal.

Teacher completes
self-assessment;
develops individual
growth plan; confers
with principal.

Using evidence,
identify area/s to
address deficiencies
in teacher's practices;
set criteria for accept-
able performance;
develop timeline for
implementation in
accord with date for
contract renewal.

By 2/1:

Principal conducts two
formal classroom teacher
observations:
*Pre-obs. conference
*Observation
*Post-obs. conference
*Written evaluation

Teacher joins and
meets with support
group and implements
growth plan.

Throughout year:

Teacher collects evidence
of practice (instructional
units, student work
portfolios; other).

Teacher enacts
growth plan and
gathers evidence of
enhanced knowledge
and skills.

Teacher enacts the plan;
meets as scheduled
with principal
to assess progress.

Unsatisfactory progress

Satisfactory progress

By 2/15:

Principal submits evaluation letter to human relations department
regarding renewal, nonrenewal, or termination.

By 6/30:

Teacher confers with
principal to review
evidence; complete
written summative
evaluation.

Teacher confers with
principal to review
growth plan outcomes.

Teacher confers with
principal; reviews
improvements; extends
action plan or returns
to summative cycle.

Annual contract status teachers

Continuing contract status teachers

FIGURE 10–3

Example of an Integrated and Differentiated Teacher Evaluation Model (Source: Adapted from *Teacher Evaluation to Enhance Professional Practice* (Figure 10–3, pp. 137–138), by Charlotte Danielson, Edited by T. L. McGreal, Alexandria, VA: ASCD. © 2007 by ASCD. Reprinted with permission. Learn more about ASCD at www.ascd.org.)

colleagues, poor teaching methods, failure to maintain discipline in the classroom, unreasonable discipline (such as intentionally hitting a student), unprofessional conduct, or a willful neglect of duty. Where incompetency exists, some states' statutes require that teachers be given an opportunity to improve themselves, and the school board must show that remediation was attempted or that the situation was irredeemable.[143]

Thus, a plan of action is a legally approved way to provide necessary remediation and documentation to protect unsatisfactorily performing teachers from unfairly losing their contract while helping them to correct their weaknesses. As long as the school board's actions in dismissing a teacher are not arbitrary or capricious, and respect the teacher's due process rights, the courts will generally not interfere.[144]

Probationary teachers, on the other hand, do not hold this property right to the teaching position. In most states, school districts are not required to give reasons for not renewing a probationary teacher's annual contract. These probationary teachers are assumed to have no expectation for employment beyond the contracted year, no right to due process, and no hearing of appeals if they do not receive a renewed annual contract.[145] How these issues are handled has a major impact on school culture.

DEVELOPING THE SCHOOL CULTURE THAT SUPPORTS EDUCATOR EVALUATION

Every school has its own culture, shaped around a unique combination of values, beliefs, and feelings. School cultures emphasize what is most important to their community as they strive to develop their knowledge base and skills in a particular direction. Although the school culture is not visible to the human eye, its symbols, artifacts, and traditions reflect special priorities.[146] An effective school leader builds a culture that positively influences teachers and other educators, who in turn, positively influence students.

In this vein, Sergiovanni (2000) has argued that shared community values and moral purposes in the organization, rather than bureaucratic processes, must be the dominant influence on professional practice.[147] "The norms of professional practitioners must drive professional practice. Each group strives to control its own professional actions yet works within a larger organization with requirements for accountability. The alternative is for rules and procedures to control practice at the expense of individual professional judgment."[148]

Evaluation needs to be more than an annual hurdle. Effective evaluation systems occur in a professional culture that requires both principals and teachers to become continuous learners. Sound principal and teacher assessment, evaluation, and professional growth processes provide schools with rich opportunities to enhance the quality of leadership, teaching, and learning. Such a culture must be planned and honored in the doing.

The culture surrounding teacher accountability influences the evaluation process. Evaluations are judgments that affect employment. As appraisals of teaching, they must be made as objectively as possible, fairly, and without favoritism. The lines of responsibility and communication must be clear and unambiguous. In contrast, professional growth suggests a more nurturing, trusting relationship between supervisor and teacher. Interactions focus on learning, and the supervisor is more coach and mentor than judge. In this formative context, the teacher can voice concerns and expect to receive assistance. When people perceive that an environment is conducive to professional learning, they experience it as profoundly different from one that generates objective evaluative—and possibly life-altering—judgments.

A collaborative culture of professional learning provides the essential soil in which growth and improved practice can occur. A collaborative culture of inquiry expects that teachers' and principals' participation in the evaluation process will be professionally rewarding. Every educator becomes part of the team working to improve the quality of adult and student learning. Novice teachers receive ongoing support and assistance through induction and mentoring programs and through invitations from experienced colleagues to observe in their classrooms and discuss strategies with them outside class. Tenured teachers are presumed to be competent (at least performing satisfactorily, unless they receive notice to the contrary) and continually learning as professionals. Evaluation in this culture carries no threats for taking professional risks, trying new strategies, and receiving constructive feedback on them—even during a formal observation.

Principals and teachers advance this culture when they engage in a process that seeks to improve teaching in every classroom. They do this by continuously analyzing learning through teacher teams, making frequent unannounced classroom visits that sample multiple lessons, supervising curriculum units in addition to individual lessons, conducting authentic conversations using real data, and offering suggestions and redirection in prompt, candid, face-to-face conversations after every classroom visit.[149] Developing and nurturing a professional learning culture in the school is an essential foundation for positive outcomes.

In such a culture, teachers who receive notice that they are not performing satisfactorily know they will receive specific assistance, time to improve their skills, and fair equitable treatment before decisions about employment become necessary. At the same time, principals are receiving training about what constitutes effective teaching behaviors and applying their refined skills to increase interrater reliability, the quality of their feedback, and their teachers' success.

Principals take the leadership role in creating and sustaining this growth-oriented environment when they visibly respect teachers as adult learners and describe evaluation and professional development as continuing processes aimed at improving instruction and student outcomes. In addition, educators improve their school culture when principals and teachers receive preparation and support to improve their skills at observing classrooms; giving detailed, frank, and honest feedback; and assessing unit plans, tests, and student learning data. The principal needs to be the "chief learner"—securing the knowledge base and facilitating study groups, article and book groups to identify strategies and perspectives that enhance professional practice, peer observations, and lesson videotapes. Likewise, teachers need to strengthen their content knowledge and instructional repertoires in ways that increase each student's mastery and to build their own adult teamwork skills in collaboration and problem solving. For the school, the goal is to create a culture in which nondefensive analysis of student learning becomes "the way we do things around here." School leadership focused on continuous improvement in teaching and learning improves their students' chances of succeeding in a high-stakes world and teachers' capacities to help get them there.

Improving teaching and learning is education's core mission. Principal and teacher evaluation and professional growth systems rely on shared professional values; ongoing, meaningful formative assessments; continuous gathering of accurate and consequential data; reflections on the data's implications; and making necessary adjustments that advance professional practice and student achievement. This process can only thrive in a culture of mutual respect, trust, collaboration, knowledge of best practices, and self-reflection. The bottom line must always be: What is best for students? Continuous adult learning and evaluation of practice serve both professional growth and accountability. Nevertheless, the fact that few of these well-regarded evaluation systems are currently in place speaks to the technical and political difficulties of such an essential undertaking.

ACTIVITY 10.7   The School Culture and Professional Evaluation

Effective professional evaluation systems occur in a culture that requires principals and teachers to become continuous learners. A collaborative culture of inquiry and a nondefensive analysis of student learning should become "the way we do things around here." Discuss as a class:

1. In the case study, what can the school district do to improve the school's culture for professional evaluation?
2. What can the principal and the assistant principal (Jim) do to improve their school's culture for evaluation?
3. What can the teachers do to improve the school's culture for evaluation?
4. How should Jim have handled the case study situation?

SUMMARY

Improving educators' performance has been a significant focus of educational reform. Evaluation serves the organization's and individual's needs for quality assurance, accountability, and growth. Summative and formative evaluations are continuous and interactive processes. A single evaluation system can successfully meet multiple evaluation purposes when the system is viewed as one component of a larger mission—advancing the organization's goals.

Most widely used educator evaluation approaches have serious conceptual, methodological, ethical, and practical limitations. Arbitrary political influences are less likely to intrude when personnel evaluation is linked with the organization's mission and uses objective, valid, reliable, and multiple data.

Although 40 years of research affirms the principal's role in strengthening teaching and learning, identifying the relevant performance expectations for principals' personnel evaluations has proved more difficult. While no one universal paradigm or theory will be valid for examining the complexity of school leader behavior in all contexts, it seems reasonable that at a minimum, some relatively generic and finite set of leadership activities is required to manage institutions. Many schools use school leadership assessment instruments that have not undergone rigorous psychometric development or yield both norm- and standard-referenced scores.

Several standards-based frames are helping educators design valid and reliable evaluation instruments and processes. The *Personnel Evaluation Standards* provides comprehensive sets of standards and practical guidelines for educator evaluation. Likewise, the Interstate School Leaders Licensure Consortium (ISLLC) produced the research-based ISLLC Standards for School Leaders, which are used in principal preparation, licensure, hiring, induction, and professional development. In addition, the National Board for Professional Teaching Standards (NBPTS) has developed a voluntary National Board Certification for Principals, which defines and validates the skills, characteristics, and behaviors of experienced and highly effective school leaders.

Current research on teaching effectiveness has moved teacher evaluation from primary attention on teacher behavior and performance (inputs) to a major focus on teaching and learning (outcomes). Research consensus exists regarding the relationship between teaching quality and student achievement. Research on teaching effectiveness is making possible comprehensive, learner-centered, classroom-based assessment systems designed to provide information useful for improving teaching and learning. Standards-based evaluation uses research-supported rubrics to create clear performance expectations for teachers. When combined with multiple data sources, standards and rubrics strengthen both feedback and objectivity and can generate a common dialogue about instruction.

Additionally, research findings on teachers' perceptions of feedback, enabling conditions, and fairness identify factors that principals can use to strengthen their teacher evaluation practices.

Effective evaluation systems occur in a professional culture that requires principals and teachers to become continuous learners. Such a culture must be planned and honored in practice.

ENDNOTES

1. Haefele, D. (1993). Evaluating teachers: A call for change. *Journal of Personnel Evaluation in Education, 7*(1), 21–31.

2. Stufflebeam, D. L. (2003). The CIPP model for evaluation. In T. Kellaghan, D. L. Stufflebeam, & L. A. Wingate (Eds.), *International handbook of educational evaluation* (Vol. 2, pp. 31–62). Dordrecht, the Netherlands: Kleuwer Academic, p. 34.

3. Huitt, W., Hummel, J., & Kaeck, D. (2001). Assessment, measurement, evaluation, and research. *Educational Psychology Interactive.* Valdosta, GA: Valdosta State University. Retrieved from http://www.edpsycinteractive.org/topics/intro/sciknow.html. *Appraisal* is a judgment about the value of something, such as professional performance. It may be used synonymously with *evaluation*.

4. Harris, B. M., & Monk, B. J. (1992). *Personnel administration in education* (3rd ed., p. 151). Needham Heights, MA: Allyn & Bacon.

5. McGreal, T. L. (1988). Evaluation for enhancing instruction: Linking teacher evaluation and staff development. In S. J. Stanley & W. J. Popham (Eds.), *Teacher evaluation: Six prescriptions for success* (pp. 1–29). Alexandria, VA: Association for Supervision and Curriculum Development.

6. Fullan, M. (1991). *The new meaning of educational change.* New York, NY: Teachers College Press.

7. Buckner, K. (2000). *Tenure and employment contracts: Evolving standards for principals. A legal memorandum* (ED450465). ERIC Educational Resources Center. Reston, VA: National Association of Secondary Schools. Retrieved from http://www.eric.ed.gov/ERICWebPortal/ Home.portal;jsessionid

=CBrfnrTTk6zfKLJNsRQvmh2DvRlw2yJkCKyy
4B4hwVT1hJG46f1p!938602629?_nfpb=true&
ERICExtSearch_SearchValue_0=ED450465&
ERICExtSearch_SearchType_0=eric_accno&_
pageLabel=ERICSearchResult&newSearch=
true&rnd=1111616479373&searchtype=keyword

8. Buckner, K. (2000). *Tenure and employment contracts: Evolving standards for principals. A legal memorandum.* Reston, VA: National Association of Secondary School Principals.

9. Hallinger, P., & Heck, R. (1996). Reassessing the principal's role in school effectiveness: A review of empirical research, 1980–1995. *Educational Administration Quarterly, 32*(1), 5–44; Heck, R., & Hallinger, P. (1999). Conceptual models, methodology, and methods for studying school leadership. In J. Murphy & K. Seashore-Louis (Eds.), *The 2nd handbook of research in educational administration.* San Francisco, CA: McCutchan; Leithwood, K. (1994). Leadership for school re-structuring. *Educational Administration Quarterly, 30*(4), 498–518; Prestine, N. A., & Nelson, B. S. (2005). How can educational leaders support and promote teaching and learning? New conceptions of learning and leading in schools. In W.A. Firestone & C. Riehl (Eds.), *A new agenda for research in educational leadership* (pp. 46–60). New York, NY: Teachers College Press.

10. Fuller, E., & Young, M. D. (2009, Summer). *Tenure and retention of newly hired principals in Texas.* Austin, TX: Texas High School Project. Leadership Initiative Issue Brief 1. Retrieved from http://www.ucea.org/storage/principal/IB%201_Principal%20Tenure%20and%20Retention%20in%20Texas%20of%20Newly%20Hired%20Principals_10_8_09.pdf

11. Fuller, E. J., Young, M. D., & Baker, B. (2007, April). *The relationship between principal character-istics, principal turnover, teacher quality, and student achievement.* Presented at the annual meeting of the American Educational Research Association, Chicago, IL; Levy, A., Fields, E., & Jablonski, E. (2006). *Overview of research: What we know and don't know about the consequences of science and math teacher turnover.* Paper presented at the NCTAF Symposium on the Scope and Consequences of K–12 Science and Mathematics Teacher Turnover.

12. Fullan, M., with Steigelbauer, S. (1991). *The new meaning of educational change.* New York, NY: Teachers College Press; McAdams, R. P. (1997). A systems approach to school reform. *Phi Delta Kappan, 79*(2), 138–142.

13. Fuller & Young. (2009). Op. cit.

14. Darling-Hammond, L., Wise, A.E. & Pease, S.R. (1983). Teacher evaluation in the organizational context. A review of the literature. Review of Educational Research, 53 (3), 285–328.

15. Fredrich, G. H. (1984, November). Supervision and evaluation: Recognizing the difference can increase value, effectiveness. *NASSP Bulletin,* 68(475), 12–18; McCarty, D. J., Kaufman, J. W., & Stafford, J. C. (1986, April). Supervision and evaluation: Two irreconcilable processes? *Clearing House,* 59(8), 351–353.

16. Petrie, T. A. (1982). Ideas that hinder evaluation—debunking the myths. *NASSP Bulletin,* 66(458), 52–55.

17. Popham, W. J. (2001). *The truth about testing: An educator's call to action* (pp. 55–65). Alexandria, VA: Association for Supervision and Curriculum Development.

18. Shufflebeam, D., & Nevo, D. (1993). Principal evaluation: New directions for improvement. *Peabody Journal of Education,* 68(2), 64–84.

19. Lipham, J. M., Rankin, R. E., & Hoch, J. A., Jr. (1985). *The principalship: Concepts, competencies, and cases.* White Plains, NY: Longman.

20. Ginsberg, R., & Berry, B. (1990). The folklore of principal evaluation. *Journal of Personnel Evaluation in Education,* 3(3), 205–230.

21. Anderson, M. E. (1991). *Principals: How to train, recruit, select, induct, and evaluate leaders for America's schools.* Eugene: ERIC Clearinghouse on Educational Management, University of Oregon.

22. Ginsberg, R., & Thompson, T. (1992). Dilemmas and solutions regarding principal evaluation. *Peabody Journal of Education,* 68(1), 58–74.

23. Hart, A. W. (1992). The social and organizational influence of principals: Evaluating principals in context. *Peabody Journal of Education,* 68(1), 37–57.

24. Drake, T. L., & Roe, W. H. (1999). *The principalship* (5th ed.). Upper Saddle River, NJ: Prentice-Hall.

25. Heck & Marcoulides. (1996). Op. cit.

26. Getzels, J. W., & Guba, E. G. (1957, Winter). Social behavior and the administrative process. *School Review, 65,* 423–441.

27. Stronge, J. H., & Helm, V. M. (1992). A performance evaluation system for professional support personnel. *Educational Evaluation and Policy Analysis, 14*(2), 175–180.

28. Duke, D. L. (1993). Removing barriers to professional growth. *Phi Delta Kappan, 74*(8), 702–712.

29. Malen, B. (1995). The micropolitics of education. In J. D. Scribner & D. H. Layton (Eds.), *The study of educational politics* (pp. 147–167). Washington, DC: Falmer, p. 148.

30. Leithwood, K. (1995). Introduction: Transforming politics in education. In K. Leithwood (Ed.), *Effective school district leadership: Transforming politics into education* (p. 2). Albany: State University of New York Press.

31. Pfeffer, J. (1992). *Managing with power* (p. 14). Boston, MA: Harvard Business School Press.

32. Lasswell, H. D. (1936). *Politics: Who gets what, when, how.* New York, NY: McGraw-Hill.

33. Davis, S. H., & Hensley, P. A. (1999). The politics of principal evaluation. *Journal of Personnel Evaluation in Education, 13*(4), 383–403.

34. Davis & Hensley. (1999). Ibid.

35. Duke, D. L. (1990). Developing teacher evaluation systems that promote professional growth. *Journal of Personnel Evaluation in Education, 4*(2), 131–144; Johnson, B. L. (1997). An organizational analysis of multiple perspectives of effective teaching. Implications for teacher evaluation. *Journal of Personnel Evaluation in Education, 11*(1), 69–87; McLoughlin, M. W. (1990). Embracing contraries: Implementing and sustaining teacher evaluation. In J. Millman & L. Darling-Hammond (Eds.), *The new handbook of teacher evaluation: Assessing elementary and secondary school teachers* (pp. 14–22). Newbury Park, CA: Sage; Poston, W. K., & Manatt, R. P. (1993). Principals as evaluators: Limiting effects on school reform. *International Journal of Educational Reform, 3*(1), 41–48; Sergiovanni, T. J., & Staratt, R. J. (1993). *Supervision: A redefinition.* New York, NY: McGraw-Hill; Stronge, J. H., & Helm, V. (1991). *Evaluating professional support personnel in education.* Newbury Park, CA: Sage.

36. Conley, D. T. (1987). Critical attributes of effective evaluation systems. *Educational Leadership, 44*(7), 60–64.

37. Scriven, M. (1995). Student ratings offer useful input to teacher evaluations. *Practical Assessment, Research and Evaluation, 4*(7). http://PAREonline. net/getvn.asp?v=4&n=7. (Accessed May 25, 2011).

38. Scriven, M. S. (1967). The methodology of evaluation. In R. Tyler, R. Gagne, & M. Scriven (Eds.), *AERA monograph review on curriculum evaluation: No. 1* (pp. 39–83). Chicago, IL: Rand McNally.

39. Stronge, J. H. (1997). Improving schools through teacher evaluation. In J. H. Stronge (Ed.), *Evaluating teachers: A guide to current thinking and implications for practice.* (pp. 1-23). Thousand Oaks, CA: Corwin Press.

40. Joint Committee on Standards for Educational Evaluation. (D. L. Stufflebeam, Chair). (1988). *The personnel evaluation standards: How to assess systems for evaluating educators.* Newbury Park, CA: Sage. Joint Committee on Standards for Educational Evaluation. (2008). *Personnel evaluation standards.* Author. Retrieved from http://www.jcsee.org/personnel-evaluation-standards. The Joint Committee is a group of educational associations that in 1988 (and revised in 2008) developed a consensus for standards in evaluating educational personnel that can be used to develop a practical, rational, and ethical system to assess principal and teacher performance.

41. Stufflebeam, D. L., & Brethower, D. M. (1987). Improving personnel evaluations through professional standards. *Journal of Personnel Evaluation in Education, 1*(2), 125–155; Stufflebeam, D. L., & Sanders, J. R. (1990). Using the Personnel Evaluation Standards to improve teacher evaluation. In J. Millman & L. Darling-Hammond (Eds.), *The new handbook of teacher evaluation: Assessing elementary and secondary school teachers* (pp. 416–428). Newbury Park, CA: Sage.

42. Helm, V. M. (1994, April). *The professional support personnel evaluation model: The use of multiple data sources in personnel evaluation.* Paper presented at the annual conference of the American Educational Research Association, New Orleans, LA. One study conducted by the Educational Research Service (1988) found that 99.8% of the public schools responding to the survey used

direct classroom observation as the primary data collection technique. See: Educational Research Service. (1988). *Teacher evaluation: Practices and procedures.* Arlington, VA: Author.

43. Beck, L., & Murphy, J. (1993). *Understanding the principalship: A metaphorical analysis from 1920–1990.* New York, NY: Teachers College Press.

44. Hallinger, P. (1992). The evolving role of American principals: From managerial to instructional to transformational leaders. *Journal of Educational Administration, 30*(3), 35–48; Leithwood, K. A. (1992). The move toward transformational leadership. *Educational Leadership, 49*(5), 8–12; Murphy, J., & Hallinger, P. (1992). The principalship in an era of transformation. *Journal of Educational Administration, 30*(3), 77–88; Murphy, J., & Louis, K. S. (1994). *Reshaping the principalship: Insights from transformational reform efforts.* Thousand Oaks, CA: Corwin.

45. Andrews, R., & Soder, R. (1987). Principal instructional leadership and school achievement. *Instructional Leadership, 44*(1), 9–11; Edmonds, R. (1979). Some schools work and more can. *Social Policy, 17*(5), 17–18; Hallinger, P., & Murphy, J. (1987). Instructional leadership in the school context. In W. Greenfield (Ed.), *Instructional leadership: Concepts, issues and controversies.* Boston, MA: Allyn & Bacon.

46. Duke & Stiggins. (1985). Op. cit.; Murphy, J., Hallinger, P., & Peterson, K. D. (1985). Supervising and evaluating principals: Lessons from effective districts. *Educational Leadership, 43*(2), 79–82; Natriella, G., Deal, T., Dornbusch, S. M., & Hong, M. (1977). *A summary of the recent literature on the evaluation of principals, teachers, and students* (Occasional Paper No. 18). Stanford, CA: Stanford University, Stanford Center for Research and Development in Teaching; Rentsch, G. L. (1976). Assessing administrator performance. *NASSP Bulletin, 60*(401), 77–83.

47. Ginsberg, R. & Berry, B. (1990). The folklore of principal evaluation. *Journal of Personnel Evaluation in Education, 3*(3), 205–230.

48. Ginsberg, R. & Thompson, T. (1992). Dilemmas and solutions regarding principal evaluation. *Peabody Journal of Education, 68*(1), 58–74.

49. Ebmeier, H. (1991, April). *The development of an instrument for client-based principal formative evaluation.* Paper presented at the annual meeting of the American Educational Research Association, Chicago, IL; Marcoulides, G. (1990). An alternative method for estimating variance components in generalizability theory. *Psychological Reports, 66*(2), 102–109; Marcoulides, G., & Heck, R. H. (1992b). Assessing instructional leadership effectiveness with generalizability theory. *International Journal of Educational Management, 6*(3), 4–13; Pitner, N., & Hocevar, D. (1987). An empirical comparison of two-factor versus multifactor theories of principal leadership: Implications for the evaluation of school principals. *Journal of Personnel Evaluation in Education, 1*(1), 93–109.

50. For a more complete discussion of these varied ways of defining the principalship, see: Ginsberg, & Thompson. (1992). Op. cit.

51. Ginsberg, R., & Berry, B. (1989). The folklore of principal evaluation. *Journal of Personnel Evaluation in Education, 3*(3), 205–230.

52. Hart, A. W. (1992). The social and organizational influence of principals: Evaluating principals in context. *Peabody Journal of Education, 68*(1), 37–57.

53. Hallinger, P., & Heck, R. H. (1996, April). *The principal's role in school effectiveness: An assessment of methodological progress, 1980–1995.* Paper presented at the AERA, New York, NY; Hallinger, P., & Heck, R. H. (1998). Exploring the principal's contribution to school effectiveness: 1980–1995. *School Effectiveness and School Improvement, 9*(2), 157–191; Leithwood, K., & Jantzi, D. (2000). Principal and teacher leadership effects: A replication. *School Leadership & Management, 20*(4), 415–434; Witziers, Bosker, & Krieger. (2003). Op. cit.

54. Witziers, Bosker, & Krieger. (2003). Op. cit.

55. Hallinger, P., & Murphy, J. (1987). Instructional leadership in the school context. In W. Greenfield (Ed.), *Instructional leadership: Concepts, issues, and controversies.* Boston, MA: Allyn & Bacon.

56. Witziers, Bosker, & Krieger. (2003). Op. cit.

57. Hallinger & Heck. (1998). Op. cit.

58. Glasman, N. S. & Heck, R. H. (1992). The changed leadership role of the principal: implications for principal assessment. *Journal of Education, 68*(1), 5–24.

59. Heck, R. H., & Marcoulides, G. A. (1992). Principal assessment: Conceptual problems,

methodological problems or both? *Peabody Journal of Education, 68*(1), 124–144.

60. Joint Committee of Standards for Educational Evaluation. (1988, 2008). *The Personnel Evaluation Standards.* Kalamazoo: Western Michigan University, The Evaluation Center.

61. Stufflebeam, D., & Nevo, D. (1993). Principal evaluation: New directions for improvement. *Peabody Journal of Education, 68*(2), 24–46.

62. Council of Chief State School Officers (CCSSO). (2008). *Educational leadership policy standards: ISLLC 2008.* As adopted by the National Policy Board for Educational Administration. Washington, DC: Author. Retrieved from http://www.ccsso.org/publications/details.cfm?PublicationID=365; Council of Chief State School Officers (CCSSO). (1996). *Interstate School Leaders Licensure Consortium Standards for School Leaders.* Washington, DC: Author.

63. Wright, G., & Gray, N. D. (2007, October). *The ISLLC standards: A unifying force in school administrators and counselor preparation.* Paper based on a program presented at the Association for Counselor Education and Supervision Conference, Columbus, OH; CCSSO. (2008). Op. cit.

64. The Principal Quality Rubric is based on Charlotte Danielson's model in *Framework for Teaching* (1996, 2007) as discussed later in this chapter. For research using PQR, see: Kaplan, L. S., Owings, W. A., & Nunnery, J. (2005). Principal quality: A Virginia study connecting Interstate School Leaders Licensure Consortium (ISLLC) standards with student achievement. NASSP Bulletin, 89(643), 28–44; Owings, W. A., Kaplan, L. S., and Nunnery, J. (2005). Principal quality, ISLLC Standards, and Student Achievement. *Journal of School Leadership,* 15 (1), 99–115.

65. Sanders, N. M. (2006, March).*Timelines and process for updating the ISLLC standards for school leaders and the ELCC/NCATE program standards.* Washington, DC: Council of Chief State School Officers. Retrieved from http://www.ccsso.org/projects/Interstate_Consortium_on_School_Leadership/

66. Fossey, R., & Shoho, A. (2006). Educational leadership preparation programs. In transition or crisis? *Journal of Cases in Educational Leadership,* 9(3), 3–11; Murphy, J. (2005, September). *Using the ISLLC standards for school leaders at the state level to strengthen school administration.* Alexandria, VA: National Association of State Boards of Education.

67. Bossert, S., Dwyer, D., Rowan, B., & Lee, G. V. (1982). The instructional management role of the principal. *Educational Administration Quarterly,* 18(3), 34–64; Bridges, E. (1982). Research on the school administrator: The state of the art, 1967–1980. *Educational Administration Quarterly,* 18(3), 12–33; Hallinger, P., & Murphy, J. (1985). Assessing the instructional leadership behavior of principals. *Elementary School Journal,* 86(2), 217–248.

68. Elliott, S. N., Goldring, E., Murphy, J., & Porter, A. (2008, March). *The VAL-ED assessment instrument: Purposes and response form.* Paper presented at the annual convention of the American Educational Research Association, New York, NY; Goldring, E., Porter, A. C., Murphy, J., Elliott, S. N., & Cravens, X. (2007, March). *Assessing learning-centered leadership. Connections to research, professional standards, and current practice.* Nashville, TN: Vanderbilt University. The School Leaders Licensure Assessment (SLLA) provides a 6-hour test (reduced to 4 hours in 2009) to assess principal candidates' decision making, analysis, and synthesis of information and problem solving on simulated work samples related to a national job analysis study and the ISLLC (Interstate School Leaders Licensure Consortium) standards. In 2009, seventeen states plus the District of Columbia and the U.S. Virgin Islands used the SLLA as a licensing requirement for their principal candidates. Unfortunately, evidence about SLLA's validity and reliability is not available. See: School Leaders Licensure Assessment (1010). (2005). Princeton, NJ: Educational Testing Service. Retrieved from http://www.ets.org/Media/Tests/PRAXIS/pdf/slla1010.pdf; Educational Testing Service. (n.d.). *The School Leadership Services Information Bulletin 2010–11.* Princeton, NJ: Author. Retrieved from http://www.ets.org/Media/Tests/SLS/pdf/15432.pdf

69. Goldring, Porter, Murphy, Elliott, & Cravens, (2007, March). Op. cit.

70. Maxwell, L. A. (2010, January 6). Review finds principal-evaluation tools a bit outdated. *Education Week,* 29(16), 8.

71. Peabody College of Education. (2008). *Development of the Vanderbilt Assessment of Leadership in Education (VAL-ED)*. Retrieved from http://peabody.vanderbilt.edu/x8451.xml; Porter, A. D., Polikoff, M. S., Goldring, E., Murphy, J., Elliott, S. N., & May, H. (2008, March). *Building a psychometrically sound assessment of educational leadership. The VAL-ED as a case study*. Paper presented at the annual convention of the American Educational Research Association, New York, NY.

72. Olson, L. (2008, January 16). Assessment to rate principal leadership to be field-tested. *Education Week, 27*(19), 1, 11.

73. Olson. (2008, January 16). Ibid.

74. Maxwell, L. A. (2009, December 16). Principals' certificate on horizon. *Education Week, 29*(15), 1, 11; National Board for Professional Teaching Standards. (2009). *National board certification for principals: A new way to develop, recognize, and retain top school leaders*. Arlington, VA: Author. Retrieved from http://www.nbpts.org/products_and_services/national_board_certifica

75. Maxwell. (2009). Ibid.

76. National Board for Professional Teaching Standards. (2009). *National Board Certification for Principals: Redefining educational leadership for the 21ˢᵗ century*. Arlington, VA: Author. Retrieved from http://www.nbpts.org/products_and_services/national_board_certifica. Nearly 7,500 educators nationwide, half of them principals, participated in the standards development process. From these concepts, stakeholders have completed the specific, detailed standards and will develop evidence-based assessments that will certify educational leaders as accomplished.

77. National Board for Professional Teaching Standards. (2009). Ibid.

78. Darling-Hammond, L. (1997). *Doing what matters most: Investing in quality teaching*. New York, NY: National Commission on Teaching and America's Future; Mendro, R. L. (1998). Student achievement and school and teacher accountability. *Journal of Personnel Evaluation in Education, 12*(3), 257–267; Stronge, J. H., & Tucker, P. D. (2000). *Teacher evaluation and student achievement*. Washington, DC: National Education Association.

79. National Commission on Excellence in Education. (1983). *A nation at risk. The imperative for educational reform*. Washington, DC: U.S. Department of Education.

80. National Commission on Teaching and America's Future. (1996, September). *What matters most: Teaching for America's future*. New York, NY: Author.

81. Danielson, C. (2001). New trends in teacher evaluation. *Educational Leadership, 58*(5), 12–15.

82. Ellett, D. C., & Teddlie, C. (2003). Teachers, teacher effectiveness and school effectiveness: Perspectives from the USA. *Journal of Personnel Evaluation in Education, 17*(1), 101–128.

83. For example, Darling-Hammond et al. (1983). Op. cit.; Ellett, C. D. (1985). Assessing minimum competencies of beginning teachers: Instrumentation, measurement issues and legal concerns. *Evaluation of teaching: The formative process. Hot topic series*. Bloomington, IN: Phi Delta Kappa; Ellett, C. D. (1987). Emerging teacher performances assessment practices: Implications for the instructional supervision role of school principals. In W. Greenfield (Ed.), *Instructional leadership: Concepts and controversies* (pp. 302–327). Boston, MA: Allyn & Bacon; Ellett, C. D., & Capie, W. (1982). *Measurement issues and procedures for establishing performance-based certification standards for teachers*. Paper presented at the annual meeting of the National Council on Measurement in Education, New York, NY; Iwanicki, E. (Ed.). (1986). *Journal of Personnel Evaluation in Education, 1*(1). Boston, MA: Kluwer Academic; Joint Committee on Standards for Educational Evaluation. (1988). *The Personnel Evaluation Standards: How to assess systems for evaluating educators*. D. Stufflebeam (Ed.). Newbury Park, CA: Corwin Press; Millman, J., & Darling-Hammond, L. (Eds.). (1990). *The new handbook of teacher evaluation: Assessing elementary and secondary school teachers*. Beverly Hills, CA: Sage; Scriven, M. (1988). Duty-based teacher evaluation. *Journal of Personnel Evaluation in Education, 1*(4), 319–334.

84. Brophy, J. (1986). Teacher influences on student achievement. *American Psychologist, 41*(10), 1069–1077; Brophy, J. (1988). Research on teacher effects: Uses and abuses. *Elementary School Journal, 89*(1), 3–22; Gage, N. L., &

Needels, M. C. (1989). Process-product research on teaching: A review of criticisms. *Elementary School Journal, 89*(3), 253–300.

85. Hall, G. E. (1983). Clinical supervision in teacher education as a research topic. *Journal of Teacher Education, 34*(4), 56–58.

86. Glickman, C. D., Gordon, S. P., & Ross-Gordon, J. M. (2001). *Supervision and instructional leadership: A developmental approach* (6th ed., pp. 316–320). Boston, MA: Allyn & Bacon/Longman; Hall, G. E. (1983). Clinical supervision in teacher education as a research topic. *Journal of Teacher Education, 34*(4), 56–58.

87. Van Der Linde, C. H. (1998). Clinical supervision in teacher evaluation: A pivotal factor in the quality management. *Education, 119*(2), 328–334.

88. Sawchuk, S. (2009, December 16). Performance-based evaluation systems face obstacles. *Education Week, 29*(15), 1, 12.

89. Wise, A. E., Darling-Hammond, L., McLaughlin, M. W., & Bernstein, H. T. (1984). *Teacher evaluation: A study of effective practices, prepared for the National Institute of Education.* Santa Monica, CA: Rand; McLaughlin, M. W., & Pfeifer, R. S. (1988). *Teacher evaluation: Improvement, accountability, and effective learning.* New York, NY: Teachers College Press; Johnson, B. L. (1997). An organizational analysis of multiple perspectives of effective teaching: Implications for teacher evaluation. *Journal of Personnel Evaluation in Education, 11*(1), 69–87; Natriello, G. (1984). Teachers' perceptions of the frequency of evaluation and assessments of their effort and effectiveness. *American Educational Research Journal, 21*(3), 579–595; Strong, J. H., & Tucker, P. D. (1999). The politics of teacher evaluation: A case study of new system design and implementation. *Journal of Personnel Evaluation in Education, 13*(4), 339–359.

90. Sawchuk, S. (2009, June 10). Grade inflation seen in evaluations of teachers, regardless of system. *Education Week, 28*(33), 6. One recent study by New York's New Teacher Project surveyed more than 15,000 teachers and 1,300 administrators across four states and 12 districts to find that more than 9 in 10 tenured teachers met local standards in recent evaluation cycles. Districts that used a binary rating system granted 99% of tenured teachers a "satisfactory" rating. In systems using more than two categories, 94% of teachers received one of the two highest ratings.

91. Sawchuk. (2009, June 10). Ibid.

92. Danielson, C., & McGreal, T. L. (2000). *Teacher evaluation to enhance professional practice.* Alexandria, VA: Association for Supervision and Curriculum Development.

93. Doyle, W. (1986). Classroom organization and management. In M. C. Wittrock (Ed.), *Handbook of research on teaching* (pp. 392–431). New York, NY: MacMillan.

94. Darling-Hammond, L. (2000). Teacher quality and student achievement: A review of state policy evidence. *Education Policy Analysis Archives, 8*(1); Hanushek, E. A. (1992). The trade-off between child quantity and quality. *Journal of Political Economy, 100*(1), 84–117; Ferguson, R. F. (1991). Paying for public education: New evidence on how and why money matters. *Harvard Journal on Legislation, 28*, 465–498; Walsh, K. (2001). *Teacher certification reconsidered: Stumbling for quality.* Baltimore, MD: Abell Foundation; Darling-Hammond, L. (2000, January 1). Teacher quality and student achievement: A review of state policy evidence. *Educational Policy Analysis Archives, 8*(1). Retrieved from http://epaa.asu.edu/epaa/v8n1; Haycock. (1998). Op. cit.; Whitehurst, G. J. (2002, March). *Scientifically based research on teacher quality: Research on teacher preparation and professional development.* Paper presented at White House Conference on Preparing Tomorrow's Teachers. Retrieved from http://www.ed.gov/inits/preparingteachersconference/whitehurst.html; Sanders, W. L., & Horn, S. P. (1995). Educational assessment reassessed: The usefulness of standardized and alternative measures of student achievement as indicators for the assessment of educational outcomes. *Education Policy Analysis Archives, 3*(6), 1–15. Retrieved from http://epaa.asu.edu/epaa/v3n6.html; Sanders, W. L., & Rivers, J. C. (1996, November). *Cumulative and residual effects of teachers on future student academic achievement.* Knoxville: University of Tennessee Value-Added Research and Assessment Center; Webster, W. J., & Mendro, R. L. (1997). The Dallas value-added accountability system. In

J. Millman (Ed.), *Grading teachers, grading schools. Is student achievement a valid evaluation measure?* (pp. 81–99). Thousand Oaks, CA: Corwin Press; Webster, W. J., Mendro, R. L., Orsak, T. H., & Weerasinghe, D. (1998a). *An application of hierarchical linear modeling to the estimation of school and teacher effect.* Dallas, TX: Dallas Independent School District. Retrieved from http://www.dallasisd.org/depts/inst_research/aer98ww2/aer98ww2.htm; Webster, W. J., Mendro, R. L., Orsak, T. H., & Weerasinghe, D. (1998b). *An application of hierarchical linear modeling to the estimation of school and teacher effects. Relevant results.* Dallas, TX: Dallas Independent School District. Retrieved from http://www.dallasisd.org/depts/inst_research/aer98ww2/aer98ww2.htm

95. Doyle, W. (1990). Themes in teacher education research. In W. R. Houston (Ed.), *Handbook of research on teacher education* (pp. 3–24). New York, NY: MacMillan; Rosenshine, B., & Stevens, R. (1986). Teaching functions. In M. C. Wittrock (Ed.), *Handbook of research on teaching* (pp. 376–391). New York, NY: MacMillan.

96. Clark, C., & Peterson, P. (1986). Teachers' thought processes. In M. C. Wittrock (Ed.), *Handbook of research on teaching* (pp. 255–296). New York, NY: MacMillan.

97. Beijaarad, D., & Verloop, N. (1995). Assessing teachers' practical knowledge. *Studies in Educational Evaluation, 22*(3), 275–286.

98. Sanders, W. L., & Horn, S. P. (1995). Educational assessment reassessed: The usefulness of standardized and alternative measures of student achievement as indicators for the assessment of educational outcomes. *Education Policy Analysis Archives, 3*(6), 1–15; Sanders, W. L., & Horn, S. P. (1998). Research findings from the Tennessee Value-Added Assessment System (TVAAS) database: Implications for educational evaluation and research. *Journal of Personnel Evaluation in Education, 12*(3), 247–257; Webster, W. J., & Mendro, R. L. (1997). The Dallas value-added accountability system. In J. Millman (Ed.), *Grading teachers, grading schools. Is student achievement a valid evaluation measure?* (pp. 81–99). Thousand Oaks, CA: Corwin Press; Webster, W. J., Mendro, R. L., Orsak, T. H., & Weerasinghe, D. (1998a). *An application of hierarchical linear modeling to the estimation of*

school and teacher effect. Dallas, TX: Dallas Independent School District. Retrieved from http://www.dallasisd.org/depts/inst_research/aer98ww2/aer98ww2.htm

99. Joint Committee on Standards for Educational Evaluation. (1988). Op. cit.

100. Bandura, A. (1997). *Self-efficacy: The exercise of control.* New York, NY: W. H. Freeman & Company.

101. McLaughlin, M. W., & Pfeifer, R. S. (1988). *Teacher evaluation: Improvement, accountability, and effective learning.* New York, NY: Teachers College Press; Stiggens, R. J., & Duke, D. L. (1988). *The case for commitment to teacher growth: Research on teacher evaluation.* Albany: State University of New York Press.

102. Gilliland, S. W., & Langdon, J. C. (1998). Creating performance management systems that promote perceptions of fairness. In J. W. Smither (Ed.), *Performance appraisal: State of the art in practice* (pp. 404–442). San Francisco, CA: Jossey-Bass; Keeping, L. M., & Levy, P. E. (2000). Performance appraisal reactions: Measurement, modeling, and method bias. *Journal of Applied Psychology, 85*(5), 708–723; Milanowski, A. T., & Heneman, H. G. (2001). Assessment of teacher reactions to a standards-based teacher evaluation system: A pilot study. *Journal of Personnel Evaluation in Education, 15*(3), 193–212.

103. Stiggens & Duke. (1988). Op. cit.

104. McLaughlin & Pfeifer. (1998). Op. cit.

105. Danielson & McGreal. (2000). Op. cit.

106. Kimball, S. M. (2002). Analysis of feedback, enabling conditions, and fairness perceptions of teachers in three school districts with new standards-based evaluation systems. *Journal of Personnel Evaluation in Education, 16*(4), 241-268.

107. Gilliland, S. W., & Landon, J. C. (1998). Creating performance management systems that promote perceptions of fairness. In J. W. Smither (Ed.), *Performance appraisal: State of the art in practice* (pp. 404–442). San Francisco, CA: Jossey-Bass.

108. Gilliland & Landon. (1998). Ibid.

109. Danielson, C. (1996). *Enhancing professional practice: A framework for teaching.* Alexandria, VA: Association for Supervision and Curriculum Development; Danielson, C. (2007). *Enhancing professional practice. A framework for teaching* (2nd ed.). Alexandria, VA: Association for

Supervision and Curriculum Development; Danielson, C. (2002). *Enhancing student achievement. A framework for school improvement.* Alexandria, VA: Association for Supervision and Curriculum Development.

110. Danielson. (1996). Ibid.
111. Danielson. (2007). Op. cit.
112. Danielson & McGreal. (2000). Op. cit.; Sawyer, L. (2001). Revamping a teacher evaluation system. *Educational Leadership, 58*(5), 44–47.
113. Marshall, K. (2005). It's time to rethink teacher supervision and evaluation. *Phi Delta Kappan, 86*(10), 722–735.
114. School districts using Danielson's framework for teaching model include Newport News, VA; Chester, NJ; Cumberland, ME; East Grand Rapids, MI; Kennett Square, PA; Columbus, IN; Dubuque, IA; Riverton, IL; Greenwood, AR; Grosse Ile, ME; Douglas County, CO; Northfield, VT; Quakertown, PA; Georgia Department of Education; among others.
115. Archibald, S. (2006). Narrowing in on educational resources that do affect student achievement. *Peabody Journal of Education, 81*(4), 23–42; Borman, G. D., & Kimball, S. M. (2005). Teacher quality and educational quality: Do teachers with higher standards-based evaluation ratings close student achievement gaps? *Elementary School Journal, 106*(1), 3–20; Gallagher, H. A. (2004). Vaughn Elementary's innovative teacher evaluation system: Are teacher evaluation scores related to growth in student achievement? *Peabody Journal of Education, 79*(4), 79–107; Kimball, S. M., White, B., Milanowski, A. T., & Borman, G. (2004). Examining the relationship between teacher evaluation and student assessment results in Washoe County. *Peabody Journal of Education, 79*(4), 54–78; Milanowski, A. T. (2004). The relationship between teacher performance evaluation scores and student achievement: Evidence from Cincinnati. *Peabody Journal of Education, 79*(4), 33–53; Milanowski, A., & Kimball, S. (2005, April). *The relationship between teacher expertise and student achievement: A synthesis of three years of data.* Paper presented at the annual meeting of the American Educational Research Association, Montreal, Quebec, Canada.

116. Kimball et al. (2004). Op. cit.; Milanowski. (2004). Op. cit.; Milanowski et al. (2005). Op. cit.
117. Kimball, S. M., & Milanowski, A. (2009). Examining teacher evaluation validity and leadership decision making within a standards-based evaluation system. *Educational Administration Quarterly, 45*(1), 34–70.
118. Peterson, K. D. (2000). *Teacher evaluation: A comprehensive guide to new directions and practice* (2nd ed.). Thousand Oaks, CA: Corwin Press.
119. Stodolsky, S. S. (1990). Classroom observation. In J. Millman & L. Darling-Hammond (Eds.), *The new handbook of teacher evaluation: Assessing elementary and secondary school teachers* (pp. 175–190). Newbury Park, CA: Sage.
120. Kimball & Milanowski. (2009). Op. cit.
121. Kimball & Milanowski. (2009). Op. cit.
122. Sawchuk. (2009). Op. cit.
123. Kimball & Milanowski. (2009). Op. cit.
124. Kimball. (2002). Op. cit. The increased administrative workload included time to learn the system, attend training sessions, conduct more frequent classroom observations with related conferences, gather more extensive evaluation evidence, and write up detailed evaluations. Teachers had additional work from compiling recommended evidence for the multiple data sources.
125. Brophy, J. (1986). Teacher influences on student achievement. *American Psychologist, 41*(10), 1069–1077; Shulman, L. S. (1987). Knowledge and teaching: Foundations of the new reform. *Harvard Educational Review, 57*(1), 1–22; Darling-Hammond, L., Wise, A. E., & Klein, S. P. (1999). *A license to teach: Raising standards for teaching.* San Francisco, CA: Jossey-Bass.
126. Nelson, B. S., & Sassi, A. (2000). Shifting approaches to supervision: The case of mathematics supervisor. *Educational Administration Quarterly, 36*(4), 553–584.
127. Viadero, D., & Honawar, V. (2008, June 18). Credential of NBPTS has impact. *Education Week, 27*(42), 1, 16. This number of NBPTS credential holders represents fewer than 3% of the nation's 3.7 million teachers.
128. Honawar, V. (2008, August 13). NBPTS expands credentialing in high-needs districts. *Education Week, 27*(45), 8.

129. National Board Certification has received recognition, support, and momentum from the American Federation of Teachers, the National Education Association, the Carnegie Foundation for the Advancement of Teaching, Columbia University's Teachers College, and the National Council for Accreditation of Teacher Education (NCATE). Some universities have incorporated the National Board standards into their teacher preparation and professional accreditation programs. Governors, state legislatures, and school boards help school districts provide a range of incentives encouraging teachers to earn NBPTS certification.

130. NBPTS. *Milestones. Raising the standard.* Retrieved from http://www.nbpts.org/about_us/background/milestones

131. Rotherham, A.J. (2004, March). Opportunity and responsibility for National Board Certified teachers. *Policy Report.* Washington, D.C.: Progressive Policy Institute. Retrieved from: http://www.ppionline.org/documents/Certified_Teachers_0304.pdf.

132. National Board for Professional Teaching Standards. (1987). *What teachers should know and be able to do.* Alexandria, VA: Author. Retrieved from http://www.nbpts.org/UserFiles/File/what_teachers.pdf; National Board for Professional Teaching Standards. (n.d.). *The five core propositions.* Alexandria, VA: Author. Retrieved from http://www.nbpts.org/the_standards/the_five_core_propositio

133. National Board for Professional Teaching Standards. (n.d.). *Standards by certificate.* Alexandria, VA: Author. Retrieved from http://www.nbpts.org/the_standards/standards_by_cert

134. Ellett, C. D., & Teddlie, C. (2003). Teacher evaluation, teacher effectiveness and school effectiveness: Perspectives from the USA. *Journal of Personnel Evaluation in Education, 17*(1), 101–128.

135. Keller, B. (2006, May 24). Under pressure, NBPTS to release full study. *Education Week, 25*(38), 5.

136. National Board of Professional Teaching Standards. (2006, Fall). *Making a difference in quality teaching and student achievement.* Retrieved from http://www.nbpts.org; Viadero & Honawar. (2008). Op. cit.

137. Bond, L., Smith, T., Baker, W. K., & Hattie, J. A. (2000, September). *Validation study: A distinction that matters.* University of North Carolina at Greensboro: Center for Educational Research and Evaluation. Retrieved from http://www.nbpts.org/UserFiles/File/validity_1_-_UNC_Greebsboro_D_-_Bond.pdf; Lustick, D., & Sykes, G. (2006, February 23). National Board Certification as professional development: What are teachers learning? *Education Policy Analysis Archives, 14*(5). Retrieved from http://epaa.asu.edu/epaa/v14n5; Sykes, G., et al. (2006, May). *National board certified teachers as organizational resource.* Grant # 61–5230. Final Report to the National Board for Professional Teaching Standards; Cohen, C. E., & Rice, J. K. (2005, August). *National Board Certification as professional development: Design and cost.* Washington, DC: U.S. Department of Education and National Science Foundation. Retrieved from http://www.nbpts.org/UserFiles/File/Complete_Study_Cohen.pdf; Viadero & Honawar. (2008). Op. cit. Goldhaber, D., & Anthony, E. (2004, March 8). *Can teacher quality be effectively assessed?* Urban Institute. Retrieved from http://www.urban.org/publications/410958.html; Vandevoort, L. G., Amrein-Beardsley, A., & Berliner, D. C. (2004, September 8). National Board Certified teachers and their students' achievement. *Education Analysis and Policy Archives, 12*(46). Retrieved from http://www.nbpts.org/UserFiles/File/National_Board_Certified_Teachers_and_Their_Students_Achievement_-_Vandevoort.pdf; Smith, T. W., Gordon, B., Colby, S. A., & Wang, J. J. (2005, April). *An examination of the relationship between depth of student learning and National Board Certification Status.* Appalachian State University: Office for Research on Teaching; Cavalluzzo, L. (2004, November). *Is National Board Certification an effective signal of teacher quality?* Alexandria, VA: CNA Corporation. Retrieved from http://www.nbpts.org/UserFiles/File/Final_Study_11204_D_Cavalluzzo_CNA_Corp.pdf

138. Sanders, W. L., Ashton, J. J., & Wright, S. P. (2005, March 7). *Comparison of the effects of NBPTS certified teachers with other teachers on the rate of student academic progress.* SAS Institute. Retrieved from http://www.nbpts.org/UserFiles/

File/SAS_final_NBPTS_report_D_Sanders.pdf; McColsky, W., Stronge, J. H., et al. (2005, June). *A comparison of National Board Certified teachers and non-National Board Certified teachers: Is there a difference between teacher effectiveness and student achievement?* University of North Carolina at Greensboro/SERVE. Retrieved from http://www .nbpts.org/UserFiles/File/Teacher_Effectiveness_ Student_Achievement_and_National_Board_ Certified_Teachers_D_-_McColskey.pdf

139. This model is adapted from Newport News Public Schools, Virginia, as cited in Danielson, C., & McGreal, T. L. (2000). *Teacher evaluation to enhance professional practice* (Appendix B, pp. 136–149). Alexandria, VA: Association for Supervision and Curriculum Development.

140. Essex, N. L. (1999). *School law and public schools. A practical guide for educational leaders* (pp. 179–202). Boston, MA: Allyn & Bacon.

141. Insubordination is generally viewed as the willful failure or inability to obey a reasonable and valid administrative directive. Insubordination may reflect a pattern of behavior or one serious violation.

142. What unprofessional conduct refers to often depends on the community norms, but may include immorality, criminal activity, sexual harassment, inappropriate relationships with students, and other teacher behaviors that the community believes set a poor example.

143. Alexander, K., & Alexander, M. D. (2003). *The law of schools, students, and teachers* (pp. 432–446). St. Paul, MN: Thomson/West.

144. Alexander & Alexander. (2003). Ibid. While school boards are not required to give a reason for denying a probationary teacher another contract, they cannot give the teacher a "bad" reason for not granting the contract.

145. Essex. (1999). Op. cit. If, however, a nontenured teacher produces evidence that a property right exists, such as when the school or district communicates damaging statements that may limit the teacher's range of future employment opportunities, due process may be instituted.

146. Hanson, M. (2001). Institutional theory and educational change. *Educational Administration Quarterly, 37*(5), 637–661.

147. Sergiovanni, T. (2000). *The lifeworld of leadership: Creating culture, community and personal meaning in our schools.* San Francisco, CA: Jossey-Bass.

148. Davis, D. R., Ellett, C. D., & Annunziata. J. (2002). Teacher evaluation, leadership, and learning organizations. *Journal of Personnel Evaluation in Education, 16*(4), 287-301.

149. Marshall, K. (2005). It's time to rethink teacher supervision and evaluation. *Phi Delta Kappan, 86*(10), 722–735.

PRINCIPAL QUALITY RUBRIC

ISLLC Standards	Unsatisfactory	Basic	Proficient	Distinguished
	There is evidence that the principal's actions have harmed the teaching and learning processes and results:	*There is evidence that the principal's actions have made little impact on teaching and learning processes or results:*	*There is clear evidence that the principal's actions have made a positive and measurable impact on teaching practice and student achievement:*	*There is clear, convincing, and consistent evidence that the principal's actions have made a significant and measurable impact on student achievement:*
Standard 1—Facilitating the development, articulation, implementation, and stewardship of a vision of learning	• Principal articulates no vision for student learning. • Principal "rationalizes" low student performance based on student SES factors.	• Principal has a written vision of learning but without faculty or community understanding, acceptance, or follow-through. • Principal recognizes the need to raise achievement in all student groups but has limited plans for doing so.	• Principal has developed, articulated, implemented, and assessed a vision of teaching and learning to the school community. • Principal's plan has strategies to raise all students' achievement. • School achievement data shows measurable improvement.	*All in Proficient PLUS:* • Principal has made these efforts systemic; teachers and community believe the vision and act upon it in the principal's absence. • School data demonstrate continuous and sustained improvement.
Standard 2—Advocating, nurturing, and sustaining a school culture and instructional program for student and staff learning	• School lacks personal and motivating student learning environment. • Large achievement gaps between student subpopulations are unaddressed or blamed on out-of-school factors. • Principal does not actively supervise instruction. • Principal does not facilitate the use of student achievement data for instructional planning. • Principal does not develop staff instructional and leadership capacity.	• Principal promotes an orderly student learning environment. • Large achievement gaps between student subpopulations are addressed with little success. • Evidence of classroom best practices is inconsistent. • Principal collects data but little evidence exists that it is used in making instructional decisions. • Principal provides some encouragement to use effective and appropriate technologies to support teaching and learning.	• Principal promotes caring, orderly, high expectations for student learning environment. • Large achievement gaps are successfully addressed and barriers to effective teaching and learning are removed. • Effective instructional practices are evident in most classrooms. • Professional development is ongoing and related to teachers' growth plans. • Principal and staff collaboratively analyze data for instructional decisions.	*All in Proficient PLUS:* • A comprehensive, rigorous, and coherent curricular program is evident. • Entire staff successfully addresses student achievement disparities and gap decreases. • Professional development is job-embedded, ongoing, collegial, and geared toward improving student achievement. • Principal, staff, and community effectively use data to monitor and evaluate the instructional program.

442

PRINCIPAL QUALITY RUBRIC

	Unsatisfactory	Basic	Proficient	Distinguished
Standard 3—Promoting and managing the organization, operations, and resources for a safe, efficient, and effective learning environment	• Principal permits frequent interruptions to instructional time. • Principal does not monitor and assess teacher performance. • Principal allocates resources in ways that do not promote student learning. • Many staff, students, and community view school as unsafe. • Principal does not allow teachers or assistant principals to take on leadership roles.	• Principal occasionally permits interruptions to interfere with instructional time. • Principal inconsistently and often ineffectively monitors and assesses teacher performance. • Principal allocates some resources to promote student learning. • Some staff, students, and community view the school as unsafe. • Principal allows some distributed leadership.	• Principal consistently enforces practices to protect instructional time. • Principal uses an effective system to monitor and assess teacher performance. • Principal routinely obtains and allocates sufficient resources to promote student learning. • Staff, students, and community view the school as safe. • Principal fosters widespread distributed leadership.	*All in Proficient PLUS:* • Teacher and organizational time focused to support quality instruction and student learning has become systemic. • Principal advocates for and obtains additional human, fiscal, and technological resources to support teaching and learning.
Standard 4—Collaborating with faculty and community members, responding to diverse community interests and needs, and mobilizing community resources	• Principal has little contact with faculty concerning the diverse community's interests and needs. • Principal has little contact with school families and community. • Principal does not collect and analyze data pertinent to educational environment.	• Principal routinely meets with faculty concerning the diverse community's interests and needs. • Principal responds to community needs in crises. • Principal collects pertinent data with minimal analysis and application.	• Principal and faculty consistently promote understanding, appreciation, and use of community's diverse cultural, social, and intellectual resources. • Principal builds and sustains positive relationships with families and caregivers. • Principal uses data effectively.	*All in Proficient PLUS:* • Principal involves appropriate stakeholders in annually developing and reviewing the school program, analyzing data, and taking responsibility for implementing strategies. • Community takes the lead in mobilizing resources for teaching and learning needs.

PRINCIPAL QUALITY RUBRIC *(continued)*

ISLLC Standards	Unsatisfactory	Basic	Proficient	Distinguished
	There is evidence that the principal's actions have harmed the teaching and learning processes and results:	*There is evidence that the principal's actions have made little impact on teaching and learning processes or results:*	*There is clear evidence that the principal's actions have made a positive and measurable impact on teaching practice and student achievement:*	*There is clear, convincing, and consistent evidence that the principal's actions have made a significant and measurable impact on student achievement:*
Standard 5—Acting with integrity and fairness, and in an ethical manner	• Principal has no system of accountability for students' academic and social success. • Principal inconsistently models self-awareness, reflective practice, transparency, and ethical behavior. • Principal makes decisions without considering and evaluating potential moral and legal consequences.	• Principal has established a minimal accountability system for students' academic and social success. • Principal routinely models self-awareness, reflective practice, transparency, and ethical behavior. • Principal generally makes decisions considering and evaluating potential moral and legal consequences.	• Principal has established an effective accountability system for students' academic and social success. • Principal consistently demonstrates integrity, fairness, and ethical behavior in speech and actions with all constituents. • Principal consistently makes decisions considering and evaluating potential moral and legal consequences.	*All in Proficient PLUS:* • Principal consistently promotes social justice and ensures that individual student needs inform all aspects of schooling.
Standard 6—Understanding, responding to, and influencing the political, social, economic, legal, and cultural contexts of learning	• Principal shows no evidence of advocating for children, families, or caregivers. • Principal does not recognize or understand how larger contexts affect teaching and learning.	• Principal shows some evidence of advocating for children, families, or caregivers. • Principal demonstrates limited understanding of how larger contexts affect teaching and learning and makes little effort to respond.	• Principal acts to influence building and district decisions affecting student learning. • Principal understands, responds to, and occasionally influences larger contexts that affect teaching and learning. • Principal assesses and analyzes emerging trends and initiatives in order to adapt leadership strategies.	*All in Proficient PLUS:* • Principal acts to influence state and national decisions affecting student learning. • Principal assesses, analyzes, and ***anticipates*** emerging trends and initiatives in order to adapt leadership strategies.

Principal Quality Scoring Sheet

Control Number: _____

Directions: Please use one score sheet for each principal you assess. *Checking only one box* (Unsatisfactory through Dinstinguished) for each of the 6 Standards, mark the scoring box below that you think best describes the principal's performance for each Standard.

PRINCIPAL QUALITY SCORING SHEET

ISLLC Standards	Unsatisfactory	Basic	Proficient	Distinguished
	There is evidence that the principal's actions have harmed the teaching and learning processes and results:	*There is evidence that the principal's actions have made little impact on teaching and learning processes or results:*	*There is clear evidence that the principal's actions have made a positive and measurable impact on teaching practice and student achievement:*	*There is clear, convincing, and consistent evidence that the principal's actions have made a significant and measurable impact on student achievement:*
Standard 1—Facilitating the development, articulation, implementation, and stewardship of a vision of learning				
Standard 2—Advocating, nurturing, and sustaining a school culture and instructional program for student and staff learning				
Standard 3—Promoting and managing the organization, operations, and resources for a safe, efficient, and effective learning environment				
Standard 4—Collaborating with faculty and community members, responding to diverse community interests and needs, and mobilizing community resources				
Standard 5—Acting with integrity and fairness, and in an ethical manner				
Standard 6—Understanding, responding to, and influencing the political, social, economic, legal, and cultural contexts of learning				

Copyright, Owings & Kaplan, 2009.

CHAPTER 11

Ethics, Integrity, and Social Justice in Leadership

Focus Questions

- How are ethics and resolving ethical dilemmas a vital part of school leadership?
- What are the general ethical perspectives and what are each one's advantages and disadvantages for ethical decision making in schools?
- How does integrating the multiple ethics paradigm assist principals in making ethical decisions?
- How do the normative leadership theories contribute to school leaders' ethical decision making? What are their limitations as guides to ethical decision making?
- How does the social justice perspective contribute to school leaders' role and ethical decision making?
- What personal qualities contribute to a school leader developing a strong ethical character?

CASE STUDY: MAKING ETHICAL DECISIONS

Dr. Eric Smith is the newly appointed superintendent of Hunt Valley County Schools, a 14,500-student district with prestigious Priceton University located in the town's center. The school board hired Smith on a split vote of 6 to 3. Dr. Smith had been the superintendent of a smaller school district for 3 years prior to the Hunt Valley appointment. In his previous positions, he was recognized for his commitment to social justice, reducing achievement gaps, and ensuring equity and equality of educational opportunity for all students. The board mentioned those qualities as essential since two high schools and several elementary and middle schools had not made adequate yearly progress (AYP).

Hunt Valley County Public Schools has three high schools: Priceton, Southern, and Western High Schools. Priceton High, a 2,000-student school located in the town limits adjoining Priceton University, is consistently ranked in *U.S. News and World Report*'s "top 10 public high schools " in the nation. Most of the professors' children attend Priceton High School. Many parents from outside the district have their children on the waiting list to attend the school and pay tuition if seats become available.

Southern High School, with its 1,200 students, is located in the southern portion of the county and is a much less affluent area than the town of Priceton. The median home value and per-capita income are less than half of that in Priceton. The 1,250-student Western High School is located in the northwestern part of the county and has an economic profile similar to Southern High.

After touring the three high schools during his first week in office, Dr. Smith observed obvious disparities in facilities, equipment, and instructional programs between Priceton High and the other two schools. He subsequently requested each school's demographic, budget, and achievement profile. The assistant superintendent told Dr. Smith that he had high school budget profiles, but the district did not track spending at the school level. The superintendent then instructed his assistant to make certain that such records were kept for all schools and let the assistant know what information was to be included.

Later in the week, Dr. Smith was given the following information (Table 1) concerning the three high schools. He distributed the information to the superintendent's leadership team (SLT) and placed the item on the next week's agenda. The eight-member SLT consisted of the superintendent, three assistant superintendents (teaching for learning, finance, and operations), and four directors (special education, human resources, public information and community involvement, and accountability).

Before the leadership team meeting, the director for accountability, Dr. Jones, mentioned to Dr. Smith that Priceton High School was a "sacred cow" to the school board, the influential community members, and the Priceton University members. Dr. Jones told his new boss that the spending for Priceton High School was way out of line but recommended not touching the issue as it might be the "third rail" to his superintendency.

At the SLT meeting, Dr. Smith commented that in his first week's school walk-throughs, he had seen some excellent elementary and middle schools. He mentioned that he understood why Priceton High School was ranked so highly by *U.S. News and World Report*. What he did not understand is elevation of one high school at the expense of the

Demographic, Budget, and Achievement Data for Hunt Valley High Schools

	Priceton High School		Southern High School		Western High School	
Students	2,251		1,616		1,607	
Administration	Principal:	$ 89,600	Principal:	$ 72,200	Principal:	$ 73,530
	Asst. Principals (6):	$ 438,398	Asst. Principals (4):	$ 209,580	Asst. Principals (4):	$ 211,614
Professional Staff	Deans (4):	$ 297,904	Deans (1):	$ 57,020	Deans (1):	$ 55,920
	Counselors (8):	$ 541,896	Counselors (5):	$ 234,535	Counselors (5):	$ 246,925
	Instructors (182):	$14,903,127	Instructors (96):	$4,107,376	Instructors (98):	$4,243,376
Classified	Secretaries (13):	$ 486,990	Secretaries (5):	$ 120,432	Secretaries (5):	$ 119,672
	Custodians (11):	$ 447,236	Custodians (5):	$ 124,904	Custodians (5):	$ 125,004
Operations and Maintenance	$ 827,542		$ 250,480		$ 239,528	
Professional Development	$ 51,840		$ 14,993		$ 12,955	
Field Trip Transportation	$ 41,765		$ 11,032		$ 12,939	
Instructional Supplies	$ 381,190		$ 82,194		$ 91,332	
Total Spending	**$18,507,488**		**$5,274,746**		**$5,432,795**	
Total Per-Student Spending	**$ 8,222**		**$ 3,264**		**$ 3,381**	
Relative Spending[1]**	$1.00		$0.397		$0.411	
Percentage of Students on Free or Reduced-Price Lunch	7%		52%		48%	
Graduation Rate	99%		81%		83%	
Students Passing All State Exams	99%		65%		66%	
Student Demographics[2]***	C = 82%; AA = 6%; L = 2%; A = 10%		C = 51%; AA = 26%; L = 21%; A = 2%		C = 53%; AA = 18%; L = 28%; A = 1%	
Notes:	International Baccalaureate program; 12.37 pupil–teacher ratio; instructors includes all professional staff not otherwise listed; 10 department chairs on 12-month contract; 2 department chairs on 11-month contract; most instructors at top end of salary scale (by calculation)		No air conditioning; 16.8 pupil–teacher ratio; instructors includes all professional staff not otherwise listed; 3 department chairs on 11-month contract; 1 department chair on 10.5-month contract; most instructors at lower end of salary scale (by calculation)		No air conditioning; 16.6 pupil–teacher ratio; instructors includes all professional staff not otherwise listed; 3 department chairs on 11- month contract; 1 department chair on 10.5-month contract; most instructors at lower end of salary scale (by calculation)	

* *For each dollar spent per pupil at Priceton, the relative per pupil spending at Southern and Western*

** *C=Caucasian; AA= African American; L=Latino; A=Asian*

other two high schools and possibly all other schools in the county. How could more than twice the per-pupil expenditure exist for Priceton than for Southern and Western?

No one in the room felt comfortable with the funding disparities. Someone noted that the previous director for accountability had mentioned this disparity at a school board meeting, and the position had been eliminated the following year. It remained vacant for 2 years; the position was reestablished only last year. The director for public information and community involvement advised Dr. Smith of the political landscape. There were nine school board members, three representing the town of Priceton, three for the Southern District, and three for the Western District. In the recent school board elections, two reelected board members from the Southern District and one board member from the Western District had come out in favor of the current funding for schools favoring Priceton, claiming that a "rising tide raises all boats" in the district.

Dr. Smith asked what was happening at Priceton that made the per-pupil costs so much higher than the other high schools. Anticipating this request, the team had been investigating the issue. The director for human resources reported that the pupil-to-teacher ratio was approximately 12.5 to 1 at Priceton and 16.5 to 1 at the other two high schools. Furthermore, Priceton had an International Baccalaureate (IB) program while the other two schools did not. Finally, from a human resources perspective, the majority of senior faculty and administration were at Priceton. The average years of teaching experience was 21.9 at Priceton versus 4.1 at the other two schools. Every teacher at Priceton had at least a master's degree while fewer than 5% of the other schools' teachers had advanced degrees.

The assistant superintendent for teaching for learning (a new title Dr. Smith had brought with him) mentioned that 6 years ago the school board had required all IB teachers to hold a master's degree. Additionally, the professional development costs were higher at Priceton since IB required intensive staff development for those teachers. The field trips for IB students also contributed to the cost differential.

Dr. Smith asked the group if it were morally right to spend so much more on one group than on the others. He asked the SLT how many of them had children who attend or attended Priceton High School, and all raised their hands. He asked if they thought Southern and Western not making AYP was a funding-related issue. The group discussed the matter with some concern for the new superintendent's tenure and suggested they all think about the issue and discuss it at the next meeting. They agreed and ended the meeting.

Less than an hour later, Dr. Smith received a phone call from the school board chair, Lucy Dinglewitt, representing the Priceton District. She stated that two of the SLT members had told her that the funding for Priceton High School had been discussed that day and the SLT planned to continue the discussion at its next meeting. Ms. Dinglewitt said that Dr. Smith was new and did not know the community well enough to make changes yet. She affirmed that the entire county was proud of Priceton High School and advised Dr. Smith to postpone any discussion or action about Priceton's funding until at least next year. Schools not making AYP should be his first concern. Besides, she said, the majority of the school board likes having such a prestigious high school in the county. She concluded by warning him to drop this issue and look into other matters or his "honeymoon" with the board might come to a premature end. Dr. Smith suggested to Ms. Dinglewitt that some schools not making AYP might be related to the Priceton funding matter. Ms. Dinglewitt ended the conversation by telling Dr. Smith he continued at his own peril.

Case Study Questions

1. What are the moral and ethical issues facing the superintendent in this situation?
2. What are Dr. Smith's choices and the consequences of those choices?
3. How would Dr. Smith's decisions differ using any of the six ethical perspectives discussed in the chapter (utilitarianism, categorical imperative, justice as fairness, communitarianism, altruism, or ethical pluralism)?
4. How could the multiple ethical paradigms help Dr. Smith decide how to best work toward creating a more equitable, just, and high-achieving school district that promotes the success of every student?
5. How do the normative leadership models offer guidance on how to create a more ethical school district culture for the Hunt Valley School District?
6. What type of leadership would be best in this situation?

INTRODUCTION

According to Joanne B. Ciulla, professor of leadership and ethics at the Unviersty of Richmond in Virginia, "Ethics is at the heart of leadership."[3] Educational leaders often face ethical dilemmas during their daily work as they try to make complex decisions in the best interests of both students and staff. Communities expect those holding leadership positions to act justly and rightly, promote good, and demonstrate moral and professional accountability. One cannot fully understand leadership without considering its ethics and morality.

Schools are supposed to serve moral purposes—nurturing young people's human, social, and intellectual growth. Likewise, educational leadership has a moral purpose.[4] In fact, principals have been called moral stewards, acknowledging that values and value judgments are central elements in school leadership.[5] All educational activities—supervising teachers, selecting curriculum, constructing a master schedule, assigning teachers and students to courses, disciplining students, monitoring budget expenses, identifying and removing health hazards, and maintaining a safe and orderly learning environment—are aimed at promoting the school's educational goals. Therefore, educators have a moral responsibility to be proactive about creating and sustaining an ethical environment in which to conduct education.

Responding ethically to situations in schools and initiating ethical behaviors to remedy inequitable circumstances are political activities. Recognizing the ethical dimensions of teaching other people's children, educational activists work to provide them with the highest quality of schooling they would desire for their own children. With a shared moral purpose, communities and educators become allies, seeking networks and teaching others to advocate for all students. In these ways, principals acting ethically become transformative leaders.

LEADERSHIP AND ETHICS

How would you recognize an ethical person? An ethical person consistently tells the truth, even when concealing the facts might be to that person's advantage. An ethical person respects all individuals for who they are and deals with others in a fair and objective manner. An ethical person cancels membership in a private club when he or she discovers racial and sexual bias in its membership criteria (if the board of directors refuses to change the criteria).

An ethical person has developed relatively mature qualities of autonomy, connectedness, and transcendence; acts as his or her own person within the supports and constraints of relationships; and behaves in ways that rise above immediate self-interest. These human and ethical sensibilities grow over a lifetime, hindered or nurtured by the significant people and circumstances in the person's life.

Defining Ethics

Ethics involves norms, values, beliefs, habits, and attitudes that we choose to follow—that we as a society impose on ourselves. As Pulitzer Prize winning author Thomas Friedman observed, "Laws regulate behavior from the outside in. Ethics regulate behavior from the inside out."[6] Professionally, ethics can be described as the rules or widely accepted standards of practice that govern members' professional conduct. Ethics are not laws imposed by the state. They are voluntary.

Ethics are about relationships. It is about "what we ought to do,"[7] requiring a judgment about a given situation. The word *ethics* is derived from the Greek word meaning "moral philosophy." The Greek word *ethos* refers to customs or usages, especially belonging to one group as apart from another. Later, ethics came to mean disposition or character, customs, and approved ways of acting. To behave ethically is to *choose* the "right" behavior whereas being moral is the ability to *practice* that right behavior. *Morals* refer to specific standards of right and wrong. Frequently, the two terms are used interchangeably. What is ethical is moral, and what is unethical is immoral.

When people find themselves in complex circumstances that require them to choose from among competing sets of principles, values, beliefs, or ideas, ethical dilemmas result. These competing sets of principles pull leaders in different directions. Complicating the situation even more, these options are not necessarily right or wrong but can involve "right versus right" or "wrong versus wrong."[8] Even determining what is right and what is wrong can be problematic.

Nonetheless, substantial agreement exists that some types of actions are better than others—better unconditionally, not solely for a particular person or in relation to a certain set of cultural norms.[9] This is because morally good acts are based on universal laws, incorporating basic values such as truth, goodness, beauty, courage, and justice. These values are found in all cultures. For example, altruism is a principle of moral behavior, highly regarded in all cultures. Societies may differ in their applications, however.[10]

The Need for Ethical Leadership in Organizations

Organizations contain people working within a structure for a common purpose. To achieve goals effectively and efficiently, organization members take on or are assigned different tasks, roles, and status levels. There are leaders and followers. Leaders are expected to provide direction, exercise control, and generally enact those functions necessary to achieve the organization's objectives. In successful organizations, leaders do more than allocate resources, monitor and direct employees, and build group cohesion. True leadership means moving followers toward achieving the vision that the leader has developed to fulfill the organization's mission. Management professors Rabindra Kanungo and Manuel Mendoncas concluded, "Without a leader, the organization is much like a rudderless ship—adrift in a turbulent environment."[11]

Questioning the role of ethics in businesses, industries, and not-for-profit organizations, including government and schools, is understandable. Businesses and organizations are started to earn profits and create wealth, not to promote morality. Yet since the ancient Greeks, people have been thinking about the purpose of government. In *Politics*, Aristotle observed that the state comes into being to provide law and order but continues for the sake of good law, good order, and noble actions. Similarly, human organizations' reasons for being are to support some "good" and meet with highest excellence. In our own time, management expert Peter Drucker noted that management must consider the impact of every business policy and action upon society to determine whether it is likely to promote the public well-being, advance the society's basic beliefs, and add to its stability, strength, and harmony.[12]

Each generation learns anew this lesson of serving the public good. Worldviews that emphasize individualism to the exclusion of responsibility to a larger public good have distinct disadvantages. To be sure, emphasis on individual accomplishment and the concept that "time is money" have created a fast-moving competitive climate with technological advancement and immense material prosperity to Western countries. But such progress with its emphasis on personal gain and winning has been bought at a heavy cost. Technological advances and geographic mobility have meant a growing sense of aloneness, lack of interdependence, and alienation. Although businesses must make money, the aftermath of 2008's near-collapse of the global financial markets and the deep worldwide recession that followed showed that the sole preoccupation with fast profit to the exclusion or neglect of other considerations is not acceptable. The unrestrained exercise of individual autonomy and freedom, and the public and private morality of corporate leaders have become significant societal concerns.

Although all organizational members are responsible for enacting their roles in a manner consistent with ideals of serving the community as they serve themselves, the organizational leader bears the primary responsibility for providing the proper direction and high performance standards. The leader presents the vision, articulates the mission, communicates the beliefs and values that shape the organization's culture and behavioral norms, and lays the foundation for organizational strategies, policies, and procedures. If these practices are to mean anything, the leader's behaviors must be congruent with the organization's beliefs and goals. In contrast, when leaders compromise their ethical standards, they do harm and create an atmosphere of ethical cynicism.[13] This is true in schools no less than in other organizations.

A greater balance between individualism and a concern for the larger community is needed if the society is to flourish. In his book, *The Duality of Human Existence* (1966), David Bakan proposed that each individual has two fundamental but opposed senses: self-protectiveness/self-assertiveness and a sense of selflessness that feels empathy with others.[14] Both orientations are essential for survival. The challenge for individuals and societies is to effectively reconcile these two polarities. Different cultures reconcile this duality in varying ways. In the West, the balance tilts in favor of self-assertiveness and individual gain. In the East, it swings in favor of communion and group advancement. Research supports the belief that a more inclusive and cooperative self can lead to greater effectiveness.[15] Additional studies in psychology have found that striving for individual achievement can often be self-defeating and counterproductive.[16] In fact, the rewards of altruism may reach well beyond good business sense to our own personal health and well-being.[17]

Organizations are human systems responsive to human needs. As human systems, organizations must develop the moral obligation to respond to the needs of their employees as well as their customers, minority groups, and others in their external environments. Within an ethical perspective, organizational leaders are truly effective only when they are motivated by a concern for others as well as for the organization—despite the risk of personal cost—and when they guide their actions primarily to achieve this purpose. That is, the most effective leaders behave in ethical, other-directed (as opposed to self-directed) ways.

Principals as Moral Stewards

School leaders perform deeply significant work that affects individual students and the larger community. As moral stewards and educators, principals do more than manage their schools' finances, teaching schedules, student discipline, and buses. As persons wishing to affect society, school leaders must be directed by a powerful array of beliefs and values anchored in issues such as justice, community, and promoting success for all children and youth. They must view their task more as a mission than a job, creating an ethical coherence and culture that bonds both leader and followers to a shared set of values, beliefs, and purposes. Principals and other school leaders must be able to see the moral implications of a thousand daily decisions.[18] In its most comprehensive and concrete form, being moral stewards means meeting the "moral imperative to provide real learning opportunities to the whole of the student population."[19] For school district superintendents, this means providing such learning opportunities to the school board, school leaders, teachers, staff, and the wider community.

Moral stewardship is also about building communities. Ideally, school leaders lead through a web of interpersonal relationships, with people rather than through them, influencing from professional expertise and moral imperative rather than by line authority. Leadership in schools depends on modeling and clarifying values and beliefs rather than on telling people what to do. And as community builders, school leaders encourage others to be leaders in their own right.

Humans consciously choose how they want to influence others, relying on persuasion, rewards, punishments, emotional appeals, rules, and other means. Having this freedom of choice makes ethical considerations a vital part of leadership. Accordingly, having a theory for practice to enact ethical behaviors helps educators frame moral situations in their workplaces and allows moral content to become more intelligible and available to their intuition. Such a theory would give school leaders a way to think ethically about their work and work environment and provide a framework to guide their decisions and actions.[20]

Examples of Ethical Dilemmas in Schools. Principals face a wide array of situations that require ethical decision making. These may be related to students, staff, finance and resources, and external relations. Frequently, ethical dilemmas involve student harassment, intimidation, or bullying. Many involve addressing conflicts between the school's values and students' home values. Monitoring staff performance may mean deciding whether to develop or dismiss an underperforming teacher or staff member. Allocating resources means choosing how to allot funds among competing areas. Ethical dilemmas also arise from external relations, resolving conflicts between central office directives, teachers, and community needs and interests.

Seeking opportunities to increase equity also creates ethical dilemmas. Should the most experienced and able teachers be assigned to work with the highest achieving students (typically more affluent) or to those students with the greatest learning needs (typically low income, minority, or disabled)? Should the curriculum focus on reading and math "test prep" to ensure that all students perform to state standards on high-stakes tests or should the arts, physical education, and opportunities for creative and critical thinking and expression be included as part of a more holistic academic education? Should prerequisites to demanding, high-status curricula be increased to create more homogeneous classes (academically and socioeconomically) or should prerequisites be reduced (and supports increased) to offer more access for highly motivated but underprepared students? Should curriculum focus on traditional academic disciplines and Western civilization or should the school infuse a multicultural curriculum that emphasizes mastering rigorous academic skills while using authentic voices from diverse communities? What should be the balance of community stakeholders on the school improvement team—between those with social, political, and financial resources and those without such resources but who hold significant influence over large groups of students in underserved communities? All these situations provide occasions for making ethical choices.

The array of possible ethical dilemmas that principals face daily is virtually endless. When making challenging decisions, should principals rely on their personal values, on their professional ethics, or on community desires? Should what is best for the individual or what is best for the group be the final arbiter for selection? How does one choose between what appear to be equally poor or equally positive alternatives? Defining and choosing the options that are in the students' best interests may not be clear-cut or unequivocal.

ACTIVITY 11.1   Identifying Moral and Ethical Issues in Schools

Case Study Question 1: What are the moral and ethical issues facing the superintendent in this situation?

The clear funding and educational disparities among the three high schools have created a dilemma for Dr. Smith, the school board, the district administrators, and the larger community. While all are extremely proud of the nationally recognized excellence and the high-quality education that Priceton High School students are receiving, students at other district schools are not making sufficient achievement gains. Resource disparity may be part of the problem. For every dollar per student the district spends at Priceton, students in the other district high schools are receiving 39 cents and 41 cents. After hearing the unfortunate history of trying to address district funding inequities and after receiving the school board chair's clear warning to tread lightly, Dr. Smith needs to thoughtfully consider his next steps. What are the moral and ethical issues facing the superintendent in this situation? Discuss as a class:

1. What do these data tell Dr. Smith about Hunt Valley School District's educational environment and the district's commitment to promoting the success of every student?
2. What are the moral and ethical issues in this situation?
3. To what extent does improving the situation for all students depend on Dr. Smith keeping his job? How does the answer to this question influence his decisions on how to address this problem?
4. How can Dr. Smith use his leadership role and the available achievement and budget data to influence the school district's organizational culture so that its beliefs, values, and purposes are aligned to equitably support all students' learning with the necessary policies, strategies, and resources?
5. How can Dr. Smith use his leadership role and the available achievement and budget data to influence the community and local business culture so they can fully support all students' learning to high levels?
6. If Dr. Smith is to show moral leadership and promote the success of every student, how might he create learning opportunities and build relationships needed to shape the organizational culture toward social justice, community, fairness, and promoting the success of all children and youth?

GENERAL ETHICAL PERSPECTIVES

Learning about well-established ethical systems can help expand school leaders' capacity to meet ethical challenges with useful cognitive tools. Utilitarianism, Kant's categorical imperative, justice as fairness, communitarianism, altruism, and ethical pluralism reflect common ethical systems. While educational leaders' ethical dilemmas may be unique, developing an informed perspective to help identify these predicaments can assist in their successful resolution.

Utilitarianism: "The Greatest Good for the Greatest Number"

Utilitarianism is founded on the idea that ethical choices should be based on their consequences. It is likely that people have always weighed the probable outcomes of their actions when deciding what to do. The process was not formalized and named, however, until the 18th and 19th centuries. English philosophers Jeremy Bentham (1748–1832) and John Stuart Mill (1806–1873) asserted that the best decisions generate the most benefits in contrast with their disadvantages and do the greatest good for the greatest number of people.[21] Utility can be based on what is best in a specific case or on what is generally best in most situations. For instance, one may decide that telling a particular lie is justified in one circumstance (such as to protect someone's reputation) but, as a general rule, believe that lying is wrong because it causes more harm than good.

Leaders often take a utilitarian approach to ethical decision making. For example, in 2010, President Barack Obama and his advisors looked at the fragile U.S. financial markets recovering from near collapse, 10% unemployment, and a record national deficit (large gap between yearly incoming tax receipts and actual spending). Tax receipts had dropped while "bailouts" of large banks, insurance firms, and U.S. auto makers; extended unemployment insurance; and outgoing stimulus dollars further emptied federal coffers. Yet, counterintuitively, the president proposed to increase spending for small business and middle-class tax cuts and new job creation. Weighing the pros and cons, the president and his advisors saw short-term advantages of forcing more money into the anemic economy as outweighing disadvantages. Working from a different perspective, others might have weighed these factors differently and drawn different conclusions.

National and school leaders are not the only persons who must find their way out of ethical dilemmas. Occasionally, teachers must decide whether to join a strike (employment walkout). They may agree with their union leaders that teachers need and deserve better salaries, increased benefits, and more accommodating work hours. They want to show allegiance and loyalty to their professional group. But they also feel a commitment to continue their students' learning, be good role models for young people, and have their principals see them as dependable employees who respect their contracts. As with others confronting an ethical dilemma, teachers in this circumstance ask themselves the following utilitarian questions:[22]

◆ What is my obligation to the organization?
◆ What is my moral obligation to colleagues in the organization?
◆ What is my ethical obligation to my profession?
◆ What will be the cost of participating in the strike to my employment, my family, and others close to me?
◆ What moral obligation do I have to myself?
◆ What is my ethical obligation to the community and to the general public?
◆ How will my action affect important values such as freedom of expression, truthfulness, courage, justice, cooperativeness, and loyalty? Which is more important to me: friendship or security?

The notion of weighing outcomes is easy to understand and apply. Focusing on outcomes encourages thinking through decisions, lessening the likelihood of making impulsive, unreasoned choices. The ultimate goal of evaluating consequences is to maximize benefits to as many people as possible. On the other hand, identifying and evaluating possible consequences can be difficult. This is especially true for leaders who represent a variety of stakeholders. For instance, suggesting national spending cuts for "discretionary budget items" may sound attractive, but when businesses and employees affected by these proposed cuts reside and vote in 49 states, their congressional delegates are likely to reject such fiscal discipline. Unanticipated consequences further complicate the choice. Restoring the budget cuts will keep people employed in the short run but may create dire financial complications and possible layoffs in the long run. Accordingly, varying budget advisors may consider these factors and recommend different decisions.

Because identifying and evaluating potential costs and benefits are difficult, decision makers who use utilitarian ethics to address the same dilemma sometimes reach dissimilar conclusions. Logical and persuasive arguments exist for each option, and decision makers may be confused or ambivalent about which decision will do the greatest good for the greatest number of people. Also, the utilitarian approach may neglect minority rights.

Kant's Categorical Imperative: "Do Right No Matter the Cost"[23]

In contrast with the utilitarians, German philosopher Immanuel Kant (1724–1804) argued that people should do what is morally right no matter what the consequences, with no exceptions.[24] His approach to moral reasoning posits that we ought to make choices based on our duty to follow universal truths that are imprinted on our consciences. Guilt is an indication that we have broken these moral laws.

According to Kant, what is right for one is right for all. If we ask ourselves, "Would I want everyone else to make the decision I did?" and the answer is yes, the choice is justified. If the answer is no, the decision is wrong. Based on this reasoning, certain behaviors such as telling the truth and helping the less fortunate are always right. Other behaviors, such as lying, cheating, and murder, are always wrong. After all, cooperation would be impossible if no one could be trusted to tell the truth.

Kant also stressed the importance of treating humanity fairly. Persons are always valuable in their own right, and should not be considered as tools to help individuals get what they want. Instead, people should respect and encourage others' capacity to think and choose for themselves. With this type of thinking, for instance, manufacturers are obligated to give those living near their factories information about possible toxic pollutants in the air and water supply so they can make informed decisions about where to live. Similarly, coercion and violence are immoral because such tactics breach freedom of choice. Failing to help a neighbor is unethical because ignoring this person's need limits his or her alternatives.

Emphasis on duty encourages persistence and consistent behavior. Certain behaviors are either right or wrong, no matter what the circumstance. Believing in these transcendent principles, people are less likely to compromise their personal ethics, despite group pressure and opposition. Seeking fairness, justice, truth, and kindness is more inspiring than seeking selfish ends. Respecting the rights of others to choose is a key guideline when making moral choices. This standard promotes the sharing of information and concern for others while condemning deception, coercion, and violence.

While Kant's categorical imperative approach to ethical decision making promotes persistence and consistency, is highly motivational, and demonstrates respect for others, it has its disadvantages. First, almost every "universal law" has its exceptions. For example, although most people disapprove of lying, many would limit or withhold the truth to save a family member or friend's life. Countries routinely justify killing during war. Next, guilt is not a guarantee of appropriate behavior. Serial killers such as Jeffrey Dahmer or Ted

Bundy did not appear to be bothered by guilt. Psychological and environmental factors, such as being raised by abusive parents, can keep a mature conscience from developing.

Despite their differences, both utilitarianism and the categorical approach involve applying universal rules or principles to specific situations. Yet dissatisfaction with rule-based approaches exists. Some modern philosophers complain that these ethical guidelines are applied to extreme situations, not the types of decisions normally made.[25] Few of us will ever be confronted with the extraordinary scenarios—such as stealing to save a life or lying to the police to protect a fugitive—used to illustrate principled decision making. Our everyday ethical challenges are far less dramatic, such as telling coworkers that we do not appreciate their telling sexist jokes or informing a friend about an unflattering new outfit without hurting his or her feelings. In addition, time pressures and ambiguity complicate our decision making. In a crisis, there is little time to carefully weigh and assess alternatives and outcomes to determine which abstract principle to follow.

Justice as Fairness: "Guaranteeing Equal Rights and Opportunities Behind the Veil of Ignorance"[26]

Many dilemmas in democratic societies center on questions of justice or fairness. Is it fair that low-poverty schools spend more money per pupil than high-poverty schools? Are curriculum tracks fair to low-income and minority students? Should schools be funded equally (the same amount of money per pupil) or equitably (the amount of money necessary to effectively educate these particular students to the level of their more affluent and less educationally needy peers)? Why should young taxpayers be required to buy health insurance when they will not get ill until much later in life?

In the late 20th century, Harvard philosopher John Rawls addressed these questions.[27] He sought to identify the principles that would foster cooperation in a society consisting of free and equal citizens who must deal with inequalities of status, resources, talents, and abilities. Rawls rejected the utilitarian principles because generating the greatest good for the greatest number could disadvantage minority populations. For example, cutting corporate taxes might spur a region's overall economic growth but most of the benefits would go to the corporate owners. Other citizens would have to pay higher taxes to make up for the lost revenues. The greatest burden would fall on those earning minimum wage.

So instead of basing decisions on cost-benefit analysis, Rawls proposed the following principles of justice be built into our social institutions:

◆ *Principle 1:* "Equal liberty"—Each person has an equal right to the same basic liberties that are compatible with similar liberties for all.
◆ *Principle 2:* Social and economic inequalities must be addressed using two principles:
   (A) "Equal opportunity"—They are to be attached to offices and positions open to all under conditions of fair equality of opportunity.
   (B) "Difference principle"—They are to provide the greatest benefit to the least advantaged members of society.[28]

The "equal liberty" principle has priority. It states that certain rights, such as the right to vote and freedom of speech, are constitutionally protected and must be equal to what others have. According to this principle, attempts to deny voting rights to minorities would be unethical. Principle 2A—"equal opportunity"—argues that everyone should have an equal opportunity to qualify for political offices and employment jobs. Discrimination based on race, gender, religion, or ethnic origin is forbidden. In addition, everyone in society ought to have access to the training and education needed to prepare for these positions. Principle 2B—"the difference principle"—recognizes that inequalities exist but priority should be given to meeting the needs of the poor, immigrants, minorities, and other marginalized groups.

Rawls presented the "veil of ignorance" theory to support his claim that his principles offer a solid foundation for a democratic society like the United States. In his view, if people were unaware of their own characteristics and societal position and were to design a set of principles to govern their society, they would choose equal liberty, equal opportunity, and the difference principle. Equal liberty would grant them the maximum amount of freedom to follow their interests. Equal opportunity would give them access to the best jobs and elected offices if they were among their society's most talented. And the difference principle would ensure that they would be cared for if they were disadvantaged. Ideally, Rawls's guidelines would guarantee that everyone has freedom of speech and thought, the right to own and sell property, and the opportunity to pursue their goals while their gains must also benefit their less fortunate neighbors. Everyone would receive adequate health care, decent housing, and high-quality education. The huge gap between the haves and have-nots would shrink.

Although the Rawls model offers a system for dealing in inequalities that touches both individual freedom and the common good, democratic values and concerns for the less fortunate, fair treatment of followers, and provides a useful guide to decision making, it also has a down side. His model applies only to liberal democratic societies and not to cultures governed by royal families or religious leaders who are granted special powers and privileges denied to others. Likewise, the more diverse democratic nations become, the more complicated it is for groups to agree on common values and principles.[29]

Then too, definitions of *justice* and *fairness* vary deeply, undermining the principles' usefulness. What one group considers fair may appear grossly unjust to others. In the past quarter century, minority groups have advocated for special consideration in college admissions to make up for generations of discrimination and to achieve equal access with Caucasians. Many Caucasians, however, believe that such standards are unfair because they deny equal opportunity and ignore legitimate differences in abilities and prior achievement. Additionally, no assurances exist that persons who step behind the "veil of ignorance" would devise the same principles as Rawls. Rather than emphasize fairness, they might use utilitarian criteria or stress certain rights. Capitalist theorists, for instance, believe that benefits should be distributed based on each person's contribution, and helping the less advantaged rewards laziness while discouraging productive people from doing their best. Because decision makers may reach different conclusions behind the veil, critics claim that Rawls's principles lack moral force.[30]

Communitarianism: "Shoulder Your Responsibilities and Seek the Common Good"[31]

Developed in the 1990s, communitarianism is a philosophical movement that seeks to shift citizens' focus from individual rights to communal responsibilities. Led by sociologist Amitai Etzioni,[32] communitarian philosophy intends to promote a moral revival. This philosophy sees American society as fragmenting and in a state of moral decline: high divorce and crime rates, campaign attack ads, and growing influence of special interest groups in politics. In this communitarian model, healthy and responsive communities consist of:[33]

◆ *Wholeness incorporating diversity.* The community's existence depends on sharing a vision of the common good or purpose that makes it possible for people to live and work together—while at the same time, segments are free to pursue their diverse and often competing interests.

◆ *A reasonable set of shared values.* Responsive communities agree on a set of core values that are reflected in written rules and laws, unwritten customs, and a shared view of the future. Important ideals include justice, equality, freedom, individual dignity, and release of human talent and energy.

◆ *Caring, trust, and teamwork.* Healthy communities foster cooperation and connection as they respect individual differences. Citizens feel a sense of belonging and responsibility, recognize minority rights, engage in effective conflict resolution, and work together on shared tasks.

◆ *Participation.* To function effectively, large, complex communities depend on their leaders' efforts dispersed throughout every segment of society.

◆ *Affirmation.* Healthy communities sustain a sense of unity through continuous reaffirmation of their shared history, symbols, and group identity.

◆ *Institutional arrangements for community maintenance.* Responsive communities ensure their survival through such structures as city and regional governments, boards of directors, and committees.

Concern for the common good is arguably the communitarian movement's most important ethical principle. Ideally, considering the broader community's needs discourages selfish, unethical behavior. By promoting the common good, the communitarian movement encourages dialogue and discussion within and between groups as they reach consensus about ethical choices.

Communitarianism offers a promising approach to leaders' moral reasoning. It addresses selfishness directly, encouraging individuals to place responsibilities above rights and to seek the common good over individual perks or power. It reminds leaders that they have obligations to immediate followers and to the entire communities in which they live. Next, communitarianism promotes the benefits of dispersed and collaborative leadership and ethical dialogue. Leaders in every segment of society—business, politics, health care, education, social service, religion—create a framework characterized by equity, openness, and honesty that encourages discussion of moral questions to solve public problems. Finally, this movement fosters the development of virtues by supporting strong families, schools, religious congregations, and governments.

Detractors disagree with these claims. First, some dislike communitarians' evangelical approach which seeks "converts." Second, others reject promoting one set of values in a pluralistic society. Different communities have different—even competing—standards and conflicting moral guidelines. For instance, who decides which values are taught in public schools? While Christians may want the Ten Commandments posted in each classroom,

Muslims, Buddhists, and other religious (and non-religious) groups may not. Still others worry that focus on community rights will weaken individual rights. Similarly, the National Collegiate Athletic Association (NCAA) has banned Native American nicknames, mascots, and logos from championship competition, viewing them as "hostile and abusive." At the same time, many fans and alumni oppose the ban, claiming the mascots are integral parts of their schools' traditions and honor Native Americans. Finally, local community standards can be oppressive and should be accountable to the larger society. For example, it took 200 years (until 1954) before the U.S. Supreme Court decided that all public schools must be racially integrated and that separate-but-equal was unconstitutional. In short, a diverse society holds varying and competing values that all demand attention and expression—which itself is a moral dilemma.

Altruism: "Love Your Neighbor"

Advocates of altruism proclaim that love of neighbor is the ultimate ethical standard. Our actions should be designed to help others, whatever the personal cost. Like communitarianism, the altruistic approach to moral reasoning shares much with virtue ethics. Many of the virtues that characterize people of high moral character—compassion, hospitality, empathy, kindness, generosity—reflect concern for other people. Virtuous leaders are other-centered, not self-centered.

Altruism appears to be a universal value advanced in cultures around the world. Tibet's Dalai Lama encourages followers to practice an ethic of compassion, and Western thought has been greatly influenced by Judaism and Christianity's altruistic teachings. In this perspective, because humans are made in God's image and God is love, individuals have an obligation to love others regardless of who they are and what their relationship is to them. Hospice volunteers provide a modern illustration of unconditional love, attending to a dying person's needs with no concern for the individual's social or religious background and expecting nothing in return.

Concern for others promotes healthy social relationships. Researchers from social psychology, economics, political science, and other fields have found that altruistic behavior is the norm, more often than not.[34] Helping family, friends, and colleagues is something individuals do every day. Altruism drives a variety of movements and organizations designed to help the less fortunate and end social problems. Doctors Without Borders, Habitat for Humanity, and the local crisis help line all began by someone motivated by altruistic aims.

Management professors Rabindra Kanungo and Manuel Mendonca believe that concern for others is even more important for leaders than it is for followers.[35] By definition, leaders exert influence on behalf of others. To succeed, leaders must understand and articulate their constituents' concerns and needs. This may require taking risks and sacrificing personal gain. According to Kanungo and Mendonca, leaders who wish to benefit followers will pursue organizational goals, rely on referent and expert power, and share power with others. In contrast, leaders intent on benefiting themselves will focus on personal achievements; rely on legitimate, coercive, and reward power; and try to control others. Table 11–1 identifies how altruistic behaviors may appear in organizations.

TABLE 11–1

Organizational Altruistic Behaviors Directed to Benefit:

Individuals	Consideration of others' needs
	Technical assistance on the job
	Job orientation in new jobs
	Training to acquire new skills
Groups	Team building
	Participative group decision making
	Protecting people from sexual harassment
	Counseling programs
	Minority advancement and achievement programs
Organizations	Organizational commitment and loyalty
	Work dedication
	Equitable compensation programs
	Whistle-blowing to maintain organizational integrity
	Protecting and conserving organizational resources
Society	Contributions to social welfare and community needs in health, education, the arts, and culture
	Lobbying for public interest legislation
	Affirmative action programs for minorities
	Training and employment for individuals with disabilities and the hard-core unemployed
	Environmental pollution control
	Ensuring product safety and customer satisfaction

Source: Adapted from Kanungo, R. N., & Conger, J. A. (1990). The quest for altruism in organizations. In S. Srivastra & D. L. Cooperrider (Eds.), *Appreciative management and leadership* (pp. 248–249). San Francisco, CA: Jossey-Bass. Reprinted with permission of the author.

Followers prefer selfless leaders to selfish ones.[36] Self-involved leaders destroy loyalty and trust and are more likely to lead their communities into disaster. By contrast, leaders who sacrifice on behalf of the group demonstrate their genuine commitment to its mission. They set a powerful example that motivates others to do the same. Higher performance often results.

However, altruism is difficult to put into practice. Some of the bitterest wars are fought in the name of religion by believers who ignore their faith's altruistic values. People also disagree about what loving behavior looks like. Cultural and personal differences mean varying behaviors called "loving."

Ethical Pluralism

Although the five ethical perspectives presented previously appear to be separate philosophies, it would be a mistake to think that individuals must select one theory and ignore the others. Overlap exists among them, and no one perspective is perfect for all ethical decisions. Each approach has its strengths and weaknesses. Recognizing this, the ethical pluralism outlook selects "what works best" from each. Ethical pluralism gives leaders a fuller array of alternatives about how to best address the problem. Table 11–2 compares these six ethical perspectives and highlights their advantages and disadvantages.

TABLE 11–2

Comparing Different Ethical Perspectives

Utilitarianism
Pros: Easy to apply to a variety of situations; weighs possible costs and benefits and seeks to do the greatest good for the most people
Cons: Outcomes are unpredictable; users frequently reach dissimilar conclusions; difficult to ascertain which decision will do the greatest good for the greatest number of people
Categorical Imperative
Pros: People are less likely to compromise their personal ethics, despite pressure and opposition; inspires people to strive towards an ideal
Cons: Does not account for exceptions; difficult to enact during a crisis
Justice as Fairness
Pros: Guarantees same basic rights and opportunities for everyone in a democratic society; advocates fair treatment for followers
Cons: Requires a democratic society; assumes agreement on common values and principles
Communitarianism
Pros: Focuses on responsibility to the larger community and the common good; disallows selfish, unethical behavior; leads to development of virtues
Cons: Considered to have an evangelical approach; rejects possibility of pluralism in developing moral guidelines
Altruism
Pros: Motivational; encourages putting others ahead of self; results in high performance
Cons: Difficult to put into practice; people disagree about what constitutes loving behavior
Ethical Pluralism
Pros: Well-established ethical systems can help set ethical priorities; applying more than one perspective to an ethical dilemma can offer varied solutions to the same problem
Cons: Two well-meaning leaders can use the same ethical theory and reach different conclusions

Source: Based on: Johnson, C. E. (2009). *Meeting the ethical challenges of leadership* (pp. 137–161). Los Angeles, CA: Sage.

ACTIVITY 11.2   Applying Varying Ethical Perspectives in Schools

Case Study Question 2: What are Dr. Smith's choices and the consequences of those choices?

Case Study Question 3: How would Dr. Smith's decisions differ using any of the six ethical perspectives discussed? Discuss in pairs and then as a class:

1. Utilitarianism as an ethical system posits that ethical choices should be based on their consequences, weighing the outcomes of each decision to maximize benefits to as many people as possible. What are some of the possible choices of action that Dr. Smith might make regarding the funding and educational inequities in his school district, and what might be some of the outcomes?

2. The categorical imperative says to do right no matter the cost. Treat people fairly, give them necessary information, and let them make choices. No exceptions. If Dr. Smith abides by this ethical system, what decisions might he make and what might be their consequences?

3. The "justice as fairness" ethical system guarantees individuals equal liberty and equal opportunity; the social and economic inequities are only justified if they create equal opportunity and provide the greatest benefit to the least advantaged. If Dr. Smith abides by this ethical system, what decisions might he make and what might be their consequences?

4. The communitarian ethical system advises leaders to shoulder their responsibilities and seek the common good over individual advancement. Leaders should consider the broader community needs and help the community share a vision for the common good and share values of justice, equality, freedom, individual dignity, and a release of human talent and energy. If Dr. Smith were to use this ethical system, what decisions might he make and what might be their consequences?

5. The altruistic ethical system advises to love your neighbor and show concern for others over self-interest and personal cost. Leaders should understand and articulate their constituents' concerns and needs. If Dr. Smith were to apply this ethical system, what decisions might he make and what might be their consequences?

6. The ethical pluralism approach advises users to select what ethical system works best in the present situation. If Dr. Smith were to rely on the ethical pluralism perspective, what approaches from the other five ethical systems might he use, what decisions would he make, and what might be their consequences?

MULTIPLE ETHICAL PARADIGMS

Although each of these six general ethical perspectives helps develop a lens by which to understand ethical behavior, a more integrated model can better aid school leaders with their daily ethical dilemmas. *Multiple ethical paradigms* is a theoretical model of problem solving that takes into account the ethics of justice, critique, care, and profession. Education professor Robert Starratt (1994) brought together the three paradigms of justice, critique, and care in an approach to ethics and schools.[37] Education professors Joan Shapiro and Jacqueline Stefkovich (2001, 2005) added the ethic of profession.[38] Working together, each ethic complements the others in making policy and practice choices. Although no one perfect ethical choice exists, the four perspectives enable educators to make decisions

FIGURE 11–1
Multiple Ethical Paradigms Model (Source: Shapiro, J. P., & Gross, S. J. (2008). *Ethical educational leadership in turbulent times. (Re)Solving moral dilemmas* (p. 7). Mahwah, NJ: Lawrence Erlbaum. Reproduced by permission of Taylor and Francis Group, LLC, a division of Informa plc.)

with the consequences more clearly defined, to move toward the "best" choice under the circumstances, or to select an option that will likely be later balanced by other choices. Figure 11–1 illustrates this model.

The Ethic of Justice

In the past, philosophers such as Aristotle, Jean Jacques Rousseau, Friedrich Hegel, Karl Marx, and John Dewey tended to see society—rather than the individual—as central to decision making. Individuals were taught how to behave throughout their lives within these same communities. Inside this tradition, justice emerged from "communal understandings."Education professor Nel Noddings (1999) added to this concept when she wrote that "in modern times, it [justice] has pointed more directly at a preferred relationship between institutions and human beings."[39]

The ethic of justice focuses on rights, laws, and policies. Part of a liberal democratic tradition, this paradigm focuses on the concepts of fairness, equality, individual freedom, and incrementalism[40] as well as faith in the legal system, and hope for progress.[41] Justice implies evenhandedness and impartiality and making decisions that respect people's equal rights.

From one ethic of justice viewpoint, passions and interests drive individuals, especially fear of harm and desire for comfort. Individuals enter into social relations to advance their own interests. Therefore, social relations are essentially artificial and governed by self-advantage. Social governance assumes a social contract in which individuals agree to give up some of their freedom in exchange for the state's protection from otherwise uncontrolled self-seeking by others. Human reason becomes the instrument that individuals use to analyze in a more or less scientific way what is to their advantage, and to calculate the obligations to social justice required by the social contract. Reason, therefore, is the instrument of morality.

A competing ethic of justice views ethics as grounded in both the individual and the community. The protection of human dignity depends on the moral quality of social relationships; this is a public and political concern. Citizenship is a shared initiative and a responsibility among persons committed to mutual care.[42] Justice and governance depend both on past tradition and on the community's present efforts to manage its affairs among competing claims between the common good and individual rights. Understanding these rival interests will never be complete, limited by inadequate traditional responses to changing circumstances and the impossibility of settling conflicting claims conclusively and totally. The choices, however, will always be made with sensitivity to the bonds that connect individuals to their communities.[43]

For schools and school governance, an ethic of justice means respecting the individual student's rights in addition to serving the common good. These issues appear in discussions, for instance, about student discipline policies, faculty and student due-process procedures, multicultural education, standardized testing and grading practices, or agreements about faculty time commitments. Each of these topics raises moral questions about individual justice in public life.

Educational leadership professor Thomas Sergiovanni (1992) has called for moral leadership and requests the principle of justice in designing "virtuous schools."[44] Sergiovanni sees school leadership as a stewardship and asks educational leaders to create institutions that are just and show deep concern for the welfare of the school as a community. Justice is at the heart of this concept in which every school member—faculty, administrators, staff, students, and families—is treated with the same equality, dignity, and fair play.

From a contemporary perspective, the ethic of justice views ethical dilemmas as opportunities for interpreting the rule of law; applying the abstract concepts of fairness, liberty, and responsibility; and weighing equality versus equity, moral absolutism versus situational ethics, and the individual's rights versus the community's greater good.[45] These are not always easy to do, however. In the United States, laws are often defined by states. What is legal in some places may be considered illegal in others. For example, corporal punishment is lawful in certain states but is unlawful elsewhere.[46] Likewise, courts often try to balance ethical issues such as due process and privacy rights against the need for civility and goodwill for the majority. Other countries and cultures also define their laws according to their unique customs and worldviews.

One of the ethic of justice's limitations is the theory's inability to determine claims in conflict.[47] What is fair for one person might not be considered fair by another. Many discussions of what is evenhanded in any given situation can tend to become trapped in rationality and objectivity, considering the minimal conditions that must be met to fulfill the claims of justice.[48] This view narrowly confines justice to its letter, rather than to its spirit.

In this context, the ethic of justice orientation leads to questions, including: Is there a law, right, or policy that would be appropriate for resolving a particular ethical dilemma? Why is this law, right, or policy the correct one for this particular case? How should the law, right, or policy be implemented? Why or why not? And if there is not a law, right, or policy, should there be one?[49] Whose views should it contain?

The Ethic of Critique

The ethic of critique considers the perspective of writers and activists, largely critical theorists who are skeptical of the justice ethic's analytic and rational approach. They consider social relationships, social customs, social institutions, and laws as grounded in structured power relationships, or in language itself. They ask: Who benefits from these arrangements? Who defines the way things are organized here? Who defines what is valued or devalued?

In answering questions of power relationships, critical theorists and others find a tension between the ethic of justice, rights, and laws and concepts such as democracy and social justice.[50] They find that no social arrangement is neutral. Uncovering which group has the advantage over the others, how things got to be the way they are, and how situations and language are structured to maintain the legitimacy of social arrangements, critical analysts expose inherent injustice or dehumanization and invite others to redress such injustice. For example, the Jim Crow laws and separate-but-equal laws supported legal racial segregation in U.S. restaurants, public transportation, theaters, and schools for a hundred years until it was ended in 1954 by *Brown vs. Board of Education*. The ethical challenge is to make these social arrangements more responsive to all citizens' human and social rights, to give those affected by social arrangements a voice in evaluating their results, and to work in the interests of the common good and of fuller participation and fairness for now-voiceless individuals.

Basing its perspective on critical theory, the ethic of critique places analysis of social class and its inequities at its center. Critical theorists argue that schools reproduce inequities similar to those in society.[51] Education favors the dominant culture's "cultural capital"—its language, values, and meanings. Schooling confirms, legitimizes, and reproduces the status quo through a process of gaining the students' passive, legitimate consent. In short, through schooling's socialization, all social and economic classes learn to accept the dominant social group's beliefs, values, and practices as right and natural. Curriculum tracking, for example, may be viewed as a way to ensure that working-class children are denied access to the resources available to more affluent children.[52] Differential access to knowledge and opportunities to learn, differential opportunities to think and use language, and differential admittance to high-quality curriculum are all part of this educational process, say critical theorists, deliberately designed to keep "less desirables" out of the cultural mainstream.

The ethic of critique challenges the school leader with the fundamental dilemma of how to construct an ethical environment in which education can occur. The ethic of critique reveals that the school as an organization in its present form is a source of unethical consequences in the educational process. The teacher evaluation practices, the homogeneous tracking systems, the labeling of children for special services (gifted or disabled), the daily interruptions of instruction by uniform time allotments for class periods, and the Eurocentric curriculum that does not respect the contributions and cultures of races other than Caucasian all contain unjustifiable assumptions and impose a disproportionate advantage to some at the expense of others. The ethic of critique calls the educational leader to a social responsibility, not simply to individuals in the school or school system or to the education profession, but to the society of whom and for whom he or she is an agent serving a high moral purpose.

Instead of accepting the values and decisions of those in authority, these critical scholars ask school leaders to challenge the status quo by using an ethic that deals with the inconsistencies, articulates the hard questions, and debates and confronts the issues. Those who practice the ethic of critique ask school leaders to rethink key concepts such as democracy and to redefine or reframe the concepts of privilege, power, culture, language, and social justice. While deconstructing the accepted concepts, they also provide educators with a language of empowerment, transformation, and possibilities.

More positively, the ethic of critique asks educators to study and wrestle with the possibilities that could enable all children—regardless of social class, race, ethnicity, gender, or ability—to have opportunities to grow, learn, and achieve. Schools contain the seeds of societal transformation. Michael Apple,[53] Henry Giroux,[54] and Peter McLaren,[55] for example, see schools' positive power for social justice. Sounding the call for pedagogical empowerment, they see the teacher's role as helping students make sense of and engage the world around them and, when necessary, change the world for the better. Schools can become the agents that raise children to question and challenge their society's limitations and failings. When students learn how to push against the status quo, they can improve their community and nation. In this way, critical theory raises educators' consciousness beyond the classroom and school yard to broader social and cultural concerns.

A shortcoming of the ethic of critique as an educational moral code, however, is that it rarely offers a blueprint for reconstructing the social order it is censuring. It highlights unethical practices in governing and managing organizations and implies ethical values such as equality, the common good, human and civil rights, and democratic participation, but it does not lay out a plan for improving school practices.

In sum, the ethic of critique inherent in critical theory intends to awaken citizens to society's inequities and injustices. It asks educators to address complex questions of power and access regarding class, race, gender, and other areas of difference. Relevant questions include: Who makes the laws, rules, or policies? Who benefits from these laws, rules, or policies? Who holds the power? Whose voices are silent? And what could make a difference to enable those who have been silenced, ignored, and oppressed to become empowered and help create a more just society?[56]

The Ethic of Care

As it does with the ethic of critique, the contemporary Western perspective often links the ethic of care with the ethic of justice. While justice aims at society and cooperative personal relationships in which people are treated fairly, with respect as equals, and receive what they are due, the ethic of care aims at a society and personal relationships in which nurturance and relationships receive high value. The ethic of care considers the interpersonal processes as well as the outcomes.

Rather than viewing a person from a contractual or legalistic perspective, the ethic of care sees relationships from a standpoint of absolute regard. Humans are persons in a relationship, each person occupying a position of unconditional value. Neither individual can be used as a means to an end. Each enjoys an intrinsic dignity and worth; given the opportunity, each will reveal genuinely loveable qualities. Individuals have a right to be who they are, and they should meet others in openness to engage them in their authentic individuality. Rather than demand intimacy, the caring relationship honors each person's dignity and the desire to enjoy a fully human life. The school as an organization should respect the well-being of persons within it, reaching beyond efficiency which uses humans as a means to some larger purpose of productivity (such as increasing in the district's average standardized test scores or lowering per-pupil costs).

Challenging the dominant ethic of justice, the ethic of care becomes more central to moral decision making and to society in general. Concepts such as loyalty, trust, and empowerment receive special attention. Similar to critical theorists, ethic of care scholars see social justice as a pivotal idea, with caring essential to education. They refer to the three Cs of caring, concern, and connection. They wish to broaden the curriculum to include both genders' experiences and the ethic of care. Similarly, they believe that education should integrate reason and emotion, self and other.[57]

To a large extent, the ethic of care finds active support from feminist scholars who point to a patriarchal cultural dynamic that favors production over reproduction.[58] Nevertheless, the ethic of care has both male and female advocates. Male ethicists including Martin Buber (1965)[59] and Thomas Sergiovanni (1992)[60] have helped to develop this paradigm, seeking to make education a fully human enterprise. Caring, as an ethical foundation, addresses concerns and needs that transcend ideological boundaries. In fact, the philosophy of utilitarianism implicitly supports the ethics of care when it espouses the greatest happiness for the greatest number, moving care into the civic arena.[61]

School leadership based on an ethic of care attends to the uniquely human issues of self-esteem, personal confidence, and respect while interacting with others. In fact, school leaders develop sensitivity to the dignity and uniqueness of each person in school and continuously monitor the school's cultural tone. Principals pay heightened notice to preventing miscommunications by not allowing negative stereotypes or defensive actions to interrupt their conversations. Instead, they ensure that teachers experience their relationship with them as one of high regard, mutual respect, and honest contact between two persons who care for each other and about their common purposes.

To develop relationships of care, school leaders initially explore with their teachers the conditions necessary to begin and maintain trust, honesty, and open communications.[62] Similarly, school leaders who practice the ethic of care will use language to facilitate the caring school culture. For instance, formal abstract language speaks from the bureaucracy and distance. In contrast, familiar imagery, metaphor, and personalized messages express the language of caring. Through visible procedures and ceremonies, school emblems, school mottoes, school songs, and other symbols, the school communicates caring, cooperation, service, and teamwork. Hearing laughter in the halls, frequently greeting each other by name, giving hand-written notes of congratulations for completing successful projects, regularly displaying student work, and publicly spotlighting pictures of student groups engaged in school activities reflect a school environment that appreciates people for who they are. Students engaged daily in such a school community learn the lessons of caring, respect, and service to each other. They learn how to fail and persist until they succeed, how to forgive and fix a bruised relationship, how to accept criticism, and how to debate different viewpoints.

If school leaders are to find the ethic of care useful when making moral decisions, they need more preparation in decision making apart from the traditional military and business models of top-down hierarchy in which principals follow the rules, policies, operating procedures, and information systems.[63] These approaches worked well when the ethic of justice, rights, and laws was the primary basis for moral decision making. Today, when leaders are working in diverse communities with multiple voices and relationships to consider in decision making, the top-down, follow-the-rules practices are inadequate.

In sum, the ethic of care offers another viewpoint and way to respond to complex moral dilemmas educational leaders face in their daily work. Focusing on concepts such as loyalty, trust, and empowerment, this ethic asks that individuals consider the consequences of their decisions and actions. It expects school leaders to ask: Who will benefit from what

I decide? Who will my actions hurt? What are the long-term effects of decisions I make today? If I am helped by someone now, what are my future obligations about giving back to this individual or the society in general?[64]

The Ethic of Profession

Hippocrates, author of what is arguably the first code of ethics, the Hippocratic oath, wrote, "First, do no harm." This is a concept that serves members of all professions well.

Professionals unite their members by common training, shared values, mutual aspirations, and collective purposes. Professional expertise confers a degree of authority and power on its holders. But professional autonomy is never without societal limits. Since every profession affects the well-being of others who depend on their skills and services, professional behaviors have both technical and moral dimensions. Society holds practitioners accountable for both aspects through a professional code of ethics.

Many professions have ethical requirements, and ethics can play a guiding role for educators' professional legitimacy. Many writers have advocated for future school leaders to have some preparation in ethics and ethical decision making.[65] There have been similar calls in the area of teacher leadership.[66] Some states have established their own ethics codes or standards.[67] Likewise, several professional education organizations have developed their own ethical codes.

Professional Codes of Ethics. *Professional codes of ethics* can be described as the rules that guide professional decisions and actions. These codes serve as both a foundation and a guide to professional behavior in morally ambiguous situations.

Society grants a profession power and privilege only if its members are willing and able to contribute to the general well-being and to conduct their affairs in a manner consistent with broad social values. The profession serves as a norm reference group for its practitioners. Its code of ethics visibly clarifies for practitioners and the general public alike the rules and norms that guide members' actions. Medicine, law, accounting, pharmacy, education, and other professions all have their own code of ethics to improve professional practice and maintain the public's confidence.

A profession's technical skills determine what its members are capable of doing while its moral dimension determines when, how well, and under what conditions members should do it. A profession's moral dimension shapes and sustains the relationship between the individual practitioner, the profession as a norm group, and those receiving the services. While the individual is responsible for his or her own behavior, the professional group accepts responsibility to direct and control that behavior. The client's trust is in both the individual practitioner and the professional group as a whole. Since the professional entity is more stable, enduring, and visible than any one practitioner, the professional group has a collective moral responsibility to ensure that its members uphold the highest standards of practice.[68]

Ethical guidelines from the National Association of Elementary School Principals (NAESP), the National Association of Secondary School Principals (NASSP), the American Association of School Administrators (AASA), and the Association of School Business Officials (ASBO) all begin with the admonition that the school leader shall, ". . . make the well being of students the fundamental value in all decision making and actions." The teaching profession's "commitment to the student" is one of two pillars of the National Education Association's (NEA) ethical framework. These can be seen as "an articulated statement of role morality as seen by members of the profession."[69]

Additionally, the American Educational Research Association (AERA) and the University Council of Educational Administration (UCEA) have recently identified social justice with its unwavering ethical focus as a new anchor for the whole education profession with "equity for all" as a new mantra.[70] The goal of ethics is to make decisions that are in the best interest of both the organization and the individuals within it.

These professional codes of ethics, however, may be somewhat removed from day-to-day personal and professional challenges that educational leaders face.[71] Plus a lack of connection may exist between educational leadership students' own personal codes and those codes advanced by their professional groups and states.[72]

ISLLC Standards.   Recognizing professional education's need for ethical training, the Interstate School Leaders Licensure Consortium (ISLLC) identifies ethics as one of the competencies necessary for school leaders. Working under the Council of Chief State School Officers sponsorship and in collaboration with the National Policy Board for Educational Administration (NPBEA), ISLLC's 1996 (revised in 2008) Standards for School Leaders presents six standards for the profession. Standard 5 reads, "An education leader promotes the success of every student by acting with integrity, fairness, and in an ethical manner."[73] This stance places the student in the center of the decision-making process with the school leader responsible to:

◆ Ensure a system of accountability for every student's academic and social success.
◆ Model principles of self-awareness, reflective practice, transparency, and ethical behavior.
◆ Safeguard the values of democracy, equity, and diversity.
◆ Consider and evaluate the potential moral and legal consequences of decision making.
◆ Promote social justice and ensure that individual student needs inform all aspects of schooling.

The ISLLC position accounts for professional standards, community ethics, the educational leaders' personal and professional codes, and the professional codes of varied educational organizations.

The ethic of profession requires that school leaders consider their own personal ethics along with the ethics of justice, critique, care, profession, and standards set by the profession. This asks them to place students at the center of the ethical decision-making process. It also expects school leaders to take the community standards into account. Additionally, it means that school leaders are responsible for establishing an ethical school environment in which education can occur.

The ethic of profession reminds principals that individual choices occur within a wider ethical context. It means having the school leader ask: What is in the students' best interests? What factors should I consider as I weigh the best interests of students whose backgrounds and needs may be diverse? What would the profession ask me to do? What is the appropriate way for a professional to act in this particular situation? What do various communities expect me to accomplish? Does a clash exist among the various codes that inform my decision making?[74]

Integrating the Multiple Paradigms

Enacting ethical beliefs and moral practices in one's life and profession is much more complex than choosing "right" or "wrong." Right and wrong are not absolutes; their meaning depends on their context. One might ask: Good or bad by whose standards? Right or wrong according to whom? Acting in ways approved by whom? Since we live in increasingly diverse communities within a globalized world, searching for a meaningful and workable theory of ethical leadership requires finding a perspective that can satisfactorily answer these questions. Ideally, educational leaders or students in training develop their professional and personal codes of ethics by considering various ethical models and integrating the ethics of justice, care, critique, and profession. These multiple ethics provide the basis for making ethical professional judgments.

Developing one's own professional code of ethics is an intricate and occasionally hazardous process. Shapiro and Stefkovich identified four possible conflicts that make this difficult.[75] First, discord may occur between an individual's personal and professional codes of ethics. For instance, a principal who strongly believes that sexual intercourse should occur only after marriage may not be able to work objectively with a minor student who is also an unmarried parent. Second, clashes may occur within the professional code itself, such as when an individual has been prepared in two or more professions which hold conflicting precepts. For example, what a school counselor deems confidential in speaking with a student may be something that a principal feels obligated to tell the parents. Third, conflict may occur between the codes of various educational leaders. Administrators in the same school may disagree about what is ethical behavior. Fourth, a leader's personal and professional code of ethics may be in conflict with those set by the community in which the leader works. Community standards vary, and what one community views as unethical (such as a teacher drinking beer at a sports bar on Saturday night) may be considered "personal preference" (and ethical) in another. These varying understandings of what is "ethical" present a good argument for including community members in the school's decision-making process.

To address the possible clashes in enacting ethical behavior, and professional ethics overall, it is important to anchor decision making in something meaningful—such as the public school's mission to prepare children to assume roles and responsibilities of citizens in a democratic society.[76] If education has a moral imperative, it is to act in the best interests of the students. This is education's counterpart of the medical assertion, "First, do no harm." At a time of increasing population diversity, when student differences encompass the cultural categories of race, ethnicity, religion, social class, gender, disability, exceptionality, and sexual orientation, this is especially vital. Similarly, this emphasis on the students' best interests fits the ethic of care, the ethic of critique, and the ethic of profession, which place students at the top of the educational hierarchy.[77]

Unfortunately, people of goodwill and the professional literature may disagree about what actually is "the best interests of students." Recent efforts have attempted to resolve this predicament.[78] Stefkovich (2006) conceptualized decisions concerning a student's best interests as those including individual rights, accepting and teaching students to accept responsibility for their actions, and respecting students.[79] This proposition notwithstanding, the concept of the students' best interests remains ambiguous.

Tying the Ethics Together.   The four ethics—justice, critique, care, and profession—are all grounded on the essential natures of human beings and human societies. Each perspective is necessary to fully develop a moral person and an ethical society. The ethic of justice assumes a rational ability to perceive injustice and a minimal level of caring about relationships in the social order. The ethic of critique assumes a viewpoint about social justice, human rights, and how communities should govern themselves. The ethic of care considers the importance of individual dignity and respect within the demands of community governance and claims that caring is the ideal fulfillment of all social relationships. The ethic of profession brings a set of standards about how practitioners should appropriately enact their knowledge and skills.

Importantly, each ethic needs the strong convictions embedded in the others. The ethic of justice needs the profound commitment to the dignity of the individual person found in the ethic of care and the insightful social analysis of the ethic of critique in order to move beyond the naïve view that the present social and educational system is fair to all. The ethic of critique requires an ethic of caring if it is to avoid the cynical and discouraging worldview. The ethic of care attends to the individual within the larger social order and fairness that the ethic of justice brings. The ethic of professionalism brings a perspective that focuses each of the others on the school's purposes and its community members' roles in its success. Each

---

ACTIVITY 11.3 Applying the Multiple Ethical Paradigm in Schools

Case Study Question 4: How could the multiple ethical paradigms help Dr. Smith decide how to best work toward creating a more equitable, just, and high-achieving school district that promotes the success of every student?

Education's moral imperative is to act in the students' best interests: in short, to do no harm. The multiple ethical paradigms—including the ethics of justice, critique, care, and profession—recognizes that no one perfect ethical choice exists. The four perspectives work together to help educators more clearly define the best choice under the circumstances.

1. How does the ethic of justice's emphasis on respecting students' individual rights while serving the common good and its assertion that the school is a community and every member should be treated with equality, dignity, and fair play influence Dr. Smith's decisions and possible outcomes? How might the ethic of justice affect school district policy and practices?

2. How does the ethic of critique's emphasis on power relationships and view of school as reproducing social inequities influence how Dr. Smith perceives the fiscal and educational inequity situation? Who benefits and who loses from the present arrangements? Whose voices are not presently heard in the school district's decision-making arena? How can Dr. Smith use the ethic of critique to construct an ethical educational environment? In what ways might Dr. Smith be able to *effectively* challenge the status quo, address the inconsistencies, and remedy the issues of unequal privilege?

3. How does the ethic of care's emphasis on developing strong and cooperative relationships influence Dr. Smith's strategies for remedying his school district's fiscal and educational inequities? In what ways can Dr. Smith model the values of loyalty, trust, honesty, empowerment, and individual dignity and worth to move the school district culture toward the success of all students?

4. How does the ethic of professionalism influence Dr. Smith's decisions about improving his district's funding and educational disparities? What decisions would be in the best interests of all students?

ethic complements the others to provide a more complete ethical environment and provide more lenses by which school leaders can make informed ethical decisions.

Ethics and Normative Leadership Theories

Over many centuries, the concept and practice of leadership have evolved. Until the 1940s, researchers believed that leaders were born, not made. Only those who inherited the essential mental and physical traits—intelligent, extroverted, tall, attractive, and almost universally male—could be leaders. This paradigm largely has been discredited.

The next leadership model was more complex. It proposed that effective leaders had to address three critical factors: the situation and the nature of the task; the followers' skills, motivations, and emotional needs; and the quality of the leader-follower relationship. These situational or contingency theories are still popular, but they contain two major limitations. They are hard to apply because they consider so many factors, and they give too much weight to contextual variables. Although situational elements are important, certain strategies can be effective across a range of settings.

More recently, normative leadership theories tell leaders how they should act.[80] Built on moral principles, they specify leader behaviors with a specific orientation toward ethical decision making and performance. Transformational leadership, servant leadership, and authentic leadership are examples of such normative leadership models.

Transformational Leadership.   The transformational approach addresses the weaknesses of both the trait and situational perspectives by isolating sets of learned behaviors that can produce positive results in many different contexts. In his 1978 book *Leadership*[81] James MacGregor Burns, a former presidential advisor and historian, introduced the concept of transformational leadership. He contrasted traditional forms of leadership, which he called "transactional," with a more powerful form of leadership, called "transforming." Transactional leaders appeal to followers' basic needs for food, shelter, and acceptance. They exchange money, benefits, recognition, and other rewards in return for followers' obedience and labor. The emphasis on compliance, however, diminishes their followers' self-worth and is highly offensive to their dignity as people.

In contrast, transformational leaders speak to followers' higher level needs for esteem, competence, self-fulfillment, and self-actualization. The leader's goal is to change the followers' core attitudes and values through empowerment strategies. This empowering experience increases the followers' self-efficacy beliefs, dignity, and capacity for self-direction as autonomous persons. Expert and referent power are sources of the transforming leader's influence, making the leader appear credible and trustworthy to followers. In this way, transforming leaders change the very nature of the groups, organizations, and cultures as a whole. Table 11–3 compares transactional and transformational leadership and their ethical implications.

TABLE 11–3

Comparing Transactional and Transformational Leadership and Their Ethical Implications

Leadership Influence Process	Transactional Leadership	Transformational Leadership
Strategies	Control	Empowerment
Leader objective in terms of behavioral outcomes	Emphasis on compliance behavior	Changing followers' core attitudes, beliefs, and values
Underlying psychological mechanism	Social exchange of valued resources	Increasing belief in self-efficacy and self-direction
Power base	Coercive, legal, reward	Expert, referent
Attitude change process and effects	Compliance, which under excessive control often leads to diminishing followers' self-worth and dignity and to their functioning as "programmed robots"	Identification and internalization leading to followers' self-growth and to their functioning as autonomous persons
Moral implication	Unethical	Ethical

Source: Kanungo, Rabindra N. (1996). *Ethical dimensions of leadership*. Thousand Oaks, CA: SAGE Publications. Copyright 1996 by SAGE Publications Inc. Books. Reproduced with permission of SAGE Publications Inc. Books in the format Textbook via Copyright Clearance Center.

Moral commitment lies at the core of Burns's transforming leadership. Burns observed that transforming leadership occurs when one or more persons engage with others in ways that raise leaders and followers to higher levels of motivation and morality. Transformational leaders focus on essential values including liberty, equality, and justice. These values mobilize and energize followers, create an action agenda, and stress instrumental values such as responsibility, fairness, and honesty, which make interactions occur smoothly.[82]

In a series of studies, leadership scholars Bernard Bass, Bruce Avolio, and their colleagues identified the factors that characterize transactional and transformational leaders.[83] They observed that transactional leadership has both active and passive elements, providing rewards and recognition depending on followers' carrying out their roles and reaching their objectives. After specifying the standards and elements of acceptable performance, transactional leaders discipline followers when they fall short. Also, transactional leaders wait for problems to arise before taking action, or they avoid taking any action at all. These leaders typically fail to provide goals and standards or to clarify expectations.

In contrast, Bass and Avolio defined transformational leadership as characterized by:

◆ *Idealized influence*. Transformational leaders become role models for followers who admire, respect, and trust them. They put their followers' needs above their own, and their behavior is consistent with the group's values and principles.

◆ *Inspirational motivation*. Transformational leaders motivate by providing meaning and challenge to the followers' tasks. They provoke team spirit, are enthusiastic and optimistic, and help followers develop desirable visions for the future.

◆ *Intellectual stimulation.* Transformational leaders stimulate innovation and creativity by encouraging followers to question assumptions, reframe situations, and approach familiar problems from new perspectives. Transforming leaders don't criticize mistakes but instead solicit solutions from followers and use setbacks as learning opportunities.

◆ *Individualized consideration.* Transformational leaders act as coaches or mentors who advance personal development. They provide learning opportunities and a supportive climate for growth. They tailor their coaching and mentoring to the followers' individual needs and wants.

While Burns believes that leaders display either transactional or transformational characteristics, Bass disagrees. In his view, transforming leadership uses both transactional and transformational elements. Abraham Lincoln, Franklin D. Roosevelt, Martin Luther King, and Ronald Reagan, for instance, were able to both "play politics" and also change their societies. In fact, empirical evidence suggests that those exhibiting transforming leadership behaviors demonstrate higher levels of moral reasoning.[84]

Transformational leadership's popularity, however, probably has more to do with its practical effectiveness than with ethical concerns.[85] Evidence from over 100 empirical studies establishes that transforming leaders are more successful than their transactional peers.[86] Their followers are more committed, form stronger bonds with colleagues, work harder, and persist in the face of obstacles. As a consequence, transforming leaders' organizations often achieve higher quality, greater profits, improved service, military victories, and better win-loss records. Many leadership scholars and authors agree.[87]

Nevertheless, transforming leaders do not always produce moral or ethical outcomes. Originally, Burns believed that the transforming leader is a moral leader because the ultimate outcome of such leadership is higher ethical standards and performance. His definition, however, did not consider that some leaders can use transformational strategies to reach immoral ends. A leader can serve as a role model, provide intellectual and motivational stimulation, and be passionate about a cause, but the leader and his or her followers may use immoral and unethical practices to reach immoral ends, and consequences can be evil. Hitler was a charismatic figure with a clear vision for Germany but whose influence led to unprecedented levels of death and destruction.[88]

Recognizing this difference between ethical and unethical transforming leaders, Bass adopted the terms *authentic* and *pseudotransformational* to separate the two categories.[89] Authentic transformational leaders are motivated by altruism and distinguished by integrity. They don't impose ethical norms but allow followers free choice, hoping that constituents will voluntarily commit themselves to moral principles. Followers are viewed as valued ends in themselves, not as a means to some other outcome. In contrast, pseudotransformational leaders are self-centered and manipulate followers in order to achieve their personal goals. Envy, greed, anger, and deception denote the groups they lead. Mahatma Gandhi, Martin Luther King Jr., and Nelson Mandela can be classified as authentic transforming leaders because they promoted universal brotherhood and peaceful approaches to societal change. In contrast, the Soviet Union's Joseph Stalin and China's Mao Zedong were pseudotransformational leaders because they encouraged followers to violently reject those who held different beliefs—religious, political, or economic. Proponents of transformational leadership, however, would like to believe that transforming leaders are probably less susceptible to ethical abuses because they (ideally) put others' needs first, treat followers respectfully, and seek worthy objectives.

Servant Leadership. Servant leadership has its roots in both Western and Eastern tradition. Jesus told his disciples that "whoever would be first among you must be slave of all."[90] Chinese philosophers encouraged leaders to be humble valleys. Taoist philosopher Lao Tzu advised that a wise leader puts his own person last.[91] In the 1970s, Robert Greenleaf, researcher and organizational consultant, coined the term *servant leadership* to describe a leadership model that puts the followers' concerns first.[92] Later he established a center to promote servant leadership. Several businesses (for example, the Container Store and Aflac supplemental insurance), nonprofit organizations, and community leadership programs have adopted this model.[93]

Basically, servant leadership believes that leaders should put their followers' or constituents' needs before their own. What happens in their followers' and constituents' lives should be the standard by which leaders are judged. According to Greenleaf, when evaluating a leader, we ought to ask, "Do those served grow as persons? Do they, while being served, become healthier, wiser, freer, more autonomous, more likely themselves to become servants?"[94] By continually reflecting on what would be best for their constituents, advocates avow, servant leaders are less likely to take advantage of their followers' trust, act inconsistently, or accumulate money and power.

Four related concepts central to servant leadership are stewardship, obligation, partnership, and elevating purpose.[95]

◆ *Stewardship*. Servant leaders act on behalf of others,[96] entrusted with special duties and opportunities for a limited time. While accountable for results, servant leaders are responsible for leading through collaboration and persuasion, protecting and nurturing their groups and organizations while ensuring that these collectives serve the common good.
◆ *Obligation*. Servant leaders take their responsibilities for their organization's present and future success seriously.[97]
◆ *Partnership*. Servant leaders view followers as partners, not subordinates. Leaders seek an equitable and just distribution of power and rewards—including sharing information, delegating authority, and encouraging employees to develop and exercise their talents.
◆ *Elevating purpose*. Servant leaders serve worthy missions, ideas, and causes. They seek to fulfill a high moral purpose and understand the role they play in the process of making work more meaningful to leaders and followers alike.

Servant leaders show four key strengths: altruism, simplicity, self-awareness, and moral sensitivity. Altruistic, they show concern for others before regard for self. Valuing simplicity, servant leaders approach their responsibilities focused on one goal: the desire to serve. They share rather than hoard power, privilege, and information. Feeling a sense of stewardship and obligation, they promote followers' and constituents' growth, and look out for the larger community's interests, lessening occasions for ethical abuses which come from placing personal interests above the group's or organization's interests. Self-aware, servant leaders listen to themselves as well as to others, take time for reflection, and recognize the value of spiritual resources. Showing moral sensitivity, servant leaders are acutely aware of the importance of seeking ethical purposes that bring meaning and fulfillment to their work. Serving a transcendent goal gives every leadership act a moral aspect.

Despite its strengths, the servant leadership model lacks universal approval. Many critics are cynical, thinking this leadership model is too good to be true: idyllic in the abstract, but not likely to work in the real world. In part, doubt about servant leadership may reflect misunderstanding service as weakness. Servant leaders cannot be weak; occasionally, the best way to serve followers and the organization is to reprimand or dismiss an inept employee. Another criticism is that servant leadership is difficult to enact in certain contexts, such as prisons, military boot camps, or in crises. In addition, servant leaders need to use careful reasoning and wise judgment to ensure that they are advancing worthy and useful goals. Finally, the word *servant* has highly negative connotations to certain groups, bringing reminders of slavery, oppression, and discrimination.[98]

Authentic Leadership. "Know thyself" is a philosophy prized since the ancient Greeks and Romans.[99] In *Hamlet*, William Shakespeare's character Polonius advises his son, "To thine own self be true" because then one cannot be false to another. Advocates of authentic leadership theory identify authenticity as the root principle undergirding all forms of positive leadership. In their view, the practice of authentic leadership leads to sustainable and actual, ethically sound organizational performance.[100]

Authenticity has four elements: awareness, unbiased (balanced) processing, action, and relational orientation.[101] *Awareness* means being conscious of and trusting in one's motives, desires, emotions, and self-concept. Self-aware people know their strengths and weaknesses, personal traits, and emotional style; and they are able to use this knowledge when interacting with others and their environments. *Unbiased (balanced) processing* describes remaining objective when receiving information from internal or external sources. Self-accepting conduct rejects the inauthentic (defensive) behaviors of denying, distorting, or ignoring feedback one wishes to evade. *Action* is acting congruently with what one believes and not changing behavior to please others, earn rewards, or avoid punishment. *Relational orientation* means seeking openness and truthfulness in close relationships. This includes allowing others to see one's attractive and less attractive aspects.[102]

Authentic leadership has a strong moral component. Authentic leaders are deeply aware of how they think and behave and are perceived by others as being aware of their own and others' values and moral perspectives, knowledge, and strengths. They are confident, hopeful, optimistic, resilient, and of high moral character. Authentic leaders are aware of the contexts in which they operate. They acknowledge the ethical responsibilities of their roles, recognize and evaluate ethical issues, and take moral actions that are thoroughly anchored in their beliefs and values. They draw on their courage, resilience, and ability to adapt when confronted by significant risk or hardship.[103]

Authentic leadership encourages ethical behaviors in followers. Followers are likely to see these leaders as role models with high ethical standards that they wish to emulate. Learning by example, they feel empowered to make their own ethical choices without the leader's input. Having built a sense of trust from witnessing the leader's consistency and honesty, followers align themselves with the organization's values and become authentic moral agents themselves. They provide feedback that reinforces the leader's behavior and self-knowledge, and reward their leaders by granting them more space to make difficult, unpopular choices. Followers who believe in their own abilities are more ready to take initiative and achieve more, even in the face of obstacles. Authentic leadership and followership are more likely to grow in organizational climates that provide the information and other resources that employees need to complete their work, encourage learning, treat each other fairly, and set clear goals and performance standards.[104]

Trigger events or critical incidents play an important role in developing an authentic leader's moral dimension.[105] Trigger experiences are often dramatic (such as facing racial or gender identity discrimination), but they can also be ordinary such as reading a thought-provoking book. Occasionally, a series of several minor successes or failures can have a cumulative effect, stimulating considerable thought. Through these experiences, leaders develop a clearer sense of who they are, including their standards of right and wrong. In the process, they build a store of moral knowledge that they can use to make better choices when confronting future ethical dilemmas.

Training and education can promote authenticity. Providing leaders with occasions to develop their moral capacity includes encouraging them to think about the possible consequences of their leadership decisions, helping them enhance their perspective, introducing them to common moral dilemmas to help them recognize ethical issues they will face in their jobs, nurturing their belief in their ability to follow through on choices, helping them develop strategies for adapting and coping with new ethical challenges, and pairing them with moral leaders so they can observe authentic and ethical behavior first hand.[106]

Nonetheless, authentic leadership as a theory has its limitations. It is still in the developmental stage, and it has yet to be supported by robust empirical research.[107] No widely used measure of authentic leadership exists. Additionally, confusion exists regarding the distinctions among authentic, transformational, and servant leadership.[108] All three theories promote concern for others and encourage growth of followers, and self-awareness is essential to both servant and authentic leadership. The theories share significant overlap. Conceptually, they may all be part of a single theory rather than three separate ones. Also of serious concern is the theory's underlying premise that authenticity is the source of all positive forms of leadership. Other sources may yet be determined, or multiple sources of ethical leadership may exist. Self-awareness cannot logically be equated with morality, despite the authentic leadership theory proponents' assertions. Similarly, being true to oneself can provoke dangerous and destructive consequences. Speaking one's mind in the heat of emotion, while authentic, can do long-term damage to relationships and to organizational productivity. Table 11–4 compares the ethical positions of the normative leadership theories.

TABLE 11–4

Comparing Ethical Positions of Normative Leadership Theory

Transformational Leadership

Pros: Has empirical evidence of its effectiveness; acknowledges that leadership reflects learning not innate capacity; appears in a variety of circumstances and cultures

Cons: Leaders may employ transforming approaches without moral precepts; depends on the leader; encourages dependent followers

Servant Leadership

Pros: Sees followers as partners; seeks pursuit of ethical purposes; exhibits concern for others

Cons: Idyllic in the abstract, but not likely to work in the real world; may reflect misunderstanding service as weakness; selectively applicable

Authentic Leadership

Pros: Stresses self-awareness, objectivity, congruence, and truthfulness; developmental in nature, through "trigger events," training, and education

Cons: Is in early stage of theory development; not clearly differentiated from related theories

Source: Based on: Johnson, C. E. (2009). *Meeting the ethical challenges of leadership* (3rd ed., pp. 167–198). Thousand Oaks, CA: Sage.

ACTIVITY 11.4   Applying Normative Leadership Models in Schools

Case Study Question 5: How do the normative leadership models offer guidance on how to create a more ethical school district culture for the Hunt Valley School District?

Case Study Question 6: What type of leadership would work best in this situation?

Normative leadership models prescribe how leaders should act. Transformational leadership theory, servant leadership theory, and authentic leadership theory all promote concern for others and contain much overlap. While each approach has limitations, aspects of each offer suggestions for how leaders can act ethically to initiate and sustain organizational change that benefits constituents and followers. Discuss as a class:

1. In adopting the transformational leadership model, how might Dr. Smith use his expert and referent power to change followers' core attitudes and values, and create organizational culture through empowerment strategies?

2. In adopting the transformational leadership model, how might Dr. Smith apply the ideas of idealized influence, inspirational motivation, intellectual stimulation, and individualized consideration to design action strategies that would lead to a more ethical school district culture and practices (and more equitable resources and expectations for all students)? How would this leadership model affect Dr. Smith's work with the community?

3. In adopting the servant leadership model, how might Dr. Smith apply the concepts of stewardship, obligation, partnership, and elevating purpose to change followers' attitudes and values and the school district's culture? How might this leadership model affect Dr. Smith's work with the community?

> **4.** In adopting the authentic leadership model, how might Dr. Smith use training and education to promote ethical thinking and acting among the school board, central office, and school leadership? How might this leadership model affect Dr. Smith's work with the community?
>
> **5.** Which type of normative leadership model do you think would work best for Dr. Smith in this situation, and why?

SCHOOL LEADERSHIP AND SOCIAL JUSTICE

Social justice has become a major concern for early 21st-century educational scholars and practitioners. This concern is driven by an array of factors, including the growing diversity of Western industrialized societies and their school-age populations, the increasing awareness of the achievement and economic gaps between mainstream and minority children,[109] and the ever more sophisticated analysis of social injustice that occurs in schools.[110] This increasing attention is part of a general shift toward a focus on school leadership's moral purpose and how to foster successful, equitable, and socially responsible learning and accountability practices for all students.[111]

Social justice in educational leadership emphasizes moral values, justice, respect, care, and equity. Many scholars advocate a critique of educational systems in terms of access, power, and privilege based on race, culture, gender, sexual orientation, language, background, ability/disability, and socioeconomic position.[112] Consciousness about the impact these variables have on schools and student learning is always central. Substantial data support this perspective. When compared to their White middle-class peers, students of color and low socioeconomic status consistently experience lower achievement test scores, teacher expectations, and resource allocations.[113] These gaps are substantial, persistent, and pervasive.

Schools' funding gap reflects this differential access to power and privilege. In a 2006 national study, the Education Trust, an educational advocacy group, determined that in 28 states, high-minority school districts received less state and local money for each child than did low-minority districts. Across the United States, schools spent $825 less per student in districts educating the most students of color as compared with districts educating the fewest students of color.[114] Similarly, a 2009 report from the Editorial Projects in Education Research Center found more than $9,000 in per-pupil spending separated the top from bottom spending states.[115] Research shows that, depending on their location, some school districts receive *eight times* as much per-pupil funding as others.[116] Consequently, wide and growing disparities in education quality appear between more affluent school districts and less affluent ones. This translates into differences in areas including teacher experience and effectiveness, class size, facilities upkeep, the level of available technology, and other factors that can affect student outcomes and, ultimately, students' life chances.

School Leaders as Public Intellectuals

As a concept, social justice is related to the ethic of critique, an application of critical theory that focuses on the educational ideas, policies, and practices that serve the dominant class's interests while simultaneously silencing and dehumanizing others. A critical stance frames the education discussion to address issues of power and privilege, weaving social justice into the fabric of educational leadership curriculum, pedagogy, programs, and policies.

Within this context, school leaders are being asked to take up the role of transformative public intellectuals who engage in critical analysis of conditions that have maintained historical inequities in schools and who work to change institutional structures and culture.[117] The critical stance recognizes and advocates for educational leaders' role as social change agents.[118] Because contemporary researchers have found that effective leaders take responsibility for their learning, share a vision for what can be, assess their own assumptions and beliefs, and understand the structural and organic nature of schools,[119] school leaders are in the position to create more socially just situations that increase students' learning as they improve students' internal and external environments.

Working for social justice in schools is a systemic, communal challenge involving not only policy and practice but also moral commitments and the courage to work for meaningful change. It involves collaborating with teachers, parents, and students to identify and remove factors that limit student learning and opportunity and instituting practices that enhance them. Social justice in schools is more than test scores and closing achievement gaps. It involves using community issues for students' literacy development, content learning, and growth of critical thinking and then applying these skills to engage students in moral thought and action within their communities. It includes considering the pedagogical value and measurable achievement benefits of using the community as a resource to study natural history, cultural journalism, action research, and other methodologies in neighborhood sites to identify local needs. This learning can occur within the current context of mandated learning standards and accountability mechanisms. It means conducting honest dialogue with varied stakeholders around the purposes of schooling.

School leadership for social justice makes the school walls more permeable.[120] Principals must build alliances inside and outside schools with others ready to act on the moral commitments that social justice expresses. Leaders' tasks are to help teachers understand these pedagogical benefits and their relationship to mandated learning standards and then enact them within the learning context.

ACTIVITY 11.5   Applying Social Justice Leadership in Schools

Case Study Question 6: What type of leadership would be best in this situation?

Social justice focuses on school leaders' moral purpose and how to foster successful, equitable, and socially responsible learning and accountability practices for all students. As a philosophy, social justice asks educational leaders to become transformative public intellectuals who engage in critical analysis of conditions that have maintained historical inequities in schools and who work to change institutional structures and culture. Discuss as a class:

1. Using a social justice framework, how would Dr. Smith describe Hunt Valley School District's culture and practices—and his role as superintendent?
2. How might Dr. Smith use a social justice perspective to build alliances inside and outside the school district to mobilize action to make the school district's structure and educational practices more equitable?
3. How might Dr. Smith use the social justice perspective in combination with normative leadership models to empower board members, school district leadership, and the community to create a more equitable school district culture and equitable educational practices?

MAINTAINING A MORAL COMPASS

Leaders' ethical responsibilities are not an addition to their regular expectations and tasks. Rather, ethical responsibilities are infused throughout them. Daily ethical dilemmas involve issues of power, privilege, information, consistency, loyalty, and responsibility. How school leaders handle these challenges determines whether they cause more good than harm.

The Practice of Ethical Leadership

Ethical leadership is a two-part process involving personal moral behavior and moral influence. Leaders act ethically when they act morally as they carry out their duties and when they shape the ethical climates of their groups, organizations, and societies.[121] Both aspects are important. Leaders must enact characteristics such as integrity, justice, humility, optimism, courage, compassion, and perspective in order to make wise decisions. They must master the ethical challenges that confront their roles. What is more, leaders are responsible for the ethical behavior of others, acting as role models for employees as they set the example. Even as they affect their climate with their own ethical behaviors, leaders reflect the ethical climates in which they work. The ethical influence goes both ways.

Ethical leaders have several critical virtues woven throughout their character. These learned attitudes and behaviors persist over time and shape the ways leaders see and interact with the world, making them more sensitive to ethical issues and encouraging them to act morally. Operating independently of the situation, these virtues—integrity, courage, humility, reverence, optimism, compassion, and justice—may be expressed differently depending on the situation.[122]

Integrity.   The term *integrity* can be defined as incorruptibility, soundness (unimpaired), and completeness (unbroken). Integrity means firm adherence to a code of moral values and is synonymous with *honesty*.[123] Leaders with integrity remain true to themselves. Their public actions and private thoughts are consistent and congruent with their moral values. They practice what they preach and are honest in their dealings with others. They are principled and cannot be bought. This reliability of belief and deed builds trust and credibility among employees and colleagues. Messages and behaviors are unswerving, rules and procedures are steady, and blaming, dishonesty, secrecy, and unjust rewards do not occur.[124] Trust encourages teamwork, cooperation, risk taking, and greater employee satisfaction. Performance suffers when trust is broken. Ethical leaders with integrity hold

FIGURE 11–2
Integrity as Central to Ethical Leadership (Source: Owings and Kaplan (authors). Based on Johannsen, R. L. (1991). Virtue ethics, character, and political communication. In R. E. Denton (Ed.), *Ethical dimensions of political communication* (pp. 69–90). New York, NY: Praeger.)

tight to their values rather than go along with the group, and they strive to create ethical environments even when faced with opposition from their superiors and subordinates. As illustrated in Figure 11–2, integrity may be considered as the hub in the wheel through which the other desirable leadership traits extend themselves, the individual's consistent, central organizing force that allows the other virtues to be expressed.

Courage. *Courage* is overcoming fear to do the right thing.[125] Courageous leaders acknowledge the dangers and anxieties they face and move forward despite the risks and costs. Courage is not necessarily physical prowess. A courageous principal, for instance, is one who suspends a star athlete with a failing semester grade point average before a state tournament and calmly faces angry parents and students. Courage is also an essential element in the capacity for the patience and persistence needed to overcome obstacles that slow or deter achievement of the vision.

Humility. True humility balances the extremes of having either an overly low or an overly high self-opinion.[126] Humility is not low self-esteem or underestimating one's abilities. Humility has three components: self-awareness, openness, and transcendence. *Self-awareness* is the ability to objectively assess one's strengths and limitations. *Openness* is receptiveness to new ideas and knowledge, including self-knowledge. *Transcendence* is the acceptance of a power greater than oneself. It keeps one's own importance in perspective while increasing the appreciation of others' worth and contributions. Because they know their limitations and are open to input, humble leaders are more willing to consider advice that promotes effective decisions.

Reverence.   Like humility, *reverence* is the capacity to feel a sense of awe, respect, and even shame when appropriate.[127] Ethical leaders serve higher causes or ideals. Awe, respect, and shame keep leaders focused on reaching common goals rather than engaging in power struggles or dwelling on winning or losing. They respect others' input, listen to followers' ideas, and rely on persuasion rather than force. Ethical leaders feel shame when they violate group norms, and this prompts them to accept the consequences of telling the truth or supporting unpopular people or ideas.

Optimism.   *Optimism* expects positive future outcomes, even amid current difficulties and disappointments.[128] More confident than pessimists (who expect things to turn out poorly), optimists are more likely to persist despite adversity. When faced with stress and defeat, optimists acknowledge the reality and take steps to improve their situation rather than escape the problem through wishful thinking, distractions, or other means. Optimism is an essential leadership quality, helping individuals—and their followers—to deal constructively with the inevitable setbacks, and they can define a positive image for the group's future.

Compassion.   *Compassion, concern, care, kindness, generosity,* and *love* all describe an orientation that places others ahead of self.[129] Persons with compassion value others whether or not they get anything in return. Compassion is an important element of altruism. An orientation toward others rather than self separates ethical from unethical leaders.[130] Recognizing that they serve the group's purposes, ethical leaders seek power and exercise influence on behalf of their followers. Unethical leaders, in contrast, put their own self-interest first.

Justice.   *Justice* has two components: a sense of obligation to the common good and treating others as equally and fairly as possible.[131] Just people feel a sense of duty and struggle to do their part as a team member—whether in a small group, organization, or society. They support equitable rules and laws and believe that everyone deserves the same rights even if they have different skills or status. Leaders have the moral obligation to consider the entire group's—and the community's—needs and interests. This means setting aside personal biases when making choices, judging others objectively, and treating them appropriately.

Perspective.   In their 1988 book, *The Power of Ethical Management,* Kenneth Blanchard and Dr. Norman Vincent Peale concluded, "Perspective is the capacity to see what is really important in any given situation."[132] The habit of reflection is critical to gaining a sense of perspective. This requires devoting some time each day to silence. Silence is more than the absence of noise. It is the inner quiet that allows one to contemplate the higher purpose, to question one's decisions in view of that purpose, and to seek strength to discern between right and wrong as one seeks to fulfill it.

Developing a Strong Ethical Character

Blending these virtues to form a strong ethical character is not easy. Individuals may make progress in some areas while showing less growth in others. Many of our greatest leaders reflect both moral strength and weakness. Developing an ethical character is a lifelong process, requiring sustained emotional, mental, and physical exertion. Some direct efforts to develop character exist, such as prominently posting lists of virtues in public places, preaching, or working with counselors to build realistic self-assessment and convert pessimism into optimism by challenging negative messages ("I am a failure") and converting them into positive thoughts ("I may have failed but I can improve"). Most virtues, however, mature indirectly or by factors that encourage developing leadership virtues. These include finding role models; learning from hardship, setbacks, mistakes, and failure; cultivating good habits; creating a personal mission statement; and clarifying values.

Leadership can often be learned by observing and imitating exemplary leaders. Role models are crucial to developing high moral character.[133] To develop worthy character, we need to see virtue lived every day. Character develops over time through a series of moral choices and actions, and assessing outcomes. Oskar Schindler, a German industrialist, risked his life and fortune to save 1,000 Jewish workers during World War II. Nelson Mandela was imprisoned for 27 years for political activities against apartheid in South Africa, yet he emerged from prison determined to unite his diverse country without violence as South Africa's first Black president.

Research has found that moral role models have three common qualities: certainty, positivity, and unity of self and moral goals.[134] They are sure of what they believe and take responsibility for acting on their convictions. They take a positive approach to life even in the face of hardship. They are optimistic about the future. Finally, moral exemplars don't separate their personal identities from their ethical beliefs. Morality is central to who they are. They believe they are successful if they are pursuing their life's mission and are helping others.

Moral capacity continues to grow well after childhood. Therefore, individuals should strive to develop their ethical capacity throughout their lives. Researchers found that working with others on important ethical tasks or projects fosters moral growth by exposing participants to different viewpoints and new moral issues—finding occasions to act upon their beliefs with an optimistic attitude in spite of setbacks or discouragement.[135]

Ethical Leadership: The Bottom Line

Leaders are their organization's heartbeat. Their behaviors send clear and unambiguous messages about ethical standards expected from employees. The organization's higher purpose is the starting point in creating an ethical environment. The higher purpose and the values it represents convey to the followers what is acceptable and unacceptable behavior. The leader develops specific codes of conduct to help employees internalize these values in action. In addition, the leader creates opportunities for employees to exchange ideas and experiences as they implement the code of conduct, identifying the difficulties they might likely meet acting in ethically-fraught situations. Some organizations hold periodic retreats or discussion forums to give employees the intellectual, emotional, and moral support they need to maintain the high ethical standards expected of them.

The bottom line for ethical leadership: While codes of conduct and related policies, procedures, and support structures are necessary to develop the organization's ethical environment, the leader's personal conduct determines its effectiveness. The organization's ethical environment is a natural outcome of the leader's genuine commitment and actions to address others' interest above the leader's own and to work to improve the organization. As moral stewards and educators, directed by beliefs and values linked to justice, caring, community, and promoting success for all children and youth, school leaders must create an ethical culture that bonds both leader and followers to a shared set of values, beliefs, and purposes enacted in a thousand daily decisions. Ethical leadership cannot merely be exhorted; it must be shared and lived.

ACTIVITY 11.6   Developing as an Ethical Leader

Ethical leadership requires both personal moral behavior and the ability to influence others to act morally. Ethical leadership takes time to develop. Discuss as a class:

1. Identify and describe behaviors you have observed in leaders that illustrate the following virtues: integrity, courage, humility, reverence, optimism, compassion, justice, and perspective.
2. What leaders (formal or informal) do you consider as moral role models?
3. What virtues have you developed that were learned from hardship, setbacks, or mistakes?
4. Which virtues do you believe you have at least moderately developed and which do you wish to develop more fully?
5. If you were the superintendent in this case study, under what conditions would you be willing to lose your job in order to take what you believe to be an ethical stand?
6. Write a 100-word statement defining the philosophy of ethical leadership that you tentatively expect to follow as an educator and school leader, using ideas discussed in this chapter. Share these with the class. As a group, discuss how you might overcome the obstacles to putting your philosophy into daily practice and how you might overcome them.

SUMMARY

Ethics are norms, values, beliefs, habits, and attitudes that we choose to follow. Ethics are about relationships—"what we ought to do"—requiring a judgment about a given situation. The terms *ethics* and *morals* are sometimes used interchangeably. When people find themselves in complex circumstances that require them to choose from among competing sets of principles, values, beliefs, or ideas, ethical dilemmas result.

Ethical leaders are motivated by a concern for others as well as for the organization—despite the risk of personal cost—and they act primarily to achieve this purpose. As moral stewards and educators, ethical school leaders are directed by beliefs anchored in values such as justice, caring, community, and promoting success for all children and youth. They must create an ethical culture that bonds both leader and followers to a shared set of values, beliefs, and purposes enacted in a thousand daily decisions.

Developing an informed perspective using well-established ethical philosophies can assist educational leaders to successfully resolve these dilemmas. Utilitarianism, Kant's categorical imperative, justice as fairness, communitarianism, and altruism are five general ethical philosophies that offer guidance on how to behave morally with individuals and groups. Each philosophy has its own strengths and weaknesses; but overlap exists, and no one perspective is perfect for all ethical decisions. By using ethical pluralism, school leaders can gain deeper and more varied insights about how to best address ethical problems.

A more integrated exemplar, the multiple ethical paradigms are tied more closely to school leadership. These paradigms include the ethics of justice, critique, care, and profession. While no one perfect ethical choice exists, the four perspectives enable educators to make decisions with more clearly defined consequences, to move toward the best choice under the circumstances, or to select an option that will likely be later balanced by other choices.

If education has a moral imperative, it is to act in the best interests of the students. At a time of increased population diversity, this is especially vital. However, people of goodwill and the professional literature may disagree about what actually is "the best interests of students."

Normative leadership theories built on moral principles orient leaders toward ethical decision making and performance. Transformational leadership, servant leadership, and authentic leadership are normative leadership models. Each approach has its strengths and limitations. Confusion exists regarding the practical and empirical distinctions among these models because they share much overlap.

Social justice in educational leadership emphasizes moral values and how to foster successful, equitable, and socially responsible learning and accountability practices for all students. Inequities in students' access to rigorous academic curricula and in schools' resources translate into large disparities in educational experiences that can affect student outcomes and life chances. School leaders are asked to become transformative public intellectuals: social change agents who engage in critical analysis of conditions that have maintained historical inequities in schools, and who work to change institutional structures and culture.

Ethical leadership involves enacting personal moral behavior and exerting moral influence. Ethical leaders have several critical virtues woven throughout their character that persist over time and shape the ways leaders see and interact with the world.

ENDNOTES

1. For each dollar spent at Priceton High School, 39.7 cents spent at Southern High School, and 41.1 cents spent at Western High School.
2. C = Caucasian; AA = African American; L = Latino; NA = Native American; A = Asian
3. Ciulla, J. (Ed.). (2008). *Ethics: The heart of leadership.* Westport, CT: Praeger.
4. Fullan, M. G. (2003). *The moral imperative of school leadership.* Thousand Oaks, CA: Corwin Press; Greenfield, W. D. (2004). Moral leadership in schools. *Journal of Educational Administration, 42*(2), 174–196.
5. Murphy, J. (2002). Reculturing the professional of educational leadership: New blueprints. *Educational Administration Quarterly, 38*(2), 176–191.
6. Friedman, T. L. (2008). *Hot, flat, and crowded. Why we need a green revolution—And how it can renew America* (p. 192). New York, NY: Ferrar, Straus, & Giroux.
7. Plato in Freakley, M., & Burgh, G. (2000). *Engaging with ethics: Ethical inquiry for teachers* (p. 97). Queensland, Australia: Social Science Press.
8. Hitt, W. D. (1990). *Ethics and leadership: Putting theory into practice.* Columbus, OH: Battelle Press.
9. Spaemann, R. (1989). *Basic moral concepts.* London, United Kingdom: Routledge.
10. Kanungo, R. K., & Mendonca, M. (1996). *Ethical dimensions of leadership.* Thousand Oaks, CA: Sage.
11. Kanungo, R. K., & Mendonca, M. (1996). *Ethical dimensions of leadership* (p. 2). Thousand Oaks, CA: Sage.

12. Drucker, P. (1968). *The practice of management* (p. 461). London, United Kingdom: Pan Books.
13. Kanungo & Mendonca. (1996). Op.cit.
14. Bakan, D. (1966). *The duality of human existence.* Chicago, IL: Rand McNally.
15. Ouchi, W. (1981). *Theory Z: How American business can meet the Japanese challenge.* Reading, MA: Addison-Wesley; Schein, E. (1980). *Organizational psychology.* Englewood Cliffs, NJ: Prentice Hall.
16. Spence, J., & Helmreich, R. (1983). Achievement-related motives and behavior. In J. Spence (Ed.), *Achievement and achievement motives: Psychological approaches* (pp. 7–74). San Francisco, CA: Freeman; Jenkins, C., Rosenman, R., & Zyzanski, S. (1974). Prediction of clinical coronary heart disease by a test for the coronary-prone behavior pattern. *New England Journal of Medicine, 290*(23), 1271–1275.
17. McClelland found a surprising link between altruism and the body's immune system. See: McClelland, D., & Burnham, D. H. (1995, January/February). Power is the great motivator. *Harvard Business Review, 73*(1), 126–139; Growald, E., & Luks, A. (1988). Beyond self. *American Health, 7*(1), 51–53.
18. Murphy, J. (2002). Reculturing the profession of educational leadership: New blueprints. *Educational Administration Quarterly, 38*(2), 176–191.
19. Osin, L., & Lesgold, A. (1996). A proposal for the reengineering of the educational system. *Review of Educational Research, 66*(4), 621–656, p. 621.
20. Starratt, R. J. (1991). Building an ethical school: A theory for practice in educational leadership. *Educational Administration Quarterly, 27*(2), 185–202.
21. Barry, V. (1978). *Personal and social ethics: Moral problems with integrated theory.* Belmont, CA: Wadsworth; Bentham, J. (1948). *An introduction to the principles of morals and legislation.* New York, NY: Hafner; DeGeorge, R. T. (1995). *Business ethics* (4th ed., chap. 3). Englewood Cliffs, NJ: Prentice Hall; Gorovitz, S. (Ed.). (1971). *Utilitarianism: Text and critical essays.* Indianapolis, IN: Bobbs-Merrill.
22. Jensen, J. V. (1996). Ethical tension points in whistle-blowing. In J. A. Jaksa & M. S. Pritchard (Eds.), *Responsible communication: Ethical issues in business, industry, and the professions* (pp. 41–51). Cresskill, NJ: Hampton.
23. *Categorical* means "without exception."
24. Kant, I. (1964). *Groundwork of the metaphysics of morals* (H. J. Ryan, Trans.). New York, NY: Harper & Row; Christians, C. G., Rotzell, K. B., & Fackler, M. (1999). *Media ethics* (3rd ed.). New York, NY: Longman; Velazquez, M. G. (1992). *Business ethics: Concepts and cases* (3rd ed., chap. 2). Englewood Cliffs, NJ: Prentice Hall.
25. Meilander, G. (1986). Virtue in contemporary religious thought. In R. J. Nehaus (Ed.), *Virtue: Public and private* (pp. 7–30). Grand Rapids, MI: Eerdmans; Alderman, H. (1997). By virtue of a virtue. In D. Statman (Ed.), *Virtue ethics* (pp. 145–164). Washington, DC: Georgetown University Press.
26. Rawls, J. (1993). Distributive justice. In T. Donaldson & P. H. Werhane (Eds.), *Ethical issues in business: A philosophical approach* (pp. 274–285). Englewood Cliffs, NJ: Prentice Hall; Rawls, J. (2001). *Justice as fairness: A restatement* (E. Kelly, Ed.). Cambridge, MA: Belknap.
27. Rawls. (1993). Ibid.
28. Rawls. (1993). Op. cit..
29. Rawls, J. (1993). *Political liberalism.* New York, NY: Columbia University Press.
30. Johnson. (2009). Op. cit.
31. Etzioni, A. (1993). *The spirit of community: The reinvention of American society.* New York, NY: Touchstone; Etzioni, A. (Ed.). (1995). *New communitarian thinking: Persons, virtues, institutions, and communities.* Charlottesville: University Press of Virginia.
32. Etzioni. (1993). Ibid.; Johnson, C. E. (2000, October). *Emerging perspectives in leadership ethics.* Selected proceedings of the 1999 annual conference of the International Leadership Association, Atlanta, GA, pp. 48–54.
33. Gardner, J. (1995). Building a responsive community. In A. Etzioni (Ed.), *Rights and the common good: The communitarian perspective* (pp. 167–178). New York, NY: St. Martin's.
34. Piliavin, J. A., & Chang, H. W. (1990). Altruism: A review of recent theory and research. *American Sociological Review, 16*(1), 27–65; Batson, C. D., Van Lange, P. A. M., Ahmad, N., & Lishner, D. A. (2003). Altruism and helping

behavior. In M. A. Hogg & J. Cooper (Eds.), *The Sage handbook of social psychology* (pp. 279–295). London, United Kingdom: Sage.

35. Kanungo, R. N., & Mendonca, M. (1996). *Ethical dimensions of leadership*. Thousand Oaks, CA: Sage.

36. Avolio, B. J., & Locke, E. E. (2002). Contrasting different philosophies of leader motivation: Altruism versus egoism. *Leadership Quarterly, 13*(2), 169–191.

37. Starratt, R. J. (1991). Building an ethical school: A theory for practice in educational leadership. *Educational Administration Quarterly, 27*(2), 185–202; Starratt, R. J. (1994). *Building an ethical school*. London, United Kingdom: Falmer Press.

38. Shapiro, J. P., & Stefkovich, J. A. (2001). *Ethical leadership and decision making in education: Applying theoretical perspectives to complex dilemmas*. Mahwah, NJ: Lawrence Erlbaum; Shapiro, J. P., & Stefkovich, J. A. (2005). *Ethical leadership and decision making in education: Applying theoretical perspectives to complex dilemmas* (2nd ed.). Mahwah, NJ: Lawrence Erlbaum.

39. Noddings, N. (1999). Care, justice and equity. In M. S. Katz, N. Noddings, & K. A. Strike (Eds.), *Justice and caring: The search for common ground in education* (pp. 7–20). New York, NY: Teachers College Press, p. 7.

40. Shapiro & Gross. (2008). Op. cit.

41. Delgado, R. (1995). *Critical race theory: The cutting edge*. Philadelphia, PA: Temple University Press.

42. Sullivan, W. M. (1986). *Reconstructing public philosophy*. Berkeley: University of California Press.

43. Starratt. (1991). Op. cit.

44. Sergiovanni, T. J. (1992). *Moral leadership: Getting to the heart of school improvement*. San Francisco, CA: Jossey-Bass.

45. Shapiro, J. P., & Gross, S. J. (2008). *Ethical educational leadership in turbulent times. (Re)Solving moral dilemmas*. Mahwah, NJ: Lawrence Erlbaum.

46. Stoddard, E. (2008, August 20). *Corporal punishment seen rife in U.S. schools*. Retrieved from http://www.reuters.com/article/idUSN1931921320080820

47. Hollenbach, D. (1979). *Claims in conflict*. New York, NY: Paulist.

48. Shapiro & Gross. (2008). Op. cit.

49. Shapiro & Gross. (2008). Op. cit.

50. For example, Apple, M. W. (1988). *Teachers and texts: A political economy of class and gender relations in education*. New York, NY: Routledge & Kegan Paul; Apple, M. W. (2000). *Official knowledge: Democratic education in a conservative age*. New York, NY: C.R. & Routledge Ashbaugh; Astuto, R. A., Clark, D. L., & Read, A. M. (Eds.). (1994). *Roots of reform: Challenging the assumptions that control education*. Bloomington, IN: Phi Delta Kappan; Freire, P. (1970). *Pedagogy of the oppressed* (M. B. Ramos, Trans.). New York, NY: Continuum; Giroux, H. A. (1994). *Educational leadership and school administrators: Rethinking the meaning of democratic public culture*. In T. M. Mulkeen, N. H. Cambron-McCabe, & B. Anderson (Eds.), *Democratic leadership: The changing context of administrative preparation*. Norwood, NJ: Ablex; Giroux, H. A. (2000). *Stealing innocence: Youth, corporate power, and politics of culture*. New York, NY: St. Martin's Press; Larson, C., & Murtadha, K. (2002). Leadership for social justice. In J. Murphy (Ed.), *The educational leadership challenge: Redefining leadership for the 21st century*. Chicago, IL: University of Chicago Press; Purpel, D. E. (1989). *The moral and spiritual crisis in education: A curriculum for justice and compassion in education*. New York, NY: Bergin & Garvey; Purpel, D. E. (2004). *Reflections on the moral and spiritual crisis of education*. New York, NY: Peter Lang; Shapiro, H. S. (2006). *Losing heart: The moral and spiritual miseducation of America's children*. Mahwah, NJ: Lawrence Erlbaum; Shapiro, J. P. (2006). Ethical decision making in turbulent times: Bridging theory with practice to prepare authentic educational leaders. *Values and Ethics in Educational Administration, 4*(2), 1–8.

51. Bourdieu, P. (1977). Cultural reproduction and social reproduction. In J. Karabel & A. H. Halsey (Eds.), *Power and ideology in education* (pp. 487–511). New York, NY: Oxford; Bourdieu, P. (2001). *Masculine domination*. Stanford, CA: Stanford University Press; Lareau, A. (1987). Social class differences in family school relationships: The importance of cultural capital. *Sociology of Education, 60*(2), 73–85; Lareau, A. (2003). *Unequal childhoods: Class, race and family life*. Berkeley: University of California Press.

52. Oakes, J. (1993). Tracking, inequality, and the rhetoric of reform: Why schools don't change. In S. H. Shapiro & D. E. Purpel (Eds.), *Critical social issues in American education: Towards the 21st century* (pp. 288–304). White Plains, NY: Longman.

53. Apple, M. (2010). *Global crises, social justice, and education.* New York, NY: Routledge; Apple, M. (2010). *The Routledge international handbook of sociology of education.* New York, NY: Routledge; Apple, M. (2004). *Ideology and curriculum. 25th anniversary* (3rd ed.). New York, NY: Routledge; Apple, M. (1996). *Cultural politics and education.* New York, NY: Teachers College Press.

54. Giroux, H. (1994, Fall). *Slack off: Border youth and postmodern education.* Retrieved from http://www.gseis.ucla.edu/courses/ed253a/Giroux/Giroux5.html; Giroux, H. (n.d.). *Doing cultural studies: Youth and the challenge of pedagogy.* Retrieved from http://www.gseis.ucla.edu/courses/ed253a/Giroux/Giroux1.html

55. McLaren, P. (1994). *Life in schools.* New York, NY: Longman; McLaren, P. (2000). White terror and oppositional agency: Toward a critical multiculturalism. In E. Duarte & S. Smith (Eds.), *Foundational perspectives in multicultural education* (pp. 213–241). Newbury Park, CA: Sage.

56. Shapiro & Gross. (2008). Op. cit.

57. Martin, R. J. (1993). Becoming educated: A journey of alienation or integration? In S. H. Shapiro & D. E. Purpel (Eds.), *Critical social issues in American education: Toward the 21st century* (pp. 137–148). White Plains, NY: Longman.

58. Beck, L. G. (1994). *Reclaiming educational administration as a caring profession.* New York, NY: Teachers College Press; Gilligan, C. (1982). *In a different voice.* Cambridge, MA: Harvard University Press; Ginsberg, A. E., Shapiro, J. P., & Brown, S. O. (2004). *Gender in urban education: Strategies for student achievement.* Portsmouth, NH: Heinemann; Grogan, M. (1996). *Voices of women aspiring to the superintendency.* Albany: State University of New York Press; Noddings, N. (1984). *Caring: A feminine approach to ethics and moral education.* Berkeley: University of California Press; Noddings, N. (1992). *The challenge to care in schools: An alternative approach to education.* New York, NY: Teachers College Press; Noddings, N. (2002). *Educating moral people: A caring alternative to character education.* New York,

NY: Teachers College Press; Noddings, N. (2003). *Caring: A feminine approach to ethics and moral education* (2nd ed.). Berkeley: University of California Press; Sernak, K. (1998). *School leadership—Balancing power with caring.* New York, NY: Teachers College Press; Shapiro, J. P., & Smith-Rosenberg, C. (1989). The "other voices" in contemporary ethical dilemmas: The value of the new scholarship on women in the teaching of ethics. *Women's Studies International Forum, 12*(2), 199–211; Shapiro, J. P., Ginsberg, A. E., & Brown, S. P. (2003). The ethic of caring in urban schools: Family and community involvement. *Leading & Managing, 9*(2), 45–50.

59. Buber, M. (1965). Education. In M. Buber (Ed.), *Between man and man* (pp. 229–252). New York, NY: Macmillan.

60. Sergiovanni, T. J. (1992). *Moral leadership: Getting to the heart of school improvement.* San Francisco, CA: Jossey-Bass.

61. Blackburn, S. (2001). *Being good: A short introduction to ethics.* Oxford, United Kingdom: Oxford University Press.

62. Hoy, W. K., & Kupersmith, W. (1984). Principal authenticity and faculty trust. *Planning and Changing, 15*(2), 80–88.

63. Bolman, L. G., & Deal, T. E. (1991). *Reframing organizations: Artistry, choice, and leadership.* San Francisco, CA; Jossey-Bass.

64. Shapiro & Gross. (2008). Op. cit.

65. For example, Beck, L. G. (1994). *Reclaiming educational administration as a caring profession.* New York, NY: Teachers College Press; Beck, L. G., & Murphy, J. (1994a). *Ethics in educational leadership programs: An expanding role.* Thousand Oaks, CA: Corwin; Beck, L. G., Murphy, J., et al. (1997). *Ethics in educational leadership programs: Emerging models.* Columbia, MO: University Council for Educational Administration; Beckner, W. (2004). *Ethics for educational leaders.* Boston, MA: Pearson Education; Begley, P. T., & Johansson, O. (1998). The values of school administration: Preferences, ethics, and conflicts. *Journal of School Leadership, 9*(4), 399–422; Begley, P. T., & Johansson, O. (Eds.). (2003). *The ethical dimensions of school leadership.* Boston, MA: Kluwer Academic; Duke, D., & Grogan, M. (1997). The moral and ethical dimensions of leadership. In L. G. Beck, J. Murphy, et al. (Eds.), *Ethics in educational*

leadership programs: Emerging models (pp. 141–160). Columbia, MO: University Council for Educational Administration; Goldring, E., & Greenfield, W. (2002). Understanding the evolving concept of leadership in education: Roles, expectations, and dilemmas. In J. Murphy (Ed.), *The educational leadership challenge: Redefining leadership for the 21st century. 101st yearbook of the National Society for the Study of Education* (pp. 1–19). Chicago, IL: University of Chicago Press; Mertz, N. T. (1997). Knowing and doing: Exploring the ethical life of educational leaders. In L. G. Beck, J. Murphy, et al. (Eds.), *Ethics in educational leadership programs: Emerging models* (pp. 77–94). Columbia, MO: University Council for Educational Administration; O'Keefe, J. (1997). Preparing ethical leaders for equitable schools. In L. G. Beck, J. Murphy, et al. (Eds.), *Ethics in educational leadership programs: Emerging models* (pp. 141–160). Columbia, MO: University Council for Educational Administration; Starratt, R. J. (1991). Building an ethical school: A theory for practice in educational leadership. *Educational Administration Quarterly, 27*(2), 185–292; Starratt, R. J. (2004). *Ethical leadership.* San Francisco, CA: Jossey-Bass; Strike, K. A., Haller, E. J., & Soltis, J. F. (Eds.). (2005). *Ethics for professionals in education: Perspectives for preparation and practice.* New York, NY: Teachers College Press..

66. Campbell, E. (2004). *The ethical teacher.* Maidenhead, United Kingdom: Open University Press; Hansen, D. T. (2001). Teaching as a moral activity. In V. Richardson (Ed.), *Handbook of research on teaching* (4th ed., pp. 57–128). Washington, DC: American Educational Research Association; Hostetler, K. D. (1997). *Ethical judgment in teaching.* Boston, MA: Allyn & Bacon; Strike, K. A., & Ternasky, P. L. (Eds.). (1993). *Ethics for professionals in education: Perspectives for preparation and practice.* New York, NY: Teachers College Press.

67. For example, *The Pennsylvania Code of Professional Practice and Conduct for Educators* (1992) and *Texas' Ethics, Standards, and Practices* (Texas Administrative Code, 1998) address the ethics of justice as well as the profession. See: Shapiro & Gross. (2008). Op. cit., p. 30.

68. Kaplan, L. S., & Owings, W. A. (2011). *American education: Building a common foundation* (pp. 232–233). Belmont, CA: Wadsworth/Cengage.

69. Beauchamp, R. L., & Childress, J. F. (1984). Morality, ethics, and ethical theories. In P. Sola (Ed.), *Ethics, education, and administrative decisions: A book of readings* (pp. 39–65). New York, NY: Peter Lang, p. 41.

70. Brown, K. W. (2004). Leadership for social justice and equity: Weaving a transformative framework and pedagogy. *Educational Administration Quarterly, 40*(1), 77–108.

71. Nash, R. J. (1996). *"Real world" ethics: Frameworks for educators and human service professionals.* New York, NY: Teachers College Press.

72. Shapiro, J. P., & Stefkovich, J. A. (2001). *Ethical leadership and decision making in education: Applying theoretical perspectives to complex dilemmas.* Mahwah, NJ: Lawrence Erlbaum; Shapiro, J. P., & Stefkovich, J. A. (2005). *Ethical leadership and decision making in education: Applying theoretical perspectives to complex dilemmas* (2nd ed.). Mahwah, NJ: Lawrence Erlbaum.

73. Interstate School Leaders Licensure Consortium (ISLLC). (1996). *Standards for school leaders.* Washington, DC: Author; Interstate School Leaders Licensure Consortium (ISLLC). (2008). *Educational leadership policy standards 2008* (p. 15). Washington, DC: Council of Chief State School Officers.

74. Shapiro, J. P., & Gross, S. J. (2008). *Ethical educational leadership in turbulent times. (Re)Solving moral dilemmas.* New York, NY: Lawrence Erlbaum.

75. Shapiro & Stefkovich. (1998). Op. cit.; Shapiro & Stefkovich. (2005). Op. cit.

76. Shapiro & Gross. (2008). Op. cit.

77. Noddings, N. (1992). *The challenge to care in schools: An alternative approach to education.* New York, NY: Teachers College Press; Noddings, N. (2003). *Caring: A feminine approach to ethics and moral education* (2nd ed.). Berkeley: University of California Press; Giroux, H. A. (1988). *Schooling and the struggle for public life: Critical pedagogy in the modern age.* Minneapolis: University of Minnesota Press; Giroux, H. A. (2003). *The abandoned generation: Democracy beyond the culture of fear.* New York, NY: Palgrave MacMillan; Weis, L., & Fine, M. (1993). *Beyond silenced voices: Class, race and gender in U.S. schools.* Albany: State University of New York Press.

78. Stefkovich, J. A. (2006). *Applying ethical constructs to legal cases: The best interests of the student.* Mahwah, NJ: Lawrence Erlbaum; Stefkovich, J. A., & O'Brien, G. M. (2004). Best interests of the student: An ethical model. *Journal of Educational Administration, 42*(2), 197–214; Walker, K. (1998). Jurisprudential and ethical perspectives of "the best interests of children." *Interchange, 29*(3), 283–304.

79. Stefkovich. (2006). Ibid.

80. Ciulla, J. B. (2004). Leadership ethics: Mapping the territory. In J. B. Ciulla (Ed.), *Ethics: The heart of leadership* (pp. 3–24). Westport, CT: Praeger.

81. Burns, J. M. (1978). *Leadership.* New York, NY: Harper & Row.

82. Burns. (1978). Ibid.

83. Bass, B. M. (1996). *A new paradigm of leadership: An inquiry into transformational leadership.* Alexandria, VA: U.S. Army Research Institute for the Behavioral and Social Sciences; Bass, B. M., Avolio, B. J., Jung, D. I., & Berson, Y. (2003). Predicting unit performance by assessing transformational and transactional leadership. *Journal of Applied Psychology, 88*(2), 207–218.

84. Turner, N., Barling, J., Epitropaki, O., Butcher, V., & Milner, C. (2002, April). Transformational leadership and moral reasoning. *Journal of Applied Psychology, 87*(2), 304–311.

85. Johnson. (2009). Op. cit.

86. Bass et al. (2003). Op. cit.; DeGroot, T., Kiker, D. S., & Cross, T. C. (2000). A meta-analysis to review organizational outcomes related to charismatic leadership. *Canadian Journal of Administrative Sciences, 17*(4), 356–371; Fiol, C. M., Harris, D., & House, R. J. (1999). Charismatic leadership: Strategies for effecting social change. *Leadership Quarterly, 10*(3), 449–482; Loew, K. B., & Kroeck, K. G. (1996). Effectiveness correlates of transformation and transactional leadership: A meta-analytic review. *Leadership Quarterly, 7*(3), 385–425.

87. Bennis, W., & Nanus, B. (2003). *Leaders: Strategies for taking charge.* New York, NY: Harper Business Essentials; Kottr, J. P. (1990). *A force for change: How leadership differs from management.* New York, NY: Free Press; Kouzes, J. M., & Posner, B. (2007). *The leadership challenge* (4th ed.). San Francisco, CA: Jossey-Bass; Nanus, B. (1992). *Visionary leadership.* San Francisco, CA: Jossey-Bass; Peters, T. (1992). *Liberation management.* New York, NY: Ballantine.

88. Bass, B. M. (1995). The ethics of transformational leadership. In J. Ciulla (Ed.), *Ethics: The heart of leadership* (pp. 169–192). Westport, CT: Praeger.

89. Bass. (1995). Ibid.

90. Mark 10:43–44, *Holy Bible.* English Standard Version. New York, NY: Crossway Bibles. Retrieved from http://bible.cc/mark/10-44.htm

91. Pay, R. (2000). *Lau Tzu. Humanistic texts.* Retrieved from http://www.humanistictexts.org/lao_tzu.htm

92. Greenleaf, R. K. (1977). *Servant leadership.* New York, NY: Paulist Press.

93. Spears, L. (1988). Introduction: Tracing the growing impact of servant-leadership. In L. C. Spears (Ed.), *Insights on leadership* (pp. 1–12). New York, NY: Wiley; Ruschman, N. L. (2002). Servant-leadership and the best companies to work for in America. In L. C. Spears & M. Lawrence (Eds.), *Focus on leadership: Servant-leadership for the twenty-first century* (pp. 123–139). New York, NY: Wiley.

94. Greenleaf. (1977). Op. cit., pp. 13–14.

95. Johnson. (2009). Op. cit., pp. 176–184.

96. Block, P. (1996). *Stewardship: Choosing service over self-interest.* San Francisco, CA: Berrett-Koehler; DePree, M. (2003). Servant-leadership: Three things necessary. In L. C. Spears & M. Lawrence (Eds.), *Focus on leadership: Servant-leadership for the 21st century.* New York, NY: Wiley.

97. In practice, this includes ensuring the stability of an organization's financial assets, relationships, and reputation; providing the organization with a legacy and future leaders; building a healthy institutional climate with openness to change and tolerance of diverse opinions; acting with maturity and rationality; providing the clear vision and research- and resource-supported strategies to create momentum toward meeting organizational goals; and effectiveness in enabling followers to reach their personal and institutional potential. These practices taken from Herman Miller, a major office furniture manufacturer, as cited in DePree, M. (1989). *Leadership is an art.* New York, NY: Doubleday.

98. Johnson. (2009). Op. cit.

99. Klenke, K. (2005). The internal theater of the authentic leader: Integrating cognitive, affective, conative, and spiritual facets of authentic leadership. In W. L. Gardner, B. J. Avolio, & F. P. Walumbwa (Eds.), *Authentic leadership theory and practice: Origins, effects and development* (pp. 48–81). Amsterdam: Elsevier.

100. Avolio, B. J., & Gardner, W. L. (2005). Authentic leadership development: Getting to the root of positive forms of leadership. *Leadership Quarterly, 16*(3), 315–340; Chan, A., Hannah, S. T., & Gardner, W. L. (2005). Veritable authentic leadership: Emergence, functioning, and impacts. In W. L. Gardner, B. Avolio, & F. O. Walumbwa (Eds.), *Authentic leadership theory and practice: Origins, effects and development* (pp. 3-41). Amsterdam: Elsevier.

101. Kernis, M. H. (2003). Toward a conceptualization of optimal self-esteem. *Psychological Inquiry, 14*(1), 1–26.

102. Kernis. (2003). Ibid.

103. May, D. R., Chan, A. Y. L., Hodges, T. D., & Avolio, B. J. (2003). Developing the moral component of authentic leadership. *Organizational Dynamics, 32*(3), 247–260; Hanna, S. T., Lester, P. B., & Vgelgesang, G. R. (2005). Moral leadership: Explicating the moral component of authentic leadership. In W. L. Gardner, B. J. Avolio, & F. O. Walumbwa (Eds.), *Authentic leadership theory and practice: Origins, effects and development* (pp. 43–81). Amsterdam: Elsevier.

104. Gardner et al. (2005). Op. cit.; Harvey, P., Martinko, M. J., & Gardner, W. L. (2006). Promoting authentic behavior in organizations: An attributional perspective. *Journal of Leadership and Organizational Studies, 12*(3), 1–11; Zhu, W., May, D. R., & Avolio, B. J. (2004). The impact of ethical leadership behavior on employee outcomes: The roles of psychological empowerment and authenticity. *Journal of Leadership and Organizational Studies, 11*(1), 16–26; Avolio, B. J., Gardner, W. L., Walumbwa, F. O., Luthans, F., & May, D. R. (2004). Unlocking the mask: A look at the process by which authentic leaders impact follower attitudes and behaviors. *Leadership Quarterly, 15*(6), 801–823.

105. Gardner, W. L., Avolio, B. J., Luthans, F., May, D. R., & Walumbwa, F. O. (2005). "Can you see the real me?" A self-based model of authentic leader and follower development. *Leadership Quarterly, 16*(3), 343–372.

106. May et al. (2005). Op. cit.; Ilies, R., Morgeson, F. P., & Nahrgang, J. D. (2005). Authentic leadership and eudemonic well-being: Understanding leader-follower outcomes. *Leadership Quarterly, 16*(3), 373–394.

107. Johnson. (2009). Op. cit.

108. Cooper, C. D., Scandura, T. A., & Schriesheim, C. A. (2005). Looking forward but learning from our past: Potential challenges to developing authentic leadership theory and authentic leaders. *Leadership Quarterly, 16*(3), 475–493.

109. Sheilds, C. M. (2003). *Good intentions are not enough: Transformative leadership for communities of difference.* Lanham, MD: Scarecrow Press.

110. Larson, C., & Ovando, C. (2001). *The color of bureaucracy: The politics of equity in multicultural school communities.* Belmont, CA: Wadsworth; McNeil, L. M. (2000). *Contradictions of school reform: Educational costs of standardized testing.* New York: Routledge; Valenzuela, A. (1999). *Subtractive schooling: U.S.-Mexican youth and the politics of caring.* Albany: State University of New York Press.

111. Furman, G. (2003). The 2002 UCDA presidential address: Toward a new scholarship of educational leadership? *UCEA Review, 45*(1), 1–6.

112. For example, Cochran-Smith, M., Albert, L., Dimattia, P., Freedman, S., Jackson, R., Mooney, J., et al. (1999). Seeking social justice: A teacher education faculty's self-study. *International Journal of Leadership in Education: Theory and Practice, 2*(3), 229–253; Grogan, M. (2000). Laying the groundwork for a reconception of the superintendency from feminist postmodern perspectives. *Educational Administration Quarterly, 36*(1), 117–142; Kincheloe, J. L., & Steinberg, S. R. (1995). The more questions we ask, the more questions we ask. In J. L. Kincheloe & S. R. Steinberg (Eds.), *Thirteen questions* (2nd ed., pp. 1–19). New York, NY: Peter Lang; Shields, C., & Oberg, S. (2000). *Year-round schooling: Promises and pitfalls.* Lanham, MD: Scarecrow/Technomics.

113. Alexander, K. L., Entwisle, D. R., & Olsen, L. S. (2001). Schools, achievement and inequality: A seasonal perspective. *Educational Evaluation and Policy Analysis, 23*(2), 171–191; Banks, J. (1997). *Educating citizens in a multicultural society.* New York, NY: Teachers College Press; Delpit, L. (1995). *Other people's children: Cultural conflict in the classroom.* New York, NY: New Press; Jencks, C., & Phillips, M. (1998). *The black-white test score gap.* Washington, DC: Brookings Institution Press; Ortiz, A. A. (1997). Learning disabilities occurring concomitantly with linguistic differences. *Journal of Learning Disabilities, 30*(3), 321–332.

114. Wiener, R., & Pristoop, E. (2006). How states shortchange the districts that need the most help. *The Education Trust, Funding Gaps 2006 Report* (pp. 5–9). Washington, DC: The Education Trust.

115. Hightower, A. M. (2009, January 8). Securing progress, striving to improve. In *Quality Counts 2009. Education Week, 28*(17), 44–47.

116. Verstegen, D. A. (2002, October). The new finance. *American School Board Journal. School Spending. The Business of Education.* Retrieved from http://www.asbj.com/schoolspending/resources1002verstegen.html

117. Burello, L. C., Lashley, C., & Beatty, E. E. (2001). *Educating all students together: How school leaders create unified systems.* Thousand Oaks, CA: Corwin Press; Dantley, M., & Tillman, L. C. (2006). Social justice and moral/transformative leadership. In C. Marshall & M. Oliva (Eds.), *Leadership for social justice: Making it happen* (pp. 16–29). Boston, MA: Allyn & Bacon; Foster, W. (2004). The decline of the local: A challenge to educational leadership. *Educational Administration Quarterly, 40*(2), 176–191; Giroux, H. A. (1997). *Pedagogy for the politics of hope: Theory, culture, and schooling.* Boulder, CO: Westview Press.

118. Brown, K. W. (2004). Leadership for social justice and equity: Weaving a transformative framework and pedagogy. *Educational Administration Quarterly, 40*(1), 77–108.

119. Argyris, C. (1990). *Overcoming organizational defenses: Facilitating organizational learning.* Englewood Cliffs, NJ: Prentice-Hall; Banks, J. (1994). *Multiethnic education: Theory and practice.*

Needham Heights, MA: Allyn & Bacon; Senge, P., Kleiner, A., Roberts, C., Ross, R., & Smith, B. (1994). *The fifth discipline fieldbook: Strategies and tools for building a learning organization.* New York, NY: Doubleday; Wheatley, M. (1992). *Leadership and the new science.* San Francisco, CA: Berrett-Koehler.

120. Smith, G. (2002). Place-based education: Learning to be where we are. *Phi Delta Kappan, 83*(8), 584–594.

121. Johnson. (2009). Op. cit.

122. Johannsen, R. L. (1991). Virtue ethics, character, and political communication. In R. E. Denton (Ed.), *Ethical dimensions of political communication* (pp. 69–90). New York, NY: Praeger.

123. Merriam Webster. (2010). *Integrity.* Retrieved from http://www.merriam-webster.com/netdict/integrity

124. Bruhn, J. G. (2001). *Trust and the health of organizations.* New York, NY: Kluwer/Plenum; Elangovan, A. R., & Shapiro, D. L. (1998). Betrayal of trust in organizations. *Academy of Management Review, 23*(3), 547–566.

125. Peterson, C., & Seligman, M. E. P. (2004). *Character strengths and virtues: A handbook and classification.* Oxford, United Kingdom: Oxford University Press.

126. Morris, J. A., Brotheridge, C. M., & Urbanski, J. C. (2005). Bringing humility to leadership: Antecedents and consequences of leader humility. *Human Relations, 58*(10), 1323–1350; Tangney, J. (2000). Humility: Theoretical perspectives, empirical findings, and directions for future research. *Journal of Social and Clinical Psychology, 19*(1), 70–82.

127. Woodruff, P. (2001). *Reverence: Renewing a forgotten virtue.* Oxford, United Kingdom: Oxford University Press.

128. Carver, C. S., & Scheier, M. R. (2005). Optimism. In C. R. Snyder & S. J. Lopez (Eds.), *Handbook of positive psychology* (pp. 231–243). Oxford, United Kingdom: Oxford University Press.

129. Peterson & Seligman. (2004). Op. cit.

130. Howell, J., & Avolio, B. J. (1992). The ethics of charismatic leadership: Submission or liberation? *Academy of Management Executive, 6*(2), 43–54.

131. Peterson & Seligman. (2004). Op. cit.; Compte-Sponville, A. (2001). *A small treatise on the great virtues: The uses of philosophy in everyday life*. New York, NY: Metropolitan; Smith, T. (1999). Justice as a personal virtue. *Social Theory & Practice, 25*(3), 361–384.

132. Blanchard, K., & Peale, N. V. (1988). *The power of ethical management* (p. 69). New York, NY: Fawcett Crest.

133. MacIntyre, A. (1984). *After virtue: A study in moral theory* (2nd ed.). Notre Dame, IN: University of Notre Dame Press; Hauerwas, S. (1981). *A community of character*. Notre Dame, IN: University of Notre Dame Press.

134. Colby, A., & Damon, W. (1992). *Some do care: Contemporary lives of moral commitment*. New York, NY: Free Press; Colby, A., & Damon, W. (1995). The development of extraordinary moral commitment. In M. Killen & D. Hart (Eds.), *Morality in everyday life: Developmental perspectives* (pp. 342–369). Cambridge, United Kingdom: Cambridge University Press.

135. Colby & Damon. (1992, 1995). Ibid.

CHAPTER

Developing as an Educational Leader

Focus Questions

- In what ways does career development concern one's whole life rather than one's occupation?

- How do Donald Super's "life-span, life-space" perspective and five career stages contribute to understanding career development?

- What is career adaptability, and why is it a central quality of adult development?

- How is the principalship a series of career stages with differing leadership and management tasks in each?

- How can effective mentoring contribute to principal recruitment, socialization, and development?

- What is reflection, and how can aspiring, novice, and mature principals use it to increase their life-span, life-space career awareness and day-to-day decisions?

CASE STUDY: THREE VISITS WITH DR. SOLOMON

Shannon Miller had finished law school, passed the bar exam, and settled into her family's midsized city law firm. Within 6 months, however, she realized that although she loved studying the law, she hated practicing it. She grew discouraged and worried how she would pay back her law school loans if she left her job. How would she tell her family that she did not want to work in the family practice? As she wondered what to do, she remembered her former high school principal, Dr. Solomon, who had mentored her so well through some difficult teen years and had become a family friend.

Dr. Solomon was delighted to hear from Shannon. Seeing each other for the first time since he had handed her a diploma, they sat down together in her high school's faculty dining room to chat. He looked a bit older, but as they talked, his eyes still had an intensity and enthusiasm for life. Shannon told him that she had made a big mistake by going to law school. She went to please her father and grandfather, whom she adored; they had attended the same law school and had made a lucrative living as lawyers. She enjoyed law school; but after 6 months, she realized that looking up cases and preparing contracts for mergers and acquisitions was not what she wanted to do for the rest of her life. Eventually, she would make partner, but she wanted to do something more meaningful.

Dr. Solomon laughed and reminded Shannon that he had told her as a student what a wonderful teacher she would be. Shannon smiled, remembering the conversations. She had never really thought about teaching as a job—it did not pay enough. Besides, she never heard her grandfather or father complain, so being a lawyer must be a good occupation. Lately, all she did was complain.

Offering some perspective, Dr. Solomon reminded Shannon that her grandfather had emigrated to America alone as a 15-year-old and had rented a room from a distant relative. He worked at night to help pay the rent while he completed high school, college, and law school. To him, work was what one did to live, eat, and provide for a family. Work was a job, an occupation. He worked to live. For him, the alternative was to starve. In contrast, her father lived to work and carry on the firm. Her life and times were different, Dr. Solomon explained. She probably wanted a career that might have various jobs with increasingly higher levels of responsibility and social meaning.

Dr. Solomon asked if teaching now made more sense. He explained that a career in education could be a series of related and increasingly responsible jobs—teacher to assistant principal to principal and so on. Shannon decided that she would consider a career in education, but she would not go back to undergraduate school for another 4 years. There had to be some other credible way to get into the classroom. Dr. Solomon helped her *explore* alternative routes into education, and after appropriate preparation, Shannon accepted a job as a high school English teacher.

For 5 years, Shannon *established* herself as an excellent high school English teacher. At that time, she was appointed department chair at her principal's encouragement, and she served as chair for 2 years. Nonetheless, Shannon began to feel restless in her teaching job. She wondered what else she might do. Her principal persuaded her to obtain a degree in educational leadership, promising to hire her as an assistant principal after she successfully completed her program.

It was now the second time to talk with her old friend, Dr. Solomon. Presently, he was the assistant superintendent for instruction in his same district. As he welcomed her into his office, she smiled at the spacious room with wall-to-wall bookcases, a conference area, and an oriental rug decorating the floor. It reminded her of her father's study. They sat around a table at the far end of the office—away from his desk.

Dr. Solomon mentioned that he had been following her career with interest. A friend in Shannon's school district had given him stellar reports about her teaching and her organizational abilities as department chair. He asked to what he owed this second visit.

Shannon referenced their last talk—about education being a career with many jobs. She told her mentor about her principal's suggestion that she get a master's degree in educational leadership and move into administration. She asked him what school administration was like. Dr. Solomon helped her **explore** the field of educational leadership—something he knew and loved well. He mentioned that her first year of high school was his first year as principal. Back then, he said, not everyone had the opportunity to be an assistant principal first. It was a "sink or swim" field—he swam! He told her that he had much anxiety about leaving the classroom. He loved teaching the students, but although he had established himself as an outstanding teacher he felt himself just ***maintaining***—continuing in a holding pattern of teaching students well. He thought about larger opportunities to make a difference one school at a time instead of one classroom at a time.

Shannon understood the mixed emotions about leaving the classroom. Would she leave teaching, where she did a very good job, to oversee books, testing, discipline, and buses? That did not seem like a good trade. She wanted to assist teachers with instructional matters so they could help students learn more effectively. Dr. Solomon responded that she might face the possibility of books, testing, and discipline, but it would be one job in her education career. He felt certain she would get her own school one day and that she would be a terrific principal.

Shannon asked Dr. Solomon why he had left the principalship after so many years. He answered that he realized the principalship today is for a younger person than he. He could not keep up the required pace. Instead, he had to ***separate himself*** from that job and move to something where he could establish himself as one who could help younger principals grow effectively in their jobs. Professionally, he moved from making one school better at a time to making one school district better at a time. Besides, he said, he wasn't getting any younger, and all responsible leaders need a succession plan.

Shannon was perceiving a cycle in employment: exploring possibilities, establishing oneself in a job until further exploration opened up new possibilities, establishing oneself there, and then starting the process again. It was like going up a spiral staircase. When she heard Dr. Solomon mention succession planning, however, she wondered if he were getting ready to step off the stairs altogether.

Shannon earned her master's degree and a doctorate in educational leadership. She spent 3 years as an assistant principal, 7 years as a principal, and the last 7 years as the assistant superintendent for curriculum and instruction for a large school district. Several major school districts were now recruiting her for the superintendent's job. The idea of such a move was intimidating. During her tenure, she had seen two effective superintendents come and go. Again, it was time to talk with her mentor.

This third time, she found Dr. Solomon at home, happily retired and looking older, but his intensity and enthusiasm for life had not changed. She asked if he had ever been recruited for a superintendency. He nodded that he had, several times. She asked why he had not tried it. He told her that he would answer her question but needed some information from her first. Did she want the superintendent's job? Did she have a "fire in her belly" for it? Shannon replied that she had always thought about what he had told her—education was a career with many jobs. Since her first year as a principal, she knew in the back of her mind that she wanted to be a superintendent.

Dr. Solomon smiled and advised her to explore the various offers and, after considering all aspects of the job, take the one that she felt was best. He told her that he never took a superintendency because he loved the principalship and never wanted to leave it. He had many satisfying opportunities to induct and mentor other principals into the role. On the other hand, he knew he eventually had to disengage from his job because he could no longer keep up the hours needed, plus he had outside interests in life that he wished to pursue. In addition, other factors kept him from seeking superintendency. All of his experience had been with one school district. Shannon's experience spanned four districts in three states. He had not been willing to relocate. She was. Dr. Solomon then confided that he had neither the temperament nor the inclination to be a superintendent. He felt confident carrying out someone else's agenda as his own and lacked the assertive self-confidence necessary to lead a school district. Now he had family, friends, and long-delayed hobbies that attracted his interest.

Shannon accepted the superintendent's job and 4 years later, she was appointed the state superintendent of public instruction. When Dr. Solomon learned of her appointment, he smiled broadly and went hiking with his granddaughter.

Case Study Questions

1. Have you ever wondered if you made a career mistake? What was it? How did you resolve that concern?
2. How did you explore the field of education before you decided to become a teacher? How did you explore the area of school leadership?
3. Does work have a different meaning to your generation than it did to your parents' generation? How?
4. As a teacher, did anyone in your school's administration encourage you to consider a position in educational leadership? What impact did that advice have on you? If no one ever encouraged you, how did that shape your decision?

5. What did Dr. Solomon mean when he said that education is a career that might have different jobs with increasingly higher levels of responsibility and social meaning?
6. Are you willing to change school districts or relocate to another region or state in order to move up into administration?
7. Dr. Solomon mentioned that he had to disengage from the principalship. How did he make that stage one of disengagement rather than disenchantment?
8. Is there someone you consider to be a mentor? What were the most meaningful aspects of that relationship? Have you started to mentor anyone?

INTRODUCTION

Work holds an important place in human behavior. Today, individuals in our society possess a degree of choice about how they will spend their time. Having a variety of occupations from which to choose and the right to decide what kind of work one will do, for whom, and when are among our culture's most highly prized freedoms.

Involvement in meaningful work—along with loving relationships—is the agent for transforming us from immaturity to maturity. Work provides a major connection to reality. Economically, work supplies the wages to provide for ourselves and our families. Through purchases and taxes, work links us to the larger community and nation. Work has a social reality, defining a person's identity and community status. An occupation is the bridge that takes us from our families to the outside world—and that shapes actions within the family. Achieving important goals on the job brings deep satisfaction and justification for our lives.

Nevertheless, the nature of work is changing. Indicators since 2000 reveal high levels of global unemployment. Corporate downsizing and jobless recoveries are commonplace. Adults are forced to recognize that although they have a job today, they may be unemployed tomorrow. Contemporary workers struggle to balance their various life role commitments as the number of work hours increase. Career paths are becoming ambiguous, and adults are anxious about how work fits within their holistic life design.[1]

Planning a career's development in a rapidly changing society can be a complicated process. Individual, contextual, economic, and social factors interact. Over the life span, persons develop themselves by interacting and integrating the roles, settings, and events in their lives.[2] Gender, ethnic origin, religion, and race also influence life roles, life settings, and life events. Accordingly, persons in education careers continue to learn and take on new roles and responsibilities, all affected by factors inside and outside the individual. When they perceive career as a lifelong process, individuals can use a career development lens to describe and understand their own work history and cultivate their ability to plan their future integration of life and work.

SCHOOL LEADERSHIP AND CAREER THEORY

Organizational behavior professors Donald Wolfe and David Kolb concluded, "Career development involves one's whole life, not just occupation. It concerns the person's needs and wants, capacities and potentials, excitements and anxieties, insights and blind spots. . . ."[3] Careers unfold and evolve every day.

Work remains a central experience for most people. What one does for a living is a key way people define their place in their community and the world.. Our choice of work tends to color the perceptual lens through which we see events and how others view us. Work identifies a person more clearly than any other single characteristic.

Yet contemporary workers cope with a different set of career development tasks than did their earlier counterparts. For example, Maccoby and Terzi (1981) predicted that adults in contemporary society would focus more on achieving personal and professional growth than being solely focused on occupational success. They described this emerging approach to work as a "self-fulfillment ethic." Those following this ethic seek work that is not so consuming that it denies opportunities for involvement in family, community, leisure, and other life roles. Rather than "living to work," many adults are more interested in "working to live." Today's workers now must assume the primary responsibility for creating the lives they live.[4]

Given the changing nature of work in our culture and the complex responsibilities that educators assume, gaining a better perspective on how careers develop over time can provide opportunities for making decisions that offer individuals more satisfying work experiences and more personally meaningful adult lifestyles.

Defining Work, Jobs, and Careers

Work can be defined broadly to encompass human activity that is initiated "for individual success and satisfaction, to express achievement strivings, to earn a living . . . to further ambitions and self-assertions . . . and to link individuals to a larger social good."[5] Work's definition depends on time, place, and culture.

Jobs and careers are both alike and different. While each involves labor, a *job* tends to be a set of specific tasks that a person carries out to accomplish a certain goal. A job may or may not be satisfying. A *career*, in contrast, is a chosen pursuit or profession, usually a progression of one's working life or professional achievements. Increasingly, however, a career is a lifestyle that includes a variety of life roles, not merely occupational roles.[6] Careers provide satisfaction and allow financial and personal advancement, generally complementing and interacting with other major life roles. A job does not include a career, whereas a career usually includes many jobs.

Career development has been described as "the unfolding of capabilities and requirements in the course of a person's interaction with environments of various kinds (home, school, play, work) across the life span."[7] Career development in education and elsewhere involves movement among positions, status levels, offices, and responsibilities. This progress has at least three characteristics: sequence, direction, and timing.[8] *Career sequence* involves the orderly, hierarchical sequence of offices, where the individual moves from lower, less important, and lower paid positions to higher positions. *Direction* traditionally meant hierarchical vertical movement up a career ladder or horizontal movement and change in function. As individuals move horizontally from department to department, they gain breadth of experience that is useful in moving to higher level positions. Today, career direction identifies vertical, horizontal, and radial movement.[9] *Vertical movement* refers to the traditional hierarchical view of movement up organizational or occupational ranks: an assistant principal is promoted to principal. *Horizontal movement* refers to the transition among functional areas or divisions, such as a principal moving from one school to another or a school counselor becoming an assistant principal. *Radial movement* refers to progression toward or away from the organization's central power structure, such as a principal taking a position in the central office, or a central office supervisor becoming a principal.

Timing refers to the formal procedures that specify when movement within the occupation or organization can occur. The organization's and individual's informal expectations about the appropriate lengths of time in positions or appropriate levels of experience necessary before moving to the next position are equally important.[10] For instance, some school districts may believe that 2 years as an assistant principal is sufficient preparation for the principalship whereas other districts expect assistant principals to spend 5 or more years in that role before becoming eligible to move into their own school. Time in educational careers is also influenced by job market and organizational change, the degree to which seniority is used to determine promotion, and family and life stage development issues.

Career stages provide a conceptual framework based on the belief that people progress through a series of distinct occupational stages during their careers, and that each stage is characterized by differences in work attitudes and behaviors, types of relationships needed, and aspects of work that are valued. People at the same career stage attempt to satisfy their work-related needs in similar ways. Career stages assume that employees and managers are likely to have different intentions, technical competencies, and dilemmas at various points in their professional cycles; and their desires to reach out for more information, knowledge, and expertise will vary accordingly.

The Changing Nature of Work and Career

Over the past century, the concept of work and career has evolved. Traditionally, careers were thought to progress in linear career sequence within the context of one or two firms. Success was defined by the organization and measured in promotions and salary increases. In contrast, by 2000, most Americans changed jobs every 4.5 years.[11] Similarly, the trend in corporate restructuring and downsizing since the 1990s (arguably to permit rapid flexibility in the face of accelerated environmental and technological change and global competition) has accelerated job losses for managers, older workers, and the more educated. Those surviving these cuts have increased job responsibilities and longer working hours plus reduced promotion opportunities. As a consequence, the psychological contract between firms and workers has altered; employees no longer exchange company loyalty for job security. Both employer-employee loyalty and job security have become problematic.[12]

Consequently, this heightened career variability has led to a change in the role work plays in people's lives. In the past, people took a significant part of their identity from their work. To their community and friends, they were farmers, shopkeepers, doctors, homemakers, or teachers. Previously, our culture's view of work's centrality in forming a person's identity reduced the ways in which nonwork life roles could contribute to self-worth and self-efficacy. Still, as contemporary workers experience periods of unemployment or lack of advancement, they face enhanced difficulty in linking work with self-worth.[13]

In response, a *self-fulfillment ethic*, which suggests that people will search for life satisfaction and self-expression in multiple life roles, has gained acceptance. As more workers focus on working to live rather than living to work, the question becomes: What is one working to live for? What other life role commitments influence one's goals that might be met through work or nonwork activities? The importance of clarifying the values one hopes to express in life roles comprising one's life structure becomes a career issue.

Also new is the view of work as an expression of self-concept. The idea that people seek out occupations that are consistent with their inner values, interests, and abilities represents one of the few areas of consensus among scholars from diverse perspectives.[14] This view reflects a radical departure from historical realities. Usually, jobs were about survival: the primary means to provide self and family with basic food and shelter. Nonetheless, as work tasks expanded and machines reduced the need for manual labor in many industries, a small minority of the human population developed vocational lives that allowed for meaningful self-expression that meshed with their interests and abilities. In truth, however, most people in the world today participate in work that is often not intrinsically interesting and may even harm their self-concepts and physical well-being.[15]

In short, the shifting nature of work points to career development as an evolutionary process: dynamic, interactive, contextual, and relational.[16] Today's workers need at least basic competence in computer skills, interpersonal skills, and lifelong learning skills. Workers must continually invest in sustaining and even upgrading their marketability. These are different competencies than those needed several decades ago. Likewise, today's careers cannot be set on "autopilot," expecting the organization to keep workers productive and employed. Instead, employees now are responsible for developing, directing, and managing their own careers as it best fits their work and economic situations, their expertise, and their priorities. Some analyses strongly encourage people to prepare themselves for change by being personally flexible, by anticipating emerging trends, and by transforming their skills and attitudes to accommodate such occupational swings.[17] Today's employees must understand the forces that are shaping the nature of work in contemporary society.

More than ever, knowledge is power. Because of the dynamic quality of work and work organizations, persons will likely engage in seven or more jobs over their work lives. This may require frequent retraining within a context of lifelong learning to manage their own career development. As shown in Table 12–1, individuals following these contemporary career patterns will require portable skills, knowledge, and abilities across multiple firms; personal identification with meaningful work; on-the-job action learning; the development of multiple networks and peer learning relationships; and individual responsibility for career management.

Clearly, coping effectively with the contemporary career milieu requires workers to develop career adaptability. Adaptability refers to "the quality of being able to change, without great difficulty, to fit new or altered circumstances."[18] The adaptability construct reflects the interplay between person and environment within the career development process across the life span. Given the rate of change occurring in the world of work and the varied demands that workers experience, conceptualizing career development from an adaptability perspective seems reasonable. As a result, career choice and development have become synonymous with human growth and development.

TABLE 12–1

Comparison of Traditional and Contemporary Career Patterns

	Traditional	Contemporary
Employment relationship:	Job security in exchange for loyalty	Employability for performance and flexibility; less job security or loyalty
Boundaries:	One or two firms	Multiple firms
Skills:	Firm specific	Transferable; continually upgraded
Responsibility for career management:	Organization	Individual
Training:	Formal programs	On-the-job, frequent retraining
Milestones:	Age-related	Learning-related
Importance of nonwork roles:	Less important	More important
Role of self-concept in career choice:	Not relevant	Very relevant

Source: Adapted from Sullivan, S. E., "The changing nature of careers: A review and research agenda," *Journal of Management, 25*(3), 457–484, p. 458, copyright © 1999. Reprinted by Permission of Sage Publications.

Finally, any discussion of contemporary career change warrants a special caution: Widespread agreement exists that the career development literature has focused almost exclusively on the White, Western, able-bodied, middle-class male. Until recently, none of the career development theories sufficiently addressed gender,[19] ethnicity, race, socioeconomic status, disability, or gender identity.[20] Additionally, some cultures view the idea of the individual who works autonomously and behaves competitively in the world of work as inconsistent with their society's collectivist norms.[21] Although it is beyond this chapter's scope to explore career development in varied American or international subpopulations, these important limitations must be noted when discussing career development theories.

ACTIVITY 12.1   The Changing Nature of Work and Careers

Case Study Question 3: Does work have a different meaning to your generation than it did to your parents' generation? How?

The nature of careers has changed significantly over the past decades. Differences now exist regarding the employment relationship (exchanging company loyalty for job security), the number of expected jobs and careers over a work life, responsibility for career advancement, need for ongoing learning, career milestones, and the importance of nonwork roles and self-concept in careers. Discuss as a class:

1. In what ways does work have a different meaning to your generation than it did to your parents' generation? How might these contrasting career expectations and experiences make it difficult to have "career advice" conversations with parents, older friends, and relatives?
2. What are the contemporary realities with which today's young adults must contend when selecting and planning their careers?
3. What are the advantages and disadvantages for young adults of today's career realities?

Donald Super's Career Development Theory

Donald E. Super, professor emeritus of psychology and education at Teachers College, Columbia University, has been one of the world's leading career development experts, formulating an innovative and comprehensive theory, testing it systematically, and using the investigations' results to design effective interventions.[22] Moving away from the psychology of occupations, which concentrated on fitting individuals into jobs, Super shifted thinking toward the psychology of careers, which focused on fitting work into individuals' lives. Additionally, Super recognized the need to incorporate interdisciplinary insights of sociologists, political scientists, and economists into discussions of career behavior to complement those of psychologists. These multiple perspectives provided awareness into career development complexities and variations across genders, socioeconomic classes, and cultures.[23] Evolving over 50 years, Super's life-span, life-space theory of careers elaborated career development theory to address more completely the intricacies of vocational behavior in varied settings and populations.

Key Contributions to Understanding Careers.   Super believed in the centrality of self-concept and self-awareness in occupational choice and career exploration. He proposed that finding a career in the postmodern era was more than matching people to jobs; rather, career development was a subjective and objective experience.

Occupational choice, in Super's view, was "an unfolding process, not a point-in-time event."[24] He proposed that individuals expand their vocational coping perspective and move into positions that provide better opportunities to use their abilities and gratify their needs.[25] From this insight, Super (1990) formulated his life-span, life-space model, which conceptually explained and operationally defined the developmental tasks and coping behaviors that fostered occupational choice and work adjustment.[26] His life-span, life-space approach to career development advanced the notion that the work role is not the only role to which career scholars, counselors, or individuals should attend. Rather, persons lived in multiple-role environments in which work roles, family roles, educational roles, and community roles varied in their demands on and importance for different persons and within different developmental periods. With this life-span, life-space perspective, career development moved beyond an event that occured in late adolescence to a lifelong process consisting of multiple transitions; shifting needs for information; and reassessment of roles, commitments, and identity as new dilemmas and questions appeared. Super's work refocused career development from what was chosen to who was doing the choosing.

Ten Propositions of Career Development.   Super stated his initial career development theory in the form of 10 propositions (which expressed the best of 1953 knowledge). Although occasionally revised, these postulates remain a useful and influential set of summary statements:[27]

◆ People differ in their abilities, interests, and personalities.
◆ These characteristics qualify them for a number of occupations.
◆ Each of these occupations requires a characteristic pattern of abilities, interests, and personality traits, with tolerances wide enough to allow some variety of occupations for each individual and some variety of individuals for each occupation.

◆ Vocational preferences and competencies, situations in which people live and work, and their self-concepts change with time and experience (although self-concepts are generally fairly stable from late adolescence until late maturity). This makes vocational choice and adjustment a continuous process.

◆ This process may be viewed as a series of life stages characterized as growth, exploration, establishment, maintenance, and disengagement. Each stage includes fantasy, tentative, and realistic phases of the exploration stage and trial and stable phases of the establishment stage.

◆ The individual's career pattern—the occupational level attained and the sequence, frequency, and duration of trial and stable jobs—is determined by the individual's parental socioeconomic level, mental ability, and personality characteristics, and by the opportunities available.

◆ Development through life stages can be guided, partly by facilitating the process of maturing abilities and interests and partly by helping in reality testing and in the development of a self-concept.

◆ The process of vocational development is essentially that of developing and implementing a self-concept. It is a compromise process in which the self-concept is a product of the interaction of inherited aptitudes, neural and endocrine makeup, opportunity to play various roles, and evaluations of the extent to which the results of role playing meet with the approval of superiors and colleagues.

◆ The process of compromise between individual and social factors, between self-concept and reality, is one of role playing, whether the role is played in fantasy, in counseling, or in real-life activities such as school classes, clubs, part-time work, and entry jobs.

◆ Work satisfactions and life satisfactions depend upon the extent to which the individual finds adequate outlets for his or her abilities, interests, personality traits, and values. They depend upon establishment in a work role that personal growth and exploratory experiences have led the individual to consider congenial and appropriate.

Super's propositions stress individuality, multipotentiality, and continuous adjustment. Individuals differ, and these variations in abilities, interest, and personalities make them eligible for many occupations. As people gain experiences in life and work, their view of themselves—their self-concept (the result of interactions among a person's genetic influences of physical, cognitive, and psychological factors in combination with environmental variables such as socioeconomic conditions and life experiences)—evolves, becoming relatively stable from late adolescence until later adulthood. People with accurate information about themselves and the world are more likely to make sound vocational decisions. As a result, occupational choice and adjustment are continuous processes. In addition, people experience careers in stages guided by their maturing interests and abilities as well as the reality testing of placing themselves into actual work roles and "testing" for goodness of fit between the work and themselves.

Updating and Expanding Super's Theory.   Super recognized that no theory in itself is enough to address the complexity of career development; contributions from others would be expected.[28] To this end, Mark L. Savickas, professor of behavioral sciences at Northeastern

Ohio University, has updated and advanced Super's career development ideas to make them more relevant to 21st-century adult careers:[29]

◆ Although vocational self-concepts become increasingly stable from late adolescence forward, providing some continuity in choice and adjustment, self-concepts and vocational preferences do change with time and experience as the situation in which people live and work changes.

◆ A minicycle of growth, exploration, establishment, management, and disengagement occurs during transitions from one career stage to the next as well as each time an individual's career is destabilized by socioeconomic and personal events such as illness and injury, plant closings and company layoffs, and job redesign and automation.

◆ Career adaptability is a psychosocial construct that denotes an individual's readiness and resources for coping with current and anticipated vocational development tasks. The adaptive fitness of attitudes, beliefs, and competencies increases along the developmental lines of concern, control, conception, and confidence.

◆ Career construction—creating meaning for one's career and life experiences—is prompted by developmental tasks, occupational transitions, and personal traumas and then produced by responses to these life changes.

Adopting a constructivist frame, Savickas has argued that careers do not "unfold"; rather, individuals "construct careers" by imposing meaning on vocational behaviors and experiences through choices that express their self-concepts and socially validate their goals in their work roles. In this context, career denotes an active process of meaning-making that imposes personal sense on past memories, present experiences, and future aspirations by weaving them into a life theme that patterns the individual's work life. Individuals use career and life roles to become who they are and live the lives they have imagined. Career adaptability and career construction, therefore, are essential to career satisfaction and effectiveness.

ACTIVITY 12.2 Understanding Your Own Occupational Choice as an Unfolding Process

Super's life-span, life-space model of careers seeks to fit work into individuals' lives. Occupational choice is an unfolding process, not a one-time event. His 10 propositions stress individuality, multipotentiality, and continuous adjustment.

1. Consider each of Super's 10 propositions of career development and identify how each one is true, or not true, of your own career experiences. Discuss your findings with a partner.
2. In what ways are self-concept and self-awareness such important players in your own career development?
3. Using Savickas's constructivist approach to updating Super's theory, identify and discuss with a partner the idea that individuals "construct their careers" and also address how this concept is true, or not true, for you.
4. How are the concepts of career adaptability and career construction essential elements to career satisfaction and effectiveness? How is this true for you or for others you know or have observed?

Stages of Career Development.   Career development is a process that continues throughout a person's life span in which the individual successively faces certain vocational developmental tasks. As depicted in Figure 12–1 and discussed in the following list, Super presented five vocational development stages: growth, exploration, establishment, maintenance, and disengagement.[30] These stages correspond with the life stages of childhood, adolescence, adulthood, middle adulthood, and later adulthood/old age and their approximate ages. Each life stage is named to reflect the nature of its major life stage task. Success in mastering tasks at one stage results in both effective functioning within that stage and preparation to address the tasks of later stages.

Updated from his original linear developmental model, Super's (1980, 1990, 1992) flexible conceptual framework accounts for the fluidity of career experiences across life roles.[31] Similarly, the ages and sequence at which people encounter each life stage's tasks vary, depending on individual biosocial development and life situations. For instance, some people will cope successfully with exploratory tasks and enter the establishment stage in their early 20s, some will continue to explore indefinitely, and others will return to exploratory tasks in their 30s or 40s in order to enter a different type of work.

◆ *Growth stage.* This is the life period (ages 4–13) when children and preadolescents explore the world around them, attend school, learn about vocations, and develop the adaptive work habits, attitudes, and positive self-esteem that give them more control over their lives and help them become future oriented. Childhood and parental influence lay the foundation for career attitudes, directions, and choices. Young people begin to develop interests and awareness of their abilities. Fantasy and play help them develop concepts of themselves in adult roles.

◆ *Exploration stage.* This is the stage from approximately ages 14–24 in which the person chooses an occupation and tries on several jobs for fit. The exploration stage has three career development tasks:[32]

  ◆ *Crystallization (ages 14–18).* The young person becomes aware of the need to make a vocational decision; accumulates data about a potential career field through classes, experiences, and hobbies; is aware of factors to consider; uses resources; identifies own interests and values; formulates a generalized but tentative career preference; and begins planning for it.

  ◆ *Specification (ages 18–21).* The young person actually selects a specific career field.

  ◆ *Implementation (ages 21–24).* The young adult trains for the selected career field and begins employment.

◆ *Establishment stage.* At approximately age 25, the individual starts to settle into a permanent job and enters the establishment stage. During this stage, the individual stabilizes, consolidates, and advances in a meaningful occupational position.

  ◆ *Stabilizing in a job (ages 25–35).* The individual becomes qualified for a stable regular job and obtains one. The individual must adapt to the organization's or profession's culture and perform the job adequately. The individual uses his or her talents in ways that demonstrate the career decision's appropriateness, occasionally changing position but rarely changing vocation.

  ◆ *Consolidating one's position in an organization (ages 35–45).* The person becomes aware of the need to become secure in one's profession and to move ahead. The worker firmly establishes him- or herself, refining and growing skills, and establishing seniority.

◆ *Advancing in a career.* Some individuals may also choose the task of advancement or promotion and seek higher levels of responsibility. In contrast, individuals may evaluate their occupation and decide to change organizations or occupations. If so, the person then recycles through the exploration and establishment stages in a minicycle. Alternatively, many workers omit the advancement task and stay in the same position the remainder of their careers.

◆ *Maintenance.* This stage (ages 45–65) is characterized by "preserving the space one has made in the world of work." Those who do not change careers or advance to roles of additional responsibility enter the maintenance stage. The tasks of this stage include holding on, keeping up (maintenance), and innovating (renewal).

◆ *Disengagement.* This is the stage (approximately ages 65 and older) in which older workers recognize that they must eventually separate themselves from their jobs by reducing their pace or workload, planning for retirement, and enjoying retirement living.

According to Super's career stages, the individual moves through life stages, each of which calls for different sorts of vocational behavior. Adolescents are essentially explorers seeking and finding a vocational direction. Young adults must translate their chosen direction into action for training, education, and job seeking. More mature adults must find their places within their vocations, and then elaborate upon them to secure or advance their position—or change organizations or occupations. Eventually, individuals will begin to separate themselves from their work by eschewing advancement or disengaging. During each phase of career development, certain behaviors are more likely to result in personal and professional growth than others. The degree to which individuals accomplish their vocational tasks depends on the adequacy with which they have performed behaviors appropriate to each developmental stage.

It is important to remember that the ages of transitions between Super's stages are flexible; individuals may recycle through stages, referred to as minicycles. This could occur as a result of a planned or unplanned change. For instance, individuals can expect to change jobs several times during their working life and can also expect to recycle through the stages several times. This conception of multiple jobs over a career and recycling through previous developmental stages makes this model relevant to today's world.

Additionally, Super acknowledged that the work role may be only one of a number of roles an individual holds at any one time. Roles interact with each other and provide each individual's life with a focus. The simultaneous combination of life roles makes up the lifestyle; their sequence and combination structures the life space and makes up the life cycle. The total structure is the career pattern. In an update of his theory, Super (1987, 1992) detailed how individuals differ in the amount of commitment and participation they devote to seven major roles—child, student, leisureite, citizen, worker, homemaker, retiree—across the career stages.[33] Choices regarding commitment to these roles cause various levels of role conflict, stress, and self-fulfillment.

Figure 12–1 demonstrates the relationships between the work role and other life roles. Arrows point to the approximate age when the role begins; it continues for more years, overlapping with many other roles. The roles interact. Role conflict may occur, however, when a less satisfying role takes time away from a more satisfying role. In contrast, roles may compensate; satisfaction not found in one role may be provided in another. Understanding the meaning and place of work in people's lives depends on its relationship to other roles.

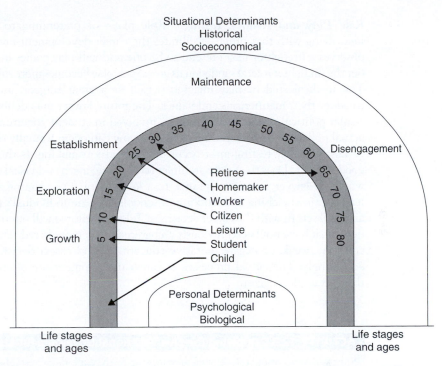

FIGURE 12–1

Super's Life-Stage, Life-Task Model and Where Each Life Role Begins (Source: Adapted from Patton, W., & McMahon, M. (2006). *Career development systems theory: Connecting theory and practice* (p. 59). Rotterdam, Netherlands: Sense Publishers.) Reprinted with permission.

Career Development and Self-Concept.   In essence, the vocational development process is one of developing and implementing a self-concept. As adults, work satisfactions occur when individuals can find sufficient expression of their abilities, interests, personality, and values; their establishment in a type of work; and a work role that they feel is suitable and agreeable.

A well-integrated individual's self-concept continually develops, shifting somewhat through life as it reconciles with experiences and reality. As individuals mature, they test themselves in many ways. The process begins as young children separate themselves from their parents and begin the search for their own identity. For instance, a toddler touches a hot stove and notices that she—not her mother—hurts. An adolescent notices the differences between self and others, becoming aware of being sociable or reserved, a strong or indifferent student, musically talented or tone deaf. An adult worker with many good ideas for product, service, or organizational improvement becomes frustrated working for supervisors who have less vision and resourcefulness than the employee, so the individual decides to look for occasions to take on more leadership responsibilities. These new functions and roles may require additional study, formal coursework, attending conferences, mentoring and coaching, and accepting increased duties and accountability within one's present role. Recognizing friction between self-concept and actual work-life experiences leads to decisions about education and work that are consistent with self-concept—or to adjustments in self-concept.

Role Play and Reality Testing. Role play—or pretending to be someone else by identifying with that other—facilitates the career development process. The youth who observes a firefighter may pretend to be one and will play games in which he or she acts out the firefighter role. As individuals grow, such play becomes more subtle and sophisticated. The medical student may imagine herself as a great surgeon and observe physicians to adopt their mannerisms and values. The future lawyer may deliberately seek extracurricular political activities and become involved in student government, debate teams, or actual political campaigns. Similar role playing can occur formally or informally.

Lastly, reality testing must occur before decision making. Is the aspiring physician a good student? Does the future architect have strong math and visual-spatial skills? Can the would-be lawyer secure acceptance to a law school? Does the prospective instructional leader enjoy teaching and working in schools? Do the individual's priorities, aspirations, and skill sets fit with the career decisions? Talents explored will often lead to talents in new fields that have not been previously recognized or even predicted. These reality factors will confirm, tweak, or negate tentative educational and career decisions and modify them accordingly. The actual processes of career development are often more complex than these examples suggest.

ACTIVITY 12.3 Applying the Five Vocational Development Stages

Super's five vocational development stages—growth, exploratory, establishment, maintenance, disengagement—are not necessarily linear stages in which success or mastery of tasks at one stage results in both effective functioning in that stage and preparation for later stages. Flexibility at transition points is key to satisfying work and life outcomes.

1. Describe the varied influences of Shannon's growth and exploratory stages that influenced her decision to become a lawyer.
2. Describe how Shannon's experiences during the establishment stage made her question and rethink her choice of professions.
3. How did Shannon's decision to enter the education profession require her to recycle through the exploratory stages of crystallization, specification, and implementation?
4. What role did Shannon's self-concept play in her career choices and career satisfactions?
5. Explain the factors that led Shannon and Dr. Solomon to make different decisions during their establishment and maintenance career stages.
6. Given the information presented in the case study, what life roles does Shannon enact? What life roles does Dr. Solomon enact? How do their life roles affect their career decisions?
7. Considering Shannon's present career stage, what are the next sets of career decisions she faces?
8. **Case Study Question 1:** Have you ever wondered if you made a career mistake? What was it? How did you resolve that concern? Use the career stages information to describe how you came to choose that occupation and explain how you resolved (or plan to resolve) it.
9. **Case Study Question 2:** How did you explore the field of education before you decided to become a teacher? How did you explore the area of school leadership?
10. **Case Study Question 5:** What did Dr. Solomon mean by education is a career that might have different jobs with increasingly higher levels of responsibility and social meaning? Use the career stages framework to explain his answer.

Adult Career Development

Although career development is a continuous process extending into midlife, attention to adult career development is relatively recent in origin. Until the late 20th century, most career theory focused on life's first two decades, not the last five.[34] As discussed, Super's theory of career stages uses a life-span approach to describe how individuals implement their self-concept through vocational choices. His maintenance and disengagement stages describe mid- and late-adult career development.

Mills (1970) expanded Super's career theory by proposing three specific tasks for adult career development: (a) the need to set one's own milestones; (b) the need to reassert control over one's self-development; and (c) the need to make adjustments to growing physical, family, and time limitations. During one's midyears, institutions no longer provide clear guidelines of progress or unmistakable markers for transition points as those provided in early years by such public events as graduation ceremonies, becoming eligible to vote, enlisting in the military services, or buying alcohol. Also, many adults feel an increased desire for taking stock of their progress and reasserting control of their future rather than passively following an earlier plan. In addition, adults experience challenges in self-acceptance as their energies fade, their relationships with family change (as children leave home, parents become grandparents, or they become caregivers for aging parents), and they realize as retirement nears that they will have fewer opportunities to accomplish their professional goals.[35]

With career paths more fluid, individual learning and skill development are essential to successfully navigate today's life and work experiences. Individuals of different ages, genders, cultures, and vocational fields will follow differing career patterns. This presents both individuals and organizations with many challenges.

Career Maturity/Adaptability.   In our present culture, a career is not a lifetime commitment to selling one's services and skills to one or two employers. Careers are mobile rather than stable, reflecting a postindustrial society's labor needs. Originally conceived as the readiness to make educational and vocational choices, career maturity has come to be generalized as adaptability across the complete life span,[36] suggesting a readiness to deal with the career development tasks appropriate to an individual's life stage, at whatever age they occur.

Super and Knasel (1981) identified adaptation as adults' central developmental process.[37] *Adaptability* means being able to change without great difficulty to fit new or changed circumstances. Especially today, individuals continually need to respond to new conditions and novel situations rather than to master a predictable linear continuum of developmental tasks. *Career adaptability* is "the individual's readiness and resources for coping with current and imminent vocational development tasks, occupational transitions, and personal traumas."[38] Career adaptability, therefore, applies to and integrates both work and life.

As a construct, adaptability uses a single idea to elegantly explain development in children, adolescents, and adults. The individual has a single motive—to adapt to one's life, one's environment, and one's self. Regardless of one's age, adaptability involves planful attitudes, self- and environmental exploration, and informed decision making. The term *adaptability* also lacks the evaluative connotations that the term *maturity* suggests.

The five principle career stages—growth, exploration, establishment, maintenance, and disengagement—compose a minicycle around each of the many transitions from school to work, from job to job, and from occupation to occupation. As each transition approaches, individuals can adapt more effectively if they meet the challenge with growing interest, focused exploration, informed decision making, trial behaviors followed by a commitment projected forward for a certain time period, active role management, and the ability to constructively anticipate slowing down and disengaging from full-time employment.

Clarifying Values.   Throughout life, clarifying one's values is an essential part of the career decision-making process. People's values—such as using one's ability, achievement, advancement, aesthetics, altruism, autonomy, creativity, cultural identity, economic rewards, economic security, prestige, risk, social interaction, variety, working conditions, personal development, and lifestyle[39]—indicate the qualities individuals seek in the "activities in which they engage, in the situations in which they live, and in the objects which they make or acquire."[40] Clarifying one's highest and lowest values can guide in-depth occupational exploration and consider whether specific career and lifestyle alternatives will satisfy individuals' high values and avoid low ones. Because values reflect the individual's goals, they offer a sense of purpose and direction in the career planning process. Although this process takes time and reflection, relatively few invest the effort to examine their values in a systematic way.[41]

Career Salience.   Super came to believe that life in the information age could not be grounded in occupational roles. Instead, he proposed shifting focus away from work roles and concentrating on the variety of life roles enacted at home, at work, and at leisure.

Super's (1982) construct of *career salience* means the importance of the work role relative to other life roles.[42] Different people hold varying ideas about the role of work and career in their lives. When salience for the work role is high, individuals see work as providing meaningful opportunities for self-expression. In these cases, people are motivated to engage in behaviors necessary for making good career decisions—they become planful, explore opportunities, and gather information. In contrast, when work role salience is low, individuals often lack motivation and career adaptability. Usually two or three core roles hold a central place and give life focus while other roles are either peripheral or absent. People's awareness of how important their career roles are to them will influence their ability to fit their lives into occupations and, at the same time, fit work into their lives.

Asking and answering clarifying questions can help individuals determine whether their career salience—the importance of work in their lives—is relatively higher or lower. These queries include: What are the life roles most and least important to me? What changes would I like to make in how I spend my time? What do I like about participating in each life role? What do I hope to accomplish in each life role? What life roles will be important to me in the future? And, what must I do to become more prepared for the life roles that will be important to me in the future?[43]

Answering these questions helps people explain and articulate their life role self-concepts. Discussing these questions makes clearer the way people want to express their values in each life role, and helps develop appropriate career options and expectations for values satisfaction within each. It also considers the person's family expectations and other cultural factors influencing their life role participation and helps identify potential barriers and supports for career transitions. By clarifying information concerning life role salience and those personal and cultural factors influencing it, people establish the foundation for making accurate self-evaluations and developing career adaptability.

Notably, career role salience becomes a critical factor for adults dissatisfied with their present career position. For example, identifying and understanding adults' varied life roles and the relative values and weights placed on each can have an impact on whether they seek career advancement, increased responsibilities, and expanded influence in their present or an alternative career field; whether they continue in their present role; or whether they give up certain career responsibilities to permit more time and energy for other life roles that they value more highly than their salaried employment.

Career Satisfaction.   Super used the construct of career satisfaction to distinguish attitudes toward the current job from attitudes toward career progress. A person might detest his or her current job, but if it is perceived as a stepping stone to a desired position, then the person can still experience high career satisfaction. This distinction is clearly evident in graduate students or assistant principals who may dislike their current position but feel very pleased about where it is taking them professionally.

Planfulness and future orientation are important in preparing for success and satisfaction in all life roles. Since not all of life's gratification comes from work, an individual's abilities, values, and interests can be implemented through many social roles in addition to the work role. Career satisfaction comes from feeling good about one's life in a variety of life roles.

Evaluating Super's Contributions

Super's theory is a well-ordered, highly systematic representation of the vocational maturation process that builds upon mainstream developmental psychology and personality theory to clarify behavior in a major realm of human activity. Refined in later versions, his theory continues to have considerable usefulness for practice and study. Most of the research generally supports his model, although some discussion exists about the specific timing of developmental tasks and the names assigned to different stages. Scholars noted—as did Super in later writings—that career development is not always linear or gain oriented.[44]

Although Super's ideas continued to evolve, critics have pointed to weaknesses in his concepts. Savickas (2001) argued that Super's original career development stages reflected traditional and outdated constructs and career patterns. It focused insufficient attention on adult and life-span career development. It made the maintenance stage look like holding on rather than a time for growth. Identity, self-concept, and coping mechanisms are better developmental indicators than age or physical maturation, and development includes losses as well as gains. Other critics contended that Super's theory ignored the learning and decision-making processes that fostered development; it reflected Western Christian values and middle-class attitudes without knowledge of cultural, gender, racial/ethnic, and personal diversity; and it disregarded advances in developmental psychology.[45] Additionally, today's psychology focuses less on maturity and more on adaptation, less on unfolding and more on interaction, and less on universal principles and more on contextual particulars.[46] More research and theory refinement are needed to include economic and social factors that may influence career decisions.[47]

Super's ideas evolved during his five-decades career. They remain relevant to career development today, both in the United States and internationally.[48]

ACTIVITY 12.4   Understanding and Applying the Adaptability and Career Salience Concepts

Adaptability has been identified as the central developmental process of adults: the quality of being able to change without great difficulty to fit new or changed circumstances. Adaptability involves planful attitudes, self- and environmental exploration, and informed decision making. Career salience is the importance of work role in relation to other life roles. Clarifying one's values is an important part of making wise and satisfying life and career choices. Discuss as a class:

1. How did adaptability and career salience influence Dr. Solomon's decision about accepting a superintendency? How did they influence Shannon's decision to not continue practicing law?
2. **Case Study Question 6:** Are you willing to change school districts or relocate to another region or state in order to move up into administration? How would you describe your degree of adaptability in your life and in your career?
3. Ask yourself the following career salience questions and share your answers with a partner:
   ◆ What are the life roles most—and least—important to me?
   ◆ What do I like most about participating in each life role?
   ◆ What changes would I like to make in how I spend my time?
   ◆ What life roles will be important to me in the future?
   ◆ What must I do to become better prepared for future life roles?
   ◆ In what combination of life roles do I expect to gain the most satisfaction?

CAREER STAGES IN SCHOOL LEADERSHIP

As discussed, career development is an ongoing process by which an individual progresses through a series of stages, each of which is characterized by a relatively unique set of issues or tasks. Principals, like other employees, are assumed to experience their career differently throughout their career cycle.[49]

It is widely accepted that entry-level principalship skills will not be enough to effectively meet the difficulties, challenges, and complications of the principal's position.[50] For instance, researchers identified self-awareness, systemic thinking, creativity, models for solving complex problems, new approaches for dealing with day-to-day difficulties, knowledge about testing and assessment of student learning, public school finance, and staff development as the capacities most needed for effective school leadership.[51] These sophisticated skills take considerable time, study, experiences, and reflection to fully mature.

Nonetheless, most theories of educational leadership overlook the principal's career stages and capacity development, even though the principal's depth of experience in the role powerfully affects the individual's ability to manage and lead the school. For example, novice principals, whose self-efficacy and managerial skills are still low, are seemingly expected to adopt instructional and even transformational leadership practices as if they were experts in this role, despite the fact that these tasks have engaged the principal for only a few weeks.[52]

Principals' Career Stages

Research on principals' career stages has been influenced by theories of adult and career development from noneducational fields.[53] It has been proposed that principals' experiences, perspectives, and behaviors may change considerably over the course of their careers. Several models depict the stages principals may experience during their career cycle.[54] These career stages include periods of stress, crisis, frustration and possible burnout, renewal, and transitions in addition to personal development.[55] Studies have found that school principals' viewpoints over their careers advance over two trends, from management to leadership, and from idealism to realism.[56] Accordingly, a principal's career should be considered flexible and fluid—rather than stable and permanent—through the years.

Specifically, the principalship goes through induction (novice), establishment, midcareer (maintenance vs. renewal),[57] and disengagement (disengagement vs. disenchantment) stages.[58]

- ◆ *Induction stage.* A new principal is socialized into the school or into the role. He or she has to confront many issues and challenges, such as achieving acceptance, learning the organizational culture, learning ways to overcome the insecurity of inexperience, and developing a reality-based sense of confidence.
- ◆ *Establishment stage.* A principal feels in control, competent, and confident to manage the school. Growth and enthusiasm characterize this stage. The principal experiences a transition from an ideal to a realistic view of the school and of the leadership and managerial roles within it.
- ◆ *Midcareer. Renewal vs. maintenance.* During the midcareer period (usually ages 40–65), principals may express high levels of self-fulfillment, enchantment, job satisfaction, and self-renewal as they seek new challenges in their role and school (renewal). In contrast, other principals may experience low opportunities for professional growth, feelings of stagnation, loss of enthusiasm, and disenchantment (maintenance). These principals may do an acceptable job without enthusiasm or pursuit of excellence and growth.
- ◆ *Disengagement. Disengagement vs. disenchantment.* This stage (approximately age 65 and over) may also have positive (disengagement) and negative (disenchantment) paths. *Disengagement* refers to making an intellectual, emotional, and eventually a physical transition to life outside the principalship, whether it is a move into another educational role, into an active professionally-involved "retirement" or next career, or to full retirement. *Disenchantment* refers to the experience of long-serving principals who feel trapped and stagnated in a post with nowhere to go. Sometimes these principals gradually become autocratic in style and respond negatively to any change initiative.

Looking more broadly, principals are both leaders of schools and agents of the central office. Not only is their entry to the principalship affected by the central office but their career opportunities are largely facilitated or limited by central office administrators. Also, a career as a principal may be the last step in an educator's profession or it may be an intermediate one, a stepping stone to central office administration, to district superintendency, to a state-level or professional association leadership position, or to a college professorship.

Criticisms of Principals' Career Stages.   Criticism of career stage models in general also apply to the principals' career stage model.[59] The models fail to address issues of gender, discrimination, culture, and ethnic groups; they lack universality;[60] the stages lack clear boundaries; and they have unclear criteria for separating one's career into stages.[61]

Similarly, careers are not necessarily linear. Principals, as with other employees, may move through the stages at different rates and some return to previous stages. Career cycles are not always experienced in the same order: Regressions, dead ends, and unpredictable changes of direction occur, occasionally sparked by new realizations. Principals will move backward and forward between stages during their career cycle for a variety of reasons related to personal, psychological, occupational, and social factors.

ACTIVITY 12.5   The Principals' Career Stages

The principalship has discrete career stages: induction, establishment, midcareer, and disengagement. Discuss in pairs and then as a class:

Case Study Question 7: Dr. Solomon mentioned that he had to disengage from the principalship. How did he make that stage one of disengagement rather than disenchantment?

1. What did Dr. Solomon do to make his midcareer stage as a principal one of renewal rather than maintenance?
2. What did Dr. Solomon do to make his disengagement stage as a principal one of disengagement rather than disenchantment?
3. In your own experiences as a student and as a teacher, what examples have you observed in principals who handled their midcareer and disengagement stages less successfully and satisfyingly? What did you see and hear?
4. In your opinion, are these career stages relevant for teachers? In what ways? What have you observed and heard to influence your opinion?

Principals' Leadership Styles at Different Career Stages

Just as the principalship has different career stages, Izhar Oplatka, an Israeli educational leadership professor, speculated that theories of educational leadership are not equally applicable to novice, established, midcareer, and disengagement stage principals alike. Instead, since the different principalship stages require different skills and responsibilities, the assumptions underlying different leadership styles are more likely to be appropriate for a principal's particular career stage, rather than for all career stages.[62]

Induction Stage.   In this initial phase of their career, principals still have to prove their competency and managerial skills. Management refers to all technical aspects of the principals' work associated with day-to-day planning, coordination, control, budgeting, and school operations in support of the instructional program and related school goals. New principals' survival and success are initially determined by their ability to be effective managers.

A range of viewpoints may help explain the novice principal's focus on management rather than leadership. First, management tasks are easily identified, are more observable, require immediate attention, and may be solved more simply than are leadership tasks. Similarly, although highly energetic and enthusiastic induction stage principals may propose an educational vision and engage in participative leadership, they may have difficulty moving their vision forward. With relatively low experience and expertise in managing a school, limited familiarity with the school culture, and few strong relationships with teachers, newly appointed principals are likely to find enacting a persuasive leadership role difficult. Even if new principals have extensive and deep experiences as successful teachers or assistant principals, they may not have enough time and skills for coping with the basic management tasks necessary for their early survival in the principal's role.

At the same time, too large a gap between the principal role's reality and what the novice principal had imagined in his or her principal preparation programs may result in stress, feelings of helplessness, and impaired functioning.[63]

Research supports these findings. Studies among beginning principals indicate that they generally experience confusion and uncertainty in their new positions. They demonstrate high personal insecurity, professional inadequacy, and lack of practical knowledge.[64] Since the new principal's arrival has been found to be a time of anxiety and fear of the unknown both for teachers and the beginning principal,[65] quite a few novice principals have difficulties in establishing rapport or trust with staff members who sometimes resist the principal's attempts to make changes in the school practices and refrain from collaborating with them.[66] New principals may be unable to implement changes before getting to know the school culture and staff better. Likewise, because most beginning principals have neither established formal authority nor expert-based authority, teachers find it difficult to perceive the novice as an instructional leader whose professional knowledge and skills can facilitate their own growth in classroom effectiveness. Then too, many studies find beginning principals have insufficient time for observing classroom work and processes because their main concern and focus on the job is directed toward managerial problems.[67] Fortunately, temporary low to moderate levels of instructional leadership do not necessarily prevent high student achievement as related to the principal's induction stage.[68]

Nevertheless, novice principals can adopt participatory forms of leadership that are more consultative, open, and democratic and involve teachers and parents in more school decision making. One of the beginning principal's major tasks is to build many relationships in order to persuade and plan to implement future changes. Establishing cooperative and participative relationships with their staff and instilling pride, faith, respect, and a sense for what is really important in their educational enterprise forms the basis for later instructional and transformational leadership. These leadership behaviors becomes more fully expressed in the establishment and midcareer stages.

Establishment Stage. Establishment behaviors generally include earning additional degrees and certifications, receiving support from others, achieving recognition for job performance, getting ahead within an organization, getting along with organizational objectives, and fitting in with coworkers. The person in this stage has generally positive feelings about his or her overall career.[69]

In the establishment stage, principals identify themselves as experts in educational management and experience their own professional development.[70] While effective management is ongoing, most experienced principals delegate management functions to subordinates while they spend more time on instructional issues. Only when principals can exhibit professional competence and create strong rapport and trust among the faculty are they able to inspire teachers' commitments to collective goals, high expectations, and mastery of the capacities needed to accomplish them. Principals' confidence and competence allow them to empower their staff, support their professional development, and delegate more responsibly, showing the staff they are valued by involving them in the work of the school.

Accordingly, establishment stage principals continue their participative leadership but can now include more instructional and transformational leadership. Instructional leadership tasks include collaboratively developing missions and goals for the school and communicating these goals to teachers, parents, and students; collecting and using data to assess organizational effectiveness and advance organizational learning; promoting and supervising quality instruction; fostering an academic learning climate by establishing and assessing positive expectations and standards; and encouraging professional development. Instructional leaders ensure that school staff understands the school goals' importance by periodically discussing and reviewing them during the year. Principals coordinate teachers' classroom objectives with those of the school and monitor classroom instruction through observation. Effectively pursuing instructional leadership responsibilities requires high levels of self-efficacy, professional confidence, and feeling control over their school, qualities characteristic of principals in the establishment stage.

Likewise, transformational leadership tasks appropriate to the establishment stage include intellectual stimulation—providing ideas that result in rethinking old ways, enabling teachers to look at problems from many angles, and resolving problems that appear stalemated. The principal can also engage in individual consideration—delegating projects to stimulate and create learning experiences, paying personal attention to teachers' needs, and treating each staff member with respect as an individual. Throughout their various actions, principals in the establishment stage become role models for their teachers, demonstrating high standards of ethical and moral conduct and considering others' needs over their own.

The literature on principal burnout suggests that principals in the establishment and midcareer stages may delegate managerial responsibilities as a way to prevent their own stagnation and burnout.[71] Undoubtedly, veteran principals have different career needs than do principals just starting out.

Midcareer Stage: Renewal vs. Maintenance. Instructional, transformational, and participative leadership models also provide appropriate roles and tasks for midcareer stage principals in the renewal path. Midcareer renewal principals are typically active, energetic, creative, and enthusiastic leaders. At this stage, many principals are capable of expressing greater sensitivity to teachers', students', and community needs, and have enough confidence to implement changes and delegate more responsibility to staff. Some principals work for self-renewal by focusing on innovations and changes rather than on day-to-day routine management tasks.

The transformational leadership style appears in the midcareer renewal stage for the following reasons. First, experienced workers in this stage have a psychological need to be a mentor. Only after principals have experienced their own professional growth and development are they sufficiently competent to serve as a positive role model for new teachers or up-and-coming school leaders. Becoming a role model, giving individual consideration to teachers and assistant principals, and providing intellectual stimulation to staff satisfy the principals' own needs for self-fulfillment and self-actualization. Plus, it helps them avoid professional obsolescence and stagnation.[72]

In the maintenance path, however, instructional, transformational, and participative leadership behaviors are less likely. Many of these principals are less willing to stimulate creativity or to move the school toward any innovation.[73] Principals in the maintenance track have been found to complain about innovation and feel stagnated in their careers.[74] And how can they actively support, empower, and consult with their staff while they are in need of support and energy to cope with their own decline?

Disengagement.   The research examining the experiences of late-career stage employees and managers is inconclusive. Two contrasting arguments appear in the literature. One vein of research finds that late-career stage employees tend to have a maturity and wisdom that enables them to anticipate problems and to respond to them calmly and confidently. This research tends to appear in the noneducational sectors. In contrast, other research suggests that late-career employees tend to be rigid, less willing to learn new ways of working, and prone to resist change and innovation. This resembles the findings in the education literature.[75] Disengagement better describes the first scenario; disenchantment more accurately characterizes the second one. These are generalities, of course, and late-career principals may appear in either category.

In disengagement, principals look beyond their offices to their next career phase. They may seek other roles in the educational system, such as becoming a task force member, head of the district or regional principals' organization, or executive director of their state school athletic association. Others may transfer attention to family and themselves, spending time with their spouses or grandchildren, reading, traveling, and participating in enrichment classes.

One study on disengagement stage principals (over age 55) reported them having a high sense of professional competence and expertise, a strong tendency toward change and innovation, a large capacity for adaptation to environmental changes, and a capacity to make adjustments in educational perspectives. These principals expressed a high level of efficiency, broad understanding of managerial work processes, substantial satisfaction about their achievements, and personal savvy related to their long years of professional experience. The high sense of professional competencies coupled with their tendency to delegate authority seemed to provide these late-career principals with much time to devote to family, hobbies, organizational roles outside schools, and themselves. In this study, their involvement with life outside work was not interpreted as the result of disappointment with school or personal burnout. Noticeably absent were the conservative attitudes toward change, a fear of decline in performance or energy, and negative attitudes toward the young generation. Methodology issues, however, including the small sample size and the use of interviews, may have contributed to these particular findings.[76]

In contrast, certain features in the disenchantment track may inhibit the principal's use of instructional, transformational, and participative leadership strategies during this stage.[77] Principals who experience stress, exhaustion, burnout, and lack of motivation are less likely to empower teachers or to facilitate the development of collegial and reciprocal norms.[78] Principals who experience decreasing levels of professional confidence, higher levels of fatigue, and more personal complaints about the "new generation" of educators and innovation overloads[79] will be less likely to find the energy and desire to promote a vision, establish an academic learning climate, monitor pupils' progress, and perform other instructional leadership tasks. For these principals, stagnation seems to be a means to stabilize and "smooth out" their career's end.

In addition, some disenchanted school leaders may become autocratic administrators. Too tired to devote energy to the long processes of decision making and empowerment, they find it faster and easier to make a decision by themselves. Their belief that they are more knowledgeable than anyone else in the school makes collaborating with teachers and community members on school issues more difficult. In contrast, a fatigued disenchantment stage principal may adopt a laissez-faire style, where teachers are allowed to be almost entirely independent while the principal shows minimal involvement and participation in the school.

ACTIVITY 12.6   Leadership Styles at Different Stages in Principals' Careers

It is suggested that principals use different leadership styles at different stages in their principalship careers. Discuss as a class:

1. In what ways was Dr. Solomon a participatory, instructional, and/or transformational leader during his various career stages?
2. What are the principal's primary leadership tasks during each career stage?
3. Why is it important for principals and teachers to recognize the appropriate—and possible—leadership roles at each stage of the principalship?

PREPARING THE NEXT GENERATION OF SCHOOL LEADERS

Changing leadership is one of the most significant events in a school's life. Principals' impact on their schools is often influenced by their predecessors and successors. Sustainable, significant school improvement—and the quality of the individual principal's career—depends on understanding and managing these transition processes over time.[80] And as stewards of their schools, principals are responsible for developing competent future leaders who can successfully lead other schools.

The professional literature disagrees about the size and characteristics of an alleged "principal shortage." Several studies found a modest to no decline in principal candidate pools and a surplus of credentialed and available administrators[81]—an excess nearly twice the number of available leadership positions.[82] With the exception of high wealth school districts, other investigators determined that the number of candidates in the early 21st century was about half to two-thirds the number it was 15 years earlier.[83]

Nonetheless, demographically-driven retirements, the difficulty of retaining leaders in urban schools, and the popular practice of moving around principals to "plug the leaks" in failing schools mean that principal turnover is accelerating. This revolving door breeds staff cynicism and undermines long-term, sustainable improvement.[84] Linked with this trend is the recognition that fewer educators are showing interest in pursuing careers as school administrators.[85]

Accordingly, it is imperative that principals and school districts plan for leadership succession, continuity, and advancement by providing more comprehensive learning opportunities for aspiring, novice, and established leaders. Various studies demonstrate that in order to meet new challenges and changing expectations for the school leader's role, future and practicing school principals need ongoing support and education to obtain new knowledge and a wide range of new skills.[86] Mentoring is an essential role that experienced principals can use to address this need.

Mentoring Future School Leaders

Much is known about the principal's value for teacher and student success, and how effective leaders create school communities in which all members are learning. Nevertheless, principals have "traditionally been thrown into their jobs without a lifejacket, and they are expected to sink or swim."[87] From a different vantage, many aspirants do not realize that the process of becoming a principal involves not only completing professional training but also engaging in personal transformation.[88]

Changing educational careers is not easy. Giving up the comfort and familiarity as a teacher or assistant principal and experiencing discomfort and uncertainty in a new, unknown role as principal is highly stressful. Into this context, a growing number of educators have discovered that mentoring can be an effective—and perhaps essential—tool for attracting, preparing, and developing effective school leaders.

Defining Mentoring.   The term *mentoring* can be defined as "the establishment of a personal relationship for the purpose of professional instruction and guidance."[89] It is an intense relationship in which a senior person oversees the career development and psychological growth of a less experienced person. Mentors impart wisdom about norms, values, and mores that are specific to the profession and the organization. Mentoring is an important part of adult learning because of its holistic, individualized, and experiential approach.

Coaching is a form of mentoring, but is more focused and usually of shorter duration. Coaching relies on job-related tasks or skills and is accomplished through instruction, demonstration, and high-impact feedback. Both mentoring and coaching are important components of leadership development. Typically, mentors are current or former administrators who work closely with their protégés, often in confidence, and are available to answer almost any type of question, personal or professional. By contrast, coaches tend to work with more than just one principal and their instruction may cover only certain aspects of the principalship. Sometimes, however, the words *mentor* and *coach* are used interchangeably.[90]

Corporations have long used mentoring as a career development strategy: Experienced executives offer developmental assistance to their less experienced protégés. Several studies confirm that more than one third of the nation's top companies have established mentoring programs. Novice teachers have also benefited from mentoring programs, and more than 30 states have implemented some form of new K–12 teacher mentoring. But relatively few principals have participated in formal mentoring programs as part of their leadership preparation.[91] A 2000 report based on a survey of current and past principals concluded that those who took part in successful internships praised mentoring for providing aspiring principals with a realistic view of the position and for better preparing them to do the job well.[92] This support, however, has not always been provided.

Socialization and Development.   Effective mentoring is a sophisticated, proactive process in which a learning contract is established between a mentor and a mentee—or protégé—to help socialize and develop the protégé for entry and success in a new role and a new organization. It is also an effective approach to acquiring new knowledge, skills, and behaviors needed to achieve career success and personal satisfaction. The mentoring process can help individuals successfully transition from one education role to another.

Mentoring benefits mentors, mentees, and school districts. The mentoring concept embeds the expectation that the mentor engages in the midlife task of generativity—showing concern for and interest in guiding the next generation. Mentoring is a form of professional stewardship, "passing the torch" from the experienced to the less experienced. Benefits for mentors include opportunities to reflect on their knowledge and practices, occasions to hear new ideas, greater overall job satisfaction, increased peer recognition, broadened opportunities for career advancement, and renewed enthusiasm for the profession.

For protégés, mentoring benefits include expanded knowledge of leadership and management practices, honest and constructive feedback about their growth in leadership skills, increased confidence about their professional competence, the ability to see theory translated into practice, the creation of a collegial support system, and a sense of belonging. Mentoring helps socialize protégés into the principal role and the educational environment. For school districts, mentoring increases staff members' motivation levels and job satisfaction, increases productivity, and establishes an attitude of lifelong learning among school leaders.[93]

Mentoring That Works

For mentoring to be effective, the mentor must be credible and qualified to comment on management and leadership performance, and the protégé must be willing and able to take on new responsibilities, accept the mentor's feedback, and incorporate it into his or her practice. In addition to these non-negotiable prerequisites, mentoring that works requires:

◆ *Authentic, mutually enhancing relationships.* Successful mentoring is grounded in a voluntary, genuine, caring professional relationship in which both parties attain goals related to personal development and career enhancement. Successful mentors and protégés must want to act in this capacity. Trust in the relationship takes time to grow before it can become truly collegial.

◆ *View as a legitimate approach to learning.* Mentoring as a good and desirable practice in which a mature colleague helps an aspiring colleague to learn one's job must be perceived as a professional virtue, not as a sign of weakness. Understanding the establishment and midcareer stages (renewal track) as a time for professional generativity offers an opportunity for mutually beneficial relationships that advantage and satisfy each party as well as contribute to their schools.

◆ *Socialization to the principal's role*. Mentors work closely with their protégés to describe policies, procedures, and normal practices in the school district, and to provide feedback concerning the extent to which the protégé has mastered the essential skills associated with effective school leadership performance. Part of this learning includes helping the protégé become more aware of his or her personal values (including moral and ethical stances) and assumptions regarding the school leader's role and deciding the extent to which one is willing to make the changes that may be necessary to become an effective school leader.

◆ *Practice in participative leadership*. Mentors must be willing to delegate and share leadership responsibilities with teachers and other aspiring and novice administrators to work on actual and meaningful school issues. Opportunities to serve as members of school leadership teams, assist with professional development, conduct teacher observations, discipline students, plan and facilitate meetings, and work with parents help mentees gain role socialization and develop leadership capacity.

◆ *Learner-centered dialogue*. Sharing information goes beyond answering questions that occur when people are trying to survive on the job. Feedback and focus should be learner centered; address issues, knowledge, and skills that the protégé can control and change; and be confidential and timely. Unlike role models, mentors are likely to prod the aspirant to learn how to do something according to his or her own personal talents, often raising more questions than providing answers.

◆ *Regular and frequent meetings*. Mentoring is an investment of time and commitment by mentor and protégé. Mentors and protégés should meet at least once every 2 weeks so they can discuss current and upcoming issues. Mentors can provide reflective conversations, emotional and moral support, and timely hands-on guidance while protégés can reflect on their actions and gain constructive feedback and affirmation.

◆ *Organizational support*. The superintendent is especially critical for ensuring a mentoring program's success. Mentors are more likely to schedule and spend time with their protégés if they know the organization values the practice.

◆ *Mentor's professional and personal skills*. Mentors must be highly skilled in communicating, listening, analyzing, providing accurate feedback, and negotiating. Mentors are able (or are educated) to ask questions in order to get their mentees to reflect and make decisions for themselves.

◆ *Mentorship training*. Mentors should receive training to build communication skills, analyze needs, and give quality feedback. Protégés should learn strategies for needs analysis, self-development using an individual growth plan, and reflection.

◆ *Flexibility*. Great principals are not necessarily great mentors. Race, gender, and culture issues also complicate forming a mentor-protégé relationship. Flexibility must exist in the mentoring program to allow for changes in matches that are not working.

Protégé Responsibilities.   From a learning perspective, future principals must be able to assess their leadership's strengths and weaknesses, reflect on these, and then make necessary adjustments. Successful protégés should demonstrate the self-direction that is characteristic of adult learners. Adult learners know their own learning needs best. At the heart of self-directed learning (and mentoring) is individual responsibility for learning. This requires that the learner accepts responsibility and accountability for setting personal learning objectives, developing strategies, finding resources, and evaluating growth. In a mentoring relationship, these tasks are mutually defined and shared.

In many instances, protégés should take the initiative in identifying, choosing, and approaching someone they respect and admire with a request for that person to become their mentor. To do this, potential mentees need to have the knowledge, skills, and dispositions that will enable them to be effective protégés. These understandings can be learned, and they include:[94]

- ◆ *Goal setting.* Developing personal awareness of their leadership capabilities and the desire to expand their influence as educators by becoming school principals. Conducting an inventory (formal or informal) of personal strengths and weaknesses forms the basis for setting goals for the mentoring relationship.[95]
- ◆ *Active listening and reflecting.* Learning and practicing the skills of thoughtful listening, seeking feedback, and refining public speaking and writing proficiencies. Experience and critical reflection work together, finding connections among existing assumptions, experiences, prior learning, and current feedback, and using these links to create personal meaning and more productive thoughts and behavior. As protégés challenge their existing assumptions, they increase self-understanding and let go of beliefs that may be self-limiting or unrealistic.
- ◆ *Essential dispositions.* A personal commitment to the mentoring experience. Protégés must be willing to learn, develop self-knowledge, take initiative, maintain confidentiality, and be aware of ethical considerations in the mentoring relationship (such as handling a breach in confidentiality, what to do if a mentor starts to take advantage of the protégé's subordinate status, how to handle such issues as cross-gender mentoring, and how to diplomatically withdraw from an unsatisfactory mentoring relationship). They also need an attitude of openness and collegiality.

ACTIVITY 12.7   Establishing a Mentoring Relationship

Mentoring is the establishment of a personal relationship for the purpose of professional instruction and guidance. Successful mentoring has identifiable characteristics and responsibilities for both mentor and mentee. Discuss in pairs and then as a class:

1. What does it mean to say that "the process of becoming a principal involves not only completing professional training but also engaging in personal transformation"? Do you agree or disagree and why?
2. What qualities of effective mentoring were in evidence in the relationship that Dr. Solomon and Shannon established and maintained?
3. What did Dr. Solomon and Shannon each gain from the mentoring relationship? What did each contribute to it?
4. **Case Study Question 4:** As a teacher, did anyone in your school's administration encourage you to consider a position in educational leadership? What impact did that advice have on you? If no one ever encouraged you, how did that shape your decision?
5. **Case Study Question 8:** Is there someone you consider to be a mentor? What were the most meaningful aspects of that relationship? Have you started to mentor anyone?

Mentoring Cautions.   While mentoring has many advantages, several issues may limit its effectiveness. Program problems include difficulties with sustaining focus, allotting sufficient time for the mentoring process, continuing availability of resources for program development, and restricting programs to limited populations. In addition, inadequate preparation of mentors and potential mentees, and a tendency among administrators to lose sight of mentoring as an important support system are concerns that directly affect principals and protégés. For instance, requiring principals to mentor aspiring principal candidates without specifying the criteria for mentoring, identifying what mentors are to do, or providing essential mentorship training, and selecting mentors based on availability rather than quality makes for poor matches and poor outcomes.

Further, weakly implemented mentoring may have harmful consequences. Mentoring can be detrimental to protégé growth if and when those being mentored become too dependent on their mentors, expecting them to provide all possible answers to all possible questions. Mentoring can also generate the unwanted side effects of stifling innovation and perpetuating the status quo. In the past, some have asserted that the "dominant culture in educational administration is androcentric, meaning informed by white, male norms."[96] Traditionally, mentoring occurred among White men, the so-called "old boys' network." Given this mindset, potential principal candidates who are highly capable but who differ from the district norm in gender, age, race, ethnicity, position, background, skill set, or other variable may be quietly (and unethically) discounted as promising school leadership prospects and candidates for mentoring.

Mentoring can occur even without formal arrangements, advice, or encouragement for aspiring leaders. Mentoring need not be a directed experience. Frequently, principal aspirants glean what is necessary for career advancement and leadership development from a variety of familial, distant, and professional sources: parents, respected friends or family members, and teachers. Constructing a "mentor" from the resources available, these aspiring principals mentally combine talents of various individuals and develop professional understandings by carefully observing leadership in action and from personally seeking information on leadership roles.[97] This approach may be particularly useful to individuals from marginalized groups typically excluded from formal mentoring programs for factors including race, ethnicity, gender, disability, sexual preference, language, religion, class, or other difference.[98]

Institutional bias in developing leadership candidates is unethical, inequitable, and harmful to schools, teachers, students, and communities. Any perception that this practice is occurring should be clarified and, if necessary, challenged.

Principals' Role in Developing Future Principals

Principals are primarily responsible for identifying and recruiting prospective candidates for the principalship. Principals are in unique positions to spot future school leaders and nurture their growth long before candidates enroll in principal preparation programs. Having close collegial relationships with the individuals gained through long-term interactions allows principals to serve as mentors in the truest sense; it also has the greatest impact on protégés' decisions to become principals and the types of principals they become.

Effective principals continually look for occasions to encourage and extend leadership throughout the school. In this way, they not only develop additional school leaders but also create means to continue school improvement. Principals develop their school's leadership pool when they:

- ◆ Identify, recruit, and develop potential leaders from their first year of teaching.
- ◆ Provide quality mentorships for teacher leaders, aspiring assistant and novice principals, and serving principals.
- ◆ Provide opportunities for aspiring leaders to take on authentic and significant leadership responsibilities and problem solving within the school without fear of censure. In private, principals offer constructive feedback to help protégés steadily improve their role performance, enhance their role and organizational socialization, and expand their professional repertoire.
- ◆ Provide constructive guidance, reflective dialogue, and honest and open communications about expectations for protégés' management and leadership behaviors.
- ◆ Inside the mentoring relationship, help aspiring principal candidates see whether they can or want to contribute at this level and facilitate their commitment to school leadership practice. Mentors help protégés check for and build career adaptability and career salience, clarify values, and monitor satisfaction with increasing leadership roles.
- ◆ Work with other principals to offer mutual learning and support in a safe and trusting environment.
- ◆ Widen the leadership pool by recognizing different routes to the school principalship.
- ◆ Partner with a university to provide appropriate field experiences for internship placements and action research for school leadership students. These supervised opportunities will help aspiring school leaders build and refine their leadership capacities and develop competent practices.

Principals thinking about their successors will not only work to develop a pool of leadership talent within their schools, they will also foster the professional culture that celebrates school improvement and accepts constructive change. When successful continuous improvement becomes embedded in the school's ethos, and a shared investment in change is widely distributed across the staff, the faculty can survive the transfer of principalship. The time to think seriously about principal succession is not the day leaders learn they are leaving their positions but the day they begin them.

Assistant principals and teacher leaders bring advantages to a future principalship in that district. They have a strong knowledge of their school and have successfully enacted leadership responsibilities. Their current work experiences give them substantial information of the school and district's culture, policies, and practices. They know their students and their parent community. Their leadership effectiveness in their present schools may have already gained them widespread staff support. If the school district values loyalty and continuity, and if the principal has been widely perceived as effective, increasing assistant principals' and teachers' leadership skills will make them desirable and attractive candidates for future school leadership openings. In contrast, if the school district prefers discontinuity in school leadership, mentoring and coaching prospective leaders on the principal's staff will make them more desirable candidates for out-of-district school leadership opportunities. Research suggests that novice principals tend to do best when they were developed within and drawn internally from schools that had become strong professional learning communities under their predecessors.[99]

Mentoring Reprise.   Socializing and developing aspiring and novice school leaders to become principals is likely to pay significant dividends for schools. Mentoring—particularly when free from traditional biases about who can provide effective leadership—supplies the essential scaffolding for effective job-embedded acculturation, professional development, and leadership capacity building. Mentoring speeds up the learning curve by affording aspiring school leaders with opportunities to test ideas, observe effective practices, participate with an experienced colleague in successfully resolving complex problems, try out leadership skills in authentic situations and receive useful feedback, and reflect on and refine their own practices. Mentoring provides the personalized guidance and real-world experiences that help prepare nascent school leaders for the principalship.

Mentoring need not be limited to would-be or novice principals. Even established school leaders can benefit from this relationship when trying to navigate the particularly complex problems that all principals face. Ongoing mentoring relationships give principals an added perspective on any issue and prepare them to become mentors in their own right, deepening the pool of experienced persons who can guide future leaders.

ACTIVITY 12.8   Planning for Leadership Succession

Planning for leadership success is an important leadership responsibility. Principals play a key role in developing future school leadership. Discuss in pairs and then as a class:

1. What actions have you observed your principal take to develop widespread leadership within the school? What opportunities have you seen your principal miss to develop leadership within the school?
2. What actions have you seen your school district take to value in-house leadership candidates for the principalship, superintendency, or central office administration?
3. Where do you suspect the most promising principalship opportunities will be for you—inside your own school district or outside your present school district? If outside, what actions does this suggest for your future planning?

PLANNING PRINCIPALS' CAREER STAGES

Leadership development is a lifelong process that requires much self-awareness. Since careers are, to some degree, expressions of personality, it is important to continually assess and reflect on where one stands relative to the work role expectations—and to one's own.

The following tables present tasks appropriate to each principalship career stage. To help you monitor and plan your own career progress and reflect on its meaning to you, review the career timetable tasks. Identify a "start date" if you have not yet begun this task or provide an "end date" if you have successfully completed that task *or* if the task is ongoing. Then reflect on the extent to which that task reflects (high, medium, or low) on your career adaptability, the salience of the principal work role to your life roles, and the degree of satisfaction that task brings you. Don't expect to complete the entire table at this point in your life since it is meant to prompt professional planning, reflection, and growth across your entire principalship career.

Stage: Exploration			Reflective Career Assessment (Rank: high, medium, or low)		
Tasks:	Start Date	End Date	Adaptability	Salience	Satisfaction
Observe principals in their leadership and management roles.					
Identify respected principal role models and ask if one is willing to serve as an unofficial mentor to help you consider whether to pursue a school leadership career.					
Accept leadership roles in school (e.g., school improvement team member or chair; club or student government sponsor).					
Ask your mentor for and seriously reflect on constructive feedback for your school leadership actions.					
Complete necessary prerequisites; apply for, begin, and complete formal coursework in an accredited principal preparation program.					
Develop at least entry-level skills in instructional leadership, school management, crisis management, finance, school law, and time management.					
Apply for and secure an assistant principal's position, learn the role, and enact it successfully.					

Stage: Induction			Reflective Career Assessment (Rank: high, medium, or low)		
Tasks:	Start Date	End Date	Adaptability	Salience	Satisfaction
Apply for and secure a principal's position.					
Enact on-the-job learning of management and leadership skills.[100]					
Learn the school and community cultures.					
Survive and learn from mistakes.					
Use your mentor to help think through, plan for, and reflect upon major responsibilities and incidents in your work life.					
Develop trust and respect in your relationships with teachers, students, parents, and community members.					
Develop and share an educational vision for your school.					

			Reflective Career Assessment (Rank: high, medium, or low)		
	Start Date	End Date	Adaptability	Salience	Satisfaction
Observe teachers and students in the classroom; demonstrate effective instructional leadership skills.					
Adopt participatory, consultative, open leadership involving teachers and parents in school decision making.					
Be visible in school when students and teachers are present—including after-school extracurricular and sports events (resist the pressure to complete required paperwork behind closed doors in your office during the school day).					
Try to separate the "urgent" from the "important."					
Learn how to do the job.					
Stage: Establishment			**Reflective Career Assessment (Rank: high, medium, or low)**		
Tasks:	Start Date	End Date	Adaptability	Salience	Satisfaction
Promote and supervise quality instruction.					
Establish positive expectations and standards for students and teachers.					
Get ahead within the organization.[101]					
Keep school improvement going: Implement organizational objectives and assess degree of effectiveness, revise if needed, reassess.					
Share educational vision with faculty, students, and community and connect to school improvement goals and activities.					
Earn additional degrees and professional certifications.					
Promote and provide professional development and intellectual stimulation to teachers, other administrators, and yourself.					
Serve as a mentor to an aspiring or novice school leader.					
Gain increased mastery of management responsibilities.					
Share leadership responsibilities with other school leaders.					
Delegate projects to stimulate and create learning experiences for teacher leaders and assistant principals.					
Become a role model who demonstrates high ethical standards and competent instructional leadership.					
Begin to think about and plan for transition to the next career or life stage.					

(continued)

Stage: Midcareer			Reflective Career Assessment (Rank: high, medium, or low)		
Tasks:	Start Date	End Date	Adaptability	Salience	Satisfaction
Work with school improvement team to continue identifying and implementing school improvement changes connected to your vision and district goals.					
Express greater sensitivity to teachers', students', and community needs.					
Serve as mentor and role model for new teachers and aspiring school leaders.					
Seek intellectual stimulation to continue own professional and personal growth.					
Use own competence and confidence to empower staff, support their professional development, and delegate more responsibility.					
If experiencing burnout, reflect on its presence and possible causes, resolve issues that are creating discouragement, and regain enthusiasm and energy—or begin transition to the next life stage.					
Begin to think about and plan for transition to the next career or life stage.					
Stage: Disengagement			Reflective Career Assessment (Rank: high, medium, or low)		
Tasks:	Start Date	End Date	Adaptability	Salience	Satisfaction
Continue to anticipate and respond to problems calmly, knowledgably, and confidently.					
Actively plan for the next life stage inside or outside education (retirement, next career, family, and hobbies).					
Continue to delegate authority to other school leaders.					
Find time to devote to other areas of personal importance (hobbies, family, organizational roles outside the principalship).					
If physically and mentally fatigued, reconsider timetable for retirement and begin transition to the next life stage.					
Enact transition to the next life stage.					

PRINCIPALS AND REFLECTION

Effective school leadership can be learned. Skilled practitioners are reflective practitioners: They use their experience as a basis for assessing and revising existing ideas of how to act so they may develop more effective action strategies. Professionals become skilled by learning from their experiences.

Defining Reflection

Reflection has been defined in various ways. *Reflection* is the continuous process of evaluating and learning from experience[102]—a mechanism for turning experience into knowledge.[103] Likewise, "reflective practice is a challenging, focused, and critical assessment of one's own behavior as a means towards developing one's own craftsmanship."[104] Reflective practice integrally links thought and action. Prompted by a problem or inconsistency between the real and the idea, or between what happened and what was expected, practitioners step back and appraise their actions and the reasons for their actions. They consider the effectiveness or legitimacy of their choices, and they use this new perception to design alternative approaches. Through this dialectic process of thought and action, practitioners actively shape their own professional growth. Reflection is accomplished "off-line" at a time when individuals can give full attention to analysis and future planning without the urgency of immediate action.

Although Donald Schon (1983) coined and popularized the term *reflective practice*,[105] its roots go back to learning theory. John Dewey, Kurt Lewin, and Jean Piaget explored experiential learning that depended on integrating experience with reflection and theory with practice. While each argued that learning could not occur without experience, they also asserted that learning could not take place without reflection. Each viewed learning as a sequential process, consisting of concrete experience, observation and reflection, formation of abstract concepts or generalizations, and active experimentation. Without reflection, the beliefs and assumptions underlying behavior cannot be revisited. Yet until new concepts, ideas, or theories of action begin to affect behavior, learning will not occur.

What Reflective Practice Accomplishes

Reflective practice challenges individuals to discover those habits of belief or behavior that reinforce the present system's inadequacies and prevent the introduction of new and better approaches. By questioning their own behavior (What am I doing? Why? With what effect?) individuals build new viewpoints about their actions from which they can make informed judgments and changes.

Bolman and Deal (1991) recommended that leaders should be reflective about their own core ethical and professional values and beliefs. Even more critical, they must be explicit and thoughtful about where they stand, what they value, and what the potential outcomes of their actions might be.[106] Moral dilemmas are commonplace in school leadership, so clearly articulating one's own and one's professional beliefs and values is key to accurately diagnosing and effectively responding to everyday school problems.

Reflective practice enhances professional practice in several ways. It increases self-awareness, develops new knowledge about professional behavior, and creates a broader and deeper understanding of the problems that practitioners face. Contradictions between what individuals do and what they hope to accomplish become clearer, as do possibilities for improvement. Reflective practice also affects the workplace environment in ways that brace organizational change and effectiveness. Research on problem solving and reflection in administrator preparation supports the idea that the interaction of reflection and behavior leads to developing expertise.[107]

Ongoing reflection is essential for building knowledge. School leadership is a complex set of behaviors. Problem solving, decision making, and complex thinking are all part of the job. Contemplating issues that arise in schools, considering the consequences of their actions, and generating alternative approaches, principals expand their repertoire of leadership skills, creating a larger array of information on which to draw for making decisions. Reflection appears to be an important tool for developing expertise and the capacity to change behavior, expanding the range and quality of available choices.

At the same time, increasing knowledge expands principals' ability to use reflection effectively and to develop as school leaders. No matter how good a decision and action, it can always be improved. To suggest that a decision or action can be made better is not to imply that the principal's judgment or responses were inferior. Instead, it engages a principal in the work of every professional: continuous self-assessment and improvement.

Reflection Is a Learned Skill

Reflection requires purposeful and mature thinking. Skilled reflection is characterized by accuracy, specificity, and ability to use the analysis in future decision making and action.[108] With experience, aspiring, novice, and mature leaders become better able to monitor and focus on what is happening at the time. They accurately recall more small events from their interactions with teachers, students, parents, and other administrators. In turn, these recollections become evidence of their decisions and responses' effectiveness. Increased skills in reflection most likely occur when the school environment feels safe and supports leadership actions that lead to increased student and teacher learning.

Smyth (1989) and Francis (1995) suggested that reflective practice requires several processing actions:[109]

◆ *Describing*. What did I do?
◆ *Informing*. What does this mean?
◆ *Confronting*. How did I come to be this way?
◆ *Reconstructing*. How might I view/do things differently?
◆ *Challenging*. What action will I take? What alternative ways are available to handle similar events (considering the action, my position, the school and societal culture, and tradition)?
◆ *Considering*. What are my personal and professional codes of ethics and how do these affect my understanding of the event and my options for action?

These reflective practices can be used in administrator preparation programs through case studies, fishbowl dialogues, reflective writing, simulations, mentor discourse with mentee/educational leadership student, developing metaphors to talk about decision-making events, reflective interviewing and shadowing, as well as by other means. Conducting group reflection, writing reflective journals, composing case studies, and reflecting on personal and professional codes of ethics are all productive approaches to learning accurate reflection.

Practitioners can also use a variety of means to aid their reflection. Since writing is itself a reflective process, principals and assistant principals can write to produce their own feedback. Daily journals (free-flowing, running accounts of important events and interactions), critical incident journals (a more structured writing response), and learning journals (loosely structured focus on thoughts about practice) are also effective means of learning and reflection. Writing one's educational leadership platform (philosophy), including stated beliefs and assumptions for guiding professional practice, likewise engages aspiring or active principals in a reflective process. Instrument feedback rating scales (such as the Myers-Briggs type indicator)[110] may be of value in sparking "surprises" for reflection. Digital and video recordings provide complete, inexpensive, and replayable records of events for reflection on actions. Shadowing and reflective interviewing are also appropriate reflection opportunities for practicing principals. All these approaches may be used separately or in combination. The intensity and duration of principals' daily responsibilities, however, do not favor such time-demanding activities.

Reflection requires that school leaders be open to experience and constructive feedback from themselves and from colleagues. Lacking defensiveness, they are not afraid to look critically at their own behaviors and seek ways to be more helpful to their assistant principals, protégés, teachers, or students. In addition, these leaders often invite comments on their leadership behaviors from other school administrators or assistant principals.

Mentors and Reflection

Although reflection is always self-analytical, others may assist the individual by providing a facilitative structure and data about the events under review. As experienced educators, mentors' caring and skilled questioning can help aspiring and beginning school leaders become more accurate, analytic, and insightful about their thoughts and practices. This dialogue can help novices learn both the essential habits of mind and a larger professional repertoire from which to make leadership decisions. The essential question is: If I had the chance to decide and respond to this again with the same group of teachers or parents, would I do it the same way or would I do it differently, and how? After a while, aspiring or novice principals become more skilled in analyzing their own actions and have additional strategies to use for decision making and implementation. Reflection becomes a habit of mind, a routine activity.

All approaches to reflection as a means for improving professional practice rest on a usually unstated assumption: The practitioner is in total control of the decision of whether to reflect and whether to change his or her behavior. Reflection is not a panacea and cannot be used as a means to improve the skills of those who choose not to use it.

If the mentor presents feedback as a "prescription," the protégé's trust and openness may be reduced, and he or she may defensively stop listening. A noncritical, nonjudgmental climate in the mentoring relationship is essential. The desire to consider feedback and the decision to use it must come from the protégé. To give advice or prescriptions for change—or to accept them—stops reflection and ends the protégé's responsibility for change.

Learning to lead is a ongoing process. Reflective practice can be a key to effective school leadership. Wanting to continually know more about themselves as leaders, reflective principals constantly improve their decision making and judgment about complex issues. Accurate reflection produces richer professional knowledge upon which to draw. Successful school leaders incorporate reflective practice into their actions as a routine facet of professional development.

ACTIVITY 12.9   Using Reflection to Develop One's Leadership Skills

Learning to lead is a continuous process. Reflection is a means of turning experience into knowledge and shaping one's own professional growth. Discuss in pairs and then as a class:

1. Using the reflective skills of describing, informing, confronting, reconstructing, challenging, and considering, identify a recent leadership decision you have made. Use reflective writing to articulate the details pertinent to each reflective skill.
2. Consider the professional incident in question 1, and ask yourself the following questions:
   ◆ If I had the chance to decide and respond to this same situation again with the same group of teachers, parents, or students, would I do the same thing or would I act differently?
   ◆ If I would do things differently, how would I do them?

SUMMARY

Work remains a central role in most people's lives. What one does for a living is a key way people define their place in the community and world. Yet contemporary workers cope with a different and broader set of career development tasks than did their earlier counterparts.

Career development has been described as "the unfolding of capabilities and requirements in the course of a person's interaction with environments of various kinds (home, school, play, work) across the life span." Careers involve movement among positions, status levels, offices, and responsibilities. Careers provide satisfaction and allow financial and personal advancement, generally complementing and interacting with other major life roles.

Today's heightened career variability has changed the role work plays in people's lives. The likelihood that persons will engage in seven or more jobs over their work lives requires career adaptability, frequent retraining, and lifelong learning in order to manage their own careers. Career choice and development have become synonymous with human growth and development.

Donald Super's "life-span, life-space" approach to career development asserts that persons live in multiple-role environments. Work roles, family roles, educational roles, and community roles vary in their demands on and importance for different persons and within different developmental periods. With this perspective, career development becomes a lifelong process of multiple transitions; shifting needs for information; and reassessment of roles, commitments, and identity as new dilemmas and questions appear. Super's 10 propositions on career development stress individuality, multipotentiality, and continuous adjustment.

The career stages concept posits that people progress through a series of distinct occupational stages during their careers. Each stage is characterized by differences in work attitudes and behaviors, types of relationships needed, and aspects of work valued. Super presented five flexible vocational development stages: growth, exploration, establishment, maintenance, and disengagement. Each stage contains several key developmental tasks. Success in mastering tasks at one stage results in both effective functioning within that stage and preparation to address the tasks of later stages

Adult career development is a relatively recent focus of theory and research. Adult career development tasks include navigating the career stages, clarifying values, monitoring career salience, and determining career satisfaction. More specifically, the principalship goes through four career stages: induction (novice), establishment, midcareer (maintenance vs. renewal), and disengagement (disengagement vs. disenchantment). Each stage requires different management and leadership skills and responsibilities.

Effective mentoring is a sophisticated, proactive process in which a mentor and a mentee—or protégé—establish a learning contract to help socialize and develop the protégé for entry and success in a new role and a new organization. Mentoring benefits both the mentor and the protégé. Effective mentoring requires certain characteristics with clear responsibilities for each party. Successful principals continually look for occasions to nurture and extend leadership throughout the school.

Effective school leadership can be learned, in part through critical reflection—the continuous process of evaluating and learning from experience.

ENDNOTES

1. Niles, S. G., Herr, E. L., & Hartung, P. J. (2002). Adult career concerns in contemporary society. In S. G. Niles (Ed.), *Adult career development: Concepts, issues, and practices* (3rd ed., pp. 3–20). Broken Arrow, OK: National Career Development Association.

2. Gysbers, N. C., Heppner, M. J., & Johnston, J. A. (1998). *Career counseling. Process, issues, and techniques.* Boston, MA: Allyn & Bacon.

3. Wolfe, D. M., & Kolb, D. A. (1980). Career development, personal growth, and experimental learning. In J. W. Springer (Ed.), *Issues in career and human resource development* (pp. 1–2). Madison, WI: American Society for Training and Development.

4. Maccoby, M., & Terzi, K. (1981). What happened to work ethic? In J. O'Toole, J. Scheiber, & L. Wood (Eds.), *Working, changes, and choices* (pp. 162–171). New York, NY: Human Services Press.

5. Richardson, M. S. (1993). Work in people's lives: A location for counseling psychologists. *Journal of Counseling Psychology, 40*(4), 425–433 (p. 428).

6. Niles, Herr, & Hartung. (2002). Op. cit.

7. Dawis, R. V. (1996). The theory of work adjustment and person-environment correspondence counseling. In D. Brown & L. Brooks (Eds.), *Career choice and development: Applying contemporary theories to practice* (3rd ed., pp. 75–120). San Francisco, CA: Jossey-Bass, p. 94.

8. Crow, G. C. (1989). The perceived opportunity structure of educational administration. *Journal of Research and Development in Education, 22*(2), 70–78.

9. Schein, E. H. (1971). The individual, the organization, and the career: A conceptual scheme. *Journal of Applied Behavioral Science, 7*(4), 401–426.

10. Martin, N. H., & Strauss, A. L. (1956). Patterns of mobility within industrial organizations.

Journal of Business, 29(2), 101–110; Rosenbaum, J. E. (1984). *Career mobility in a corporate hierarchy.* Orlando, FL: Academic.

11. Sullivan, S. E. (1999). The changing nature of careers: A review and research agenda. *Journal of Management, 25*(3), 457–484.

12. Sullivan. (1999). Op. cit.

13. Niles, Herr, & Hartung. (2002). Op. cit.

14. Brown, D., & Brooks, L. (Eds.). (1996). *Career choice and development* (3rd ed.). San Francisco, CA: Jossey-Bass.

15. Blustein, D. L. (2001). Extending the reach of vocational psychology: Toward an inclusive and integrative psychology of working. *Journal of Vocational Behavior, 59*(2), 171–182; Smith, E. J. (1983). Issues in racial minorities' career behavior. In W. B. Walsh & S. H. Osipow (Eds.), *Handbook of vocational psychology, 1* (pp. 161–222). Hillsdale, NJ: Erlbaum; Thomas, K. (1999). *The Oxford book of work.* Oxford, United Kingdom: Oxford University Press.

16. Niles, Herr, & Hartung. (2002). Op. cit.

17. Hall, D. T., et al. (Eds.). (1996). *The career is dead—long live the career: A relationship approach to careers.* San Francisco, CA: Jossey-Bass.

18. Savickas, M. (1997). Career adaptability: An integrative construct for life-span, life-space theory. *Career Development Quarterly, 45*(3), 247–259 (p. 254).

19. Theory-building and empirical study of women's career behavior has increased in the past three decades. Although women's career development does not fundamentally differ from that of men, it is demonstrably more complex due to a socialization process that emphasizes the separation of work and family. See: Fitzgerald, L. F., & Weitzman, L. M. (1992). Women's career development: Theory and practice from a feminist perspective. In H. D. Lea & Z. B. Leibowitz (Eds.), *Adult career development: Concepts, issues, and practice* (pp. 124–160). Alexandra, VA: National Career Development Association.

20. Alfred, M. V. (2001). Expanding theories of career development: Adding the voices of African American women in the White academy. *Adult Education Quarterly, 51*(2), 108–127; Betz, N. E. (2005). Women's career development. In S. D. Brown & R. W. Lent (Eds.), *Career development and counseling: Putting theory and research to work* (pp. 253–277). Hoboken, NJ: John Wiley & Sons; Phillips, S. D., & Imhoff, A. R. (1997). Women and career development: A decade of research. *Annual Review of Psychology, 48*(1), 31–59.

21. Carter, R. T., & Cook, D. A. (1992). A culturally relevant perspective for understanding the career paths of visible racial/ethnic group people. In H. D. Lea & Z. B. Leibowitz (Eds.), *Adult career development: Concepts, issues, and practice* (pp. 192–217). Alexandria, VA: National Career Development Association.

22. Bingham, W. C. (2001). Donald Super: A personal view of the man and his work. *International Journal for Educational and Vocational Guidance, 1*(1–2), 21–19.

23. Super, D. E. (1990). A life-span, life-space approach to career development. In D. Brown, L. Brooks, et al. (Eds.), *Career choice and development: Applying contemporary theories to practice* (2nd ed., pp. 197–261). San Francisco, CA: Jossey-Bass.

24. Super, D. E., Savickas, M. L., & Super, C. M. (1996). The life-span, life-space approach to careers. In D. Brown, L. Brooks, et al. (Eds.), *Career choice and development* (3rd ed., pp. 121–178). San Francisco, CA: Jossey-Bass, p. 122.

25. Super, D. E. (1953). A theory of vocational development. *American Psychologist, 8*(4), 185–190.

26. Super, D. E. (1990). A life-span, life-space approach to career development. In D. Brown, L. Brooks, et al. (Eds.), *Career choice and development: Applying contemporary theories to practice* (2nd ed., pp. 197–261). San Francisco, CA: Jossey-Bass; Herr, E. L. (1997). Super's life-span, life-space approach and its outlook for refinement. *Career Development Quarterly, 45*(3), 238–246; Herr, E. L., & Cramer, S. H. (1996). *Career guidance and counseling through the lifespan. Systematic approaches* (5th ed.). New York, NY: Harper Collins.

27. Super. (1953). Op. cit.

28. Super. (1990). Op. cit.

29. Savickas. (2001). Op. cit.; Savickas, M. L. (2005). The theory and practice of career construction. In S. D. Brown & R. W. Lent (Eds.),

Career development and counseling: Putting theory and research to work (pp. 42–70). Hoboken, NJ: John Wiley & Sons.

30. Super preferred to use the term *decline* as the last developmental stage in earlier versions of his career development model. See: Super, 1992; Super, Savickas, & Super, 1996.

31. Super, D. E. (1980). A life-span, life-space approach to career development. *Journal of Vocational Behavior, 16*(3), 282–298; Super, D. E. (1990). A life-span, life-space approach to career development. In D. Brown, L. Brooks, et al. (Eds.), *Career choice and development: Applying contemporary theories to practice* (2nd ed., pp. 197–261). San Francisco, CA: Jossey-Bass; Super, D. E. (1992). Toward a comprehensive theory of career development. In D. H. Montross & C. J. Shinkman (Eds.), *Career development: Theory and practice* (pp. 35–64). Springfield, IL: Thomas.

32. Osipow, S.J. (1973). Theories of career development (2nd ed.). Englewood Cliffs, NJ: Prentice Hall.

33. Super, D. E. (1987). Life career roles: Self-realization in work and leisure. In D. T. Hall et al. (Eds.), *Career development in organizations* (pp. 95–119). San Francisco, CA: Jossey-Bass; Super, D. E. (1992). Toward a comprehensive theory of career development. In D. H. Montross & C. J. Shinkman (Eds.), *Career development: Theory and practice* (pp. 35–64). Springfield, IL: Charles C. Thomas.

34. Herr, & Cramer (1996). Op cit.

35. Mills, E. W. (1970). Career development in middle life. In W. E. Bartlett (Ed.), *Evolving religious careers* (pp. 181–198). Washington, DC: CARA.

36. Super, D. E. (1984). Career and life development. In D. Brown, L. Brooks, et al. (Eds.), *Career choice and development: Applying contemporary theories to practice* (pp. 192–234). San Francisco, CA: Jossey-Bass; Savickas, M. L. (1997). Career adaptability: An integrative construct for life-span, life-space theory. *Career Development Quarterly, 45*(3), 247–259; Savickas, M. L. (2001). Towards a comprehensive theory of career development: Dispositions, concerns, and narratives. In F. T. L. Leong & A. Barak (Eds.), *Contemporary models in vocational psychology: A volume in honor of Samuel H. Osipow* (pp. 295–320). Mahwah, NJ: Erlbaum.

37. Super, D. E., & Knasel, E. G. (1981). Career development in adulthood: Some theoretical problems. *British Journal of Guidance and Counseling, 9*(2), 194–201.

38. Savickas. (1997). Op. cit., p. 254.

39. Super, D. E., & Nevill, D. D. (1986). *The values scale.* Palo Alto, CA: Consulting Psychologists Press.

40. Super, D. E. (1970). *The work values inventory* (p. 4). Boston, MA: Houghton-Mifflin.

41. Harrington, T. (1996). Is job satisfaction related to changing values? In R. Feler & G. Walz (Eds.), *Career transitions in turbulent times* (pp. 155–161). Greensboro, NC: ERIC/CASS.

42. Super, D. E. (1982). The relative importance of work. *Counseling Psychologist, 10*(4), 95–103.

43. Niles, S. G. (2001). Using Super's career development assessment and counseling (C-DAC) model to link theory to practice. *International Journal for Educational and Vocational Guidance, 1*(1–2), 131–139.

44. Savickas., (2001). Op. cit. Baltes, P. B., Staudinger, U. N., & Lindenberger, U. (1999). Lifespan psychology: Theory and application to intellectual functioning. *Annual Review of Psychology, 50*(1), 471–507.

45. Savickas. (2001). Op. cit.

46. Vondracek, F. W., Lerner, R. M., & Schulenberg, J. E. (1986). *Savickas.* Hillsdale, NJ: Erlbaum.

47. Osipow. (1973). Op. cit.

48. Sverko, B. (2001). Life roles and values in international perspective: Super's contribution through the work importance study. *International Journal for Educational and Vocational Guidance, 1*(1–2), 121–130.

49. Day, C., & Bakioglu, A. (1996). Development and disenchantment in the professional lives of headteachers. In I. Goodson & A. Hargreaves (Eds.), *Teachers' professional lives* (pp. 123–138). London, United Kingdom: Falmer Press; Earley, P., & Weindling, D. (2004). *Understanding school leadership.* London, United Kingdom: Paul Chapman; Ribbins, P. (1999). Understanding leadership: Developing headteachers. In R. Vush, L. Bell, R. Bolam, R. Glatter, & P. Ribbins (Eds.), *Educational management: Redefining theory, policy, practice* (pp. 77–89). London, United Kingdom: Paul Chapman.

50. Crow, G. (2006). Complexity and the beginning principal in the US: Perspective on socialization.

Journal of Educational Administration, *44*(4), 310–325; Daresh, J., & Male, T. (2000). Crossing the border in leadership: Experiences of newly appointed British head teachers and American principals. *Educational Management and Administration*, *28*(1), 89–101; Oplatka, I. (2001). Types of difficulties in the induction stage: Retrospective voices of women principals. *Planning and Changing*, *32*(1–2), 1–12; Orr, M. T. (2005). Learning advanced leadership. *Educational Management, Administration & Leadership*, *35*(3), 327–347.

51. Grey, C., & French, R. (1997. Rethinking management education: An introduction. In R. French & C. Grey (Eds.), *Rethinking management education* (pp. 94–110). London, United Kingdom: Sage; Van Velsor, E., McCauley, C. D., & Moxley, R. S. (1998). Our view of leadership development. In C. D. McCauley, R. S. Moxley, & E. Van Velsor (Eds.), *Handbook of leadership development* (pp. 1–25). San Francisco, CA: Jossey-Bass; Wallace, R. C. (1994). Linking practice and the preparation of school administrators. In T. A. Mulkeen, F. H. Cambron-McCabe, & B. J. Anderson (Eds.), *Democratic leadership: The changing context of administrative preparation* (pp. 189–200). Norwood, NJ: Ablex.

52. Oplatka, I. (2004). The principal's career stage: An absent element in leadership perspectives. *International Journal of Leadership in Education*, *7*(1), 43–55.

53. Hall, D. T. (1986). Breaking career routines: Midcareer choice and identity development. In D. T. Hall (Ed.), *Career development in organization* (pp. 120–159). San Francisco, CA: Jossey-Bass; Super, D. E. (1992). Toward a comprehensive theory of career development. In D. A. Montross & C. H. Shinkman (Eds.), *Career development: Theory and practice* (pp. 35–64). Springfield, IL: Charles & Thomas.

54. Day & Bakioglu. (1996). Op. cit.; Hart, A. W. (1993). *Principal succession: Establishing leadership in schools*. New York: State University of New York; Kremer-Hayon, L., & Fessler, D. (1992). The inner world of school headteachers: Reflections on career life stages. *International Review of Education*, *38*(1), 35–45; Ribbins. (1999). Op. cit.; Weindling. (1999). Op. cit.

55. Oplatka, I. (2009). Learning the principal's future internal career experiences in a principal preparation program. *International Journal of Educational Management*, *23*(2), 129–144.

56. Kremer-Hayon, L., & Fessler, R. (1992). The inner world of school principals: Reflections on career life stages. *International Review of Education*, *38*(1), 35–45.

57. Daresh, J. C. (1986). Support for beginning principals: First hurdles are highest. *Theory into Practice*, *25*(3), 168–173; Parkay, F. W., Currie, G. D., & Rhodes, J. (1992). Professional socialization: A longitudinal study of first-time high school principals. *Educational Administration Quarterly*, *28*(1), 43–75; Oplatka, I., Bargal, D., & Inbar, D. (2001). The process of self-renewal among women headteachers in mid-career. *Journal of Educational Administration*, *39*(1), 77–94; Oplatka, I. (2004). The principal's career stage: An absent element in leadership perspectives. *International Journal of Leadership in Education*, *7*(1), 43–55 Weindling, D., & Earley, P. (1987). *Secondary headship: The first years*. London, United Kingdom: NFER-Nelson.;

58. Depson, D. A., & Dickson, G. L. (2003). Continuity in life-span career development: Career exploration as a precursor to career establishment. *Career Development Quarterly*, *51*(3), 217–233.

59. Wrightsman, L. S. (1988). *Personality development in adulthood*. Newbury Park, CA: Sage; Gallos, J. V. (1989). Exploring women's development: Implications for career theory, practice, and research. In B. A. Arthur, D. T. Hall, & B. S. Lawrence (Eds.), *Handbook of career theory* (pp. 110–132). New York, NY: Cambridge University Press; Leong, D., & Brown, G. (1995). Theoretical issues in cross-cultural career development: Cultural validity and cultural specificity. In W. B. Walsh & S. H. Osipow (Eds.), *Handbook of vocational psychology* (pp. 143–180). Mahwah, NJ: Erlbaum.

60. Gallos. (1989). Op. cit.; Leong & Brown. (1995). Op. cit.

61. Wrightsman. (1988). Op. cit.

62. Oplatka. (2004). Ibid.

63. Pines, A., & Kafri, D. (1978). Occupational tedium in the social services. *Social Work*, *12*(6), 499–507.

64. Parkey & Rhodes. (1992). Op. cit.; Robbins & Alvy. (1995). Op. cit.; Day & Bakioglu. (1996). Op. cit.; Dunning. (1996). Op. cit.; Daresh & Male (2000). Op. cit. Oplatka. (2001). Op. cit.

65. Daresh. (1986). Op. cit.; Weindling & Earley. (1987). Op. cit.

66. Daresh, J., & Playko, M. A. (1995). The arrival of the new principal: Reactions of staff. *People and Education, 3*(3), 322–332; Robbins & Alvy. (1995). Op. cit.

67. Kremer-Hayon & Fessler. (1992). Op. cit.; Day & Bakioglu. (1996). Op. cit.; Robbins, P., & Alvy, H. B. (1995). *The principal's companion: Strategies and hints to make the job easier.* Thousand Oaks, CA: Sage; Dunning. (1996). Op. cit.

68. Oplatka. (2004). Op. cit.

69. Jepson, D. A., & Dickson, G. L. (2003). Continuity of life-span career development: Career exploration as a precursor to career establishment. *Career Development Quarterly, 51*(3), 217–233.

70. Crow, G. M. (1993). Reconceptualizing the school administrator's role: Socialization and mid-career. *School Effectiveness and School Improvement, 4*(2), 131–152; Ribbin. (1999). Op. cit.

71. Sarros, J. C. (1988). Administrator burnout: Findings and future directions. *Journal of Educational Administration, 26*(2), 184–196; Torelli, J. A., & Gmelch, W. H. (1993). Occupational stress and burnout in educational administration. *People and Education, 1*(4), 363–381; Friedman, J. A. (1999). Turning our schools into a healthier workplace: Bridging between professional self-efficacy and professional demands. In R. Vanderberghe & A. M. Huberman (Eds.), *Understanding and preventing teacher burnout* (pp. 166–175). Cambridge, United Kingdom: Cambridge University Press; Oplatka, I. (2002). Women principals and the concept of burnout: An alternative voice? *International Journal of Leadership in Education, 5*(3), 211–226.

72. Hall, D. T. (1986). Breaking career routines: Mid-career choice and identity development. In D. T. Hall (Ed.), *Career development in organization* (pp. 120–159). San Francisco, CA: Jossey-Bass; Oplatka et al. (2001). Op. cit.

73. Day & Bakioglu. (1996). Op. cit.

74. Ribbins. (1999). Op. cit.

75. Oplatka, I. (2007). The school principal in late career: An explorative inquiry into career issues and experiences in the pre-retirement years. *Leadership and Policy in Schools, 6*(4), 345–369.

76. Oplatka. (2007). Ibid.

77. Oplatka. (2004). Op. cit.; Gibson, D. E. (2003). Developing the professional self-concept: Role model construals in early, middle, and late career stages. *Organizational Science, 14*(4), 591–610; Hall, D. T. (2002). *Careers in and out of organizations.* Thousand Oaks, CA: Sage; Kabacoff, R. I. (2002). *Leadership: What has age got to do with it?* New York, NY: Research Release. Management Research Group; Lahn, L. C. (2003). Competence and learning in late career. *European Educational Research Journal, 2*(1), 126–140.

78. Kremer-Hayon & Fessler. (1992). Op. cit.; Day & Bakioglu. (1996). Op. cit.; Weindling. (1999). Op. cit.

79. Day & Bakioglu. (1996). Op. cit; Weindling. (1999). Op. cit.

80. Hargreaves, A., & Fink, D. (2003). Sustaining leadership. *Phi Delta Kappan, 84*(9), 693–700.

81. Davis, S. H. (2005). *School leadership study: Developing successful principals.* Stanford, CA: Stanford Educational Leadership Institute; National Association of Secondary School Principals. (1998). Salaries paid principals and assistant principals. Arlington, VA: Educational Research Service; Portin, B. S., Shen, J., & Williams, R. C. (1998). The changing principalship and its impact: Voices from principals. *NASSP Bulletin, 82,* 1–8.

82. Gajda, R., & Militello, M. (2008). Recruiting and retaining school principals: What we can learn from practicing administrators. *AASA Journal of Scholarship and Practice, 5*(1), 14–20.

83. Cusick, P. (2003). *A study of Michigan's school principal shortage* (Policy Report No. 12). East Lansing: Education Policy Center, Michigan State University; Whitaker, (2001). Op. cit.

84. Hargreaves, A. (2005, Winter). Leadership succession. *Educational Forum, 69,* 163–173.

85. Daresh, J. (2004). Mentoring school leaders: Professional promise or predictable problems? *Educational Administration Quarterly, 40*(4), 495–517.

86. Jackson, B. L., & Kelley, C. (2002). Exceptional and innovative programs in educational leadership. *Educational Administration Quarterly, 38*(2),

192–212; Kelley, C., & Peterson, K. (2000, November). *The work of principals and their preparation: Addressing critical needs for the 21st century.* Paper presented at the annual meeting of the University Council for Educational Administration, Albuquerque, NM.

87. NAESP & Brown University. (2003). *Making the case for principal mentoring* (p. 8). Alexandria, VA and Providence, RI: National Association of Elementary Principals and the Education Alliance at Brown University. Retrieved from http://www.alliance.brown.edu/pubs/pln/prncpalmntrg.pdf

88. Brown-Ferigno, T. (2003). Becoming a principal: Role conception, initial socialization, role-identity transformation, purposeful engagement. *Educational Administration Quarterly, 39*(4), 468–503; Brown & Ferigno, T., & Muth, R. (2004). Leadership mentoring in clinical practice: Role socialization, professional development, and capacity building. *Educational Administration Quarterly, 40*(4), 468–494; Crow, G. M., & Glascock, C. (1995). *Finding one's way: How mentoring can lead to dynamic leadership.* Thousand Oaks, CA: Corwin Press; White, E., & Crow, G. M. (1993, April). *Rites of passage: The role perceptions of interns in the preparation for principalship.* Paper presented at the annual meeting of the American Educational Research Association, Atlanta, GA.

89. Ashburn, E. A., Mann, M., & Purdue, P. A. (1987, April). *Teacher mentoring: ERIC clearinghouse on teacher education* (p. 2). Paper presented at the annual meeting of the American Educational Research Association, Washington, DC.

90. Gray, W. A. (1988). Developing a planned mentoring program to facilitate career development. *Career Planning and Adult Development Journal, 4*(2), 9–16.

91. NAESP & Brown University. (2003). Ibid.

92. Educational Research Service. (2000). *The principal, keystone of a high-achieving school: Attracting and keeping the leaders we need.* Arlington, VA: Author, National Association of Elementary School Principals (NAESP), National Association of Secondary School Principals (NASSP).

93. Daresh, J. (2001). *Leaders helping leaders: A practical guide to administrative mentoring* (2nd ed.). Thousand Oaks, CA: Corwin Press.

94. See for resources: Daresh & Playko. (1995). Op. cit.; Searby & Tripses. (2006). Op. cit.; Zachary, L.

(2000). *The mentor's guide: Facilitating effective learning relationships.* San Francisco, CA: Jossey-Bass.

95. Formal self-assessments, such as the National Association of Secondary School Principals' *21st Century School Administrator Skills* can assist the self-assessment and reflection process and provide direction for professional growth. See: National Association of Secondary School Principals (NASSP). (2007). *Changing role of the middle level and high school leader: Learning from the past—preparing for the future.* Reston, VA: Author.

96. Gardiner, M. E., Enomoto, E. K., & Grogan, M. (2000). *Coloring outside the lines* (p. 1). Albany: State University of New York Press; Johnsrud, L. K. (1991). Administrative promotion: The power of gender. *Journal of Higher Education, 62*(2), 119–149; Ortiz, F. L. (1982). *Career patterns in education: Women, men and minorities in public school administration.* New York, NY: Praeger; Valverde, L. A. (1989). *Succession socialization: Its influence on school administrative candidates and its implications to the exclusion of minorities from administration* (Final report). Washington, DC: National Institute of Education; Wesley, C. L. (1997). *Mentoring in the superintendency: Effects of gender, race/ethnicity, and position on career and psychosocial functions* (Unpublished doctoral dissertation). University of Cincinnati.

97. Mendez-Morse, S. (2004). Constructing mentors: Latino educational leaders' role models and mentors. *Educational Administration Quarterly, 40*(4), 561–590.

98. Grogan, M., & Crow, G. (2004). Mentoring in the context of educational leadership preparation and development—Old win in new bottles? Introduction to a special issue. *Educational Administration Quarterly, 40*(4), 463–467.

99. Hargreaves et al. (2003). Op. cit.

100. Principals' responsibilities include: management (planning, coordination, control, budgeting, school operations in support of instructional program and related school goals) and leadership (setting instructional direction, teamwork, sensitivity, resolving complex problems, sound judgment, results orientation, organizational ability, oral and written communication skills, developing self and others. See: NASSP. (2004). Op. cit.

101. Get ahead within the organization by doing your job well, attending school district meetings, sharing important information with central office supervisors, raising student achievement, gaining teacher and community support, and serving on district committees.

102. Pinsky, L. E., Monson, D., & Irby, D. M. (1998, November). How excellent teachers are made: Reflecting on success to improve teaching. *Advances in Health Sciences Education, 3*(3), 207–215; Schon, D. A. (1983). *The reflective practitioner. How professionals think in action.* New York, NY: Basic Books.

103. McAlpine, L., & Weston, C. (2000, September). Reflection: Issues related to improving professional teaching and student learning. *Instructional Science, 28*(5), 363–385.

104. Osterman, K. F. (1990). Reflective practice: A new agenda for education. *Education and Urban Society, 22*(2), 133–152 (p. 133).

105. Schon. (1983). Op. cit.

106. Bolman, L. G., & Deal, T. E. (1991). *Reframing organizations.* San Francisco, CA: Jossey-Bass.

107. Chi, M. T. H., Feltovich, P. J., & Glaser, R. (1981). Categorization and representation of physics problems by experts and novices. *Cognitive Science, 5*(2), 121–152; Fredericksen, N. (1984). Implications of cognitive theory for instruction in problem solving. *Review of Educational Research, 54*(3), 363–407; Larkin, J., McDermott, J., & Simon, H. A. (1980). Expert and novice performance in solving physics problems. *Science, 208*(4450), 1335–1342; Lesgold, A. M. (1984). Acquiring expertise. In J. R. Anderson & S. M. Kosslyn (Eds.), *Tutorials in learning and memory: Essays in honor of Gordon Bower* (pp. 140–162). San Francisco, CA: Freeman; Rabinowitz, M., & Glaser, R. (1986). *Cognitive structure and process in highly competent performance.* Pittsburgh, PA: University of Pittsburgh, Learning Research and Development Center; Short, P. M., & Rinehart, J. S. (1993). Reflection as a means of developing expertise. *Educational Administration Quarterly, 29*(4), 501–521.

108. Danielson. (2007). Op. cit

109. Smyth, J. (1989). Developing and sustaining critical reflection in teacher education. *Journal of Teacher Education, 10*(2), 2–9; Francis, D. (1995). The reflective journal: A window to preservice teachers' practical knowledge. *Teaching and Teacher Education, 11*(3), 229–241.

110. Myers, I. B., & McCauley, M. H. (1985). *Manual: A guide to the development and use of the Myers-Briggs type indicator.* Palo Alto, CA: Consulting Psychologist Press.

Index